PICK-UPS AND BRONCO
1987-96 REPAIR MANUAL

CHILTON'S

Covers all U.S. and Canadian models of
Ford F-150, F-250, F-350 and F-Super Duty Pick-Ups,
Bronco, Chassis Cab, Commercial Chassis and
F-Series Motor Home Chassis; 2 and 4 wheel drive,
gasoline and diesel engines

by Jaffer A. Ahmad

CHILTON *Automotive Books*

PUBLISHED BY HAYNES NORTH AMERICA. Inc.

Manufactured in USA
© 1997 Haynes North America, Inc.
ISBN 0-8019-8828-4
Library of Congress Catalog Card No. 97-85115
0123456789 9876543210

Haynes Publishing Group
Sparkford Nr Yeovil
Somerset BA22 7JJ England

Haynes North America, Inc
861 Lawrence Drive
Newbury Park
California 91320 USA

ABCDE
FG

12D2

Contents

Contents

DRIVE TRAIN 7

SUSPENSION AND STEERING 8

BRAKES 9

BODY AND TRIM 10

GLOSSARY

MASTER INDEX

SAFETY NOTICE

Proper service and repair procedures are vital to the safe, reliable operation of all motor vehicles, as well as the personal safety of those performing repairs. This manual outlines procedures for servicing and repairing vehicles using safe, effective methods. The procedures contain many NOTES, CAUTIONS and WARNINGS which should be followed, along with standard procedures to eliminate the possibility of personal injury or improper service which could damage the vehicle or compromise its safety.

It is important to note that repair procedures and techniques, tools and parts for servicing motor vehicles, as well as the skill and experience of the individual performing the work vary widely. It is not possible to anticipate all of the conceivable ways or conditions under which vehicles may be serviced, or to provide cautions as to all possible hazards that may result. Standard and accepted safety precautions and equipment should be used when handling toxic or flammable fluids, and safety goggles or other protection should be used during cutting, grinding, chiseling, prying, or any other process that can cause material removal or projectiles.

Some procedures require the use of tools specially designed for a specific purpose. Before substituting another tool or procedure, you must be completely satisfied that neither your personal safety, nor the performance of the vehicle will be endangered.

Although information in this manual is based on industry sources and is complete as possible at the time of publication, the possibility exists that some car manufacturers made later changes which could not be included here. While striving for total accuracy, the authors or publishers cannot assume responsibility for any errors, changes or omissions that may occur in the compilation of this data.

PART NUMBERS

Part numbers listed in this reference are not recommendations by Haynes North America, Inc. for any product brand name. They are references that can be used with interchange manuals and aftermarket supplier catalogs to locate each brand supplier's discrete part number.

SPECIAL TOOLS

Special tools are recommended by the vehicle manufacturer to perform their specific job. Use has been kept to a minimum, but where absolutely necessary, they are referred to in the text by the part number of the tool manufacturer. These tools can be purchased, under the appropriate part number, from your local dealer or regional distributor, or an equivalent tool can be purchased locally from a tool supplier or parts outlet. Before substituting any tool for the one recommended, read the SAFETY NOTICE at the top of this page.

ACKNOWLEDGMENTS

This publication contains material that is reproduced and distributed under a license from Ford Motor Company. No further reproduction of distribution of the Ford Motor Company material is allowed without the express written permission from Ford Motor Company.

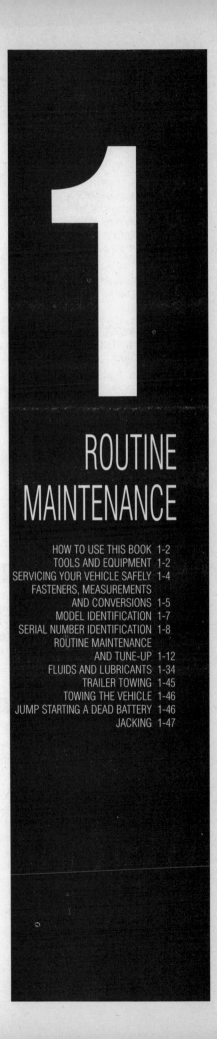

1

ROUTINE MAINTENANCE

HOW TO USE THIS BOOK

This Chilton's Total Car Care manual for Ford Trucks is intended to help you learn more about the inner workings of your vehicle while saving you money on its upkeep and operation.

The beginning of the book will likely be referred to the most, since that is where you will find information for maintenance and tune-up. The other sections deal with the more complex systems of your vehicle. Systems (from engine through brakes) are covered to the extent that the average do-it-yourselfer can attempt. This book will not explain such things as rebuilding a differential because the expertise required and the special tools necessary make this uneconomical. It will, however, give you detailed instructions to help you change your own brake pads and shoes, replace spark plugs, and perform many more jobs that can save you money and help avoid expensive problems.

A secondary purpose of this book is a reference for owners who want to understand their vehicle and/or their mechanics better.

Where to Begin

Before removing any bolts, read through the entire procedure. This will give you the overall view of what tools and supplies will be required. So read ahead and plan ahead. Each operation should be approached logically and all procedures thoroughly understood before attempting any work.

If repair of a component is not considered practical, we tell you how to remove the part and then how to install the new or rebuilt replacement. In this way, you at least save labor costs.

Avoiding Trouble

Many procedures in this book require you to "label and disconnect . . ." a group of lines, hoses or wires. Don't be think you can remember where everything goes—you won't. If you hook up vacuum or fuel lines incorrectly, the vehicle may run poorly, if at all. If you hook up electrical wiring incorrectly, you may instantly learn a very expensive lesson.

You don't need to know the proper name for each hose or line. A piece of masking tape on the hose and a piece on its fitting will allow you to assign your own label. As long as you remember your own code, the lines can be reconnected by matching your tags. Remember that tape will dissolve in gasoline or solvents; if a part is to be washed or cleaned, use another method of identification. A permanent felt-tipped marker or a metal scribe can be very handy for marking metal parts. Remove any tape or paper labels after assembly.

Maintenance or Repair?

Maintenance includes routine inspections, adjustments, and replacement of parts which show signs of normal wear. Maintenance compensates for wear or deterioration. Repair implies that something has broken or is not working. A need for a repair is often caused by lack of maintenance. for example: draining and refilling automatic transmission fluid is maintenance recommended at specific intervals. Failure to do this can shorten the life of the transmission/transaxle, requiring very expensive repairs. While no maintenance program can prevent items from eventually breaking or wearing out, a general rule is true: MAINTENANCE IS CHEAPER THAN REPAIR.

Two basic mechanic's rules should be mentioned here. First, whenever the left side of the vehicle or engine is referred to, it means the driver's side. Conversely, the right side of the vehicle means the passenger's side. Second, screws and bolts are removed by turning counterclockwise, and tightened by turning clockwise unless specifically noted.

Safety is always the most important rule. Constantly be aware of the dangers involved in working on an automobile and take the proper precautions. Please refer to the information in this section regarding SERVICING YOUR VEHICLE SAFELY and the SAFETY NOTICE on the acknowledgment page.

Avoiding the Most Common Mistakes

Pay attention to the instructions provided. There are 3 common mistakes in mechanical work:

1. Incorrect order of assembly, disassembly or adjustment. When taking something apart or putting it together, performing steps in the wrong order usually just costs you extra time; however, it CAN break something. Read the entire procedure before beginning. Perform everything in the order in which the instructions say you should, even if you can't see a reason for it. When you're taking apart something that is very intricate, you might want to draw a picture of how it looks when assembled in order to make sure you get everything back in its proper position. When making adjustments, perform them in the proper order. One adjustment possibly will affect another.

2. Overtorquing (or undertorquing). While it is more common for overtorquing to cause damage, undertorquing may allow a fastener to vibrate loose causing serious damage. Especially when dealing with aluminum parts, pay attention to torque specifications and utilize a torque wrench in assembly. If a torque figure is not available, remember that if you are using the right tool to perform the job, you will probably not have to strain yourself to get a fastener tight enough. The pitch of most threads is so slight that the tension you put on the wrench will be multiplied many times in actual force on what you are tightening.

There are many commercial products available for ensuring that fasteners won't come loose, even if they are not torqued just right (a very common brand is Loctite®). If you're worried about getting something together tight enough to hold, but loose enough to avoid mechanical damage during assembly, one of these products might offer substantial insurance. Before choosing a threadlocking compound, read the label on the package and make sure the product is compatible with the materials, fluids, etc. involved.

3. Crossthreading. This occurs when a part such as a bolt is screwed into a nut or casting at the wrong angle and forced. Crossthreading is more likely to occur if access is difficult. It helps to clean and lubricate fasteners, then to start threading the bolt, spark plug, etc. with your fingers. If you encounter resistance, unscrew the part and start over again at a different angle until it can be inserted and turned several times without much effort. Keep in mind that many parts have tapered threads, so that gentle turning will automatically bring the part you're threading to the proper angle. Don't put a wrench on the part until it's been tightened a couple of turns by hand. If you suddenly encounter resistance, and the part has not seated fully, don't force it. Pull it back out to make sure it's clean and threading properly.

Be sure to take your time and be patient, and always plan ahead. Allow yourself ample time to perform repairs and maintenance.

TOOLS AND EQUIPMENT

▶ **See Figures 1 thru 15**

Without the proper tools and equipment it is impossible to properly service your vehicle. It would be virtually impossible to catalog every tool that you would need to perform all of the operations in this book. It would be unwise for the amateur to rush out and buy an expensive set of tools on the theory that he/she may need one or more of them at some time.

The best approach is to proceed slowly, gathering a good quality set of those tools that are used most frequently. Don't be misled by the low cost of bargain tools. It is far better to spend a little more for better quality. Forged wrenches, 6 or 12-point sockets and fine tooth ratchets are by far preferable to their less expensive counterparts. As any good mechanic can tell you, there are few worse experiences than trying to work on a vehicle with bad tools. Your monetary savings will be far outweighed by frustration and mangled knuckles.

Begin accumulating those tools that are used most frequently: those associated with routine maintenance and tune-up. In addition to the normal assortment of screwdrivers and pliers, you should have the following tools:

- Wrenches/sockets and combination open end/box end wrenches in sizes 1/8–3/4 in. and/or 3mm–19mm 13/16 in. or 5/8 in. spark plug socket (depending on plug type).

➡ **If possible, buy various length socket drive extensions. Universal-joint and wobble extensions can be extremely useful, but be careful when using them, as they can change the amount of torque applied to the socket.**

- Jackstands for support.
- Oil filter wrench.
- Spout or funnel for pouring fluids.

• Grease gun for chassis lubrication (unless your vehicle is not equipped with any grease fittings)

• Hydrometer for checking the battery (unless equipped with a sealed, maintenance-free battery).

• A container for draining oil and other fluids.

• Rags for wiping up the inevitable mess.

In addition to the above items there are several others that are not absolutely necessary, but handy to have around. These include an equivalent oil absorbent gravel, like cat litter, and the usual supply of lubricants, antifreeze and fluids. This is a basic list for routine maintenance, but only your personal needs and desire can accurately determine your list of tools.

After performing a few projects on the vehicle, you'll be amazed at the other tools and non-tools on your workbench. Some useful household items are: a large turkey baster or siphon, empty coffee cans and ice trays (to store parts), a ball of twine, electrical tape for wiring, small rolls of colored tape for tagging lines or hoses, markers and pens, a note pad, golf tees (for plugging vacuum lines), metal coat hangers or a roll of mechanic's wire (to hold things out of the way), dental pick or similar long, pointed probe, a strong magnet, and a small mirror (to see into recesses and under manifolds).

A more advanced set of tools, suitable for tune-up work, can be drawn up easily. While the tools are slightly more sophisticated, they need not be outrageously expensive. There are several inexpensive tach/dwell meters on the market that are every bit as good for the average mechanic as a professional model. Just be sure that it goes to a least 1200–1500 rpm on the tach scale and that it works on 4, 6 and 8-cylinder engines. The key to these purchases is to make them with an eye towards adaptability and wide range. A basic list of tune-up tools could include:

• Tach/dwell meter.
• Spark plug wrench and gapping tool.
• Feeler gauges for valve adjustment.
• Timing light.

The choice of a timing light should be made carefully. A light which works on the DC current supplied by the vehicle's battery is the best choice; it should have a xenon tube for brightness. On any vehicle with an electronic ignition sys-

Fig. 1 All but the most basic procedures will require an assortment of ratchets and sockets

TCCS1200

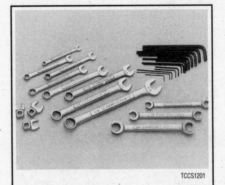

Fig. 2 In addition to ratchets, a good set of wrenches and hex keys will be necessary

TCCS1201

Fig. 3 A hydraulic floor jack and a set of jackstands are essential for lifting and supporting the vehicle

TCCS1202

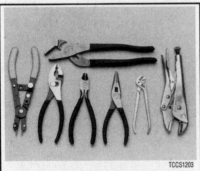

Fig. 4 An assortment of pliers, grippers and cutters will be handy for old rusted parts and stripped bolt heads

TCCS1203

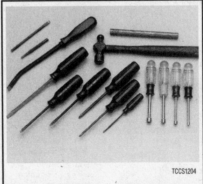

Fig. 5 Various drivers, chisels and prybars are great tools to have in your toolbox

TCCS1204

Fig. 6 Many repairs will require the use of a torque wrench to assure the components are properly fastened

TCCS1205

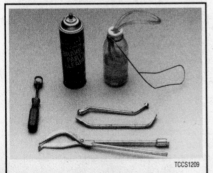

Fig. 7 Although not always necessary, using specialized brake tools will save time

TCCS1209

Fig. 8 A few inexpensive lubrication tools will make maintenance easier

TCCS1210

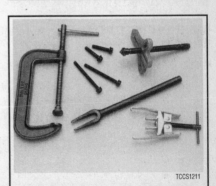

Fig. 9 Various pullers, clamps and separator tools are needed for many larger, more complicated repairs

TCCS1211

Fig. 10 A variety of tools and gauges should be used for spark plug gapping and installation

TCCS1212

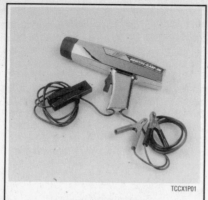

Fig. 11 Inductive type timing light

TCCX1P01

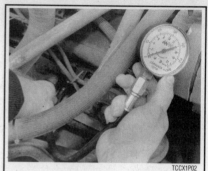

Fig. 12 A screw-in type compression gauge is recommended for compression testing

TCCX1P02

Fig. 13 A vacuum/pressure tester is necessary for many testing procedures

TCCX1P03

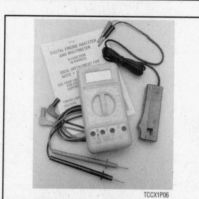

Fig. 14 Most modern automotive multimeters incorporate many helpful features

TCCX1P06

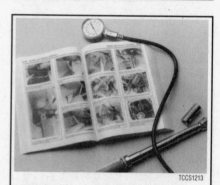

Fig. 15 Proper information is vital, so always have a Chilton Total Car Care manual handy

TCCS1213

tem, a timing light with an inductive pickup that clamps around the No. 1 spark plug cable is preferred.

In addition to these basic tools, there are several other tools and gauges you may find useful. These include:

• Compression gauge. The screw-in type is slower to use, but eliminates the possibility of a faulty reading due to escaping pressure.
• Manifold vacuum gauge.
• 12V test light.
• A combination volt/ohmmeter
• Induction Ammeter. This is used for determining whether or not there is current in a wire. These are handy for use if a wire is broken somewhere in a wiring harness.

As a final note, you will probably find a torque wrench necessary for all but the most basic work. The beam type models are perfectly adequate, although the newer click types (breakaway) are easier to use. The click type torque wrenches tend to be more expensive. Also keep in mind that all types of torque wrenches should be periodically checked and/or recalibrated. You will have to decide for yourself which better fits your pocketbook, and purpose.

Special Tools

Normally, the use of special factory tools is avoided for repair procedures, since these are not readily available for the do-it-yourself mechanic. When it is possible to perform the job with more commonly available tools, it will be pointed out, but occasionally, a special tool was designed to perform a specific function and should be used. Before substituting another tool, you should be convinced that neither your safety nor the performance of the vehicle will be compromised.

Special tools can usually be purchased from an automotive parts store or from your dealer. In some cases special tools may be available directly from the tool manufacturer.

SERVICING YOUR VEHICLE SAFELY

▶ See Figures 16, 17 and 18

It is virtually impossible to anticipate all of the hazards involved with automotive maintenance and service, but care and common sense will prevent most accidents.

The rules of safety for mechanics range from "don't smoke around gasoline," to "use the proper tool(s) for the job." The trick to avoiding injuries is to develop safe work habits and to take every possible precaution.

Do's

• Do keep a fire extinguisher and first aid kit handy.
• Do wear safety glasses or goggles when cutting, drilling, grinding or prying, even if you have 20–20 vision. If you wear glasses for the sake of vision, wear safety goggles over your regular glasses.
• Do shield your eyes whenever you work around the battery. Batteries contain sulfuric acid. In case of contact with, flush the area with water or a mixture of water and baking soda, then seek immediate medical attention.
• Do use safety stands (jackstands) for any undervehicle service. Jacks are for raising vehicles; jackstands are for making sure the vehicle stays raised until you want it to come down.
• Do use adequate ventilation when working with any chemicals or hazardous materials. Like carbon monoxide, the asbestos dust resulting from some brake lining wear can be hazardous in sufficient quantities.
• Do disconnect the negative battery cable when working on the electrical system. The secondary ignition system contains EXTREMELY HIGH VOLTAGE. In some cases it can even exceed 50,000 volts.
• Do follow manufacturer's directions whenever working with potentially hazardous materials. Most chemicals and fluids are poisonous.

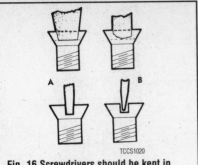

Fig. 16 Screwdrivers should be kept in good condition to prevent injury or damage which could result if the blade slips from the screw

Fig. 17 Using the correct size wrench will help prevent the possibility of rounding off a nut

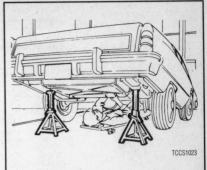

Fig. 18 NEVER work under a vehicle unless it is supported using safety stands (jackstands)

• Do properly maintain your tools. Loose hammerheads, mushroomed punches and chisels, frayed or poorly grounded electrical cords, excessively worn screwdrivers, spread wrenches (open end), cracked sockets, slipping ratchets, or faulty droplight sockets can cause accidents.

• Likewise, keep your tools clean; a greasy wrench can slip off a bolt head, ruining the bolt and often harming your knuckles in the process.

• Do use the proper size and type of tool for the job at hand. Do select a wrench or socket that fits the nut or bolt. The wrench or socket should sit straight, not cocked.

• Do, when possible, pull on a wrench handle rather than push on it, and adjust your stance to prevent a fall.

• Do be sure that adjustable wrenches are tightly closed on the nut or bolt and pulled so that the force is on the side of the fixed jaw.

• Do strike squarely with a hammer; avoid glancing blows.

• Do set the parking brake and block the drive wheels if the work requires a running engine.

Don'ts

• Don't run the engine in a garage or anywhere else without proper ventilation—EVER! Carbon monoxide is poisonous; it takes a long time to leave the human body and you can build up a deadly supply of it in your system by simply breathing in a little at a time. You may not realize you are slowly poisoning yourself. Always use power vents, windows, fans and/or open the garage door.

• Don't work around moving parts while wearing loose clothing. Short sleeves are much safer than long, loose sleeves. Hard-toed shoes with neoprene soles protect your toes and give a better grip on slippery surfaces. Watches and jewelry is not safe working around a vehicle. Long hair should be tied back under a hat or cap.

• Don't use pockets for toolboxes. A fall or bump can drive a screwdriver deep into your body. Even a rag hanging from your back pocket can wrap around a spinning shaft or fan.

• Don't smoke when working around gasoline, cleaning solvent or other flammable material.

• Don't smoke when working around the battery. When the battery is being charged, it gives off explosive hydrogen gas.

• Don't use gasoline to wash your hands; there are excellent soaps available. Gasoline contains dangerous additives which can enter the body through a cut or through your pores. Gasoline also removes all the natural oils from the skin so that bone dry hands will suck up oil and grease.

• Don't service the air conditioning system unless you are equipped with the necessary tools and training. When liquid or compressed gas refrigerant is released to atmospheric pressure it will absorb heat from whatever it contacts. This will chill or freeze anything it touches.

• Don't use screwdrivers for anything other than driving screws! A screwdriver used as an prying tool can snap when you least expect it, causing injuries. At the very least, you'll ruin a good screwdriver.

• Don't use an emergency jack (that little ratchet, scissors, or pantograph jack supplied with the vehicle) for anything other than changing a flat! These jacks are only intended for emergency use out on the road; they are NOT designed as a maintenance tool. If you are serious about maintaining your vehicle yourself, invest in a hydraulic floor jack of at least a 1½ ton capacity, and at least two sturdy jackstands.

FASTENERS, MEASUREMENTS AND CONVERSIONS

Bolts, Nuts and Other Threaded Retainers

▶ **See Figures 19 and 20**

Although there are a great variety of fasteners found in the modern car or truck, the most commonly used retainer is the threaded fastener (nuts, bolts, screws, studs, etc.). Most threaded retainers may be reused, provided that they are not damaged in use or during the repair. Some retainers (such as stretch bolts or torque prevailing nuts) are designed to deform when tightened or in use and should not be reinstalled.

Whenever possible, we will note any special retainers which should be replaced during a procedure. But you should always inspect the condition of a retainer when it is removed and replace any that show signs of damage. Check all threads for rust or corrosion which can increase the torque necessary to achieve the desired clamp load for which that fastener was originally selected. Additionally, be sure that the driver surface of the fastener has not been compromised by rounding or other damage. In some cases a driver surface may become only partially rounded, allowing the driver to catch in only one direction. In many of these occurrences, a fastener may be installed and tightened, but the driver would not be able to grip and loosen the fastener again.

If you must replace a fastener, whether due to design or damage, you must ALWAYS be sure to use the proper replacement. In all cases, a retainer of the

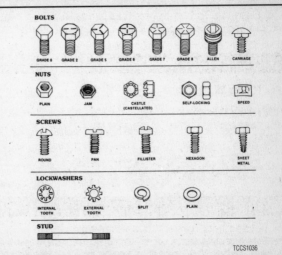

Fig. 19 There are many different types of threaded retainers found on vehicles

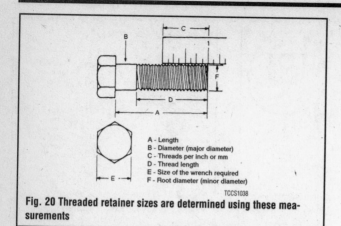

A - Length
B - Diameter (major diameter)
C - Threads per inch or mm
D - Thread length
E - Size of the wrench required
F - Root diameter (minor diameter)

TCCS1038

Fig. 20 Threaded retainer sizes are determined using these measurements

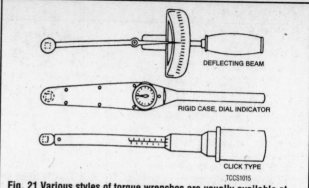

TCCS1015

Fig. 21 Various styles of torque wrenches are usually available at your local automotive supply store

same design, material and strength should be used. Markings on the heads of most bolts will help determine the proper strength of the fastener. The same material, thread and pitch must be selected to assure proper installation and safe operation of the vehicle afterwards.

Thread gauges are available to help measure a bolt or stud's thread. Most automotive and hardware stores keep gauges available to help you select the proper size. In a pinch, you can use another nut or bolt for a thread gauge. If the bolt you are replacing is not too badly damaged, you can select a match by finding another bolt which will thread in its place. If you find a nut which threads properly onto the damaged bolt, then use that nut to help select the replacement bolt.

⁂ WARNING

Be aware that when you find a bolt with damaged threads, you may also find the nut or drilled hole it was threaded into has also been damaged. If this is the case, you may have to drill and tap the hole, replace the nut or otherwise repair the threads. NEVER try to force a replacement bolt to fit into the damaged threads.

Torque

Torque is defined as the measurement of resistance to turning or rotating. It tends to twist a body about an axis of rotation. A common example of this would be tightening a threaded retainer such as a nut, bolt or screw. Measuring torque is one of the most common ways to help assure that a threaded retainer has been properly fastened.

When tightening a threaded fastener, torque is applied in three distinct areas, the head, the bearing surface and the clamp load. About 50 percent of the measured torque is used in overcoming bearing friction. This is the friction between the bearing surface of the bolt head, screw head or nut face and the base material or washer (the surface on which the fastener is rotating). Approximately 40 percent of the applied torque is used in overcoming thread friction. This leaves only about 10 percent of the applied torque to develop a useful clamp load (the force which holds a joint together). This means that friction can account for as much as 90 percent of the applied torque on a fastener.

TORQUE WRENCHES

♦ See Figure 21

In most applications, a torque wrench can be used to assure proper installation of a fastener. Torque wrenches come in various designs and most automotive supply stores will carry a variety to suit your needs. A torque wrench should be used any time we supply a specific torque value for a fastener. Again, the general rule of "if you are using the right tool for the job, you should not have to strain to tighten a fastener" applies here.

Beam Type

The beam type torque wrench is one of the most popular types. It consists of a pointer attached to the head that runs the length of the flexible beam (shaft) to a scale located near the handle. As the wrench is pulled, the beam bends and the pointer indicates the torque using the scale.

Click (Breakaway) Type

Another popular design of torque wrench is the click type. To use the click type wrench you pre-adjust it to a torque setting. Once the torque is reached, the wrench has a reflex signaling feature that causes a momentary breakaway of the torque wrench body, sending an impulse to the operator's hand.

Pivot Head Type

♦ See Figure 22

Some torque wrenches (usually of the click type) may be equipped with a pivot head which can allow it to be used in areas of limited access. BUT, it must be used properly. To hold a pivot head wrench, grasp the handle lightly, and as you pull on the handle, it should be floated on the pivot point. If the handle comes in contact with the yoke extension during the process of pulling, there is a very good chance the torque readings will be inaccurate because this could alter the wrench loading point. The design of the handle is usually such as to make it inconvenient to deliberately misuse the wrench.

➡It should be mentioned that the use of any U-joint, wobble or extension will have an effect on the torque readings, no matter what type of wrench you are using. For the most accurate readings, install the socket directly on the wrench driver. If necessary, straight extensions (which hold a socket directly under the wrench driver) will have the least effect on the torque reading. Avoid any extension that alters the length of the wrench from the handle to the head/driving point (such as a crow's foot). U-joint or wobble extensions can greatly affect the readings; avoid their use at all times.

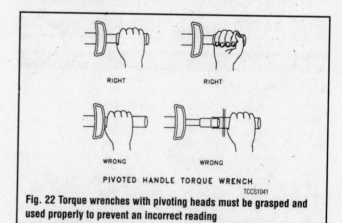

RIGHT   RIGHT

WRONG   WRONG

PIVOTED HANDLE TORQUE WRENCH

TCCS1041

Fig. 22 Torque wrenches with pivoting heads must be grasped and used properly to prevent an incorrect reading

Rigid Case (Direct Reading)

A rigid case or direct reading torque wrench is equipped with a dial indicator to show torque values. One advantage of these wrenches is that they can be held at any position on the wrench without affecting accuracy. These wrenches are often preferred because they tend to be compact, easy to read and have a great degree of accuracy.

TORQUE ANGLE METERS

Because the frictional characteristics of each fastener or threaded hole will vary, clamp loads which are based strictly on torque will vary as well. In most applications, this variance is not significant enough to cause worry. But, in certain applications, a manufacturer's engineers may determine that more precise clamp loads are necessary (such is the case with many aluminum cylinder heads). In these cases, a torque angle method of installation would be specified. When installing fasteners which are torque angle tightened, a predetermined seating torque and standard torque wrench are usually used first to remove any compliance from the joint. The fastener is then tightened the specified additional portion of a turn measured in degrees. A torque angle gauge (mechanical protractor) is used for these applications.

Standard and Metric Measurements

▶ See Figure 23

Throughout this manual, specifications are given to help you determine the condition of various components on your vehicle, or to assist you in their installation. Some of the most common measurements include length (in. or cm/mm), torque (ft. lbs., inch lbs. or Nm) and pressure (psi, in. Hg, kPa or mm Hg). In most cases, we strive to provide the proper measurement as determined by the manufacturer's engineers.

Though, in some cases, that value may not be conveniently measured with what is available in your toolbox. Luckily, many of the measuring devices which are available today will have two scales so the Standard or Metric measurements may easily be taken. If any of the various measuring tools which are available to you do not contain the same scale as listed in the specifications, use the accompanying conversion factors to determine the proper value.

The conversion factor chart is used by taking the given specification and multiplying it by the necessary conversion factor. For instance, looking at the first line, if you have a measurement in inches such as "free-play should be 2 in." but your ruler reads only in millimeters, multiply 2 in. by the conversion factor of 25.4 to get the metric equivalent of 50.8mm. Likewise, if the specification was given only in a Metric measurement, for example in Newton Meters (Nm), then look at the center column first. If the measurement is 100 Nm, multiply it by the conversion factor of 0.738 to get 73.8 ft. lbs.

CONVERSION FACTORS

LENGTH–DISTANCE

Inches (in.)	x 25.4	= Millimeters (mm)	x .0394	= Inches
Feet (ft.)	x .305	= Meters (m)	x 3.281	= Feet
Miles	x 1.609	= Kilometers (km)	x .0621	= Miles

VOLUME

Cubic Inches (in3)	x 16.387	= Cubic Centimeters	x .061	= in3
IMP Pints (IMP pt.)	x .568	= Liters (L)	x 1.76	= IMP pt.
IMP Quarts (IMP qt.)	x 1.137	= Liters (L)	x .88	= IMP qt.
IMP Gallons (IMP gal.)	x 4.546	= Liters (L)	x .22	= IMP gal.
IMP Quarts (IMP qt.)	x 1.201	= US Quarts (US qt.)	x .833	= IMP qt.
IMP Gallons (IMP gal.)	x 1.201	= US Gallons (US gal.)	x .833	= IMP gal.
Fl. Ounces	x 29.573	= Milliliters	x .034	= Ounces
US Pints (US pt.)	x .473	= Liters (L)	x 2.113	= Pints
US Quarts (US qt.)	x .946	= Liters (L)	x 1.057	= Quarts
US Gallons (US gal.)	x 3.785	= Liters (L)	x .264	= Gallons

MASS–WEIGHT

Ounces (oz.)	x 28.35	= Grams (g)	x .035	= Ounces
Pounds (lb.)	x .454	= Kilograms (kg)	x 2.205	= Pounds

PRESSURE

Pounds Per Sq. In. (psi)	x 6.895	= Kilopascals (kPa)	x .145	= psi
Inches of Mercury (Hg)	x .4912	= psi	x 2.036	= Hg
Inches of Mercury (Hg)	x 3.377	= Kilopascals (kPa)	x .2961	= Hg
Inches of Water (H₂O)	x .07355	= Inches of Mercury	x 13.783	= H₂O
Inches of Water (H₂O)	x .03613	= psi	x 27.684	= H₂O
Inches of Water (H₂O)	x .248	= Kilopascals (kPa)	x 4.026	= H₂O

TORQUE

Pounds–Force Inches (in–lb)	x .113	= Newton Meters (N·m)	x 8.85	= in–lb
Pounds–Force Feet (ft–lb)	x 1.356	= Newton Meters (N·m)	x .738	= ft–lb

VELOCITY

Miles Per Hour (MPH)	x 1.609	= Kilometers Per Hour (KPH)	x .621	= MPH

POWER

Horsepower (Hp)	x .745	= Kilowatts	x 1.34	= Horsepower

FUEL CONSUMPTION*

Miles Per Gallon IMP (MPG)	x .354	= Kilometers Per Liter (Km/L)	
Kilometers Per Liter (Km/L)	x 2.352	= IMP MPG	
Miles Per Gallon US (MPG)	x .425	= Kilometers Per Liter (Km/L)	
Kilometers Per Liter (Km/L)	x 2.352	= US MPG	

*It is common to covert from miles per gallon (mpg) to liters/100 kilometers (1/100 km), where mpg (IMP) x 1/100 km = 282 and mpg (US) x 1/100 km = 235.

TEMPERATURE

Degree Fahrenheit (°F) = (°C x 1.8) + 32
Degree Celsius (°C) = (°F − 32) x .56

TCCS1044

Fig. 23 Standard and metric conversion factors chart

MODEL IDENTIFICATION

▶ See Figure 24

The F-Series vehicles covered by this manual are all variations on the basic full-size pick-up body style. The model (or line), series, chassis, cab or body type information is found in digits five, six and seven of the Vehicle Identification Number (VIN). (See diagram).

Common design parameters include a front engine, rear wheel (primary) or 4-wheel drive layout. All pick-ups are equipped with some sort of pick-up box behind the cab, whereas certain Crew Cab (heavy duty) models and the Stripped Motorhome Chassis came with bare frame rails, ready to accept the owner's choice of bed or camper compartment, as the case may be. The Bronco, in typical sport utility vehicle fashion, is essentially a pick-up with a passenger compartment built in the short bed, the roof extended and no partition where the rear of the cab is on the rest of the F-Series vehicles.

Gasoline and diesel engines were available for 1987–96 F-Series vehicles in a range of displacements with either 6-cylinders or 8-cylinders. For the gasoline engines, the inline-6-cylinder, 4.9L (300 CID) engine is the standard powerplant for most models. Optional larger displacement engines are all V8's, and include the 5.0L (302 CID), 5.8L (351 CID) and 7.5L (460 CID) engines. In 1987 there was a 6.9L (420 CID) 8-cylinder diesel engine available for certain heavy duty models. Then in 1988, the engine's displacement was increased to 7.3L (445 CID), which size was carried through to 1996.

VIN POSITIONS 5, 6 AND 7

1FT E [F25] H 5 T L A00001

VIN CODE	LINE	SERIES	CHASSIS TYPE	CAR OR BODY TYPE	VEHICLE TYPE
U15	BRONCO	XL	4x4	BRONCO	MPV

NOTE: ONE OF THE FOLLOWING OPTIONAL EXTERIOR NAMEPLATES (INDICATING HIGHER TRIM LEVELS) MAY ALSO BE AFFIXED TO THE VEHICLE IN ADDITION TO THE BRONCO NAMEPLATE:
• XLT • EDDIE BAUER

REGULAR CAB	SUPER CAB OR CREW CAB		XL		CAR OR BODY TYPE	VEHICLE TYPE
F14	X14	F-SERIES	F150	4x4	PICKUP – REGULAR CAB/SUPER CAB	TRUCK
F15	X15	F-SERIES	F150	4x2	PICKUP – REGULAR CAB/SUPER CAB	TRUCK
F25	X25	F-SERIES	F250	4x2	PICKUP – REGULAR CAB/SUPER CAB	TRUCK
F26	X26	F-SERIES	F250	4x4	PICKUP – REGULAR CAB/SUPER CAB	TRUCK
—	W25	F-SERIES	F250	4x2	PICKUP – CREW CAB*	
—	W26	F-SERIES	F250	4x4	PICKUP – CREW CAB*	
F35	X35/W35	F-SERIES	F350	4x2	PICKUP – REGULAR CAB/SUPER CAB/ CREW CAB	TRUCK
F37		F-SERIES	F350	4x2	REGULAR CAB (CHASSIS CAB)	IV
F36	W36	F-SERIES	F350	4x4	PICKUP – REGULAR CAB/CREW CAB	TRUCK
F38		F-SERIES	F350	4x4	REGULAR CAB (CHASSIS CAB)	IV
F47		F-SERIES	F-SUPER DUTY	4x2	REGULAR CAB (CHASSIS CAB)	IV
F53		F-SERIES	F-SUPER DUTY	4x2	MOTOR HOME STRIPPED CHASSIS	IV

* PICKUP BOX DELETE AVAILABLE
NOTE: MPV MEANS MULTI-PURPOSE PASSENGER VEHICLE. IV MEANS INCOMPLETE VEHICLE.
NOTE: ONE OF THE FOLLOWING OPTIONAL EXTERIOR NAMEPLATES (INDICATING HIGHER TRIM LEVELS) MAY ALSO BE AFFIXED TO THE VEHICLE IN ADDITION TO THE F-SERIES NAMEPLATES:
• XLT • 4x4
NOTE: SPECIAL ORDER (DSO) UNITS WILL BE CODED WITH THE APPROPRIATE SERIES VIN CODES LISTED ABOVE.

88281G08

Fig. 24 Model identification information found in VIN digits five, six and seven—1996 example shown, others similar

SERIAL NUMBER IDENTIFICATION

Vehicle

▶ See Figures 25, 26, 27, 28 and 29

The Vehicle Identification Number (VIN) is located on the left side of the dash panel behind the windshield and may also be found on a sticker affixed to the door jamb.

Fig. 25 The VIN (as well as other crucial information) is found on this door jamb sticker

Fig. 26 By law, the VIN appears on a plate visible through the windshield

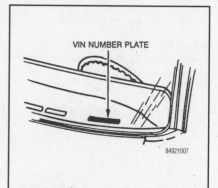

Fig. 27 The VIN is located on the driver's side of the dash

A seventeen digit combination of numbers and letters forms the VIN. Refer to the illustration for VIN details.

Vehicle Safety Compliance Certification Label

The Vehicle Safety Compliance Certification label is attached to the driver's door lock pillar. The label contains the name of the manufacturer, the month and

year of the vehicle, certification statement and VIN. The label also contains gross vehicle weight and tire data.

Engine

▶ See Figures 30 and 31

There are several ways to determine engine type supplied with the vehicle. The Vehicle Emission Control Information (VECI) decal mounted under the hood is perhaps the simplest way to identify the vehicle's engine. Another way is to refer to the 10th digit of the VIN along with the necessary chart to determine the meaning of that digit (engine code). And there is also a specific engine identification label (or tag) attached to the engine.

The engine identification tag identifies the cubic inch displacement of the engine, the model year, the year and month in which the engine was built, where it was built and the change level number. The change level is usually the number one (1), unless there are parts on the engine that will not be completely interchangeable and will require minor modification.

The engine identification tag is located under the ignition coil attaching bolt on most engines except the 6.9L and 7.3L diesels. The diesel engine I.D. number is stamped on the front of the block, in front of the left cylinder head.

1FTBF25G5 [H] LA00001

VIN Code	Year
H	1987
J	1988
K	1989
L	1990

Fig. 28 Vehicle model year is the 10th position

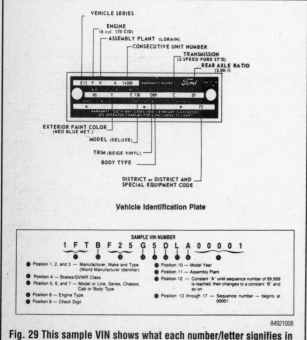

Fig. 29 This sample VIN shows what each number/letter signifies in the VIN

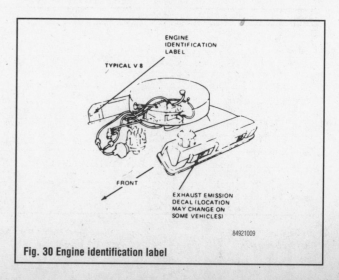

Fig. 30 Engine identification label

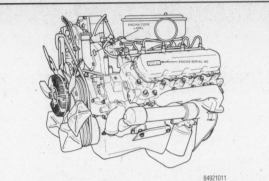

Fig. 31 Diesel engine serial number and identification label locations

Transmission

♦ **See Figure 32**

The transmission identification letter is located on a metal tag or plate attached to the case or it is stamped directly on the transmission case. Also, the transmission code is located on the Safety Certification Decal. Refer to the "Transmission Application" chart in this section.

Drive Axle

♦ **See Figure 33**

The drive axle code is found stamped on a flat surface on the axle tube, next to the differential housing, or, on a tag secured by one of the differential housing cover bolts. A separate limited-slip tag is attached to the differential housing cover bolt. The letters L-S signifies a limited-slip differential.

Transfer Case

A tag is affixed to the case mounting bolts. The information on the tag is needed when ordering service parts. If the tag is removed for any reason, make sure it is reinstalled.

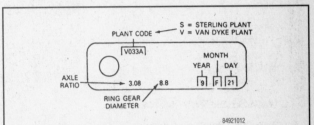

Fig. 33 Differential identification label. Limited slip units have a separate tag secured by a cover bolt

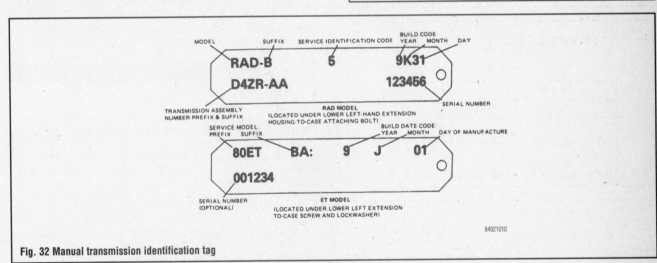

Fig. 32 Manual transmission identification tag

VEHICLE IDENTIFICATION CHART

Code	Liters	Cu. In. (cc)	Cyl.	Fuel Sys.	Eng. Mfg.
C	7.3	444 (7270)	8	IDI	Navistar
F	7.3	444 (7270)	8	DI	Navistar
G	7.5	460 (7536)	8	MFI/SFI	Ford
H	5.8	351 (5766)	8	4 BBL	Ford
H	5.8	351 (5766)	8	MFI/SFI	Ford
I	6.9	420 (6886)	8	DSL	Navistar
K	7.3	444 (7270)	8	IDI	Navistar
L	7.5	460 (7536)	8	4 BBL	Ford
M	7.3	444 (7270)	8	DSL	Navistar
N	5.0	302 (4942)	8	MFI/SFI	Ford
R	5.8	351 (5766)	8	MFI	Ford
Y	4.9	300 (4917)	6	MFI/SFI	Ford

Code	Year
H	1987
J	1988
K	1989
L	1990
M	1991
N	1992
P	1993
R	1994
S	1995
T	1996

MFI - Multi-port Fuel Injection
BBL - Barrel carburetor
DI - Direct Injection (turbo diesel)
DSL - Diesel
IDI - Indirect Injection (turbo diesel)
SFI - Sequential Fuel Injection

ENGINE IDENTIFICATION
All measurements are given in inches.

Year	Model	Engine Displacement Liters (cc)	Engine Series (ID/VIN)	Fuel System	No. of Cylinders	Engine Type
1987	Bronco	4.9L (4917)	Y	MFI	6	OHV
	Bronco	5.0L (4942)	N	MFI	8	OHV
	Bronco	5.8L (5766)	H	4 BBL	8	OHV
	F-150	4.9L (4917)	Y	MFI	6	OHV
	F-150	5.0L (4942)	N	MFI	8	OHV
	F-150	5.8L (5766)	H	4 BBL	8	OHV
	F-250	4.9L (4917)	Y	MFI	6	OHV
	F-250	5.0L (4942)	N	MFI	8	OHV
	F-250	5.8L (5766)	H	4 BBL	8	OHV
	F-250	6.9L (6886)	—	DSL	8	OHV
	F-250	7.5L (7536)	L	4 BBL	8	OHV
	F-350	4.9L (4917)	Y	MFI	6	OHV
	F-350	5.8L (5766)	H	4 BBL	8	OHV
	F-350	6.9L (6886)	—	DSL	8	OHV
	F-350	7.5L (7536)	L	4 BBL	8	OHV
1988	Bronco	4.9L (4917)	Y	MFI	6	OHV
	Bronco	5.0L (4942)	N	MFI	8	OHV
	Bronco	5.8L (5766)	H	MFI	8	OHV
	F-150	4.9L (4917)	Y	MFI	6	OHV
	F-150	5.0L (4942)	N	MFI	8	OHV
	F-150	5.8L (5766)	H	MFI	8	OHV
	F-250	4.9L (4917)	Y	MFI	6	OHV
	F-250	5.0L (4942)	N	MFI	8	OHV
	F-250	5.8L (5766)	H	MFI	8	OHV
	F-250	7.3L (7270)	M	DSL	8	OHV
	F-250	7.5L (7536)	G	MFI	8	OHV
	F-350	4.9L (4917)	Y	MFI	6	OHV
	F-350	5.8L (5766)	H	MFI	8	OHV
	F-350	7.3L (7270)	M	DSL	8	OHV
	F-350	7.5L (7536)	G	MFI	8	OHV
	F-Super Duty	7.3L (7270)	M	DSL	8	OHV
	F-Super Duty	7.5L (7536)	G	MFI	8	OHV
1989	Bronco	4.9L (4917)	Y	MFI	6	OHV
	Bronco	5.0L (4942)	N	MFI	8	OHV
	Bronco	5.8L (5766)	H	MFI	8	OHV
	F-150	4.9L (4917)	Y	MFI	6	OHV
	F-150	5.0L (4942)	N	MFI	8	OHV
	F-150	5.8L (5766)	H	MFI	8	OHV
	F-250	4.9L (4917)	Y	MFI	6	OHV
	F-250	5.0L (4942)	N	MFI	8	OHV
	F-250	5.8L (5766)	H	MFI	8	OHV
	F-250	7.3L (7270)	M	DSL	8	OHV
	F-250	7.5L (7536)	G	MFI	8	OHV
	F-350	4.9L (4917)	Y	MFI	6	OHV
	F-350	5.8L (5766)	H	MFI	8	OHV
	F-350	7.3L (7270)	M	DSL	8	OHV
	F-350	7.5L (7536)	G	MFI	8	OHV
	F-Super Duty	7.3L (7270)	M	DSL	8	OHV
	F-Super Duty	7.5L (7536)	G	MFI	8	OHV

88281C01

ENGINE IDENTIFICATION
All measurements are given in inches.

Year	Model	Engine Displacement Liters (cc)	Engine Series (ID/VIN)	Fuel System	No. of Cylinders	Engine Type
1990	Bronco	4.9L (4917)	Y	MFI	6	OHV
	Bronco	5.0L (4942)	N	MFI	8	OHV
	Bronco	5.8L (5766)	H	MFI	8	OHV
	F-150	4.9L (4917)	Y	MFI	6	OHV
	F-150	5.0L (4942)	N	MFI	8	OHV
	F-150	5.8L (5766)	H	MFI	8	OHV
	F-250	4.9L (4917)	Y	MFI	6	OHV
	F-250	5.0L (4942)	N	MFI	8	OHV
	F-250	5.8L (5766)	H	MFI	8	OHV
	F-250	7.3L (7270)	M	DSL	8	OHV
	F-250	7.5L (7536)	G	MFI	8	OHV
	F-350	4.9L (4917)	Y	MFI	6	OHV
	F-350	5.8L (5766)	H	MFI	8	OHV
	F-350	7.3L (7270)	M	DSL	8	OHV
	F-350	7.5L (7536)	G	MFI	8	OHV
	F-Super Duty	7.3L (7270)	M	DSL	8	OHV
	F-Super Duty	7.5L (7536)	G	MFI	8	OHV
1991	Bronco	4.9L (4917)	Y	MFI	6	OHV
	Bronco	5.0L (4942)	N	MFI	8	OHV
	Bronco	5.8L (5766)	H	MFI	8	OHV
	F-150	4.9L (4917)	Y	MFI	6	OHV
	F-150	5.0L (4942)	N	MFI	8	OHV
	F-150	5.8L (5766)	H	MFI	8	OHV
	F-250	4.9L (4917)	Y	MFI	6	OHV
	F-250	5.0L (4942)	N	MFI	8	OHV
	F-250	5.8L (5766)	H	MFI	8	OHV
	F-250	7.3L (7270)	M	DSL	8	OHV
	F-250	7.5L (7536)	G	MFI	8	OHV
	F-350	4.9L (4917)	Y	MFI	6	OHV
	F-350	5.8L (5766)	H	MFI	8	OHV
	F-350	7.3L (7270)	M	DSL	8	OHV
	F-350	7.5L (7536)	G	MFI	8	OHV
	F-Super Duty	7.3L (7270)	M	DSL	8	OHV
	F-Super Duty	7.5L (7536)	G	MFI	8	OHV
1992	Bronco	4.9L (4917)	Y	MFI	6	OHV
	Bronco	5.0L (4942)	N	MFI	8	OHV
	Bronco	5.8L (5766)	H	MFI	8	OHV
	F-150	4.9L (4917)	Y	MFI	6	OHV
	F-150	5.0L (4942)	N	MFI	8	OHV
	F-150	5.8L (5766)	H	MFI	8	OHV
	F-250	4.9L (4917)	Y	MFI	6	OHV
	F-250	5.0L (4942)	N	MFI	8	OHV
	F-250	5.8L (5766)	H	MFI	8	OHV
	F-250	7.3L (7270)	M	DSL	8	OHV
	F-250	7.5L (7536)	G	MFI	8	OHV
	F-350	4.9L (4917)	Y	MFI	6	OHV
	F-350	5.8L (5766)	H	MFI	8	OHV
	F-350	7.3L (7270)	M	DSL	8	OHV
	F-350	7.5L (7536)	G	MFI	8	OHV
	F-Super Duty	7.3L (7270)	G	DSL	8	OHV
	F-Super Duty	7.5L (7536)	G	MFI	8	OHV

88281C02

ENGINE IDENTIFICATION

All measurements are given in inches.

Year	Model	Engine Displacement Liters (cc)	Engine Series (ID/VIN)	Fuel System	No. of Cylinders	Engine Type
1995	F-250	4.9L (4917)	Y	MFI	6	OHV
	F-250	5.0L (4942)	N	MFI ②	8	OHV
	F-250	5.8L (5766)	H	MFI ①	8	OHV
	F-250	7.3L (7270)	F	DI	8	OHV
	F-250	7.5L (7536)	G	MFI	8	OHV
	F-350	4.9L (4917)	Y	MFI ②	6	OHV
	F-350	5.8L (5766)	H	MFI ②	8	OHV
	F-350	7.3L (7270)	F	DI	8	OHV
	F-350	7.5L (7536)	G	MFI	8	OHV
	F-Super Duty	7.3L (7270)	F	DI	8	OHV
	F-Super Duty	7.5L (7536)	G	MFI	8	OHV
1996	Bronco	5.0L (4942)	N	MFI	8	OHV
	Bronco	5.8L (5766)	H	SFI	8	OHV
	F-150	4.9L (4917)	Y	SFI	6	OHV
	F-150	5.0L (4942)	N	SFI	8	OHV
	F-150	5.8L (5766)	H	SFI	8	OHV
	F-250	4.9L (4917)	Y	SFI	6	OHV
	F-250	5.0L (4942)	N	SFI	8	OHV
	F-250	5.8L (5766)	H	SFI ③	8	OHV
	F-250	7.3L (7270)	F	DI	8	OHV
	F-250	7.5L (7536)	G	MFI ②	8	OHV
	F-350	4.9L (4917)	Y	SFI	6	OHV
	F-350	5.8L (5766)	H	SFI	8	OHV
	F-350	7.3L (7270)	F	DI	8	OHV
	F-350	7.5L (7536)	G	MFI ②	8	OHV
	F-Super Duty	7.3L (7270)	F	DI	8	OHV
	F-Super Duty	7.5L (7536)	G	MFI ②	8	OHV

BBL - Barrel carburetor
DI - Direct Injection (turbo diesel)
DSL - Diesel

IDI - Indirect Injection (turbo diesel)
MFI - Multi-port Fuel Injection
SFI - Sequential Fuel Injection

OHV - Overhead valve
① SFI with automatic transmission
② SFI in California

② MFI on vehicles over 8500 lbs. GVWR

88281C04

ENGINE IDENTIFICATION

All measurements are given in inches.

Year	Model	Engine Displacement Liters (cc)	Engine Series (ID/VIN)	Fuel System	No. of Cylinders	Engine Type
1993	Bronco	5.0L (4942)	N	MFI	8	OHV
	Bronco	5.8L (5766)	H	MFI	8	OHV
	F-150	4.9L (4917)	Y	MFI	6	OHV
	F-150	5.0L (4942)	N	MFI	8	OHV
	F-150	5.8L (5766)	H	MFI	8	OHV
	F-150 Lightning	5.8L (5766)	R	MFI	8	OHV
	F-250	4.9L (4917)	Y	MFI	6	OHV
	F-250	5.0L (4942)	N	MFI	8	OHV
	F-250	5.8L (5766)	H	MFI	8	OHV
	F-250	7.3L (7270)	M	DSL	8	OHV
	F-250	7.3L (7270)	C	IDI	8	OHV
	F-250	7.5L (7536)	G	MFI	8	OHV
	F-350	4.9L (4917)	Y	MFI	6	OHV
	F-350	5.8L (5766)	H	MFI	8	OHV
	F-350	7.3L (7270)	M	DSL	8	OHV
	F-350	7.3L (7270)	C	IDI	8	OHV
	F-350	7.5L (7536)	G	MFI	8	OHV
	F-Super Duty	7.3L (7270)	M	DSL	8	OHV
	F-Super Duty	7.3L (7270)	C	IDI	8	OHV
	F-Super Duty	7.5L (7536)	G	MFI	8	OHV
1994	Bronco	5.0L (4942)	N	MFI	8	OHV
	Bronco	5.8L (5766)	H	MFI	8	OHV
	F-150	4.9L (4917)	Y	DI	6	OHV
	F-150	5.0L (4942)	N	MFI	8	OHV
	F-150	5.8L (5766)	H	MFI	8	OHV
	F-150 Lightning	5.8L (5766)	R	MFI	8	OHV
	F-250	4.9L (4917)	Y	MFI	6	OHV
	F-250	5.0L (4942)	N	MFI	8	OHV
	F-250	5.8L (5766)	H	MFI	8	OHV
	F-250	7.3L (7270)	K	DSL	8	OHV
	F-250	7.3L (7270)	M	MFI	8	OHV
	F-250	7.5L (7536)	G	MFI	8	OHV
	F-350	4.9L (4917)	Y	MFI	6	OHV
	F-350	5.8L (5766)	H	MFI	8	OHV
	F-350	7.3L (7270)	F	DI	8	OHV
	F-350	7.3L (7270)	K	IDI	8	OHV
	F-350	7.3L (7270)	M	DSL	8	OHV
	F-350	7.5L (7536)	G	MFI	8	OHV
	F-Super Duty	7.3L (7270)	F	DI	8	OHV
	F-Super Duty	7.3L (7270)	K	IDI	8	OHV
	F-Super Duty	7.3L (7270)	M	DSL	8	OHV
	F-Super Duty	7.5L (7536)	G	MFI	8	OHV
1995	Bronco	5.0L (4942)	N	MFI ①	8	OHV
	Bronco	5.8L (5766)	H	MFI ②	8	OHV
	F-150	4.9L (4917)	Y	MFI	6	OHV
	F-150	5.0L (4942)	N	MFI ①	8	OHV
	F-150	5.8L (5766)	H	MFI ②	8	OHV
	F-150 Lightning	5.8L (5766)	R	MFI	8	OHV

88281C03

ROUTINE MAINTENANCE AND TUNE-UP

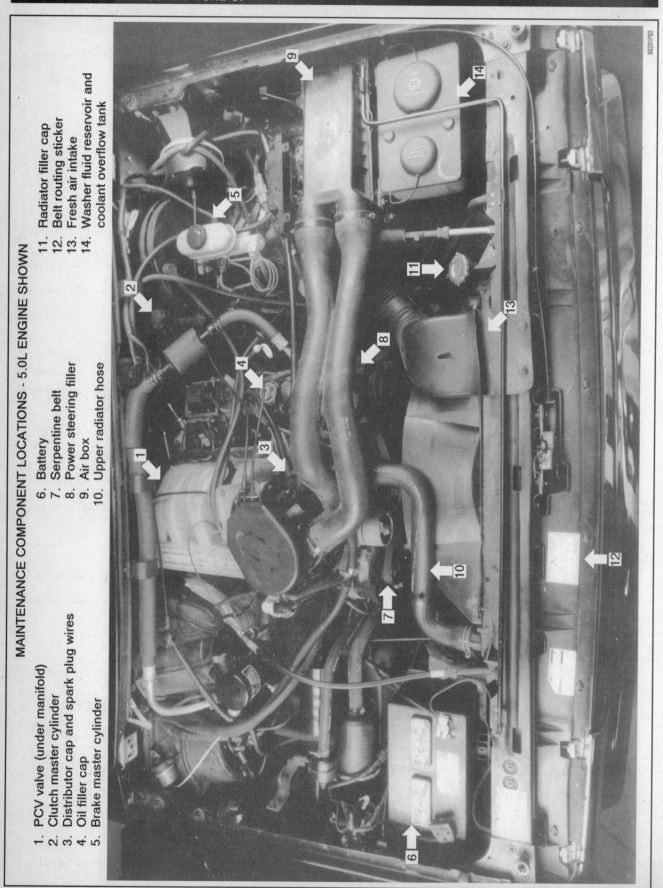

MAINTENANCE COMPONENT LOCATIONS - 5.0L ENGINE SHOWN

1. PCV valve (under manifold)
2. Clutch master cylinder
3. Distributor cap and spark plug wires
4. Oil filler cap
5. Brake master cylinder
6. Battery
7. Serpentine belt
8. Power steering filler
9. Air box
10. Upper radiator hose
11. Radiator filler cap
12. Belt routing sticker
13. Fresh air intake
14. Washer fluid reservoir and coolant overflow tank

→All maintenance procedures included in this section refer to both gasoline and diesel engines, except where noted.

Proper maintenance and tune-up is the key to long and trouble-free vehicle life, and the work can yield its own rewards. Studies have shown that a properly tuned and maintained vehicle can achieve better gas mileage than an out-of-tune vehicle. As a conscientious owner and driver, set aside a Saturday morning, say once a month, to check or replace items which could cause major problems later. Keep your own personal log to jot down which services you performed, how much the parts cost you, the date, and the exact odometer reading at the time. Keep all receipts for such items as engine oil and filters, so that they may be referred to in case of related problems or to determine operating expenses. As a do-it-yourselfer, these receipts are the only proof you have that the required maintenance was performed. In the event of a warranty problem, these receipts will be invaluable.

The literature provided with your vehicle when it was originally delivered includes the factory recommended maintenance schedule. If you no longer have this literature, replacement copies are usually available from the dealer. A maintenance schedule is provided later in this section, in case you do not have the factory literature.

Air Cleaner

♦ See Figures 34 thru 39

The air cleaner is a paper element type.

The paper cartridge should be replaced according to the Preventive Maintenance Schedule at the end of this section.

→Check the air filter more often if the vehicle is operated under severe dusty conditions and replace or clean it as necessary.

REPLACEMENT

Carbureted Engines

1. Open the engine compartment hood.
2. Remove the wingnut holding the air cleaner assembly to the top of the carburetor.

Fig. 34 Clean out the air cleaner body before installing the new filter

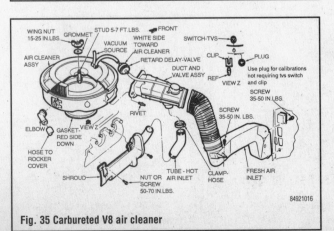

Fig. 35 Carbureted V8 air cleaner

3. Disconnect the crankcase ventilation hose at the air cleaner and remove the entire air cleaner assembly from the carburetor.
4. Remove and discard the old filter element, and inspect the condition of the air cleaner mounting gasket. Replace the gasket as necessary.

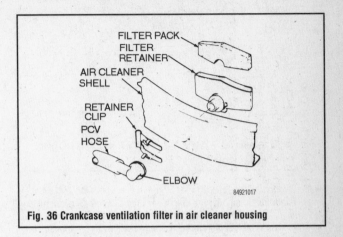

Fig. 36 Crankcase ventilation filter in air cleaner housing

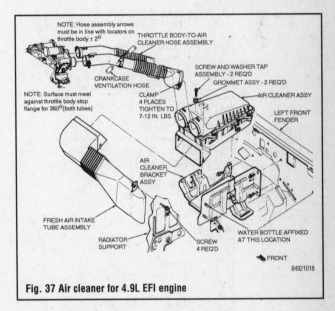

Fig. 37 Air cleaner for 4.9L EFI engine

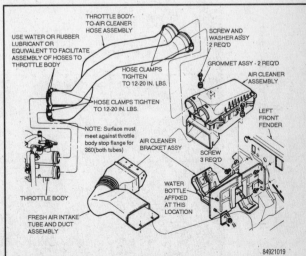

Fig. 38 Air cleaner for F-150, F-250 and Bronco with 5.0L and 5.8L EFI engines

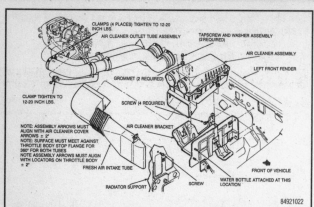

Fig. 39 Air cleaner for F-250HD, F-350 and F-Super Duty Chassis Cab with 7.5L EFI engine

A crankcase ventilation filter is located in the side of the air cleaner body. The filter should be replaced rather than cleaned. Simply pull the old filter out of the body every 20,000 miles (32,206 km), or more frequently if the vehicle has been used in extremely dusty conditions, and push a new filter into place.

5. Install the air cleaner body on the carburetor so that the word **FRONT** faces toward the front of the vehicle.

6. Place the new filter element in the air cleaner body and install the cover and tighten the wingnut. If the word **TOP** appears on the element, make sure that the side that the word appears on is facing up when the element is in place.

7. Connect the crankcase ventilation hose to the air cleaner.

Fuel Injected Gasoline Engines

▶ **See Figures 40 and 41**

1. Loosen the two clamps that secure the hose assembly to the air cleaner.
2. Remove the two screws that attach the air cleaner to the bracket.
3. Disconnect the hose and inlet tube from the air cleaner.
4. Remove the screws attaching the air cleaner cover.
5. Remove the air filter and tubes.

To install:

6. Install the air filter and tubes.
7. Install the screws attaching the air cleaner cover. Don't overtighten the hose clamps! A torque of 12–15 inch lbs. (1.36–1.69 Nm) is sufficient.
8. Connect the hose and inlet tube to the air cleaner.
9. Install the two screws that attach the air cleaner to the bracket.
10. Tighten the two clamps that secure the hose assembly to the air cleaner.

Diesel Engines

1. Open the engine compartment hood.
2. Remove the wingnut holding the air cleaner assembly.
3. Remove and discard the old filter element, and inspect the condition of the air cleaner mounting gasket. Replace the gasket as necessary.

4. Place the new filter element in the air cleaner body and install the cover and tighten the wingnut.

Fuel Filter

REPLACEMENT

✳✳ CAUTION

Observe all applicable safety precautions when working around fuel. Whenever servicing the fuel system, always work in a well ventilated area. Do not allow fuel spray or vapors to come in contact with a spark or open flame. Keep a dry chemical fire extinguisher near the work area. Always keep fuel in a container specifically designed for fuel storage; also, always properly seal fuel containers to avoid the possibility of fire or explosion.

Carbureted Engines

▶ **See Figures 42 and 43**

A carburetor mounted gas filter is used. These filters screw into the float chamber. To replace one of these filters:

1. Wait until the engine is cold.
2. Remove the air cleaner assembly.
3. Place some absorbent rags under the filter.
4. Remove the hose clamp and slide the rubber hose from the filter.

✳✳ CAUTION

It is possible for gasoline to spray in all directions when removing the hose! This rarely happens, but it is possible, so protect your eyes!

5. Move the fuel line out of the way and unscrew the filter from the carburetor.

To install:

6. Coat the threads of the new filter with non-hardening, gasoline-proof sealer and screw it into place by hand. Tighten it snugly with the wrench.

✳✳ WARNING

Do not overtighten the filter! The threads in the carburetor bowl are soft metal and are easily stripped! You don't want to damage these threads!

7. Connect the hose to the new filter. Most replacement filters come with a new hose and clamps. Use them.

8. Remove the fuel-soaked rags, wipe up any spilled fuel and start the engine. Check the filter connections for leaks.

CHILTON TIP: The problem with the screw-in type filter used with the above engines is the possibility of stripping the soft threads in the carburetor float bowl when replacing the filter. Such an occurrence is disastrous! To avoid this possibility, discard the screw-in filter and replace

Fig. 40 Remove the retaining screws to the airbox lid

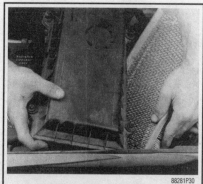

Fig. 41 Maneuver the air cleaner element from the airbox

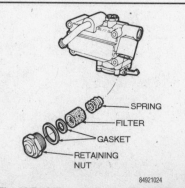

Fig. 42 Fuel filter—Holley model 4180C 4-bbl. carburetor

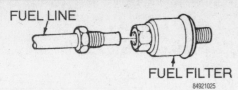

FUEL LINE

FUEL FILTER

84921025

Fig. 43 Some models have the screw-in type fuel filter which threads into the carburetor

it in the float bowl with a brass fitting having a 5/16 in. OD nipple. To this, attach a length of 5/16 in. ID fuel hose, with a similar length of hose attached to the steel fuel line. Between these 2 hoses you can use an inline type fuel filter such as a Fram G2 or equivalent. Now, filter replacement is simply a matter of removing the inline filter from the hoses. Always use the spring-type hose clamps supplied with the new filter at all hose connection points. Use enough hose to avoid stretching, but not too much, to avoid movement of the filter against nearby components.

Fuel Injected Gasoline Engines

1987–89 ENGINES

The inline filter is mounted on the same bracket as the fuel supply pump on the frame rail under the truck, back by the fuel tank. To replace the filter:
1. Raise and support the rear end on jackstands.
2. With the engine off, properly depressurize the fuel system. See Section 5.
3. Remove the quick-disconnect fittings at both ends of the filter. See Section 5.
4. Remove the filter and retainer from the bracket.
5. Remove the rubber insulator ring from the filter.
6. Remove the filter from the retainer.

To install:
7. Install the new filter into the retainer, noting the direction of the flow arrow.
8. Install a new rubber insulator ring.
9. Install the retainer and filter on the bracket and tighten the screws to 60 inch lbs. (6.75 Nm).
10. Install the fuel lines using new retainer clips.
11. Start the engine and check for leaks.

1990–94 ENGINES

The filter, with these engines, is located amidships on the left frame rail. The filter should be changed either every 15,000 mi. (24,000 km), or 15 months, whichever comes first. The filter should also be changed whenever a fuel delivery module is replaced.

❄❄ CAUTION

To prevent siphoning of fuel from the tank when the filter is removed, raise and support the front end of the truck above the level of the tank.

1. Relieve fuel system pressure. See Section 5. When working in hot weather, work quickly to complete filter replacement before the fuel pressure rebuilds!
2. Unsnap the filter canister from the retaining clips.
3. Disconnect the quick-connect couplings and remove the filter.

❄❄ WARNING

Be careful to avoid kinking the fuel lines!

To install:
4. Noting the direction-of-flow arrow on the new filter, connect the fuel lines.
5. Snap the filter into the clips.
6. Turn the ignition switch to RUN several times—without starting the engine—and check for leaks.

1995–96 ENGINES—IN-LINE FILTER

▶ See Figures 44, 45 and 46

1. Relieve fuel system pressure. See Section 5.

➡ When the battery is disconnected and reconnected, some abnormal drive symptoms may appear temporarily. Do not be unduly concerned. The vehicle must be driven for at least 10 miles to allow the engine management computer to relearn its adaptive strategy.

2. Disconnect the negative battery cable.
3. Raise and safely support the vehicle.
4. Remove the filter-to-fuel line retainer clips.
5. Disconnect the quick-connect couplings from both ends of the filter.
6. Remove the two nuts from the filter studs and remove the fuel filter bracket.

❄❄ WARNING

Be careful to avoid kinking the fuel lines!

To install:

➡ Note the direction-of-flow arrow on the new filter. The arrow should point to the tab of the fuel filter bracket against which the filter rests.

7. Install the filter assembly and the two nuts. Tighten the nuts to 6–7 ft. lbs. (8–10 Nm).
8. Install the push-connect fittings to the filter ends.
9. Snap the filter into the clips.
10. Lower the vehicle and connect the negative battery cable.
11. Turn the ignition switch to RUN several times—without starting the engine—and check for leaks.

1995–96 ENGINES—FUEL TANK FILTER

The in-tank fuel filter is integral with the venturi pump (part of the fuel delivery module) and is not independently serviceable.

The filter is made of nylon and mounts to the mouth of the venturi pump to prevent dirt and particles from entering the system. The filter has no capability to prevent water in the tank from passing through to the system.

88281P03

Fig. 44 A standard fuel injected engine in-line fuel filter—1990 F-150 shown

88281P04

Fig. 45 Remove the retaining clip and set in a safe place

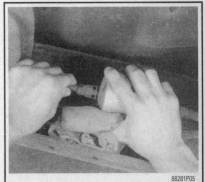

88281P05

Fig. 46 Use a shop towel to minimize fuel spillage when disconnecting the lines

Diesel Engines

The 6.9L and 7.3L diesel engines use a one-piece spin-on fuel filter. Do not add fuel to the new fuel filter. Allow the engine to draw fuel through the filter.

1. Remove the spin-on filter by unscrewing it counterclockwise with your hands or a strap wrench.
2. Clean the filter mounting surface.
3. Coat the gasket or the replacement filter with clean diesel fuel. This helps ensure a good seal.
4. Tighten the filter by hand until the gasket touches the filter mounting surface.
5. Tighten the filter an additional ½ turn.

➡ After changing the fuel filter, the engine will purge the trapped air as it runs. The engine may run roughly and smoke excessively until the air is cleared from the system.

PCV Valve

REMOVAL & INSTALLATION

Gasoline Engines Only

♦ See Figures 47, 48, 49 and 50

➡ Some models require the removal of the upper intake manifold in order to remove the PCV valve.

Check the PCV valve according to the Preventive Maintenance Schedule at the end of this section to see if it is free and not gummed up, stuck or blocked. To check the valve, remove it from the engine and work the valve by sticking a screwdriver in the crankcase side of the valve. It should move. It is possible to clean the PCV valve by soaking it in a solvent and blowing it out with compressed air. This can restore the valve to some level of operating order. This should be used only as an emergency measure. Otherwise the valve should be replaced.

1. Disconnect the oil separator hose from the PCV valve.
2. Remove the PCV valve from the grommet in the crankcase.
3. Inspect the grommet for deterioration.
To install:
4. If necessary, replace the crankcase grommet.
5. Install the PCV valve.
6. Install the hose.

Evaporative Canister

SERVICING

Gasoline Engines Only

The fuel evaporative emission control canister should be inspected for damage or leaks at the hose fittings every 24,000 miles. Repair or replace any old or cracked hoses. Replace the canister if it is damaged in any way. The canister is located under the hood, to the right of the engine.

For more detailed canister service, see Section 4.

Battery

GENERAL MAINTENANCE

All batteries, regardless of type, should be carefully secured by a battery hold-down device. If this is not done, the battery terminals or casing may crack from stress applied to the battery during vehicle operation. A battery which is not secured may allow acid to leak out, making it discharge faster; such leaking corrosive acid can also eat away components under the hood. A battery that is not sealed must be checked periodically for electrolyte level. You cannot add water to a sealed maintenance-free battery (though not all maintenance-free batteries are sealed), but a sealed battery must also be checked for proper electrolyte level as indicated by the color of the built-in hydrometer "eye."

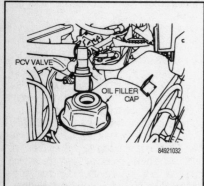

Fig. 47 PCV valve location—carbureted V8 engines

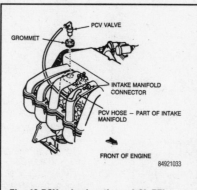

Fig. 48 PCV valve location—4.9L EFI engine

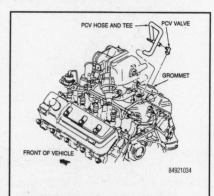

Fig. 49 PCV valve location—7.5L EFI engine

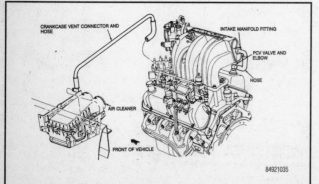

Fig. 50 PCV valve location—5.0L and 5.8L EFI engines

Keep the top of the battery clean, as a film of dirt can help completely discharge a battery that is not used for long periods. A solution of baking soda and water may be used for cleaning, but be careful to flush this off with clear water. DO NOT let any of the solution into the filler holes. Baking soda neutralizes battery acid and will deactivate a battery cell.

✳✳ CAUTION

Always use caution when working on or near the battery. Never allow a tool to bridge the gap between the negative and positive battery terminals. Also, be careful not to allow a tool to provide a ground between the positive cable/terminal and any metal component on the vehicle. Either of these conditions will cause a short circuit leading to sparks and possible personal injury.

Batteries in vehicles which are not operated on a regular basis can fall victim to parasitic loads (small current drains which are constantly drawing current from the battery). Normal parasitic loads may drain a battery on a vehicle that is in storage and not used for 6–8 weeks. Vehicles that have additional accessories such as a cellular phone, an alarm system or other devices that increase parasitic load may discharge a battery sooner. If the vehicle is to be stored for 6–8 weeks in a secure area and the alarm system, if present, is not necessary, the negative battery cable should be disconnected at the onset of storage to protect the battery charge.

Remember that constantly discharging and recharging will shorten battery life. Take care not to allow a battery to be needlessly discharged.

BATTERY FLUID

▶ See Figures 51, 52 and 53

✳✳ CAUTION

Battery electrolyte contains sulfuric acid. If you should splash any on your skin or in your eyes, flush the affected area with plenty of clear water. If it lands in your eyes, get medical help immediately.

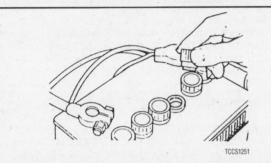

Fig. 51 On non-maintenance free batteries, the level can be checked through the case on translucent batteries; the cell caps must be removed on other models

Fig. 52 Check the specific gravity of the battery's electrolyte with a hydrometer

The fluid (sulfuric acid solution) contained in the battery cells will tell you many things about the condition of the battery. Because the cell plates must be kept submerged below the fluid level in order to operate, maintaining the fluid level is extremely important. And, because the specific gravity of the acid is an indication of electrical charge, testing the fluid can be an aid in determining if the battery must be replaced. A battery in a vehicle with a properly operating charging system should require little maintenance, but careful, periodic inspection should reveal problems before they leave you stranded.

Fluid Level

Check the battery electrolyte level at least once a month, or more often in hot weather or during periods of extended vehicle operation. On non-sealed batteries, the level can be checked either through the case on translucent batteries or by removing the cell caps on opaque-cased types. The electrolyte level in each cell should be kept filled to the split ring inside each cell, or the line marked on the outside of the case.

If the level is low, add only distilled water through the opening until the level is correct. Each cell is separate from the others, so each must be checked and filled individually. Distilled water should be used, because the chemicals and minerals found in most drinking water are harmful to the battery and could significantly shorten its life.

If water is added in freezing weather, the vehicle should be driven several miles to allow the water to mix with the electrolyte. Otherwise, the battery could freeze.

Although some maintenance-free batteries have removable cell caps for access to the electrolyte, the electrolyte condition and level on all sealed maintenance-free batteries must be checked using the built-in hydrometer "eye." The exact type of eye varies among battery manufacturers, but most apply a sticker to the battery itself explaining the possible readings. When in doubt, refer to the battery manufacturer's instructions to interpret battery condition using the built-in hydrometer.

➡**Although the readings from built-in hydrometers found in sealed batteries may vary, a green eye usually indicates a properly charged battery with sufficient fluid level. A dark eye is normally an indicator of a battery with sufficient fluid, but one which may be low in charge. And a light or yellow eye is usually an indication that electrolyte supply has dropped below the necessary level for battery (and hydrometer) operation. In this last case, sealed batteries with an insufficient electrolyte level must usually be discarded.**

Specific Gravity

As stated earlier, the specific gravity of a battery's electrolyte level can be used as an indication of battery charge. At least once a year, check the specific gravity of the battery. It should be between 1.20 and 1.26 on the gravity scale. Most auto supply stores carry a variety of inexpensive battery testing hydrometers. These can be used on any non-sealed battery to test the specific gravity in each cell.

The battery testing hydrometer has a squeeze bulb at one end and a nozzle at the other. Battery electrolyte is sucked into the hydrometer until the float is lifted from its seat. The specific gravity is then read by noting the position of the float. If gravity is low in one or more cells, the battery should be slowly charged and checked again to see if the gravity has come up. Generally, if after charging, the specific gravity between any two cells varies more than 50 points (0.50), the battery should be replaced as it can no longer produce sufficient voltage to guarantee proper operation.

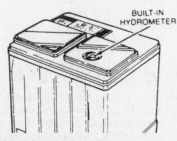

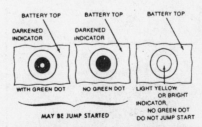

Check the appearance of the charge indicator on top of the battery before attempting a jump start; if it's not green or dark, do not jump start the car

Fig. 53 A typical sealed (maintenance-free) battery with a built-in hydrometer—NOTE that the hydrometer eye may vary among battery manufacturers; always refer to the battery's label

On sealed batteries, the built-in hydrometer is the only way of checking specific gravity. Again, check with your battery's manufacturer for proper interpretation of its built-in hydrometer readings.

CABLES

▶ **See Figures 54, 55, 56, 57 and 58**

Once a year (or as necessary), the battery terminals and the cable clamps should be cleaned. Loosen the clamps and remove the cables, negative cable first. On batteries with posts on top, the use of a puller specially made for this purpose is recommended. These are inexpensive and available in most auto parts stores. Side terminal battery cables are secured with a small bolt.

Clean the cable clamps and the battery terminal with a wire brush, until all corrosion, grease, etc., is removed and the metal is shiny. It is especially important to clean the inside of the clamp (an old knife is useful here) thoroughly, since a small deposit of foreign material or oxidation there will prevent a sound electrical connection and inhibit either starting or charging. Special tools are available for cleaning these parts, one type for conventional top post batteries and another type for side terminal batteries.

Before installing the cables, loosen the battery hold-down clamp or strap, remove the battery and check the battery tray. Clear it of any debris, and check it for soundness (the battery tray can be cleaned with a baking soda and water solution). Rust should be wire brushed away, and the metal given a couple coats of anti-rust paint. Install the battery and tighten the hold-down clamp or strap securely. Do not overtighten, as this can crack the battery case.

After the clamps and terminals are clean, reinstall the cables, negative cable last; DO NOT hammer the clamps onto post batteries. Tighten the clamps securely, but do not distort them. Give the clamps and terminals a thin external coating of grease after installation, to retard corrosion.

Check the cables at the same time that the terminals are cleaned. If the cable insulation is cracked or broken, or if the ends are frayed, the cable should be replaced with a new cable of the same length and gauge.

CHARGING

A battery should be charged at a slow rate to keep the plates inside from getting too hot. However, if some maintenance-free batteries are allowed to discharge until they are almost "dead," they may have to be charged at a high rate to bring them back to "life." Always follow the charger manufacturer's instructions on charging the battery.

REPLACEMENT

When it becomes necessary to replace the battery, select one with a rating equal to or greater than the battery originally installed. Deterioration and just plain aging of the battery cables, starter motor, and associated wires makes the battery's job harder in successive years. The slow increase in electrical resistance over time makes it prudent to install a new battery with a greater capacity than the old.

Belts

INSPECTION

▶ **See Figures 59, 60, 61, 62 and 63**

Inspect the belts for signs of glazing or cracking. A glazed belt will be perfectly smooth from slippage, while a good belt will have a slight texture of fabric

Fig. 54 Maintenance is performed with household items and with special tools like this post cleaner

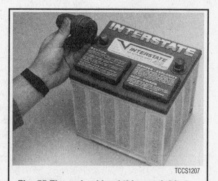

Fig. 55 The underside of this special battery tool has a wire brush to clean post terminals

Fig. 56 Place the tool over the terminals and twist to clean the post

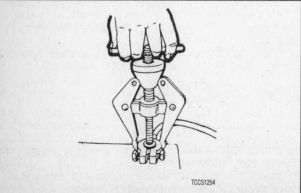

Fig. 57 A special tool is available to pull the clamp from the post

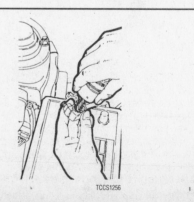

Fig. 58 The cable ends should be cleaned as well

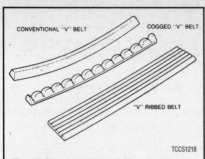

Fig. 59 There are typically 3 types of accessory drive belts found on vehicles today

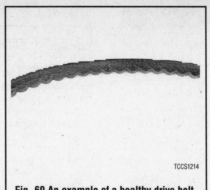

Fig. 60 An example of a healthy drive belt

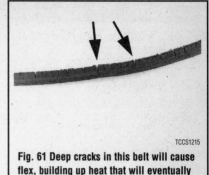

Fig. 61 Deep cracks in this belt will cause flex, building up heat that will eventually lead to belt failure

Fig. 62 The cover of this belt is worn, exposing the critical reinforcing cords to excessive wear

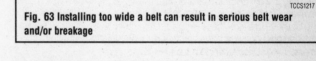

Fig. 63 Installing too wide a belt can result in serious belt wear and/or breakage

visible. Cracks will usually start at the inner edge of the belt and run outward. All worn or damaged drive belts should be replaced immediately. It is best to replace all drive belts at one time, as a preventive maintenance measure, during this service operation.

ADJUSTMENT—EXCEPT SERPENTINE BELT

Alternator (Fan Drive) Belt

1. Position the ruler perpendicular to the drive belt at its longest straight run. Test the tightness of the belt by pressing it firmly with your thumb. The deflection should not exceed ¼ in. (6mm).
2. If the deflection exceeds ¼ in. (6mm), loosen the alternator mounting and adjusting arm bolts.
3. Place a 1 in. open-end or adjustable wrench on the adjusting ridge cast on the body, and pull on the wrench until the proper tension is achieved.
4. Holding the alternator in place to maintain tension, tighten the adjusting arm bolt. Recheck the belt tension. When the belt is properly tensioned, tighten the alternator mounting bolt.

Power Steering Drive Belt

4.9L ENGINE

1. Hold a ruler perpendicularly to the drive belt at its longest run, test the tightness of the belt by pressing it firmly with your thumb. The deflection should not exceed ¼ in. (6mm).
2. To adjust the belt tension, loosen the adjusting and mounting bolts on the front face of the steering pump cover plate (hub side).
3. Using a pry bar or broom handle on the pump hub, move the power steering pump toward or away from the engine until the proper tension is reached. Do not pry against the reservoir as it is relatively soft and easily deformed.
4. Holding the pump in place, tighten the adjusting arm bolt and then recheck the belt tension. When the belt is properly tensioned tighten the mounting bolts.

V8 MODELS

1. Position a ruler perpendicular to the drive belt at its longest run. Test the tightness of the belt by pressing it firmly with your thumb. The deflection should be about ¼ in. (6mm).
2. To adjust the belt tension, loosen the three bolts in the three elongated adjusting slots at the power steering pump attaching bracket.
3. Turn the steering pump drive belt adjusting nut as required until the proper deflection is obtained. Turning the adjusting nut clockwise will increase tension and decrease deflection; counterclockwise will decrease tension and increase deflection.
4. Without disturbing the pump, tighten the three attaching bolts.

Air Conditioning Compressor Drive Belt

1. Position a ruler perpendicular to the drive belt at its longest run. Test the tightness of the belt by pressing it firmly with your thumb. The deflection should not exceed ¼ in. (6mm).
2. If the engine is equipped with an idler pulley, loosen the idler pulley adjusting bolt, insert a pry bar between the pulley and the engine (or in the idler pulley adjusting slot), and adjust the tension accordingly. If the engine is not equipped with an idler pulley, the alternator must be moved to accomplish this adjustment, as outlined under Alternator (Fan Drive) Belt.
3. When the proper tension is reached, tighten the idler pulley adjusting bolt (if so equipped) or the alternator adjusting and mounting bolts.

Thermactor® Air Pump Drive Belt

1. Position a ruler perpendicular to the drive belt at its longest run. Test the tightness of the belt by pressing it firmly with your thumb. The deflection should be about ¼ in. (6mm).
2. To adjust the belt tension, loosen the adjusting arm bolt slightly. If necessary, also loosen the mounting belt slightly.
3. Using a pry bar or broom handle, pry against the pump rear cover to move the pump toward or away from the engine as necessary.

❊❊ CAUTION

Do not pry against the pump housing itself, as damage to the housing may result.

4. Holding the pump in place, tighten the adjusting arm bolt and recheck the tension. When the belt is properly tensioned, tighten the mounting bolt.

ADJUSTMENT—SERPENTINE (SINGLE) BELT

▶ **See Figures 64, 65, 66, 67 and 68**

Most models feature a single, wide, ribbed V-belt that drives the water pump, alternator, and (on some models) the air conditioner compressor. The spring powered tensioner eliminates the need for periodic adjustments.

REMOVAL & INSTALLATION—EXCEPT SERPENTINE BELT

Alternator (Fan Drive) Belt

▶ **See Figures 69, 70 and 71**

1. Remove any component or belt that obstructs the removal of the alternator belt, if applicable.
2. Loosen the alternator mounting and adjusting arm bolts to allow sufficient slack in the belt.
3. Remove the alternator belt.

To install:

4. Install the alternator belt on the pulleys.
5. Holding the alternator in place to maintain tension, tighten the adjusting arm bolt. Recheck the belt tension. When the belt is properly tensioned, tighten the alternator mounting bolt.
6. Install any component or belt that was removed to allow this procedure.

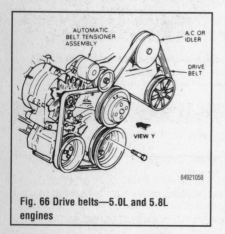

Fig. 64 Belt removal instructions (and routing information) may be found on a sticker under the hood

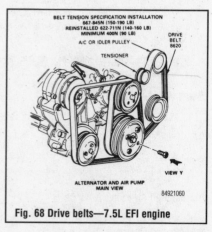

Fig. 65 Drive belts—4.9L EFI engine

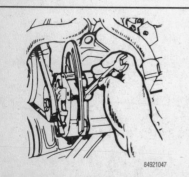

Fig. 66 Drive belts—5.0L and 5.8L engines

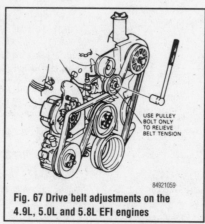

Fig. 67 Drive belt adjustments on the 4.9L, 5.0L and 5.8L EFI engines

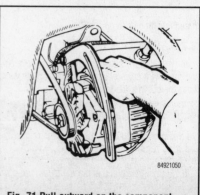

Fig. 68 Drive belts—7.5L EFI engine

Fig. 69 To adjust belt tension or to change belts, first loosen the component's mounting and adjusting bolts slightly

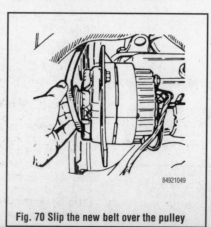

Fig. 70 Slip the new belt over the pulley

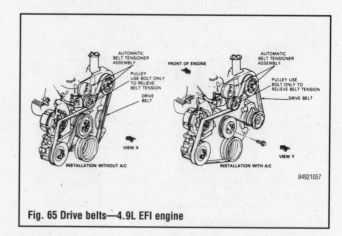

Fig. 71 Pull outward on the component and tighten the mounting bolts

Power Steering Drive Belt

4.9L ENGINE

1. Remove any component or belt that obstructs the removal of the power steering drive belt, if applicable.
2. Loosen the adjusting and mounting bolts on the front face of the steering pump cover plate (hub side).
3. Remove the power steering drive belt.

To install:

4. Install the power steering drive belt.
5. Using a pry bar or broom handle on the pump hub, move the power steering pump toward or away from the engine until the proper tension is reached. Do not pry against the reservoir as it is relatively soft and easily deformed.
6. Holding the pump in place, tighten the adjusting arm bolt and then recheck the belt tension. When the belt is properly tensioned tighten the mounting bolts.
7. Install any component or belt that was removed to allow this procedure.

V8 MODELS

1. Remove any component or belt that obstructs the removal of the power steering drive belt, if applicable.
2. Loosen the three bolts in the three elongated adjusting slots at the power steering pump attaching bracket.
3. Remove the power steering drive belt.

To install:

4. Install the power steering drive belt.
5. Turn the steering pump drive belt adjusting nut as required until the proper deflection is obtained. Turning the adjusting nut clockwise will increase tension and decrease deflection; counterclockwise will decrease tension and increase deflection.
6. Without disturbing the pump, tighten the three attaching bolts.
7. Install any component or belt that was removed to allow this procedure.

Air Conditioning Compressor Drive Belt

1. Remove any component or belt that obstructs the removal of the air conditioning compressor belt, if applicable.
2. If the engine is equipped with an idler pulley, loosen the idler pulley adjusting bolt.
3. Remove the air conditioning compressor belt.

To install:

4. Install the air conditioning compressor belt.
5. Insert a pry bar between the pulley and the engine (or in the idler pulley adjusting slot), and adjust the tension accordingly. If the engine is not equipped with an idler pulley, the alternator must be moved to accomplish this adjustment, as outlined under Alternator (Fan Drive) Belt.
6. When the proper tension is reached, tighten the idler pulley adjusting bolt (if so equipped) or the alternator adjusting and mounting bolts.
7. Install any component or belt that was removed to allow this procedure.

Thermactor® Air Pump Drive Belt

1. Remove any component or belt that obstructs the removal of the air conditioning compressor belt, if applicable.
2. Loosen the adjusting arm bolt slightly. If necessary, also loosen the mounting belt slightly.
3. Remove the Thermactor® air pump drive belt.

To install:

4. Install the Thermactor® air pump drive belt.
5. Using a pry bar or broom handle, pry against the pump rear cover to move the pump toward or away from the engine as necessary.

❋❋ CAUTION

Do not pry against the pump housing itself, as damage to the housing may result.

6. Holding the pump in place, tighten the adjusting arm bolt and recheck the tension. When the belt is properly tensioned, tighten the mounting bolt.
7. Install any component or belt that was removed to allow this procedure.

REMOVAL & INSTALLATION—SERPENTINE (SINGLE) BELT

▶ See Figure 72

The serpentine belt drives the water pump, alternator, and (on some models) the air conditioner compressor.

❋❋ WARNING

Check to make sure that the V-ribbed belt is located properly in all drive pulleys before applying tensioner pressure.

1. Loosen the bracket lock bolt, retract the belt tensioner with a pry bar and slide the old belt off of the pulleys.

To install:

➡**The spring powered tensioner automatically adjusts the belt to the proper tension.**

2. Install the belt and release the tensioner. Tighten the lockbolt.

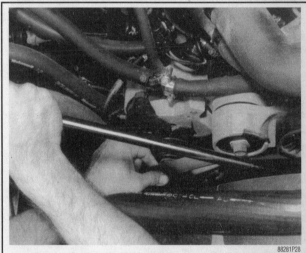

88281P28

Fig. 72 Pry back the serpentine belt tensioner and remove the belt from the pulleys

Hoses

INSPECTION

▶ See Figures 73, 74, 75 and 76

Upper and lower radiator hoses along with the heater hoses should be checked for deterioration, leaks and loose hose clamps at least every 15,000 miles (24,000 km). It is also wise to check the hoses periodically in early spring

TCCS1219

Fig. 73 The cracks developing along this hose are a result of age-related hardening

Fig. 74 A hose clamp that is too tight can cause older hoses to separate and tear on either side of the clamp

TCCS1220

Fig. 75 A soft spongy hose (identifiable by the swollen section) will eventually burst and should be replaced

TCCS1221

Fig. 76 Hoses are likely to deteriorate from the inside if the cooling system is not periodically flushed

TCCS1222

and at the beginning of the fall or winter when you are performing other maintenance. A quick visual inspection could discover a weakened hose which might have left you stranded if it had remained unrepaired.

Whenever you are checking the hoses, make sure the engine and cooling system are cold. Visually inspect for cracking, rotting or collapsed hoses, and replace as necessary. Run your hand along the length of the hose. If a weak or swollen spot is noted when squeezing the hose wall, the hose should be replaced.

REMOVAL & INSTALLATION

1. Remove the radiator pressure cap.

❊❊ CAUTION

Never remove the pressure cap while the engine is running, or personal injury from scalding hot coolant or steam may result. If possible, wait until the engine has cooled to remove the pressure cap. If this is not possible, wrap a thick cloth around the pressure cap and turn it slowly to the stop. Step back while the pressure is released from the cooling system. When you are sure all the pressure has been released, use the cloth to turn and remove the cap.

2. Position a clean container under the radiator and/or engine draincock or plug, then open the drain and allow the cooling system to drain to an appropriate level. For some upper hoses, only a little coolant must be drained. To remove hoses positioned lower on the engine, such as a lower radiator hose, the entire cooling system must be emptied.

❊❊ CAUTION

When draining coolant, keep in mind that cats and dogs are attracted by ethylene glycol antifreeze, and are quite likely to drink any that is left in an uncovered container or in puddles on the ground. This will prove fatal in sufficient quantity. Always drain coolant into a sealable container. Coolant may be reused unless it is contaminated or several years old.

3. Loosen the hose clamps at each end of the hose requiring replacement. Clamps are usually either of the spring tension type (which require pliers to squeeze the tabs and loosen) or of the screw tension type (which require screw or hex drivers to loosen). Pull the clamps back on the hose away from the connection.

4. Twist, pull and slide the hose off the fitting, taking care not to damage the neck of the component from which the hose is being removed.

➡**If the hose is stuck at the connection, do not try to insert a screwdriver or other sharp tool under the hose end in an effort to free it, as the connection and/or hose may become damaged. Heater connections especially may be easily damaged by such a procedure. If the hose is to be replaced, use a single-edged razor blade to make a slice along the portion of the hose which is stuck on the connection, perpendicular to the end of the hose. Do not cut too deep to prevent damaging the connection. The hose can then be peeled from the connection and discarded.**

5. Clean both hose mounting connections. Inspect the condition of the hose clamps and replace them, if necessary.
To install:
6. Dip the ends of the new hose into clean engine coolant to ease installation.

7. Slide the clamps over the replacement hose, then slide the hose ends over the connections into position.

8. Position and secure the clamps at least ¼ in. (6.35mm) from the ends of the hose. Make sure they are located beyond the raised bead of the connector.

9. Close the radiator or engine drains and properly refill the cooling system with the clean drained engine coolant or a suitable mixture of ethylene glycol coolant and water.

10. If available, install a pressure tester and check for leaks. If a pressure tester is not available, run the engine until normal operating temperature is reached (allowing the system to naturally pressurize), then check for leaks.

❊❊ CAUTION

If you are checking for leaks with the system at normal operating temperature, BE EXTREMELY CAREFUL not to touch any moving or hot engine parts. Once temperature has been reached, shut the engine OFF, and check for leaks around the hose fittings and connections which were removed earlier.

CV-Boots

INSPECTION

◗ **See Figures 77 and 78**

The CV (Constant Velocity) boots should be checked for damage each time the oil is changed and any other time the vehicle is raised for service. These boots keep water, grime, dirt and other damaging matter from entering the CV-joints. Any of these could cause early CV-joint failure which can be expensive to

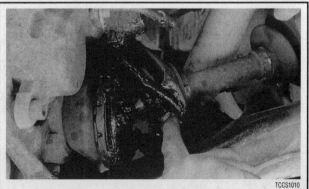

TCCS1010

Fig. 77 CV-boots must be inspected periodically for damage

Fig. 78 A torn boot should be replaced immediately

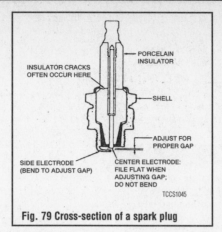

Fig. 79 Cross-section of a spark plug

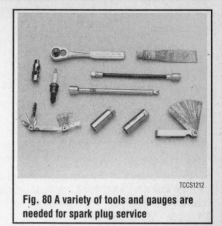

Fig. 80 A variety of tools and gauges are needed for spark plug service

repair. Heavy grease thrown around the inside of the front wheel(s) and on the brake caliper/drum can be an indication of a torn boot. Thoroughly check the boots for missing clamps and tears. If the boot is damaged, it should be replaced immediately. Please refer to Section 7 for procedures.

Spark Plugs

▶ See Figures 79 and 80

A typical spark plug consists of a metal shell surrounding a ceramic insulator. A metal electrode extends downward through the center of the insulator and protrudes a small distance. Located at the end of the plug and attached to the side of the outer metal shell is the side electrode. The side electrode bends in at a 90⁻ angle so that its tip is just past and parallel to the tip of the center electrode. The distance between these two electrodes (measured in thousandths of an inch or hundredths of a millimeter) is called the spark plug gap.

The spark plug does not produce a spark, but instead provides a gap across which the current can arc. The coil produces anywhere from 20,000 to 50,000 volts (depending on the type and application) which travels through the wires to the spark plugs. The current passes along the center electrode and jumps the gap to the side electrode, and in doing so, ignites the air/fuel mixture in the combustion chamber.

SPARK PLUG HEAT RANGE

▶ See Figure 81

Spark plug heat range is the ability of the plug to dissipate heat. The longer the insulator (or the farther it extends into the engine), the hotter the plug will operate; the shorter the insulator (the closer the electrode is to the block's cooling passages) the cooler it will operate. A plug that absorbs little heat and remains too cool will quickly accumulate deposits of oil and carbon since it is not hot enough to burn them off. This leads to plug fouling and consequently to misfiring. A plug that absorbs too much heat will have no deposits but, due to the excessive heat, the electrodes will burn away quickly and might possibly

lead to preignition or other ignition problems. Preignition takes place when plug tips get so hot that they glow sufficiently to ignite the air/fuel mixture before the actual spark occurs. This early ignition will usually cause a pinging during low speeds and heavy loads.

The general rule of thumb for choosing the correct heat range when picking a spark plug is: if most of your driving is long distance, high speed travel, use a colder plug; if most of your driving is stop and go, use a hotter plug. Original equipment plugs are generally a good compromise between the 2 styles and most people never have the need to change their plugs from the factory-recommended heat range.

REMOVAL & INSTALLATION

▶ See Figures 82 and 83

A set of spark plugs usually requires replacement after about 20,000–30,000 miles (32,000–48,000 km), depending on your style of driving. In normal operation plug gap increases about 0.001 in. (0.025mm) for every 2500 miles (4000 km). As the gap increases, the plug's voltage requirement also increases. It requires a greater voltage to jump the wider gap and about two to three times as much voltage to fire the plug at high speeds than at idle. The improved air/fuel ratio control of modern fuel injection combined with the higher voltage output of modern ignition systems will often allow an engine to run significantly longer on a set of standard spark plugs, but keep in mind that efficiency will drop as the gap widens (along with fuel economy and power).

When you're removing spark plugs, work on one at a time. Don't start by removing the plug wires all at once, because, unless you number them, they may become mixed up. Take a minute before you begin and number the wires with tape.

1. Disconnect the negative battery cable, and if the vehicle has been run recently, allow the engine to thoroughly cool.

2. Carefully twist the spark plug wire boot to loosen it, then pull upward and remove the boot from the plug. Be sure to pull on the boot and not on the wire, otherwise the connector located inside the boot may become separated.

3. Using compressed air, blow any water or debris from the spark plug well to assure that no harmful contaminants are allowed to enter the combustion

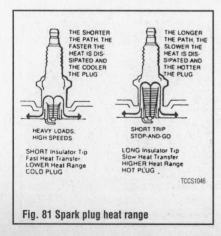

Fig. 81 Spark plug heat range

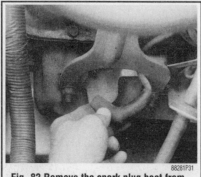

Fig. 82 Remove the spark plug boot from the plug—pull the boot, do not pull on the wire itself

Fig. 83 Remove the spark plug for inspection or replacement

chamber when the spark plug is removed. If compressed air is not available, use a rag or a brush to clean the area.

→Remove the spark plugs when the engine is cold, if possible, to prevent damage to the threads. If removal of the plugs is difficult, apply a few drops of penetrating oil or silicone spray to the area around the base of the plug, and allow it a few minutes to work.

4. Using a spark plug socket that is equipped with a rubber insert to properly hold the plug, turn the spark plug counterclockwise to loosen and remove the spark plug from the bore.

✳✳ WARNING

Be sure not to use a flexible extension on the socket. Use of a flexible extension may allow a shear force to be applied to the plug. A shear force could break the plug off in the cylinder head, leading to costly and frustrating repairs.

To install:

5. Inspect the spark plug boot for tears or damage. If a damaged boot is found, the spark plug wire must be replaced.

6. Using a wire feeler gauge, check and adjust the spark plug gap. When using a gauge, the proper size should pass between the electrodes with a slight drag. The next larger size should not be able to pass while the next smaller size should pass freely.

7. Carefully thread the plug into the bore by hand. If resistance is felt before the plug is almost completely threaded, back the plug out and begin threading again. In small, hard to reach areas, an old spark plug wire and boot could be used as a threading tool. The boot will hold the plug while you twist the end of the wire and the wire is supple enough to twist before it would allow the plug to crossthread.

✳✳ WARNING

Do not use the spark plug socket to thread the plugs. Always carefully thread the plug by hand or using an old plug wire boot to prevent the possibility of crossthreading and damaging the cylinder head.

8. Carefully tighten the spark plug. If the plug you are installing is equipped with a crush washer, seat the plug, then tighten about ¼ turn to crush the washer. If you are installing a tapered seat plug, tighten the plug to specifications provided by the vehicle or plug manufacturer.

9. Apply a small amount of silicone dielectric compound to the end of the spark plug lead or inside the spark plug boot to prevent sticking, then install the boot to the spark plug and push until it clicks into place. The click may be felt or heard, then gently pull back on the boot to assure proper contact.

INSPECTION & GAPPING

▶ See Figures 84, 85, 86 and 87

Check the plugs for deposits and wear. If they are not going to be replaced, clean the plugs thoroughly. Remember that any kind of deposit will decrease

the efficiency of the plug. Plugs can be cleaned on a spark plug cleaning machine, which can sometimes be found in service stations, or you can do an acceptable job of cleaning with a stiff brush. If the plugs are cleaned, the electrodes must be filed flat. Use an ignition points file, not an emery board or the like, which will leave deposits. The electrodes must be filed perfectly flat with sharp edges; rounded edges reduce the spark plug voltage by as much as 50%.

Check spark plug gap before installation. The ground electrode (the L-shaped one connected to the body of the plug) must be parallel to the center electrode and the specified size wire gauge (please refer to the Tune-Up Specifications chart for details) must pass between the electrodes with a slight drag.

→NEVER adjust the gap on a used platinum type spark plug.

Always check the gap on new plugs as they are not always set correctly at the factory. Do not use a flat feeler gauge when measuring the gap on a used plug, because the reading may be inaccurate. A round-wire type gapping tool is the best way to check the gap. The correct gauge should pass through the electrode gap with a slight drag. If you're in doubt, try one size smaller and one larger. The smaller gauge should go through easily, while the larger one shouldn't go through at all. Wire gapping tools usually have a bending tool attached. Use that to adjust the side electrode until the proper distance is obtained. Absolutely never attempt to bend the center electrode. Also, be careful not to bend the side electrode too far or too often as it may weaken and break off within the engine, requiring removal of the cylinder head to retrieve it.

Spark Plug Wires

TESTING

▶ See Figures 88 and 89

At every tune-up/inspection, visually check the spark plug cables for burns, cuts, or breaks in the insulation. Check the boots and the nipples on the distributor cap and/or coil. Replace any damaged wiring.

Every 50,000 miles (80,000 Km) or 60 months, the resistance of the wires should be checked with an ohmmeter. Wires with excessive resistance will cause misfiring, and may make the engine difficult to start in damp weather.

To check resistance, an ohmmeter should be used on each wire to test resistance between the end connectors. Remove and install/replace the wires in order, one-by-one.

Resistance on these wires must not exceed 5,000ω per foot. To properly measure this, remove the wires from the plugs, and remove the distributor cap. Measure the resistance through the distributor cap at that end. Do not pierce any ignition wire for any reason. Measure only from the two ends.

→Whenever the high tension wires are removed from the plugs, coil, or distributor, silicone grease must be applied to the boot before reconnection. Use a clean small screwdriver blade to coat the entire interior surface with Ford silicone grease D7AZ–19A331–A, Dow Corning #111, or General Electric G–627.

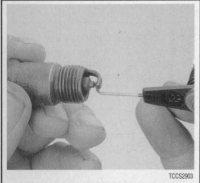

TCCS2903

Fig. 84 Checking the spark plug gap with a feeler gauge

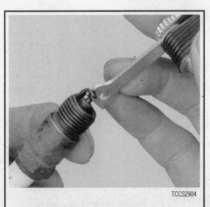

TCCS2904

Fig. 85 Adjusting the spark plug gap

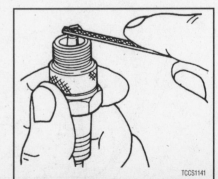

TCCS1141

Fig. 86 If the standard plug is in good condition, the electrode may be filed flat—WARNING: do not file platinum plugs

A normally worn spark plug should have light tan or gray deposits on the firing tip.

A carbon fouled plug, identified by soft, sooty, black deposits, may indicate an improperly tuned vehicle. Check the air cleaner, ignition components and engine control system.

This spark plug has been **left in the engine too long,** as evidenced by the extreme gap- Plugs with such an extreme gap can cause misfiring and stumbling accompanied by a noticeable lack of power.

An oil fouled spark plug indicates an engine with worn poston rings and/or bad valve seals allowing excessive oil to enter the chamber.

A physically damaged spark plug may be evidence of severe detonation in that cylinder. Watch that cylinder carefully between services, as a continued detonation will not only damage the plug, but could also damage the engine.

A bridged or almost bridged spark plug, identified by a build-up between the electrodes caused by excessive carbon or oil build-up on the plug.

TCCA1P40

Fig. 87 Inspect the spark plug to determine engine running conditions

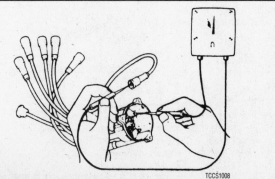
TCCS1008

Fig. 88 Checking plug wire resistance through the distributor cap with an ohmmeter

REMOVAL & INSTALLATION

1. If the wires are to be re-used, label all the wires prior to removal.
2. If the wires are being replaced, remove and replace them one-by-one.
3. In all cases, use a spark plug removal tool to grasp the protective boot at the connector. Do not pull on the wires. Grasp and twist the boot to remove the wire.

➡ **Whenever the high tension wires are removed from the plugs, coil, or distributor, silicone grease must be applied to the boot before reconnection. Use a clean small screwdriver blade to coat the entire interior surface with Ford silicone grease D7AZ–19A331–A, Dow Corning #111, or General Electric G–627.**

Fig. 89 Checking individual plug wire resistance with a digital ohmmeter

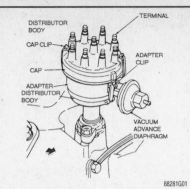

Fig. 90 Distributor assembly. Arrow points to front

Fig. 91 Mark the cap, if necessary to take the guesswork out of reinstallation

Distributor Cap and Rotor

REMOVAL

Carbureted Engines (DuraSpark II)

▶ See Figures 90 and 91

1. Remove the air cleaner assembly, taking note of the hose locations.
2. Disconnect the distributor wiring connector from the vehicle wiring harness.
3. Noting the position of the vacuum line(s) on the distributor diaphragm, disconnect the lines at the diaphragm. Unsnap the two distributor cap retaining clamps and remove the cap, rotor and adapter.

Fuel Injected Engines (TFI-IV Systems)

1. Disconnect the primary wiring connector from the distributor.
2. Mark the position of the cap's No. 1 terminal on the distributor base.
3. Unclip and remove the cap. Remove the adapter.
4. Remove the rotor.

INSTALLATION—CRANKSHAFT OR CAMSHAFT NOT ROTATED

Carbureted Engines (DuraSpark II)

1. Install the distributor cap and wires.
2. Connect the distributor wiring connector to the wiring harness. Tighten the hold-down bolt.
3. Install the air cleaner, if removed.

Fuel Injected Engines (TFI-IV Systems)

To install:
1. Install the rotor.

➡ Coat the brass portions of the rotor with a 1/32 in. (0.8mm) thick coating of silicone dielectric compound.

2. Install the cap and adapter (as necessary). Install the wires and start the engine.

INSTALLATION—CRANKSHAFT OR CAMSHAFT ROTATED

Carbureted Engines (DuraSpark II)

If the engine is cranked (disturbed) with the distributor removed, it will now be necessary to re-time the engine.
1. Rotate the engine so that No. 1 piston is at TDC of the compression stroke.
2. Align the timing marks to the correct initial timing shown on the underhood decal.

3. Install the distributor with the rotor in the No. 1 firing position and any armature pole aligned with the stator pole.

➡ Make sure that the oil pump intermediate shaft properly engages the distributor shaft. It may be necessary to crank the engine after the distributor gear is partially engaged in order to engage the oil pump intermediate shaft and fully seat the distributor in the block.

4. If it was necessary to rotate the engine to align the oil pump, repeat Steps 1, 2 and 3.
5. Install the hold-down bolt finger-tight.
6. Install the distributor cap and wires.
7. Connect the distributor wiring connector to the wiring harness. Tighten the hold-down bolt.
8. Install the air cleaner, if removed.
9. Check the ignition timing, as outlined later in this section.
10. When everything is set, tighten the hold-down bolt to 25 ft. lbs. (34 Nm).

Fuel Injected Engines (TFI-IV Systems)

If the engine is cranked (disturbed) with the distributor removed, it will now be necessary to re-time the engine.
1. Rotate the engine so that No. 1 piston is at TDC of the compression stroke.
2. Align the timing marks to the correct initial timing shown on the underhood decal.
3. Install the rotor on the shaft and rotate the shaft so that the rotor tip points to the No. 1 mark made on the distributor base.
4. Continue rotating the shaft so that the leading edge of the vane is centered on the vane switch assembly.
5. Position the distributor in the block and rotate the distributor body to align the leading edge of the vane and vane switch. Verify that the rotor tip points to the No. 1 mark on the body.
6. Install and finger-tighten the hold-down bolt.
7. Connect the TFI and primary wiring.
8. Install the rotor, if not already done.
9. Install the cap and adapter (as necessary). Install the wires and start the engine.
10. Check and set the initial timing.
11. Tighten the hold-down bolt to 25 ft. lbs. (34 Nm).

INSPECTION

1. Remove the distributor cap and rotor.
2. Wash the inside and outside of the cap and wash the rotor with soap and water, then dry them thoroughly with compressed air or a lint-free cloth.
3. Look closely at the distributor cap, inspecting it for signs of deterioration such as cracks, broken carbon button or carbon tracks.
4. Inspect the terminals for dirt or corrosion.
5. Inspect the rotor for carbon build-up, cracks or damage to the blade or spring.
6. If damage is found, replace the distributor cap and/or rotor.

Ignition Timing

GENERAL INFORMATION

Ignition timing is the measurement, in degrees of crankshaft rotation, of the point at which the spark plugs fire in each of the cylinders. It is measured in degrees before or after Top Dead Center (TDC) of the compression stroke.

Ideally, the air/fuel mixture in the cylinder will be ignited by the spark plug just as the piston passes TDC of the compression stroke. If this happens, the piston will be beginning the power stroke just as the compressed and ignited air/fuel mixture starts to expand. The expansion of the air/fuel mixture then forces the piston down on the power stroke and turns the crankshaft.

Because it takes a fraction of a second for the spark plug to ignite the mixture in the cylinder, the spark plug must fire a little before the piston reaches TDC. Otherwise, the mixture will not be completely ignited as the piston passes TDC and the full power of the explosion will not be used by the engine.

The timing measurement is given in degrees of crankshaft rotation before the piston reaches TDC (BTDC, or Before Top Dead Center). If the setting for the ignition timing is 5°BTDC, each spark plug must fire 5° before each piston reaches TDC. This only holds true, however, when the engine is at idle speed.

As the engine speed increases, the piston go faster. The spark plugs have to ignite the fuel even sooner if it is to be completely ignited when the piston reaches TDC.

With the Dura Spark II system, the distributor has a means to advance the timing of the spark as the engine speed increases. This is accomplished by centrifugal weights within the distributor and a vacuum diaphragm mounted on the side of the distributor. It is necessary to disconnect the vacuum lines from the diaphragm when the ignition timing is being set.

With the TFI-IV system, ignition timing is calculated at all phases of vehicle operation by the TFI module.

If the ignition is set too far advanced (BTDC), the ignition and expansion of the fuel in the cylinder will occur too soon and tend to force the piston down while it is still traveling up. This causes engine ping. If the ignition spark is set too far retarded after TDC (ATDC), the piston will have already passed TDC and started on its way down when the fuel is ignited. This will cause the piston to be forced down for only a portion of its travel. This will result in poor engine performance and lack of power.

The timing must be checked with a timing light. This device is connected in series with the No. 1 spark plug. The current that fires the spark plug also causes the timing light to flash.

There is a notch on the crankshaft pulley on 6-cylinder engines. A scale of degrees of crankshaft rotation is attached to the engine block in such a position that the notch will pass close by the scale.

On V8 engines, the scale is located on the crankshaft pulley and a pointer is attached to the engine block so that the scale will pass close by. When the engine is running, the timing light is aimed at the mark on the crankshaft pulley and the scale.

INSPECTION AND ADJUSTMENT

Dura Spark II Systems

With the Dura Spark II system, only an initial timing adjustment is possible. Ignition timing is not considered to be a part of tune-up or routine maintenance.

To inspect the adjustment, perform the following:
1. Locate the timing marks on the crankshaft pulley and the front of the engine.
2. Clean the timing marks so that you can see them.
3. Mark the timing marks with a piece of chalk or with paint. Color the mark on the scale that will indicate the correct timing when it is aligned with the mark on the pulley or the pointer. It is also helpful to mark the notch in the pulley or the tip of the pointer with a small dab of color.
4. Attach a tachometer to the engine.
5. Attach a timing light according to the manufacturer's instructions. If the timing light has three wires, one is attached to the No. 1 spark plug with an adapter. The other wires are connected to the battery. The red wire goes to the positive side of the battery and the black wire is connected to the negative terminal of the battery.
6. Disconnect the vacuum line to the distributor at the distributor and plug the vacuum line. A golf tee does a fine job.

7. Check to make sure that all of the wires clear the fan and then start the engine.
8. Adjust the idle to the correct setting.
9. Aim the timing light at the timing marks. If the marks that you put on the flywheel or pulley and the engine are aligned with the light flashes, the timing is correct. Turn off the engine and remove the tachometer and the timing light. If the mark are not in alignment, replace the ignition module.

TFI-IV System

With the TFI-IV system no ignition timing adjustment is possible and none should be attempted.

Valve Lash Adjustment

Valve adjustment determines how far the valves enter the cylinder and how long they stay open and closed.

If the valve clearance is too large, part of the lift of the camshaft will be used in removing the excessive clearance. Consequently, the valve will not be opening as far as it should. This condition has two effects: the valve train components will emit a tapping sound as they take up the excessive clearance and the engine will perform poorly because the valves don't open fully and allow the proper amount of gases to flow into and out of the engine.

If the valve clearance is too small, the intake valve and the exhaust valves will open too far and they will not fully seal on the cylinder head when they close. When a valve seats itself on the cylinder head, it does two things: it seals the combustion chamber so that none of the gases in the cylinder escape and it cools itself by transferring some of the heat it absorbs from the combustion in the cylinder to the cylinder head and to the engine's cooling system. If the valve clearance is too small, the engine will run poorly because of the gases escaping from the combustion chamber. The valves will also become overheated and will warp, since they cannot transfer heat unless they are touching the valve seat in the cylinder head.

➡**While all valve adjustments must be made as accurately as possible, it is better to have the valve adjustment slightly loose than slightly tight as a burned valve may result from overly tight adjustments.**

4.9L ENGINE

◆ See Figures 92 and 93

1. Rotate the crankshaft by hand so that No. 1 piston is at TDC of the compression stroke. Make a chalk mark on the damper at that point, then, make 2 more chalk marks about 120° apart, dividing the damper into 3 equal parts.
2. With No. 1 at TDC, tighten the rocker arm bolts on No. 1 cylinder intake and exhaust to 17–23 ft. lbs. (23–31 Nm). Then, slowly apply pressure, using

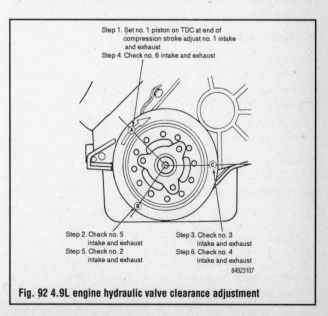

Fig. 92 4.9L engine hydraulic valve clearance adjustment

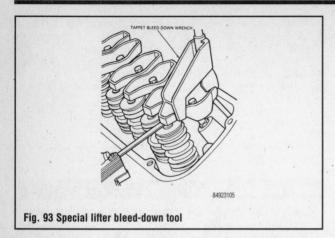

Fig. 93 Special lifter bleed-down tool

Lifter Bleed-down wrench T70P-6513-A, or equivalent, to completely bottom the lifter. Take care to avoid excessive pressure that might bend the pushrod. Hold the lifter in this position and check the clearance between the rocker arm and the valve stem tip. Allowable clearance is 2.5–5.0mm (0.10–0.20 in.) with a desired clearance of 3.0–4.5mm (0.125–0.175 in.).

3. If the clearance is less than specified, install a shorter pushrod. If the clearance is greater than specified, install a longer pushrod.

4. Rotate the crankshaft clockwise (as viewed from the front) until the next chalk mark is aligned with the timing pointer. Repeat the procedure for No. 5 intake and exhaust.

5. Rotate the crankshaft to the next chalk mark and repeat the procedure for No. 3 intake and exhaust.

6. Repeat the rotation/checking procedure for the remaining valves in firing order, that is: 6–2–4.

5.0L ENGINE

▶ See Figures 93 and 94

1. Rotate the crankshaft by hand so that No. 1 piston is at TDC of the compression stroke. Make a chalk mark on the damper at that point, then, make 2 more chalk marks about 90° apart in a clockwise direction.

2. With No. 1 at TDC, slowly apply pressure, using Lifter Bleed-down wrench T70P-6513-A, or equivalent, to completely bottom the lifter, on the following valves:
- No. 1 intake and exhaust
- No. 7 intake
- No. 5 exhaust
- No. 8 intake
- No. 4 exhaust

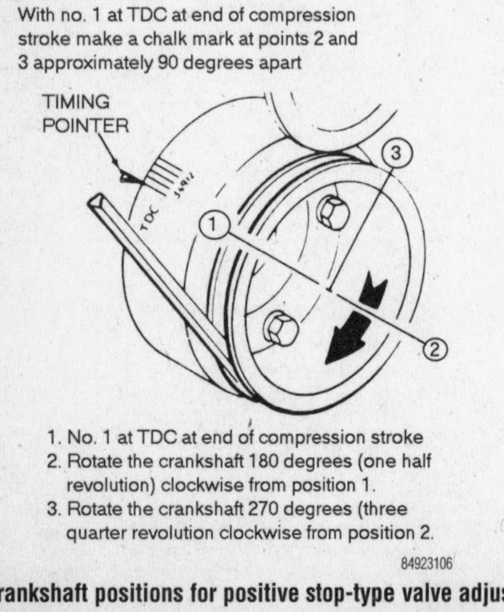

With no. 1 at TDC at end of compression stroke make a chalk mark at points 2 and 3 approximately 90 degrees apart

TIMING POINTER

1. No. 1 at TDC at end of compression stroke
2. Rotate the crankshaft 180 degrees (one half revolution) clockwise from position 1.
3. Rotate the crankshaft 270 degrees (three quarter revolution clockwise from position 2.

84923106

Fig. 94 Crankshaft positions for positive stop-type valve adjustment — 5.0L engine

Take care to avoid excessive pressure that might bend the pushrod. Hold the lifter in this position and check the clearance between the rocker arm and the valve stem tip. Allowable clearance is 1.8—4.9mm (0.071—0.193 in.) with a desired clearance of 2.4—4.2mm (0.096—0.165 in.).

3. If the clearance is less than specified, install a shorter pushrod. If the clearance is greater than specified, install a longer pushrod.

4. Rotate the crankshaft clockwise—as viewed from the front—180°, until the next chalk mark is aligned with the timing pointer. Repeat the procedure for:
- No. 5 intake
- No. 2 exhaust
- No. 4 intake
- No. 6 exhaust

5. Rotate the crankshaft to the next chalk mark—90°—and repeat the procedure for:
- No. 2 intake
- No. 7 exhaust
- No. 3 intake and exhaust
- No. 6 intake
- No. 8 exhaust

5.8L ENGINE

▶ See Figure 94

1. Rotate the crankshaft by hand so that No. 1 piston is at TDC of the compression stroke. Make a chalk mark on the damper at that point, then, make 2 more chalk marks about 90° apart in a clockwise direction.

2. With No. 1 at TDC, slowly apply pressure, using Lifter Bleed-down wrench T70P-6513-A, or equivalent, to completely bottom the lifter, on the following valves:
- No. 1 intake and exhaust
- No. 4 intake
- No. 3 exhaust
- No. 8 intake
- No. 7 exhaust

Take care to avoid excessive pressure that might bend the pushrod. Hold the lifter in this position and check the clearance between the rocker arm and the valve stem tip. Allowable clearance is 2.5–5.0mm (0.098–0.198 in.) with a desired clearance of 3.1–4.4mm (0.123–0.173 in.).

3. If the clearance is less than specified, install a shorter pushrod. If the clearance is greater than specified, install a longer pushrod.

4. Rotate the crankshaft clockwise—viewed from the front—180°, until the next chalk mark is aligned with the timing pointer. Repeat the procedure for:
- No. 3 intake
- No. 2 exhaust
- No. 7 intake
- No. 6 exhaust

5. Rotate the crankshaft to the next chalk mark—90°—and repeat the procedure for:
- No. 2 intake
- No. 4 exhaust
- No. 5 intake and exhaust
- No. 6 intake
- No. 8 exhaust

7.5L ENGINE

▶ See Figure 93

1. Rotate the crankshaft by hand so that No. 1 piston is at TDC of the compression stroke. Make a chalk mark on the damper at that point.

2. With No. 1 at TDC, slowly apply pressure, using Lifter Bleed-down wrench T70P-6513-A, or equivalent, to completely bottom the lifter, on the following valves:
- No. 1 intake and exhaust
- No. 3 intake
- No. 4 exhaust
- No. 7 intake
- No. 5 exhaust
- No. 8 intake and exhaust

Take care to avoid excessive pressure that might bend the pushrod. Hold the lifter in this position and check the clearance between the rocker arm and the valve stem tip. Allowable clearance is 1.9–4.4mm (0.075–0.175 in.) with a desired clearance of 2.5–3.8mm (0.100-0.150 in.).

3. If the clearance is less than specified, install a shorter pushrod. If the clearance is greater than specified, install a longer pushrod.

4. Rotate the crankshaft clockwise—viewed from the front—360°, until the chalk mark is once again aligned with the timing pointer. Repeat the procedure for:

- No. 2 intake and exhaust
- No. 4 intake
- No. 3 exhaust
- No. 5 intake
- No. 7 exhaust
- No. 6 intake and exhaust

Idle Speed and Mixture Adjustments

CARBURETED ENGINES

▶ **See Figure 95**

1. Block the wheels and firmly apply parking brake.
2. Run engine until normal operating temperature is reached.
3. Place the vehicle in Park or Neutral, A/C in OFF position, and set parking brake.
4. Remove air cleaner.
5. Disconnect and plug the decel throttle control kicker diaphragm vacuum hose.
6. Connect a slave vacuum hose from an engine manifold vacuum source to the decel throttle control kicker.
7. Run engine at approximately 2,500 rpm for 15 seconds, then release the throttle.
8. If the decel throttle control rpm is not within 50 rpm of specification, adjust the kicker.
9. Disconnect the slave vacuum hose and allow engine to return to curb idle.
10. Adjust curb idle, if necessary, using the curb idle adjusting screw.
11. Rev the engine momentarily, recheck curb idle and adjust if necessary.
12. Reconnect the decel throttle control vacuum hose to the diaphragm.
13. Reinstall the air cleaner.

FUEL INJECTED ENGINES

These engines have idle speed controlled by the TFI-IV/EEC-IV system and no adjustment is possible.

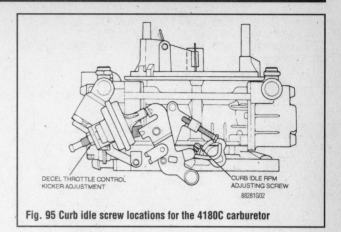

DECEL THROTTLE CONTROL KICKER ADJUSTMENT

CURB IDLE RPM ADJUSTING SCREW

88281G02

Fig. 95 Curb idle screw locations for the 4180C carburetor

6.9L AND 7.3L DIESEL ENGINES

Curb Idle Adjustment

1. Bring the engine up to normal operating temperature.
2. Place the transmission in Neutral or Park. Firmly set the parking brake.

➡**Idle speed is measured with manual transmission in Neutral and automatic transmission in Drive, with the wheels blocked and parking brake ON.**

3. Check the curb idle speed, using a magnetic pickup tachometer suitable for diesel engines. The part number of the Ford tachometer is Rotunda 99–0001. Adjust the idle speed to 600–700 rpm.

➡**Always check the underhood emissions control information sticker for the latest idle and adjustment specifications.**

4. Place the transmission in Neutral or Park and momentarily speed up the engine. Allow the rpm to drop to idle and recheck the idle speed. Readjust if necessary.

Fast Idle Adjustment

1. Start the engine and bring up to normal operating temperatures.
2. Place the transmission in Neutral or Park.
3. Disconnect the wire from the fast idle solenoid.

DIESEL ENGINE TUNE-UP SPECIFICATIONS

Year	Engine ID/VIN	Engine Displacement cu. in. (cc)	Valve Clearance Intake (in.)	Valve Clearance Exhaust (in.)	Intake Valve Opens (deg.)	Injection Pump Setting (deg.)	Injection Nozzle Pressure (psi) New	Injection Nozzle Pressure (psi) Used	Idle Speed (rpm)	Cranking Compression Pressure (psi)
1987	I	6.9L (6886)	HYD	HYD	–	1.5A	1875	1425	①	195-440 ②
1988	M	7.3L (7270)	HYD	HYD	–	6.5B ③	1875	1425	①	195-440 ②
1989	M	7.3L (7270)	HYD	HYD	–	8.5B ③	1875	1425	①	195-440 ②
1990	M	7.3L (7270)	HYD	HYD	–	8.5B ③	1875	1425	①	195-440 ②
1991	M	7.3L (7270)	HYD	HYD	–	8.5B ③	1875	1425	①	195-440 ②
1992	M	7.3L (7270)	HYD	HYD	–	8.5B ③	1875	1425	①	195-440 ②
1993	C	7.3L (7270)	HYD	HYD	–	8.5B ③	1875	1425	①	195-440 ②
	M	7.3L (7270)	HYD	HYD	–	8.5B ③	1875	1425	①	195-440 ②
1994	M	7.3L (7270)	HYD	HYD	–	8.5B ③	1900	1450	①	195-440 ②
	F	7.3L (7270)	HYD	HYD	–	④	1900	1450	①	195-440 ②
	K	7.3L (7270)	HYD	HYD	–	④	1900	1450	①	195-440 ②
1995	F	7.3L (7270)	HYD	HYD	–	④	1900	1450	①	195-440 ②
1996	F	7.3L (7270)	HYD	HYD	–	④	1900	1450	①	195-440 ②

NOTE: The Vehicle Emission Control Information label often reflects specification changes made during production. The label figures must be used if they differ from those in this chart.

HYD - Hydraulic

B - Before top dead center
A - After top dead center

① Curb idle speed is specified on the Vehicle Emission Control Information label
② Compression pressure in the lowest cylinder must be at least 75% of the highest cylinder

③ At 2000 rpm
④ PCM controlled

88281C15

4. Apply battery voltage to activate the solenoid plunger.
5. Speed up the engine momentarily to set the plunger.
6. The fast idle should be between 850–900 rpm. Adjust the fast idle by turning the solenoid plunger in or out.

7. Speed up the engine momentarily and recheck the fast idle. Readjust if necessary.
8. Remove the battery voltage from the solenoid and reconnect the solenoid wire.

GASOLINE ENGINE TUNE-UP SPECIFICATIONS

Year	Engine ID/VIN	Engine Displacement Liters (cc)	Spark Plugs Gap (in.)	Ignition Timing (deg.) MT	Ignition Timing (deg.) AT	Fuel Pump (psi)	Idle Speed (rpm) MT	Idle Speed (rpm) AT	Valve Clearance In.	Valve Clearance Ex.
1987	Y	4.9L (4917)	0.044	10B	10B	50-60 ①	700	575	HYD	HYD
	N	5.0L (4942)	0.044	10B	10B	35-45 ①	700	650	HYD	HYD
	H	5.8L (5766)	0.044	–	10B	6-8	–	600	HYD	HYD
	L	7.5L (7536)	0.044	8B	8B	6-8	775	675	HYD	HYD
1988	Y	4.9L (4917)	0.044	10B	10B	50-60 ①	700	575	HYD	HYD
	N	5.0L (4942)	0.044	10B	10B	35-45 ①	700	650	HYD	HYD
	H	5.8L (5766)	0.044	10B	10B	35-45 ①	650	650	HYD	HYD
	G	7.5L (7536)	0.044	10B	10B	35-45 ①	650	650	HYD	HYD
1989	Y	4.9L (4917)	0.044	10B	10B	50-60 ①	700	575	HYD	HYD
	N	5.0L (4942)	0.044	10B	10B	35-45 ①	700	650	HYD	HYD
	H	5.8L (5766)	0.044	10B	10B	35-45 ①	650	650	HYD	HYD
	G	7.5L (7536)	0.044	10B	10B	35-45 ①	650	650	HYD	HYD
1990	Y	4.9L (4917)	0.044	10B	10B	50-60 ①	700	575	HYD	HYD
	N	5.0L (4942)	0.044	10B	10B	35-45 ①	700	650	HYD	HYD
	H	5.8L (5766)	0.044	10B	10B	35-45 ①	650	650	HYD	HYD
	G	7.5L (7536)	0.044	10B	10B	35-45 ①	650	650	HYD	HYD
1991	Y	4.9L (4917)	0.044	10B	10B	50-60 ①	700	575	HYD	HYD
	N	5.0L (4942)	0.044	10B	10B	35-45 ①	700	650	HYD	HYD
	H	5.8L (5766)	0.044	10B	10B	35-45 ①	650	650	HYD	HYD
	G	7.5L (7536)	0.044	10B	10B	35-45 ①	650	650	HYD	HYD
1992	Y	4.9L (4917)	0.044	10B	10B	50-60 ①	700	575	HYD	HYD
	N	5.0L (4942)	0.044	10B	10B	35-45 ①	700	650	HYD	HYD
	H	5.8L (5766)	0.044	10B	10B	35-45 ①	650	650	HYD	HYD
	G	7.5L (7536)	0.044	10B	10B	35-45 ①	650	650	HYD	HYD
1993	Y	4.9L (4917)	0.044	10B	10B	50-60 ①	700	575	HYD	HYD
	N	5.0L (4942)	0.044	10B	10B	35-45 ①	700	650	HYD	HYD
	H	5.8L (5766)	0.044	10B	10B	35-45 ①	650	650	HYD	HYD
	R	5.8L (5766)	0.044	–	10B	35-45 ①	–	675	HYD	HYD
	G	7.5L (7536)	0.044	10B	10B	35-45 ①	650	650	HYD	HYD
1994	Y	4.9L (4917)	0.044	10B	10B	50-60 ①	700	575	HYD	HYD
	N	5.0L (4942)	0.044	10B	10B	35-45 ①	700	650	HYD	HYD
	H	5.8L (5766)	0.044	10B	10B	35-45 ①	650	650	HYD	HYD
	R	5.8L (5766)	0.044	–	10B	35-45 ①	–	675	HYD	HYD
	G	7.5L (7536)	0.044	10B	10B	35-45 ①	650	650	HYD	HYD
1995	Y	4.9L (4917)	0.044	10B	10B	50-60 ①	700	575	HYD	HYD
	N	5.0L (4942)	0.044	10B	10B	35-45 ①	700	650	HYD	HYD
	H	5.8L (5766)	0.044	10B	10B	35-45 ①	650	650	HYD	HYD
	R	5.8L (5766)	0.044	–	10B	35-45 ①	–	675	HYD	HYD
	G	7.5L (7536)	0.044	10B	10B	35-45 ①	650	650	HYD	HYD
1996	Y	4.9L (4917)	0.044	10B	10B	50-60 ①	700	575	HYD	HYD
	N	5.0L (4942)	0.044	10B	10B	35-45 ①	700	650	HYD	HYD
	H	5.8L (5766)	0.044	10B	10B	35-45 ①	650	650	HYD	HYD
	G	7.5L (7536)	0.044	10B	10B	35-45 ①	650	650	HYD	HYD

NOTE: The Vehicle Emission Control Information label often reflects specification changes made during production. The label figures must be used if they differ from those in this chart.

B - Before top dead center

HYD - Hydraulic

① Key on, engine off

88281C14

Air Conditioning System

SYSTEM SERVICE & REPAIR

➡️**It is recommended that the A/C system be serviced by an EPA Section 609 certified automotive technician utilizing a refrigerant recovery/recycling machine.**

The do-it-yourselfer should not service his/her own vehicle's A/C system for many reasons, including legal concerns, personal injury, environmental damage and cost.

According to the U.S. Clean Air Act, it is a federal crime to service or repair (involving the refrigerant) a Motor Vehicle Air Conditioning (MVAC) system for money without being EPA certified. It is also illegal to vent R-12 and R-134a refrigerants into the atmosphere. State and/or local laws may be more strict than the federal regulations, so be sure to check with your state and/or local authorities for further information.

➡️**Federal law dictates that a fine of up to $25,000 may be levied on people convicted of venting refrigerant into the atmosphere.**

When servicing an A/C system you run the risk of handling or coming in contact with refrigerant, which may result in skin or eye irritation or frostbite. Although low in toxicity (due to chemical stability), inhalation of concentrated refrigerant fumes is dangerous and can result in death; cases of fatal cardiac arrhythmia have been reported in people accidentally subjected to high levels of refrigerant. Some early symptoms include loss of concentration and drowsiness.

➡️**Generally, the limit for exposure is lower for R-134a than it is for R-12. Exceptional care must be practiced when handling R-134a.**

Also, some refrigerants can decompose at high temperatures (near gas heaters or open flame), which may result in hydrofluoric acid, hydrochloric acid and phosgene (a fatal nerve gas).

It is usually more economically feasible to have a certified MVAC automotive technician perform A/C system service on your vehicle.

R-12 REFRIGERANT CONVERSION

If your vehicle still uses R-12 refrigerant, one way to save A/C system costs down the road is to investigate the possibility of having your system converted to R-134a. The older R-12 systems can be easily converted to R-134a refrigerant by a certified automotive technician by installing a few new components and changing the system oil.

The cost of R-12 is steadily rising and will continue to increase, because it is no longer imported or manufactured in the United States. Therefore, it is often possible to have an R-12 system converted to R-134a and recharged for less than it would cost to just charge the system with R-12.

If you are interested in having your system converted, contact local automotive service stations for more details and information.

PREVENTIVE MAINTENANCE

Although the A/C system should not be serviced by the do-it-yourselfer, preventive maintenance should be practiced to help maintain the efficiency of the vehicle's A/C system. Be sure to perform the following:

• The easiest and most important preventive maintenance for your A/C system is to be sure that it is used on a regular basis. Running the system for five minutes each month (no matter what the season) will help ensure that the seals and all internal components remain lubricated.

➡️**Some vehicles automatically operate the A/C system compressor whenever the windshield defroster is activated. Therefore, the A/C system would not need to be operated each month if the defroster was used.**

• In order to prevent heater core freeze-up during A/C operation, it is necessary to maintain proper antifreeze protection. Be sure to properly maintain the engine cooling system.

• Any obstruction of or damage to the condenser configuration will restrict air flow which is essential to its efficient operation. Keep this unit clean and in proper physical shape.

➡️**Bug screens which are mounted in front of the condenser (unless they are original equipment) are regarded as obstructions.**

• The condensation drain tube expels any water which accumulates on the bottom of the evaporator housing into the engine compartment. If this tube is obstructed, the air conditioning performance can be restricted and condensation buildup can spill over onto the vehicle's floor.

SYSTEM INSPECTION

Although the A/C system should not be serviced by the do-it-yourselfer, system inspections should be performed to help maintain the efficiency of the vehicle's A/C system. Be sure to perform the following:

The easiest and often most important check for the air conditioning system consists of a visual inspection of the system components. Visually inspect the system for refrigerant leaks, damaged compressor clutch, abnormal compressor drive belt tension and/or condition, plugged evaporator drain tube, blocked condenser fins, disconnected or broken wires, blown fuses, corroded connections and poor insulation.

A refrigerant leak will usually appear as an oily residue at the leakage point in the system. The oily residue soon picks up dust or dirt particles from the surrounding air and appears greasy. Through time, this will build up and appear to be a heavy dirt impregnated grease.

For a thorough visual and operational inspection, check the following:
• Check the surface of the radiator and condenser for dirt, leaves or other material which might block air flow.
• Check for kinks in hoses and lines. Check the system for leaks.
• Make sure the drive belt is properly tensioned. During operation, make sure the belt is free of noise or slippage.
• Make sure the blower motor operates at all appropriate positions, then check for distribution of the air from all outlets.

➡️**Remember that in high humidity, air discharged from the vents may not feel as cold as expected, even if the system is working properly. This is because moisture in humid air retains heat more effectively than dry air, thereby making humid air more difficult to cool.**

Windshield Wipers

ELEMENT (REFILL) CARE & REPLACEMENT

▶ **See Figures 96, 97 and 98**

For maximum effectiveness and longest element life, the windshield and wiper blades should be kept clean. Dirt, tree sap, road tar and so on will cause streaking, smearing and blade deterioration if left on the glass. It is advisable to wash the windshield carefully with a commercial glass cleaner at least once a month. Wipe off the rubber blades with the wet rag afterwards. Do not attempt to move wipers across the windshield by hand; damage to the motor and drive mechanism will result.

To inspect and/or replace the wiper blade elements, place the wiper switch in the **LOW** speed position and the ignition switch in the **ACC** position. When the wiper blades are approximately vertical on the windshield, turn the ignition switch to **OFF**.

Examine the wiper blade elements. If they are found to be cracked, broken or torn, they should be replaced immediately. Replacement intervals will vary with usage, although ozone deterioration usually limits element life to about one year. If the wiper pattern is smeared or streaked, or if the blade chatters across the glass, the elements should be replaced. It is easiest and most sensible to replace the elements in pairs.

If your vehicle is equipped with aftermarket blades, there are several different types of refills and your vehicle might have any kind. Aftermarket blades and arms rarely use the exact same type blade or refill as the original equipment.

Regardless of the type of refill used, be sure to follow the part manufacturer's instructions closely. Make sure that all of the frame jaws are engaged as the refill is pushed into place and locked. If the metal blade holder and frame are allowed to touch the glass during wiper operation, the glass will be scratched.

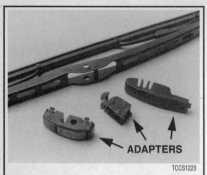

Fig. 96 Most aftermarket blades are available with multiple adapters to fit different vehicles

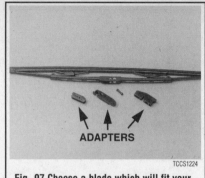

Fig. 97 Choose a blade which will fit your vehicle, and that will be readily available next time you need blades

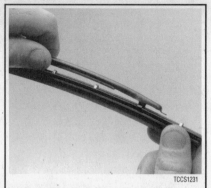

Fig. 98 When installed, be certain the blade is fully inserted into the backing

Tires and Wheels

Common sense and good driving habits will afford maximum tire life. Make sure that you don't overload the vehicle or run with incorrect pressure in the tires. Either of these will increase tread wear. Fast starts, sudden stops and sharp cornering are hard on tires and will shorten their useful life span.

→For optimum tire life, keep the tires properly inflated, rotate them often and have the wheel alignment checked periodically.

Inspect your tires frequently. Be especially careful to watch for bubbles in the tread or sidewall, deep cuts or underinflation. Replace any tires with bubbles in the sidewall. If cuts are so deep that they penetrate to the cords, discard the tire. Any cut in the sidewall of a radial tire renders it unsafe. Also look for uneven tread wear patterns that may indicate the front end is out of alignment or that the tires are out of balance.

TIRE ROTATION

▶ See Figure 99

Tires must be rotated periodically to equalize wear patterns that vary with a tire's position on the vehicle. Tires will also wear in an uneven way as the front steering/suspension system wears to the point where the alignment should be reset.

Rotating the tires will ensure maximum life for the tires as a set, so you will not have to discard a tire early due to wear on only part of the tread. Regular rotation is required to equalize wear.

When rotating "unidirectional tires," make sure that they always roll in the same direction. This means that a tire used on the left side of the vehicle must not be switched to the right side and vice-versa. Such tires should only be rotated front-to-rear or rear-to-front, while always remaining on the same side of the vehicle. These tires are marked on the sidewall as to the direction of rotation; observe the marks when reinstalling the tire(s).

Some styled or "mag" wheels may have different offsets front to rear. In these cases, the rear wheels must not be used up front and vice-versa. Furthermore, if these wheels are equipped with unidirectional tires, they cannot be rotated unless the tire is remounted for the proper direction of rotation.

→The compact or space-saver spare is strictly for emergency use. It must never be included in the tire rotation or placed on the vehicle for everyday use.

TIRE DESIGN

▶ See Figure 100

For maximum satisfaction, tires should be used in sets of four. Mixing of different brands or types (radial, bias-belted, fiberglass belted) should be avoided. In most cases, the vehicle manufacturer has designated a type of tire on which the vehicle will perform best. Your first choice when replacing tires should be to use the same type of tire that the manufacturer recommends.

When radial tires are used, tire sizes and wheel diameters should be selected to maintain ground clearance and tire load capacity equivalent to the original specified tire. Radial tires should always be used in sets of four.

✳✳ CAUTION

Radial tires should never be used on only the front axle.

When selecting tires, pay attention to the original size as marked on the tire. Most tires are described using an industry size code sometimes referred to as P-Metric. This allows the exact identification of the tire specifications, regardless of the manufacturer. If selecting a different tire size or brand, remember to check the installed tire for any sign of interference with the body or suspension while the vehicle is stopping, turning sharply or heavily loaded.

Snow Tires

Good radial tires can produce a big advantage in slippery weather, but in snow, a street radial tire does not have sufficient tread to provide traction and control. The small grooves of a street tire quickly pack with snow and the tire behaves like a billiard ball on a marble floor. The more open, chunky tread of a snow tire will self-clean as the tire turns, providing much better grip on snowy surfaces.

To satisfy municipalities requiring snow tires during weather emergencies, most snow tires carry either an M + S designation after the tire size stamped on the sidewall, or the designation "all-season." In general, no change in tire size is necessary when buying snow tires.

Most manufacturers strongly recommend the use of 4 snow tires on their vehicles for reasons of stability. If snow tires are fitted only to the drive wheels, the opposite end of the vehicle may become very unstable when braking or turning on slippery surfaces. This instability can lead to unpleasant endings if the driver can't counteract the slide in time.

Note that snow tires, whether 2 or 4, will affect vehicle handling in all non-snow situations. The stiffer, heavier snow tires will noticeably change the turning and braking characteristics of the vehicle. Once the snow tires are installed, you must re-learn the behavior of the vehicle and drive accordingly.

→Consider buying extra wheels on which to mount the snow tires. Once done, the "snow wheels" can be installed and removed as needed. This

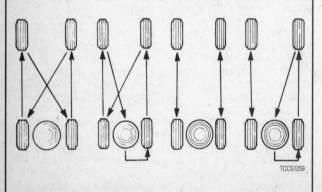

Fig. 99 Common tire rotation patterns for 4 and 5-wheel rotations

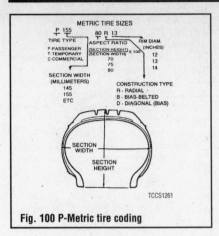

Fig. 100 P-Metric tire coding

Fig. 101 Tires with deep cuts, or cuts which bulge, should be replaced immediately

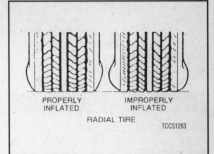

Fig. 102 Radial tires have a characteristic sidewall bulge; don't try to measure pressure by looking at the tire. Use a quality air pressure gauge

eliminates the potential damage to tires or wheels from seasonal removal and installation. Even if your vehicle has styled wheels, see if inexpensive steel wheels are available. Although the look of the vehicle will change, the expensive wheels will be protected from salt, curb hits and pothole damage.

TIRE STORAGE

If they are mounted on wheels, store the tires at proper inflation pressure. All tires should be kept in a cool, dry place. If they are stored in the garage or basement, do not let them stand on a concrete floor; set them on strips of wood, a mat or a large stack of newspaper. Keeping them away from direct moisture is of paramount importance. Tires should not be stored upright, but in a flat position.

INFLATION & INSPECTION

▶ See Figures 101 thru 106

The importance of proper tire inflation cannot be overemphasized. A tire employs air as part of its structure. It is designed around the supporting strength of the air at a specified pressure. For this reason, improper inflation drastically reduces the tire's ability to perform as intended. A tire will lose some air in day-to-day use; having to add a few pounds of air periodically is not necessarily a sign of a leaking tire.

Two items should be a permanent fixture in every glove compartment: an accurate tire pressure gauge and a tread depth gauge. Check the tire pressure (including the spare) regularly with a pocket type gauge. Too often, the gauge on the end of the air hose at your corner garage is not accurate because it suffers too much abuse. Always check tire pressure when the tires are cold, as

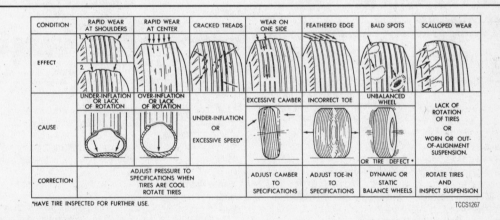

Fig. 103 Common tire wear patterns and causes

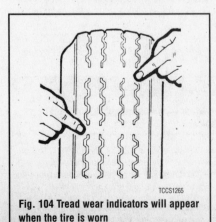

Fig. 104 Tread wear indicators will appear when the tire is worn

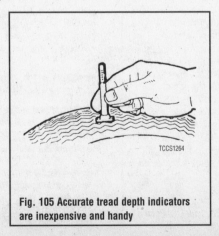

Fig. 105 Accurate tread depth indicators are inexpensive and handy

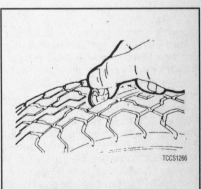

Fig. 106 A penny works well for a quick check of tread depth

pressure increases with temperature. If you must move the vehicle to check the tire inflation, do not drive more than a mile before checking. A cold tire is generally one that has not been driven for more than three hours.

A plate or sticker is normally provided somewhere in the vehicle (door post, hood, tailgate or trunk lid) which shows the proper pressure for the tires. Never counteract excessive pressure build-up by bleeding off air pressure (letting some air out). This will cause the tire to run hotter and wear quicker.

❄ CAUTION

Never exceed the maximum tire pressure embossed on the tire! This is the pressure to be used when the tire is at maximum loading, but it is rarely the correct pressure for everyday driving. Consult the owner's manual or the tire pressure sticker for the correct tire pressure.

Once you've maintained the correct tire pressures for several weeks, you'll be familiar with the vehicle's braking and handling personality. Slight adjustments

in tire pressures can fine-tune these characteristics, but never change the cold pressure specification by more than 2 psi. A slightly softer tire pressure will give a softer ride but also yield lower fuel mileage. A slightly harder tire will give crisper dry road handling but can cause skidding on wet surfaces. Unless you're fully attuned to the vehicle, stick to the recommended inflation pressures.

All automotive tires have built-in tread wear indicator bars that show up as ½ in. (13mm) wide smooth bands across the tire when 1/16 in. (1.5mm) of tread remains. The appearance of tread wear indicators means that the tires should be replaced. In fact, many states have laws prohibiting the use of tires with less than this amount of tread.

You can check your own tread depth with an inexpensive gauge or by using a Lincoln head penny. Slip the Lincoln penny (with Lincoln's head upside-down) into several tread grooves. If you can see the top of Lincoln's head in 2 adjacent grooves, the tire has less than 1/16 in. (1.5mm) tread left and should be replaced. You can measure snow tires in the same manner by using the "tails" side of the Lincoln penny. If you can see the top of the Lincoln memorial, it's time to replace the snow tire(s).

FLUIDS AND LUBRICANTS

Fluid Disposal

Used fluids such as engine oil, transmission fluid, antifreeze and brake fluid are hazardous wastes and must be disposed of properly. Before draining any fluids, consult with the local authorities; in many areas, waste oil, etc. is being accepted as part of recycling programs. A number of service stations and auto parts stores are also accepting waste fluids for recycling.

Be sure of the recycling center's policies before draining any fluids, as many will not accept different fluids that have been mixed together, such as oil and antifreeze.

Fuel and Oil Recommendations

GASOLINE ENGINES

Fuel

All 1987–96 Ford pickups and Broncos must use lead-free gasoline with an (R+M)/2 minimum anti-knock index rating of at least 87. The 5.8L Lightening engine requires 91 octane during towing or carrying heavy loads. Use of gasoline with an anti-knock index rating lower than specified can cause persistent, heavy spark knock which can lead to engine damage.

Engine Oil

▶ **See Figure 107**

The recommended oil viscosities for sustained temperatures ranging from below 0°F (−18°C) to above 32°F (0°C) are listed in this section. They are broken down into multi-viscosity and single viscosities. Multi-viscosity oils are recommended because of their wider range of acceptable temperatures and driving conditions.

When adding oil to the crankcase or changing the oil or filter, it is important that oil of an equal quality to original equipment be used in your truck. The use of inferior oils may void the warranty, damage your engine, or both.

The Society of Automotive Engineers (SAE) grade number of oil indicates the viscosity of the oil (its ability to lubricate at a given temperature). The lower the SAE number, the lighter the oil; the lower the viscosity, the easier it is to crank the engine in cold weather but the less the oil will lubricate and protect the engine in high temperatures. This number is marked on every oil container.

Oil viscosities should be chosen from those oils recommended for the lowest anticipated temperatures during the oil change interval. Due to the need for an oil that embodies both good lubrication at high temperatures and easy cranking in cold weather, multigrade oils have been developed. Basically, a multigrade oil is thinner at low temperatures and thicker at high temperatures. For example, a 10W–40 oil (the W stands for winter) exhibits the characteristics of a 10 weight (SAE 10) oil when the truck is first started and the oil is cold. Its lighter weight allows it to travel to the lubricating surfaces quicker and offer less resistance to starter motor cranking than, say, a straight 30 weight (SAE 30) oil.

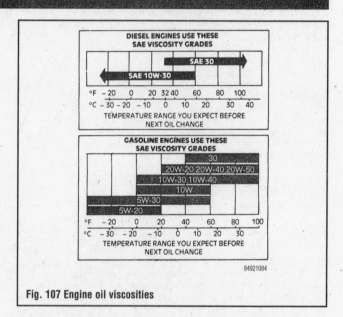

Fig. 107 Engine oil viscosities

But after the engine reaches operating temperature, the 10W–40 oil begins acting like straight 40 weight (SAE 40) oil, its heavier weight providing greater lubrication with less chance of foaming than a straight 30 weight oil.

The API (American Petroleum Institute) designations, also found on the oil container, indicates the classification of engine oil used under certain given operating conditions. Only oils designated for use Service SH heavy duty detergent should be used in your truck. Oils of the SH type perform may functions inside the engine besides their basic lubrication. Through a balanced system of metallic detergents and polymeric dispersants, the oil prevents high and low temperature deposits and also keeps sludge and dirt particles in suspension. Acids, particularly sulfuric acid, as well as other by-products of engine combustion are neutralized by the oil. If these acids are allowed to concentrate, they can cause corrosion and rapid wear of the internal engine parts.

❄ CAUTION

Non-detergent motor oils or straight mineral oils should not be used in your Ford gasoline engine.

Synthetic Oil

There are many excellent synthetic and fuel-efficient oils currently available that can provide better gas mileage, longer service life, and in some cases better engine protection. These benefits do not come without a few hitches, however; the main one being the price of synthetic oils, which can be three or four times the price per quart of conventional oil.

Synthetic oil is not necessarily for every truck and every type of driving, so you should consider your engine's condition and your type of driving. Also, check your truck's warranty conditions regarding the use of synthetic oils.

Depending on the type of synthetic oil, brand new engines and older, high mileage engines can be the wrong candidates for synthetic oil. In some cases, the synthetic oil is so slippery that it can prevent the proper break-in of new engines. With the exception of vehicles that are equipped with certain brands of sysnthetic oil from the factory, most manufacturers recommend that you wait until the engine is properly broken in (3000 miles) before using synthetic oil. Older engines with wear have a different problem with some synthetics: they "use" (consume during operation) more oil as they age. Slippery synthetic oils get past these worn parts easily. If your engine is "using" conventional oil, it may use synthetics much faster. Also, if your truck is leaking oil past old seals you'll have a much greater leak problem with synthetics.

Consider your type of driving, and consult someone knowledgeable on the particular brand of oil you are thinking of using. If most of your accumulated mileage is high speed, highway type driving, the more expensive synthetic oils may be a benefit. Extended highway driving gives the engine a chance to warm up, accumulating less acids in the oil and putting less stress on the engine over the long run. Under these conditions, the oil change interval can be extended (as long as your oil filter can last the extended life of the oil) up to the advertised mileage claims of the synthetics. Trucks with synthetic oils may show increased fuel economy in highway driving, due to less internal friction. However, many automotive experts agree that 50,000 miles (80,000 km) is too long to keep any oil in your engine.

Trucks used under harder circumstances, such as stop-and-go, city type driving, short trips, or extended idling, should be serviced more frequently. For the engines in these trucks, the much greater cost of synthetic or fuel-efficient oils may not be worth the investment. Internal wear increase much quicker on these trucks, causing greater oil consumption and leakage.

➡Read the label of the synthetic oil before you contemplate mixing it with conventional oils; not all synthetic and conventional oils are compatible. If you are using synthetic oil, it might be wise to carry two or three quarts with you no matter where you drive, as not all service stations carry this type of lubricant. Non-detergent or straight mineral oils must never be used.

DIESEL ENGINES

Diesel Fuel

Fuel makers produce two grades of diesel fuel, No. 1 and No. 2, for use in automotive diesel engines. Generally speaking, No. 2 fuel is recommended over No. 1 for driving in temperatures above 20°F (−7°C). In fact, in many areas, No. 2 diesel is the only fuel available. By comparison, No. 2 diesel fuel is less volatile than No. 1 fuel, and gives better fuel economy. No. 2 fuel is also a better injection pump lubricant.

Two important characteristics of diesel fuel are its cetane number and its viscosity.

The cetane number of a diesel fuel refers to the ease with which a diesel fuel ignites. High cetane numbers mean that the fuel will ignite with relative ease or that it ignites well at low temperatures. Naturally, the lower the cetane number, the higher the temperature must be to ignite the fuel. Most commercial fuels have cetane numbers that range from 35 to 65. No. 1 diesel fuel generally has a higher cetane rating than No. 2 fuel.

Viscosity is the ability of a liquid, in this case diesel fuel, to flow. Using straight No. 2 diesel fuel below 20°F (−7°C) can cause problems, because this fuel tends to become cloudy, meaning wax crystals begin forming in the fuel. 20°F (−7°C) is often call the cloud point for No. 2 fuel. In extremely cold weather, No. 2 fuel can stop flowing altogether. In either case, fuel flow is restricted, which can result in no start condition or poor engine performance. Fuel manufacturers often winterize No. 2 diesel fuel by using various fuel additives and blends (no. 1 diesel fuel, kerosene, etc.) to lower its winter time viscosity. Generally speaking, though, No. 1 diesel fuel is more satisfactory in extremely cold weather.

➡No. 1 and No. 2 diesel fuels will mix and burn with no ill effects, although the engine manufacturer recommends one or the other. Consult the owner's manual for information.

Depending on local climate, most fuel manufacturers make winterized No. 2 fuel available seasonally.

Many automobile manufacturers publish pamphlets giving the locations of diesel fuel stations nationwide. Contact the local dealer for information.

Do not substitute home heating oil for automotive diesel fuel. While in some cases, home heating oil refinement levels equal those of diesel fuel, many times they are far below diesel engine requirements. The result of using dirty home heating oil will be a clogged fuel system, in which case the entire system may have to be dismantled and cleaned.

One more word on diesel fuels. Don't thin diesel fuel with gasoline in cold weather. The lighter gasoline, which is more explosive, will cause rough running at the very least, and may cause extensive damage to the fuel system if enough is used.

Engine Oil

♦ See Figure 107

Diesel engines require different engine oil from those used in gasoline engines. Besides doing the things gasoline engine oil does, diesel oil must also deal with increased engine heat and the diesel blow-by gases, which create sulfuric acid, a high corrosive.

Under the American Petroleum Institute (API) classifications, gasoline engine oil codes begin with an **S**, and diesel engine oil codes begin with a **C**. This first letter designation is followed by a second letter code which explains what type of service (heavy, moderate, light) the oil is meant for. For example, the top of a typical oil can will include: API SERVICES SH, CD. This means the oil in the can is a superior, heavy duty engine oil when used in a diesel engine.

Many diesel manufacturers recommend an oil with both gasoline and diesel engine API classifications.

➡Ford specifies the use of an engine oil conforming to API service categories of both SH and CD. DO NOT use oils labeled as only SH or only CD as they could cause engine damage.

OPERATION IN FOREIGN COUNTRIES

If you plan to drive your truck outside the United States or Canada, there is a possibility that fuels will be too low in anti-knock quality and could produce engine damage. It is wise to consult with local authorities upon arrival in a foreign country to determine the best fuels available.

OIL LEVEL CHECK

♦ See Figure 108

Check the engine oil level every time you fill the gas tank. The oil level should be above the ADD mark and not above the FULL mark on the dipstick. Make sure that the dipstick is inserted into the crankcase as far as possible and that the vehicle is resting on level ground. Also, allow a few minutes after turn-

88281P42

Fig. 108 Pull the dipstick to check engine oil level

ing off the engine for the oil to drain into the pan or an inaccurate reading will result.

1. Open the hood and remove the engine oil dipstick.
2. Wipe the dipstick with a clean, lint-free rag and reinsert it. Be sure to insert it all the way.
3. Pull out the dipstick and note the oil level. It should be between the **SAFE** (MAX) mark and the **ADD** (MIN) mark.
4. If the level is below the lower mark, replace the dipstick and add fresh oil to bring the level within the proper range. Do not overfill.
5. Recheck the oil level and close the hood.

➡**Use a multi-grade oil with API classification SH.**

OIL AND FILTER CHANGE

♦ **See Figures 109 thru 114**

➡**The engine oil and oil filter should be changed at the same time, at the recommended intervals on the maintenance schedule chart.**

The oil should be changed more frequently if the vehicle is being operated in very dusty areas. Before draining the oil, make sure that the engine is at operating temperature. Hot oil will hold more impurities in suspension and will flow better, allowing the removal of more oil and dirt.

1. Place a suitable receptacle beneath the oil drain plug.
2. Loosen the drain plug with a wrench, then, unscrew the plug with your fingers, using a rag or rubber gloves, to shield your fingers from the heat.
3. Push in on the plug as you unscrew it so you can feel when all of the screw threads are out of the hole. You can then remove the plug quickly with the minimum amount of oil running down your arm and you will also have the plug in your hand and not in the bottom of a pan of hot oil.

➡**The oil filter is located on the left side of all the engines installed in Ford trucks. For longest engine life, it should be changed every time the oil is changed.**

4. To remove the filter, make sure that you have a pan under the filter before you start to remove it from the engine
5. Loosen the filter with the filter wrench.

➡**A filter wrench can be obtained at an auto parts store and is well worth the investment, since it will save you a lot of grief.**

6. With a rag wrapped around the filter, unscrew the filter from the boss on the side of the engine. Be careful of hot oil that will run down the side of the filter.
7. Wipe the base of the mounting boss with a clean, dry cloth. When you install the new filter, smear a small amount of oil on the gasket with your finger, just enough to coat the entire surface, where it comes in contact with the mounting plate.
8. Install the filter. Tighten the filter only a half turn after it comes in contact with the mounting boss.

Manual Transmission

FLUID RECOMMENDATIONS

Manual Transmissions:
- All 4-speed transmissions—SAE 85W/90 gear oil
- All 5-speed transmissions—MERCON® (Dexron®II) ATF

LEVEL CHECK

♦ **See Figure 115**

The fluid level should be checked every 6 months/6,000 miles, whichever comes first.

1. Park the truck on a level surface, turn off the engine, apply the parking brake and block the wheels.
2. Remove the filler plug from the side of the transmission case with a proper size wrench. The fluid level should be even with the bottom of the filler hole.

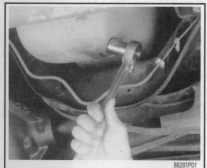

Fig. 109 Loosen, but do not remove, the drain plug at the bottom of the oil pan. Get your drain pan ready

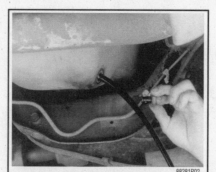

Fig. 110 Unscrew the plug (keeping inward pressure on the plug so oil won't escape until it is removed)

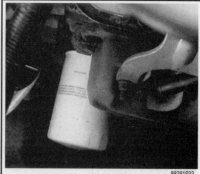

Fig. 111 Location of the oil filter—5.0L EFI engine

Fig. 112 Use a strap wrench only to remove—install by hand to prevent over-tightening

Fig. 113 Before installing a new oil filter, lightly coat the rubber gasket with clean oil

Fig. 114 Add oil through the filler cap in the valve cover

Fig. 115 Manual transmission filler location

Fig. 116 This 1990 model manual transmission has its drain plug clearly marked

Fig. 117 Note the metal (steel) particle that cling to this magnetic drain plug bolt

3. If additional fluid is necessary, add it through the filler hole using a siphon pump or squeeze bottle.

4. Replace the filler plug; do not overtighten.

DRAIN AND REFILL

▶ **See Figures 116 and 117**

1. Place a suitable drain pan under the transmission.
2. Remove the drain plug and allow the gear lube to drain out.
3. Replace the drain plug, remove the filler plug and fill the transmission to the proper level with the required fluid.
4. Reinstall the filler plug.

Automatic Transmission

FLUID RECOMMENDATIONS

- All models—MERCON® (Dexron®II) ATF

LEVEL CHECK

▶ **See Figures 118, 119 and 120**

It is very important to maintain the proper fluid level in an automatic transmission. If the level is either too high or too low, poor shifting operation and internal damage are likely to occur. For this reason a regular check of the fluid level is essential.

1. Drive the vehicle for 15–20 minutes to allow the transmission to reach operating temperature.
2. Park the truck on a level surface, apply the parking brake and leave the engine idling. Shift the transmission and engage each gear, then place the gear selector in **P** (PARK).
3. Wipe away any dirt in the areas of the transmission dipstick to prevent it from falling into the filler tube. Withdraw the dipstick, wipe it with a clean, lint-free rag and reinsert it until it seats.

4. Withdraw the dipstick and note the fluid level. It should be between the upper (FULL) mark and the lower (ADD) mark.

5. If the level is below the lower mark, use a funnel and add fluid in small quantities through the dipstick filler neck. Keep the engine running while adding fluid and check the level after each small amount. Do not overfill.

DRAIN AND REFILL

▶ **See Figures 121, 122, 123, 124 and 125**

1. Raise the truck and support on jackstands.
2. Place a drain pan under the transmission.
3. Loosen the pan attaching bolts and drain the fluid from the transmission.
4. When the fluid has drained to the level of the pan flange, remove the remaining pan bolts working from the rear and both sides of the pan to allow it to drop and drain slowly.
5. When all of the fluid has drained, remove the pan and clean it thoroughly. Discard the pan gasket.
6. Place a new gasket on the pan, and install the pan on the transmission. Tighten the attaching bolts to 12–16 ft. lbs. (16–22 Nm).
7. Add three quarts of fluid to the transmission through the filler tube.
8. Lower the vehicle. Start the engine and move the gear selector through shift pattern. Allow the engine to reach normal operating temperature.
9. Check the transmission fluid. Add fluid, if necessary, to maintain correct level.

Transfer Case

FLUID LEVEL CHECK

Position the vehicle on level ground. Remove the transfer case fill plug located on the left side of the transfer case. The fluid level should be up to the fill hole. If lubricant doesn't run out when the plug is removed, add lubricant until it does run out and then replace the fill plug. Use Ford MERCON® or Dexron®II ATF.

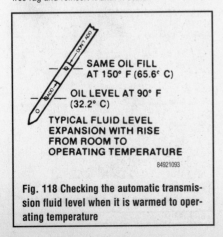

Fig. 118 Checking the automatic transmission fluid level when it is warmed to operating temperature

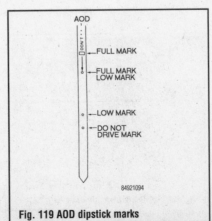

Fig. 119 AOD dipstick marks

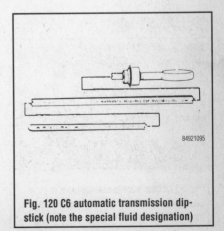

Fig. 120 C6 automatic transmission dipstick (note the special fluid designation)

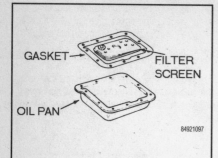

Fig. 121 Automatic transmission filters are found above the transmission oil pan

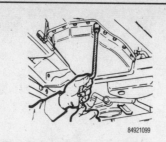

Fig. 122 Many late model vehicles have no drain plug. Loosen the pan bolts and allow one corner of the pan to hang, so that the fluid will drain out

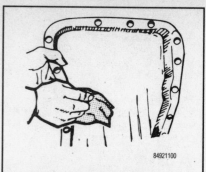

Fig. 123 Clean the pan thoroughly with a safe solvent and allow it to air dry

Fig. 124 Install a new pan gasket

Fig. 125 Fill the transmission with the required amount of fluid. Do not overfill

Fig. 126 Loosen, but do not remove, the transfer case drain plug

DRAIN AND REFILL

▶ See Figures 126, 127 and 128

The transfer case is serviced at the same time and in the same manner as the transmission. Clean the area around the filler and drain plugs and remove the filler plug on the side of the transfer case. Remove the drain plug on the bottom of the transfer case and allow the lubricant to drain completely.

Clean and install the drain plug. Add the proper lubricant. See the section on level checks.

Drive Axle—Front (4WD) and Rear

FLUID LEVEL CHECK

▶ See Figure 129

Clean the area around the fill plug, which is located in the housing cover, before removing the plug. The lubricant level should be maintained to the bottom of the fill hole with the axle in its normal running position. If lubricant does not appear at the hole when the plug is removed, additional lubricant should be added. Use hypoid gear lubricant SAE 80 or 90.

➡ If the differential is of the limited slip type, be sure and use special limited slip differential additive.

DRAIN AND REFILL

Drain and refill the front and rear axle housing every 24,000 miles, or every day if the vehicle is operated in deep water. The best way to drain a Ford or Dana rear axle is to remove the cover. If desired, you may also remove the oil with a suction gun. Refill the axle housings with the proper oil. Be sure and clean the area around the drain plug before removing the plug. See the section on level checks.

Cooling System

FLUID RECOMMENDATIONS

Completely draining and refilling the cooling system every two years at least will remove accumulated rust, scale and other deposits. Coolant in late model

Fig. 127 Make sure the receptacle is properly positioned before you unscrew the transfer case drain plug

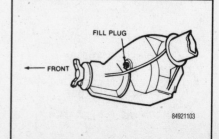

Fig. 128 Refill the transfer case with the approved lubricant

Fig. 129 Differential fill plug location, 2-wheel drive shown. The 4X4 front axle is similar

trucks is a 50/50 mixture of ethylene glycol and water for year round use. Use a good quality antifreeze with water pump lubricants, rust inhibitors and other corrosion inhibitors along with acid neutralizers.

Additionally, whenever servicing the cooling system, the pressure cap should be looked at for signs of age or deterioration. Fan belt and other drive belts should be inspected and adjusted to the proper tension. (See checking belt tension).

Hose clamps should be tightened, and soft or cracked hoses replaced. Damp spots, or accumulations of rust or dye near hoses, water pump or other areas, indicate possible leakage, which must be corrected before filling the system with fresh coolant.

LEVEL CHECK

▶ **See Figure 130**

❊❊ CAUTION

Never remove the radiator cap under any conditions while the engine is running! Failure to follow these instructions could result in damage to the cooling system or engine and/or personal injury. To avoid having scalding hot coolant or steam blow out of the radiator, use extreme care when removing the radiator cap from a hot radiator. Wait until the engine has cooled, then wrap a thick cloth around the radiator cap and turn it slowly to the first stop. Step back while the pressure is released from the cooling system. When you are sure the pressure has been released, press down on the radiator cap (still have the cloth in position) turn and remove the radiator cap.

1. Allow the engine to cool and remove the radiator cap. Because a coolant recovery (overflow) tank is used, the coolant level should be at the cap seal in the filler neck. The coolant should be clear green or clear blue in color (depending on the brand of coolant used).

2. Examine the fluid color:
• If the coolant is a very light green or blue, there is less than a 50/50 mixture and the system should be drained and refilled.
• If the coolant is muddy brown in color, it is likely that an unapproved stop-leak has caused the discoloration. This may eventually plug the system and cause overheating. The best course of action would be to empty the system, repair the leak and refill with the correct 50/50 mixture of ethylene glycol and water.
• If the coolant is reddish brown, there is rust in the system. The entire cooling system should be flushed and refilled.
• If there is an iridescent sheen floating on top of the coolant, there is likely a small amount of engine oil leaking into the system. Check the oil dipstick to look for drops of greenish coolant or whether the oil is milky in appearance. If the oil checks out normal, the sheen on top of the coolant may not be an immediate problem, but be advised it may grow worse and should be closely monitored during routine maintenance.
• If the coolant is milky brown (like coffee with heavy cream) engine oil is entering the cooling system. On 7.3L diesel and 7.5L gasoline engines, the oil cooler is the most likely cause of the problem and should

be checked first. Next check in order: the head gasket, cylinder block and cylinder head. Check also the transmission for traces of coolant (the transmission fluid will be milky). If found, the transmission should be flushed and refilled.

3. Assuming the coolant is normal, add fluid as necessary.

➡**While you are checking the coolant level, check the radiator cap for a worn or cracked gasket. It the cap doesn't seal properly, fluid will be lost and the engine will overheat. Worn caps should be replaced with a new one of the same pressure rating.**

CLEAN RADIATOR OF DEBRIS

▶ **See Figure 131**

Periodically clean any debris—leaves, paper, insects, etc.—from the radiator fins. Pick the large pieces off by hand. The smaller pieces can be washed away with water pressure from a hose.

Carefully straighten any bent radiator fins with a pair of needle nose pliers. Be careful—the fins are very soft. Don't wiggle the fins back and forth too much. Straighten them once and try not to move them again.

DRAIN AND REFILL THE COOLING SYSTEM

▶ **See Figures 132, 133, 134, 135 and 136**

1. Drain the existing antifreeze coolant. Open the radiator petcock and remove the engine drain plugs, or disconnect the bottom radiator hose, at the radiator outlet.

➡**Before opening the radiator petcock, spray it with some penetrating lubricant.**

❊❊ CAUTION

When draining the coolant, keep in mind that cats and dogs are attracted by the ethylene glycol antifreeze, and are quite likely to drink any that is left in an uncovered container or in puddles on the ground. This will prove fatal in sufficient quantity. Always drain the coolant into a sealable container. Coolant should be reused unless it is contaminated or several years old.

2. Close the petcock or reconnect the lower hose and fill the system with water.
3. Add a can of quality radiator flush.
4. Place the heater control in the HOT position.
5. Idle the engine until the upper radiator hose gets hot.
6. Drain the system again.
7. Repeat this process until the drained water is clear and free of scale.
8. Close all petcocks and connect all the hoses.
9. If equipped with a coolant recovery system, flush the reservoir with water and leave empty.
10. Determine the capacity of your coolant system (see the Capacities specification chart). Add a 50/50 mix of quality antifreeze (ethylene glycol) and water to provide the desired protection.

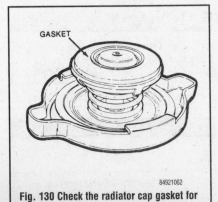

Fig. 130 Check the radiator cap gasket for cracks or wear

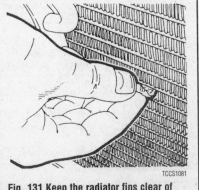

Fig. 131 Keep the radiator fins clear of debris for maximum cooling

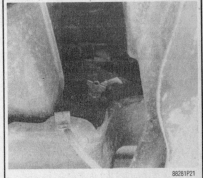

Fig. 132 Location of the radiator draincock—F-150 shown

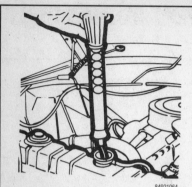

Fig. 133 Check antifreeze protection with an inexpensive tester

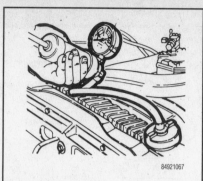

Fig. 134 The system should be pressure tested once a year

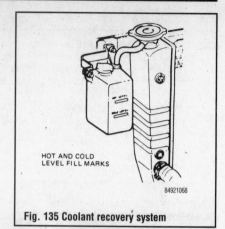

HOT AND COLD
LEVEL FILL MARKS

Fig. 135 Coolant recovery system

Fig. 136 Fill the cooling system with the correct mixture and amount of coolant

Fig. 137 Add clean brake fluid to the brake master cylinder reservoir as necessary

11. Run the engine to operating temperature.
12. Stop the engine and check the coolant level.
13. Check the level of protection with an antifreeze tester, replace the cap and check for leaks.

Brake Master Cylinder

FLUID RECOMMENDATIONS

Use Ford Heavy-Duty Brake Fluid, Ford specification No. ESA–M6C25–A, or equivalent; do not overfill.

LEVEL CHECK

▶ See Figure 137

The master cylinder reservoir is located under the hood, on the left side firewall. There is a rubber diaphragm in the top of the master cylinder cap. As the fluid level lowers in the reservoir due to normal brake shoe wear or leakage, the diaphragm takes up the space. This is to prevent the loss of brake fluid out the vented cap and contamination by dirt.
1. Before removing the master cylinder reservoir cap, make sure the vehicle is resting on level ground and clean all dirt away from the top of the master cylinder.
2. On early models, pry off the retaining clip or unscrew the hold-down bolt and remove the cap.
3. On later models, simply unscrew the cap.
4. The brake fluid level should be within ¼ in. (6mm) of the top of the reservoir, on cast iron cylinders, or, at the level mark on plastic reservoirs.

➡ If the level of the brake fluid is less than half the volume of the reservoir, it is advised that you check the brake system for leaks. Leaks in the hydraulic brake system most commonly occur at the wheel cylinder.

5. After filling the master cylinder to the proper level with heavy duty brake fluid, but before replacing the cap, fold the rubber diaphragm up into the cap, then replace the cap in the reservoir and tighten the retaining bolt or snap the retaining clip into place.

Clutch Master Cylinder

FLUID RECOMMENDATIONS

Keep the reservoir topped up with Ford Heavy-Duty Brake fluid Ford specification No. ESA–M6C25–A, or equivalent; do not overfill.

LEVEL CHECK

The hydraulic fluid reservoirs on these systems are mounted on the firewall. Fluid level checks are performed like those on the brake hydraulic system. The proper fluid level is indicated by a step on the reservoir.

✵✵ CAUTION

Carefully clean the top and sides of the reservoir before opening, to prevent contamination of the system with dirt, etc. Remove the reservoir diaphragm before adding fluid, and replace after filling.

See the illustration of the hydraulic clutch assembly in Section 7.

Power Steering Pump

FLUID RECOMMENDATIONS

Use Ford Premium Power Steering Fluid, or an equivalent power steering fluid that meets Ford specification ESW–M2C33–F.

LEVEL CHECK

▶ **See Figures 138, 139 and 140**

1. Position the vehicle on level ground. Run the engine until the fluid is at normal operating temperature.
2. Turn the steering wheel all the way to the left and right several times.
3. Position the wheels in the straight ahead position, then shut off the engine.
4. Check the fluid level on the dipstick which is attached to the reservoir cap. The level should be between the ADD and FULL marks on the dipstick.
5. Add fluid if necessary. Do not overfill. Use an approved power steering fluid.

Manual Steering Gear

LUBRICANT RECOMMENDATIONS

Use Ford Steering Gear Grease, C3AZ–1957B–A (ESW–M1C87–A), or equivalent.

LEVEL CHECK

2-Wheel Drive Models

1. Center the steering wheel.
2. Remove the steering gear housing filler plug.
3. Remove the lower cover-to-housing attaching bolt.
4. With a clean punch or similar object, clean out or push the loose lubricant in the filler plug hole and cover-to-housing attaching bolt hole inward.
5. Slowly turn the steering wheel to the left until the linkage reaches its stop. Lubricant should rise within the cover lower bolt hole.
6. Slowly turn the steering wheel to the right until the linkage reaches its stop. Lubricant should rise within the filler plug hole.
7. If lubricant does not rise in both of the holes, add steering gear lubricant until it comes out both the holes during the check.
8. Install the lower cover-to-housing attaching bolt and the filler plug.

4-Wheel Drive Models

1. Remove the filler plug from the sector shaft cover.
2. Check to see if the lubricant level is visible in the filler plug tower. If the lubricant is visible, install the filler plug. If the lubricant is not visible, add steering gear lubricant until the lubricant is visible about 1 in. (25mm) from the top of the hole in the filler plug tower.
3. Replace the filler plug.

Chassis Greasing

KNUCKLES AND STEERING LINKAGE

The lubrication chart indicates where the grease fittings are located. The vehicle should be greased according to the intervals in the Preventive Maintenance Schedule at the end of this section. Fittings are usually located on the ball joints, steering linkage and driveshaft(s). In some cases, a threaded plug will be found which will have to be removed to allow the installation of a fitting. Fittings are available at most auto parts stores.

Using a grease gun loaded with multi-purpose chassis lube, pump grease through the fitting until some grease is forced from the ball stud or joint being serviced.

Wipe the fitting clean before applying the grease gun and wipe off the excess grease after servicing.

➡ **The grease fitting inside the double cardan joint on the driveshaft, will require a special needle adapter for the grease gun**

PARKING BRAKE LINKAGE

Use chassis grease on the parking brake cable where it contacts the cable guides, levers and linkage.

AUTOMATIC TRANSMISSION LINKAGE

Apply a small amount of clean engine oil to the kickdown and shift linkage points at 7,500 mile intervals.

Body Lubrication And Maintenance

LOCK CYLINDERS

Apply graphite lubricant sparingly through the key slot. Insert the key and operate the lock several times to be sure that the lubricant is worked into the lock cylinder.

HOOD LATCH AND HINGES

Clean the latch surfaces and apply clean engine oil to the latch pilot bolts and the spring anchor. Also lubricate the hood hinges with engine oil. Use a chassis grease to lubricate all the pivot points in the latch release mechanism.

DOOR HINGES

The gas tank filler door and truck doors should be wiped clean and lubricated with clean engine oil once a year. The door lock cylinders and latch mech-

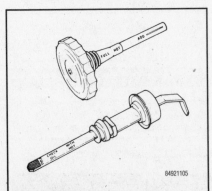

Fig. 138 Typical power steering pump reservoir dipsticks

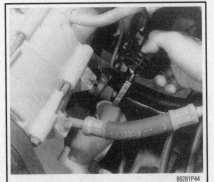

Fig. 139 Check the power steering fluid against the markings on the dipstick

Fig. 140 Add power steering fluid as necessary

anisms should be lubricated periodically with a few drops of graphite lock lubricant or a few shots of silicone spray.

BODY DRAIN HOLES

Be sure that the drain holes in the doors and rocker panels are cleared of obstruction. A small punch or a length cut from a wire coat hanger can be used to clear them of any debris.

2-Wheel Drive Front Wheel Bearings

PRECAUTIONS

Before handling the bearings, there are a few things that you should remember to do and not to do.

DO the following:
- Remove all outside dirt from the housing before exposing the bearing.
- Treat a used bearing as gently as you would a new one.
- Work with clean tools in clean surroundings.
- Use clean, dry canvas gloves, or at least clean, dry hands.
- Clean solvents and flushing fluids are a must.
- Use clean paper when laying out the bearings to dry.
- Protect disassembled bearings from rust and dirt. Cover them up.
- Use clean rags to wipe bearings.
- Keep the bearings in oil-proof paper when they are to be stored or are not in use.
- Clean the inside of the housing before replacing the bearing.

DO NOT do the following:
- Do not work in dirty surroundings.
- Do not use dirty, chipped or damaged tools.
- Do not work on wooden work benches or use wooden mallets.
- Do not handle bearings with dirty or moist hands.
- Do not use gasoline for cleaning; use a safe solvent.
- Do not spin-dry bearings with compressed air. They will be damaged.
- Do not spin dirty bearings.
- Do not use cotton waste or dirty cloths to wipe bearings.
- Do not scratch or nick bearing surfaces.
- Do not allow the bearing to come in contact with dirt or rust at any time.

REMOVAL, REPACKING, AND INSTALLATION

✳✳ WARNING

Before proceeding with any work on the front wheel bearings, read the precautions listed at the beginning of this section.

1. Raise and support the front end on jackstands.
2. Remove the wheel cover. Remove the wheel.
3. Remove the caliper from the disc and wire it to the underbody to prevent damage to the brake hose. See Section 9

4. Remove the grease cap from the hub. Then, remove the cotter pin, nut lock, adjusting nut and flat washer from the spindle. Remove the outer bearing assembly from the hub.
5. Pull the hub and disc assembly off the wheel spindle.
6. Remove and discard the old grease retainer. Remove the inner bearing cone and roller assembly from the hub.
7. Clean all grease from the inner and outer bearing cups with solvent. Inspect the cups for pits, scratches, or excessive wear. If the cups are damaged, remove them with a drift.
8. Clean the inner and outer cone and roller assemblies with solvent and shake them dry. If the cone and roller assemblies show excessive wear or damage, replace them with the bearing cups as a unit.
9. Clean the spindle and the inside of the hub with solvent to thoroughly remove all old grease.
10. Covering the spindle with a clean cloth, brush all loose dirt and dust from the brake assembly. Remove the cloth carefully so as to not get dirt on the spindle.
11. If the inner and/or outer bearing cups were removed, install the replacement cups on the hub. Be sure that the cups seat properly in the hub.
12. It is imperative that all old grease be removed from the bearings and surrounding surfaces before repacking. The new lithium-based grease is not compatible with the sodium base grease used in the past.
13. Install the hub and disc on the wheel spindle. To prevent damage to the grease retainer and spindle threads, keep the hub centered on the spindle.
14. Install the outer bearing cone and roller assembly and the flat washer on the spindle. Install the adjusting nut.
15. Adjust the wheel bearings by tightening the adjusting nut to 17–25 ft. lbs. (23–38 Nm) with the wheel rotating to seat the bearing. Then back off the adjusting nut ½ turn. Retighten the adjusting nut to 10–15 inch lbs. (1.1–1.7 Nm). Install the locknut so that the castellations are aligned with the cotter pin hole. Install the cotter pin. Bend the ends of the cotter pin around the castellations of the locknut to prevent interference with the radio static collector in the grease cap. Install the grease cap.

➡**New bolts MUST be used when servicing floating caliper units. The upper bolt must be tightened first. For caliper service see Section 9.**

16. Install the wheels.
17. Install the wheel cover.

ADJUSTMENT

◆ **See Figures 141, 142, 143 and 144**

The front wheels each rotate on a set of opposed, tapered roller bearings as shown in the accompanying illustration. The grease retainer at the inside of the hub prevents lubricant from leaking into the brake drum.

1987–89 F-150, F-250, F-350

1. Raise and support the front end on jackstands.
2. Remove the grease cap and remove excess grease from the end of the spindle.
3. Remove the cotter pin and nut lock shown in the illustration.
4. Back off the adjusting nut 2-3 turns.

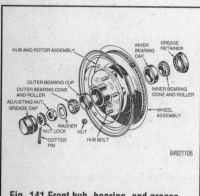

Fig. 141 Front hub, bearing, and grease seal with disc brakes—2-wheel drive

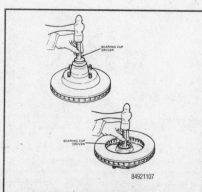

Fig. 142 2-wheel drive front wheel bearing race removal using a driver

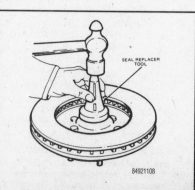

Fig. 143 2-wheel drive front wheel bearing grease seal installation

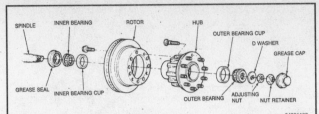

Fig. 144 Front hub, rotor, bearings and related parts for the F-Super Duty

5. Rotate the wheel, hub and rotor assembly while tightening the adjusting nut to 22–25 ft. lbs. (30–34 Nm) in order to seat the bearings.

6. Back off the adjusting nut ⅛ turn.

7. Locate the nut lock on the adjusting nut so that the castellations on the lock are lined up with the cotter pin hole in the spindle. Try to avoid turning the adjusting nut.

8. Install the new cotter pin, bending the ends of the cotter pin around the castellated flange of the nut lock. If possible, check the bearing end-play. Proper end-play should be 0.001–0.010 in. (0.025–0.254mm).

9. Check the wheel for proper rotation, then install the grease cap. If the wheel still does not rotate properly, inspect and clean or replace the wheel bearings and cups.

1990–96 F-150, F-250, F-350 and All F-Super Duty Chassis Cab

1. Raise and support the front end on jackstands.

2. Remove the grease cap and remove excess grease from the end of the spindle.

3. Remove the cotter pin and nut lock shown in the illustration.

4. Loosen the adjusting nut 3 full turns. Obtain a clearance between the brake rotor and brake pads by rocking the wheel in and out several times to push the pads away from the rotor. If that doesn't work, you'll have to remove the caliper (see Section 9). The rotor must turn freely.

5. Tighten the adjusting nut to 17–25 ft. lbs. (23–34 Nm) while rotating the brake rotor in the opposite direction.

6. Back off the adjusting nut 120–180° (⅓–½ turn).

7. Tighten the nut to 18–20 inch lbs. (2.03–2.26 Nm) while rotating the brake rotor in the opposite direction.

8. Install the retainer and cotter pin without additional movement of the locknut.

9. If a dial indicator is available, check the end-play at the hub. End-play should be 0.00024–0.0050 in. (0.006–0.127mm).

10. Install the grease cap.

11. If removed, install the caliper.

F-Super Duty Stripped Chassis Motor Home Chassis

1. Raise and support the front end on jackstands.

2. Remove the grease cap and remove excess grease from the end of the spindle.

3. Remove the cotter pin and nut lock shown in the illustration.

4. Loosen the adjusting nut 3 full turns. Obtain a clearance between the brake rotor and brake pads by rocking the wheel in and out several times to push the pads away from the rotor. If that doesn't work, you'll have to remove the caliper (see Section 9). The rotor must turn freely.

5. Tighten the adjusting nut to 17–25 ft. lbs. (23–34 Nm) while rotating the brake rotor in the opposite direction.

6. Back off the adjusting nut 120–180° (⅓–½ turn).

7. Tighten the adjusting nut to 18–20 inch lbs. (2–2.26 Nm) while rotating the brake rotor.

8. If a dial indicator is available, check the end-play at the hub. End-play should be 0.00024–0.0050 in. (0.006–0.127mm). The torque required to turn the hub should be 10–25 inch lbs. (1.13–2.8 Nm).

9. Install the locknut, cotter pin and grease cap.

10. If removed, install the caliper.

11. Install the wheel. Tighten the lug nuts to 140 ft. lbs. (190 Nm). After 500 miles, retighten the lug nuts.

Front Axle Locking Hubs (4x4 only)

The front axle hubs should be disassembled, cleaned and repacked with new grease approximately every 30,000 miles. Refer to Section 7 for removal and installation procedures.

4-Wheel Drive Front Wheel Bearings

PRECAUTIONS

Before handling the bearings, there are a few things that you should remember to do and not to do.

DO the following:

• Remove all outside dirt from the housing before exposing the bearing.
• Treat a used bearing as gently as you would a new one.
• Work with clean tools in clean surroundings.
• Use clean, dry canvas gloves, or at least clean, dry hands.
• Clean solvents and flushing fluids are a must.
• Use clean paper when laying out the bearings to dry.
• Protect disassembled bearings from rust and dirt. Cover them up.
• Use clean rags to wipe bearings.
• Keep the bearings in oil-proof paper when they are to be stored or are not in use.
• Clean the inside of the housing before replacing the bearing.

DO NOT do the following:

• Do not work in dirty surroundings.
• Do not use dirty, chipped or damaged tools.
• Do not work on wooden work benches or use wooden mallets.
• Do not handle bearings with dirty or moist hands.
• Do not use gasoline for cleaning; use a safe solvent.
• Do not spin-dry bearings with compressed air. They will be damaged.
• Do not spin dirty bearings.
• Do not use cotton waste or dirty cloths to wipe bearings.
• Do not scratch or nick bearing surfaces.
• Do not allow the bearing to come in contact with dirt or rust at any time.

REMOVAL, REPACKING AND INSTALLATION

With Manual Locking Hubs

▶ **See Figures 145, 146, 147, 148 and 149**

✳ WARNING

Before proceeding with any work on the front wheel bearings, read the precautions listed at the beginning of this section.

Fig. 145 Remove the bearing adjusting nut from the manual locking hub—F-150 shown

Fig. 146 As you remove components, organize them for cleaning and inspection

Fig. 147 Slide the hub and disc assembly off of the spindle

Fig. 148 Remove the seal/retainer to expose the inner bearings inside the hub and disc assembly

Fig. 149 Gently drive in the new cup (seal) using a suitable tool and mallet

1. Raise the vehicle and install jackstands.
2. Refer to Manual Locking Hub Removal and Installation and remove the hub assemblies.
3. On Bronco, F-150 and F-250 LD with the Dana 44 axle: apply inward pressure on the bearing adjusting nut, using a socket made for that purpose, available at most auto parts stores, to disengage the adjusting nut locking splines, while turning it counterclockwise to remove it. On F-250 HD (Dana 50 axle) and F-350, use the hub nut tool to unscrew the outer locking nut. Then, remove the lock ring from the bearing adjusting nut. This can be done with your finger tips or an O-ring pick. Use the locknut socket to remove the bearing adjusting nut.
4. Remove the caliper and suspend it out of the way. See Section 9.
5. Slide the hub and disc assembly off of the spindle. The outer wheel bearing will slide out as the hub is removed, so be prepared to catch it.
6. Lay the hub on a clean work surface. Carefully drive the inner bearing cone and grease seal out of the hub using Tool T69L–1102–A, or equivalent.
7. Inspect the bearing cups for pits or cracks. If necessary, remove them with a drift. If new cups are installed, install new bearings.
8. Lubricate the bearings with Multi-Purpose Lubricant Ford Specification, ESA–MIC7–B or equivalent. Clean all old grease from the hub. Pack the cones and rollers. If a bearing packer is not available, work as much lubricant as possible between the rollers and the cages.
9. Drive new cups into place with a driver, making sure that they are fully seated.
10. Position the inner bearing cone and roller in the inner cup and install the grease retainer.
11. Carefully position the hub and disc assembly on the spindle.
12. Install the outer bearing cone and roller, and the adjusting nut.

On Bronco, F-150 and F-250 LD with the Dana 44 axle:
   a. Make sure the metal stamping on the adjusting nut faces inboard and the inner diameter key on the nut enters the spindle keyway.
   b. Apply inward pressure on the hub nut wrench and tighten the adjusting nut to 70 ft. lbs. (95 Nm) while rotating the hub back and forth to seat the bearings.
   c. Apply inward pressure on the wrench and back off the nut about 90° then, re-tighten the nut to 15–20 ft. lbs. (20–27 Nm).
   d. Remove the wrench. End-play of the hub/rotor assembly should be 0 (zero) and the torque required to rotate the hub assembly should not exceed 20 inch lbs. (2.26 Nm).
13. Install the outer bearing cone and roller, and the adjusting nut.

On the F-250 HD (Dana 50 axle) and F-350:

➡ **The adjusting nut has a small dowel on one side. This dowel faces outward to engage the locking ring.**

   a. Using the hub nut socket and a torque wrench, tighten the bearing adjusting nut to 50 ft. lbs. (68 Nm), while rotating the wheel back and forth to seat the bearings.
   b. Back off the adjusting nut approximately 90°.
   c. Install the lock ring by turning the nut to the nearest hole and inserting the dowel pin.

✳✳ WARNING

The dowel pin must seat in a lock ring hole for proper bearing adjustment and wheel retention!

   d. Install the outer lock nut and tighten to 160–205 ft. lbs. (217–278 Nm). Final end-play of the wheel on the spindle should be 0–0.004 in. (0–0.15mm).
14. Assemble the hub parts.
15. Install the caliper.
16. Remove the jackstands and lower the vehicle.

With Automatic Locking Hubs

✳✳ WARNING

Before proceeding with any work on the front wheel bearings, read the precautions listed at the beginning of this section.

1. Raise the vehicle and install jackstands.
2. Refer to Automatic Locking Hub Removal and Installation and remove the hub assemblies.
3. Using a socket made for that purpose, available at most auto parts stores, use the hub nut tool to unscrew the outer locking nut.
4. Remove the lock ring from the bearing adjusting nut. This can be done with your finger tips or a screwdriver.
5. Use the locknut socket to remove the bearing adjusting nut.
6. Remove the caliper and suspend it out of the way. See Section 9.
7. Slide the hub and disc assembly off of the spindle. The outer wheel bearing will slide out as the hub is removed, so be prepared to catch it.

8. Lay the hub on a clean work surface. Carefully drive the inner bearing cone and grease seal out of the hub using Tool T69L–1102–A, or equivalent.

9. Inspect the bearing cups for pits or cracks. If necessary, remove them with a drift. If new cups are installed, install new bearings.

10. Lubricate the bearings with Multi-Purpose Lubricant Ford Specification, ESA–MIC7–B or equivalent. Clean all old grease from the hub. Pack the cones and rollers. If a bearing packer is not available, work as much lubricant as possible between the rollers and the cages.

11. Drive new cups into place with a driver, making sure that they are fully seated.

12. Position the inner bearing cone and roller in the inner cup and install the grease retainer.

13. Carefully position the hub and disc assembly on the spindle.

14. Install the outer bearing cone and roller, and the adjusting nut.

➡️**The adjusting nut has a small dowel on one side. This dowel faces outward to engage the locking ring.**

15. Using the hub nut socket and a torque wrench, tighten the bearing adjusting nut to 50 ft. lbs. (68 Nm), while rotating the wheel back and forth to seat the bearings.

16. Back off the adjusting nut approximately 90°.

17. Install the lock ring by turning the nut to the nearest hole and inserting the dowel pin.

➡️**The dowel pin must seat in a lock ring hole for proper bearing adjustment and wheel retention.**

18. Install the outer lock nut and tighten to 160–205 ft. lbs. (217–278 Nm). Final end-play of the wheel on the spindle should be 0–0.004 in. (0–0.15mm).

19. Assemble the hub parts.

20. Install the caliper.

21. Remove the jackstands and lower the vehicle.

TRAILER TOWING

Factory trailer towing packages are available on most trucks. However, if you are installing a trailer hitch and wiring on your truck, there are a few thing that you ought to know.

Trailer Weight

Trailer weight is the first, and most important, factor in determining whether or not your vehicle is suitable for towing the trailer you have in mind. The horsepower-to-weight ratio should be calculated. The basic standard is a ratio of 35:1. That is, 35 pounds of GVW for every horsepower.

To calculate this ratio, multiply you engine's rated horsepower by 35, then subtract the weight of the vehicle, including passengers and luggage. The resulting figure is the ideal maximum trailer weight that you can tow. One point to consider: a numerically higher axle ratio can offset what appears to be a low trailer weight. If the weight of the trailer that you have in mind is somewhat higher than the weight you just calculated, you might consider changing your rear axle ratio to compensate.

Hitch (Tongue) Weight

There are three kinds of hitches: bumper mounted, frame mounted, and load equalizing.

Bumper mounted hitches are those which attach solely to the vehicle's bumper. Many states prohibit towing with this type of hitch, when it attaches to the vehicle's stock bumper, since it subjects the bumper to stresses for which it was not designed. Aftermarket rear step bumpers, designed for trailer towing, are acceptable for use with bumper mounted hitches.

Frame mounted hitches can be of the type which bolts to two or more points on the frame, plus the bumper, or just to several points on the frame. Frame mounted hitches can also be of the tongue type, for Class I towing, or, of the receiver type, for Classes II and III.

Load equalizing hitches are usually used for large trailers. Most equalizing hitches are welded in place and use equalizing bars and chains to level the vehicle after the trailer is hooked up.

The bolt-on hitches are the most common, since they are relatively easy to install.

Check the gross weight rating of your trailer. Tongue weight is usually figured as 10% of gross trailer weight. Therefore, a trailer with a maximum gross weight of 2,000 lb. will have a maximum tongue weight of 200 lb. Class I trailers fall into this category. Class II trailers are those with a gross weight rating of 2,000–3,500 lb., while Class III trailers fall into the 3,500–6,000 lb. category. Class IV trailers are those over 6,000 lb. and are for use with fifth wheel trucks, only.

When you've determined the hitch that you'll need, follow the manufacturer's installation instructions, exactly, especially when it comes to fastener torques. The hitch will subjected to a lot of stress and good hitches come with hardened bolts. Never substitute an inferior bolt for a hardened bolt.

Wiring

Wiring the truck for towing is fairly easy. There are a number of good wiring kits available and these should be used, rather than trying to design your own. All trailers will need brake lights and turn signals as well as tail lights and side marker lights. Most states require extra marker lights for overly wide trailers. Also, most states have recently required backup lights for trailers, and most trailer manufacturers have been building trailers with backup lights for several years.

Additionally, some Class I, most Class II and just about all Class III trailers will have electric brakes.

Add to this number an accessories wire, to operate trailer internal equipment or to charge the trailer's battery, and you can have as many as seven wires in the harness.

Determine the equipment on your trailer and buy the wiring kit necessary. The kit will contain all the wires needed, plus a plug adapter set which included the female plug, mounted on the bumper or hitch, and the male plug, wired into, or plugged into the trailer harness.

When installing the kit, follow the manufacturer's instructions. The color coding of the wires is standard throughout the industry.

One point to note, some domestic vehicles, and most imported vehicles, have separate turn signals. On most domestic vehicles, the brake lights and rear turn signals operate with the same bulb. For those vehicles with separate turn signals, you can purchase an isolation unit so that the brake lights won't blink whenever the turn signals are operated, or, you can go to your local electronics supply house and buy four diodes to wire in series with the brake and turn signal bulbs. Diodes will isolate the brake and turn signals. The choice is yours. The isolation units are simple and quick to install, but far more expensive than the diodes. The diodes, however, require more work to install properly, since they require the cutting of each bulb's wire and soldering in place of the diode.

One final point, the best kits are those with a spring loaded cover on the vehicle mounted socket. This cover prevents dirt and moisture from corroding the terminals. Never let the vehicle socket hang loosely. Always mount it securely to the bumper or hitch.

Cooling

ENGINE

Overflow Tank

One of the most common, if not THE most common, problem associated with trailer towing is engine overheating.

With factory installed trailer towing packages, a heavy duty cooling system is usually included. Heavy duty cooling systems are available as optional equipment on most trucks, with or without a trailer package. If you have one of these extra-capacity systems, you shouldn't have any overheating problems.

If you have a standard cooling system, without an expansion tank, you'll definitely need to get an aftermarket expansion tank kit, preferably one with at least a 2 quart capacity. These kits are easily installed on the radiator's overflow hose, and come with a pressure cap designed for expansion tanks.

Flex Fan

Another helpful accessory is a Flex Fan. These fan are large diameter units are designed to provide more airflow at low speeds, with blades that have deeply cupped surfaces. The blades then flex, or flatten out, at high speed, when less cooling air is needed. These fans are far lighter in weight than stock fans, requiring less horsepower to drive them. Also, they are far quieter than stock fans.

If you do decide to replace your stock fan with a flex fan, note that if your truck has a fan clutch, a spacer between the flex fan and water pump hub will be needed.

Oil Cooler

Aftermarket engine oil coolers are helpful for prolonging engine oil life and reducing overall engine temperatures. Both of these factors increase engine life.

While not absolutely necessary in towing Class I and some Class II trailers, they are recommended for heavier Class II and all Class III towing.

Engine oil cooler systems consist of an adapter, screwed on in place of the oil filter, a remote filter mounting and a multi-tube, finned heat exchanger, which is mounted in front of the radiator or air conditioning condenser.

TRANSMISSION

An automatic transmission is usually recommended for trailer towing. Modern automatics have proven reliable and, of course, easy to operate, in trailer towing.

The increased load of a trailer, however, causes an increase in the temperature of the automatic transmission fluid. Heat is the worst enemy of an automatic transmission. As the temperature of the fluid increases, the life of the fluid decreases.

TOWING THE VEHICLE

If your truck has to be towed by a tow truck, it can be towed forward for any distance with the driveshaft connected as long as it is done fairly slowly. Otherwise disconnect the driveshaft at the rear axle and tie it up. On a truck with a full-floating rear axle, the rear axle shafts can be removed and the hub covered

JUMP STARTING A DEAD BATTERY

♦ See Figure 150

Whenever a vehicle is jump started, precautions must be followed in order to prevent the possibility of personal injury. Remember that batteries contain a small amount of explosive hydrogen gas which is a by-product of battery charging. Sparks should always be avoided when working around batteries, especially when attaching jumper cables. To minimize the possibility of accidental sparks, follow the procedure carefully.

✳✳ CAUTION

NEVER hook the batteries up in a series circuit or the entire electrical system will go up in smoke, including the starter!

Vehicles equipped with a diesel engine may utilize two 12 volt batteries. If so, the batteries are connected in a parallel circuit (positive terminal to positive terminal, negative terminal to negative terminal). Hooking the batteries up in parallel circuit increases battery cranking power without increasing total battery voltage output. Output remains at 12 volts. On the other hand, hooking two 12

It is essential, therefore, that you install an automatic transmission cooler.

The cooler, which consists of a multi-tube, finned heat exchanger, is usually installed in front of the radiator or air conditioning compressor, and hooked inline with the transmission cooler tank inlet line. Follow the cooler manufacturer's installation instructions.

Select a cooler of at least adequate capacity, based upon the combined gross weights of the truck and trailer.

Cooler manufacturers recommend that you use an aftermarket cooler in addition to, and not instead of, the present cooling tank in your truck's radiator. If you do want to use it in place of the radiator cooling tank, get a cooler at least two sizes larger than normally necessary.

➡A transmission cooler can, sometimes, cause slow or harsh shifting in the transmission during cold weather, until the fluid has a chance to come up to normal operating temperature. Some coolers can be purchased with or retrofitted with a temperature bypass valve which will allow fluid flow through the cooler only when the fluid has reached operating temperature, or above.

Handling A Trailer

Towing a trailer with ease and safety requires a certain amount of experience. It's a good idea to learn the feel of a trailer by practicing turning, stopping and backing in an open area such as an empty parking lot.

to prevent lubricant loss. If your 4-wheel drive truck has to be towed backward, remove the front axle driving hubs, or disengage the lock-out hubs to prevent the front differential from rotating. If the drive hubs are removed, improvise a cover to keep out dust and dirt.

volt batteries up in a series circuit (positive terminal to negative terminal, positive terminal to negative terminal) increases total battery output to 24 volts (12 volts plus 12 volts).

Jump Starting Precautions

- Be sure that both batteries are of the same voltage. Vehicles covered by this manual and most vehicles on the road today utilize a 12 volt charging system.
- Be sure that both batteries are of the same polarity (have the same terminal, in most cases NEGATIVE grounded).
- Be sure that the vehicles are not touching or a short could occur.
- On serviceable batteries, be sure the vent cap holes are not obstructed.
- Do not smoke or allow sparks anywhere near the batteries.
- In cold weather, make sure the battery electrolyte is not frozen. This can occur more readily in a battery that has been in a state of discharge.
- Do not allow electrolyte to contact your skin or clothing.

Single Battery Gasoline Engines

PROCEDURE

1. Make sure that the voltages of the 2 batteries are the same. Most batteries and charging systems are of the 12 volt variety.
2. Pull the jumping vehicle (with the good battery) into a position so the jumper cables can reach the dead battery and that vehicle's engine. Make sure that the vehicles do NOT touch.
3. Place the transmissions of both vehicles in **Neutral** (MT) or **P** (AT), as applicable, then firmly set their parking brakes.

➡If necessary for safety reasons, the hazard lights on both vehicles may be operated throughout the entire procedure without significantly increasing the difficulty of jumping the dead battery.

```
MAKE CONNECTIONS IN NUMERICAL ORDER
        ①  FIRST JUMPER CABLE
DO NOT ALLOW
VEHICLES TO TOUCH
           DISCHARGED
           BATTERY
        ④  SECOND JUMPER CABLE
           MAKE LAST
           CONNECTION ON
           ENGINE, AWAY
           FROM BATTERY
                            ③
           BATTERY IN VEHICLE
           WITH CHARGED BATTERY
                            ②
                      TCCS1080
```

Fig. 150 Connect the jumper cables to the batteries and engine in the order shown

4. Turn all lights and accessories OFF on both vehicles. Make sure the ignition switches on both vehicles are turned to the **OFF** position.

5. Cover the battery cell caps with a rag, but do not cover the terminals.

6. Make sure the terminals on both batteries are clean and free of corrosion or proper electrical connection will be impeded. If necessary, clean the battery terminals before proceeding.

7. Identify the positive (+) and negative (–) terminals on both batteries.

8. Connect the first jumper cable to the positive (+) terminal of the dead battery, then connect the other end of that cable to the positive (+) terminal of the booster (good) battery.

9. Connect one end of the other jumper cable to the negative (–) terminal on the booster battery and the final cable clamp to an engine bolt head, alternator bracket or other solid, metallic point on the engine with the dead battery. Try to pick a ground on the engine that is positioned away from the battery in order to minimize the possibility of the 2 clamps touching should one loosen during the procedure. DO NOT connect this clamp to the negative (–) terminal of the bad battery.

✳✳ CAUTION

Be very careful to keep the jumper cables away from moving parts (cooling fan, belts, etc.) on both engines.

10. Check to make sure that the cables are routed away from any moving parts, then start the donor vehicle's engine. Run the engine at moderate speed for several minutes to allow the dead battery a chance to receive some initial charge.

11. With the donor vehicle's engine still running slightly above idle, try to start the vehicle with the dead battery. Crank the engine for no more than 10 seconds at a time and let the starter cool for at least 20 seconds between tries. If the vehicle does not start in 3 tries, it is likely that something else is also wrong or that the battery needs additional time to charge.

12. Once the vehicle is started, allow it to run at idle for a few seconds to make sure that it is operating properly.

13. Turn ON the headlights, heater blower and, if equipped, the rear defroster of both vehicles in order to reduce the severity of voltage spikes and subsequent risk of damage to the vehicles' electrical systems when the cables are disconnected. This step is especially important to any vehicle equipped with computer control modules.

14. Carefully disconnect the cables in the reverse order of connection. Start with the negative cable that is attached to the engine ground, then the negative cable on the donor battery. Disconnect the positive cable from the donor battery and finally, disconnect the positive cable from the formerly dead battery. Be careful when disconnecting the cables from the positive terminals not to allow the alligator clips to touch any metal on either vehicle or a short and sparks will occur.

Dual Battery Diesel Engines

PROCEDURE

▶ **See Figure 151**

Ford pickups equipped with the 6.9L or 7.3L V8 diesel utilize two 12 volt batteries, one on either side of the engine compartment. The batteries are con-

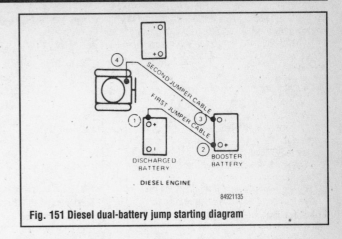

Fig. 151 Diesel dual-battery jump starting diagram

nected in a parallel circuit (positive terminal to positive terminal, negative terminal to negative terminal). Hooking the batteries up in parallel circuit increases battery cranking power without increasing total battery voltage output. Output remains at 12 volts. On the other hand, hooking two 12 volt batteries up in a series circuit (positive terminal to negative terminal, positive terminal to negative terminal) increases total battery output to 24 volts (12 volts plus 12 volts).

✳✳ CAUTION

NEVER hook the batteries up in a series circuit or the entire electrical system will go up in smoke, especially the starter.

In the event that a diesel pick-up needs to be jump started, use the following procedure.

1. Turn all lights off.

2. Turn on the heater blower motor to remove transient voltage.

3. Connect one jumper cable to the passenger side battery positive (+) terminal and the other cable clamp to the positive (+) terminal to the booster (good) battery.

4. Connect one end of the other jumper cable to the negative (–) terminal of the booster (good) battery and the other cable clamp to an engine bolt head, alternator bracket or other solid, metallic point on the diesel engine. DO NOT connect this clamp to the negative (–) terminal of the bad battery.

✳✳ CAUTION

Be very careful to keep the jumper cables away from moving parts (cooling fan, belts, etc.) on both engines.

5. Start the engine of the donor truck and run it at moderate speed.

6. Start the engine of the diesel.

7. When the diesel starts, remove the cable from the engine block before disconnecting the positive terminal.

JACKING

▶ **See Figures 152, 153, 154, 155 and 156**

Your vehicle was supplied with a jack for emergency road repairs. This jack is fine for changing a flat tire or other short term procedures not requiring you to go beneath the vehicle. If it is used in an emergency situation, carefully follow the instructions provided either with the jack or in your owner's manual. Do not attempt to use the jack on any portions of the vehicle other than specified by Ford Motor Co. Always block the diagonally opposite wheel when using a jack.

A more convenient way of jacking is the use of a garage or floor jack.

Never place the jack under the radiator, engine or transmission components. Severe and expensive damage will result when the jack is raised. Additionally, never jack under the floorpan or bodywork; the metal will deform.

It is very important to be careful about running the engine on vehicles equipped with limited slip differentials, while the vehicle is up on the

jack. This is because when the drive train is engaged, power is transmitted to the wheel with the best traction and the vehicle will drive off the jack if one drive wheel is in contact with the floor, resulting in possible damage or injury.

Whenever you plan to work under the vehicle, you must support it on jackstands or ramps. Never use cinder blocks or stacks of wood to support the vehicle, even if you're only going to be under it for a few minutes. Never crawl under the vehicle when it is supported only by the tire-changing jack or other floor jack.

Jacking Precautions

The following safety points cannot be overemphasized:

• Always block the opposite wheel or wheels to keep the vehicle from rolling off the jack.

Fig. 152 A sturdy floor jack under the rear axle is a good way to get the rear up in the air safely and quickly

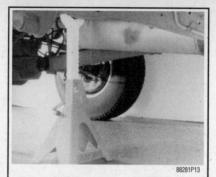

Fig. 153 The frame rail is another safe jacking point in the rear under which to place a jackstand

Fig. 154 Raise the front end using approved jacking points

Fig. 155 The front end may be supported under the frame rail

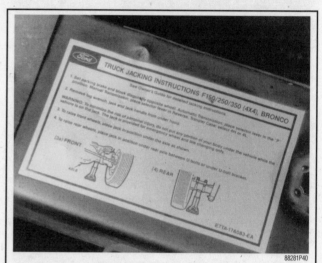

Fig. 156 Jacking instructions for the emergency use jack may be found under the hood

- When raising the front of the vehicle, firmly apply the parking brake.
- When the drive wheels are to remain on the ground, leave the vehicle in gear or **P** to help prevent it from rolling.

- Always use jackstands to support the vehicle when you are working underneath. Place the stands beneath the vehicle's jacking brackets. Before climbing underneath, rock the vehicle a bit to make sure it is firmly supported.

PREVENTIVE MAINTENANCE SCHEDULE

Model/Interval	Item — Gasoline Engine Models	Service
Every 6 months or 6,000 miles	Crankcase	change oil & filter
	Carbureted idle speed and TSP-off speed	adjust
	Chassis fittings	lubricate
	4 x 4 power cylinder	lubricate
	Clutch linkage	inspect and oil
	Exhaust system heat shields	inspect
	Transmission, automatic	check level
Every 15 months or 15,000 miles	Spark plugs	replace
	Exhaust control valve	check & lubricate
	Drive belts	check and adjust
	Air cleaner temperature control	check
	Choke system	check
	Thermactor system	check
	Crankcase breather cap	clean
	EGR system	clean and inspect
	PCV system	clean and inspect
Every 30 months or 30,000 miles	PCV valve	replace
	Air cleaner element	replace
	Air cleaner crankcase filter	replace
	Fuel vapor system	replace
	Brake master cylinder	check
	Brakes	inspect
	Free-running hubs	clean and repack
	Front wheel bearings	clean and repack
	Rear wheel bearings, Dana axles	clean and repack
Every 6 months or 5,000 miles	Crankcase	change oil and filter
	Idle speed	check and adjust
	Throttle linkage	check operation
	Fuel/water separator	drain water
	U-joints	lubricate
	Front axle spindles	lubricate
Every 6 months or 15,000 miles	Fuel filter	replace
	Drive belts	check/adjust
	Steering linkage	lubricate
Every year	Coolant	check condition/replace
	Cooling hoses, clamps	check condition/replace

88281C16

CAPACITIES

Year	Model	Engine ID/VIN	Engine Displacement Liters (cc)	Oil with Filter (qts.)	Engine Transmission (pts.) 4-Spd	5-Spd	Auto.	Transfer Case (pts.)	Drive Axle Front (pts.)	Rear (pts.)	Fuel Tank (gal.)	Cooling System (qts.)
1987	Bronco	Y	4.9L (4942)	6.0	—	—	27.0	4.0	3.8	5.5	32.0	[9]
	Bronco	N	5.0L (4942)	6.0	[1]	—	[7]	4.0	3.8	5.5	32.0	[9]
	Bronco	H	5.8L (5766)	6.0	—	—	27.0	4.0	3.8	5.5	32.0	[7]
	F-150	Y	4.9L (4917)	6.0	[1]	—	[9]	[2]	3.8	5.5	32.0	[9]
	F-150	N	5.0L (4942)	6.0	[1]	—	[9]	[2]	3.8	5.5	[13]	[9]
	F-150	H	5.8L (5766)	6.0	[1]	—	[9]	[2]	3.8	5.5	[13]	[9]
	F-150	Y	4.9L (4917)	6.0	[1]	—	[9]	[2]	[11]	7.5	[13]	[9]
	F-250	N	5.0L (4942)	6.0	[1]	—	[9]	[2]	[11]	7.5	[13]	[9]
	F-250	H	5.8L (5766)	6.0	[1]	—	[9]	[2]	[11]	7.5	[13]	[9]
	F-250	H	6.9L (6886)	10.0	[1]	—	[9]	[2]	[11]	7.5	[13]	29.0
	F-250	L	7.5L (7536)	6.0	[1]	—	[9]	[2]	[11]	7.5	[13]	18.0
	F-350	Y	4.9L (4917)	6.0	[1]	—	[9]	[2]	[11]	7.5	[13]	[9]
	F-350	H	5.8L (5766)	6.0	[1]	—	[9]	[2]	[11]	7.5	[13]	[9]
	F-350	I	6.9L (6886)	10.0	[1]	—	[9]	[2]	[11]	7.5	[13]	29.0
	F-350	L	7.5L (7536)	6.0	[1]	—	[9]	[2]	[11]	7.5	[13]	18.0
1988	Bronco	Y	4.9L (4917)	6.0	[10]	[9]	27.0	4.0	3.8	5.5	32.0	[9]
	Bronco	N	5.0L (4942)	6.0	[10]	[9]	27.0	4.0	3.8	5.5	32.0	[7]
	Bronco	H	5.8L (5766)	6.0	—	[9]	[9]	[2]	3.8	5.5	32.0	[9]
	F-150	Y	4.9L (4917)	6.0	[10]	[9]	[9]	[2]	3.8	5.5	[13]	[9]
	F-150	N	5.0L (4942)	6.0	[10]	[9]	[9]	[2]	3.8	5.5	[13]	[9]
	F-250	H	5.8L (5766)	6.0	[10]	[9]	[9]	[2]	[11]	7.5	[13]	[9]
	F-250	Y	4.9L (4917)	6.0	[10]	[9]	[9]	[2]	[11]	7.5	[13]	[9]
	F-250	N	5.0L (4942)	6.0	[10]	[9]	[9]	[2]	[11]	7.5	[13]	[9]
	F-250	H	5.8L (5766)	6.0	[10]	[9]	[9]	[2]	[11]	7.5	[13]	[9]
	F-250	M	7.3L (7270)	10.0	[10]	[9]	[9]	[2]	[11]	7.5	[13]	31.0
	F-250	G	7.5L (7536)	6.0	[10]	[9]	[9]	[2]	[11]	7.5	[13]	18.0
	F-350	Y	4.9L (4917)	6.0	[10]	[9]	[9]	[2]	[11]	7.5	[13]	[9]
	F-350	H	5.8L (5766)	6.0	[10]	[9]	[9]	[2]	[11]	7.5	[13]	[9]
	F-350	M	7.3L (7270)	10.0	[10]	[9]	[9]	[2]	[11]	7.5	[13]	31.0
	F-350	G	7.5L (7536)	6.0	[10]	[9]	[9]	[2]	[11]	7.5	[13]	18.0
	F-Super Duty	M	7.3L (7270)	10.0	—	[9]	[9]	—	—	8.3	[13]	31.0
	F-Super Duty	G	7.5L (7536)	6.0	—	[9]	[9]	—	—	8.3	[13]	18.0
1989	Bronco	Y	4.9L (4917)	6.0	[10]	[9]	27.0	4.0	3.8	5.5	32.0	[9]
	Bronco	N	5.0L (4942)	6.0	[10]	[9]	[3]	4.0	3.8	5.5	32.0	[6]
	Bronco	H	5.8L (5766)	6.0	—	[9]	27.0	4.0	3.8	5.5	32.0	[7]
	F-150	Y	4.9L (4917)	6.0	[10]	[9]	[4]	[2]	3.8	5.5		[9]
	F-150	N	5.0L (4942)	6.0	[10]	[9]	[4]	[2]	3.8	5.5		[9]
	F-150	H	5.8L (5766)	6.0	[10]	[9]	[4]	[2]	3.8	5.5		[9]
	F-250	Y	4.9L (4917)	6.0	[10]	[9]	[4]	[2]	[11]	7.5		[9]
	F-250	N	5.0L (4942)	6.0	[10]	[9]	[4]	[2]	[11]	7.5		[9]
	F-250	H	5.8L (5766)	6.0	[10]	[9]	[4]	[2]	[11]	7.5		[9]
	F-250	M	7.3L (7270)	10.0	[10]	[9]	[4]	[2]	[11]	7.5		31.0
	F-250	G	7.5L (7536)	6.0	[10]	[9]	[4]	[2]	[11]	7.5		18.0
	F-350	Y	4.9L (4917)	6.0	[10]	[9]	[4]	[2]	[11]	7.5		[9]
	F-350	H	5.8L (5766)	6.0	[10]	[9]	[4]	[2]	[11]	7.5		[9]
	F-350	M	7.3L (7270)	10.0	[10]	[9]	[4]	[2]	[11]	7.5		31.0
	F-350	G	7.5L (7536)	6.0	[10]	[9]	[4]	[2]	[11]	7.5		18.0
	F-Super Duty	M	7.3L (7270)	10.0	—	[9]	27.0	4.0		8.3	32.0	31.0
	F-Super Duty	G	7.5L (7536)	6.0	—	[9]	27.0	4.0		8.3	32.0	18.0
1990	Bronco	Y	4.9L (4942)	6.0	[10]	[9]	[4]	4.0	3.8	5.5	32.0	[9]
	Bronco	N	5.0L (4942)	6.0	[10]	[9]	[4]	4.0	3.8	5.5	32.0	[6]
	Bronco	H	5.8L (5766)	6.0	[10]	[9]	[4]	4.0	3.8	5.5	32.0	[7]

88281C17

CAPACITIES

Year	Model	Engine ID/VIN	Engine Displacement Liters (cc)	Oil with Filter (qts.)	Engine Transmission (pts.) 4-Spd	5-Spd	Auto.	Transfer Case (pts.)	Drive Axle Front (pts.)	Rear (pts.)	Fuel Tank (gal.)	Cooling System (qts.)
1993	F-150 Lightning	R	5.8L (5766)	6.0						5.5		
	F-250	Y	4.9L (4917)	6.0						7.5		
	F-250	N	5.0L (4942)	6.0						7.5		
	F-250	H	5.8L (5766)	6.0						7.5		
	F-250	M	7.3L (7270)	10.0						7.5		31.0
	F-250	C	7.5L (7536)	10.0						7.5		29.0
	F-250	G	7.5L (7536)	6.0						7.5		18.0
	F-350	Y	4.9L (4917)	6.0						7.5		
	F-350	H	5.8L (5766)	6.0						7.5		
	F-350	M	7.3L (7270)	10.0						7.5		31.0
	F-350	C	7.3L (7270)	10.0						7.5		29.0
	F-350	C	7.5L (7536)	10.0						7.5		18.0
	F-Super Duty	M	7.3L (7270)	10.0						8.3		
	F-Super Duty	G	7.5L (7536)	10.0						8.3		
	F-Super Duty	C	7.3L (7270)	6.0						8.3		18.0
1994	Bronco	N	5.0L (4942)	6.0					3.8	5.5	32.0	
	Bronco	H	5.8L (5766)	6.0					3.8	5.5	32.0	
	F-150	Y	4.9L (4917)	6.0					3.8	5.5		
	F-150	N	5.0L (4942)	6.0					3.8	5.5		
	F-150	H	5.8L (5766)	6.0						5.5		
	F-150 Lightning	R	5.8 (5766)	6.0						5.5		
	F-250	Y	4.9L (4917)	6.0						7.5		
	F-250	N	5.0L (4942)	6.0						7.5		
	F-250	H	5.8L (5766)	6.0						7.5		
	F-250	F	7.3L (7270)	14.0						7.5		23.0
	F-250	K	7.3L (7270)	10.0						7.5		
	F-250	G	7.5L (7536)	10.0						7.5		
	F-350	Y	4.9L (4917)	6.0						7.5		
	F-350	H	5.8L (5766)	6.0						7.5		19.8
	F-350	F	7.3L (7270)	14.0						8.3		
	F-350	K	7.3L (7270)	10.0						8.3		
	F-350	M	7.5L (7536)	10.0						8.3		
	F-Super Duty	G	7.5L (7536)	6.0						8.3		
	F-Super Duty	F	7.3L (7270)	14.0						8.3		
	F-Super Duty	K	7.3L (7270)	10.0						8.3		19.8
	F-Super Duty	G	7.5L (7536)	6.0						8.3		
1995	Bronco	N	5.0L (4942)	6.0					3.8	5.5	32.0	23.0
	Bronco	H	5.8L (5766)	6.0					3.8	5.5	32.0	
	F-150	Y	4.9L (4917)	6.0					3.8	5.5		
	F-150	N	5.0L (4942)	6.0					3.8	5.5		19.8
	F-150	H	5.8L (5766)	6.0					3.8	5.5		
	F-150 Lightning	R	5.8 (5766)	6.0						5.5		23.0
	F-250	Y	4.9L (4917)	6.0						7.5		
	F-250	N	5.0L (4942)	6.0						7.5		19.8
	F-250	H	5.8L (5766)	6.0						7.5		
	F-250	F	7.3L (7270)	14.0						7.5		23.0
	F-350	Y	4.9L (4917)	6.0						7.5		19.8
	F-350	H	5.8L (5766)	6.0						7.5		
	F-350	F	7.3L (7270)	14.0						7.5		23.0

88281C19

CAPACITIES

Year	Model	Engine ID/VIN	Engine Displacement Liters (cc)	Oil with Filter (qts.)	Engine Transmission (pts.) 4-Spd	5-Spd	Auto.	Transfer Case (pts.)	Drive Axle Front (pts.)	Rear (pts.)	Fuel Tank (gal.)	Cooling System (qts.)
1990	F-150	Y	4.9L (4917)	6.0					3.8	5.5		
	F-150	N	5.0L (4942)	6.0					3.8	5.5		
	F-150	H	5.8L (5766)	6.0					3.8	5.5		
	F-250	Y	4.9L (4917)	6.0						7.5		
	F-250	N	5.0L (4942)	6.0						7.5		
	F-250	H	5.8L (5766)	6.0						7.5		
	F-250	M	7.3L (7270)	10.0						7.5		31.0
	F-250	G	7.5L (7536)	6.0						7.5		18.0
	F-350	Y	4.9L (4917)	6.0						7.5		
	F-350	H	5.8L (5766)	6.0						7.5		
	F-350	M	7.3L (7270)	10.0						7.5		
	F-Super Duty	M	7.3L (7270)	10.0						8.3		
	F-Super Duty	G	7.5L (7536)	6.0						8.3		18.0
1991	Bronco	Y	4.9L (4917)	6.0					3.8	5.5	32.0	
	Bronco	N	5.0L (4942)	6.0					3.8	5.5	32.0	
	Bronco	H	5.8L (5766)	6.0					3.8	5.5	32.0	
	F-150	Y	4.9L (4917)	6.0					3.8	5.5		
	F-150	N	5.0L (4942)	6.0					3.8	5.5		
	F-150	H	5.8L (5766)	6.0						5.5		
	F-250	Y	4.9L (4917)	6.0						7.5		
	F-250	N	5.0L (4942)	6.0						7.5		
	F-250	H	5.8L (5766)	6.0						7.5		
	F-250	M	7.3L (7270)	10.0						7.5		31.0
	F-250	G	7.5L (7536)	6.0						7.5		18.0
	F-350	Y	4.9L (4917)	6.0						7.5		
	F-350	H	5.8L (5766)	6.0						7.5		31.0
	F-350	M	7.3L (7270)	10.0						7.5		
	F-350	G	7.5L (7536)	6.0						7.5		18.0
	F-Super Duty	M	7.3L (7270)	10.0						8.3		
	F-Super Duty	G	7.5L (7536)	6.0						8.3		
1992	Bronco	Y	4.9L (4917)	6.0					3.8	5.5	32.0	
	Bronco	N	5.0L (4942)	6.0					3.8	5.5	32.0	
	Bronco	H	5.8L (5766)	6.0					3.8	5.5	32.0	
	F-150	Y	4.9L (4917)	6.0					3.8	5.5		
	F-150	N	5.0L (4942)	6.0					3.8	5.5		
	F-250	H	5.8L (5766)	6.0						7.5		
	F-250	M	7.3L (7270)	10.0						7.5		
	F-250	G	7.5L (7536)	6.0						7.5		
	F-350	Y	4.9L (4917)	6.0						7.5		
	F-350	H	5.8L (5766)	6.0						7.5		
	F-350	M	7.3L (7270)	10.0						7.5		
	F-350	G	7.5L (7536)	6.0						7.5		
	F-Super Duty	M	7.3L (7270)	10.0						8.3		
	F-Super Duty	G	7.5L (7536)	6.0						8.3		
1993	Bronco	N	5.0L (4942)	6.0					3.8	5.5	32.0	23.0
	Bronco	H	5.8L (5766)	6.0					3.8	5.5	32.0	19.8
	F-150	Y	4.9L (4917)	6.0					3.8	5.5		
	F-150	N	5.0L (4942)	6.0					3.8	5.5		
	F-150	H	5.8L (5766)	6.0						5.5		23.0

88281C18

ENGLISH TO METRIC CONVERSION: MASS (WEIGHT)

Current mass measurement is expressed in pounds and ounces (lbs. & ozs.). The metric unit of mass (or weight) is the kilogram (kg). Even although this table does not show conversion of masses (weights) larger than 15 lbs, it is easy to calculate larger units by following the data immediately below.

To convert ounces (oz.) to grams (g): multiply th number of ozs. by 28
To convert grams (g) to ounces (oz.): multiply the number of grams by .035

To convert pounds (lbs.) to kilograms (kg): multiply the number of lbs. by .45
To convert kilograms (kg) to pounds (lbs.): multiply the number of kilograms by 2.2

lbs	kg	oz	kg	oz	kg
0.1	0.04	0.1	0.003	0.9	0.024
0.2	0.09	0.2	0.005	1	0.03
0.3	0.14	0.3	0.008	2	0.06
0.4	0.18	0.4	0.011	3	0.08
0.5	0.23	0.5	0.014	4	0.11
0.6	0.27	0.6	0.017	5	0.14
0.7	0.32	0.7	0.020	10	0.28
0.8	0.36	0.8	0.023	15	0.42
0.9	0.41				
1	0.4				
2	0.9				
3	1.4				
4	1.8				
5	2.3				
10	4.5				
15	6.8				

ENGLISH TO METRIC CONVERSION: TEMPERATURE

To convert Fahrenheit (°F) to Celsius (°C): take number of °F and subtract 32; multiply result by 5; divide result by 9
To convert Celsius (°C) to Fahrenheit (°F): take number of °C and multiply by 9; divide result by 5; add 32 to total

Fahrenheit (°F)	Celsius (°C)	Celsius (°C)	Fahrenheit (°F)	Fahrenheit (°F)	Celsius (°C)	Celsius (°C)	Fahrenheit (°F)	Fahrenheit (°F)	Celsius (°C)	Celsius (°C)	Fahrenheit (°F)
-40	-40	-38	-36.4	80	26.7	18	64.4	215	101.7	80	176
-35	-37.2	-36	-32.8	85	29.4	20	68	220	104.4	85	185
-30	-34.4	-34	-29.2	90	32.2	22	71.6	225	107.2	90	194
-25	-31.7	-32	-25.6	95	35.0	24	75.2	230	110.0	95	202
-20	-28.9	-30	-22	100	37.8	26	78.8	235	112.8	100	212
-15	-26.1	-28	-18.4	105	40.6	28	82.4	240	115.6	105	221
-10	-23.3	-26	-14.8	110	43.3	30	86	245	118.3	110	230
-5	-20.6	-24	-11.2	115	46.1	32	89.6	250	121.1	115	239
0	-17.8	-22	-7.6	120	48.9	34	93.2	255	123.9	120	248
1	-17.2	-20	-4	125	51.7	36	96.8	260	126.6	125	257
2	-16.7	-18	-0.4	130	54.4	38	100.4	265	129.4	130	266
3	-16.1	-16	3.2	135	57.2	40	104	270	132.2	135	275
4	-15.6	-14	6.8	140	60.0	42	107.6	275	135.0	140	284
5	-15.0	-12	10.4	145	62.8	44	112.2	280	137.8	145	293
10	-12.2	-10	14	150	65.6	46	114.8	285	140.6	150	302
15	-9.4	-8	17.6	155	68.3	48	118.4	290	143.3	155	311
20	-6.7	-6	21.2	160	71.1	50	122	295	146.1	160	320
25	-3.9	-4	24.8	165	73.9	52	125.6	300	148.9	165	329
30	-1.1	-2	28.4	170	76.7	54	129.2	305	151.7	170	338
35	1.7	0	32	175	79.4	56	132.8	310	154.4	175	347
40	4.4	2	35.6	180	82.2	58	136.4	315	157.2	180	356
45	7.2	4	39.2	185	85.0	60	140	320	160.0	185	365
50	10.0	6	42.8	190	87.8	62	143.6	325	162.8	190	374
55	12.8	8	46.4	195	90.6	64	147.2	330	165.6	195	383
60	15.6	10	50	200	93.3	66	150.8	335	168.3	200	392
65	18.3	12	53.6	205	96.1	68	154.4	340	171.1	205	401
70	21.1	14	57.2	210	98.9	70	158	345	173.9	210	410
75	23.9	16	60.8	212	100.0	75	167	350	176.7	215	414

CAPACITIES

Year	Model	Engine ID/VIN	Engine Displacement Liters (cc)	Oil with Filter (qts.)	Engine Transmission (pts.) 4-Spd	Engine Transmission (pts.) 5-Spd	Engine Transmission (pts.) Auto.	Transfer Case (pts.)	Axle Front (pts.)	Axle Rear (pts.)	Drive Fuel Tank (gal.)	Cooling System (qts.)
1995	F-350	G	7.5L (7536)	6.0	-	⑧	⑥	②	⑪	7.5	⑭	19.8
	F-Super Duty	F	7.3L (7270)	14.0	-	⑧	⑥	②		8.3	⑭	23.0 ㉑
	F-Super Duty	G	7.5L (7536)	6.0	-	⑧	⑥	②		8.3	⑭	19.8
1996	Bronco	N	5.0L (4942)	6.0	①	⑧	⑥	④	3.8	5.5	32.0	⑯
	Bronco	H	5.8L (5766)	6.0		⑧	⑥	④	3.8	5.5	32.0	⑰
	F-150	Y	4.9L (4917)	6.0		⑧	⑥	④	3.8	5.5		⑰
	F-150	N	5.0L (4942)	6.0		⑧	⑥	②	3.8	5.5		⑬
	F-150	H	5.8L (5766)	6.0		⑧	⑥	②	3.8	5.5		⑱
	F-250	Y	4.9L (4917)	6.0		⑧	⑥	②		7.5		⑰
	F-250	N	5.0L (4942)	6.0		⑧	⑥	②		7.5		⑰
	F-250	H	5.8L (5766)	6.0		⑧	⑥	②		7.5		⑰
	F-250	F	7.3L (7270)	14.0		⑧	⑥	②		7.5		23.0
	F-250	G	7.5L (7536)	6.0		⑧	⑥	②		7.5		19.8
	F-350	Y	4.9L (4917)	6.0		⑧	⑥	②		7.5 ⑰		⑰
	F-350	H	5.8L (5766)	6.0		⑧	⑥	②		7.5 ⑰		⑰
	F-350	F	7.3L (7270)	14.0		⑧	⑥	②		7.5		23.0
	F-350	G	7.5L (7536)	6.0		⑧	⑥	②		7.5		19.8
	F-Super Duty	F	7.3L (7270)	14.0		⑧	⑥	②		8.3		23.0
	F-Super Duty	G	7.5L (7536)	6.0		⑧	⑥	②		8.3		19.8

NOTES: Exact automatic transmission fill level determined by use of the dipstick. Motorhome fuel capacity approx. 75 gallons. For limited slip differentials, add the following amounts of
Friction Modifier Additive: Dana front axle: 2 oz., Dana rear axle: 4 oz. Ford 8.8 in. rear axle: 4 oz. Ford 10.25 in. rear axle 8 oz., 1993-95 Lightning and F-150 w/4.10 axle ratio: 5 oz.

A/C - Air Conditioning
A/T - Automatic Transmission
M/T - Manual Transmission
LWB - Long Wheelbase
SWB - Short Wheelbase

① Warner T-18, T-19: 7.0 pts.
NP-435 with extension housing: 7.0 pts.
NP-435 without extension housing: 6.5 pts.
② Ford 4-speed overdrive: 4.5 pts.
New Process: 9 pts.
BW 1345: 6.5 pts.
BW 1356: 4 pts.
③ Add 4.1 qts. to capacity shown if a transfer case mounted power take off (PTO) is used.
C6 and E4OD: 27.0 pts.
④ AOD: 24.6 pts.
⑤ C5: 22 pts.
⑥ AOD (2WD): 24.6 pts.
AOD (4WD): 24.6 pts.
C6 (2WD): 24.0 pts.
C6 (4WD): 27.0 pts.
E4OD (2WD): 15.5 pts.
E4OD (4WD): 16.0 pts.
⑦ Standard: 13 pts.

⑧ M/T with Standard Cooling: 13.0 qts.
M/T with A/C or Super Cooling: 14 qts.
A/T (except below): 14 qts.
A/T with A/C: 15.5 qts.
⑨ A/T or M/T with A/C and Super Cooling: 15.6 qts.
M/T with Standard Cooling: 15.7 qts.
A/T with Standard Cooling: 16.5 qts.
A/T or M/T with A/C: 16.4 qts.
⑩ M/T with Standard Cooling: 18.3 qts.
A/T with Standard Cooling: 15.7 qts.
A/T with Standard Cooling: 16.4 qts.
A/T or M/T with A/C: 16.4 qts.
⑪ Dana 44: 3.8 pts.
Dana 50: 3.9 pts.
Dana 50: 5.8 pts.
⑫ M/T with Standard Cooling: 15.0 qts.
A/T with Standard Cooling: 16.0 qts.
M/T or A/T with Super Cooling: 17.0 qts.
⑬ Front tank (SWB F-150): 16.5 gal.
Front tank (LWB): 19.0 gal.
Rear tank (early): 19.0 gal.
Rear tank (late): 17.5 gal.
⑭ Front tank (SWB F-150): 16.5 gal.
Front tank (LWB gas): 19.0 gal.
Front tank (LWB diesel): 20.0 to 22.0 gal. (varies with model)
Rear tank (exc. Chassis Cab and Super Duty): 18.2 gal.
Rear tank (Chassis Cab and Super Duty): 19 gal.

⑮ Mazda transmission: 7.6 pts.
ZF transmission: 6.8 pts.
⑯ Standard: 13.0 qts.
M/T with A/C or Super Cooling: 14 qts.
A/T with A/C: 15 qts.
A/T with Super Cooling: 14 qts.
⑰ M/T or A/T with A/C and Super Cooling: 15 qts.
Commercial stripped chassis: 8.3 pts.
⑱ M/T with Standard Cooling: 13.0 qts.
M/T with A/C or Super Cooling: 14 qts.
A/T (except listed below): 14.0 qts.
A/T with A/C and Super Cooling: 14 qts.
A/T with A/C: 15.0 qts.
⑲ AOD (2WD): 12.3 qts.
AOD (4WD): 12.3 qts.
C6 (2WD): 12.0 qts.
C6 (4WD): 13.5 qts.
E4OD (2WD): 16.7 qts.
E4OD (4WD): 16.2 qts.
4R70W: 14.0 qts.
⑳ F-Series: 29 qts.
F-Series Commercial Stripped Chassis: 31 qts.
㉑ Includes 1.5 quarts of coolant additive (FW 15 or equivalent)

TCCS1C01

88281C20

ENGLISH TO METRIC CONVERSION: TORQUE

Torque is now expressed as either foot-pounds (ft./lbs.) or inch-pounds (in./lbs.). The metric measurement unit for torque is the Newton-meter (Nm). This unit—the Nm—will be used for all SI metric torque references, both the present ft. lbs. and in./lbs.

ft lbs	N-m	ft lbs	N-m	ft lbs	N-m	ft lbs	N-m
0.1	0.1	33	44.7	74	100.3	115	155.9
0.2	0.3	34	46.1	75	101.7	116	157.3
0.3	0.4	35	47.4	76	103.0	117	158.6
0.4	0.5	36	48.8	77	104.4	118	160.0
0.5	0.7	37	50.7	78	105.8	119	161.3
0.6	0.8	38	51.5	79	107.1	120	162.7
0.7	1.0	39	52.9	80	108.5	121	164.0
0.8	1.1	40	54.2	81	109.8	122	165.4
0.9	1.2	41	55.6	82	111.2	123	166.8
1	1.3	42	56.9	83	112.5	124	168.1
2	2.7	43	58.3	84	113.9	125	169.5
3	4.1	44	59.7	85	115.2	126	170.8
4	5.4	45	61.0	86	116.6	127	172.2
5	6.8	46	62.4	87	118.0	128	173.5
6	8.1	47	63.7	88	119.3	129	174.9
7	9.5	48	65.1	89	120.7	130	176.2
8	10.8	49	66.4	90	122.0	131	177.6
9	12.2	50	67.8	91	123.4	132	179.0
10	13.6	51	69.2	92	124.7	133	180.3
11	14.9	52	70.5	93	126.1	134	181.7
12	16.3	53	71.9	94	127.4	135	183.0
13	17.6	54	73.2	95	128.8	136	184.4
14	18.9	55	74.6	96	130.2	137	185.7
15	20.3	56	75.9	97	131.5	138	187.1
16	21.7	57	77.3	98	132.9	139	188.5
17	23.0	58	78.6	99	134.2	140	189.8
18	24.4	59	80.0	100	135.6	141	191.2
19	25.8	60	81.4	101	136.9	142	192.5
20	27.1	61	82.7	102	138.3	143	193.9
21	28.5	62	84.1	103	139.6	144	195.2
22	29.8	63	85.4	104	141.0	145	196.6
23	31.2	64	86.8	105	142.4	146	198.0
24	32.5	65	88.1	106	143.7	147	199.3
25	33.9	66	89.5	107	145.1	148	200.7
26	35.2	67	90.8	108	146.4	149	202.0
27	36.6	68	92.2	109	147.8	150	203.4
28	38.0	69	93.6	110	149.1	151	204.7
29	39.3	70	94.9	111	150.5	152	206.1
30	40.7	71	96.3	112	151.8	153	207.4
31	42.0	72	97.6	113	153.2	154	208.8
32	43.4	73	99.0	114	154.6	155	210.2

TCCS1C03

ENGLISH TO METRIC CONVERSION: LENGTH

To convert inches (ins.) to millimeters (mm): multiply number of inches by 25.4
To convert millimeters (mm) to inches (ins.): multiply number of millimeters by .04

Inches	Decimals	Milli-meters		Inches	Decimals	mm
1/64	0.015625	0.3969		33/64	0.515625	13.0969
	0.03125	0.7937	17/32		0.53125	13.4937
3/64	0.046875	1.1906		35/64	0.546875	13.8906
1/16	0.0625	1.5875	9/16		0.5625	14.2875
5/64	0.078125	1.9844		37/64	0.578125	14.6844
	0.09375	2.3812	19/32		0.59375	15.0812
7/64	0.109375	2.7781		39/64	0.609375	15.4781
1/8	0.125	3.1750	5/8		0.625	15.8750
9/64	0.140625	3.5719		41/64	0.640625	16.2719
	0.15625	3.9687	21/32		0.65625	16.6687
11/64	0.171875	4.3656		43/64	0.671875	17.0656
3/16	0.1875	4.7625	11/16		0.6875	17.4625
13/64	0.203125	5.1594		45/64	0.703125	17.8594
	0.21875	5.5562	23/32		0.71875	18.2562
15/64	0.234375	5.9531		47/64	0.734375	18.6531
1/4	0.25	6.3500	3/4		0.75	19.0500
17/64	0.265625	6.7469		49/64	0.765625	19.4469
	0.28125	7.1437	25/32		0.78125	19.8437
19/64	0.296875	7.5406		51/64	0.796875	20.2406
5/16	0.3125	7.9375	13/16		0.8125	20.6375
21/64	0.328125	8.3344		53/64	0.828125	21.0344
	0.34375	8.7312	27/32		0.84375	21.4312
23/64	0.359375	9.1281		55/64	0.859375	21.8281
3/8	0.375	9.5250	7/8		0.875	22.2250
25/64	0.390625	9.9219		57/64	0.890625	22.6219
	0.40625	10.3187	29/32		0.90625	23.0187
27/64	0.421875	10.7156		59/64	0.921875	23.4156
7/16	0.4375	11.1125	15/16		0.9375	23.8125
29/64	0.453125	11.5094		61/64	0.953125	24.2094
	0.46875	11.9062	31/32		0.96875	24.6062
31/64	0.484375	12.3031		63/64	0.984375	25.0031
1/2	0.5	12.7000				

Inches to millimeters

inches	mm	inches	mm
0.0001	0.00254	0.6	15.24
0.0002	0.00508	0.7	17.78
0.0003	0.00762	0.8	20.32
0.0004	0.01016	0.9	22.86
0.0005	0.01270	1	25.4
0.0006	0.01524	2	50.8
0.0007	0.01778	3	76.2
0.0008	0.02032	4	101.6
0.0009	0.02286	5	127.0
0.001	0.0254	6	152.4
0.002	0.0508	7	177.8
0.003	0.0762	8	203.2
0.004	0.1016	9	228.6
0.005	0.1270	10	254.0
0.006	0.1524	11	279.4
0.007	0.1778	12	304.8
0.008	0.2032	13	330.2
0.009	0.2286	14	355.6
0.01	0.254	15	381.0
0.02	0.508	16	406.4
0.03	0.762	17	431.8
0.04	1.016	18	457.2
0.05	1.270	19	482.6
0.06	1.524	20	508.0
0.07	1.778	21	533.4
0.08	2.032	22	558.8
0.09	2.286	23	584.2
0.1	2.54	24	609.6
0.2	5.08	25	635.0
0.3	7.62	26	660.4
0.4	10.16	27	685.8
0.5	12.70		

ENGLISH TO METRIC CONVERSION: TORQUE

To convert foot-pounds (ft. lbs.) to Newton-meters: multiply the number of ft. lbs. by 1.3
To convert inch-pounds (in. lbs.) to Newton-meters: multiply the number of in. lbs. by .11

in lbs	N-m	in lbs	N-m	in lbs	N-m	in lbs	N-m	in lbs	N-m
0.1	0.01	1	0.11	10	1.13	19	2.15	28	3.16
0.2	0.02	2	0.23	11	1.24	20	2.26	29	3.28
0.3	0.03	3	0.34	12	1.36	21	2.37	30	3.39
0.4	0.04	4	0.45	13	1.47	22	2.49	31	3.50
0.5	0.06	5	0.56	14	1.58	23	2.60	32	3.62
0.6	0.07	6	0.68	15	1.70	24	2.71	33	3.73
0.7	0.08	7	0.78	16	1.81	25	2.82	34	3.84
0.8	0.09	8	0.90	17	1.92	26	2.94	35	3.95
0.9	0.10	9	1.02	18	2.03	27	3.05	36	4.0

TCCS1C02

2

ENGINE
ELECTRICAL

ELECTRONIC DISTRIBUTOR IGNITION SYSTEM

➡**All fuel injected engines use the TFI-IV system. All carbureted engines use the Dura Spark II system.**

Dura Spark II System

GENERAL INFORMATION

♦ **See Figures 1 and 2**

With the ignition switch **ON**, the primary circuit is on and the ignition coil is energized. When the armature spokes approach the magnetic pickup coil assembly, they induce the voltage which tells the amplifier to turn the coil primary current off. A timing circuit in the amplifier module will turn the current on again after the coil field has collapsed. When the current is on, it flows from the battery through the ignition switch, the primary windings of the ignition coil, and through the amplifier module circuits to ground. When the current is off, the magnetic field built up in the ignition coil is allowed to collapse, inducing a high voltage into the secondary windings of the coil. High voltage is produced each time the field is thus built up and collapsed. When DuraSpark is used in conjunction with the EEC, the EEC computer tells the DuraSpark module when to turn the coil primary current off or on. In this case, the armature position is only a reference signal of engine timing, used by the EEC computer in combination with other reference signals to determine optimum ignition spark timing.

The high voltage flows through the coil high tension lead to the distributor cap where the rotor distributes it to one of the spark plug terminals in the distributor cap. This process is repeated for every power stroke of the engine.

Ignition system troubles are caused by a failure in the primary and/or the secondary circuit, incorrect ignition timing or incorrect distributor advance. Circuit failures may be caused by shorts, corroded or dirty terminals, loose connections, defective wire insulation, cracked distributor cap or rotor, defective pick-up coil assembly or amplifier module, defective distributor points or fouled spark plugs.

If an engine starting or operating trouble is attributed to the ignition system, start the engine and verify the complaint. On engines that will not start, be sure that there is gasoline in the fuel tank and the fuel is reaching the carburetor. Then locate the ignition system problem using the following procedures.

DIAGNOSIS AND TESTING

♦ **See Figures 3, 4, 5 and 6**

The following procedures can be used to determine whether the ignition system is working or not. If these procedures fail to correct the problem, a full troubleshooting procedure should be performed.

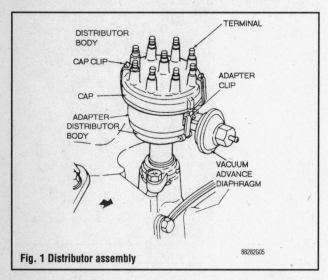

Fig. 1 Distributor assembly

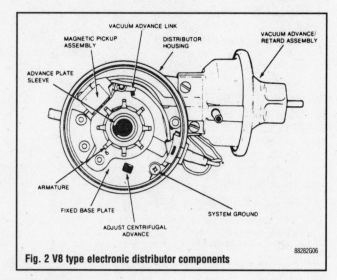

Fig. 2 V8 type electronic distributor components

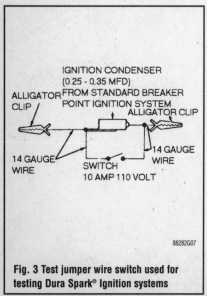

Fig. 3 Test jumper wire switch used for testing Dura Spark® Ignition systems

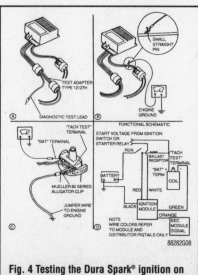

Fig. 4 Testing the Dura Spark® ignition on models with EEC

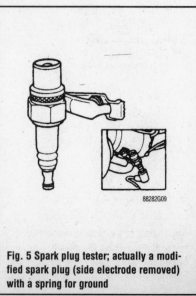

Fig. 5 Spark plug tester; actually a modified spark plug (side electrode removed) with a spring for ground

Preliminary Checks

1. Check the battery's state of charge and connections.
2. Inspect all wires and connections for breaks, cuts, abrasions, or burned spots. Repair as necessary.
3. Unplug all connectors one at a time and inspect for corroded or burned contacts. Repair and plug connectors back together. DO NOT remove the dielectric compound in the connectors.
4. Check for loose or damaged spark plug or coil wires. A wire resistance check is given at the end of this section. If the boots or nipples are removed on 8mm ignition wires, recoat the inside of each with new silicone dielectric compound (Motorcraft WA-10).

Special Tools

▶ See Figures 7 thru 12

To perform the following tests, two special tools are needed; the ignition test jumper shown in the illustration and a modified spark plug. Use the illustration to assembly the ignition test jumper. The test jumper must be used when performing the following tests. The modified spark plug is basically a spark plug with the side electrode removed. Ford makes a special tool called a Spark Tester for this purpose, which besides not having a side elec-

trode is equipped with a spring clip so that it can be grounded to engine metal. It is recommended that the Spark Tester be used as there is less chance of being shocked.

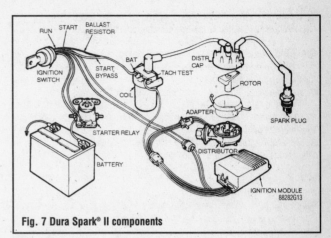

Fig. 7 Dura Spark® II components

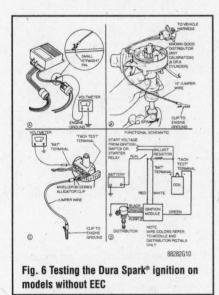

Fig. 6 Testing the Dura Spark® ignition on models without EEC

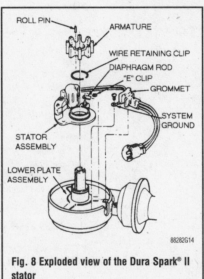

Fig. 8 Exploded view of the Dura Spark® II stator

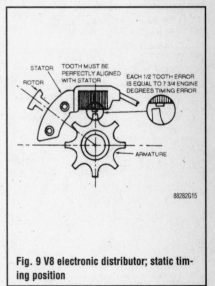

Fig. 9 V8 electronic distributor; static timing position

Fig. 10 Unplug the module connectors where shown—leave the module side alone (on right) to prevent short-out

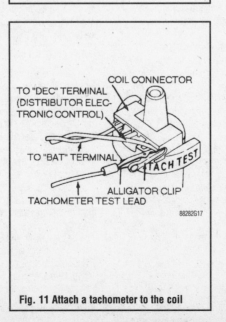

Fig. 11 Attach a tachometer to the coil

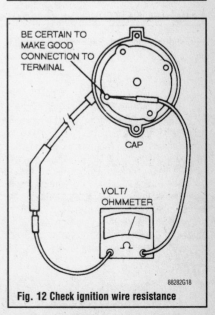

Fig. 12 Check ignition wire resistance

Run Mode Spark Test

→The wire colors given here are the main colors of the wires, not the dots or hash marks.

STEP 1

1. Remove the distributor cap and rotor from the distributor.
2. With the ignition off, turn the engine over by hand until one of the teeth on the distributor armature aligns with the magnet in the pickup coil.
3. Remove the coil wire from the distributor cap. Install the modified spark plug (see Special Tools, above) in the coil wire terminal and using heavy gloves and insulated pliers, hold the spark plug shell against the engine block.
4. Turn the ignition to **RUN** (not START) and tap the distributor body with a screwdriver handle. There should be a spark at the modified spark plug or at the coil wire terminal.
5. If a good spark is evident, the primary circuit is OK: perform the Start Mode Spark Test. If there is no spark, proceed to STEP 2.

STEP 2

1. Unplug the module connector(s) which contain(s) the green and black module leads.
2. In the harness side of the connector(s), connect the special test jumper (see Special Tools, above) between the leads which connect to the green and black leads of the module pig tails. Use paper clips on connector socket holes to make contact. Do not allow clips to ground.
3. Turn the ignition switch to **RUN** (not START) and close the test jumper switch. Leave closed for about 1 second, then open. Repeat several times. There should be a spark each time the switch is opened.
4. If there is no spark, the problem is probably in the primary circuit through the ignition switch, the coil, the green lead or the black lead, or the ground connection in the distributor; Perform STEP 3. If there is a spark, the primary circuit wiring and coil are probably OK. The problem is probably in the distributor pick-up, the module red wire, or the module: perform STEP 6.

STEP 3

1. Disconnect the test jumper lead from the black lead and connect it to a good ground. Turn the test jumper switch on and off several times as in STEP 2.
2. If there is no spark, the problem is probably in the green lead, the coil, or the coil feed circuit: perform STEP 5.
3. If there is spark, the problem is probably in the black lead or the distributor ground connection: perform STEP 4.

STEP 4

1. Connect an ohmmeter between the black lead and ground. With the meter on its lowest scale, there should be no measurable resistance in the circuit. If there is resistance, check the distributor ground connection and the black lead from the module. Repair as necessary, remove the ohmmeter, plug in all connections and repeat STEP 1.
2. If there is no resistance, the primary ground wiring is OK: perform STEP 6.

STEP 5

1. Disconnect the test jumper from the green lead and ground and connect it between the TACH-TEST terminal of the coil and a good ground to the engine.
2. With the ignition switch in the **RUN** position, turn the jumper switch on. Hold it on for about 1 second then turn it off as in Step 2. Repeat several times. There should be a spark each time the switch in turned off. If there is no spark, the problem is probably in the primary circuit running through the ignition switch to the coil BAT terminal, or in the coil itself. Check coil resistance (test given later in this section), and check the coil for internal shorts or opens. Check the coil feed circuit for opens, shorts, or high resistance. Repair as necessary, reconnect all connectors and repeat STEP 1. If there is spark, the coil and its feed circuit are OK. The problem could be in the green lead between the coil and the module. Check for an open or short, repair as necessary, reconnect all connectors and repeat STEP 1.

STEP 6

To perform this step, a voltmeter which is not combined with a dwell meter is needed. The slight needle oscillations ($FR1/2v) you'll be looking for may not be detectable on the combined voltmeter/dwell meter unit.
1. Connect a voltmeter between the orange and purple leads on the harness side of the module connectors.

2. Set the voltmeter on its lowest scale and crank the engine. The meter needle should oscillate slightly (about $FR1/2v). If the meter does not oscillate, check the circuit through the magnetic pick-up in the distributor for open, shorts, shorts to ground and resistance. Resistance between the orange and purple leads should be 400–1,000 ohms, and between each lead and ground should be more than 70,000 ohms. Repair as necessary, reconnect all connectors and repeat STEP 1.
   If the meter oscillates, the problem is probably in the power feed to the module (red wire) or in the module itself: proceed to STEP 7.

STEP 7

1. Remove all meters and jumpers and plug in all connectors.
2. Turn the ignition switch to the **RUN** position and measure voltage between the battery positive terminal and engine ground. It should be 12 volts.
3. Next, measure voltage between the red lead of the module and engine ground. To mark this measurement, it will be necessary to pierce the red wire with a straight pin and connect the voltmeter to the straight pin and to ground. DO NOT ALLOW THE STRAIGHT PIN TO GROUND ITSELF!
4. The two readings should be within one volt of each other. If not within one volt, the problem is in the power feed to the red lead. Check for shorts, open, or high resistance and correct as necessary. After repairs, repeat Step 1. If the readings are within one volt, the problem is probably in the module. Replace it with a good module and repeat STEP 1. If this corrects the problem, reconnect the old module and repeat STEP 1. If the problem returns, permanently install the new module.

Start Mode Spark Test

→The wire colors given here are the main colors of the wires, not the dots or hash marks.

1. Remove the coil wire from the distributor cap. Install the modified spark plug mentioned under Special Tools, above, in the coil wire and ground it to engine metal either by its spring clip (Spark Tester) or by holding the spark plug shell against the engine block with insulated pliers.

→See CAUTION under STEP 6 of Run Mode Spark Test, above.

2. Have an assistant crank the engine using the ignition switch and check for spark. If there is good spark, the problem is probably in distributor cap, rotor, ignition cables or spark plugs. If there is no spark, proceed to Step 3.
3. Measure the battery voltage. Next, measure the voltage at the white wire of the module while cranking the engine. To mark this measurement, it will be necessary to pierce the white wire with a straight pin and connect the voltmeter to the straight pin and to ground. DO NOT ALLOW THE STRAIGHT PIN TO GROUND ITSELF. The battery voltage and the voltage at the white wire should be within 1 volt of each other. If the readings are not within 1 volt of each other, check and repair the feed through the ignition switch to the white wire. Recheck for spark (Step 1). If the readings are within 1 volt of each other, or if there is still no spark after the power feed to white wire is repaired, proceed to Step 4.
4. Measure the coil BAT terminal voltage while cranking the engine. The reading should be within 1 volt of battery voltage. If the readings are not within 1 volt of each other, check and repair the feed through the ignition switch to the coil. If the readings are within 1 volt of each other, the problem is probably in the ignition module. Substitute another module and repeat the test for spark (Step 1).

TFI-IV System

GENERAL INFORMATION

▶ **See Figure 13**

The Thick Film Integrated (TFI-IV) ignition system uses a camshaft driven distributor with no centrifugal or vacuum advance. The distributor has a diecast base, incorporating a Hall effect stator assembly. The TFI-IV system module is mounted on the distributor base, it has 6 pins and uses an E-Core ignition coil, named after the shape of the laminations making up the core.

The TFI-IV module supplies voltage to the Profile Ignition Pick-up (PIP) sensor, which sends the crankshaft position information to the TFI-IV module. The TFI-IV module then sends this information to the EEC-IV module, which determines the spark timing and sends an electronic signal to the TFI-IV ignition module to turn off the coil and produce a spark to fire the spark plug.

The operation of the universal distributor is accomplished through the Hall effect stator assembly, causing the ignition coil to be switched off and on by the EEC-IV computer and TFI-IV modules. The vane switch is an encapsulated package consisting of a Hall sensor on one side and a permanent magnet on the other side.

A rotary vane cup, made of ferrous metal, is used to trigger the Hall effect switch. When the window of the vane cup is between the magnet and the Hall effect device, a magnetic flux field is completed from the magnet through the Hall effect device back to the magnet. As the vane passes through the opening, the flux lines are shunted through the vane and back to the magnet. A voltage is produced while the vane passes through the opening. When the vane clears the opening, the window causes the signal to go to 0 volts. The signal is then used by the EEC-IV system for crankshaft position sensing and the computation of the desired spark advance based on the engine demand and calibration. The voltage distribution is accomplished through a conventional rotor, cap and ignition wires.

GENERAL TESTING

Spark Plug Wire Resistance

See Section 1.

Adjustments

The air gap between the armature and magnetic pick-up coil in the distributor is not adjustable, nor are there any adjustment for the amplifier module. Inoperative components are simply replaced. Any attempt to connect components outside the vehicle may result in component failure.

TROUBLESHOOTING THE TFI-IV SYSTEM

➡ **After performing any test which requires piercing a wire with a straight pin, remove the straight pin and seal the holes in the wire with silicone sealer.**

Wiring Harness

1. Disconnect the wiring harness connector from the TFI module; the connector tabs must be PUSHED to disengage the connector. Inspect the connector for damage, dirt, and corrosion.
2. Attach the negative lead of a voltmeter to the base of the distributor. Attach the other voltmeter lead to a small straight pin. With the ignition switch in the **RUN** position, insert the straight pin into the No. 1 terminal of the TFI module connector. Note the voltage reading. With the ignition switch in the **RUN** position, move the straight pin to the No. 2 connector terminal. Again, note the voltage reading. Move the straight pin to the No. 3 connector terminal, then turn the ignition switch to the **START** position. Note the voltage reading then turn the ignition **OFF**.
3. The voltage readings should all be at least 90 percent of the available battery voltage. If the readings are okay, proceed to the Stator Assembly and Module test. If any reading is less than 90 percent of the battery voltage, inspect the wiring, connectors, and/or ignition switch for defects. if the voltage is low only at the No. 1 terminal, proceed to the ignition coil primary voltage test.

Stator Assembly and Module

1. Remove the distributor from the engine.
2. Remove the TFI module from the distributor.
3. Inspect the distributor terminals, ground screw, and stator wiring for damage. Repair as necessary.
4. Measure the resistance of the stator assembly, using an ohmmeter. If the ohmmeter reading is 800–975 ohms, the stator is okay, but the TFI module must be replaced. If the ohmmeter reading is less than 800 ohms or more than 975 ohms; the TFI module is okay, but the stator module must be replaced.
5. Repair as necessary and install the TFI module and the distributor.

Primary Circuit Continuity

This test is performed in the same manner as the previous Wiring Harness test, but only the No. 1 terminal conductor is tested (ignition switch in Run position). If the voltage is less than 90 percent of the available battery voltage, proceed to the coil primary voltage test.

Ignition Coil

TESTING

Ignition Coil Test

The ignition coil must be diagnosed separately from the rest of the ignition system.

1. Primary resistance is measured between the two primary (low voltage) coil terminals, with the coil connector disconnected and the ignition switch off. Primary resistance should be 0.3–1.0 ohms.
2. On Dura Spark ignitions, the secondary resistance is measured between the BATT and high voltage (secondary) terminals of the ignition coil with the ignition **OFF**, and the wiring from the coil disconnected. Secondary resistance must be 8,000–11,500 ohms.
3. If resistance tests are okay, but the coil is still suspected, test the coil on a coil tester by following the test equipment manufacturer's instructions for a standard coil. If the reading differs from the original test, check for a defective wiring harness.

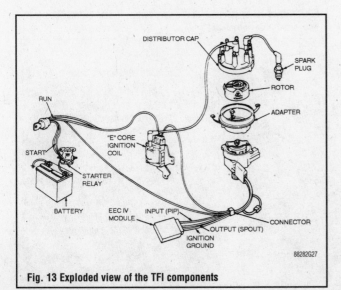

Fig. 13 Exploded view of the TFI components

88282G27

Ignition Coil Primary Circuit Switching

1. Insert a small straight pin in the wire which runs from the coil negative (–) terminal to the TFI module, about 1 in. (25mm) from the module.

❊❊ WARNING

The pin must not touch ground!

2. Connect a 12 VDC test lamp between the straight pin and an engine ground.
3. Crank the engine, noting the operation of the test lamp. If the test lamp flashes, proceed to the next test. If the test lamp lights but does not flash, proceed to the Wiring Harness test. If the test lamp does not light at all, proceed to the Primary Circuit Continuity test.

Ignition Coil Resistance

Refer to the General Testing for an explanation of the resistance tests. Replace the ignition coil if the resistance is out of the specification range.

Ignition Coil Secondary Voltage

1. Disconnect the secondary (high voltage) coil wire from the distributor cap and install a spark tester between the coil wire and ground.
2. Crank the engine. A good, strong spark should be noted at the spark tester. If spark is noted, but the engine will not start, check the spark plugs, spark plug wiring, and fuel system. If there is no spark at the tester: Check the ignition coil secondary wire resistance; it should be no more than 5,000 ohms per foot. Inspect the ignition coil for damage and/or carbon tracking. With the distributor cap removed, verify that the distributor shaft turns with the engine; if it does not, repair the engine as required. If the fault was not found proceed to the Ignition Coil Primary Voltage test.

Ignition Coil Primary Voltage

1. Attach the negative lead of a voltmeter to the distributor base.
2. Turn the ignition switch **ON** and connect the positive voltmeter lead to the negative (–) ignition coil terminal. Note the voltage reading and turn the ignition **OFF**. If the voltmeter reading is less than 90 percent of the available battery voltage, inspect the wiring between the ignition module and the negative (–) coil terminal, then proceed to the Ignition Coil Supply Voltage test.

Ignition Coil Supply Voltage

1. Attach the negative lead of a voltmeter to the distributor base.
2. Turn the ignition switch **ON** and connect the positive voltmeter lead to the positive (+) ignition coil terminal. Note the voltage reading then turn the ignition **OFF**. If the voltage reading is at least 90 percent of the battery voltage,

yet the engine will still not run; first, check the ignition coil connector and terminals for corrosion, dirt, and/or damage; second, replace the ignition switch if the connectors and terminal are okay.

3. Connect any remaining wiring.

REMOVAL & INSTALLATION

Carbureted Engines

1. Disconnect the battery ground.
2. Disconnect the two small and one large wires from the coil.
3. Disconnect the condenser connector from the coil, if equipped.
4. Unbolt and remove the coil.
5. Installation is the reverse of removal.

Fuel Injected Engines

▶ See Figures 14, 15, 16 and 17

1. Pulling on the connector boot, disconnect the high tension lead at the coil.
2. Disconnect the wiring at the ignition coil.
3. Remove the ignition coil-to-bracket attaching screws, then remove the coil.

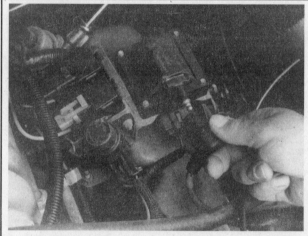

Fig. 14 Disengage the high tension wire by pulling on the connector boot—fuel injected engines

Fig. 15 Separate the wiring harness connection at the coil

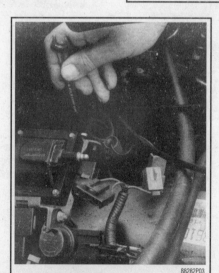

Fig. 16 Unscrew the coil from its bracket mount

Fig. 17 Remove the coil from the engine

To install:
4. Install the coil, tightening the screws to 25–35 inch lbs. (2.8–4.0 Nm).
5. Connect the ignition coil wiring harness and the high tension lead.

Ignition Module

REMOVAL & INSTALLATION

1. Remove the distributor cap from the distributor, and set it aside (spark plug wires still connected).
2. Disconnect the harness connector.
3. Remove the distributor.
4. Remove the TFI module retaining screws.

✴ WARNING

Step 5 must be followed EXACTLY; failure to do so will result in damage to the distributor module connector pins.

5. To disengage the TFI module's terminals from the distributor base connector, pull the right side of the module down the distributor mounting flange and then back up. Carefully pull the module toward the flange and away from the distributor.
6. Coat the TFI module baseplate with a thin layer of silicone grease (FD7AZ–19A331–A or its equivalent).
7. Place the TFI module on the distributor base mounting flange. Position the module assembly toward the distributor bowl and carefully engage the distributor connector pins. Install and torque the two TFI module retaining screws to 9–16 inch lbs.
8. Install the distributor assembly.
9. Install the distributor cap and check the engine timing.

Distributor

REMOVAL

Carbureted Engines (DuraSpark II)

▶ **See Figure 18**

1. Remove the air cleaner assembly, taking note of the hose locations.
2. Disconnect the distributor wiring connector from the vehicle wiring harness.

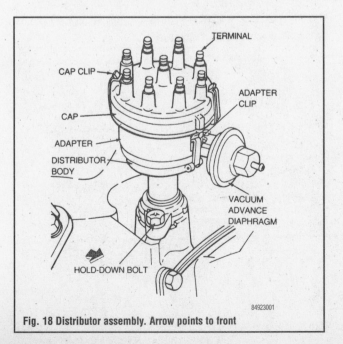

Fig. 18 Distributor assembly. Arrow points to front

3. Noting the position of the vacuum line(s) on the distributor diaphragm, disconnect the lines at the diaphragm. Unsnap the two distributor cap retaining clamps and remove the cap, rotor and adapter.

➡**If it is necessary to disconnect ignition wires from the cap to get enough room to remove the distributor, make sure to label every wire and the cap for easy and accurate reinstallation.**

4. Rotate the engine to align any pole on the armature with the pole on the stator.
5. Install the rotor. Using chalk or paint, carefully mark the position of the distributor rotor in relation to the distributor housing and mark the position of the distributor housing in relation to the engine block. When this is done, you should have a line on the distributor housing directly in line with the tip of the rotor and another line on the engine block directly in line with the mark on the distributor housing. This is very important because the distributor must be installed in the exact same location from which it was removed, if correct ignition timing is to be maintained.
6. Remove the distributor hold-down bolt and clamp. Remove the distributor from the engine. Make sure that the oil pump (intermediate) driveshaft does not come out with the distributor. If it does, remove it from the distributor shaft, coat its lower end with heavy grease, and reinsert it, making sure that it fully engages the oil pump drive.

➡**Do not disturb the engine while the distributor is removed. If you turn the engine over with the distributor removed, you will have to re-time the engine.**

INSTALLATION—ENGINE NOT ROTATED

Carbureted Engines (DuraSpark II)

1. If the engine was not cranked (disturbed) when the distributor was removed, position the distributor in the block with the armature and stator poles aligned, the rotor aligned with the mark previously scribed on the distributor body and the marks on the distributor body and cylinder block in alignment. Install the distributor hold-down bolt and clamp finger-tight.
2. If the stator and armature poles cannot be aligned by rotating the distributor, pull the distributor out just far enough to disengage the drive gear and rotate the distributor shaft to engage a different gear tooth.
3. Install the distributor cap and wires.
4. Connect the distributor wring connector to the wiring harness. Tighten the hold-down bolt.
5. Install the air cleaner, if removed.
6. Check the ignition timing, as outlined in Section 1.

INSTALLATION—CRANKSHAFT OR CAMSHAFT ROTATED

Carbureted Engines (DuraSpark II)

If the engine is cranked (disturbed) with the distributor removed, it will now be necessary to re-time the engine.
1. Rotate the engine so that No. 1 piston is at TDC of the compression stroke.
2. Align the timing marks to the correct initial timing shown on the underhood decal.
3. Install the distributor with the rotor in the No. 1 firing position and any armature pole aligned with the stator pole.

➡**Make sure that the oil pump intermediate shaft properly engages the distributor shaft. It may be necessary to crank the engine after the distributor gear is partially engaged in order to engage the oil pump intermediate shaft and fully seat the distributor in the block.**

4. If it was necessary to rotate the engine to align the oil pump, repeat Steps 1, 2 and 3.
5. Install the hold-down bolt finger tight.
6. Install the distributor cap and wires.
7. Connect the distributor wring connector to the wiring harness. Tighten the hold-down bolt.

8. Install the air cleaner, if removed.
9. Check the ignition timing.
10. When everything is set, tighten the hold-down bolt to 25 ft. lbs. (34 Nm).

REMOVAL

Fuel Injected Engines (TFI-IV Systems)

▶ See Figures 19 and 20

1. Disconnect the primary wiring connector from the distributor.
2. Mark the position of the cap's No. 1 terminal on the distributor base.
3. Unclip and remove the cap. Remove the adapter.
4. Remove the rotor.
5. Remove the TFI connector.
6. Matchmark the distributor base and engine for installation reference.
7. Remove the hold-down bolt and lift out the distributor.

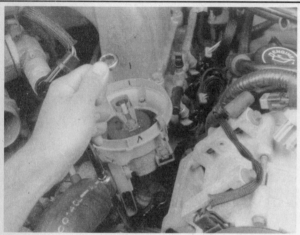

88282P10

Fig. 19 Remove the hold-down bolt to the distributor—fuel injected engine shown

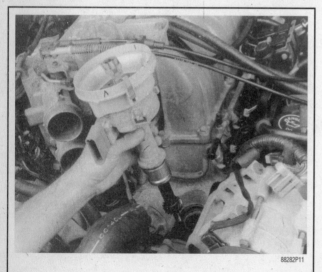

88282P11

Fig. 20 Remove the distributor from the engine

INSTALLATION

Fuel Injected Engines (TFI-IV System)

1. Rotate the engine so that the No. 1 piston is at TDC of the compression stroke.
2. Align the timing marks so that the engine is set at the initial timing shown on the underhood sticker.
3. Install the rotor on the shaft and rotate the shaft so that the rotor tip points to the No. 1 mark made on the distributor base.
4. Continue rotating the shaft so that the leading edge of the vane is centered on the vane switch assembly.
5. Position the distributor in the block and rotate the distributor body to align the leading edge of the vane and vane switch. Verify that the rotor tip points to the No. 1 mark on the body.

➡If the vane and vane switch cannot be aligned by rotating the distributor body in the engine, pull the distributor out just far enough to disengage the gears and rotate the shaft to engage a different gear tooth. Repeat Steps 3, 4 and 5.

6. Install and finger tighten the hold-down bolt.
7. Connect the TFI and primary wiring.
8. Install the rotor, if not already done.

➡Coat the brass portions of the rotor with a $FR1/32 in. (0.8mm) thick coating of silicone dielectric compound.

9. Install the cap and adapter (as necessary). Install the wires and start the engine.
10. Check and set the initial timing.
11. Tighten the hold-down bolt to 25 ft. lbs. (34 Nm).

INSPECTION

1. Remove the distributor cap and rotor.
2. Wash the inside and outside of the cap and wash the rotor with soap and water, then dry them thoroughly with compressed air or a lint-free cloth.
3. Look closely at the distributor cap, inspecting it for signs of deterioration such as cracks, broken carbon button or carbon tracks.
4. Inspect the terminals for dirt or corrosion.
5. Inspect the rotor for carbon build-up, cracks or damage to the blade or spring.
6. If damage is found, replace the distributor cap and/or rotor.

STATOR ASSEMBLY REPLACEMENT

Carbureted Engines

1. Disconnect the battery ground cable.
2. Remove the distributor cap.
3. Remove the rotor.
4. Unclip and remove the upper distributor body.
5. Remove the retaining screw and remove the wire harness from the distributor.
6. Using a small gear puller, remove the stator from the distributor shaft. As the stator is pulled up on the shaft, take care to hold on to the roll pin so that it doesn't fall into the distributor.
   To install:
7. Place the new stator on the shaft, press or dive it down slightly, insert the roll pin and drive it into place inside the stator.
8. Using a deep socket, or similar tool, drive the stator down until it bottoms. Check occasionally to be sure that the roll pin stays in place.
9. Install the wiring harness, upper body, rotor and cap.

Fuel Injected Engines

V8 ENGINES

1. Remove the distributor assembly from the engine; refer to the procedure in this section.
2. Remove the ignition rotor from the distributor shaft.
3. Mark the armature and distributor drive gear with a felt tip pen or equivalent, to note their orientation. While holding the distributor gear, remove the 2 armature retaining screws and remove the armature.

➡️**Do not hold the armature to loosen the screws.**

4. Use a suitable punch to remove the roll pin from the distributor drive gear; discard the roll pin.
5. Position the distributor upside down in a suitable press. Using a press plate and suitable driver, press off the distributor drive gear.
6. Use a file and/or emery paper to remove any burrs or deposits from the distributor shaft, that would keep the shaft from sliding freely from the distributor housing. Remove the shaft assembly.
7. Remove the 2 stator assembly retaining screws.
8. Remove the octane rod and screw.
9. Remove the stator assembly.
10. Inspect the base bushing for wear or signs of excess heat concentration. If damage is evident, the entire distributor assembly must be replaced.
11. Inspect the base O-ring for cuts or damage and replace, as necessary.
12. Inspect the base for cracks and wear. Replace the entire distributor assembly if the base is damaged.
To install:
13. Position the stator assembly over the bushing and press down to seat.
14. Position the stator connector. The tab should fit in the notch on the base and the fastening eyelets should be aligned with the screw holes. Be sure the wires are positioned out of the way of moving parts.
15. Install the 2 stator retaining screws and tighten to 15–35 inch lbs. (1.7–4.0 Nm). Install the octane rod.
16. Apply a thin coat of clean engine oil to the distributor shaft below the armature. Insert the shaft into the distributor base.
17. Place a ½ in. deep well socket over the distributor shaft, invert the assembly and place on the press plate.
18. Position the distributor drive gear on the end of the distributor shaft, aligning the marks on the armature and gear. Make sure the holes in the shaft and drive gear are aligned, so the roll pin can be installed.
19. Place a ⅝ in. deep well socket over the shaft and gear and press the gear until the holes are aligned.

➡️**If the shaft and gear holes do not align, the gear must be removed and repressed. Do not attempt to use a drift punch to align the holes.**

20. Drive a new roll pin through the gear and shaft.
21. Install the armature and tighten the screws to 25–35 inch lbs. (2.8–4.0 Nm).
22. Check that the distributor shaft moves freely over full rotation. If the armature contacts the stator, the entire distributor must be replaced.
23. Make sure the back of the TFI-IV module and the distributor mounting face are clean. Apply silicone dielectric compound to the back of the module, spreading thinly and evenly.
24. Turn the distributor base upside down, so the stator connector is in full view.
25. Install the ignition rotor onto the distributor shaft. Install the distributor as described in this section.

4.9L ENGINE

1. Remove the distributor assembly from the engine; refer to the procedure in this section.
2. Remove the ignition rotor from the distributor shaft.
3. Mark the armature and distributor drive gear with a felt tip pen or equivalent, to note their orientation. While holding the distributor gear, remove the 2 armature retaining screws and remove the armature.

➡️**Do not hold the armature to loosen the screws.**

4. Use a suitable punch to remove the roll pin from the distributor drive gear; discard the roll pin.

5. Position the distributor upside down in a suitable arbor press. Using a press plate and suitable driver, press off the distributor drive gear.
6. Remove the thrust washer and save it.
7. Use a file and/or emery paper to remove any burrs or deposits from the distributor shaft, that would keep the shaft from sliding freely from the distributor housing.
8. Remove the shaft assembly.
9. Remove the 2 stator assembly retaining screws.
10. Remove the octane rod and screw.
11. Remove the stator assembly.
12. Inspect the base bushing for wear or signs of excess heat concentration. If damage is evident, the entire distributor assembly must be replaced.
13. Inspect the base O-ring for cuts or damage and replace, as necessary.
14. Inspect the base for cracks and wear. Replace the entire distributor assembly if the base is damaged.
To install:
15. Position the stator assembly over the bushing and press down to seat.
16. Position the stator connector. The tab should fit in the notch on the base and the fastening eyelets should be aligned with the screw holes. Be sure the wires are positioned out of the way of moving parts.
17. Install the 2 stator retaining screws and tighten to 15–35 inch lbs. (1.7–4.0 Nm). Install the octane rod.
18. Apply a thin coat of clean engine oil to the distributor shaft below the armature. Insert the shaft into the distributor base. Install the thrust washer.
19. Place a ½ in. deep well socket over the distributor shaft, invert the assembly and place on the press plate.
20. Position the distributor drive gear on the end of the distributor shaft, aligning the marks on the armature and gear. Make sure the holes in the shaft and drive gear are aligned, so the roll pin can be installed.
21. Place a ⅝ in. deep well socket over the shaft and gear and press the gear until the holes are aligned.

➡️**If the shaft and gear holes do not align, the gear must be removed and repressed. Do not attempt to use a drift punch to align the holes.**

22. Drive a new roll pin through the gear and shaft.
23. Install the armature and tighten the screws to 25–35 inch lbs. (2.8–4.0 Nm).
24. Check that the distributor shaft moves freely over full rotation. If the armature contacts the stator, the entire distributor must be replaced.
25. Make sure the back of the TFI-IV module and the distributor mounting face are clean. Apply silicone dielectric compound to the back of the module, spreading thinly and evenly.
26. Turn the distributor base upside down, so the stator connector is in full view.
27. Install the ignition rotor onto the distributor shaft. Install the distributor, as described in this section.

VACUUM DIAPHRAGM ASSEMBLY REPLACEMENT

1. Disconnect the diaphragm assembly vacuum hose(s).
2. Remove the C-clip securing the diaphragm rod to the base plate pin. Lift the diaphragm rod off the base plate pin.
3. Remove the 2 diaphragm assembly attaching screws and identification tag.
4. Remove the diaphragm assembly from the distributor base.
To install:
5. Adjust the new diaphragm assembly per manufacturer's instructions included with the new diaphragm.
6. Install the diaphragm on the distributor base. Attach the diaphragm assembly and identification tag to the distributor base with the 2 attaching screws and tighten to 15 inch lbs. (1.7 Nm).
7. Place diaphragm rod on the pin and install the C-clip.
8. Reconnect the vacuum hose(s).

Camshaft Position Sensor

Please refer to Section 4 for information regarding the Camshaft Position Sensor.

FIRING ORDERS

▶ **See Figures 21, 22, 23 and 24**

➡**To avoid confusion, remove and tag the spark plug wires one at a time, for replacement.**

If a distributor is not keyed for installation with only one orientation, it could

have been removed previously and rewired. The resultant wiring would hold the correct firing order, but could change the relative placement of the plug towers in relation to the engine. For this reason it is imperative that you label all wires before disconnecting any of them. Also, before removal, compare the current wiring with the accompanying illustrations. If the current wiring does not match, make notes in your book to reflect how your engine is wired.

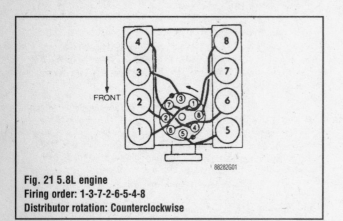

Fig. 21 5.8L engine
Firing order: 1-3-7-2-6-5-4-8
Distributor rotation: Counterclockwise

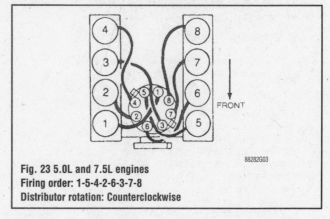

Fig. 23 5.0L and 7.5L engines
Firing order: 1-5-4-2-6-3-7-8
Distributor rotation: Counterclockwise

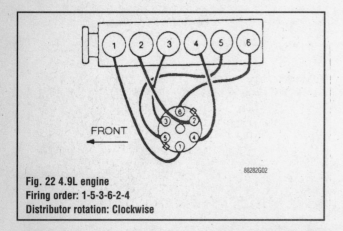

Fig. 22 4.9L engine
Firing order: 1-5-3-6-2-4
Distributor rotation: Clockwise

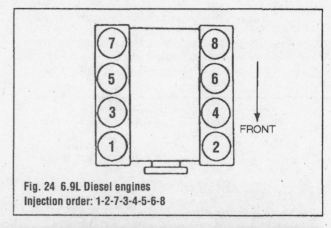

Fig. 24 6.9L Diesel engines
Injection order: 1-2-7-3-4-5-6-8

CHARGING SYSTEM

Alternator Precautions

To prevent damage to the alternator and regulator, the following precautions should be taken when working with the electrical system.

1. Never reverse the battery connections.
2. Booster batteries for starting must be connected properly: positive-to-positive and negative-to-ground.
3. Disconnect the battery cables before using a fast charger; the charger has a tendency to force current through the diodes in the opposite direction for which they were designed. This burns out the diodes.
4. Never use a fast charger as a booster for starting the vehicle.
5. Never disconnect the voltage regulator while the engine is running.
6. Avoid long soldering times when replacing diodes or transistors. Prolonged heat is damaging to AC generators.
7. Do not use test lamps of more than 12 volts (V) for checking diode continuity.
8. Do not short across or ground any of the terminals on the AC generator.
9. The polarity of the battery, generator, and regulator must be matched and considered before making any electrical connections within the system.
10. Never operate the alternator on an open circuit. Make sure that all connections within the circuit are clean and tight.
11. Disconnect the battery terminals when performing any service on the electrical system. This will eliminate the possibility of accidental reversal of polarity.
12. Disconnect the battery ground cable if arc welding is to be done on any part of the car.

Alternator

IDENTIFICATION

There are 4 different types of alternators found on the years and model ranges covered in this manual:

1. Rear Terminal, External Regulator, External Fan Alternator
2. Side Terminal, Internal Regulator, External Fan Alternator
3. Leece-Neville 165 Ampere Alternator
4. Integral Rear Mount Regulator, Internal Fan Alternator

Rear Terminal, External Regulator, External Fan Alternator

This unit utilizes a separate, external electronic regulator. The regulator is non-adjustable. The rear terminal alternator was standard equipment on 1987 trucks, and can be found on some 1992 motor home chassis models equipped with the 7.3L diesel or 7.5L gasoline engine.

Side Terminal, Internal Regulator, External Fan Alternator

This unit was optional on 1987, standard on all 1988–92 models and standard on 1993–96 models equipped with the 4.9L and 7.5L engines. The regulator in integrated within the alternator body and is not adjustable.

Integral Rear Mount Regulator, Internal Fan Alternator

This alternator is standard equipment on all 1993–96 models equipped with 5.0L, 5.8L gasoline engines and 7.3L diesel engines (except the 1996 F-Super Duty models).

Leece-Neville 165 Ampere Alternator

This unit is optional equipment on some 1989–94 trucks and ambulance packages. A separate, electronic, fully adjustable regulator is employed in this system.

Mitsubishi 215 Ampere Alternator

This unit is found on 1996 F-Super Duty models equipped with the 7.3L diesel engine. The regulator is integral and the fan is external.

TESTING

Voltage Test

1. Make sure the engine is **OFF**, and turn the headlights on for 15–20 seconds to remove any surface charge from the battery.
2. Using a DVOM set to volts DC, probe across the battery terminals.
3. Measure the battery voltage.
4. Write down the voltage reading and proceed to the next test.

No-Load Test

1. Connect a tachometer to the engine.

> ✳✳ **CAUTION**

Ensure that the transmission is in PARK and the emergency brake is set. Blocking a wheel is optional and an added safety measure.

2. Turn off all electrical loads (radio, blower motor, wipers, etc.)
3. Start the engine and increase engine speed to approximately 1500 rpm.
4. Measure the voltage reading at the battery with the engine holding a steady 1500 rpm. Voltage should have raised at least 0.5 volts, but no more than 2.5 volts.
5. If the voltage does not go up more than 0.5 volts, the alternator is not charging. If the voltage goes up more than 2.5 volts, the alternator is overcharging.

➡Usually under and overcharging is caused by a defective alternator, or its related parts (regulator), and replacement will fix the problem; however, faulty wiring and other problems can cause the charging system to malfunction. Further testing, which is not covered by this book, will reveal the exact component failure. Many automotive parts stores have alternator bench testers available for use by customers. An alternator bench test is the most definitive way to determine the condition of your alternator.

6. If the voltage is within specifications, proceed to the next test.

Load Test

1. With the engine running, turn on the blower motor and the high beams (or other electrical accessories to place a load on the charging system).
2. Increase and hold engine speed to 2000 rpm.
3. Measure the voltage reading at the battery.
4. The voltage should increase at least 0.5 volts from the voltage test. If the voltage does not meet specifications, the charging system is malfunctioning.

➡Usually under and overcharging is caused by a defective alternator, or its related parts (regulator), and replacement will fix the problem; however, faulty wiring and other problems can cause the charging system to malfunction. Further testing, which is not covered by this book, will reveal the exact component failure. Many automotive parts stores have alternator bench testers available for use by customers. An alternator

bench test is the most definitive way to determine the condition of your alternator.

REMOVAL & INSTALLATION

▶ **See Figures 25, 26, 27 and 28**

1. Disconnect the battery ground cable.
2. Remove the adjusting arm bolt.
3. Remove the alternator through-bolt. Remove the drive belt from the alternator pulley and lower the alternator.

➡**Some engines are equipped with a ribbed, K-section belt and automatic tensioner. A suitable tool must be made to remove the tension from the tensioner arm. Loosen the idler pulley pivot and adjuster bolts before using the tool..**

4. Label all of the leads to the alternator so that you can install them correctly and disconnect the leads from the alternator.
5. Remove the alternator from the vehicle.
6. To install, reverse the above procedure. Observe the following torques:
- Pivot bolt: 58 ft. lbs. (78 Nm)
- Adjusting bolt: 25 ft. lbs. (34 Nm)
- Wire terminal nuts: 60–90 inch lbs. (6.8–10.1 Nm)

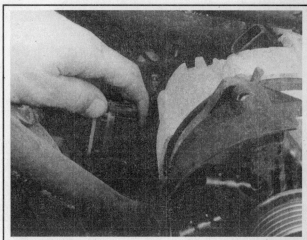

Fig. 25 Disengage all wiring harness connections from the alternator

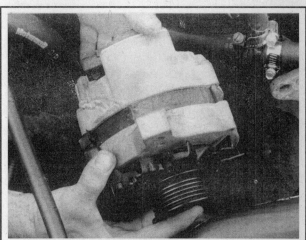

Fig. 26 Once it is unbolted, maneuver the alternator from the engine compartment

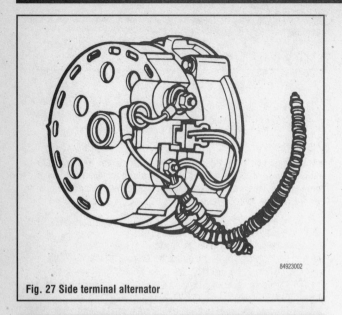

Fig. 27 Side terminal alternator

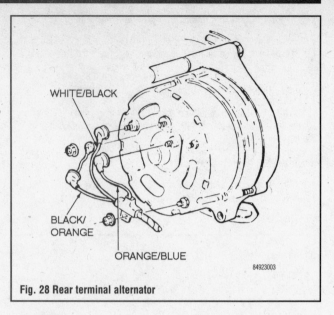

Fig. 28 Rear terminal alternator

Regulator

REMOVAL & INSTALLATION

Leece-Neville Alternator

The regulator is mounted on the back of the alternator.
1. Disconnect the diode trio lead from the regulator terminal.
2. Remove the 2 nuts retaining the regulator and the jumper leads.
3. Carefully pull the regulator from its holder.

➡ **The brushes will snap together when the regulator is removed. They can now be checked for length. Brush length minimum is 0.188 in. (4.76mm).**

STARTING SYSTEM

Starter

TESTING

Voltage Drop Test

➡ **The battery must be in good condition and fully charged prior to performing this test.**

1. Disable the ignition system by unplugging the coil pack. Verify that the vehicle will not start.
2. Connect a voltmeter between the positive terminal of the battery and the starter **B+** circuit.
3. Turn the ignition key to the **START** position and note the voltage on the meter.
4. If voltage reads 0.5 volts or more, there is high resistance in the starter cables or the cable ground, repair as necessary. If the voltage reading is ok, proceed to the next step.
5. Connect a voltmeter between the positive terminal of the battery and the starter **M** circuit.
6. Turn the ignition key to the **START** position and note the voltage on the meter.
7. If voltage reads 0.5 volts or more, there is high resistance in the starter. Repair or replace the starter as necessary.

➡ **Many automotive parts stores have starter bench testers available for use by customers. A starter bench test is the most definitive way to determine the condition of your starter.**

To install:
4. Push the brushes back into their holders and insert a $FR1/32 inch pin through the hole provided in the housing. This will hold the brushes in place.
5. Carefully push the regulator into place and **just start** the retaining nuts. Remove the brush holding pin and **then** tighten the retaining nuts.
6. Connect the diode trio leads.

Rear Terminal Alternators

This unit is located on the fender liner, adjacent to the alternator.
1. Disconnect the battery ground.
2. Remove the regulator mounting screws.
3. Disconnect the wiring harness from the regulator.
4. Installation is the reverse of removal.

REMOVAL & INSTALLATION

Gasoline Engines

▶ **See Figures 29, 30, 31 and 32**

1. Disconnect the negative battery cable.
2. Raise the front of the truck and install jackstands beneath the frame. Firmly apply the parking brake and place blocks in back of the rear wheels.
3. Tag and disconnect the wiring at the starter.
4. If necessary, turn the front wheels fully to the right. On some later models it will be necessary to remove the frame brace.
5. Remove the starter mounting bolts and remove the starter.
To install:
Observe the following torque specifications:
• Mounting bolts: 12–15 ft. lbs. (16–20 Nm) on starters with 3 mounting bolts and 15–20 ft. lbs. (20–27 Nm) on starters with 2 mounting bolts.
• Idler arm retaining bolts to 28–35 ft. lbs. (38–47 Nm), if removed.
6. Install the starter.
7. If removed, install the steering idler arm.
8. If removed, install the frame brace.
9. Connect the starter wiring. Make sure that the nut securing the heavy cable to the starter is snugged down tightly.
10. Lower the vehicle and connect the negative battery cable.

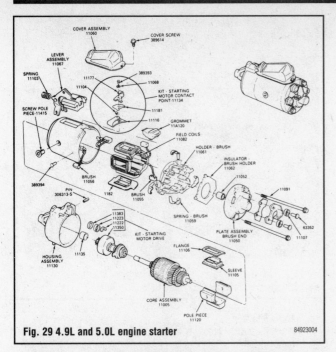

Fig. 29 4.9L and 5.0L engine starter

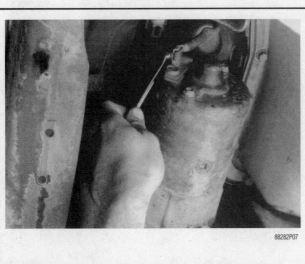

Fig. 30 Remove the wiring from the starter—5.0L engine shown

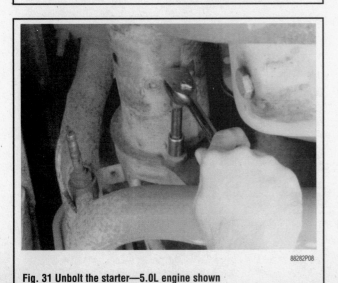

Fig. 31 Unbolt the starter—5.0L engine shown

Diesel Engines

▶ **See Figure 33**

1. Disconnect the battery ground cable.
2. Raise the vehicle and disconnect the cables and wires at the starter solenoid.
3. If necessary, turn the front wheels to the right and remove the two bolts attaching the steering idler arm to the frame.
4. Remove the starter mounting bolts and remove the starter.

To install:

5. Install the starter. Torque the mounting bolts to 20 ft. lbs. (27 Nm).
6. If removed, install the idler arm.
7. Connect the starter wiring.
8. Connect the negative battery cable.

RELAY REPLACEMENT

Fender Mounted Solenoid

▶ **See Figures 34 and 35**

1. Disconnect the positive battery cable from the battery terminal. With dual batteries, disconnect the connecting cable at both ends.
2. Remove the nut securing the positive battery cable to the relay.
3. Remove the positive cable and any other wiring under that cable.
4. Tag and remove the push-on wires from the front of the relay.

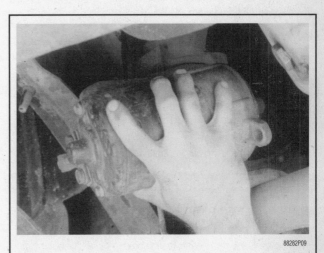

Fig. 32 Remove the detached starter from the vehicle—5.0L engine shown

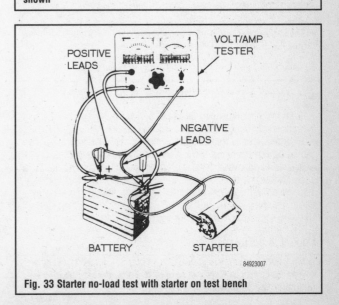

Fig. 33 Starter no-load test with starter on test bench

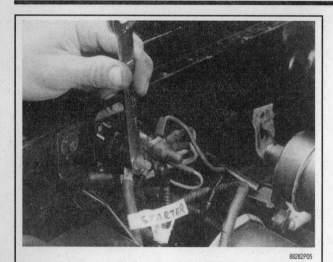

Fig. 34 Tag the wires prior to their removal—fender mounted solenoid

5. Remove the nut and disconnect the cable from the starter side of the relay.
6. Remove the relay attaching bolts and remove the relay.
7. Installation is the reverse of removal.

Starter Mounted Solenoid

1. Disconnect the negative battery cable.

SENDING UNITS AND SENSORS

The sensors covered in this section are NOT related to electronic engine control. These are basic sensors designed to monitor certain vital functions of the vehicle's operation in order to alert the driver of a malfunction. Please refer to Section 4 for information regarding electronic engine controls.

Coolant Temperature Sending Unit

OPERATION

When coolant temperature is low, the resistance of the sending unit is high, restricting the flow of current through the gauge and moving the pointer only a short distance. As coolant temperature rises, the resistance of the sending unit decreases, causing a proportional increase in current flow through the sending unit and corresponding movement of the gauge pointer.

The sending unit may only be tested for operation. There is no calibration, adjustment or maintenance required.

TESTING

▶ See Figures 36, 37, 38 and 39

1. Remove the sender from the vehicle.
2. Immerse the tip of the sensor in container of water.
3. Connect a digital ohmmeter to the two terminals of the sensor.
4. Using a calibrated thermometer, compare the resistance of the sensor to the temperature of the water. Refer to the engine coolant sensor temperature vs. resistance illustration.
5. Repeat the test at two other temperature points, heating or cooling the water as necessary.
6. If the sensor does not meet specification, it must be replaced.

REMOVAL & INSTALLATION

For the location of your unit, see the accompanying illustrations.
1. Disconnect the negative battery cable.

Fig. 35 Unbolt and remove the relay from the fender

2. Remove the starter.
3. Remove the positive brush connector from the solenoid M terminal.
4. Remove the solenoid retaining screws and remove the solenoid.
5. Attach the solenoid plunger rod to the slot in the lever and tighten the solenoid retaining screws to 45–54 inch lbs. (5.1–6.1 Nm).
6. Attach the positive brush connector to the solenoid M terminal and tighten the retaining nut to 80–120 inch lbs. (9.0–13.5 Nm).
7. Install the starter and connect the negative battery terminal.

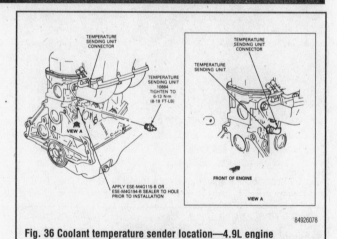

Fig. 36 Coolant temperature sender location—4.9L engine

2. Drain the cooling system into a suitable container.

❊❊ CAUTION

When draining the coolant, keep in mind that cats and dogs are attracted by ethylene glycol antifreeze, and are quite likely to drink any that is left in an uncovered container or in puddles on the ground. This will prove fatal in sufficient quantity. Always drain the coolant into a sealable container. Coolant should be reused unless it is contaminated or several years old.

3. Disengage the electrical connector at the temperature sender.
4. Remove the temperature sender.
To install:
5. Apply pipe sealant or Teflon® tape to the threads of the new sender.
6. Install the temperature sender and connect the electrical connector.
7. Connect the negative battery cable. Fill the cooling system.
8. Run the engine and check for leaks.

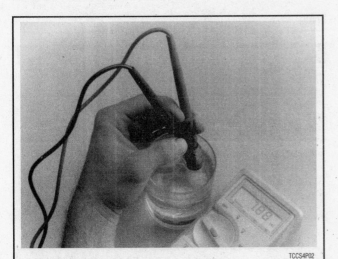

Fig. 37 Coolant temperature sending unit—5.0L/5.8L engine shown, 7.5L engine similar

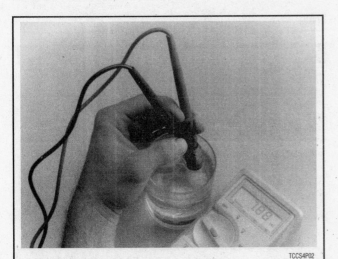

Fig. 38 Submerge the end of the coolant temperature sender in cold or hot water and check the resistance

ENGINE COOLANT SENSOR

TEMPERATURE VS. RESISTANCE VALUES (APPROXIMATE)

°C	°F	OHMS
100	212	177
90	194	241
80	176	332
70	158	467
60	140	667
50	122	973
45	113	1188
40	104	1459
35	95	1802
30	86	2238
25	77	2796
20	68	3520
15	59	4450
10	50	5670
5	41	7280
0	32	9420
-5	23	12300
-10	14	16180
-15	5	21450
-20	-4	28680
-30	-22	52700
-40	-40	100700

88282G29

Fig. 39 Coolant temperature sender temperature vs. resistance values

Oil Pressure Indicator Lamp Sending Unit

▶ See Figures 40, 41 and 42

1. Unscrew the unit.
2. Coat the threads with electrically conductive sealer and screw the unit into place. The torque should be 10–18 ft. lbs. (14–24 Nm).
   For the location of your unit, see the accompanying illustrations.
3. Disconnect the wiring at the unit.

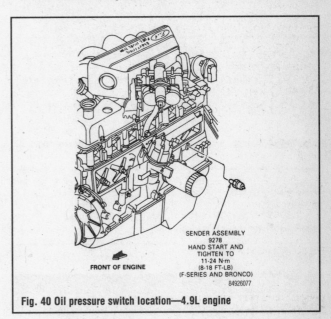

Fig. 40 Oil pressure switch location—4.9L engine

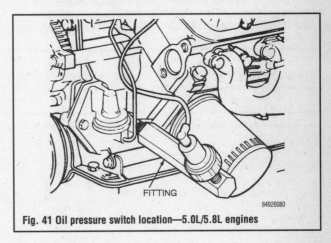

Fig. 41 Oil pressure switch location—5.0L/5.8L engines

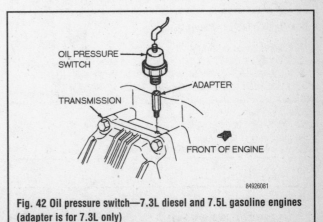

Fig. 42 Oil pressure switch—7.3L diesel and 7.5L gasoline engines (adapter is for 7.3L only)

OPERATION

A single terminal oil pressure switch is used on vehicles equipped with an oil pressure lamp.

If the pressure is detected to be at an unsafe level, a red indicator lamp will glow on the dashboard. The light should come on when the engine is off but the ignition is in the **RUN** position. Once the engine is started, the light should go out.

The lamp is connected between the oil pressure switch unit (mounted on the engine and the coil terminal of the ignition switch.

TESTING

1. Turn the ignition to the **RUN** position with the engine not running. The indicator lamp should come on.

2. If the indicator lamp does not come on, disconnect the wire from the oil pressure switch terminal and ground the wire.

3. If the indicator light comes on, the pressure switch is inoperative. Replace the switch.

4. If the indicator light fails to come on, either the bulb is burned out, there is no power to the bulb, or the circuit is open somewhere between the bulb and the oil pressure switch.

5. If the lamp stays on with the engine running and the engine has adequate oil pressure, disconnect the wire to the switch. If the lamp goes out, replace the oil pressure switch. If the lamp does not go out, correct the short in the wiring between the switch and lamp.

REMOVAL & INSTALLATION

▶ See Figure 43

✳✳ WARNING

The pressure switch used with the oil pressure warning light is not interchangeable with the sending unit used with the oil pressure gauge. If the incorrect part is installed the oil pressure indicating system will be inoperative and the sending unit or gauge will be damaged.

1. Unplug the connector at the unit and unscrew it from its mounting.

2. To install the unit, apply pipe sealant or Teflon® tape to the threads of the new switch and screw it in to its mount. Tighten it to 8–18 ft. lbs. (11–24 Nm).

3. Connect the wiring to the unit.

4. Run the engine and check for leaks and proper operation.

Oil Pressure Gauge Sending Unit

OPERATION

The oil pressure sending unit is a variable resistance type magnetic unit that works in conjunction with the magnetic operation of the gauge system.

The sensing unit may only be tested for operation. There is no calibration, adjustment or maintenance required.

TESTING

1. With the key in the **RUN** position and the engine off, unplug the wiring at the switch. The gauge should read on the LOW graduation or below.

2. Attach the wiring connector to the engine block (ground). The gauge should read just slightly above mid-scale.

3. If the oil pressure gauge tests within specification, replace the oil pressure switch.

4. If the gauge still tests out of calibration, replace the oil pressure gauge.

REMOVAL & INSTALLATION

✳✳ WARNING

The pressure switch used with the oil pressure warning light is not interchangeable with the sending unit used with the oil pressure gauge. If the incorrect part is installed the oil pressure indicating system will be inoperative and the sending unit or gauge will be damaged.

1. Unplug the connector at the unit and unscrew it from its mounting.

2. To install the unit, apply pipe sealant or Teflon® tape to the threads of the new switch and screw it in to its mount. Tighten it to 8–18 ft. lbs. (11–24 Nm).

3. Connect the wiring to the unit.

4. Run the engine and check for leaks and proper operation.

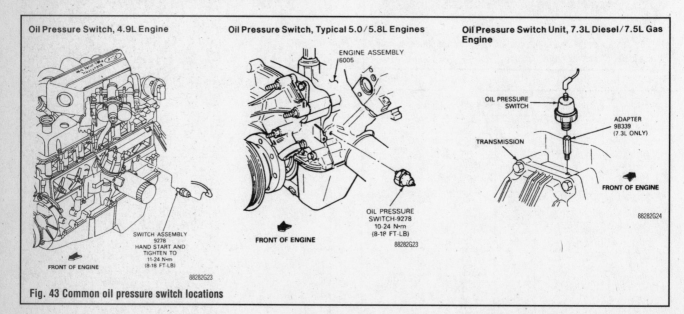

Fig. 43 Common oil pressure switch locations

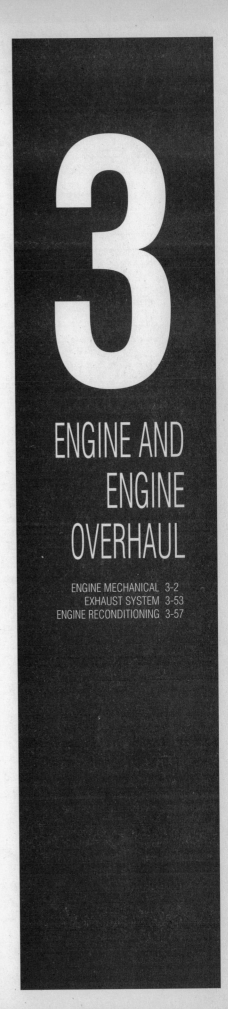

3

ENGINE AND ENGINE OVERHAUL

ENGINE MECHANICAL

GENERAL ENGINE SPECIFICATIONS

Year	Engine ID/VIN	Engine Displacement Liters (cc)	Fuel System Type	Net Horsepower @ rpm	Net Torque @ rpm (ft. lbs.)	Bore x Stroke (In.)	Compression Ratio	Oil Pressure @ rpm
1987	Y	4.9L (4917)	MFI	150@3400	260@2000	4.00x3.98	8.8:1	40-60@2000
	N	5.0L (4942)	MFI	185@3800	270@2400	4.00x3.00	9.0:1	40-60@2000
	H	5.8L (5766)	4 BBL	210@3800	315@2800	4.00x3.50	8.8:1	40-65@2000
	I	6.9L (6886)	DSL	170@3300	315@1400	4.00x4.18	21.5:1	40-70@3300
	L	7.5L (7536)	4 BBL	230@3600	390@2000	4.36x3.85	8.5:1	40-65@2000
1988	Y	4.9L (4917)	MFI	150@3400 ④	260@2000 ⑤	4.00x3.98	8.8:1	40-60@2000
	N	5.0L (4942)	MFI	185@3800	270@2400	4.00x3.00	9.0:1	40-60@2000
	H	5.8L (5766)	MFI	210@3800	315@2800 ①	4.00x3.50	8.8:1	40-65@2000
	M	7.3L (7270)	DSL	180@3300 ②	345@1400 ③	4.11x4.18	21.5:1	40-70@3300
	G	7.5L (7536)	MFI	230@3600	390@2000	4.36x3.85	8.5:1	40-65@2000
1989	Y	4.9L (4917)	MFI	150@3400 ④	260@2000 ⑤	4.00x3.98	8.8:1	40-60@2000
	N	5.0L (4942)	MFI	185@3800	270@2400	4.00x3.00	9.0:1	40-60@2000
	H	5.8L (5766)	MFI	210@3800	315@2800 ①	4.00x3.50	8.8:1	40-65@2000
	M	7.3L (7270)	DSL	180@3300 ②	345@1400 ③	4.11x4.18	21.5:1	40-70@3300
	G	7.5L (7536)	MFI	230@3600	390@2000	4.36x3.85	8.5:1	40-65@2000
1990	Y	4.9L (4917)	MFI	150@3400 ④	260@2000 ⑤	4.00x3.98	8.8:1	40-60@2000
	N	5.0L (4942)	MFI	185@3800	270@2400	4.00x3.00	9.0:1	40-60@2000
	H	5.8L (5766)	MFI	210@3800	315@2800 ①	4.00x3.50	8.8:1	40-65@2000
	M	7.3L (7270)	DSL	180@3300 ②	345@1400 ③	4.11x4.18	21.5:1	40-70@3300
	G	7.5L (7536)	MFI	230@3600	390@2200	4.36x3.85	8.5:1	40-88@2000
1991	Y	4.9L (4917)	MFI	150@3400 ④	260@2000 ⑤	4.00x3.98	8.8:1	40-60@2000
	N	5.0L (4942)	MFI	185@3800	270@2400	4.00x3.00	9.0:1	40-60@2000
	H	5.8L (5766)	MFI	210@3800	315@2800 ①	4.00x3 50	8.8:1	40-65@2000
	M	7.3L (7270)	DSL	180@3300 ②	345@1400 ③	4.11x4.18	21.5:1	40-70@3300
	G	7.5L (7536)	MFI	230@3600	390@2200	4.36x3.85	8.5:1	40-88@2000
1992	Y	4.9L (4917)	MFI	150@3400 ④	260@2000 ⑤	4.00x3.98	8.8:1	40-60@2000
	N	5.0L (4942)	MFI	185@3800	270@2400	4.00x3.00	9.0:1	40-60@2000
	H	5.8L (5766)	MFI	200@3800	300@2800	4.00x3.50	8.8:1	40-65@2000
	M	7.3L (7270)	DSL	180@3300 ②	345@1400 ③	4.11x4.18	21.5:1	40-70@3300
	G	7.5L (7536)	MFI	230@3600	390@2200	4.36x3.85	8.5:1	40-88@2000
1993	Y	4.9L (4917)	MFI	150@3400 ④	260@2000 ⑤	4.00x3.98	8.8:1	40-60@2000
	N	5.0L (4942)	MFI	185@3800	270@2400	4.00x3.00	9.0:1	40-60@2000
	H	5.8L (5766)	MFI	200@3800	310@2800	4.00x3.50	8.8:1	40-65@2000
	R	5.8L (5766)	MFI	240@4200	340@3200	4.00x3.50	8.8:1	40-65@2000
	C	7.3L (7270)	IDI	190@3000	395@1400	4.11x4.18	21.5:1	40-70@3300
	M	7.3L (7270)	DSL	185@3000 ⑩	360@1400 ⑪	4.11x4.18	21.5:1	40-70@3300
	G	7.5L (7536)	MFI	230@3600	390@2200	4.36x3.85	8.5:1	40-88@2000
1994	Y	4.9L (4917)	MFI	150@3400 ④	260@2000 ⑤	4.00x3.98	8.8:1	40-60@2000
	N	5.0L (4942)	MFI	185@3800	270@2400	4.00x3.00	9.0:1	40-60@2000
	H	5.8L (5766)	MFI	200@3800	310@2800	4.00x3.50	8.8:1	40-65@2000
	R	5.8L (5766)	MFI	240@4200	340@3200	4.00x3.50	8.8:1	40-65@2000
	F	7.3L (7270)	DI	210@3000	425@2000	4.11x4.18	17.5:1	40-70@3300
	K	7.3L (7270)	IDI	190@3000	395@1400	4.11x4.18	21.5:1	40-70@3300
	M	7.3L (7270)	DSL	185@3000 ⑩	360@1400 ⑪	4.11x4.18	21.5:1	40-70@3300
	G	7.5L (7536)	MFI	230@3600	390@2200	4.36x3.85	8.5:1	40-88@2000
1995	Y	4.9L (4917)	MFI ⑥	150@3400 ④	260@2000 ⑤	4.00x3.98	8.8:1	40-60@2000
	N	5.0L (4942)	MFI ⑦	205@4000 ⑧	275@3000 ⑧	4.00x3.00	9.0:1	40-60@2000
	H	5.8L (5766)	MFI ⑥	210@3600 ⑭	325@2800 ⑮	4.00x3.50	8.8:1	40-65@2000
	R	5.8L (5766)	MFI	240@4200	340@3200	4.00x3.50	8.8:1	40-65@2000
	F	7.3L (7270)	DI	210@3000	425@2000	4.11x4.18	17.5:1	40-70@3300
	G	7.5L (7536)	MFI	245@4000 ⑫	400@2200 ⑬	4.36x3.85	8.5:1	40-88@2000

88283C25

VALVE SPECIFICATIONS

Year	Engine ID/VIN	Engine Displacement Liters (cc)	Seat Angle (deg.)	Face Angle (deg.)	Spring Test Pressure (lbs. @ in.)	Spring Installed Height (in.)	Stem-to-Guide Clearance Intake (in.)	Stem-to-Guide Clearance Exhaust (in.)	Stem Diameter Intake (in.)	Stem Diameter Exhaust (in.)
1987	Y	4.9L (4917)	45	44	⑥	①	0.0010-0.0027	0.0010-0.0032	0.3416-0.3423	0.3416-0.3423
	N	5.0L (4942)	45	44	⑦	②	0.0010-0.0027	0.0015-0.0032	0.3423	0.3423
	H	5.8L (5766)	45	44	200@1.20		0.0010-0.0027	0.0015-0.0032	0.3416-0.3423	0.3411-0.3418
	I	6.9L (6886)	④	④	80@1.83		0.0012-0.0029	0.0012-0.0029	0.3716-0.3723	0.3716-0.3723
	L	7.5L (7536)	45	44	229@1.33	1.80	0.0010-0.0027	0.0010-0.0027	0.3416-0.3423	0.3416-0.3423
1988	Y	4.9L (4917)	45	44	⑥	①	0.0010-0.0027	0.0010-0.0027	0.3416-0.3423	0.3416-0.3423
	N	5.0L (4942)	45	44	⑦	②	0.0010-0.0027	0.0015-0.0032	0.3423	0.3423
	H	5.8L (5766)	45	44	200@1.20	③	0.0010-0.0027	0.0015-0.0032	0.3416-0.3423	0.3411-0.3418
	M	7.3L (7270)	④	④	80@1.83	④	0.0055 MAX	0.0055 MAX	0.3716	0.3723
	G	7.5L (7536)	45	44	229@1.33	1.80	0.0010-0.0027	0.0010-0.0027	0.3416-0.3423	0.3416-0.3423
1989	Y	4.9L (4917)	45	44	⑥	①	0.0010-0.0027	0.0010-0.0027	0.3416-0.3423	0.3416-0.3423
	N	5.0L (4942)	45	44	⑦	②	0.0010-0.0027	0.0015-0.0032	0.3423	0.3423
	H	5.8L (5766)	45	44	200@1.20	③	0.0010-0.0027	0.0015-0.0032	0.3416-0.3423	0.3411-0.3418
	M	7.3L (7270)	④	④	80@1.83	④	0.0055 MAX	0.0055 MAX	0.3716	0.3723
	G	7.5L (7536)	45	44	229@1.33	1.80	0.0010-0.0027	0.0010-0.0027	0.3415-0.3423	0.3415-0.3423
1990	Y	4.9L (4917)	45	44	⑥	①	0.0010-0.0027	0.0010-0.0027	0.3416-0.3423	0.3416-0.3423
	N	5.0L (4942)	45	44	⑦	②	0.0010-0.0027	0.0015-0.0032	0.3423	0.3423
	H	5.8L (5766)	45	44	200@1.20	③	0.0010-0.0027	0.0015-0.0032	0.3416-0.3423	0.3411-0.3418
	M	7.3L (7270)	④	④	80@1.83	④	0.0055 MAX	0.0055 MAX	0.3716	0.3723
	G	7.5L (7536)	45	44	229@1.33	1.80	0.0010-0.0027	0.0010-0.0027	0.3415-0.3423	0.3415-0.3423
1991	Y	4.9L (4917)	45	44	⑥	①	0.0010-0.0027	0.0010-0.0027	0.3416-0.3423	0.3416-0.3423
	N	5.0L (4942)	45	44	⑦	②	0.0010-0.0027	0.0015-0.0032	0.3423	0.3423
	H	5.8L (5766)	45	44	200@1.20	③	0.0010-0.0027	0.0015-0.0032	0.3416-0.3423	0.3411-0.3418
	M	7.3L (7270)	④	④	80@1.83	④	0.0055 MAX	0.0055 MAX	0.3716	0.3723
	G	7.5L (7536)	45	44	229@1.33	1.80	0.0010-0.0027	0.0010-0.0027	0.3415-0.3423	0.3415-0.3423

88283C27

GENERAL ENGINE SPECIFICATIONS

Year	Engine ID/VIN	Engine Displacement Liters (cc)	Fuel System Type	Net Horsepower @ rpm	Net Torque @ rpm (ft. lbs.)	Bore x Stroke (in.)	Compression Ratio	Oil Pressure @ rpm
1996	Y	4.9L (4917)	SFI	150@3400 ④	260@2000 ⑤	4.00x3.98	8.8:1	40-60@2000
	N	5.0L (4942)	SFI	199@4200	270@2400	4.00x3.00	9.0:1	40-60@2000
	H	5.8L (5766)	SFI ②	210@3600	325@2800	4.00x3.50	8.8:1	40-65@2000
	F	7.3L (7270)	DI	210@3000	425@2000	4.11x4.18	17.5:1	40-70@3300
	G	7.5L (7536)	MFI ⑥	245@4000 ⑦	400@2200 ⑩	4.36x3.85	8.5:1	40-88@2000

DSL - Diesel
DI - Direct Injection (turbo diesel)
IDI - Indirect Injection (turbo diesel)
MFI - Multi-port Fuel Injection
SFI - Sequential Fuel Injection
① Over 8500 lbs. GVWR: 150@3300 rpm
② High altitude: 150@3300 rpm
③ High altitude: 305@1400 rpm

④ Except Bronco, F-150 with 2730.08 axle ratio or F-150/F-250 w/E4OD: 145@3400
⑤ Except Bronco, F-150 with 2730.08 axle ratio or F-150/F-250 w/E4OD: 265@2000
⑥ SFI in California
⑦ SFI with automatic transmission
⑧ M/T shown.
⑨ A/T: 195 hp@4000
 270 ft. lbs.@2000

⑩ MFI on vehicles over 8500 lbs. GVWR
⑪ High altitude: 165@2000
⑫ High altitude: 325@1600
⑬ F-Super Duty: 325@4000
⑭ F-Super Duty: 255@4000
⑮ F-Super Duty: 405@2400
⑯ California E4OD: 255@3600
⑰ California E4OD: 330@2600

88283C26

VALVE SPECIFICATIONS

Year	Engine ID/VIN	Engine Displacement Liters (cc)	Seat Angle (deg.)	Face Angle (deg.)	Spring Test Pressure (lbs. @ in.)	Spring Installed Height (in.)	Stem-to-Guide Clearance (in.) Intake	Stem-to-Guide Clearance (in.) Exhaust	Stem Diameter (in.) Intake	Stem Diameter (in.) Exhaust
1995	G	7.5L (7536)	45	44	229@1.33	1.80	0.0010-0.0027	0.0010-0.0027	0.3415-0.3423	0.3415-0.3423
1996	Y	4.9L (4917)	45	44	⑦	⑧	0.0010-0.0027	0.0010-0.0027	0.3415-0.3423	0.3415-0.3423
	N	5.0L (4942)	45	44	⑦	⑧	0.0010-0.0027	0.0015-0.0032	0.3415-0.3423	0.3410-0.3418
	H	5.8L (5766)	45	44	200@1.20	⑧	0.0010-0.0027	0.0010-0.0032	0.3415-0.3423	0.3410-0.3418
	F	7.3L (7270)	④	④	213@1.35	⑤	0.0055 MAX	0.0055 MAX	0.3119-0.3126	0.3119-0.3126
	G	7.5L (7536)	45	44	229@1.33	1.80	0.0010-0.0027	0.0010-0.0027	0.3415-0.3423	0.3415-0.3423

MAX - Maximum
① Intake: 1.64 in. Exhaust: 1.47 in.
② Intake: 1.68 in. Exhaust: 1.59 in.
③ Intake: 1.78 in. Exhaust: 1.59 in.
④ Intake: 30 degrees Exhaust: 37.5 degrees
⑤ Intake: 1.77 in. Exhaust: 1.83 in.
⑥ Intake: 166-164 lbs.@1.24 in. Exhaust: 166-184 lbs.@1.07 in.
⑦ Intake: 196-212 lbs.@1.36 in. Exhaust: 190-210 lbs.@1.20 in.
⑧ Intake: 1.75-1.81 in.
⑨ 0.0055 in. MAX

88283C29

VALVE SPECIFICATIONS

Year	Engine ID/VIN	Engine Displacement Liters (cc)	Seat Angle (deg.)	Face Angle (deg.)	Spring Test Pressure (lbs. @ in.)	Spring Installed Height (in.)	Stem-to-Guide Clearance (in.) Intake	Stem-to-Guide Clearance (in.) Exhaust	Stem Diameter (in.) Intake	Stem Diameter (in.) Exhaust
1992	Y	4.9L (4917)	45	44	⑥	①	0.0010-0.0027	0.0010-0.0027	0.3416-0.3423	0.3416-0.3423
	N	5.0L (4942)	45	44	⑦	②	0.0010-0.0027	0.0015-0.0032	0.3416-0.3423	0.3416-0.3418
	H	5.8L (5766)	45	44	200@1.20	③	0.0010-0.0027	0.0015-0.0032	0.3416-0.3423	0.3411-0.3418
	M	7.3L (7270)	④	④	80@1.83	⑧	0.0010-MAX	0.0055 MAX	0.3716-0.3723	0.3716-0.3723
	G	7.5L (7536)	45	44	229@1.33	1.80	0.0010-0.0027	0.0010-0.0032	0.3415-0.3423	0.3415-0.3423
1993	Y	4.9L (4917)	45	44	⑥	①	0.0010-0.0027	0.0010-0.0027	0.3416-0.3423	0.3416-0.3423
	N	5.0L (4942)	45	44	⑦	⑧	0.0010-0.0027	0.0015-0.0032	0.3415-0.3423	0.3410-0.3418
	H	5.8L (5766)	45	44	200@1.20	⑧	0.0010-0.0027	0.0015-0.0032	0.3415-0.3423	0.3410-0.3418
	R	5.8L (5766)	45	44	200@1.20	⑧	0.0010-0.0027	0.0015-0.0032	0.3415-0.3423	0.3410-0.3418
	C	7.3L (7270)	④	④	80@1.83	⑧	0.0010-0.0027	0.0055 MAX	0.3716-0.3723	0.3716-0.3723
	M	7.3L (7270)	④	④	80@1.83	⑧	0.0055 MAX	0.0055 MAX	0.3716-0.3723	0.3716-0.3723
	G	7.5L (7536)	45	44	229@1.33	1.80	0.0010-0.0027	0.0010-0.0027	0.3415-0.3423	0.3415-0.3423
1994	Y	4.9L (4917)	45	44	⑥	①	0.0010-0.0027	0.0010-0.0027	0.3415-0.3423	0.3415-0.3423
	N	5.0L (4942)	45	44	⑦	⑧	0.0010-0.0027	0.0010-0.0027	0.3415-0.3423	0.3410-0.3418
	H	5.8L (5766)	45	44	200@1.20	⑧	0.0010-0.0027	0.0015-0.0032	0.3415-0.3423	0.3410-0.3418
	R	5.8L (5766)	45	44	200@1.20	⑧	0.0010-0.0027	0.0010-0.0027	0.3415-0.3423	0.3410-0.3418
	F	7.3L (7270)	④	④	200@1.40	⑤	0.0010-0.0027	0.0010-0.0027	0.3119-0.3126	0.3119-0.3126
	K	7.3L (7270)	④	④	200@1.40	⑤	0.0055 MAX	0.0055 MAX	0.3716-0.3723	0.3716-0.3723
	M	7.3L (7270)	④	④	200@1.40	⑤	0.0055 MAX	0.0055 MAX	0.3716-0.3723	0.3716-0.3723
	G	7.5L (7536)	45	44	229@1.33	1.80	0.0010-0.0027	0.0010-0.0027	0.3415-0.3423	0.3415-0.3423
1995	Y	4.9L (4917)	45	44	⑥	①	0.0010-0.0027	0.0010-0.0027	0.3415-0.3423	0.3415-0.3423
	N	5.0L (4942)	45	44	⑦	⑧	0.0010-0.0027	0.0015-0.0032	0.3415-0.3423	0.3410-0.3418
	H	5.8L (5766)	45	44	200@1.20	⑧	0.0010-0.0027	0.0010-0.0027	0.3415-0.3423	0.3410-0.3418
	R	5.8L (5766)	45	44	200@1.20	⑧	0.0010-0.0027	0.0015-0.0032	0.3415-0.3423	0.3410-0.3418
	F	7.3L (7270)	④	④	213@1.35	⑤	0.0055 MAX	0.0055 MAX	0.3119-0.3126	0.3119-0.3126

88283C28

CAMSHAFT SPECIFICATIONS
All measurements given in inches.

Year	Engine ID/VIN	Engine Displacement Liters (cc)	Journal Diameter 1	2	3	4	5	Elevation In.	Ex.	Bearing Clearance	Camshaft End Play
1992	Y	4.9L (4917)	2.0170-2.0180	2.0170-2.0180	2.0170-2.0180	2.0170-2.0180	NA	0.2490①	0.2490①	0.0010-0.0030	0.0010-0.0070
	N	5.0L (4942)	2.0805-2.0815	2.0655-2.0665	2.0505-2.0515	2.0355-2.0365	2.0205-2.0215	0.2375	0.2474	0.0010-0.0030	0.0010-0.0070
	H	5.8L (5766)	2.0805-2.0815	2.0655-2.0665	2.0505-2.0515	2.0355-2.0365	2.0205-2.0215	0.2780	0.2830	0.0010-0.0030	0.0010-0.0070
	M	7.3L (7270)	2.0990-2.1000	2.0990-2.1000	2.0990-2.1000	2.0990-2.1000	2.0990-2.1000	NA	NA	0.0015-0.0035	0.0020-0.0090
	G	7.5L (7536)	2.1238-2.1248	2.1238-2.1248	2.1238-2.1248	2.1238-2.1248	2.1238-2.1248	0.2520	0.2780	0.0010-0.0030	0.0010-0.0060
1993	Y	4.9L (4917)	2.0170-2.0180	2.0170-2.0180	2.0170-2.0180	2.0170-2.0180	NA	0.2490①	0.2490①	0.0010-0.0030	0.0010-0.0070
	N	5.0L (4942)	2.0805-2.0815	2.0655-2.0665	2.0505-2.0515	2.0355-2.0365	2.0205-2.0215	0.2375	0.2474	0.0010-0.0030	0.0010-0.0070
	H	5.8L (5766)	2.0805-2.0815	2.0655-2.0665	2.0505-2.0515	2.0355-2.0365	2.0205-2.0215	0.2780	0.2830	0.0010-0.0030	0.0010-0.0070
	R	5.8L (5766)	2.0805-2.0815	2.0655-2.0665	2.0505-2.0515	2.0355-2.0365	2.0205-2.0215	0.2600	0.2780	0.0010-0.0030	0.0010-0.0070
	C	7.3L (7270)	2.0990-2.1000	2.0990-2.1000	2.0990-2.1000	2.0990-2.1000	2.0990-2.1000	NA	NA	0.0015-0.0035	0.0020-0.0090
	M	7.3L (7270)	2.0990-2.1000	2.0990-2.1000	2.0990-2.1000	2.0990-2.1000	2.0990-2.1000	NA	NA	0.0015-0.0035	0.0010-0.0070
	G	7.5L (7536)	2.1238-2.1248	2.1238-2.1248	2.1238-2.1248	2.1238-2.1248	2.1238-2.1248	0.2520	0.2780	0.0010-0.0030	0.0010-0.0060
1994	Y	4.9L (4917)	2.0170-2.0180	2.0170-2.0180	2.0170-2.0180	2.0170-2.0180	NA	0.2490①	0.2490①	0.0010-0.0030	0.0010-0.0070
	N	5.0L (4942)	2.0805-2.0815	2.0655-2.0665	2.0505-2.0515	2.0355-2.0365	2.0205-2.0215	0.2375	0.2474	0.0010-0.0030	0.0010-0.0070
	H	5.8L (5766)	2.0805-2.0815	2.0655-2.0665	2.0505-2.0515	2.0355-2.0365	2.0205-2.0215	0.2780	0.2830	0.0010-0.0030	0.0010-0.0070
	R	5.8L (5766)	2.0805-2.0815	2.0655-2.0665	2.0505-2.0515	2.0355-2.0365	2.0205-2.0215	0.2600	0.2780	0.0010-0.0030	0.0010-0.0070
	F	7.3L (7270)	2.0990-2.1000	2.0990-2.1000	2.0990-2.1000	2.0990-2.1000	2.0990-2.1000	NA	NA	0.0020-0.0040	0.0010-0.0070
	K	7.3L (7270)	2.0990-2.1000	2.0990-2.1000	2.0990-2.1000	2.0990-2.1000	2.0990-2.1000	NA	NA	0.0160	0.0120
	M	7.3L (7270)	2.0990-2.1000	2.0990-2.1000	2.0990-2.1000	2.0990-2.1000	2.0990-2.1000	NA	NA	0.0015-0.0035	0.0010-0.0090
	G	7.5L (7536)	2.1238-2.1248	2.1238-2.1248	2.1238-2.1248	2.1238-2.1248	2.1238-2.1248	0.2520	0.2780	0.0010-0.0030	0.0010-0.0060
1995	Y	4.9L (4917)	2.0170-2.0180	2.0170-2.0180	2.0170-2.0180	2.0170-2.0180	NA	0.2490①	0.2490①	0.0010-0.0030	0.0010-0.0070
	N	5.0L (4942)	2.0805-2.0815	2.0655-2.0665	2.0505-2.0515	2.0355-2.0365	2.0205-2.0215	0.2780	0.2830	0.0010-0.0030	0.0010-0.0070
	H	5.8L (5766)	2.0805-2.0815	2.0655-2.0665	2.0505-2.0515	2.0355-2.0365	2.0205-2.0215	0.2780	0.2830	0.0010-0.0030	0.0010-0.0070
	R	5.8L (5766)	2.0805-2.0815	2.0655-2.0665	2.0505-2.0515	2.0355-2.0365	2.0205-2.0215	0.2600	0.2780	0.0010-0.0030	0.0010-0.0070
	M	7.3L (7270)	2.0990-2.1000	2.0990-2.1000	2.0990-2.1000	2.0990-2.1000	2.0990-2.1000	NA	NA	0.0010-0.0030	0.0010-0.0070
	F	7.5L (7536)	2.1238-2.1248	2.1238-2.1248	2.1238-2.1248	2.1238-2.1248	2.1238-2.1248	0.2535	0.2531	0.0020-0.0160	0.0010-0.0080

88283C31

CAMSHAFT SPECIFICATIONS
All measurements given in inches.

Year	Engine ID/VIN	Engine Displacement Liters (cc)	Journal Diameter 1	2	3	4	5	Elevation In.	Ex.	Bearing Clearance	Camshaft End Play
1987	Y	4.9L (4917)	2.0170-2.0180	2.0170-2.0180	2.0170-2.0180	2.0170-2.0180	NA	0.2490①	0.2490①	0.0010-0.0030	0.0010-0.0070
	N	5.0L (4942)	2.0805-2.0815	2.0655-2.0665	2.0505-2.0515	2.0355-2.0365	2.0205-2.0215	0.2375	0.2474	0.0010-0.0030	0.0010-0.0070
	H	5.8L (5766)	2.0805-2.0815	2.0655-2.0665	2.0505-2.0515	2.0355-2.0365	2.0205-2.0215	0.2780	0.2830	0.0010-0.0030	0.0010-0.0070
	I	6.9L (6886)	2.0990-2.1000	2.0990-2.1000	2.0990-2.1000	2.0990-2.1000	2.0990-2.1000	NA	NA	0.0020-0.0065	0.0010-0.0090
	L	7.5L (7536)	2.1238-2.1248	2.1238-2.1248	2.1238-2.1248	2.1238-2.1248	2.1238-2.1248	0.2520	0.2780	0.0010-0.0030	0.0010-0.0060
1988	Y	4.9L (4917)	2.0170-2.0180	2.0170-2.0180	2.0170-2.0180	2.0170-2.0180	NA	0.2490①	0.2490①	0.0010-0.0030	0.0010-0.0070
	N	5.0L (4942)	2.0805-2.0815	2.0655-2.0665	2.0505-2.0515	2.0355-2.0365	2.0205-2.0215	0.2375	0.2474	0.0010-0.0030	0.0010-0.0070
	H	5.8L (5766)	2.0805-2.0815	2.0655-2.0665	2.0505-2.0515	2.0355-2.0365	2.0205-2.0215	0.2780	0.2830	0.0010-0.0030	0.0010-0.0070
	M	7.3L (7270)	2.0990-2.1000	2.0990-2.1000	2.0990-2.1000	2.0990-2.1000	2.0990-2.1000	NA	NA	0.0015-0.0035	0.0010-0.0070
	G	7.5L (7536)	2.1238-2.1248	2.1238-2.1248	2.1238-2.1248	2.1238-2.1248	2.1238-2.1248	0.2520	0.2780	0.0010-0.0030	0.0010-0.0060
1989	Y	4.9L (4917)	2.0170-2.0180	2.0170-2.0180	2.0170-2.0180	2.0170-2.0180	NA	0.2490①	0.2490①	0.0010-0.0030	0.0010-0.0070
	N	5.0L (4942)	2.0805-2.0815	2.0655-2.0665	2.0505-2.0515	2.0355-2.0365	2.0205-2.0215	0.2375	0.2474	0.0010-0.0030	0.0010-0.0070
	H	5.8L (5766)	2.0805-2.0815	2.0655-2.0665	2.0505-2.0515	2.0355-2.0365	2.0205-2.0215	0.2780	0.2830	0.0010-0.0030	0.0010-0.0070
	M	7.3L (7270)	2.0990-2.1000	2.0990-2.1000	2.0990-2.1000	2.0990-2.1000	2.0990-2.1000	NA	NA	0.0015-0.0035	0.0010-0.0070
	G	7.5L (7536)	2.1238-2.1248	2.1238-2.1248	2.1238-2.1248	2.1238-2.1248	2.1238-2.1248	0.2520	0.2780	0.0010-0.0030	0.0010-0.0060
1990	Y	4.9L (4917)	2.0170-2.0180	2.0170-2.0180	2.0170-2.0180	2.0170-2.0180	NA	0.2490①	0.2490①	0.0010-0.0030	0.0010-0.0070
	N	5.0L (4942)	2.0805-2.0815	2.0655-2.0665	2.0505-2.0515	2.0355-2.0365	2.0205-2.0215	0.2375	0.2474	0.0010-0.0030	0.0010-0.0070
	H	5.8L (5766)	2.0805-2.0815	2.0655-2.0665	2.0505-2.0515	2.0355-2.0365	2.0205-2.0215	0.2780	0.2830	0.0010-0.0030	0.0010-0.0070
	M	7.3L (7270)	2.0990-2.1000	2.0990-2.1000	2.0990-2.1000	2.0990-2.1000	2.0990-2.1000	NA	NA	0.0015-0.0035	0.0010-0.0070
	G	7.5L (7536)	2.1238-2.1248	2.1238-2.1248	2.1238-2.1248	2.1238-2.1248	2.1238-2.1248	0.2520	0.2780	0.0010-0.0030	0.0010-0.0060
1991	Y	4.9L (4917)	2.0170-2.0180	2.0170-2.0180	2.0170-2.0180	2.0170-2.0180	NA	0.2490①	0.2490①	0.0010-0.0030	0.0010-0.0070
	N	5.0L (4942)	2.0805-2.0815	2.0655-2.0665	2.0505-2.0515	2.0355-2.0365	2.0205-2.0215	0.2375	0.2474	0.0010-0.0030	0.0010-0.0070
	H	5.8L (5766)	2.0805-2.0815	2.0655-2.0665	2.0505-2.0515	2.0355-2.0365	2.0205-2.0215	0.2780	0.2830	0.0010-0.0030	0.0010-0.0070
	M	7.3L (7270)	2.0990-2.1000	2.0990-2.1000	2.0990-2.1000	2.0990-2.1000	2.0990-2.1000	NA	NA	0.0015-0.0035	0.0010-0.0090
	G	7.5L (7536)	2.1238-2.1248	2.1238-2.1248	2.1238-2.1248	2.1238-2.1248	2.1238-2.1248	0.2520	0.2780	0.0010-0.0030	0.0010-0.0060

88283C30

CRANKSHAFT AND CONNECTING ROD SPECIFICATIONS
All measurements are given in inches.

Year	Engine ID/VIN	Engine Displacement Liters (cc)	Crankshaft Main Brg. Journal Dia.	Main Brg. Oil Clearance	Shaft End-play	Thrust on No.	Connecting Rod Journal Diameter	Oil Clearance	Side Clearance
1987	Y	4.9L (4917)	2.3982-2.3990	0.0010-0.0028	0.0040-0.0080	5	2.1228-2.1236	0.0007-0.0024	0.0060-0.0130
	N	5.0L (4942)	2.2482-2.2490	⊕	0.0040-0.0080	3	2.1228-2.1236	0.0008-0.0015	0.0100-0.0200
	H	5.8L (5766)	2.9994-3.0002	0.0008-0.0015	0.0040-0.0080	3	2.3103-2.3111	0.0008-0.0015	0.0100-0.0200
	I	6.9L (6686)	3.1228-3.1236	0.0018-0.0036	0.0020-0.0090	3	2.4980-2.4990	0.0011-0.0026	0.0120-0.0240
	L	7.5L (7536)	2.9994-3.0002	0.0008-0.0015	0.0040-0.0080	3	2.4992-2.5000	0.0008-0.0015	0.0100-0.0200
1988	Y	4.9L (4917)	2.3982-2.3990	0.0010-0.0028	0.0040-0.0080	5	2.1228-2.1236	0.0007-0.0024	0.0060-0.0130
	N	5.0L (4942)	2.2452-2.2490	⊕	0.0040-0.0080	3	2.1228-2.1236	0.0008-0.0015	0.0100-0.0200
	H	5.8L (5766)	2.9994-3.0002	0.0008-0.0015	0.0040-0.0080	3	2.3103-2.3111	0.0008-0.0015	0.0100-0.0200
	M	7.3L (7270)	3.1226-3.1236	0.0018-0.0036	0.0025-0.0085	3	2.4980-2.4990	0.0011-0.0036	0.0120-0.0240
	G	7.5L (7536)	2.9994-3.0002	0.0008-0.0015	0.0040-0.0080	3	2.4992-2.5000	0.0008-0.0015	0.0100-0.0200
1989	Y	4.9L (4917)	2.3982-2.3990	0.0010-0.0028	0.0040-0.0080	5	2.1228-2.1236	0.0007-0.0024	0.0060-0.0130
	N	5.0L (4942)	2.2482-2.2490	⊕	0.0040-0.0080	3	2.1228-2.1236	0.0008-0.0015	0.0100-0.0200
	H	5.8L (5766)	2.9994-3.0002	0.0008-0.0015	0.0040-0.0080	3	2.3103-2.3111	0.0008-0.0015	0.0100-0.0200
	M	7.3L (7270)	3.1228-3.1236	0.0018-0.0036	0.0025-0.0085	3	2.4980-2.4990	0.0011-0.0036	0.0120-0.0240
	G	7.5L (7536)	2.9994-3.0002	0.0008-0.0015	0.0040-0.0080	3	2.4992-2.5000	0.0008-0.0015	0.0100-0.0200
1990	Y	4.9L (4917)	2.3982-2.3990	0.0010-0.0028	0.0040-0.0080	5	2.1228-2.1236	0.0007-0.0024	0.0060-0.0130
	N	5.0L (4942)	2.2482-2.2490	⊕	0.0040-0.0080	3	2.1228-2.1236	0.0008-0.0015	0.0100-0.0200
	H	5.8L (5766)	2.9994-3.0002	0.0008-0.0015	0.0040-0.0080	3	2.3103-2.3111	0.0008-0.0015	0.0100-0.0200
	M	7.3L (7270)	3.1228-3.1236	0.0018-0.0036	0.0025-0.0085	3	2.4980-2.4990	0.0011-0.0036	0.0120-0.0240
	G	7.5L (7536)	2.9994-3.0002	0.0008-0.0015	0.0040-0.0080	3	2.4992-2.5000	0.0008-0.0015	0.0100-0.0200
1991	Y	4.9L (4917)	2.3982-2.3990	0.0010-0.0028	0.0040-0.0080	5	2.1226-2.1236	0.0007-0.0024	0.0060-0.0130
	N	5.0L (4942)	2.2482-2.2490	⊕	0.0040-0.0080	3	2.1228-2.1236	0.0008-0.0015	0.0100-0.0200
	H	5.8L (5766)	2.9994-3.0002	0.0008-0.0015	0.0040-0.0080	3	2.3103-2.3111	0.0008-0.0015	0.0100-0.0200
	M	7.3L (7270)	3.1228-3.1236	0.0018-0.0036	0.0025-0.0085	3	2.4980-2.4990	0.0011-0.0036	0.0120-0.0240
	G	7.5L (7536)	2.9994-3.0002	0.0008-0.0015	0.0040-0.0080	3	2.4992-2.5000	0.0008-0.0015	0.0100-0.0200

88283C33

CAMSHAFT SPECIFICATIONS
All measurements given in inches.

Year	Engine ID/VIN	Engine Displacement Liters (cc)	Journal Diameter 1	2	3	4	5	Elevation In.	Ex.	Bearing Clearance	Camshaft End Play
1995	G	7.5L (7536)	2.1238-2.1248	2.1238-2.1248	2.1238-2.1248	2.1238-2.1248	2.1238-2.1248	0.2520	0.2780	0.0010-0.0030	0.0010-0.0060
1996	Y	4.9L (4917)	2.0170-2.0180	2.0170-2.0180	2.0170-2.0180	2.0170-2.0180	NA	0.2490①	0.2490①	0.0010-0.0030	0.0010-0.0070
	N	5.0L (4942)	2.0805-2.0815	2.0655-2.0665	2.0505-2.0515	2.0355-2.0365	2.0205-2.0215	0.2780	0.2830	0.0010-0.0030	0.0010-0.0070
	H	5.8L (5766)	2.0805-2.0815	2.0655-2.0665	2.0505-2.0515	2.0355-2.0365	2.0205-2.0215	0.2780	0.2830	0.0010-0.0030	0.0010-0.0070
	F	7.3L (7270)	2.0990-2.1000	2.0990-2.1000	2.0990-2.1000	2.0990-2.1000	2.0990-2.1000	0.2535	0.2531	0.0020-0.0160	0.0020-0.0080
	G	7.5L (7536)	2.1238-2.1248	2.1238-2.1248	2.1238-2.1248	2.1238-2.1248	2.1238-2.1248	0.2520	0.2780	0.0010-0.0030	0.0010-0.0060

NA - Not Available
① F-150 2WD with 2.47:1 or 2.75:1 axle ratio (49 state emissions) use 0.247 in.

88283C32

CRANKSHAFT AND CONNECTING ROD SPECIFICATIONS
All measurements are given in inches.

Year	Engine ID/VIN	Engine Displacement Liters (cc)	Crankshaft Main Brg. Journal Dia.	Main Brg. Oil Clearance	Shaft End-play	Thrust on No.	Connecting Rod Journal Diameter	Oil Clearance	Side Clearance
1995	G	7.5L (7536)	2.9994-3.0002	②	0.0040-0.0080	3	2.4992-2.5000	0.0008-0.0015	0.0100-0.0200
1996	Y	4.9L (4917)	2.3982-2.3990	0.0009-0.0028	0.0040-0.0080	5	2.1228-2.1236	0.0009-0.0027	0.0060-0.0130
	N	5.0L (4942)	2.2482-2.2490	0.0005-0.0015	0.0040-0.0080	3	2.1228-2.1236	0.0008-0.0015	0.0100-0.0200
	H	5.8L (5766)	2.9994-3.0002	0.0008-0.0015	0.0040-0.0080	3	2.3103-2.3111	0.0008-0.0015	0.0100-0.0200
	F	7.3L (7270)	3.1228-3.1236	0.0018-0.0036	0.0025-0.0085	5	2.4980-2.4990	0.0011-0.0036	0.0120-0.0240
	G	7.5L (7536)	2.9994-3.0002	②	0.0040-0.0080	3	2.4992-2.5000	0.0008-0.0015	0.0100-0.0200

① No. 1 bearing: 0.0001-0.0015 in. Nos. 2-5 bearings: 0.0005-0.0015 in.

② No. 1 bearing: 0.0004-0.0022 in. Nos. 2-5 bearings: 0.0009-0.0027 in.

88283C35

CRANKSHAFT AND CONNECTING ROD SPECIFICATIONS
All measurements are given in inches.

Year	Engine ID/VIN	Engine Displacement Liters (cc)	Crankshaft Main Brg. Journal Dia.	Main Brg. Oil Clearance	Shaft End-play	Thrust on No.	Connecting Rod Journal Diameter	Oil Clearance	Side Clearance
1992	Y	4.9L (4917)	2.3982-2.3990	0.0010-0.0028	0.0040-0.0080	5	2.1228-2.1236	0.0007-0.0024	0.0060-0.0130
	N	5.0L (4942)	2.2482-2.2490	①	0.0040-0.0080	3	2.1228-2.1236	0.0008-0.0015	0.0100-0.0200
	H	5.8L (5766)	2.9994-3.0002	0.0008-0.0015	0.0040-0.0080	3	2.3103-2.3111	0.0008-0.0015	0.0100-0.0200
	M	7.3L (7270)	3.1228-3.1236	0.0018-0.0036	0.0025-0.0085	3	2.4980-2.4990	0.0011-0.0036	0.0120-0.0240
	G	7.5L (7536)	2.9994-3.0002	0.0008-0.0015	0.0040-0.0080	3	2.4992-2.5000	0.0008-0.0015	0.0100-0.0200
1993	Y	4.9L (4917)	2.3982-2.3990	0.0010-0.0028	0.0040-0.0080	5	2.1228-2.1236	0.0007-0.0024	0.0060-0.0130
	N	5.0L (4942)	2.2482-2.2490	0.0008-0.0015	0.0040-0.0080	3	2.1228-2.1236	0.0008-0.0015	0.0100-0.0200
	H	5.8L (5766)	2.9994-3.0002	0.0008-0.0015	0.0040-0.0080	3	2.3103-2.3111	0.0008-0.0015	0.0100-0.0200
	R	5.8L (5766)	2.9994-3.0002	0.0008-0.0015	0.0040-0.0080	3	2.3103-2.3111	0.0011-0.0036	0.0120-0.0240
	C	7.3L (7270)	3.1228-3.1236	0.0018-0.0036	0.0025-0.0085	3	2.4980-2.4990	0.0011-0.0036	0.0120-0.0240
	M	7.3L (7270)	3.1228-3.1236	0.0018-0.0036	0.0025-0.0085	3	2.4980-2.4990	0.0011-0.0036	0.0120-0.0240
	G	7.5L (7536)	2.9994-3.0002	0.0008-0.0015	0.0040-0.0080	3	2.4992-2.5000	0.0008-0.0015	0.0100-0.0200
1994	Y	4.9L (4917)	2.3982-2.3990	0.0009-0.0028	0.0040-0.0080	5	2.1228-2.1236	0.0008-0.0027	0.0060-0.0130
	N	5.0L (4942)	2.2482-2.2490	0.0008-0.0015	0.0040-0.0080	3	2.1228-2.1236	0.0008-0.0015	0.0100-0.0200
	H	5.8L (5766)	2.9994-3.0002	0.0008-0.0015	0.0040-0.0080	3	2.3103-2.3111	0.0008-0.0015	0.0100-0.0200
	R	5.8L (5766)	2.9994-3.0002	0.0008-0.0015	0.0040-0.0080	3	2.3103-2.3111	0.0008-0.0015	0.0100-0.0200
	F	7.3L (7270)	3.1228-3.1236	0.0018-0.0036	0.0025-0.0085	5	2.4980-2.4990	0.0011-0.0036	0.0120-0.0240
	K	7.3L (7270)	3.1228-3.1236	0.0018-0.0036	0.0025-0.0085	3	2.4980-2.4990	0.0011-0.0036	0.0120-0.0240
	M	7.3L (7270)	3.1228-3.1236	0.0018-0.0036	0.0025-0.0085	3	2.4980-2.4990	0.0011-0.0036	0.0120-0.0240
	G	7.5L (7536)	2.9994-3.0002	②	0.0040-0.0080	3	2.4992-2.5000	0.0008-0.0015	0.0100-0.0200
1995	Y	4.9L (4917)	2.3982-2.3990	0.0009-0.0028	0.0040-0.0080	5	2.1228-2.1236	0.0009-0.0027	0.0060-0.0130
	N	5.0L (4942)	2.2482-2.2490	0.0008-0.0015	0.0040-0.0080	3	2.1228-2.1236	0.0008-0.0015	0.0100-0.0200
	H	5.8L (5766)	2.9994-3.0002	0.0008-0.0015	0.0040-0.0080	3	2.3103-2.3111	0.0008-0.0015	0.0100-0.0200
	R	5.8L (5766)	2.9994-3.0002	0.0008-0.0015	0.0040-0.0080	3	2.3103-2.3111	0.0008-0.0015	0.0100-0.0200
	F	7.3L (7270)	3.1228-3.1236	0.0018-0.0036	0.0025-0.0085	5	2.4980-2.4990	0.0011-0.0036	0.0120-0.0240

88283C34

PISTON AND RING SPECIFICATIONS
All measurements are given in inches.

Year	Engine ID/VIN	Engine Displacement Liters (cc)	Piston Clearance	Ring Gap Top Compression	Ring Gap Bottom Compression	Ring Gap Oil Control	Ring Side Clearance Top Compression	Ring Side Clearance Bottom Compression	Ring Side Clearance Oil Control
1992	Y	4.9L (4917)	0.0010-0.0018	0.0100-0.0200	0.0100-0.0200	0.0150-0.0550	0.0019-0.0036	0.0020-0.0040	SNUG
	N	5.0L (4942)	0.0014-0.0022	0.0100-0.0200	0.0100-0.0200	0.0150-0.0550	0.0013-0.0033	0.0020-0.0040	SNUG
	H	5.8L (5766)	0.0018-0.0026	0.0100-0.0200	0.0100-0.0200	0.0150-0.0550	0.0020-0.0040	0.0020-0.0040	SNUG
	M	7.3L (7270)	⊖	0.0130-0.0450	0.0600-0.0850	NA	0.0040	0.0040	0.0010-0.0030
	G	7.5L (7536)	0.0022-0.0030	0.0100-0.0200	0.0100-0.0200	0.0100-0.0350	0.0025-0.0045	0.0025-0.0045	SNUG
1993	Y	4.9L (4917)	0.0010-0.0018	0.0100-0.0200	0.0100-0.0200	0.0150-0.0550	0.0019-0.0036	0.0020-0.0040	SNUG
	N	5.0L (4942)	0.0014-0.0022	0.0100-0.0200	0.0180-0.0280	0.0100-0.0400	0.0013-0.0033	0.0013-0.0033	SNUG
	H	5.8L (5766)	0.0018-0.0026	0.0100-0.0200	0.0100-0.0200	0.0150-0.0550	0.0020-0.0040	0.0020-0.0040	SNUG
	R	5.8L (5766)	0.0015-0.0023	0.0100-0.0200	0.0180-0.0280	0.0100-0.0400	0.0013-0.0033	0.0013-0.0033	SNUG
	C	7.3L (7270)	⊖	0.0130-0.0450	0.0600-0.0850	NA	0.0020-0.0040	0.0020-0.0040	0.0010-0.0030
	M	7.3L (7270)	⊖	0.0130-0.0450	0.0600-0.0850	NA	0.0020-0.0040	0.0020-0.0040	0.0010-0.0030
1994	G	7.5L (7536)	0.0022-0.0030	0.0100-0.0200	0.0100-0.0200	0.0100-0.0350	0.0025-0.0045	0.0025-0.0045	SNUG
	Y	4.9L (4917)	0.0010-0.0014	0.0100-0.0200	0.0100-0.0200	0.0100-0.0350	0.0019-0.0036	0.0020-0.0040	SNUG
	N	5.0L (4942)	0.0014-0.0022	0.0100-0.0200	0.0180-0.0280	0.0100-0.0350	0.0013-0.0033	0.0013-0.0033	SNUG
	H	5.8L (5766)	0.0015-0.0023	0.0100-0.0200	0.0180-0.0280	0.0100-0.0400	0.0013-0.0033	0.0013-0.0033	SNUG
	R	5.8L (5766)	0.0015-0.0023	0.0100-0.0200	0.0180-0.0280	0.0100-0.0400	0.0013-0.0033	0.0013-0.0033	SNUG
	F	7.3L (7270)	0.0036-0.0049	0.0140-0.0240	0.0620-0.0720	0.0120-0.0240	0.0020-0.0040	0.0020-0.0040	NA
	K	7.3L (7270)	0.0055-0.0085	0.0130-0.0450	0.0600-0.0850	0.0100-0.0240	0.0036	0.0040	NA
	M	7.3L (7270)	0.0055-0.0085	0.0130-0.0450	0.0600-0.0850	NA	0.0040	0.0040	NA
1995	G	7.5L (7536)	0.0014-0.0022	0.0150	0.0110	0.0100-0.0300	0.0012-0.0022	0.0012-0.0022	SNUG
	Y	4.9L (4917)	0.0010-0.0018	0.0100-0.0200	0.0100-0.0200	0.0150-0.0350	0.0019-0.0036	0.0020-0.0040	SNUG
	N	5.0L (4942)	0.0014-0.0022	0.0100-0.0200	0.0180-0.0280	0.0100-0.0400	0.0013-0.0033	0.0013-0.0033	SNUG
	H	5.8L (5766)	0.0015-0.0023	0.0100-0.0200	0.0180-0.0280	0.0100-0.0400	0.0013-0.0033	0.0013-0.0033	SNUG
	R	5.8L (5766)	0.0015-0.0023	0.0100-0.0200	0.0180-0.0280	0.0100-0.0400	0.0013-0.0033	0.0020-0.0040	SNUG
	F	7.3L (7270)	0.0044-0.0057	0.0140-0.0240	0.0620-0.0720	0.0120-0.0240	NA	0.0020-0.0040	NA

88283C37

PISTON AND RING SPECIFICATIONS
All measurements are given in inches.

Year	Engine ID/VIN	Engine Displacement Liters (cc)	Piston Clearance	Ring Gap Top Compression	Ring Gap Bottom Compression	Ring Gap Oil Control	Ring Side Clearance Top Compression	Ring Side Clearance Bottom Compression	Ring Side Clearance Oil Control
1987	Y	4.9L (4917)	0.0010-0.0018	0.0100-0.0200	0.0100-0.0200	0.0150-0.0550	0.0019-0.0036	0.0020-0.0040	SNUG
	N	5.0L (4942)	0.0013-0.0030	0.0100-0.0200	0.0100-0.0200	0.0150-0.0550	0.0013-0.0033	0.0020-0.0040	SNUG
	H	5.8L (5766)	0.0018-0.0026	0.0100-0.0200	0.0100-0.0200	0.0150-0.0550	0.0013-0.0033	0.0020-0.0040	SNUG
	I	6.9L (6886)	0.0055-0.0075	0.0140-0.0240	0.0600-0.0700	0.0100-0.0240	0.0020-0.0040	0.0020-0.0040	0.0010-0.0030
	L	7.5L (7536)	0.0022-0.0030	0.0100-0.0200	0.0100-0.0200	0.0100-0.0350	0.0025-0.0045	0.0025-0.0045	SNUG
1988	Y	4.9L (4917)	0.0010-0.0018	0.0100-0.0200	0.0100-0.0200	0.0150-0.0550	0.0019-0.0036	0.0020-0.0040	SNUG
	N	5.0L (4942)	0.0013-0.0030	0.0100-0.0200	0.0100-0.0200	0.0150-0.0550	0.0013-0.0033	0.0020-0.0040	SNUG
	H	5.8L (5766)	0.0018-0.0026	0.0100-0.0200	0.0100-0.0200	0.0150-0.0550	0.0013-0.0033	0.0020-0.0040	SNUG
	M	7.3L (7270)	⊖	0.0130-0.0450	0.0600-0.0850	NA	0.0020-0.0040	0.0020-0.0040	0.0010-0.0030
	G	7.5L (7536)	0.0022-0.0030	0.0100-0.0200	0.0100-0.0200	0.0100-0.0350	0.0025-0.0045	0.0025-0.0045	SNUG
1989	Y	4.9L (4917)	0.0010-0.0018	0.0100-0.0200	0.0100-0.0200	0.0150-0.0550	0.0019-0.0036	0.0020-0.0040	SNUG
	N	5.0L (4942)	0.0013-0.0030	0.0100-0.0200	0.0100-0.0200	0.0150-0.0550	0.0013-0.0033	0.0020-0.0040	SNUG
	H	5.8L (5766)	0.0018-0.0026	0.0100-0.0200	0.0100-0.0200	0.0150-0.0550	0.0013-0.0033	0.0020-0.0040	SNUG
	M	7.3L (7270)	⊖	0.0130-0.0450	0.0600-0.0850	NA	0.0020-0.0040	0.0020-0.0040	0.0010-0.0030
	G	7.5L (7536)	0.0022-0.0030	0.0100-0.0200	0.0100-0.0200	0.0100-0.0350	0.0025-0.0045	0.0025-0.0045	SNUG
1990	Y	4.9L (4917)	0.0010-0.0018	0.0100-0.0200	0.0100-0.0200	0.0150-0.0550	0.0019-0.0036	0.0020-0.0040	SNUG
	N	5.0L (4942)	0.0013-0.0030	0.0100-0.0200	0.0100-0.0200	0.0150-0.0550	0.0013-0.0033	0.0020-0.0040	SNUG
	H	5.8L (5766)	0.0018-0.0026	0.0100-0.0200	0.0100-0.0200	0.0150-0.0550	0.0013-0.0033	0.0020-0.0040	SNUG
	M	7.3L (7270)	⊖	0.0130-0.0450	0.0600-0.0850	NA	0.0020-0.0040	0.0020-0.0040	0.0010-0.0030
	G	7.5L (7536)	0.0022-0.0030	0.0100-0.0200	0.0100-0.0200	0.0100-0.0350	0.0025-0.0045	0.0025-0.0045	SNUG
1991	Y	4.9L (4917)	0.0010-0.0018	0.0100-0.0200	0.0100-0.0200	0.0150-0.0550	0.0019-0.0036	0.0020-0.0040	SNUG
	N	5.0L (4942)	0.0014-0.0022	0.0100-0.0200	0.0100-0.0200	0.0150-0.0550	0.0013-0.0033	0.0020-0.0040	SNUG
	H	5.8L (5766)	0.0018-0.0026	0.0100-0.0200	0.0100-0.0200	0.0150-0.0550	0.0013-0.0033	0.0020-0.0040	SNUG
	M	7.3L (7270)	⊖	0.0130-0.0450	0.0600-0.0850	NA	0.0020-0.0040	0.0020-0.0040	0.0010-0.0030
	G	7.5L (7536)	0.0022-0.0030	0.0100-0.0200	0.0100-0.0200	0.0100-0.0350	0.0025-0.0045	0.0025-0.0045	SNUG

88283C36

PISTON AND RING SPECIFICATIONS
All measurements are given in inches.

Year	Engine ID/VIN	Engine Displacement Liters (cc)	Piston Clearance	Ring Gap Top Compression	Ring Gap Bottom Compression	Ring Gap Oil Control	Ring Side Clearance Top Compression	Ring Side Clearance Bottom Compression	Ring Side Clearance Oil Control
1995	G	7.5L (7536)	0.0014-0.0022	0.0100-0.0150	0.0110-0.0210	0.0100-0.0300	0.0012-0.0022	0.0012-0.0022	SNUG
1996	Y	4.9L (4917)	0.0010-0.0022	0.0100-0.0150	0.0100-0.0210	0.0100-0.0300	0.0019-0.0022	0.0020-0.0040	SNUG
	N	5.0L (4942)	0.0010-0.0018	0.0200	0.0200	0.0350	0.0036	0.0040	SNUG
	N	5.8L (5766)	0.0012-0.0020	0.0100-0.0200	0.0180-0.0280	0.0100-0.0400	0.0013-0.0033	0.0013-0.0033	SNUG
	H	7.3L (7270)	0.0015-0.0023	0.0100-0.0200	0.0180-0.0280	0.0100-0.0400	0.0013-0.0033	0.0013-0.0033	SNUG
	F	7.3L (7270)	0.0044-0.0057	0.0140-0.0240	0.0620-0.0720	0.0120-0.0240	NA	0.0020-0.0040	NA
	G	7.5L (7536)	0.0014-0.0022	0.0100-0.0150	0.0110-0.0210	0.0100-0.0300	0.0012-0.0022	0.0012-0.0022	SNUG

① Bores 1-6: 0.0055-0.0085 in.
② Bores 7-8: 0.0060-0.0085 in.

88283C38

TORQUE SPECIFICATIONS
All readings in ft. lbs.

Year	Engine ID/VIN	Engine Displacement Liters (cc)	Cylinder Head Bolts	Main Bearing Bolts	Rod Bearing Bolts	Crankshaft Damper Bolts	Flywheel Bolts	Manifold Intake	Manifold Exhaust ②	Spark Plugs	Lug Nut ②
1987	Y	4.9L (4917)	①	60-70	40-45	130-150	75-85	22-32	22-32	10-15	②
	N	5.0L (4942)	③	60-70	19-24	70-90	75-85	23-25	18-24	10-15	②
	H	5.8L (5766)	⑰	95-105	40-45	70-90	75-85	23-25	18-24	10-15	②
	I	6.9L (6886)	④	②	41-45	90	47	24	28-33	5-10	②
	L	7.5L (7536)	⑦	95-105	40-45	90	75-85	24	22-30	10-15	②
1988	Y	4.9L (4917)	③	60-70	41-45	130-150	75-85	22-32	22-32	10-15	②
	N	5.0L (4942)	③	60-70	19-24	70-90	75-85	23-25	18-24	10-15	②
	H	5.8L (5766)	⑩	95-105	40-45	70-90	75-85	23-25	18-24	10-15	②
	M	7.3L (7536)	⑦	95-105	41-45	90	47	⑩	22-30	5-10	②
1989	Y	4.9L (4917)	①	60-70	41-45	130-150	75-85	22-32	22-32	10-15	②
	N	5.0L (4942)	③	60-70	19-24	70-90	75-85	23-25	18-24	10-15	②
	H	5.8L (5766)	⑰	95-105	40-45	70-90	75-85	23-25	18-24	10-15	②
	M	7.3L (7270)	④	95-105	40-45	90	47	②	22-44	②	②
1990	G	7.5L (7536)	①	95-105	41-45	70-90	75-85	22-32	22-32	5-10	②
	Y	4.9L (4917)	③	60-70	19-24	130-150	75-85	23-25	18-24	10-15	②
	N	5.0L (4942)	⑩	60-70	40-45	70-90	75-85	23-25	18-24	10-15	②
	H	5.8L (5766)	⑩	95-105	40-45	70-90	75-85	23-25	18-24	10-15	②
	M	7.3L (7270)	⑩	95-105	41-45	90	47	⑩	22-44	5-10	②
1991	G	7.5L (7536)	①	60-70	40-45	130-150	75-85	22-32	22-32	10-15	②
	Y	4.9L (4917)	③	60-70	19-24	70-90	75-85	23-25	18-24	10-15	②
	N	5.0L (4942)	⑩	95-105	40-45	70-90	75-85	23-25	18-24	10-15	②
	H	5.8L (5766)	⑩	95-105	41-45	90	47	②	22-44	5-10	②
	M	7.3L (7270)	⑦	95-105	41-45	90	47	②	22-45	5-10	②
1992	Y	4.9L (4917)	①	60-70	41-45	130-150	75-85	22-32	22-32	10-15	②
	N	5.0L (4942)	③	60-70	19-24	70-90	75-85	23-25	18-24	10-15	②
	H	5.8L (5766)	⑰	95-105	40-45	70-90	75-85	23-25	18-24	10-15	②
	M	7.3L (7270)	⑩	95-105	41-45	90	47	②	22-45	5-10	②
1993	G	7.5L (7536)	①	60-70	41-45	130-150	75-85	22-32	22-32	10-15	②
	Y	4.9L (4917)	③	60-70	19-24	70-90	75-85	23-25	18-24	10-15	②
	N	5.0L (4942)	⑰	95-105	40-45	70-90	75-85	23-25	18-24	10-15	②
	H	5.8L (5766)	⑩	95-105	40-45	90	47	②	22-45	-	②
	R	7.3L (7270)	⑩	60-70	19-24	90	47	24	20	-	②
	C	7.3L (7270)	⑩	60-70	40-45	90	47	24	20	-	②
	M	7.5L (7536)	⑦	95-105	41-45	90	47	②	22-45	5-10	②
1994	Y	4.9L (4917)	①	60-70	41-45	130-150	75-85	22-32	22-30	10-15	②
	N	5.0L (4942)	③	60-70	19-24	70-90	75-85	23-25	18-24	10-15	②
	H	5.8L (5766)	⑰	95-105	40-45	70-90	75-85	23-25	18-24	10-15	②
	R	7.3L (7270)	⑩	95-105	40-45	90	47	②	18-24	10-15	②
	F	7.3L (7270)	⑳	95	②	212	89	24	45	-	②
	K	7.3L (7270)	⑩	②	②	90	47	24	20	-	②
	M	7.3L (7270)	⑦	95-105	②	90	90	24	20	5-10	②
1995	G	7.5L (7536)	⑦	95-105	45-50	70-90	75-85	22-32	38-48	5-10	②
	Y	4.9L (4917)	⑲	60-70	40-45	130-150	70-90	23-25	22-32	10-15	②
	N	5.0L (4942)	⑩	60-70	19-24	70-90	75-85	23-25	18-24	10-15	②
	H	5.8L (5766)	⑩	95-105	40-45	70-90	75-85	23-25	18-24	10-15	②

88283C39

TORQUE SPECIFICATIONS
All readings in ft. lbs.

Year	Engine ID/VIN	Engine Displacement Liters (cc)	Cylinder Head Bolts	Main Bearing Bolts	Rod Bearing Bolts	Crankshaft Damper Bolts	Flywheel Bolts	Manifold ㉕ Intake	Manifold ㉕ Exhaust	Spark Plugs	Lug Nut
1995	R	5.8L (5766)	⑪	95-105	40-45	70-90	75-85	23-25 ⑱	18-24	10-15	②
	F	7.3L (7270)	㉓	95		㉔	212	89		⑧ 45	-	②
	G	7.5L (7536)	⑭	95-105	40-45	70-90	75-85		⑲ 38-48	5-10	②
1996	Y	4.9L (4917)	⑯	60-69	40-45	130-150	75-85	22-32	22-32	10-15	②
	N	5.0L (4942)	⑩	60-70	19-24	70-90	75-85	23-25 ⑱	26-32	10-15	②
	H	5.8L (5766)	⑪	95-105	40-45	70-90	75-85	23-25 ⑱	26-32	10-15	②
	F	7.3L (7270)	㉓	95	70	212	89	⑧	45	-	②
	G	7.5L (7536)	⑭	95-105	40-45	70-90	75-85		⑲ 25-35	5-10	②

① Step 1: 50-55 ft. lbs.
Step 2: 60-65 ft. lbs.
Step 3: 70-85 ft. lbs.
② Bronco, F-150: 100 ft. lbs.
F-250, F-350 with single rear wheels: 140 ft. lbs.
F350 with dual rear wheels: 140 ft. lbs.
③ Step 1: 55-65 ft. lbs.
Step 2: 65-72 ft. lbs.
④ Step 1: 40 ft. lbs.
Step 2: 70 ft. lbs.
Step 3: 80 ft. lbs.
Step 4: 80 ft. lbs.
⑤ Step 1: 75 ft. lbs.
Step 2: 95 ft. lbs.
⑥ Step 1: 38 ft. lbs.
Step 2: 50-55 ft. lbs.
⑦ Step 1: 80 ft. lbs.
Step 2: 110 ft. lbs.
Step 3: 130-140 ft. lbs.
⑧ Intake manifold cover bolts: 18 ft. lbs.

⑨ Step 1: 65 ft. lbs.
Step 2: 90 ft. lbs.
Step 3: 100 ft. lbs.
⑩ With flanged head bolts:
Step 1: 25-35 ft. lbs.
Step 2: 40-55 ft. lbs.
Step 3: Plus 1/4 turn
With hex head bolts:
Step 1: 55-65 ft. lbs.
Step 2: 65-72 ft. lbs.
⑪ Step 1: 95-105 ft. lbs.
Step 2: 105-112 ft. lbs.
⑫ Step 1: 95 ft. lbs.
Step 2: plus 45 degrees
⑬ Step 1: 47 ft. lbs.
Step 2: plus 45 degrees
⑭ Step 1: 70-80 ft. lbs.
Step 2: 100-110 ft. lbs.
Step 3: 130-140 ft. lbs.
⑮ Step 1: 25-35 ft. lbs.
Step 2: 48-55 ft. lbs.
Step 3: plus 80-100 degrees

⑯ Step 1: 45-55 ft. lbs.
Step 2: plus 80-100 degrees
⑰ Step 1: 85 ft. lbs.
Step 2: 95 ft. lbs.
Step 3: 105-112 ft. lbs.
⑱ Tighten bolts and studs in steps to figure shown. Tighten nut to 8-10 ft. lbs.
⑲ Step 1: 8-12 ft. lbs.
Step 2: 12-22 ft. lbs.
Step 3: 22-35 ft. lbs.
⑳ Step 1: 35 ft. lbs.
Step 2: 35 ft. lbs.
㉑ Step 1: 38 ft. lbs.
Step 2: 51 ft. lbs.
㉒ Step 1: 24 ft. lbs.
Step 2: 24 ft. lbs.
㉓ Step 1: 65 ft. lbs.
Step 2: 85 ft. lbs.
Step 3: 105 ft. lbs.
㉔ Step 1: 52 ft. lbs.
Step 2: 80 ft. lbs.
㉕ Manifold to cylinder head

88283C40

Engine

REMOVAL & INSTALLATION

▶ See Figure 1

In the process of removing the engine, you will come across a number of steps which call for the removal of a separate component or system, such as "disconnect the exhaust system" or "remove the radiator." In most instances, a detailed removal procedure can be found elsewhere in this manual.

It is virtually impossible to list each individual wire and hose which must be disconnected, simply because so many different model and engine combinations have been manufactured. Careful observation and common sense are the best possible additions to any repair procedure. Be absolutely sure to tag any wire or hose before it is disconnected, so that you can be assured of proper reconnection during installation.

❉❉ WARNING

Disconnect the negative battery cable(s) before beginning any work. Always label all disconnected hoses, vacuum lines and wires, to prevent incorrect reassembly. Do not disconnect any air conditioning lines unless you are thoroughly familiar with air conditioning systems and the hazards involved; escaping refrigerant will freeze any surface it contacts, including skin and eyes. Have the system discharged professionally before required repairs are started.

1. Drain the cooling system and the crankcase into suitable containers.

❉❉ CAUTION

When draining the coolant, keep in mind that cats and dogs are attracted by ethylene glycol antifreeze and are quite likely to drink any that is left in an uncovered container or in puddles on the ground. This will prove fatal in sufficient quantity. Always drain the coolant into a sealable container. Coolant should be reused unless it is contaminated or several years old.

2. Use an indelible felt tip pen to enscribe around the hood bolts, then remove the hood.

TCCS3111

Fig. 1 When removing nuts, bolts and other parts, place them in a tray or other container

3. Remove the throttle body inlet tubes.

4. Disconnect the battery and alternator cables.

✳ CAUTION

The EPA warns that prolonged contact with used engine oil may cause a number of skin disorders, including cancer! You should make every effort to minimize your exposure to used engine oil. Protective gloves should be worn when changing the oil. Wash your hands and any other exposed skin areas as soon as possible after exposure to used engine oil. Soap and water, or waterless hand cleaner should be used.

5. If so equipped, have the air conditioning system discharged by an MVAC certified automotive technician.

6. Disconnect the refrigerant lines at the compressor. Cap all openings at once.

7. Remove the compressor.

8. Disconnect the refrigerant lines at the condenser. Cap all openings at once.

9. Remove the condenser.

10. Disconnect the heater hose from the water pump and coolant outlet housing.

11. Remove the radiator.

12. Disconnect the speed control cable, if so equipped.

13. On the 5.0L and 5.8L Engines:

   a. On carbureted engines, remove the air cleaner and intake duct assembly, plus the crankcase ventilation hose.

   b. On fuel injected engines, remove the PCV tube and carbon canister hose.

   c. Disconnect the fuel tank-to-pump fuel line at the fuel pump and plug the line.

   d. On trucks with EFI, disconnect the chassis fuel line at the fuel rails.

   e. On EFI models, disconnect the throttle bracket from the upper intake manifold and swing it out of the way with the cables still attached.

   f. Remove the wiring harness from the left rocker arm cover and position the wires out of the way.

   g. Disconnect the air conditioning compressor clutch wire.

14. On the 7.5L Engine:

   a. Disconnect the engine oil cooler lines at the oil filter adapter.

✳ WARNING

Don't disconnect the lines at the quick-connect fittings behind or at the oil cooler. Disconnecting them may permanently damage them.

   b. Remove the transmission fluid filler tube attaching bolt from the right side valve cover and position the tube out of the way.

   c. Disconnect all vacuum lines at the rear of the intake manifold.

   d. Remove the coil and bracket assembly from the intake manifold. Make sure no other component interferes with the engine removal.

15. Disconnect the ground strap from the cylinder block.

16. Disconnect the automatic transmission kick-down rod and remove the return spring, if so equipped.

17. Disconnect the oil pressure sending unit lead from the sending unit.

18. Remove the fan shroud, fan, water pump pulley and fan belt.

19. Disconnect the accelerator cable.

20. Remove the power steering pump from the engine and position it to one side. Do not disconnect the fluid lines.

21. Disconnect the brake booster vacuum hose at the intake manifold.

22. On trucks with automatic transmission, disconnect the transmission kickdown rod at the bell crank assembly.

23. Disconnect the exhaust pipe from the exhaust manifold.

24. Disconnect the Electronic Engine Control (EEC) harness from all the sensors.

25. Disconnect the body ground strap and the negative battery cable from the engine.

26. Disconnect the engine wiring harness at the ignition coil, the coolant temperature sending unit and the oil pressure sending unit. Position the wiring harness out of the way.

27. Remove the alternator mounting bolts and position the alternator out of the way.

28. Remove the power steering pump from the mounting brackets and move it to one side, leaving the lines attached.

29. Raise and support the truck on jackstands.

30. Remove the starter.

31. Remove the automatic transmission filler tube bracket, if so equipped.

32. Remove the rear engine plate upper right bolt.

33. On manual transmission equipped trucks:

   a. Remove the flywheel housing lower attaching bolts.

   b. Disconnect the clutch return spring.

34. On automatic transmission equipped trucks:

   a. Remove the converter housing access cover assembly.

   b. Remove the flywheel-to-converter attaching nuts.

   c. Secure the converter in the housing.

   d. Remove the transmission oil cooler lines from the retaining clip at the engine.

   e. Remove the lower converter housing-to-engine attaching bolts.

35. Remove the nut from each of the two front engine mounts.

36. Lower the vehicle and position a jack under the transmission and support it.

37. Remove the remaining bell housing-to-engine attaching bolts. Make sure no other component interferes with the engine removal.

38. Attach an engine lifting device and raise the engine slightly and carefully pull it from the transmission. Lift the engine out of the vehicle.

To install:

39. Remove the engine mount brackets from the frame. Attach them to the engine mounts, making the nuts just tight enough to hold the brackets securely to the mounts.

40. Place a new gasket on the muffler inlet pipe.

41. Lower the engine carefully into the transmission. Make sure that the dowels in the engine block engage the holes in the bell housing through the rear cover plate. If the engine hangs up after the transmission input shaft enters the clutch disc (manual transmission only), turn the crankshaft with the transmission in gear until the input shaft splines mesh with the clutch disc splines.

42. On automatic transmission equipped trucks, start the converter pilot into the crankshaft. Secure the converter in the housing.

43. Install the engine mount nuts and washers. Tighten the nuts to 80 ft. lbs. (108 Nm) on the 4.9L, 5.0L, and 5.8L engines, and 74 ft. lbs. (100 Nm) on the 7.5L engine.

44. Tighten the bracket-to-frame bolts to 70 ft. lbs. (95 Nm) on the 4.9L, 5.0L, and 5.8L engines, and 70 ft. lbs. (95 Nm) on the 7.5L engine.

45. Install the bell housing bolts. Tighten the bolts to 50 ft. lbs. (68 Nm).

46. Remove the engine lifting device.

47. Remove the jack supporting the transmission.

48. The balance of installation is the reverse of removal.

6.9L and 7.3L Diesel Engines

1. Use an indelible felt tip pen to enscribe around the hood bolts, then remove the hood.

2. Disconnect both negative battery cables.

3. Drain the cooling system.

✳ CAUTION

When draining the coolant, keep in mind that cats and dogs are attracted by ethylene glycol antifreeze and are quite likely to drink any that is left in an uncovered container or in puddles on the ground. This will prove fatal in sufficient quantity. Always drain the coolant into a sealable container. Coolant should be reused unless it is contaminated or several years old.

4. Remove the air cleaner and intake duct assembly and cover the air intake opening with a clean rag to keep out the dirt.

5. Remove the upper grille support bracket and upper air conditioning condenser mounting bracket.

6. On vehicles equipped with air conditioning, the system MUST be discharged to remove the condenser.

✳ WARNING

DO NOT attempt to do this yourself, unless you are familiar with air conditioning repair and have the appropriate equipment (see Section 1).

7. Remove the radiator fan shroud halves.

8. Remove the fan and clutch assembly as described under water pump removal in this section.

9. Detach the radiator hoses and the transmission cooler lines, if so equipped.

10. Remove the condenser. Cap all openings at once!

11. Remove the radiator.

12. Remove the power steering pump and position it out of the way.

13. Disconnect the fuel supply line heater and alternator wires at the alternator.

14. Disconnect the oil pressure sending unit wire at the sending unit, remove the sender from the firewall and lay it on the engine.

15. Disconnect the accelerator cable and the speed control cable, if so equipped, from the injection pump. Remove the cable bracket with the cables attached, from the intake manifold and position it out of the way.

16. Disconnect the transmission kickdown rod from the injection pump, if so equipped.

17. Disconnect the main wiring harness connector from the right side of the engine and the ground strap from the rear of the engine.

18. Remove the fuel return hose from the left rear of the engine.

19. Remove the two upper transmission-to-engine attaching bolts.

20. Disconnect the heater hoses.

21. Disconnect the water temperature sender wire.

22. Disconnect the overheat light switch wire and position the wire out of the way.

23. Raise the truck and support on it on jackstands.

24. Disconnect the starter cables from the starter.

25. Remove the fuel inlet line and plug the fuel line at the fuel pump.

26. Detach the exhaust pipe at the exhaust manifold.

27. Disconnect the engine insulators from the no. 1 crossmember.

28. Remove the flywheel inspection plate and the four converter-to-flywheel attaching nuts, if equipped with automatic transmission.

29. Remove the jackstands and lower the truck.

30. Supporting the transmission on a jack, remove the four lower transmission attaching bolts.

31. Make sure no other component interferes with the engine removal.

32. Attach an engine lifting sling and remove the engine from the truck.

To install:

33. Lower the engine into truck.

34. Align the converter to the flexplate and the engine dowels to the transmission.

35. Install the engine mount bolts and tighten them to 80 ft. lbs. (108 Nm).

36. Remove the engine lifting sling.

37. Install the four lower transmission attaching bolts. Tighten the bolts for automatic transmissions to 41–56 ft. lbs. (56–76 Nm). Tighten the bolts for manual transmissions to 40–50 ft. lbs. (48–68 Nm).

38. Remove transmission jack.

39. The balance of installation is the reverse of removal.

Rocker Arm (Valve) Cover

REMOVAL & INSTALLATION

4.9L Engine

1. Disconnect the inlet hose at the crankcase filler cap.

2. Remove the throttle body inlet tubes.

3. Disconnect the accelerator cable at the throttle body. Remove the cable retracting spring. Remove the accelerator cable bracket from the upper intake manifold and position the cable and bracket out of the way.

4. Remove the fuel line from the fuel rail. Be careful not to kink the line.

5. Remove the upper intake manifold and throttle body assembly (see Section 5).

6. Remove the ignition coil and wires.

7. Remove the rocker arm cover.

8. Remove and discard the gasket.

To install:

9. Clean the mating surfaces for the cover and head thoroughly.

10. Place the new gasket on the head with the locating tabs downward. The use of gasket sealer is not necessary.

11. Place the cover on the head making sure the gasket is evenly seated. Tighten the bolts for 1987–91 models to 48–84 inch lbs. (5–9 Nm). For 1992–96 models, tighten the bolts to 70–124 inch lbs. (8–14 Nm).

12. The balance of installation is the reverse of removal.

5.0L and 5.8L Engines

▶ **See Figures 2, 3, 4, 5 and 6**

1. Disconnect the negative battery cable.

2. Remove the air cleaner and inlet duct.

3. Remove the coil.

4. For the right cover, remove the lifting eye (except Lightning engine) and Thermactor® tube; for the left cover, remove the oil filler pipe attaching bolt and, on Lightning engine, the lifting eye.

5. Mark and remove the spark plug wires. On the Lightning engine, remove the upper intake manifold.

6. Remove any vacuum lines, wires or pipes in the way. Make sure that you tag them for identification.

7. Remove the cover bolts and lift off the cover. It may be necessary to break the cover loose by rapping on it with a rubber mallet. NEVER pry the cover off!

To install:

8. Thoroughly clean the mating surfaces of both the cover and head.

9. Place the new gasket(s) in the cover(s) with the locating tabs engaging the slots.

10. Place the cover on the head making sure the gasket is evenly seated.

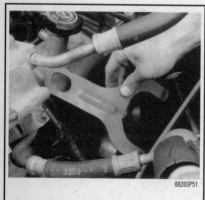

Fig. 2 Remove the lifting eye

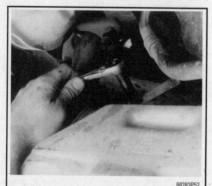

Fig. 3 Re-position any pipes that interfere with the removal

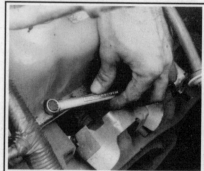

Fig. 4 Unbolt the valve cover from the cylinder head

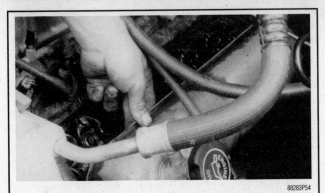

Fig. 5 Maneuver the valve cover away from the cylinder head when detached

Fig. 6 Remove and discard the valve cover gasket

Tighten the bolts to 12–15 ft. lbs. (16–20 Nm). After 2 minutes, retighten the bolts to the same specifications.

11. The balance of installation is the reverse of removal.

7.5L Engine

1. Disconnect the negative battery cable(s).
2. Remove the air cleaner and inlet duct.
3. Remove the Thermactor® air supply control valve and bracket.
4. Remove the coil.
5. Disconnect the MTA hose at the Thermactor® valve. Disconnect the Thermactor® air control valve-to-air pump hose and tube.
6. Mark and remove the spark plug wires.
7. Remove any vacuum lines, wires or pipes in the way. Make sure that you tag them for identification.
8. Remove the cover bolts and lift off the cover. It may be necessary to break the cover loose by rapping on it with a rubber mallet. NEVER pry the cover off!

To install:
9. Thoroughly clean the mating surfaces of both the cover and head.
10. Place the new cover seal(s) in the cover(s) with the locating tab engaging the slot.
11. Place the cover on the head. Tighten the bolts to 6–9 ft. lbs. (8–12 Nm) from right to left.
12. The balance of installation is the reverse of removal.

1987–93 6.9L and 7.3L Diesel Engines

1. Disconnect both negative battery cables.
2. Remove the dipstick tube and valve cover bracket.
3. Remove the transmission filler tube, if applicable.
4. Raise and safely support the front of the vehicle on jackstands.
5. Remove the nuts attaching the right hand engine mount to the frame.
6. Place a jack under the engine in a suitable location and raise the engine until the fuel filter header touches the vehicle sheet metal. Place a wooden block in the gap and lower the engine so it rests on the block.
7. Lower the vehicle.
8. Remove the cover bolts and lift off the covers. It may be necessary to break the covers loose by rapping on them with a rubber mallet. NEVER pry a cover off!

To install:
9. Clean the mating surfaces of the covers and heads thoroughly, place new gaskets in the covers, position the covers on the heads and tighten the bolts to 72 inch lbs. (8 Nm).
10. Raise and safely support the front of the vehicle on jackstands.
11. Raise the engine by jacking from a suitable jacking point and remove the wooden block. Install the engine mount fasteners. Tighten to specification, if required.
12. Lower the vehicle.

13. Install the transmission filler tube and install the dipstick, if applicable.
14. Install the oil tube and dipstick.
15. Connect both negative battery cables.

1994–96 7.3L Diesel Engine

RIGHT COVER

1. Disconnect both negative battery cables.
2. Remove the alternator bolt and move the heater hose out of the way.
3. Remove the drive belt.
4. Remove the alternator.
5. Remove the oil level indicator bracket and dipstick.
6. Remove the fuel injector harness clip and disengage the engine harness connectors from the cover gasket.
7. Remove the cover bolts and lift off the covers. It may be necessary to break the covers loose by rapping on them with a rubber mallet. NEVER pry a cover off!
8. Disconnect the fuel injectors and glow plugs.
9. Remove the valve cover gasket.

To install:
10. Clean the mating surfaces of the cover and head thoroughly. Install a new gasket.
11. Connect the fuel injectors and glow plugs.
12. Install the valve cover. Tighten the bolts to 8 ft. lbs. (11 Nm).
13. The balance of installation is the reverse of removal.

LEFT COVER

1. Disconnect both negative battery cables.
2. Remove the air inlet duct assembly between the turbocharger and air cleaner.
3. Remove the crankcase breather assembly.
4. Remove the intake duct and retaining nuts.
5. Remove the vacuum pump hose at the pump.
6. Remove the cover bolts and lift off the covers. It may be necessary to break the covers loose by rapping on them with a rubber mallet. NEVER pry a cover off!
7. Disconnect the fuel injectors and glow plugs.
8. Remove the valve cover gasket.

To install:
9. Clean the mating surfaces of the cover and head thoroughly. Install a new gasket.
10. Connect the fuel injectors and glow plugs.
11. Install the valve cover. Tighten the bolts to 8 ft. lbs. (11 Nm).
12. Connect the vacuum pump hose to the pump.
13. Install the intake duct bracket.
14. Install the crankcase breather assembly.
15. Install the intake duct tube assembly.
16. Connect both negative battery cables.

Rocker Arms

REMOVAL & INSTALLATION

4.9L Engine

▶ See Figure 7

1. Remove the rocker arm cover.
2. If necessary, remove the spark plug wires and distributor cap.
3. If applicable, remove the pushrod cover (engine side cover).
4. Loosen the rocker arm bolts, then remove the rocker arms. KEEP THE PUSHRODS IN ORDER, FOR INSTALLATION!

To install:

5. Engage the rocker arms with the pushrods and tighten the rocker arm bolts enough to hold the pushrods in place.
6. Adjust the valve clearance, if necessary.
7. If applicable, install the pushrod cover (engine side cover).
8. If removed, install the distributor cap and spark plug wires.
9. Install the rocker arm cover.

5.0L and 5.8L Engines

▶ See Figures 8 and 9

1. Remove the rocker arm covers.
2. Loosen the rocker arm fulcrum bolts, fulcrum seats and rocker arms. KEEP ALL PARTS IN ORDER FOR INSTALLATION!

To install:

3. Apply multi-purpose grease to the valve stem tips, the fulcrum seats and sockets.
4. Install the fulcrum guides, rocker arms, seats and bolts. Tighten the bolts to 18–25 ft. lbs. (24–34 Nm).
5. Install the rocker arm covers.

7.5L Engine

▶ See Figure 10

1. Remove the rocker arm covers.
2. Loosen the rocker arm fulcrum bolts, fulcrum, oil deflector, seat and rocker arms: KEEP EVERYTHING IN ORDER FOR INSTALLATION!

To install:

3. Coat each end of each pushrod with multi-purpose grease.
4. Coat the top of the valve stems, the rocker arms and the fulcrum seats with multi-purpose grease.
5. Rotate the crankshaft by hand until No. 1 piston is at TDC of compression. The firing order marks on the damper will be aligned at TDC with the timing pointer.
6. Install the rocker arms, seats, deflectors and bolts on the following valves:
   - No. 1 intake and exhaust
   - No. 3 intake
   - No. 8 exhaust
   - No. 7 intake
   - No. 5 exhaust
   - No. 8 intake
   - No. 4 exhaust

Engage the rocker arms with the pushrods and tighten the rocker arm fulcrum bolts to 18–25 ft. lbs.

7. Rotate the crankshaft one full turn (360°) and re-align the TDC mark and pointer. Install the parts and tighten the bolts on the following valves:
   - No. 2 intake and exhaust
   - No. 4 intake
   - No. 3 exhaust
   - No. 5 intake
   - No. 6 exhaust
   - No. 6 intake
   - No. 7 exhaust

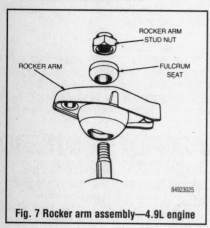

Fig. 7 Rocker arm assembly—4.9L engine

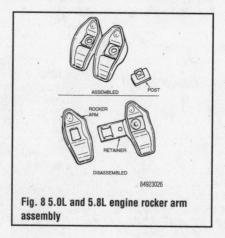

Fig. 8 5.0L and 5.8L engine rocker arm assembly

Fig. 9 A piece of cardboard makes an excellent organizer for the pushrods

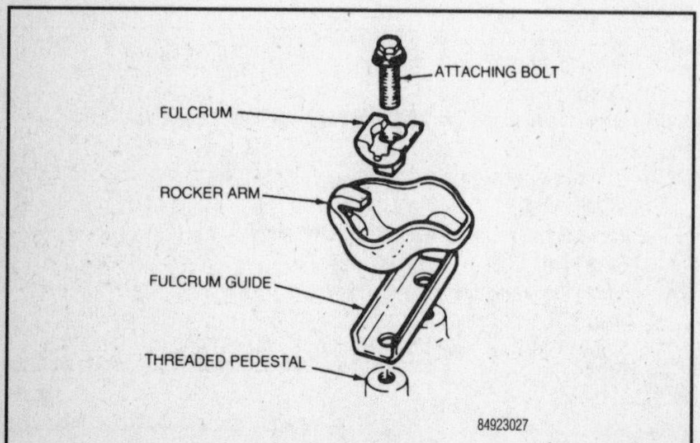

8. Install the rocker arm covers.
9. Check the valve clearance as described in this section.

Diesel Engines

▶ See Figure 11

1. Disconnect both negative battery cables.
2. Remove both valve covers.
3. Remove the valve rocker arm post mounting bolts. Remove the rocker arms and posts in order and mark them with tape so they can be installed in their original positions.
4. If the cylinder heads are to be removed, then the pushrods can now be removed. Make a holder for the pushrods out of a piece of wood or cardboard and remove the pushrods in order. It is very important that the pushrods be reinstalled in their original order. The pushrods can remain in position if no further disassembly is required.
5. If the pushrods were removed, install them in their original locations. Make sure they are fully seated in the tappet seats.

Fig. 10 7.5L engine rocker arm assembly

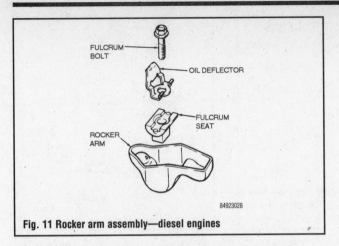

FULCRUM
BOLT

OIL DEFLECTOR

FULCRUM
SEAT

ROCKER
ARM

84923028

Fig. 11 Rocker arm assembly—diesel engines

➡ **The copper colored end of the pushrod goes toward the rocker arm.**

6. Apply a polyethylene grease to the valve stem tips. Install the rocker arms and posts in their original positions.

7. Turn the engine over by hand until the valve timing mark is at the 11 o'clock position, as viewed from the front of the engine. Install all of the rocker arm post attaching bolts and tighten to 20 ft. lbs. (27 Nm).

8. Install new valve cover gaskets and install the valve cover. Connect both battery cables, start the engine and check for leaks.

Thermostat

REMOVAL & INSTALLATION

➡ **It is a good practice to check the operation of a new thermostat before it is installed in an engine. Place the thermostat in a pan of boiling water. If it does not open more than ¼ in. (6mm), do not install it in the engine.**

4.9L Engine

▶ See Figure 12

1. Drain the cooling system below the level of the coolant outlet housing. Use the petcock valve at the bottom of the radiator to drain the system. It is not necessary to remove any of the hoses.

✳✳ CAUTION

When draining the coolant, keep in mind that cats and dogs are attracted by ethylene glycol antifreeze and are quite likely to drink any that is left in an uncovered container or in puddles on the ground. This will prove fatal in sufficient quantity. Always drain the coolant into a sealable container. Coolant should be reused unless it is contaminated or several years old.

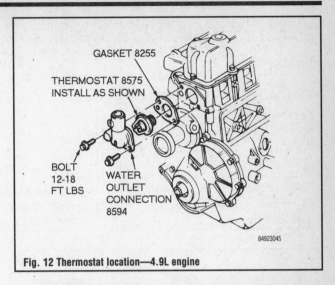

GASKET 8255

THERMOSTAT 8575
INSTALL AS SHOWN

BOLT
12-18
FT LBS

WATER
OUTLET
CONNECTION
8594

84923045

Fig. 12 Thermostat location—4.9L engine

2. Remove the coolant outlet housing retaining bolts and slide the housing with the hose attached to one side.

3. Remove the thermostat and gasket from the cylinder head and clean both mating surfaces.

4. To install the thermostat, coat a new gasket with water resistant sealer and position it on the outlet of the engine. The gasket must be in place before the thermostat is installed.

5. Install the thermostat with the bridge (opposite end of the spring) inside the elbow connection.

6. Position the elbow connection onto the mounting surface of the outlet, so that the thermostat flange is resting on the gasket and install the retaining bolts. Tighten the bolts to 15 ft. lbs. (20 Nm).

7. Fill the radiator and operate the engine until it reaches operating temperature. Check the coolant level and adjust if necessary.

5.0L, 5.8L and 7.5L Engine

▶ See Figures 13 thru 19

The gasoline-powered 5.0L and 5.8L engine thermostat is mounted vertically on the front of engine, the 7.5L engine thermostat is positioned vertically.

1. Drain the cooling system below the level of the coolant outlet housing. Use the petcock valve at the bottom of the radiator to drain the system. It is not necessary to remove any of the hoses.

✳✳ CAUTION

When draining the coolant, keep in mind that cats and dogs are attracted by ethylene glycol antifreeze and are quite likely to drink any that is left in an uncovered container or in puddles on the ground. This will prove fatal in sufficient quantity. Always drain the coolant into a sealable container. Coolant should be reused unless it is contaminated or several years old.

88283P44

Fig. 13 Unbolt the thermostat housing

88283P45

Fig. 14 Pull away the thermostat from the housing

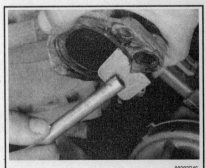

88283P46

Fig. 15 Scrape the gasket material taking care not to gouge the aluminum mating surfaces

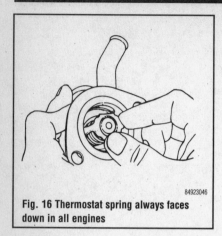

Fig. 16 Thermostat spring always faces down in all engines

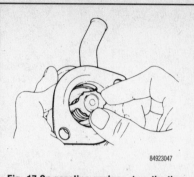

Fig. 17 On gasoline engines, turn the thermostat CLOCKWISE to lock it into position on the flats in the outlet elbow

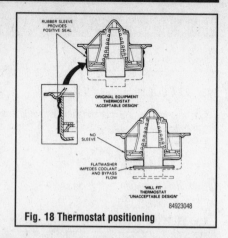

Fig. 18 Thermostat positioning

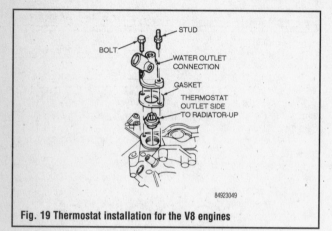

Fig. 19 Thermostat installation for the V8 engines

2. Disconnect the bypass hoses at the water pump and intake manifold.
3. Remove the bypass tube.
4. Remove the coolant outlet housing retaining bolts, bend the hose and lift the housing with the hose attached to one side.
5. Remove the thermostat and gasket from the intake manifold and clean both mating surfaces.

To install:

6. For 5.0L and 5.8L engines, coat a new gasket with water resistant sealer and position it on the outlet of the engine. The gasket must be in place before the thermostat is installed. Install the thermostat with the bridge (opposite end of the spring) inside the elbow connection and the thermostat flange positioned in the recess in the manifold.
7. For the 7.5L engine, install the thermostat in the recess, then coat the gasket with a water resistant sealer and position the gasket on top of the thermostat.
8. Position the elbow connection onto the mounting surface of the outlet. Tighten the bolts to 18 ft. lbs. (24 Nm) on the 5.0L and 5.8L engines; 28 ft. lbs. (38 Nm) on the 7.5L engine.
9. Install the bypass tube and hoses.
10. Fill the radiator and operate the engine until it reaches operating temperature. Check the coolant level and adjust if necessary.

6.9L and 7.3L Diesel Engines

➡The diesel engine thermostat is on the front side of the intake manifold

1987–93 ENGINES

✳✳ CAUTION

When draining the coolant, keep in mind that cats and dogs are attracted by ethylene glycol antifreeze and are quite likely to drink any that is left in an uncovered container or in puddles on the ground. This will prove fatal in sufficient quantity. Always drain the coolant into a sealable container. Coolant should be reused unless it is contaminated or several years old.

✳✳ WARNING

The factory specified thermostat does not contain an internal bypass. On these engines, an internal bypass is located in the block. The use of any replacement thermostat other than that meeting the manufacturer's specifications will result in engine overheating! Use only thermostats meeting the specifications of Ford part number E5TZ–8575–C or Navistar International part number 1807945–C1.

1. Disconnect both negative battery cables.
2. Drain the coolant to a point below the thermostat housing.
3. Remove the alternator and vacuum pump belt(s)
4. Remove the alternator.
5. Remove the vacuum pump and bracket.
6. Remove all but the lowest vacuum pump/alternator mounting casting bolt.
7. Loosen that lowest bolt and pivot the casting outboard of the engine.
8. Remove the thermostat housing attaching bolts, bend the hose and lift the housing up and to one side.
9. Remove the thermostat and gasket.

To install:

10. Clean the thermostat housing and block surfaces thoroughly.
11. Coat a new gasket with waterproof sealer and position the gasket on the manifold outlet opening.
12. Install the thermostat in the manifold opening with the spring element end downward and the flange positioned in the recess in the manifold.
13. Place the outlet housing into position and install the bolts. Tighten the bolts to 20 ft. lbs. (27 Nm).
14. Reposition the casting.
15. Install the vacuum pump and bracket.
16. Install the alternator.
17. Adjust the drive belt(s).
18. Fill and bleed the cooling system.
19. Connect both battery cables.
20. Run the engine and check for leaks.

1994–96 ENGINES

1. Disconnect both negative battery cables.
2. Drain the coolant to a point below the thermostat housing.
3. Remove the drive belt.
4. Disconnect the upper radiator hose.
5. Remove the thermostat housing, its O-ring and the thermostat.

To install:

6. Install the thermostat and the thermostat housing O-ring in the hose connection.
7. Place the outlet housing into position and install the screws. Tighten the screws to 15 ft. lbs. (20 Nm).
8. Install the upper radiator hose.
9. Install the drive belt.
10. Fill and bleed the cooling system.
11. Connect both battery cables.
12. Run the engine and check for leaks.

Intake Manifold

REMOVAL & INSTALLATION

1987–93 4.9L Engine

The intake and exhaust manifolds on these engines are known as combination manifolds and are serviced as a unit. See Combination Manifold Removal and Installation.

1994–96 4.9L Engine

UPPER INTAKE MANIFOLD

1. Disconnect the negative battery cable.
2. Tag and disengage the electrical connectors and vacuum lines that interfere with the removal of the manifold.
3. Disconnect the PCV hose on the underside of the manifold.
4. Disconnect the throttle linkage and position the loose cable out of the way.
5. Disconnect the air cleaner outlet tube from the throttle body.
6. Disconnect the EGR valve tube from the manifold.
7. Remove the secondary air bypass tube.
8. If applicable, disconnect any other component that interferes with the removal.
9. Disconnect the upper manifold from the lower manifold.
10. Remove the seven studs retaining the upper manifold.
11. Remove the upper manifold and throttle body as an assembly from the lower manifold.

To install:

12. Clean the mounting surfaces as necessary and install a new gasket on the lower manifold half. Position the gasket correctly on the dowels.
13. Install the upper manifold onto the lower manifold, again using the dowels to locate the manifold halves together. Install the seven studs and hand tighten them.
14. Tighten the seven studs to 12–18 ft. lbs. (16–24 Nm).
15. Position the upper intake manifold support onto the boss of the upper intake located under the throttle body. install the screws, tightening them to 22–32 ft. lbs. (30–43 Nm).
16. Install the EGR valve. The tube should be routed between the No. 5 and No. 6 intake runners. Tighten both fittings to 25–35 ft. lbs. (34–47 Nm).
17. The balance of installation is the reverse of removal.

LOWER INTAKE MANIFOLD

The lower intake manifold and exhaust manifolds for the 1994–96 4.9L engine must be removed together. To remove the lower intake manifold, refer to the appropriate Combination Manifold Removal and Installation procedure.

1987 5.8L Engine With 4-Bbl. Carburetor

▶ See Figures 20, 21 and 22

1. Drain the cooling system, remove the air cleaner and the intake duct assembly.
2. Disconnect the accelerator rod from the carburetor and remove the accelerator retracting spring. Disconnect the automatic transmission kickdown rod at the carburetor, if so equipped.
3. Disconnect the high tension lead and all other wires from the ignition coil.
4. Disconnect the spark plug wires from the spark plugs by grasping the rubber boots and twisting and pulling at the same time. Remove the wires from the brackets on the rocker covers. Remove the distributor cap and spark plug wire assembly.
5. Remove the carburetor fuel inlet line and the distributor vacuum line from the carburetor.
6. Remove the distributor lockbolt and remove the distributor and vacuum line.
7. Disconnect the upper radiator hose from the coolant outlet housing and the temperature sending unit wire at the sending unit. Remove the heater hose from the intake manifold.
8. Loosen the clamp on the water pump bypass hose at the coolant outlet housing and slide the hose off the outlet housing.

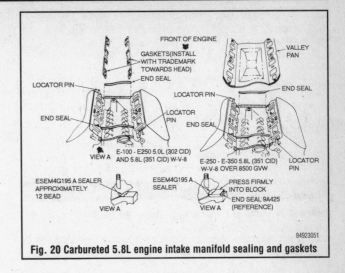

Fig. 20 Carbureted 5.8L engine intake manifold sealing and gaskets

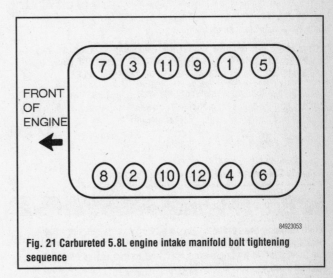

Fig. 21 Carbureted 5.8L engine intake manifold bolt tightening sequence

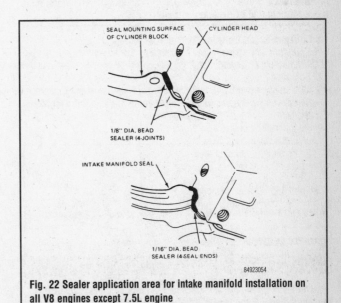

Fig. 22 Sealer application area for intake manifold installation on all V8 engines except 7.5L engine

9. Disconnect the PCV hose at the rocker cover.
10. If the engine is equipped with the Thermactor® exhaust emission control system, remove the air pump to cylinder head air hose at the air pump and

position it out of the way. Also remove the air hose at the backfire suppressor valve. Remove the air hose bracket from the valve cover and position the air hose out of the way.

11. If applicable, disconnect any other component that interferes with the removal.

12. Remove the intake manifold and carburetor as an assembly. It may be necessary to pry the intake manifold from the cylinder head. Remove all traces of the intake manifold-to-cylinder head gaskets and the two end seals from both the manifold and the other mating surfaces of the engine.

To install:

13. Clean the mating surfaces of the intake manifold, cylinder heads and block with lacquer thinner or similar solvent. Apply a ⅛ in. (3mm) bead of sili-cone-rubber RTV sealant at the points shown in the accompanying diagram.

✴✴ WARNING

Do not apply sealer to the waffle portions of the seals as the sealer will rupture the end seal material.

14. Position new seals on the block and press the seal locating extensions into the holes in the mating surfaces.

15. Apply a 1/16 in. (1.5mm) bead of sealer to the outer end of each manifold seal for the full length of the seal (4 places). As before, do not apply sealer to the waffle portion of the end seals.

➡ **This sealer sets in about 15 minutes, depending on brand, so work quickly but carefully. DO NOT DROP ANY SEALER INTO THE MANIFOLD CAVITY. IT WILL FORM AND SET AND PLUG THE OIL GALLERY.**

16. Position the manifold gasket onto the block and heads with the alignment notches under the dowels in the heads. Be sure gasket holes align with head holes.

17. Install the manifold and related equipment in reverse order of removal.

1987 7.5L Engine With 4-Bbl. Carburetor

◗ **See Figures 23 and 24**

1. Drain the cooling system and remove the air cleaner assembly.

✴✴ CAUTION

When draining the coolant, keep in mind that cats and dogs are attracted by ethylene glycol antifreeze and are quite likely to drink any that is left in an uncovered container or in puddles on the ground. This will prove fatal in sufficient quantity. Always drain the coolant into a sealable container. Coolant should be reused unless it is contaminated or several years old.

2. Disconnect the upper radiator hose at the engine.

3. Disconnect the heater hoses at the intake manifold and the water pump. Position them out of the way. Loosen the water pump by-pass hose clamp at the intake manifold.

4. Disconnect the PCV valve and hose at the right valve cover. Disconnect all of the vacuum lines at the rear of the intake manifold and tag them for proper reinstallation.

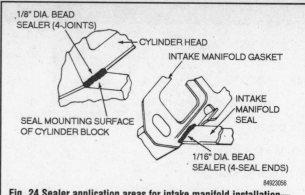

Fig. 24 Sealer application areas for intake manifold installation— 7.5L engine

5. Disconnect the wires at the spark plugs and remove the wires from the brackets on the valve cover. Disconnect the high tension wire from the coil and remove the distributor cap and wires as an assembly.

6. Disconnect all of the distributor vacuum lines at the carburetor and vac-uum control valve and tag them for proper installation. Remove the distributor and vacuum lines as an assembly.

7. Disconnect the accelerator linkage at the carburetor. Remove the speed control linkage bracket, if so equipped, from the manifold and carburetor.

8. Remove the bolts holding the accelerator linkage bell crank, then position the linkage and return springs out of the way.

9. Disconnect the fuel line at the carburetor.

10. Disconnect the wiring harness at the coil battery terminal, engine tem-perature sending unit, oil pressure sending until and other connections as nec-essary. Disconnect the wiring harness from the clips at the left valve cover and position the harness out of the way.

11. Remove the coil and bracket assembly.

12. Remove the intake manifold attaching bolts and lift the manifold and carburetor from the engine as an assembly. It may be necessary to pry the mani-fold away from the cylinder heads. Do not damage the gasket sealing surfaces.

Installation is as follows:

13. Clean the mating surfaces of the intake manifold, cylinder heads and block with lacquer thinner or similar solvent. Apply a ⅛ in. (3mm) bead of sili-cone-rubber RTV sealant at the points shown in the accompanying diagram.

✴✴ WARNING

Do not apply sealer to the waffle portions of the seals as the sealer will rupture the end seal material.

14. Position the new seals on the block and press the seal locating exten-sions into the holes in the mating surfaces.

15. Apply a 1/16 in. (1.5mm) bead of sealer to the outer end of each manifold seal for the full length of the seal (4 places). As before, do not apply sealer to the waffle portion of the end seals.

➡ **This sealer sets in about 15 minutes, depending on brand, so work quickly but carefully. DO NOT DROP ANY SEALER INTO THE MANIFOLD CAVITY. IT WILL FORM AND SET AND PLUG THE OIL GALLERY.**

16. Position the manifold gasket onto the block and heads with the alignment notches under the dowels in the heads. Be sure gasket holes align with head holes.

17. Install the manifold and related equipment in reverse order of removal.

Fuel Injected 5.0L, 5.8L and 7.5L Engines—Except 5.8L Lightning

➡ **Discharge the fuel system pressure before starting any work that involves disconnecting fuel system lines. See Section 5.**

UPPER INTAKE MANIFOLD

◗ **See Figures 25, 26, 27 and 28**

1. Remove the air cleaner. Disengage the electrical connectors at the idle air control valve, throttle position sensor and EGR position sensor.

2. Disconnect the throttle linkage at the throttle ball and the AOD transmis-

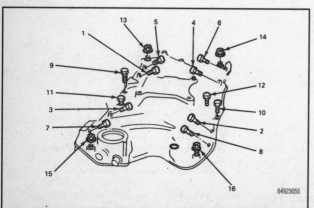

Fig. 23 Carbureted 7.5L intake manifold bolt tightening sequence

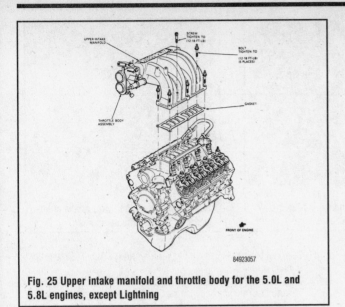

Fig. 25 Upper intake manifold and throttle body for the 5.0L and 5.8L engines, except Lightning

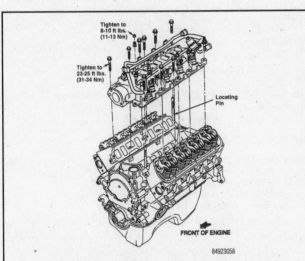

Fig. 26 Lower intake manifold and throttle body for the 5.0L and 5.8L engines, except Lightning

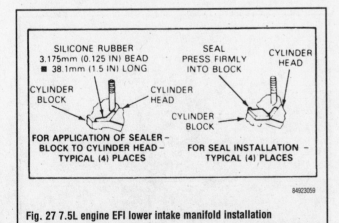

Fig. 27 7.5L engine EFI lower intake manifold installation

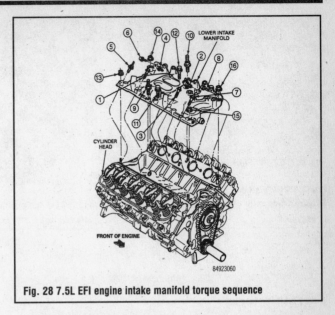

Fig. 28 7.5L EFI engine intake manifold torque sequence

4. Disconnect the PCV system by disconnecting the hose from the fitting at the rear of the upper manifold.

5. Remove the two canister purge lines from the fittings at the throttle body.

6. Disconnect the EGR tube from the EGR valve by loosening the flange nut.

7. If applicable, disconnect any other component that interferes with the removal.

8. Remove the bolt from the upper intake support bracket to upper manifold. Remove the upper manifold retaining bolts and remove the upper intake manifold and throttle body as an assembly.

9. Clean and inspect all mounting surfaces of the upper and lower intake manifolds.

To install:

10. Position a new mounting gasket on the lower intake manifold.

11. Install the upper intake manifold and throttle body as an assembly. Install the upper manifold retaining bolts and install the bolt at the upper intake support bracket. Mounting bolts are torqued to 12–18 ft. lbs. (16–24 Nm).

12. The balance of installation is the reverse of removal.

LOWER INTAKE MANIFOLD

▶ See Figures 29, 30 and 31

1. Remove the upper manifold and throttle body.

2. Drain the cooling system.

3. Remove the distributor assembly, cap and wires.

4. Disengage the electrical connectors at the engine, coolant temperature sensor and sending unit, at the air charge temperature sensor and at the knock sensor.

5. Disconnect the injector wiring harness from the main harness assembly. Remove the ground wire from the intake manifold stud. The ground wire must be installed at the same position it was removed from.

6. Disconnect the fuel supply and return lines from the fuel rails.

7. Remove the upper radiator hose from the thermostat housing. Remove the bypass hose. Remove the heater outlet hose at the intake manifold.

8. Remove the air cleaner mounting bracket. Remove the intake manifold mounting bolts and studs. Pay attention to the location of the bolts and studs for reinstallation. Remove the lower intake manifold assembly.

To install:

9. Clean and inspect the mounting surfaces of the heads and manifold.

10. Apply a 1/16 in. (1.5mm) bead of RTV sealer to the ends of the manifold seal (the junction point of the seals and gaskets). Install the end seals and intake gaskets on the cylinder heads. The gaskets must interlock with the seal tabs.

11. Install locator bolts at opposite ends of each head and carefully lower the intake manifold into position. Install and tighten the mounting bolts and studs to 23–25 ft. lbs. (31–34 Nm).

12. Install the lower intake manifold assembly. Install the intake manifold

sion linkage from the throttle body. Remove the bolts that secure the bracket to the intake and position the bracket and cables out of the way.

3. Disconnect the upper manifold vacuum fitting connections by removing all the vacuum lines at the vacuum tree (label lines for position identification). Remove the vacuum lines to the EGR valve and fuel pressure regulator.

Fig. 29 With all components, hoses and wiring detached, unbolt the lower intake manifold

Fig. 30 Lift the manifold away from the engine—5.0L engine shown

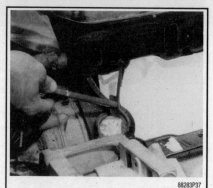

Fig. 31 Scrape off the lower intake manifold seal with a suitable scraper

mounting bolts and studs. Pay attention to the location of the bolts. Install the air cleaner mounting bracket.

13. The balance of installation is the reverse of removal.

5.8L Lightning Engine

UPPER INTAKE MANIFOLD

♦ **See Figure 32**

1. Disconnect the negative battery cable.
2. Remove the air intake tube.
3. Remove the snow/ice shield from the throttle body.
4. Disengage the electrical connectors at:
- Throttle position sensor
- Idle air control valve
- EVP sensor
- Emission vacuum control secondary regulator
- Secondary air injection bypass/secondary air injection diverter solenoids
5. Disconnect the vacuum lines from:
- EGR external pressure valve
- EVP sensor
- AIRB/AIRD solenoids
- Vacuum tree
6. Disconnect the PCV fresh air tube from the throttle body and oil fill tube.
7. Loosen the radiator cap.
8. Disconnect and plug the coolant hoses at the EGR spacer.
9. Using a prytool, carefully pry the throttle cable from the ball stud. DO NOT PULL IT OFF BY HAND!

10. Reach up behind the upper intake manifold and pull the PCV valve from the lower intake manifold.
11. Disconnect the vacuum line from the brake booster.
12. Remove the mounting bolts, lift the upper manifold up and pull it forward to gain access to the vacuum hoses located below it. Disconnect the hoses and remove the upper manifold.

To install:

13. Clean all gasket surfaces thoroughly and carefully. Don't allow any gasket material to fall into the lower manifold.
14. Position a new gasket on the lower manifold.
15. Place the upper manifold onto the lower and connect all the vacuum hoses.
16. Install the bolts and tighten them, in the sequence shown, to 12–18 ft. lbs. (16–24 Nm).
17. The balance of installation is the reverse of removal.

LOWER INTAKE MANIFOLD

♦ **See Figure 33**

1. Remove the upper intake manifold and throttle body.
2. Drain the cooling system.
3. Remove the distributor assembly, cap and wires.
4. Disengage the electrical connectors at the engine, coolant temperature sensor and sending unit, at the air charge temperature sensor and at the knock sensor.
5. Disconnect the injector wiring harness from the main harness assembly. Remove the ground wire from the intake manifold stud. The ground wire must be installed at the same position it was removed from.
6. Disconnect the fuel supply and return lines from the fuel rails.

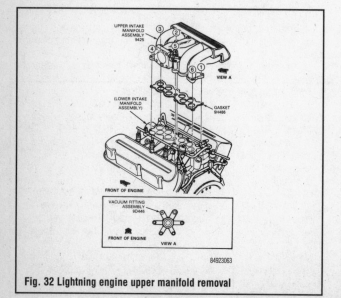

Fig. 32 Lightning engine upper manifold removal

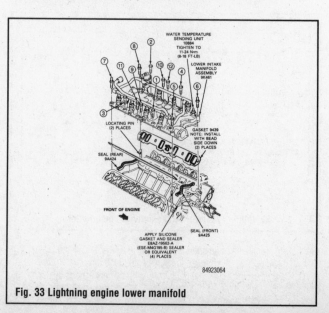

Fig. 33 Lightning engine lower manifold

7. Remove the upper radiator hose from the thermostat housing. Remove the bypass hose. Remove the heater outlet hose at the intake manifold.

8. Remove the air cleaner mounting bracket. Remove the intake manifold mounting bolts and studs. Pay attention to the location of the bolts and studs for reinstallation. Remove the lower intake manifold assembly.

To install:

9. Clean and inspect the mounting surfaces of the heads and manifold.

10. Apply a ¹⁄₁₆ in. (1.5mm) bead of RTV sealer to the ends of the manifold seal (the junction point of the seals and gaskets). Install the end seals and intake gaskets on the cylinder heads. The gaskets must interlock with the seal tabs.

11. Install locator bolts at opposite ends of each head and carefully lower the intake manifold into position. Install and tighten the mounting bolts and studs to 23–25 ft. lbs. (31–34 Nm).

12. The balance of installation is the reverse of removal.

6.9L and 7.3L Diesel Engines

1987–93 ENGINES

▶ See Figures 34 and 35

1. Disconnect both negative battery cables.

2. Remove the air cleaner and install clean rags into the air intake of the intake manifold. It is important that no dirt or foreign objects get into the diesel intake.

3. Remove the injection pump as described in Section 5 under Diesel Fuel System.

4. Remove the fuel return hose from No. 7 and No. 8 rear nozzles and remove the return hose to the fuel tank.

5. Label the positions of the wires and remove the engine wiring harness from the engine.

➡The engine harness ground cables must be removed from the back of the left cylinder head.

6. If applicable, disconnect any other component that interferes with the removal.

7. Remove the bolts attaching the intake manifold to the cylinder heads and remove the manifold.

8. Remove the CDR tube grommet from the valley pan.

9. Remove the bolts attaching the valley pan strap to the front of the engine block and remove the strap.

10. Remove the valley pan drain plug and remove the valley pan.

11. Apply a ⅛ in. (3mm) bead of RTV sealer to each end of the cylinder block as shown in the accompanying illustration.

➡The RTV sealer should be applied immediately prior to the valley pan installation.

12. Install the valley pan drain plug, CDR tube and new grommet into the valley pan.

13. Install a new O-ring and new back-up ring on the CDR valve.

14. Install the valley pan strap on the front of the valley pan.

15. Install the intake manifold and tighten the bolts to 24 ft. lbs. (32 Nm) using the sequence shown in the illustration.

16. The balance of installation is the reverse of removal.

➡If necessary, purge the nozzle high pressure lines of air by loosening the connector one half to one turn and cranking the engine until solid stream of fuel, devoid of any bubbles, flows from the connection.

✳✳ CAUTION

Keep eyes and hands away from the nozzle spray. Fuel spraying from the nozzle under high pressure can penetrate the skin.

17. Check and adjust the injection pump timing, as described in Section 5 under Diesel Fuel System.

1994–96 ENGINES

▶ See Figure 36

1. Disconnect both negative battery cables.

2. Remove the air cleaner and install clean rags into the air intake to keep dirt or foreign objects out of the manifold.

3. Remove the turbocharger assembly.

4. Remove the injection pump.

5. Remove the fuel return hose from No. 7 and No. 8 rear nozzles and remove the return hose to the fuel tank.

6. Label the positions of the wires and remove the engine wiring harness from the engine.

➡The engine harness ground cables must be removed from the back of the left cylinder head.

7. Remove the two retaining bolts from the crankcase breather switch and remove the switch.

8. Remove the bolts attaching the intake manifold to the cylinder heads and remove the manifold.

9. Remove the crankcase breather tube grommet from the valley pan.

10. Remove the bolts attaching the valley pan strap to the front of the engine block, and remove the strap.

11. Remove the valley pan drain plug and remove the valley pan.

To install:

12. Apply a ⅛ in. (3mm) bead of RTV sealer to each end of the cylinder block.

➡The RTV sealer should be applied immediately prior to the valley pan installation.

13. Install the valley pan drain plug, crankcase breather tube and new grommet into the valley pan.

14. Install a new O-ring and new back-up ring on the crankcase breather valve.

15. Install the valley pan strap on the front of the valley pan.

16. Install the intake manifold and torque the bolts as follows:

   a. Torque to 33 ft. lbs. (45 Nm) in the numbered sequence, working from the center of the manifold towards the ends.

   b. Torque to 33 ft. lbs. (45 Nm) in the line sequence, working from front-to-rear of the right bank and rear-to-front of the left bank.

17. The balance of installation is the reverse of removal.

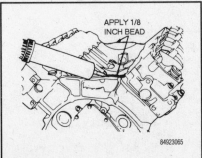

Fig. 34 Apply sealer to the diesel cylinder block-to-intake manifold mating surfaces on each end

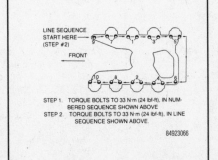

Fig. 35 Diesel engine intake manifold bolt tightening sequence—1987–93 engines

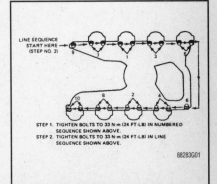

Fig. 36 Intake manifold tightening sequence—1994–96 diesel engines

→If necessary, bleed injection lines of air by loosening them at the injector and cranking the engine until solid stream of fuel flows from the connection.

❋❋ CAUTION

Keep eyes and hands away from the nozzle spray. Fuel spraying from the nozzle under high pressure can penetrate the skin.

18. Check and adjust the injection pump timing, if necessary.

Exhaust Manifold

REMOVAL & INSTALLATION

5.0L, 5.8L and 7.5L Engines

▶ **See Figures 37, 38, 39 and 40**

1. Remove the air cleaner if the manifold being removed has the carburetor heat stove attached to it.
2. On the 5.0L, remove the dipstick bracket.
3. Remove the lifting eye, if applicable.
4. Disconnect the exhaust pipe or catalytic converter from the exhaust manifold. Remove and discard the doughnut gasket.
5. Remove any shield that may interfere with the removal.
6. Remove the exhaust manifold attaching screws and remove the manifold from the cylinder head.
To install:
7. Clean all gasket mating surfaces thoroughly, then install a new gasket.

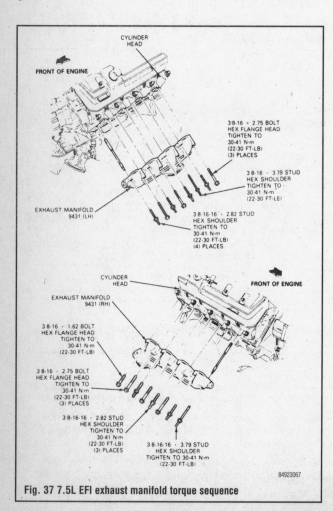

Fig. 37 7.5L EFI exhaust manifold torque sequence

8. Bolt on the exhaust manifold. Working from the center to the ends. Tighten the bolts to specification.
9. Place a new gasket, if equipped, on the muffler inlet pipes. Position the inlet pipe(s) and exhaust heat control valve, if so equipped, into the manifold. Install and fasten the hardware to specification
10. The rest of the installation is the reverse of the removal.

6.9L and 7.3L Diesel Engines

▶ **See Figure 41**

1. Disconnect both negative battery cables.
2. Raise and safely support the vehicle with jackstands.
3. Disconnect the muffler inlet pipe from the exhaust manifolds.
4. Lower the truck to remove the right manifold.
5. To remove the left manifold, jack the truck up again. Bend the tabs on the manifold attaching bolts, then remove the bolts and manifold.
To install:
6. Before installing, clean all mounting surfaces on the cylinder heads and the manifold. Apply an anti-seize compound on the manifold bolt threads and install the left manifold, using a new gasket and new locking tabs.
7. Tighten the bolts to specifications and bend the tabs over the flats on the bolt heads to prevent the bolts from loosening.
8. Raise the truck to install the left manifold. Install the right manifold by first lowering the truck.
9. Connect the inlet pipes to the manifold and tighten. Lower the truck, connect the batteries and run the engine to check for exhaust leaks.

Combination Manifold

REMOVAL & INSTALLATION

4.9L Engine

1987–93 ENGINES

▶ **See Figure 42**

1. Disconnect the negative battery cable.
2. Remove the air inlet hose at the crankcase filter cap.
3. Remove the throttle body inlet hoses.
4. Disconnect the accelerator cable at the throttle body.
5. Remove the cable retracting spring.
6. Remove the cable bracket from the upper intake manifold.
7. Disconnect the fuel inlet line at the fuel rail. Don't kink the line!
8. Remove the upper intake and throttle body as an assembly (see Section 5).
9. Tag and disconnect all vacuum lines attached to the parts in question.
10. Disconnect the inlet pipe from the exhaust manifold.
11. Disconnect the power brake vacuum line, if so equipped.
12. Remove the bolts and nuts attaching the manifolds to the cylinder head. Lift the manifold assemblies from the engine. Remove and discard the gaskets.
13. To separate the manifold, remove the nuts joining the intake and exhaust manifolds.
To install:
14. Clean the mating surfaces of the cylinder head and the manifolds.
15. If the intake and exhaust manifolds have been separated, coat the mating surfaces lightly with graphite grease and place the exhaust manifold over the studs on the intake manifold. Install the lockwashers and nuts. Tighten them finger tight.
16. Install a new intake manifold gasket.
17. Coat the mating surfaces lightly with graphite grease. Place the manifold assemblies in position against the cylinder head. Make sure that the gaskets have not become dislodged. Install the attaching nuts and bolts in the proper sequence to 26 ft. lbs. (35 Nm). If the intake and exhaust manifolds were separated, tighten the nuts joining them.
18. Position a new gasket on the muffler inlet pipe and connect the inlet pipe to the exhaust manifold.
19. The balance of installation is the reverse of removal.

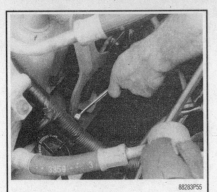

Fig. 38 If the lifting eye is on the side you are working on, remove it

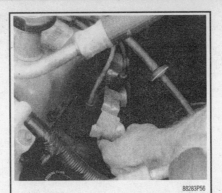

Fig. 39 Remove the heat shield (if applicable)—1990 5.0L engine shown

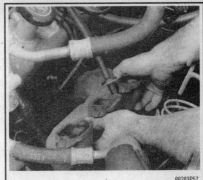

Fig. 40 Once unbolted, carefully lift away the exhaust manifold

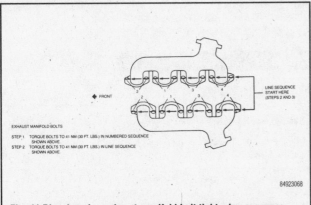

Fig. 41 Diesel engine exhaust manifold bolt tightening sequence

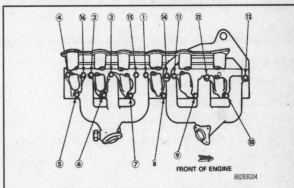

Fig. 43 Intake/exhaust (combination) manifold tightening sequence—1994–96 4.9L engine

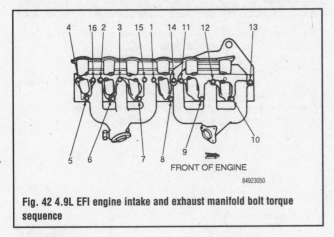

Fig. 42 4.9L EFI engine intake and exhaust manifold bolt torque sequence

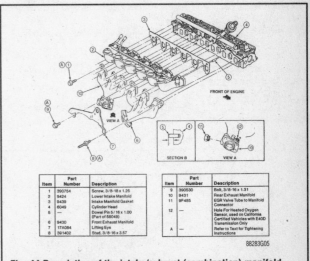

Fig. 44 Description of the intake/exhaust (combination) manifold components—1994–96 4.9L engine

1994–96 ENGINES

▶ See Figures 43 and 44

1. Disconnect the negative battery cable.
2. Remove the upper intake manifold and throttle body.
3. Remove the two clips and the intake manifold shield.
4. Remove the drive belt.
5. Remove the alternator.
6. Remove the air pump.
7. Remove the alternator bracket.
8. Disconnect the Y-pipe and EGR valve.
9. Disconnect the power brake vacuum line.
10. Remove the manifold, rear exhaust manifold and lower intake manifold to the cylinder head. Lift the manifolds from the engine. Remove and discard the gaskets.

To install:

11. Before installing, clean all mounting surfaces on the cylinder heads and the manifold. Apply an anti-seize compound on the manifold bolt threads.

➡The EGR valve tube is only on the rear exhaust manifold. If the rear manifold is to be replaced, remove the tube fittings from the discarded manifold as required.

12. On SFI-equipped engines, if either exhaust manifold is to be replaced, remove the heated oxygen sensor from the old manifold and install in the new one.

13. Make sure the dowel pin is in place.

14. Install the rear exhaust manifold with bolts in holes 15 and 16. Tighten the bolts to 22–32 ft. lbs. (30–43 Nm).

15. Install the front exhaust manifold and lifting eye with the stud in hole 13 and bolt in hole 14. Snug the stud and tighten the bolt to 22–32 ft. lbs. (30–43 Nm).

16. Install the intake manifold gasket over the dowel pin and line up the port openings in the cylinder head and intake manifold gasket.

17. Install the lower intake manifold onto the dowel pins, then install the remaining bolts.

18. Tighten the bolts to 22–32 ft. lbs. (30–43 Nm) using the proper sequence (see illustration).

19. Connect the power brake vacuum line.

20. Connect the dual converter Y-pipe to the front and rear exhaust manifolds. Tighten the lockwashers and nuts to 25–36 ft. lbs. (34–49 Nm).

21. The balance of installation is the reverse of removal.

Turbocharger

REMOVAL & INSTALLATION

1994–96 7.3L Diesel Engine

▶ See Figure 45

1. Remove the two duct tube assembly bolts, the clamp at the turbo and at the air cleaner and duct tube assembly.

2. Remove the exhaust outlet clamp from the turbo.

3. Raise the vehicle and disconnect the exhaust outlet pipe bolt from the transmission case.

4. Remove the nuts and bolts securing the exhaust outlet pipe to the catalytic converter.

5. Remove the two lower bolts retaining the turbo exhaust inlet pipe to the left exhaust manifold.

6. Remove the lower retaining bolts at the turbo exhaust inlet pipe and turbo collector.

7. Remove the two lower bolts retaining the turbo exhaust inlet pipe to the right exhaust manifold.

8. Remove the lower bolt retaining the right turbo exhaust inlet pipe to the turbo collector.

9. Lower the vehicle.

10. Remove the upper bolt retaining the left and right turbo exhaust inlet pipe to the turbo collector.

11. Remove the right side engine lift hook and bolt.

12. Loosen the four intake manifold hose clamps, and the one clamp retaining the compressor to the turbo.

13. Remove the compressor.

14. Remove the four turbo pedestal bolts. Disconnect the electrical connectors and remove the turbo assembly.

15. Remove the used oil galley O-rings.

To install:

16. Replace the oil galley O-rings with new ones.

17. Install the turbo assembly. Tighten the pedestal bolts to 18 ft. lbs. (24 Nm).

18. Install, but do not tighten, the bolts retaining the right and left turbo exhaust inlet pipe to the turbo collector.

19. Install the compressor assembly including the hoses and clamps.

20. Install the engine hooks.

21. Raise and support the vehicle.

22. Tighten the bolts retaining the right and left turbo exhaust inlet pipe to the turbo collector to 36 ft. lbs. (49 Nm).

23. Tighten the four inlet pipe the exhaust manifold pipe bolts to 18 ft. lbs. (24 Nm).

24. Install the catalytic converter to the exhaust outlet pipe.

25. Lower the vehicle.

26. Install the exhaust outlet clamp to the turbo.

27. Install the duct tube assembly and tighten the clamps.

Radiator

REMOVAL & INSTALLATION

▶ See Figures 46 thru 55

All gasoline-engine equipped trucks use a cross-flow radiator. In this type, the coolant flows horizontally from a radiator inlet tank to a radiator outlet tank.

Most diesel engines are equipped with copper core downflow (vertical flow) radiators. The 7.3L diesel engine copper core radiator was phased out during the 1995 model year and was replaced with an aluminum downflow radiator.

1. Drain the cooling system.

✸✸ CAUTION

When draining the coolant, keep in mind that cats and dogs are attracted by ethylene glycol antifreeze and are quite likely to drink any that is left in an uncovered container or in puddles on the ground. This will prove fatal in sufficient quantity. Always drain the coolant into a sealable container. Coolant should be reused unless it is contaminated or several years old.

2. Disconnect the transmission cooling lines from the bottom of the radiator, if so equipped.

Item	Part Number	Description
1	—	Turbine Housing (Part of 6K682)
2	—	Exhaust Back Pressure Housing (Part of 6K682)
3	—	Compressor Housing (Part of 6K682)
4	—	Crossover Flange Clamp (Part of 6K682)
5	—	Duct Elbow (Part of 6K682)
6	6K854	Inlet Turbo Pipe
7	6K864	Air Inlet Bracket
8	—	Compressor Manifold

Item	Part Number	Description
9	—	Compressor Outlet (Part of 6K682)
10	—	Exhaust Inlet Flange (Part of 6K682)
11	—	Back Pressure Control Linkage (Part of 6K682)
12	6F089	Bypass Valve Actuator
13	—	Back Pressure Control Valve (Part of 6K682)
14	—	Pedestal Assembly (Part of 6K682)
15	—	Exhaust Back Pressure Housing (Part of 6K682)

88283G02

Fig. 45 Turbocharger components—1994–96 7.3L diesel engine

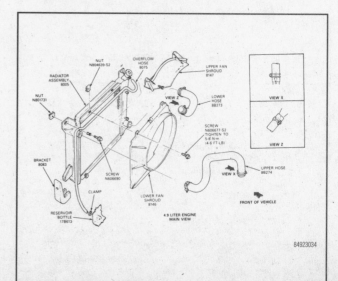

84923034

Fig. 46 4.9L engine radiator

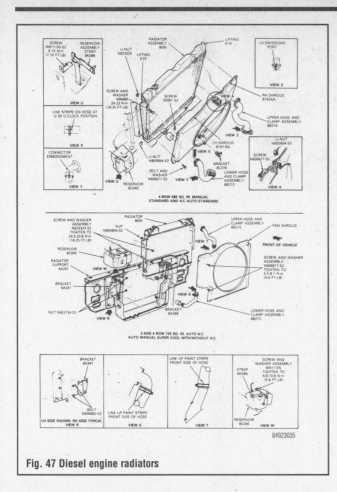

Fig. 47 Diesel engine radiators

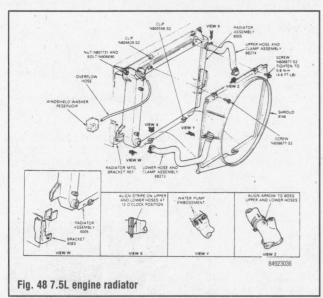

Fig. 48 7.5L engine radiator

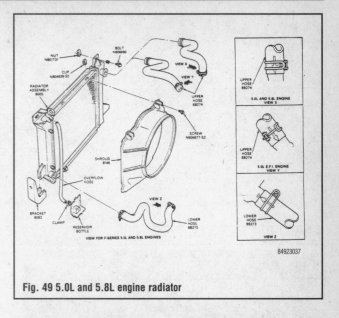

Fig. 49 5.0L and 5.8L engine radiator

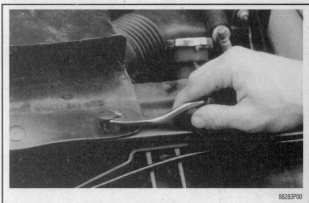

Fig. 50 Remove the air intake duct if applicable

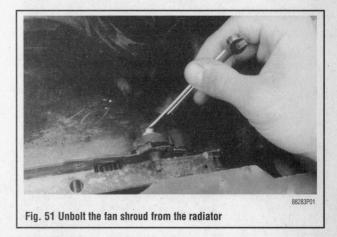

Fig. 51 Unbolt the fan shroud from the radiator

3. If applicable, use a suitable prytool (see photo) to remove the push-in fasteners that retain the air intake duct, then remove the duct from its mounting on the radiator support.

4. Remove the retaining bolts at each of the four corners of the shroud, if so equipped and position the shroud over the fan, clear of the radiator.

5. Disconnect the upper and lower hoses from the radiator.

6. Remove the radiator retaining bolts or the upper supports and lift the radiator from the vehicle.

To install:

7. Lower the radiator into the vehicle. Install the radiator retaining bolts or the upper supports.

8. Connect the upper and lower hoses at the radiator.

9. Install the shroud, if so equipped.

10. If applicable, install the air intake duct.

11. Connect the transmission cooling lines at the bottom of the radiator.

12. Fill the cooling system.

Fig. 52 Lift out the unbolted fan shroud to access the radiator

Fig. 53 Loosen the hose clamps and detach the radiator hoses from the radiator

Fig. 54 Unbolt the radiator from the radiator support

Fig. 55 Lift out the radiator taking care not to damage the cooling fins—do not lay it flat; set it upright

Engine Fan and Fan Clutch

REMOVAL & INSTALLATION

4.9L Engine

▸ See Figures 56 and 57

1. Remove the fan shroud.
2. Remove one of the fan-to-clutch bolts, to access the clutch-to-hub nut.
3. Turn the large fan clutch-to-hub nut COUNTERCLOCKWISE to remove the fan and clutch from the hub. Use holding tool T84T-6312-C and nut wrench T84T-6312-D, or equivalent.
4. If the fan and clutch have to be separated, remove the remaining fa-to-clutch bolts.

To install:

5. Attach the fan to the clutch using all but one of the bolts. The bolts are tightened to 18 ft. lbs. (24 Nm).
6. Install the assembly on the hub and tighten the hub nut to 30–100 ft. lbs. (41–135 Nm).
7. Install and tighten the last fan-to-clutch bolt.
8. Install the shroud.

5.0L, 5.8L and 7.5L Engines

▸ See Figures 58 and 59

1. If you need the clearance, remove the fan shroud and, if necessary, the radiator.
2. Remove the four fan clutch-to-water pump hub bolts and lift off the fan/clutch assembly.
3. Remove the four fan-to-clutch bolts and separate the fan from the clutch.
4. Installation is the reverse of removal. Tighten all the bolts to 18 ft. lbs. (24 Nm).

6.9L and 7.3L Diesel Engines

▸ See Figure 60

1. Remove the fan shroud.
2. Turn the large fan clutch-to-hub nut CLOCKWISE (left-handed threads) to remove the fan and clutch from the hub. There are 2 tools made for this purpose, holding tool T84T-6312-A and nut wrench T84T-6312-B.
3. If the fan and clutch have to be separated, remove the fan-to-clutch bolts.

To install:

4. Attach the fan to the clutch. Tighten the bolts to 18 ft. lbs. (24 Nm).
5. Install the assembly on the hub and tighten the hub nut to a maximum of 113 ft. lbs. (153 Nm). Remember, the nut is left-handed. Tighten it by turning it COUNTERCLOCKWISE.
6. Install the fan shroud.

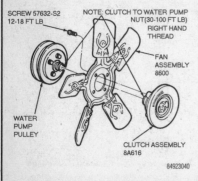

Fig. 56 Fan and clutch assembly for the 4.9L engine

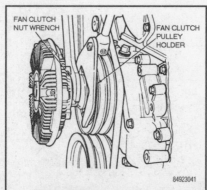

Fig. 57 Loosening the fan clutch on the 4.9L engine

Fig. 58 Remove the four bolts holding the fan clutch to the water pump hub—5.0L,

Fig. 59 Remove the engine fan from the vehicle

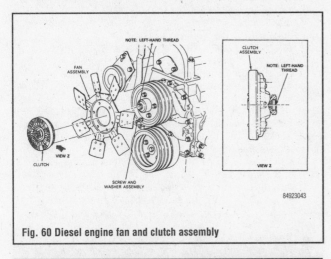

Fig. 60 Diesel engine fan and clutch assembly

Water Pump

REMOVAL & INSTALLATION

4.9L Engine

1. Drain the cooling system.

✳✳ CAUTION

When draining the coolant, keep in mind that cats and dogs are attracted by ethylene glycol antifreeze and are quite likely to drink any that is left in an uncovered container or in puddles on the ground. This will prove fatal in sufficient quantity. Always drain the coolant into a sealable container. Coolant should be reused unless it is contaminated or several years old.

2. Disconnect the lower radiator hose from the water pump.
3. Remove the drive belt, fan, fan spacer, fan shroud, if so equipped and water pump pulley.
4. Remove the alternator pivot arm from the pump.
5. Disconnect the heater hose at the water pump.
6. Remove the water pump.

To install:

7. Before installing the old water pump, clean the gasket mounting surfaces on the pump and on the cylinder block. If a new water pump is being installed, remove the heater hose fitting from the old pump and install it on the new one.
8. Coat the new gaskets with sealer on both sides and install the water pump. Tighten the mounting bolts to 18 ft. lbs. (24 Nm).
9. Connect the heater hose at the water pump.
10. Install the alternator pivot arm on the pump.
11. Install the water pump pulley fan shroud, fan spacer, fan and drive belt.
12. Connect the lower radiator hose at the water pump.
13. Fill the cooling system.

5.0L, 5.8L and 7.5L Engines

▶ See Figures 61, 62, 63, 64 and 65

1. Drain the cooling system.

✳✳ CAUTION

When draining the coolant, keep in mind that cats and dogs are attracted by ethylene glycol antifreeze and are quite likely to drink any that is left in an uncovered container or in puddles on the ground. This will prove fatal in sufficient quantity. Always drain the coolant into a sealable container. Coolant should be reused unless it is contaminated or several years old.

2. Remove the bolts securing the fan shroud to the radiator, if so equipped and position the shroud over the fan.
3. Disconnect the lower radiator hose, heater hose and by-pass hose at the water pump. Remove the drive belt(s), fan, fan spacer and pulley. Remove the fan shroud, if so equipped.
4. Loosen the alternator pivot bolt and the bolt attaching the alternator adjusting arm to the water pump. If applicable, remove the power steering pump bracket from the water pump and position it out of the way.

➡ It may be easier to remove the pulley from the water pump shaft by using belt tension to hold the pulley prior to removal.

5. Remove the bolts securing the water pump to the timing chain cover and remove the water pump.

To install:

6. Coat a new gasket with sealer and install the water pump. Tighten the bolts to 18 ft. lbs. (24 Nm).
7. Install the power steering pump bracket.
8. Connect the lower radiator hose, heater hose and by-pass hose at the water pump.

Fig. 61 Removing the pulley from the water pump shaft may be easier if you use belt tension to hold the pulley

Fig. 62 Loosen the clamp and remove the hoses at the water pump

Fig. 63 Unbolt the water pump from the timing chain cover

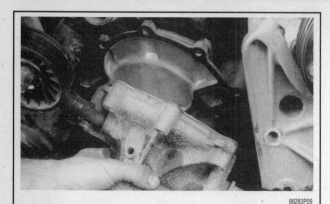

Fig. 64 Remove the water pump from the timing chain cover

Fig. 65 Make sure the gasket mating surfaces are clean and dry

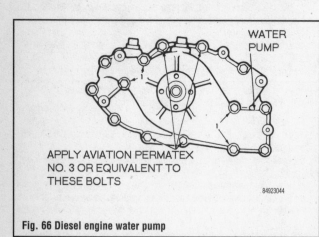

WATER PUMP

APPLY AVIATION PERMATEX NO. 3 OR EQUIVALENT TO THESE BOLTS

Fig. 66 Diesel engine water pump

9. Install the fan shroud, if so equipped.
10. Install the pulley, fan spacer, fan and drive belt(s).
11. Fill the cooling system.

6.9L and 7.3L Diesel Engines

▶ See Figure 66

1. Disconnect both negative battery cables.

✳✳ CAUTION

When draining the coolant, keep in mind that cats and dogs are attracted by ethylene glycol antifreeze and are quite likely to drink any that is left in an uncovered container or in puddles on the

ground. This will prove fatal in sufficient quantity. Always drain the coolant into a sealable container. Coolant should be reused unless it is contaminated or several years old.

2. Drain the cooling system.
3. Remove the radiator shroud halves.
4. Remove the fan clutch and fan.

➡The fan clutch bolts are left-hand thread. Remove them by turning them CLOCKWISE.

5. Remove the power steering pump belt.
6. Remove the air conditioning compressor belt.
7. Remove the vacuum pump drive belt.
8. Remove the alternator drive belt.
9. Remove the water pump pulley.
10. Disconnect the heater hose at the water pump.
11. If you're installing a new pump, remove the heater hose fitting from the old pump at this time.
12. Remove the alternator adjusting arm and bracket.
13. Unbolt the air conditioning compressor and position it out of the way. DO NOT DISCONNECT THE REFRIGERANT LINES!
14. Remove the air conditioning compressor brackets.
15. Unbolt the power steering pump and bracket and position it out of the way. DO NOT DISCONNECT THE POWER STEERING FLUID LINES!
16. Remove the bolts attaching the water pump to the front cover and lift off the pump.
17. Thoroughly clean the mating surfaces of the pump and front cover.
18. Get a hold of two dowel pins—anything that will fit into 2 mounting bolt holes in the front cover. You'll need these to ensure proper bolt hole alignment when you're installing the water pump.
19. Using a new gasket, position the water pump over the dowel pins and into place on the front cover.
20. Install the attaching bolts. The two top center and two bottom center bolts must be coated with RTV silicone sealant prior to installation. See the illustration. Also, the four bolts marked No. 1 in the illustration are a different length than the other bolts. Tighten the bolts to 14 ft. lbs. (19 Nm).
21. Install the water pump pulley.
22. Wrap the heater hose fitting threads with Teflon® tape and screw it into the water pump. Torque it to 18 ft. lbs.
23. Connect the heater hose to the pump.
24. Install the power steering pump and bracket. Install the belt.
25. Install the air conditioning compressor bracket.
26. Install the air conditioning compressor. Install the belt.
27. Install the alternator adjusting arm and install the belt.
28. Install the vacuum pump drive belt.
29. Adjust all the drive belt(s).
30. Install the fan and clutch. Remember that the bolts are left-hand thread. Turn them COUNTERCLOCKWISE to tighten them. Tighten them to 113 ft. lbs. (153 Nm).
31. Install the fan shroud halves.
32. Fill and bleed the cooling system.
33. Connect both negative battery cables.
34. Start the engine and check for leaks.

Cylinder Head

REMOVAL & INSTALLATION

4.9L Engine

▶ See Figure 67

1. Disconnect the negative battery cable.
2. Drain the cooling system.
3. If extra working space is desired, remove the hood.
4. Remove the throttle body inlet tubes.
5. Remove the air conditioning compressor.
6. Remove the condenser.
7. Disconnect the heater hoses from the water pump and coolant outlet housing.

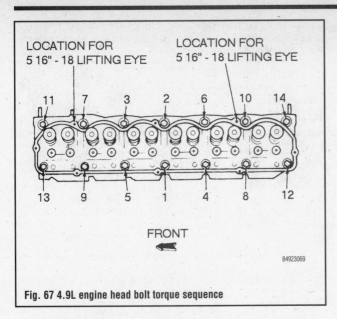

LOCATION FOR 5 16" - 18 LIFTING EYE

LOCATION FOR 5 16" - 18 LIFTING EYE

11   7   3   2   6   10   14

13   9   5   1   4   8   12

FRONT

84923069

Fig. 67 4.9L engine head bolt torque sequence

8. Remove the radiator.

9. Remove the engine fan and fan drive, the water pump pulley and the drive belt.

10. Disconnect the accelerator cable and retracting spring.

11. Disconnect the power brake hose at the manifold.

12. Disconnect the transmission kickdown rod on trucks with automatic transmission.

13. Disconnect the muffler inlet pipe at the exhaust manifold. Pull the muffler inlet pipe down. Remove the gasket.

14. Disconnect the EEC harness from all the sensors.

15. Tag and disconnect all remaining wiring from the head and related components.

16. Remove the alternator, leaving the wires connected and position it out of the way.

17. Remove the air pump and bracket.

18. Remove the power steering pump and position it out of the way with the hoses still connected.

19. If the truck is equipped with an air compressor, bleed the two pressure lines and remove the compressor and bracket.

20. Remove the valve cover.

21. Loosen the rocker arm bolts so they can be pivoted out of the way. Remove the pushrods in sequence so that they can be identified and reinstalled in their original positions.

22. Disconnect the spark plug wires at the spark plugs.

23. Remove the cylinder head bolts and remove the cylinder head. Do not pry between the cylinder head and the block as the gasket surfaces maybe damaged.

To install:

24. Clean the head and block gasket surfaces. If the cylinder head was removed for a gasket change, check the flatness of the cylinder head and block.

25. Position the gasket on the cylinder block.

26. Install a new gasket on the flange of the muffler inlet pipe.

27. Lift the cylinder head above the cylinder block and lower it into position using two head bolts installed through the head as guides.

28. Coat the threads of the Nos. 1 and 6 bolts for the right side of the cylinder head with a small mount of water-resistant sealer. Oil the threads of the remaining bolts. Install, but do not tighten, two bolts at the opposite ends of the head to hold the head and gasket in position.

29. For 1987–94 models, the cylinder head bolts are tightened in 3 progressive steps. Tighten them in the proper sequence as follows:
- Step 1: 50–55 ft. lbs. (68–75 Nm)
- Step 2: 60–65 ft. lbs. (81–88 Nm)
- Step 3: 70–85 ft. lbs. (95–115 Nm)

30. For 1995 models, tighten all bolts in numerical sequence in three steps:
- Step 1: 25–35 ft. lbs. (34–47 Nm)
- Step 2: 48–55 ft. lbs. (65–74 Nm)
- Step 3: Rotate all bolts an additional 80–100°

31. For 1996 models, tighten all bolts in numerical sequence in two steps:
- Step 1: 45–55 ft. lbs. (61–74 Nm)

- Step 2: Rotate all bolts an additional 80–100°

32. Apply Lubriplate® to both ends of the pushrods and install them in their original positions.

33. Apply Lubriplate® to both the fulcrum and seat and position the rocker arms on the valves and pushrods.

34. Adjust the valves, as outlined below.

35. Install the valve cover.

36. The balance of installation is the reverse of removal.

1987 5.8L Engine With 4-Bbl. Carburetor

1. Drain the cooling system.

2. Remove the intake manifold and carburetor.

3. Remove the rocker arm cover(s).

4. If the right cylinder head is to be removed, loosen the alternator adjusting arm bolt and remove the alternator mounting bracket bolt and spacer. Swing the alternator down and out of the way. Remove the air cleaner inlet duct from the right cylinder head assembly.

➡**If the left cylinder head is being removed, remove the bolts fastening the accelerator shaft assembly at the front of the cylinder head. On vehicles equipped with air conditioning, the system must be discharged and the compressor removed. The procedure is best left to an air conditioning specialist. Persons not familiar with air conditioning systems can be easily injured when working on the systems.**

5. Disconnect the exhaust manifold(s) from the muffler inlet pipe(s).

6. Loosen the rocker arm stud nuts so that the rocker arms can be rotated to the side. Remove the pushrods and identify them so that they can be reinstalled in their original positions.

7. Remove the cylinder head bolts and lift the cylinder head from the block.

To install the cylinder head(s):

8. Clean the cylinder head, intake manifold, the valve cover and the head gasket surfaces.

9. A specially treated composition head gasket is used. Do not apply sealer to a composition gasket. Position the new gasket over the locating dowels on the cylinder block. Then, position the cylinder head on the block and install the attaching bolts.

10. The cylinder head bolts are tightened in progressive steps. Tighten all the bolts in the proper sequence to:
- Step 1: 85 ft. lbs. (115 Nm)
- Step 2: 95 ft. lbs. (128 Nm)
- Step 3: 105–112 ft. lbs. (142–151 Nm)

11. Clean the pushrods. Blow out the oil passage in the rods with compressed air. Check the pushrods for straightness by rolling them on a piece of glass. Never try to straighten a bent pushrod; always replace it.

12. Apply Lubriplate® to the ends of the pushrods and install them in their original positions.

13. Apply Lubriplate® to the rocker arms and their fulcrum seats and install the rocker arms. Adjust the valves.

14. Position a new gasket(s) on the muffler inlet pipe(s) as necessary. Connect the exhaust manifold(s) at the muffler inlet pipe(s).

15. If the right cylinder head was removed, install the alternator, ignition coil and air cleaner duct on the right cylinder head. Adjust the drive belt.

16. If the left cylinder head was removed, install the accelerator shaft assembly at the front of the cylinder head.

17. Clean the valve cover and the cylinder head gasket surfaces. Place the new gaskets in the covers, making sure that the tabs of the gasket engage the notches provided in the cover. Install the compressor, evaluate, charge and leak test the system. Let an air conditioning specialist do this.

18. Install the intake manifold and related parts.

19. Fill and bleed the cooling system.

5.0L and 5.8L Fuel Injected Engines

▶ **See Figures 68, 69, 70, 71 and 72**

1. Drain the cooling system.

2. Remove the intake manifold and EFI throttle body.

3. Remove the rocker arm cover(s).

4. If the right cylinder head is to be removed, lift the tensioner and remove the drive belt. Loosen the alternator adjusting arm bolt and remove the alternator mounting bracket bolt and spacer. Swing the alternator down and out of the way. Remove the air cleaner inlet duct.

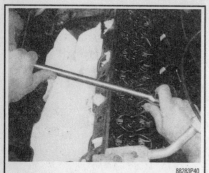

Fig. 68 Use a long breaker bar to ease removal of the cylinder head bolts—5.0L engine shown

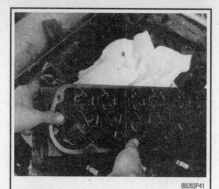

Fig. 69 Lift off the cylinder head from the block and set in a safe location

Fig. 70 Stuff rags in the open cylinders before scraping mating surfaces completely clean

Fig. 71 Use a torque wrench to tighten the cylinder head bolts to the proper torque specification

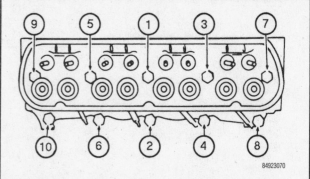

Fig. 72 Cylinder head bolt tightening sequence—all V8 gasoline engines

If the left cylinder head is being removed, remove the air conditioning compressor (see Section 1). Persons not familiar with air conditioning systems should exercise extreme caution, perhaps leaving this job to a professional. Remove the oil dipstick and tube. Remove the cruise control bracket.

5. Disconnect the exhaust manifold(s) from the muffler inlet pipe(s).

6. Loosen the rocker arm stud nuts so that the rocker arms can be rotated to the side. Remove the pushrods and identify them so that they can be reinstalled in their original positions.

7. Disconnect the Thermactor® air supply hoses at the check valves. Cover the check valve openings.

8. Remove the cylinder head bolts and lift the cylinder head from the block. Remove the discard the gasket.

To install the cylinder head(s):

9. Clean the cylinder head, intake manifold, the valve cover and the head gasket surfaces.

10. A specially treated composition head gasket is used. Do not apply sealer to a composition gasket. Position the new gasket over the locating dowels on the cylinder block. Then, position the cylinder head on the block and install the attaching bolts.

11. For 1987–91 models, the cylinder head bolts are tightened in progressive steps. Tighten all the bolts in the proper sequence to:

5.0L Engines
- Step 1: 55–65 ft. lbs. (75–88 Nm)
- Step 2: 66–72 ft. lbs. (89–97 Nm)

5.8L Engines
- Step 1: 85 ft. lbs. (115 Nm)
- Step 2: 95 ft. lbs. (129 Nm)
- Step 3: 105–112 ft. lbs. (142–151 Nm)

➡All 1995–96 5.0L engines came with the flanged type of bolt only.

12. For 1992–96 models, the cylinder head bolts are tightened in progressive steps. Tighten all the bolts in the proper sequence to:

5.0L engines with FLANGED head bolts
- Step 1: 25–35 ft. lbs. (34–47 Nm)

- Step 2: 45–55 ft. lbs. (61–75 Nm)
- Step 3: Rotate all bolts an additional 85–95°

5.0L engines with HEX head bolts
- Step 1: 55–65 ft. lbs. (75–88 Nm)
- Step 2: 65–72 ft. lbs. (88–98 Nm)

5.8L engines
- Step 1: 95–105 ft. lbs. (129–142 Nm)
- Step 3: 105–112 ft. lbs. (142–151 Nm)

13. Clean the pushrods. Blow out the oil passage in the rods with compressed air. Check the pushrods for straightness by rolling them on a piece of glass. Never try to straighten a bent pushrod; always replace it.

14. Apply Lubriplate® to the ends of the pushrods and install them in their original positions.

15. Apply Lubriplate® to the rocker arms and their fulcrum seats and install the rocker arms. Adjust the valves.

16. Position a new gasket(s) on the muffler inlet pipe(s) as necessary. Connect the exhaust manifold(s) at the muffler inlet pipe(s).

17. The balance of installation is the reverse of removal.

18. Fill and bleed the cooling system.

7.5L Engine With 4-Bbl. Carburetor

1. Drain the cooling system.

2. Remove the intake manifold and carburetor as an assembly.

3. Disconnect the exhaust pipe from the exhaust manifold.

4. Loosen the air conditioning compressor drive belt, if so equipped.

5. Loosen the alternator attaching bolts and remove the bolt attaching the alternator bracket to the right cylinder head.

6. Disconnect the air conditioning compressor from the engine and move it aside, out of the way. Do not discharge the air conditioning system.

7. Remove the bolts securing the power steering reservoir bracket to the left cylinder head. Position the reservoir and bracket out of the way.

8. Remove the valve covers. Remove the rocker arm bolts, rocker arms, oil deflectors, fulcrums and pushrods in sequence so that they can be reinstalled in their original positions.

9. Remove the cylinder head bolts and lift the head and exhaust manifold off the engine. If necessary, pry at the forward corners of the cylinder head against the casting bosses provided on the cylinder block. Do not damage the gasket mating surfaces of the cylinder head and block by prying against them.

10. Remove all gasket material from the cylinder head and block. Clean all gasket material from the mating surfaces of the intake manifold. If the exhaust manifold was removed, clean the mating surfaces of the cylinder head and exhaust manifold. Apply a thin coat of graphite grease to the cylinder head exhaust port areas and install the exhaust manifold.

11. Position two long cylinder head bolts in the two rear lower bolt holes of the left cylinder head. Place a long cylinder head bolt in the rear lower bolt hole of the right cylinder head. Use rubber bands to keep the bolts in position until the cylinder heads are installed on the cylinder block.

12. Position new cylinder head gaskets on the cylinder block dowels. Do not apply sealer to the gaskets, heads, or block.

13. Place the cylinder heads on the block, guiding the exhaust manifold studs into the exhaust pipe connections. Install the remaining cylinder head bolts. The longer bolts go in the lower row of holes.

14. Tighten all the cylinder head attaching bolts in the proper sequence in three stages: 75 ft. lbs. (102 Nm), 105 ft. lbs. (142 (Nm) and finally to 135 ft. lbs. (183 Nm). When this procedure is used, it is not necessary to retighten the heads after extended use.

15. Make sure that the oil holes in the pushrods are open and install the pushrods in their original positions. Place a dab of Lubriplate® to the ends of the pushrods before installing them.

16. Lubricate and install the valve rockers. Make sure that the pushrods remain seated in their lifters.

17. Connect the exhaust pipes to the exhaust manifolds.

18. Install the intake manifold and carburetor assembly. Tighten the intake manifold attaching bolts in the proper sequence to 25–30 ft. lbs. (34–41 Nm)

19. The balance of installation is the reverse of removal.

20. Fill the radiator with coolant.

21. Start the engine and check for leaks.

Fuel Injected 7.5L Engine

1. Drain the cooling system.

2. Remove the upper and lower intake manifolds (see above and Section 5).

3. Disconnect the exhaust pipe from the exhaust manifold.

4. Loosen the air conditioning compressor drive belt, if so equipped.

5. Loosen the alternator attaching bolts and remove the bolt attaching the alternator bracket to the right cylinder head.

6. Disconnect the air conditioning compressor from the engine and move it aside, out of the way. Do not discharge the air conditioning system.

7. Remove the bolts securing the power steering reservoir bracket to the left cylinder head. Position the reservoir and bracket out of the way. On motor home chassis, remove the oil filler tube.

8. Remove the valve covers. Remove the rocker arm bolts, rocker arms, oil deflectors, fulcrums and pushrods in sequence so that they can be reinstalled in their original positions.

9. Remove the cylinder head bolts and lift the head and exhaust manifold off the engine. If necessary, pry at the forward corners of the cylinder head against the casting bosses provided on the cylinder block. Do not damage the gasket mating surfaces of the cylinder head and block by prying against them.

10. Remove all gasket material from the cylinder head and block. Clean all gasket material from the mating surfaces of the intake manifold. If the exhaust manifold was removed, clean the mating surfaces of the cylinder head and exhaust manifold. Apply a thin coat of graphite grease to the cylinder head exhaust port areas and install the exhaust manifold.

11. Position two long cylinder head bolts in the two rear lower bolt holes of the left cylinder head. Place a long cylinder head bolt in the rear lower bolt hole of the right cylinder head. Use rubber bands to keep the bolts in position until the cylinder heads are installed on the cylinder block.

12. Position new cylinder head gaskets on the cylinder block dowels. Do not apply sealer to the gaskets, heads, or block.

13. Place the cylinder heads on the block, guiding the exhaust manifold studs into the exhaust pipe connections. Install the remaining cylinder head bolts. The longer bolts go in the lower row of holes.

14. Tighten all the cylinder head attaching bolts in the proper sequence in three stages: 80–90 ft. lbs. (108–122 Nm), 100–110 ft. lbs. (135–149 Nm) and

finally to 130–140 ft. lbs. (176–190 Nm). When this procedure is used, it is not necessary to retighten the heads after extended use.

15. Make sure that the oil holes in the pushrods are open and install the pushrods in their original positions. Place a dab of Lubriplate® to the ends of the pushrods before installing them.

16. Lubricate and install the valve rockers. Make sure that the pushrods remain seated in their lifters.

17. Connect the exhaust pipes to the exhaust manifolds.

18. Install the upper and lower intake manifolds.

19. Install the air conditioning compressor.

20. Install the power steering reservoir.

21. Apply oil-resistant sealer to one side of the new valve cover gaskets and lay the cemented side in place in the valve cover. Install the covers.

22. Install the alternator. If applicable, adjust the drive belt.

23. Adjust the air conditioning compressor drive belt tension.

24. On motor home chassis, install the oil filler tube.

25. Fill and bleed the cooling system.

26. Start the engine and check for leaks.

1987–93 6.9L and/or 7.3L Diesel Engines

▶ See Figures 73, 74 and 75

1. Disconnect both negative battery cables.

2. Drain the cooling system and remove the radiator fan shroud halves.

3. Remove the radiator fan and clutch assembly using special tool T83T–6312–A and B, or equivalent.

➡This tool (T83T–6312–A and B) is available through Ford Dealers and through many tool rental shops.

➡The fan clutch uses a left-hand thread and must be removed by turning the nut CLOCKWISE.

4. Label and disconnect the wiring from the alternator.

5. Remove the adjusting bolts and pivot bolts from the alternator and the vacuum pump and remove both units.

6. Remove the alternator and vacuum pump.

7. Remove the heater hose from the cylinder head.

8. Remove the fuel injection pump as described in Section 5 under Diesel Fuel System.

9. Remove the intake manifold and valley cover.

10. Jack up the truck and safely support it with jackstands.

11. Disconnect the exhaust pipes from the exhaust manifolds.

12. Remove the clamp holding the engine oil dipstick tube in place and the bolt attaching the transmission oil dipstick to the cylinder head.

13. Lower the truck.

14. Remove the engine oil dipstick tube.

15. Remove the valve covers, rocker arms and pushrods. Keep the pushrods in order so they can be returned to their original positions.

16. Remove the nozzles and glow plugs as described in Section 5 under Diesel Fuel System.

17. Remove the cylinder head bolts and attach lifting eyes, using special tool T70P–6000 or equivalent, to each end of the cylinder heads.

18. Carefully lift the cylinder heads out of the engine compartment and remove the head gaskets.

➡The cylinder head pre-chambers may fall out of the heads upon removal.

To install:

19. Position the cylinder head gasket on the engine block and carefully lower the cylinder head in place.

➡Use care in installing the cylinder heads to prevent the pre-chambers from falling out into the cylinder bores.

20. Install the cylinder head bolt and torque in 4 steps using the sequence shown in the illustration.

➡Lubricate the threads and the mating surfaces of the bolt heads and washers with engine oil.

21. Dip the pushrod ends in clean engine oil and install the pushrods with the copper colored ends toward the rocker arms, making sure the pushrods are fully seated in the tappet pushrod seats.

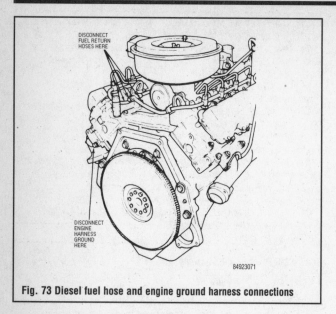

DISCONNECT
FUEL RETURN
HOSES HERE

DISCONNECT
ENGINE
HARNESS
GROUND
HERE

84923071

Fig. 73 Diesel fuel hose and engine ground harness connections

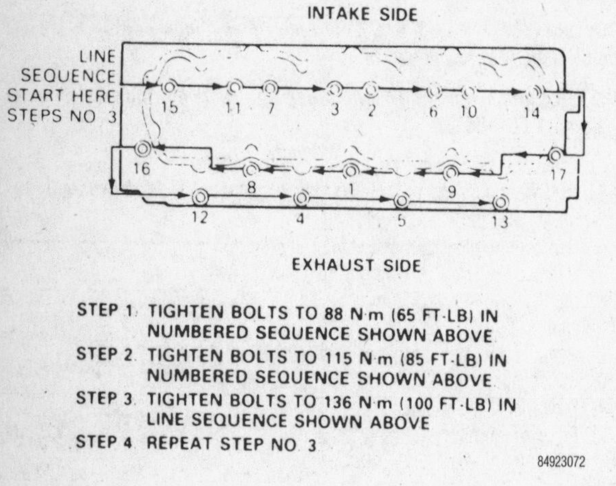

INTAKE SIDE

LINE
SEQUENCE
START HERE
STEPS NO 3

15 11 7   3 2   6 10   14

16   17

8   1   9

12   4   5   13

EXHAUST SIDE

STEP 1 TIGHTEN BOLTS TO 88 N·m (65 FT·LB) IN
         NUMBERED SEQUENCE SHOWN ABOVE

STEP 2 TIGHTEN BOLTS TO 115 N·m (85 FT·LB) IN
         NUMBERED SEQUENCE SHOWN ABOVE

STEP 3 TIGHTEN BOLTS TO 136 N·m (100 FT·LB) IN
         LINE SEQUENCE SHOWN ABOVE

STEP 4 REPEAT STEP NO 3

84923072

Fig. 74 7.3L diesel engine head bolt torque sequence

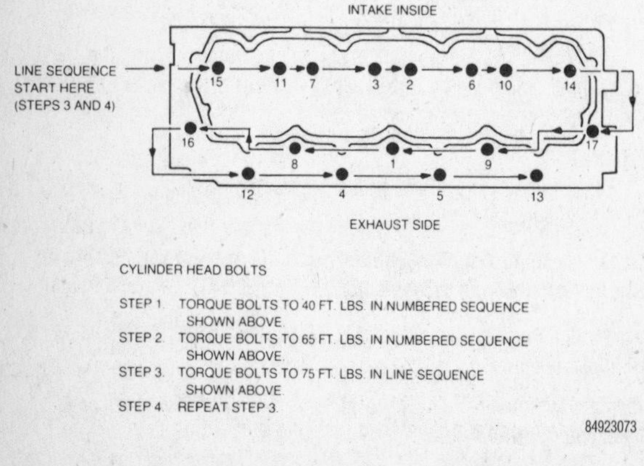

INTAKE INSIDE

LINE SEQUENCE
START HERE
(STEPS 3 AND 4)

15 11 7   3 2   6 10   14

16   17

8   1   9

12   4   5   13

EXHAUST SIDE

CYLINDER HEAD BOLTS

STEP 1 TORQUE BOLTS TO 40 FT. LBS. IN NUMBERED SEQUENCE
         SHOWN ABOVE

STEP 2 TORQUE BOLTS TO 65 FT. LBS. IN NUMBERED SEQUENCE
         SHOWN ABOVE

STEP 3 TORQUE BOLTS TO 75 FT. LBS. IN LINE SEQUENCE
         SHOWN ABOVE

STEP 4 REPEAT STEP 3

84923073

Fig. 75 6.9L diesel engine cylinder head bolt tightening sequence

22. Install the rocker arms and posts in their original positions. Apply Lubriplate® grease to the valve stem tips. Turn the engine over by hand until the timing mark is at the 11 o'clock position as viewed from the front. Install the rocker arm posts, bolts and tighten to 27 ft. lbs. (37 Nm). Install the valve covers.

23. Install the valley pan and the intake manifold.

24. Install the fuel injection pump as described in Section 5 under Diesel Fuel System.

25. Connect the heater hose to the cylinder head.

26. Install the fuel filter, alternator, vacuum pump and their drive belt(s).

27. Install the engine oil and transmission dip stick.

28. Connect the exhaust pipe to the exhaust manifolds.

29. Reconnect the alternator wiring harness and replace the air cleaner. Connect both negative battery cables.

30. Refill and bleed the cooling system.

31. Run the engine and check for fuel, coolant and exhaust leaks.

➡ If necessary, purge the high pressure fuel lines of air by loosening the connector one half to one turn and cranking the engine until a solid stream of fuel, free from any bubbles, flows from the connections.

32. Check the injection pump timing. Refer to Section 5 for these procedures.

33. Install the radiator fan and clutch assembly using special tools T83T–6312A and B or equivalent.

➡ The fan clutch uses a left-hand thread. Tighten by turning the nut COUNTERCLOCKWISE. Install the radiator fan shroud halves.

1994–96 7.3L DI Turbo Diesel Engine

RIGHT CYLINDER HEAD

▶ See Figures 76, 77, 78, 79 and 80

1. Disconnect both negative battery cables.

2. Drain the cooling system.

3. Remove the radiator.

4. Remove the turbocharger assembly.

5. Disconnect the fuel lines by disconnecting them from the rear of both cylinder heads and the fuel pump.

6. Label and disconnect the wiring from the alternator.

7. Remove the adjusting bolts and pivot bolts from the alternator and the vacuum pump and remove both units.

8. Remove the alternator and its bracket.

9. Remove the engine oil dipstick tube.

10. Remove the MAP sensor and position it aside.

11. Remove the valve cover.

12. Remove the connectors from the injectors and glow plugs.

13. Remove the valve cover gasket.

14. Remove the high pressure oil pump supply line to the right cylinder head.

15. Remove the exhaust back pressure line.

16. Remove the three glow plug relay bracket nuts and the ground wire.

17. Disconnect the heater hose from the cylinder head.

18. Remove the outer half of the heater distribution box.

19. Remove the four outboard fuel injector hold-down bolts, retaining screws and four oil deflectors.

⁂ WARNING

Remove the oil drain plugs prior to removing the injectors or oil could enter the combustion chamber which could result in hydrostatic lock and severe engine damage.

20. Remove the oil rail drain plugs.

21. Remove the fuel injectors using Injector Remover No. T94T–9000–AH1, or equivalent. Position the tool's fulcrum beneath the fuel injector hold-down plate and over the edge of the cylinder head. Install the remover screw in the threaded hole of the fuel injector plate (see illustration). Tighten the screw to lift out the injector from its bore. Place the injector in a suitable protective sleeve such as Rotunda Injector Protective Sleeve, No. 014–00933–2, and set the injector in a suitable holding rack.

22. Use a suitable vacuum tool, such as Rotunda Vacuum Pump, No. 021–00037, or equivalent to remove the oil and fuel left over in the injector bores.

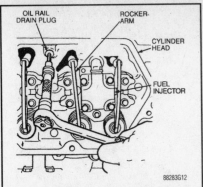

Fig. 76 Remove the oil rail drain plug as shown—7.3L DI turbo diesel engine

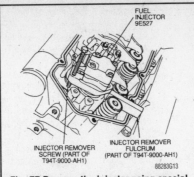

Fig. 77 Remove the injector using special tools as shown—7.3L DI turbo diesel engine

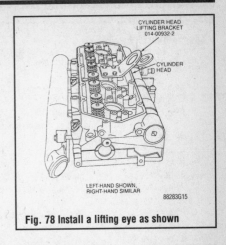

Fig. 78 Install a lifting eye as shown

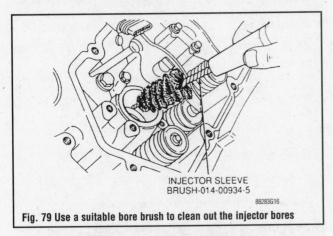

Fig. 79 Use a suitable bore brush to clean out the injector bores

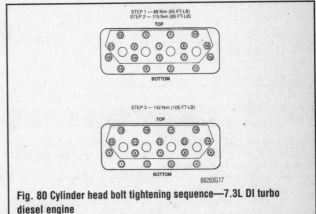

Fig. 80 Cylinder head bolt tightening sequence—7.3L DI turbo diesel engine

23. Remove the rocker arms and pushrods, KEEP EVERYTHING IN ORDER.
24. Remove the four glow plugs.
25. Remove the right turbo exhaust inlet pipe.
26. Remove the ground strap from the rear of the cylinder head.
27. Disconnect the fuel return line at the front of the cylinder head.
28. Remove the four inboard fuel injector shoulder bolts.
29. Remove the cylinder head bolts and attach a Rotunda Cylinder Head Lifting Bracket, 014–00932–2, or equivalent.
30. Carefully lift the cylinder head out of the engine compartment and remove the head gaskets.

To install:

➡ **To prepare a good seat for the fuel injector O-rings, use a suitable injector sleeve brush to clean any debris from the bore.**

31. Carefully clean the cylinder block and head mating surfaces.
32. Position the cylinder head gasket on the engine block and carefully lower the cylinder head in place.
33. Install the cylinder head bolt and torque in 3 steps using the sequence shown in the illustration.

➡ **Lubricate the threads and the mating surfaces of the bolt heads and washers with engine oil.**

34. Connect the fuel return line to the cylinder head.
35. Install the four inboard injector shoulder bolts. Tighten them to 9 ft. lbs. (12 Nm).
36. Install the fuel injectors using special tools as follows:
    a. Lubricate the injectors with clean engine oil. Using new copper washers, carefully push the injectors square into the bore using hand pressure only to seat the O-rings.
    b. Position the open end of Injector Replacer, No. T94T–9000–AH2, or equivalent between the fuel injector body and injector hold-down plate, while positioning the opposite end of the tool over the edge of the cylinder head.
    c. Align the hole in the tool with the threaded hole in the cylinder head and install the bolt from the tool kit. Tighten the bolt to fully seat the injector, then remove the bolt and tool.

37. Install the four outboard fuel injector hold-down bolts, the four oil deflectors and retaining screws. Tighten them to 9 ft. lbs. (12 Nm).
38. Dip the pushrod ends in clean engine oil and install the pushrods with the copper colored ends toward the rocker arms, making sure the pushrods are fully seated in the tappet pushrod seats.
39. Install the rocker arms and posts in their original positions. Apply Lubriplate® grease to the valve stem tips. Turn the engine over by hand until the timing mark is at the 11 o'clock position as viewed from the front. Install the rocker arm posts, bolts and tighten to 27 ft. lbs. (37 Nm). Install the valve covers.
40. Install the fuel rail drain plugs, tightening them to 8 ft. lbs. (11 Nm).
41. Install the oil rail drain plugs, tightening them to 53 inch lbs. (6 Nm).
42. Install the heater distribution box.
43. Install the heater hose to the cylinder head.
44. Install the glow plug relay bracket and ground wire.
45. Install the exhaust back pressure line.
46. Install the oil supply line to the cylinder head, tightening it to 19 ft. lbs. (26 Nm).
47. Install the dipstick tube.
48. Install the MAP sensor and screws.
49. Install the valve cover gasket.
50. Connect the wiring to the fuel injectors and glow plugs.
51. Install the valve cover, tightening the bolts to 8 ft. lbs. (11 Nm).
52. Connect the injector wiring harness to the valve cover gasket.
53. Install the alternator, tightening the bracket bolts to 40–55 ft. lbs. (54–75 Nm).
54. Connect the alternator wiring and install the drive belt.
55. The remainder of the installation is the reverse of the removal. Tighten the fuel pump-to-fuel line banjo bolt to 40 ft. lbs. (54 Nm).
56. Connect both negative battery cables.
57. Refill and bleed the cooling system.
58. Run the engine and check for fuel, coolant and exhaust leaks.

LEFT CYLINDER HEAD

▶ **See Figures 76 thru 80**

1. Disconnect both negative battery cables.
2. Drain the cooling system.
3. Remove the radiator.
4. Remove the turbocharger assembly.
5. Remove the two crankcase breather screws and the breather.
6. Disconnect the wiring from the air conditioning compressor.
7. Remove the four left accessory bracket bolts.
8. Disconnect the vacuum hose at the brake vacuum pump.
9. Disconnect the A/C lines from the compressor.
10. Remove the power steering lines from the pump.
11. Remove the left accessory bracket and accessories as an assembly.
12. Remove the valve cover
13. Disconnect the fuel line assembly between the cylinder heads and fuel pump.
14. Remove the fuel line nut from the intake manifold stud.
15. Disconnect the fuel return line from the cylinder head.
16. Remove the high pressure oil pump supply line from the cylinder head.
17. Raise the vehicle and support it safely on jackstands.
18. Remove the left turbo exhaust pipe from the manifold.
19. Lower the vehicle.
20. Remove the oil rail drain plugs.
21. Remove the four outboard fuel injector hold-down bolts, retaining screws and four oil deflectors.

✱✱ WARNING

Remove the oil drain plugs prior to removing the injectors or oil could enter the combustion chamber which could result in hydrostatic lock and severe engine damage.

22. Remove the oil rail drain plugs.
23. Remove the fuel injectors using Injector Remover No. T94T–9000–AH1, or equivalent. Position the tool's fulcrum beneath the fuel injector hold-down plate and over the edge of the cylinder head. Install the remover screw in the threaded hole of the fuel injector plate (see illustration). Tighten the screw to lift out the injector from its bore. Place the injector in a suitable protective sleeve such as Rotunda Injector Protective Sleeve, No. 014–00933–2, and set the injector in a suitable holding rack.
24. Use a suitable vacuum tool, such as Rotunda Vacuum Pump, No. 021–00037, or equivalent to remove the oil and fuel left over in the injector bores.
25. Remove the rocker arms and pushrods, KEEP EVERYTHING IN ORDER.
26. Remove the four glow plugs.
27. Remove the left turbo exhaust inlet pipe.
28. Remove the main engine harness connectors in the left fender well and position the harness aside.
29. Remove the four inboard fuel injector shoulder bolts.
30. Remove the cylinder head bolts and attach a Rotunda Cylinder Head Lifting Bracket, 014–00932–2, or equivalent.
31. Carefully lift the cylinder head out of the engine compartment and remove the head gaskets.

To install:

➡ **To prepare a good seat for the fuel injector O-rings, use a suitable injector sleeve brush to clean any debris from the bore.**

32. Carefully clean the cylinder block and head mating surfaces.
33. Position the cylinder head gasket on the engine block and carefully lower the cylinder head in place.
34. Install the cylinder head bolt and torque in 3 steps using the sequence shown in the illustration.

➡ **Lubricate the threads and the mating surfaces of the bolt heads and washers with engine oil.**

35. Apply anti-seize paste and install the glow plugs, tightening them to 14 ft. lbs. (19 Nm).
36. Install the four outboard fuel injector hold-down bolts, the four oil deflectors and retaining screws. Tighten them to 9 ft. lbs. (12 Nm).
37. Dip the pushrod ends in clean engine oil and install the pushrods with the copper colored ends toward the rocker arms, making sure the pushrods are fully seated in the tappet pushrod seats.
38. Install the rocker arms and posts in their original positions. Apply Lubriplate® grease to the valve stem tips. Turn the engine over by hand until the timing mark is at the 11 o'clock position as viewed from the front. Install the rocker arm posts, bolts and tighten to 27 ft. lbs. (37 Nm). Install the valve covers.
39. Install the four inboard injector shoulder bolts. Tighten them to 9 ft. lbs. (12 Nm).
40. Install the fuel injectors using special tools as follows:
   a. Lubricate the injectors with clean engine oil. Using new copper washers, carefully push the injectors square into the bore using hand pressure only to seat the O-rings.
   b. Position the open end of Injector Replacer, No. T94T–9000–AH2, or equivalent between the fuel injector body and injector hold-down plate, while positioning the opposite end of the tool over the edge of the cylinder head.
   c. Align the hole in the tool with the threaded hole in the cylinder head and install the bolt from the tool kit. Tighten the bolt to fully seat the injector, then remove the bolt and tool.
41. Install the fuel rail drain plugs, tightening them to 8 ft. lbs. (11 Nm).
42. Install the oil rail drain plugs, tightening them to 53 inch lbs. (6 Nm).
43. Install the heater distribution box.
44. Install the valve cover gasket.
45. Connect the wiring to the fuel injectors and glow plugs.
46. Install the valve cover, tightening the bolts to 8 ft. lbs. (11 Nm).
47. Connect the engine wiring harness.
48. Raise and safely support the vehicle on jackstands.
49. Loosely install the turbo exhaust pipe to the manifold.
50. Lower the vehicle.
51. The remainder of the installation is the reverse of the removal. Tighten the fuel pump-to-fuel line banjo bolt to 40 ft. lbs. (54 Nm).
52. Connect both negative battery cables.
53. Refill and bleed the cooling system.
54. Run the engine and check for fuel, coolant and exhaust leaks.

Valve Lifters

REMOVAL & INSTALLATION

▶ **See Figures 81, 82, 83 and 84**

4.9L Engine

1. Disconnect the inlet hose at the crankcase filler cap.
2. Remove the throttle body inlet tubes.
3. Disconnect the accelerator cable at the throttle body. Remove the cable retracting spring. Remove the accelerator cable bracket from the upper intake manifold and position the cable and bracket out of the way.
4. Remove the fuel line from the fuel rail. Be careful not to kink the line.
5. Remove the upper intake manifold and throttle body assembly (see Section 5).
6. Remove the ignition coil and wires.
7. Remove the rocker arm cover.
8. Remove the spark plug wires.
9. Remove the distributor cap.
10. Remove the pushrod cover (engine side cover).
11. Loosen the rocker arm bolts until the pushrods can be removed. KEEP THE PUSHRODS IN ORDER, FOR INSTALLATION!
12. Using a magnetic lifter removal tool, remove the lifters. Wipe clean the exterior of each lifter as it's removed and mark it with an indelible marker, so that it can be installed in its original bore.

To install:

13. Coat the bottom surface of each lifter with multi-purpose grease and coat the rest of the lifter with clean engine oil.
14. Install each lifter in its original bore using the magnetic tool.
15. Coat each end of each pushrod with multi-purpose grease and install each in its original position. Make sure that each pushrod is properly seated in the lifter socket.
16. Engage the rocker arms with the pushrods and tighten the rocker arm bolts enough to hold the pushrods in place.

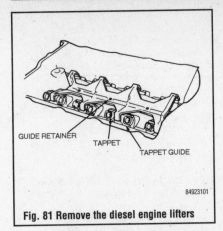

GUIDE RETAINER   TAPPET   TAPPET GUIDE

84923101

Fig. 81 Remove the diesel engine lifters

88283P28

Fig. 82 Remove the lifter from its bore—5.0L engine shown

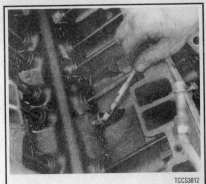

TCCS3812

Fig. 83 A magnet is useful in removing lifters from their bores

TCCS3813

Fig. 84 Stuck lifters must be freed using a slide hammer type lifter removal tool

17. Adjust the valve clearance.
18. Install the pushrod cover (engine side cover).
19. Install the distributor cap.
20. Install the spark plug wires.
21. Install the rocker arm cover.
22. Install the ignition coil and wires.
23. Install the upper intake manifold and throttle body assembly (see Section 5).
24. Install the fuel line at the fuel rail.
25. Install the accelerator cable bracket at the upper intake manifold. Install the cable retracting spring. Connect the accelerator cable at the throttle body.
26. Install the throttle body inlet tubes.
27. Connect the inlet hose at the crankcase filler cap.

5.0L and 5.8L Engines

➡The 1993–96 5.0L engine uses roller lifters.

1. Remove the intake manifold.
2. Disconnect the Thermactor® air supply hose at the pump.
3. Remove the rocker arm covers.
4. Loosen the rocker arm fulcrum bolts until the rocker arms can be rotated off the pushrods.
5. Remove the pushrods. KEEP THE PUSHRODS IN ORDER, FOR INSTALLATION!

6. Using a magnetic lifter removal tool, remove the lifters. Wipe clean the exterior of each lifter as it's removed and mark it with an indelible marker, so that it can be installed in its original bore.

To install:
7. Coat the bottom surface of each lifter with multi-purpose grease and coat the rest of the lifter with clean engine oil.
8. Install each lifter in its original bore using the magnetic tool.
9. Coat each end of each pushrod with multi-purpose grease and install each in its original position. Make sure that each pushrod is properly seated in the lifter socket.
10. Engage the rocker arms with the pushrods and tighten the rocker arm fulcrum bolts to 18–25 ft. lbs. (24–34 Nm). No valve adjustment should be necessary, however, if there is any question as to post-assembly collapsed lifter clearance, see the "Valve Lash" procedure in Section 1.
11. Install the rocker arm covers.
12. Connect the Thermactor® air supply hose at the pump.
13. Install the intake manifold.

7.5L Engine

1. Remove the intake manifold.
2. Remove the rocker arm covers.
3. Loosen the rocker arm fulcrum bolts until the rocker arms can be rotated off the pushrods.
4. Remove the pushrods. KEEP THE PUSHRODS IN ORDER, FOR INSTALLATION!
5. Using a magnetic lifter removal tool, remove the lifters. Wipe clean the exterior of each lifter as it's removed and mark it with an indelible marker, so that it can be installed in its original bore.

To install:
6. Coat the bottom surface of each lifter with multi-purpose grease and coat the rest of the lifter with clean engine oil.
7. Install each lifter in it original bore using the magnetic tool.
8. Coat each end of each pushrod with multi-purpose grease and install each in its original position. Make sure that each pushrod is properly seated in the lifter socket.
9. Rotate the crankshaft by hand until No. 1 piston is at TDC of compression. The firing order marks on the damper will be aligned at TDC with the timing pointer.
10. Engage the rocker arms with the pushrods and tighten the rocker arm fulcrum bolts to 18–25 ft. lbs. (24–34 Nm) in the following sequence:
- No. 1 intake and exhaust
- No. 3 intake
- No. 8 exhaust
- No. 7 intake
- No. 5 exhaust
- No. 8 intake
- No. 4 exhaust
11. Rotate the crankshaft on full turn — 360° — and re-align the TDC mark and pointer. Tighten the fulcrum bolt on the following valves:
- No. 2 intake and exhaust
- No. 4 intake
- No. 3 exhaust

- No. 5 intake
- No. 6 exhaust
- No. 6 intake
- No. 7 exhaust

12. Check the valve clearance as described under "Valve Lash" in Section 1.
13. Install the intake manifold.
14. Install the rocker arm covers.

Diesel Engine

1. Remove the intake manifold.
2. Remove the CDR tube and grommet from the valley pan.
3. Remove the valley pan strap from the front of the block.
4. Remove the valley pan drain plug and lift out the valley pan.
5. Remove the rocker arm covers.
6. Remove the rocker arms. KEEP THEM IN ORDER FOR INSTALLATION!
7. Remove the pushrods. KEEP THEM IN ORDER FOR INSTALLATION!
8. Remove the lifter guide retainer.
9. Using a magnetic lifter removal tool, remove the lifters. Wipe clean the exterior of each lifter as it's removed and mark it with an indelible marker, so that it can be installed in its original bore.

To install:

10. Coat the bottom surface of each lifter with multi-purpose grease and coat the rest of the lifter with clean engine oil.
11. Install each lifter in it original bore using the magnetic tool.
12. Install the lifter guide retainer.
13. Install the pushrods, copper colored end up, into their original locations, making sure that they are firmly seated in the lifters.
14. Coat the valve stem tips with multi-purpose grease and install the rocker arms and posts in their original positions.
15. Turn the crankshaft by hand, until the timing mark is at the 11 o'clock position (viewed from the front).
16. Install all the rocker arm post bolts and tighten them to 20 ft. lbs. (27 Nm).
17. Install the rocker arm covers.
18. Clean all old RTV gasket material from the block and run a ⅛ in. (3mm) bead of new RTV gasket material at each end of the block. Within 15 minutes, install the valley pan. Install the pan drain plug.
19. Install the CDR tube, new grommet and new O-ring.
20. Install the intake manifold and related parts.

Oil Pan

REMOVAL & INSTALLATION

4.9L Engine

1. Drain the crankcase.

❊❊ CAUTION

The EPA warns that prolonged contact with used engine oil may cause a number of skin disorders, including cancer! You should make every effort to minimize your exposure to used engine oil. Protective gloves should be worn when changing the oil. Wash your hands and any other exposed skin areas as soon as possible after exposure to used engine oil. Soap and water, or waterless hand cleaner should be used.

2. Drain the cooling system.

❊❊ CAUTION

When draining the coolant, keep in mind that cats and dogs are attracted by ethylene glycol antifreeze and are quite likely to drink any that is left in an uncovered container or in puddles on the ground. This will prove fatal in sufficient quantity. Always drain the coolant into a sealable container. Coolant should be reused unless it is contaminated or several years old.

3. On 1987–93 models, remove the upper intake manifold and throttle body (see Section 5).

4. Remove the starter.
5. Remove the engine front support insulator to support bracket nuts and washers on both supports. Raise the front of the engine with a transmission jack and wood block and place 1 in. (25mm) thick wood blocks between the front support insulators and support brackets. Lower the engine and remove the transmission jack.
6. Remove the oil pan attaching bolts and lower the pan to the crossmember. Remove the two oil pump inlet tube and screw assembly bolts and drop the assembly in the pan. Remove the oil pan. Remove the oil pump inlet tube attaching bolts. Remove the inlet tube and screen assembly from the oil pump and leave it in the bottom of the oil pan. Remove the oil pan gaskets. Remove the inlet tube and screen from the oil pan.

To install:

7. Clean the gasket surfaces of the oil pump, oil pan and cylinder block. Remove the rear main bearing cap to oil pan seal and cylinder front cover to oil pan seal. Clean the seal grooves.
8. Apply oil-resistant sealer in the cavities between the bearing cap and cylinder block. Install a new seal in the rear main bearing cap and apply a bead of oil-resistant sealer to the tapered ends of the seal.
9. Install new side gaskets on the oil pan with oil-resistant sealer. Position a new oil pan to cylinder front cover seal on the oil pan.
10. Clean the inlet tube and screen assembly and place it in the oil pan.
11. Position the oil pan under the engine. Install the inlet tube and screen assembly on the oil pump with a new gasket. Tighten the screws to 5–7 ft. lbs. (7–9 Nm). Position the oil pan against the cylinder block and install the attaching bolts. Tighten the bolts in sequence to 10–12 ft. lbs. (13–16 Nm).
12. Raise the engine with a transmission jack and remove the wood blocks from the engine front supports. Lower the engine until the front support insulators are positioned on the support brackets. Install the washers and nuts on the insulator studs and tighten the nuts.
13. Install the starter and connect the starter cable.
14. Install the intake manifold and throttle body, if removed.
15. Fill the crankcase and cooling system.
16. Start the engine and check for coolant and oil leaks.

1987 5.8L Engine With 4-Bbl. Carburetor

1. Remove the oil dipstick (on pan entry models only).
2. Remove the bolts attaching the fan shroud to the radiator and position the shroud over the fan.
3. Remove the nuts and lockwashers attaching the engine support insulators to the chassis bracket.
4. If equipped with an automatic transmission, disconnect the oil cooler line at the left side of the radiator.
5. Raise the engine and place wood blocks under the engine supports.
6. Drain the crankcase.

❊❊ CAUTION

The EPA warns that prolonged contact with used engine oil may cause a number of skin disorders, including cancer! You should make every effort to minimize your exposure to used engine oil. Protective gloves should be worn when changing the oil. Wash your hands and any other exposed skin areas as soon as possible after exposure to used engine oil. Soap and water, or waterless hand cleaner should be used.

7. Remove the oil pan attaching bolts and lower the oil pan onto the crossmember.
8. Remove the two bolts attaching the oil pump pickup tube to the oil pump. Remove nut attaching oil pump pickup tube to the number 3 main bearing cap stud. Lower the pick-up tube and screen into the oil pan.
9. Remove the oil pan from the vehicle.
10. Clean oil pan, inlet tube and gasket surfaces. Inspect the gasket sealing surface for damages and distortion due to overtightening of the bolts. Repair and straighten as required.
11. Position a new oil pan gasket and seal to the cylinder block.
12. Position the oil pick-up tube and screen to the oil pump and install the lower attaching bolt and gasket loosely. Install nut attaching to number 3 main bearing cap stud.
13. Place the oil pan on the crossmember. Install the upper pick-up tube bolt. Tighten the pick-up tube bolts.

14. Position the oil pan to the cylinder block and install the attaching bolts. Tighten to 10–12 ft. lbs. (13–16 Nm).

Fuel Injected 5.0L and 5.8L Engines

▶ See Figures 85 thru 95

1. Drain the cooling system.

❊❊ CAUTION

When draining the coolant, keep in mind that cats and dogs are attracted by ethylene glycol antifreeze and are quite likely to drink any that is left in an uncovered container or in puddles on the ground. This will prove fatal in sufficient quantity. Always drain the coolant into a sealable container. Coolant should be reused unless it is contaminated or several years old.

2. Remove the bolts attaching the fan shroud to the radiator and position the shroud over the fan.

3. Remove the upper intake manifold and throttle body (see Section 5).

4. Remove the nuts and lockwashers attaching the engine support insulators to the chassis bracket.

5. If equipped with an automatic transmission, disconnect the oil cooler line at the left side of the radiator.

6. Remove the exhaust system.

7. Raise the engine and place wood blocks under the engine supports.

8. Drain the crankcase.

❊❊ CAUTION

The EPA warns that prolonged contact with used engine oil may cause a number of skin disorders, including cancer! You should make every effort to minimize your exposure to used engine oil. Protective gloves should be worn when changing the oil. Wash your hands and any other exposed skin areas as soon as possible after exposure to used engine oil. Soap and water, or waterless hand cleaner should be used.

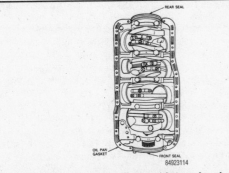

Fig. 85 5.0L and 5.8L engine oil pan gaskets and seals

Fig. 86 Unbolt the engine mounts to allow the oil pan removal—fuel injected 5.0L and 5.8L engines

Fig. 87 Raise the engine slightly—note load dispersing wood block on the jack pad

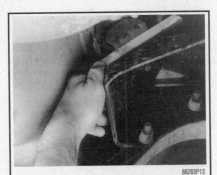

Fig. 88 Insert a wooden block to maintain the clearance gained by jacking up the engine

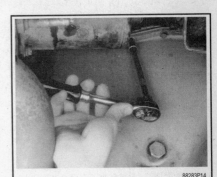

Fig. 89 Remove all the fasteners from the oil pan and set them where they won't get lost

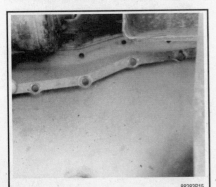

Fig. 90 Remove the stiffener from the pan when unbolted

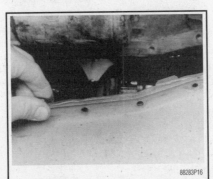

Fig. 91 Lower the pan to access the oil pump pickup tube—fuel injected 5.0L and 5.8L engines

Fig. 92 Remove the two bolts attaching the oil pump pickup tube to the oil pump

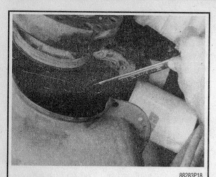

Fig. 93 Remove the nut attaching the oil pump pickup tube to the No. 3 main bearing cap stud

Fig. 94 Lower the pickup tube and screen into the oil pan, then lower the pan from the engine

Fig. 95 Thoroughly scrape and clean the oil pan gasket mating surfaces

9. Support the transmission with a floor jack and remove the transmission crossmember.

10. Remove the oil pan attaching bolts and lower the oil pan onto the crossmember.

11. Remove the two bolts attaching the oil pump pickup tube to the oil pump. Remove the nut attaching the oil pump pickup tube to the No. 3 main bearing cap stud. Lower the pickup tube and screen into the oil pan.

12. Remove the oil pan from the vehicle.

To install:

13. Clean the oil pan, inlet tube and gasket surfaces. Inspect the gasket sealing surface for damages and distortion due to overtightening of the bolts. Repair and straighten as required.

14. Position a new oil pan gasket and seal to the cylinder block.

15. Position the oil pick-up tube and screen to the oil pump and install the lower attaching bolt and gasket loosely. Install nut attaching to number 3 main bearing cap stud.

16. Place the oil pan on the crossmember. Install the upper pick-up tube bolt. Tighten the pick-up tube bolts.

17. Position the oil pan to the cylinder block and install the attaching bolts. Tighten to 10–12 ft. lbs. (13–16 Nm).

18. Install the transmission crossmember.

19. Raise the engine and remove the blocks under the engine supports. Bolt the engine to the supports.

20. Install the exhaust system.

21. If equipped with an automatic transmission, connect the oil cooler line at the left side of the radiator.

22. Install the nuts and lockwashers attaching the engine support insulators to the chassis bracket.

23. Install the upper intake manifold and throttle body (see Section 5).

24. Install the fan shroud.

25. Fill the crankcase.

26. Fill and bleed the cooling system.

1987 7.5L Engine With 4-Bbl. Carburetor

1. Raise and support the truck on jackstands. Remove the oil dipstick.

2. Remove the bolts attaching the fan shroud and position it over the fan.

3. Remove the engine support insulators-to-chassis bracket attaching nuts and washers. Disconnect the exhaust pipe at the manifolds.

4. If the vehicle is equipped with an automatic transmission, disconnect the oil cooler line at the left side of the radiator.

5. Raise the engine with a jack placed under the crankshaft damper and a block of wood to act as a cushion. Place wood blocks under the engine supports.

6. Drain the crankcase. Remove the oil filter.

✳✳ CAUTION

The EPA warns that prolonged contact with used engine oil may cause a number of skin disorders, including cancer! You should make every effort to minimize your exposure to used engine oil. Protective gloves should be worn when changing the oil. Wash your

hands and any other exposed skin areas as soon as possible after exposure to used engine oil. Soap and water, or waterless hand cleaner should be used.

7. Remove the oil pan attaching screws and lower the oil pan onto the crossmember. Remove the two bolts attaching the oil pump pick-up tube to the oil pump. Lower the assembly from the oil pump. Leave it on the bottom of the oil pan. Remove the oil pan and gaskets. Remove the inlet tube and screen from the oil pan.

To install:

8. In preparation for installation, clean the gasket surfaces of the oil pump, oil pan and cylinder block. Remove the rear main bearing cap-to-oil pan seal and engine front cover-to-oil pan seal. Clean the seal grooves.

9. Position the oil pan front and rear seal on the engine front cover and the rear main bearing cap, respectively. Be sure that the tabs on the seals are over the oil pan gasket.

10. Clean the inlet tube and screen assembly and place it in the oil pan.

11. Position the oil pan under the engine and install the inlet tube and screen assembly on the oil pump with a new gasket. Using new gaskets, position the oil pan against the cylinder block and install the retaining bolts.

12. Install the oil filter.

13. Remove the wood blocks and lower the engine.

14. If the vehicle is equipped with an automatic transmission, connect the oil cooler line at the left side of the radiator.

15. Install the engine support insulators-to-chassis bracket attaching nuts and washers. Connect the exhaust pipe at the manifolds.

16. Install the fan shroud.

17. Install the oil dipstick.

18. Fill the crankcase with oil.

Fuel Injected 7.5L Engine

1. Remove the hood.

2. Disconnect the negative battery cable.

3. Drain the cooling system.

✳✳ CAUTION

When draining the coolant, keep in mind that cats and dogs are attracted by ethylene glycol antifreeze and are quite likely to drink any that is left in an uncovered container or in puddles on the ground. This will prove fatal in sufficient quantity. Always drain the coolant into a sealable container. Coolant should be reused unless it is contaminated or several years old.

4. Remove the air intake tube and air cleaner assembly.

5. Disconnect the throttle linkage at the throttle body.

6. Disconnect the power brake vacuum line at the manifold.

7. Disconnect the fuel lines at the fuel rail.

8. Disconnect the air tubes at the throttle body.

9. Remove the radiator.

10. Remove the power steering pump and position it out of the way without disconnecting the lines.

11. Remove the oil dipstick tube. On motor home chassis, remove the oil filler tube.

12. Remove the front engine mount through-bolts.

13. Position the air conditioner refrigerant hoses so that they are clear of the firewall. If necessary, discharge the system and remove the compressor (see Section 1).

14. Remove the upper intake manifold and throttle body (see Section 5).

15. Drain the crankcase. Remove the oil filter.

✲✲ CAUTION

The EPA warns that prolonged contact with used engine oil may cause a number of skin disorders, including cancer! You should make every effort to minimize your exposure to used engine oil. Protective gloves should be worn when changing the oil. Wash your hands and any other exposed skin areas as soon as possible after exposure to used engine oil. Soap and water, or waterless hand cleaner should be used.

16. Disconnect the exhaust pipe at the manifolds.

17. Disconnect the transmission linkage at the transmission.

18. Remove the driveshaft(s).

19. Remove the transmission fill tube.

20. Raise the engine with a jack placed under the crankshaft damper and a block of wood to act as a cushion. Raise the engine until the transmission contacts the underside of the floor. Place wood blocks under the engine supports. The engine MUST remain centralized at a point at least 4 in. (102mm) above the mounts, to remove the oil pan!

21. Remove the oil pan attaching screws and lower the oil pan onto the crossmember. Remove the two bolts attaching the oil pump pick-up tube to the oil pump. Lower the assembly from the oil pump. Leave it on the bottom of the oil pan. Remove the oil pan and gaskets. Remove the inlet tube and screen from the oil pan.

To install:

22. Clean the gasket surfaces of the oil pan and cylinder block.

23. Apply a coating of gasket adhesive on the block mating surface and stick the one-piece silicone gasket on the block.

24. Clean the inlet tube and screen assembly and place on the pump.

25. Position the oil pan against the cylinder block and install the retaining bolts. Torque all bolts to 10 ft. lbs. (13 Nm).

26. Lower the engine and bolt it in place.

27. Install the transmission fill tube.

28. Install the driveshaft(s).

29. Connect the transmission linkage at the transmission.

30. Connect the exhaust pipe at the manifolds.

31. Install the oil filter.

32. Install the upper intake manifold and throttle body (see Section 5).

33. Install the compressor or reposition the hoses.

34. Install the oil dipstick tube. On motor home chassis, install the oil filler tube.

35. Install the power steering pump.

36. Install the radiator.

37. Connect the air tubes at the throttle body.

38. Connect the fuel lines at the fuel rail.

39. Connect the power brake vacuum line at the manifold.

40. Connect the throttle linkage at the throttle body.

41. Install the air intake tube and air cleaner assembly.

42. Fill and bleed the cooling system.

43. Fill the crankcase.

44. Connect the negative battery cable.

45. Install the hood.

6.9L and 7.3L Diesel Engines

1. Disconnect both negative battery cables.

2. Remove the engine oil dipstick.

3. Remove the transmission oil dipstick.

4. Remove the air cleaner and cover the intake opening.

5. Remove the fan and fan clutch.

➡**The fan uses left-hand threads. Remove by turning CLOCKWISE.**

6. Drain the cooling system.

✲✲ CAUTION

When draining the coolant, keep in mind that cats and dogs are attracted by ethylene glycol antifreeze and are quite likely to drink any that is left in an uncovered container or in puddles on the ground. This will prove fatal in sufficient quantity. Always drain the coolant into a sealable container. Coolant should be reused unless it is contaminated or several years old.

7. Disconnect the lower radiator hose.

8. Disconnect the power steering return hose and plug the line and pump.

9. Disconnect the alternator wiring harness.

10. Disconnect the fuel line heater connector from the alternator.

11. Raise and support the front end on jackstands.

12. On trucks with automatic transmission, disconnect the transmission cooler lines at the radiator and plug them.

13. Disconnect and plug the fuel pump inlet line.

14. Drain the crankcase and remove the oil filter.

✲✲ CAUTION

The EPA warns that prolonged contact with used engine oil may cause a number of skin disorders, including cancer! You should make every effort to minimize your exposure to used engine oil. Protective gloves should be worn when changing the oil. Wash your hands and any other exposed skin areas as soon as possible after exposure to used engine oil. Soap and water, or waterless hand cleaner should be used.

15. Remove the engine oil filler tube.

16. Disconnect the exhaust pipes at the manifolds.

17. Disconnect the muffler inlet pipe from the muffler and remove the pipe.

18. Remove the upper inlet mounting stud from the right exhaust manifold.

19. Unbolt the engine from the No. 1 crossmember.

20. Lower the vehicle.

21. Install lifting brackets on the front of the engine.

22. Raise the engine until the transmission contact the body.

23. Install wood blocks between the engine insulators and crossmember: 2¾ in. (70mm) on the left side; 2 in. (50mm) on the right side.

24. Lower the engine onto the blocks.

25. Raise and support the front end on jackstands.

26. Remove the flywheel inspection plate.

27. Position fuel pump inlet line No. 1 rearward of the crossmember and position the oil cooler lines out of the way.

28. Remove the oil pan bolts.

29. Lower the oil pan.

➡**The oil pan is sealed to the crankcase with RTV silicone sealant in place of a gasket. It may be necessary to separate the pan from the crankcase with a utility knife.**

➡**The crankshaft may have to be turned to allow the pan to clear the crankshaft throws.**

30. Clean the pan and crankcase mating surfaces thoroughly.

To install:

31. Apply a ⅛ in. (3mm) bead of RTV silicone sealant to the pan mating surfaces and a ¼ in. (6mm) bead on the front and rear covers and in the corners. You have 15 minutes within which to install the pan!

32. Install locating dowels (which you supply) into position as shown.

33. Position the pan on the engine and install the pan bolts loosely.

34. Remove the dowels.

35. Tighten the pan bolts to 7 ft. lbs. (9 Nm) for ¼ in.—20 bolts; 14 ft. lbs. (19 Nm) for ⁵⁄₁₆ in.—18 bolts; 24 ft. lbs. (32 Nm) for ⅜ in.—16 bolts.

36. Install the flywheel inspection cover.

37. Lower the truss.

38. Raise the engine and remove the wood blocks.

39. Lower the engine onto the crossmember and remove the lifting brackets.

40. Raise and support the front end on jackstands.

41. Tighten the engine-to-crossmember nuts to 70 ft. lbs. (95 Nm).

42. Install the upper inlet pipe mounting stud.

43. Install the inlet pipe, using a new gasket.

44. Install the transmission oil filler tube, using a new gasket.
45. Install the oil pan drain plug.
46. Install a new oil filter.
47. Connect the fuel pump inlet line. Make sure that the clip is installed on the crossmember.
48. Connect the transmission cooler lines.
49. Lower the truck.
50. Connect all wiring.
51. Connect the power steering return line.
52. Connect the lower radiator hose.
53. Install the fan and fan clutch.

➡ **The fan uses left-hand threads. Install by turning COUNTERCLOCK-WISE.**

54. Remove the cover and install the air cleaner.
55. Install the dipsticks.
56. Fill the crankcase.
57. Fill and bleed the cooling system.
58. Fill the power steering reservoir.
59. Connect the batteries.
60. Run the engine and check for leaks.
61. Remove the cover and install the air cleaner.
62. Install the dipsticks.
63. Fill the crankcase.
64. Fill and bleed the cooling system.
65. Fill the power steering reservoir.
66. Connect the batteries.
67. Run the engine and check for leaks.

Oil Pump

REMOVAL & INSTALLATION

Gasoline Engines

1. Remove the oil pan.
2. Remove the oil pump inlet tube and screen assembly.
3. Remove the oil pump attaching bolts and remove the oil pump gasket and intermediate driveshaft.
   To install:
4. Before installing the oil pump, prime it by filling the inlet and outlet port with engine oil and rotating the shaft of the pump to distribute it.
5. Position the intermediate driveshaft into the distributor socket.
6. Position the new gasket on the pump body and insert the intermediate driveshaft into the pump body.
7. Install the pump and intermediate driveshaft as an assembly. Do not force the pump if it does not seal readily. The driveshaft may be misaligned with the distributor shaft. To align it, rotate the intermediate driveshaft into a new position.
8. Install the oil pump attaching bolts. Tighten them on 6-cylinder engines to 12–15 ft. lbs. (16–20 Nm). For 8-cylinder engines, tighten the bolts to 22–32 ft. lbs. (30–43 Nm).
9. Install the oil pan.

Diesel Engines

▶ **See Figures 96 and 97**

1. Remove the oil pan.
2. Remove the oil pick-up tube from the pump.
3. Unbolt and remove the oil pump.
   To install:
4. Assemble the pick-up tube and pump. Use a new gasket.
5. Install the oil pump and tighten the bolts to 14 ft. lbs. (19 Nm).
6. Install the oil pan.

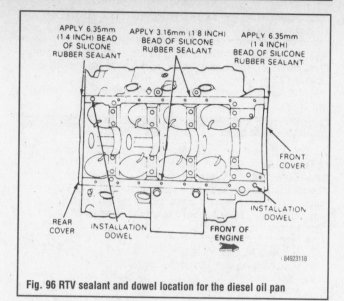

APPLY 6.35mm (1 4 INCH) BEAD OF SILICONE RUBBER SEALANT   APPLY 3.16mm (1 8 INCH) BEAD OF SILICONE RUBBER SEALANT   APPLY 6.35mm (1 4 INCH) BEAD OF SILICONE RUBBER SEALANT

FRONT COVER
INSTALLATION DOWEL
REAR COVER   INSTALLATION DOWEL   FRONT OF ENGINE

84923118

Fig. 96 RTV sealant and dowel location for the diesel oil pan

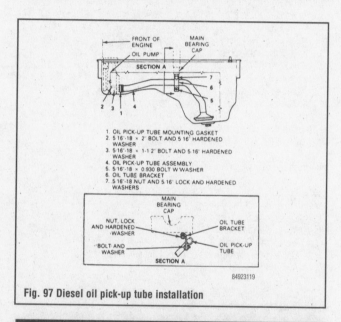

FRONT OF ENGINE   MAIN BEARING CAP
OIL PUMP
SECTION A

1. OIL PICK-UP TUBE MOUNTING GASKET
2. 5 16-18 × 2" BOLT AND 5 16" HARDENED WASHER
3. 5 16-18 × 1-1 2" BOLT AND 5 16" HARDENED WASHER
4. OIL PICK-UP TUBE ASSEMBLY
5. 5 16-18 × 0.930 BOLT W WASHER
6. OIL TUBE BRACKET
7. 5 16-18 NUT AND 5 16" LOCK AND HARDENED WASHERS

MAIN BEARING CAP
NUT, LOCK AND HARDENED WASHER   OIL TUBE BRACKET
BOLT AND WASHER   OIL PICK-UP TUBE
SECTION A

84923119

Fig. 97 Diesel oil pick-up tube installation

Crankshaft Damper

REMOVAL & INSTALLATION

Gasoline Engines

▶ **See Figures 98 thru 106**

1. Remove the fan shroud, if required.
2. If necessary, drain the cooling system and remove the radiator.
3. Remove the drive belt from the pulley.

❊❊ CAUTION

When draining the coolant, keep in mind that cats and dogs are attracted by ethylene glycol antifreeze and are quite likely to drink any that is left in an uncovered container or in puddles on the ground. This will prove fatal in sufficient quantity. Always drain the

coolant into a sealable container. Coolant should be reused unless it is contaminated or several years old.

4. On those engines with a separate pulley, matchmark the pulley to its mount, then remove the retaining bolts to separate the pulley from the vibration damper.

5. Remove the vibration damper/pulley retaining bolt from the crankshaft end.

6. Using a puller, remove the damper/pulley from the crankshaft.

To install:

7. Align the key slot of the pulley hub to the crankshaft key, then install the damper, tightening the retaining hardware to specification.

8. Install the drive belt.

9. Install the radiator and fan shroud.

Diesel Engines

▶ See Figure 107

1. Drain the cooling system.
2. Remove the upper radiator hose.
3. Detach the coolant reservoir hose at the radiator.
4. Remove the fan and clutch assembly using Clutch Nut Wrench T83T–6312–B and Fan Clutch Pulley Holder T94T–6312–AH, or their equivalents. Turn the nut COUNTERCLOCKWISE, it is right-hand threaded. Rest the assembly in the fan shroud until the shroud is removed.
5. Remove the fan shroud and fan and clutch assembly.
6. Remove the radiator.
7. Raise the vehicle and safely support it with jackstands.
8. Remove the flywheel housing cover.

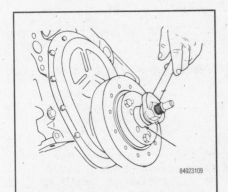

Fig. 98 Vibration damper installation on all gasoline V8 engines

Fig. 99 Removing the front crankshaft seal on all gasoline V8 engines

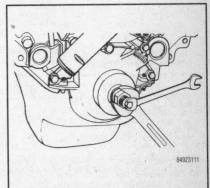

Fig. 100 Install the front crankshaft seal on gasoline V8

Fig. 101 Unbolt the pulley from the crankshaft damper

Fig. 102 White paint makes a good mark to ease installation in the same position

Fig. 103 Remove the pulley from the damper hub

Fig. 104 Remove the crankshaft damper retaining bolt

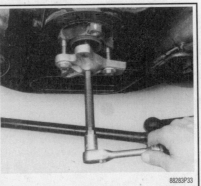

Fig. 105 Use a suitable puller to remove the crankshaft damper

Fig. 106 Once free, remove the crankshaft damper

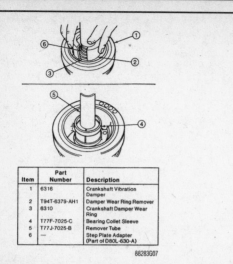

Item	Part Number	Description
1	6316	Crankshaft Vibration Damper
2	T94T–6379–AH1	Damper Wear Ring Remover
3	6310	Crankshaft Damper Wear Ring
4	T77F–7025–C	Bearing Collet Sleeve
5	T77J–7025–B	Remover Tube
6	—	Step Plate Adapter (Part of D80L–630–A)

88283G07

Fig. 107 Special tools used in the removal of the crankshaft damper wear ring—diesel engines

9. Using a breaker bar to prevent the crankshaft from rotating, remove the crankshaft pulley bolt and washer.

10. Remove the crankshaft vibration damper using a suitable puller.

11. Remove the crankshaft damper wear ring by assembling Step Plate Adapter D80L–630–A, Damper Wear Ring Remover T94T–6379–AH1, Bearing Collet Sleeve T77F–7025–C, Remover Tube T77J–7025–B and Forcing Screw T84T–7025–B, or their equivalents to the crankshaft damper. Tighten the forcing screw until the damper wear ring is pulled free from the hub (see illustration).

To install:

12. Assemble Driver Handle T80T–4000–W to Damper Wear Ring Replacer T94T–6379–AH2. Insert the crankshaft damper wear ring into the Damper Wear Ring Replacer T94T–6379–AH2 and position the tool assembly onto the vibration damper.

13. Use a ball peen hammer to seat the wear ring into the hub. Use Loctite® 271, or equivalent to the inside diameter of the wear sleeve to prevent oil from traveling through.

14. Install a new crankshaft front seal.

15. Apply RTV sealant to the damper keyway, then drive on the damper using a suitable installation tool set.

16. Position a breaker bar to prevent the crankshaft from turning, then install the crankshaft pulley bolt and washer, tightening them to specification.

17. Install the radiator, the fan and clutch and fan shroud assembly.

18. Refill and bleed the cooling system.

19. Check the oil level and refill as necessary.

Timing Chain Cover and Seal

REMOVAL & INSTALLATION

5.0L and 5.8L Engines

1. Drain the cooling system and the crankcase.

❖❖❖ CAUTION

The EPA warns that prolonged contact with used engine oil may cause a number of skin disorders, including cancer! You should make every effort to minimize your exposure to used engine oil. Protective gloves should be worn when changing the oil. Wash your hands and any other exposed skin areas as soon as possible after exposure to used engine oil. Soap and water, or waterless hand cleaner should be used.

2. Disconnect the upper and lower radiator hoses from the water pump, transmission oil cooler lines from the radiator and remove the radiator.

3. Disconnect the heater hose from the water pump. Slide the water pump by-pass hose clamp toward the water pump.

4. Loosen the alternator pivot bolt and the bolt which secures the alternator adjusting arm to the water pump. Position the alternator out of the way.

5. Remove the power steering pump and air conditioning compressor from their mounting brackets, if so equipped.

6. Remove the bolts holding the fan shroud to the radiator, if so equipped. Remove the fan, spacer, pulley and drive belt(s).

7. Remove the crankshaft pulley from the crankshaft damper. Remove the damper attaching bolt and washer and remove the damper with a puller.

8. Disconnect the fuel pump outlet line at the fuel pump. Disconnect the vacuum inlet and outlet lines from the fuel pump. Remove the fuel pump attaching bolts and lay the pump to one side with the fuel inlet line still attached.

9. Remove the oil level dipstick and the bolt holding the dipstick tube to the exhaust manifold on the 5.0L.

10. Remove the oil pan-to-cylinder front cover attaching bolts. Use a sharp, thin cutting blade to cut the oil pan gasket flush with the cylinder block. Remove the front cover and water pump as an assembly.

11. Discard the front cover gasket.

To install:

12. Place the front seal removing tool (Ford part no. T70P–6B070–A or equivalent) into the front cover plate and over the front of the seal as shown in the illustration. Tighten the two through bolts to force the seal puller under the seal flange, then alternately tighten the four puller bolts a half turn at a time to pull the oil seal from the cover.

13. Coat a new front cover oil seal with Lubriplate® or equivalent and place it onto the front oil seal alignment and installation tool (Ford part no. T70P–6B070–A or equivalent) as shown in the illustration. Place the tool and the seal onto the end of the crankshaft and push it toward the engine until the seal starts into the front cover.

14. Place the installation screw, washer and nut onto the end of the crankshaft, then thread the screw into the crankshaft. Tighten the nut against the washer and tool to force the seal into the front cover plate. Remove the tool.

15. Apply Lubriplate® or equivalent to the oil seal rubbing surface of the vibration damper inner hub to prevent damage to the seal. Coat the front of the crankshaft with engine oil for damper installation.

16. To install the damper, line up the damper keyway with the key on the crankshaft, then install the damper onto the crankshaft. Install the cap screw and washer and tighten the screw to 80 ft. lbs. (108 Nm). Install the crankshaft pulley.

17. Install the fan, spacer, pulley and drive belt(s).

18. Install the bolts holding the fan shroud to the radiator, if so equipped.

19. Install the power steering pump and air conditioning compressor.

20. Position and tighten the alternator.

21. Connect the heater hose at the water pump.

22. Install the radiator.

23. Connect the upper and lower radiator hoses and transmission oil cooler lines.

24. Fill the cooling system and the crankcase.

7.5L Engine

◆ See Figures 108 and 109

1. Drain the cooling system and crankcase.

❖❖❖ CAUTION

The EPA warns that prolonged contact with used engine oil may cause a number of skin disorders, including cancer! You should make every effort to minimize your exposure to used engine oil. Protective gloves should be worn when changing the oil. Wash your hands and any other exposed skin areas as soon as possible after exposure to used engine oil. Soap and water, or waterless hand cleaner should be used.

2. Remove the radiator shroud and fan.

3. Disconnect the upper and lower radiator hoses and the automatic transmission oil cooler lines from the radiator.

4. Remove the radiator upper support and remove the radiator.

5. Loosen the alternator attaching bolts and air conditioning compressor idler pulley and remove the drive belt(s) with the water pump pulley. Remove the bolts attaching the compressor support to the water pump and remove the bracket (support), if so equipped.

6. Remove the crankshaft pulley from the vibration damper. Remove the

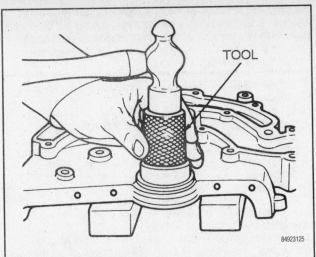

Fig. 108 Installing the oil seal into the 7.5L engine front cover. The tool makes it easier to drive in the seal evenly

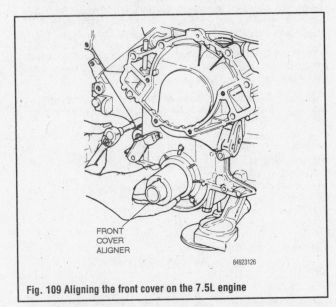

Fig. 109 Aligning the front cover on the 7.5L engine

bolt and washer attaching the crankshaft damper and remove the damper with a puller. Remove the woodruff key from the crankshaft.

7. Loosen the by-pass hose at the water pump and disconnect the heater return tube at the water pump.

8. Disconnect and plug the fuel inlet and outlet lines at the fuel pump and remove the fuel pump.

9. Remove the bolts attaching the front cover to the cylinder block. Cut the oil pan seal flush with the cylinder block face with a thin knife blade prior to separating the cover from the cylinder block. Remove the cover and water pump as an assembly. Discard the front cover gasket and oil pan seal.

To install:

10. Transfer the water pump if a new cover is going to be installed. Clean all of the gasket sealing surfaces on both the front cover and the cylinder block.

11. Coat the gasket surface of the oil pan with sealer. Cut and position the required sections of a new seal on the oil pan. Apply sealer to the corners.

12. Drive out the old front cover oil seal with a pin punch. Clean out the seal recess in the cover. coat a new seal with Lubriplate® or equivalent grease. Install the seal, making sure the seal spring remains in the proper position. A front cover seal tool, Ford part no. T72J–117 or equivalent, makes installation easier.

13. Coat the gasket surfaces of the cylinder block and cover with sealer and position the new gasket on the block.

14. Position the front cover on the cylinder block. Use care not to damage the seal and gasket or misplace them.

15. Coat the front cover attaching screws with sealer and install them.

➤It may be necessary to force the front cover downward to compress the oil pan seal in order to install the front cover attaching bolts. Use a prytool or drift to engage the cover screw holes through the cover and pry downward.

16. Install the fuel pump.

17. Connect the fuel inlet and outlet lines at the fuel pump.

18. Tighten the by-pass hose at the water pump.

19. Connect the heater return tube at the water pump.

20. Install the woodruff key from the crankshaft.

21. Install the damper.

22. Install the crankshaft pulley on the vibration damper.

23. Install the compressor support on the water pump and install the bracket (support), if so equipped.

24. Install the drive belt(s) with the water pump pulley.

25. Install the radiator and upper support.

26. Connect the upper and lower radiator hoses and the automatic transmission oil cooler lines.

27. Install the radiator shroud and fan.

28. Fill the cooling system and crankcase.

Observe the following torques:

- Front cover bolts — 15–20 ft. lbs. (20–27 Nm)
- Water pump attaching screws — 12–15 ft. lbs. (16–20 Nm)
- Crankshaft damper — 70–90 ft. lbs. (95–122 Nm)
- Crankshaft pulley — 35–50 ft. lbs. (47–68 Nm).
- Fuel pump — 19–27 ft. lbs. (26–37 Nm)
- Oil pan bolts — 9–11 ft. lbs. (12–15 Nm) for the 5/16 in. screws and to 7–9 ft. lbs. (9–12 Nm) for the 1/4 in. screws
- Alternator pivot bolt — 45–57 ft. lbs. (61–77 Nm)

Timing Chain Cover and Seal

REMOVAL & INSTALLATION

5.0L, 5.8L and 7.5L Engines

1. Refer to the Water Pump removal procedure and perform all steps except removal of the pump. Leave it attached to the front cover.

2. Remove the crankshaft pulley and vibration damper using a suitable pulley.

3. Remove the oil pan-to-cylinder block front cover attaching bolts. Use a thin bladed knife to cut the oil pan gasket flush with the face of the block prior to separating the cover from the block. Remove the cylinder front cover and water pump as an assembly.

To install:

4. Coat the gasket surface of the oil pan with sealer, then cut and position a new gasket on the oil pan and apply sealer at the corners. Coat the gasket surfaces of the block and cover with Ford Perfect Seal Sealing Compound, or equivalent. Position a new gasket on the block.

5. Position the front cover on the block. Be careful not to damage the seal or dislocate the gasket.

6. Install the cylinder front cover-to-seal alignment using Front Cover Aligner tool No. T61P–6019–B, or equivalent.

7. You may have to force the cover downward to slightly compress the pan gasket. This can be done by using a suitable tool at the front cover attaching hole locations.

8. Coat the threads of the attaching crews with Ford Perfect Seal Sealing Compound, or equivalent, and install the screws. While pushing on the alignment tool, tighten the oil pan-to-front cover attaching screws to 12–18 ft. lbs. (16–24 Nm). Tighten the cover-to-cylinder block attaching screws to 12–18 ft. lbs. (16–24 Nm). Remove the alignment tool.

9. Apply a suitable multi-purpose grease to the oil seal rubbing surface of the vibration damper inner hub to prevent damage to the seal and to the front of the crankshaft for damper installation.

10. Line up the vibration damper keyway with the key on the crankshaft. Install the vibration damper on the crankshaft using Damper Removal/Replacer tool No. T79T–6316–A, or equivalent. Install the capscrew and washer and tighten to 70–90 ft. lbs. (95–122 Nm). Install the crankshaft pulley.

11. Complete the remaining installation steps as found under Water Pump.

12. Fill and bleed the cooling system.

13. Operate the engine at fast idle then shut off the engine. Check the coolant level and for oil leaks. Check and adjust the ignition timing according to the specification on the engine decal.

14. Install the air cleaner and intake duct assembly, including the crankcase ventilation hose.

Timing Gear Cover and Seal

REMOVAL & INSTALLATION

4.9L Engine

▶ See Figure 110

1. Drain the cooling system and disconnect the radiator upper hose at the coolant outlet elbow and remove the two upper radiator retaining bolts.

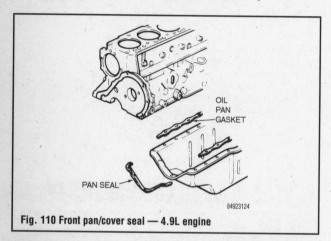

Fig. 110 Front pan/cover seal — 4.9L engine

⁂ CAUTION

When draining the coolant, keep in mind that cats and dogs are attracted by ethylene glycol antifreeze and are quite likely to drink any that is left in an uncovered container or in puddles on the ground. This will prove fatal in sufficient quantity. Always drain the coolant into a sealable container. Coolant should be reused unless it is contaminated or several years old.

2. Raise the vehicle and drain the crankcase.

⁂ CAUTION

The EPA warns that prolonged contact with used engine oil may cause a number of skin disorders, including cancer! You should make every effort to minimize your exposure to used engine oil. Protective gloves should be worn when changing the oil. Wash your hands and any other exposed skin areas as soon as possible after exposure to used engine oil. Soap and water, or waterless hand cleaner should be used.

3. Remove the splash shield and the automatic transmission oil cooling lines, if so equipped, then remove the radiator.

4. Loosen and remove the fan belt, fan and pulley.

5. Use a gear puller to remove the crankshaft pulley damper.

6. Remove the cylinder front cover retaining bolts and gently pry the cover away from the block. Remove the gasket.

7. Drive out the old seal with a pin punch from the rear of the cover. Clean out the recess in the cover.

To install:

8. Coat the new seal with grease and drive it into the cover until it is fully seated. Check the seal to make sure that the spring around the seal is in the proper position.

9. Clean the cylinder front cover and the gasket surface of the cylinder block. Apply an oil-resistant sealer to the new front cover gasket and install the gasket onto the cover.

10. Position the front cover assembly over the end of the crankshaft and against the cylinder block. Start, but do not tighten, the cover and pan attaching screws. Slide a front cover alignment tool (Ford part no. T68P–6019–A or equivalent) over the crank stub and into the seal bore of the cover. Tighten all front cover and oil pan attaching screws to 12–18 ft. lbs. (26–24 Nm) front cover; 10–15 ft. lbs. (13–19 Nm) oil pan, tightening the oil pan screws first.

➡**Trim away the exposed portion of the old oil pan gasket flush with the front of the engine block. Cut and position the required portion of a new gasket to the oil pan and apply sealer to both sides.**

11. Lubricate the hub of the crankshaft damper pulley with Lubriplate® to prevent damage to the seal during installation or on initial starting of the engine.

12. Install the fan belt, fan and pulley.

13. Install the radiator.

14. Install the splash shield and the automatic transmission oil cooling lines, if so equipped.

15. Fill the crankcase.

16. Connect the radiator upper hose at the coolant outlet elbow and install the two upper radiator retaining bolts.

17. Fill and bleed the cooling system.

18. Start the engine and check for leaks.

6.9L and 7.3L Diesel Engines

▶ See Figures 111 thru 118

1. Disconnect both negative battery cables. Drain the cooling system.

⁂ CAUTION

When draining the coolant, keep in mind that cats and dogs are attracted by ethylene glycol antifreeze and are quite likely to drink any that is left in an uncovered container or in puddles on the

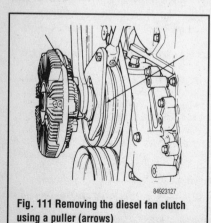

Fig. 111 Removing the diesel fan clutch using a puller (arrows)

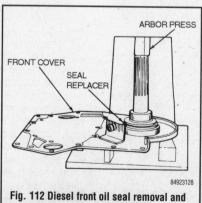

Fig. 112 Diesel front oil seal removal and installation using an arbor press

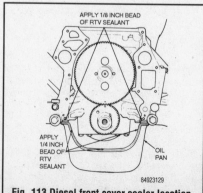

Fig. 113 Diesel front cover sealer location

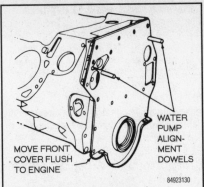

Fig. 114 Front cover installation on diesels, showing the alignment dowels

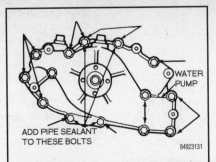

Fig. 115 Water pump-to-front cover installation on the diesel. The two top pump bolts must be no more than 1¼ in. (31.75mm) long

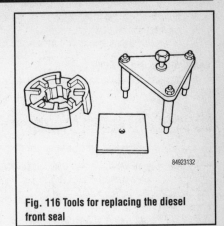

Fig. 116 Tools for replacing the diesel front seal

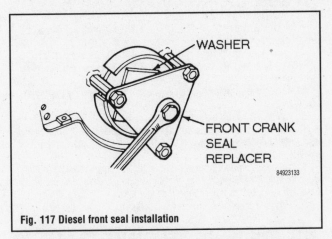

Fig. 117 Diesel front seal installation

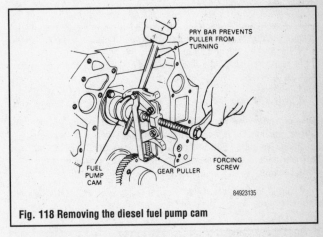

Fig. 118 Removing the diesel fuel pump cam

ground. This will prove fatal in sufficient quantity. Always drain the coolant into a sealable container. Coolant should be reused unless it is contaminated or several years old.

2. Remove the air cleaner and cover the air intake on the manifold with clean rags. Do not allow any foreign material to enter the intake.

3. Remove the radiator fan shroud halves.

4. Remove the fan and fan clutch assembly. You will need a puller or Ford tool No. T83T–6312–A for this.

➡The nut is a left-hand thread; remove by turning the nut CLOCKWISE.

5. Remove the injection pump as described in Section 5 under Diesel Fuel System.

6. Remove the water pump.

7. Jack up the truck and safely support it with jackstands.

8. Remove the crankshaft pulley and vibration damper as described in this section.

9. Remove the engine ground cables at the front of the engine.

10. Remove the five bolts attaching the engine front cover to the engine block and oil pan.

11. Lower the truck.

12. Remove the front cover.

➡The front cover oil seal on the diesel must be driven out with an arbor press and a 3¼ in. (82.5mm) spacer. Take the cover to a qualified machinist or engine specialist for this procedure. See also steps 14 and 15.

To install:

13. Remove all old gasket material from the front cover, engine block, oil pan sealing surfaces and water pump surfaces.

14. Coat the new front oil seal with Lubriplate® or equivalent grease.

15. The new seal must be installed using a seal installation tool, Ford part no. T83T–6700–A or an arbor press. A qualified machinist or engine specialist can handle seal installation as well as removal. When the seal bottoms out on the front cover surface, it is installed at the proper depth.

16. Install alignment dowels into the engine block to align the front cover and gaskets. These can be made out of round stock. Apply a gasket sealer to the engine block sealing surfaces, then install the gaskets on the block.

17. Apply a ⅛ in. (3mm) bead of RTV sealer on the front of the engine block as shown in the illustration. Apply a ¼ in. (6mm) bead of RTV sealer on the oil pan as shown.

18. Install the front cover immediately after applying RTV sealer. The sealer will begin to cure and lose its effectiveness unless the cover is installed quickly.

19. Install the water pump gasket on the engine front cover. Apply RTV sealer to the four water pump bolts illustrated. Install the water pump and hand tighten all bolts.

✳✳ WARNING

The two top water pump bolts must be no more than 1¼ in. (31.75mm) long bolts any longer will interfere with (hit) the engine drive gears.

20. Tighten the water pump bolts to 19 ft. lbs. (25 Nm). Tighten the front cover bolts to specifications according to bolt size (see Torque Specifications chart).

21. Install the injection pump adapter and injection pump as described in Section 5 under Diesel Fuel System.

22. Install the heater hose fitting in the pump using pipe sealant and connect the heater hose to the water pump.

23. Jack up the truck and safely support it with jackstands.

24. Lubricate the front of the crankshaft with clean engine oil. Apply RTV sealant to the engine side of the retaining bolt washer to prevent oil seepage past the keyway. Install the crankshaft vibration damper using Ford Special tools T83T–6316B, or equivalent. Tighten the damper-to-crankshaft bolt to 90 ft. lbs. (122 Nm).

25. Install the fan and fan clutch assembly.

➡The nut is a left-hand thread; Install by turning the nut CLOCKWISE.

26. Install the radiator fan shroud halves.

27. Install the air cleaner.
28. Connect both negative battery cables.
29. Fill the cooling system.

CRANKSHAFT DRIVE GEAR

1. Complete the front cover removal procedures.
2. Install the crankshaft drive gear remover Tool T83T–6316–A, or equivalent, and using a breaker bar to prevent crankshaft rotation, or flywheel holding Tool T74R–6375–A, or equivalent, remove the crankshaft gear.
3. Install the crankshaft gear using Tool T83T–6316–B, or equivalent, aligning the crankshaft drive gear timing mark with the camshaft drive gear timing mark.

➡The gear may be heated to 300–350°F (149–260°C) for ease of installation. Heat it in an oven. Do not use a torch.

4. Complete the front cover installation procedures.

INJECTION PUMP DRIVE GEAR AND ADAPTER

1. Disconnect both negative battery cables.
2. Remove the air cleaner and install an intake opening cover.
3. Remove the injection pump. Remove the bolts attaching the injection pump adapter to the engine block and remove the adapter.
4. Remove the engine front cover. Remove the drive gear.
5. Clean all gasket and sealant surfaces of the components removed with a suitable solvent and dry them thoroughly.
   To install:
6. Install the drive gear in position, aligning all the drive gear timing marks.

➡To determine that the No. 1 piston is at TDC of the compression stroke, position the injection pump drive gear dowel at the 4 o'clock position. The scribe line on the vibration damper should be at TDC. Use extreme care to avoid disturbing the injection pump drive gear, once it is in position.

7. Install the engine front cover. Apply a ⅛ in. (3mm) bead of RTV Sealant along the bottom surface of the injection pump adapter.

➡RTV should be applied immediately prior to adapter installation.

8. Install the injection pump adapter. Apply sealer to the bolt threads before assembly.

➡With the injection pump adapter installed, the injection pump drive gear cannot jump timing.

9. Install all removed components. Run the engine and check for leaks.

➡If necessary, purge the high pressure fuel lines of air by loosening the connector one half to one turn and crank the engine until a solid flow of fuel, free of air bubbles, flows from the connection.

CAMSHAFT DRIVE GEAR, FUEL PUMP CAM, SPACER AND THRUST PLATE

♦ See Figures 119 thru 125

1. Complete the front cover removal procedures.
2. Remove the camshaft Allen screw.
3. Install a gear puller, Tool T83T–6316–A, or equivalent, and remove the gear. Remove the fuel supply pump, if necessary.
4. Install a gear puller, Tool T77E–4220–B and shaft protector T83T–6316–A, or their equivalents, and remove the fuel pump cam and spacer, if necessary.
5. Remove the bolts attaching the thrust plate and remove the thrust plate, if necessary.
6. Install a new thrust plate, if removed.
7. Install the spacer and fuel pump cam against the camshaft thrust flange, using installation sleeve and replacer Tool T83T–6316–B, or equivalent, if removed.
8. Install the camshaft drive gear against the fuel pump cam, aligning the timing mark with the timing mark on the crankshaft drive gear, using installation sleeve and replacer Tool T83T–6316–B, or equivalent.
9. Install the camshaft Allen screw and tighten to 18 ft. lbs. (24 Nm).

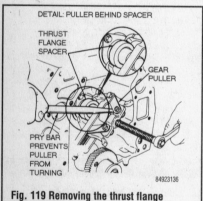

Fig. 119 Removing the thrust flange spacer on diesel engines

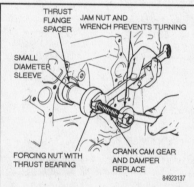

Fig. 120 Installing the thrust flange spacer on diesel engines

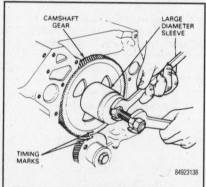

Fig. 121 Installing the diesel camshaft gear

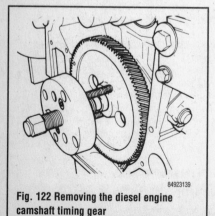

Fig. 122 Removing the diesel engine camshaft timing gear

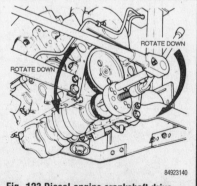

Fig. 123 Diesel engine crankshaft drive gear removal — engine out of truck

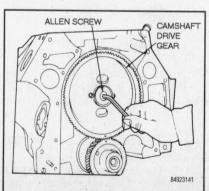

fig. 124 Diesel engine camshaft timing gear installation

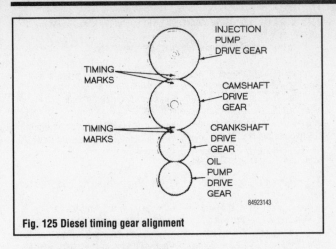

Fig. 125 Diesel timing gear alignment

10. Install the fuel pump, if removed.
11. Install the front cover, following the previous procedure.

CAMSHAFT END-PLAY MEASUREMENT

▶ **See Figures 126 and 127**

The camshaft gears used on some engines are easily damaged if pried upon while the valve train load is on the camshaft. Loosen the rocker arm nuts or rocker arm shaft support bolts before checking the camshaft end-play.

Push the camshaft toward the rear of engine, install and zero a dial indicator, then pry between the camshaft gear and the block to pull the camshaft forward. If the end-play is excessive, check for correct installation of the spacer. If the spacer is installed correctly, replace the thrust plate.

Timing Chain

REMOVAL & INSTALLATION

5.0L, 5.8L and 7.5L Engines

▶ **See Figures 128, 129, 130, 131 and 132**

1. Remove the front cover.
2. Rotate the crankshaft COUNTERCLOCKWISE to take up the slack on the left side of the chain.
3. Establish a reference point on the cylinder block and measure from this point to the chain.
4. Rotate the crankshaft in the opposite direction to take up the slack on the right side of the chain.
5. Force the left side of the chain out with your fingers and measure the distance between the reference point and the chain. The timing chain deflection is the difference between the two measurements. If the deflection exceeds ½ in. (13mm), replace the timing chain and sprockets.

To replace the timing chain and sprockets:

6. Turn the crankshaft until the timing marks on the sprockets are aligned vertically.
7. Remove the camshaft sprocket retaining screw and remove the fuel pump eccentric and washers.
8. Alternately slide both of the sprockets and timing chain off the crankshaft and camshaft until free of the engine.
9. Position the timing chain on the sprockets so that the timing marks on the sprockets are aligned vertically. Alternately slide the sprockets and chain onto the crankshaft and camshaft sprockets.
10. Install the fuel pump eccentric washers and attaching bolt on the camshaft sprocket. Tighten to 40–45 ft. lbs. (54–61 Nm).
11. Install the front cover.

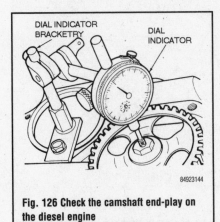

Fig. 126 Check the camshaft end-play on the diesel engine

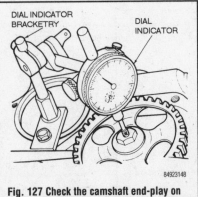

Fig. 127 Check the camshaft end-play on gasoline V8 engine

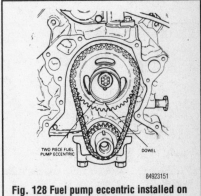

Fig. 128 Fuel pump eccentric installed on the 5.0L and 5.8L engines

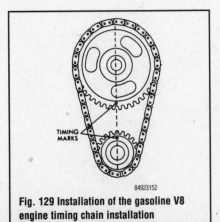

Fig. 129 Installation of the gasoline V8 engine timing chain installation

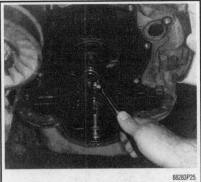

Fig. 130 Unbolt the upper timing chain sprocket

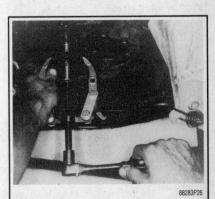

Fig. 131 Use a suitable puller to remove the lower timing chain sprocket

Fig. 132 Keep the timing chain and sprockets together as an assembly

CHECKING TIMING CHAIN DEFLECTION

▶ See Figure 133

To measure timing chain deflection, rotate the crankshaft CLOCKWISE to take up slack on the left side of chain. Choose a reference point and measure the distance from this point and the chain. Rotate the crankshaft in the opposite direction to take up slack on the right side of the chain. Force the left (slack) side of the chain out and measure the distance to the reference point chosen earlier. The difference between the two measurements is the deflection.

The timing chain should be replaced if the deflection measurement exceeds ½ in. (13mm).

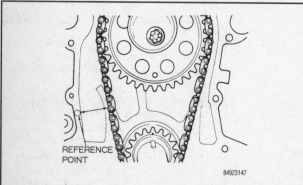

Fig. 133 Check for excessive timing chain deflection—gasoline V8 engines

Timing Gears

REMOVAL & INSTALLATION

4.9L Engine

▶ See Figures 134, 135, 136, 137 and 138

1. Drain the cooling system and remove the front cover.

✷✷ CAUTION

When draining the coolant, keep in mind that cats and dogs are attracted by ethylene glycol antifreeze and are quite likely to drink any that is left in an uncovered container or in puddles on the ground. This will prove fatal in sufficient quantity. Always drain the coolant into a sealable container. Coolant should be reused unless it is contaminated or several years old.

2. Crank the engine until the timing marks on the camshaft and crankshaft gears are aligned.
3. Use a gear puller to removal both of the timing gears.
   To install:
4. Before installing the timing gears, be sure that the key and spacer are properly installed. Align the gear key way with the key and install the gear on the camshaft. Be sure that the timing marks line up on the camshaft and the crankshaft gears and install the crankshaft gear.
5. Install the front cover and assemble the rest of the engine in the reverse order of disassembly. Fill the cooling system.

6.9L and 7.3L Diesel Engines

1. Follow the procedures for timing gear cover removal and installation and remove the front cover.
2. To remove the crankshaft gear, install gear puller (Ford part) no. T83T–6316–A or equivalent and using a breaker bar to prevent the crankshaft from rotating, remove the crankshaft gear. To install the crankshaft gear use tool (Ford part) no. T83T–6316–B or equivalent while aligning the timing marks as shown in the illustration and press the gear into place.
3. The camshaft gear may be removed by taking out the Allen screw and installing a gear puller, Ford part no. T83T–6316–A or equivalent and removing the gear. The gear may be replaced by using tool (Ford part) no. T83T–6316–B or equivalent. Tighten the Allen head screw to 12–18 ft. lbs. (16–24 Nm).

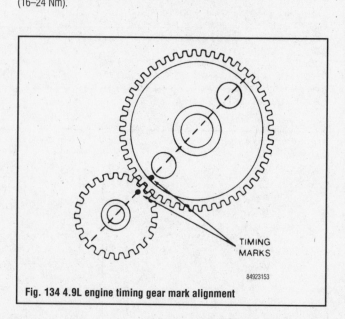

Fig. 134 4.9L engine timing gear mark alignment

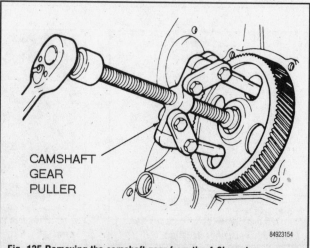

Fig. 135 Removing the camshaft gear from the 4.9L engine

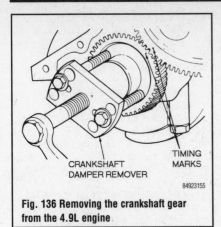

Fig. 136 Removing the crankshaft gear from the 4.9L engine

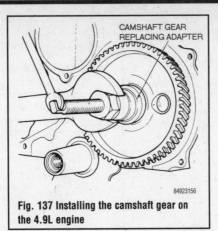

Fig. 137 Installing the camshaft gear on the 4.9L engine

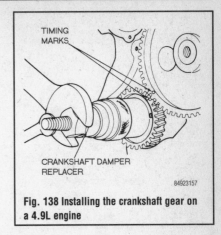

Fig. 138 Installing the crankshaft gear on a 4.9L engine

MEASURING TIMING GEAR BACKLASH

▶ See Figures 139 and 140

Use a dial indicator installed on block to measure timing gear backlash. Hold the gear firmly against the block while making the measurement. If excessive backlash exists, replace both gears.

Camshaft and Bearings

REMOVAL & INSTALLATION

▶ See Figure 141

4.9L Engine

1. Remove the grille, radiator, air conditioner condenser and timing cover.
2. Remove the distributor.
3. Align the timing marks. Unbolt the camshaft thrust plate, working through the holes in the camshaft gear.
4. Loosen the rocker arms, remove the pushrods, take off the side cover and remove the valve lifter with a magnet.
5. Remove the camshaft very carefully to prevent nicking the bearings.

To install:

6. Oil the camshaft bearing journals and use Lubriplate®, or equivalent, on the lobes. Install the camshaft, gear and thrust plate, aligning the gear marks. Tighten down the thrust plate. Make sure that the camshaft end-play is not excessive.
7. Install the distributor. The rotor should be at the firing position for No. 1 cylinder, with the timing gear marks aligned.

8. Install the fan shroud, radiator and air conditioning condenser.
9. Fill the crankcase with oil. Fill the cooling system.

Except 4.9L Engine

▶ See Figure 142

➡On diesel engines, Ford recommends removing the engine for camshaft removal.

1. Remove the intake manifold and valley pan, if so equipped.
2. Remove the rocker covers and either remove the rocker arm shafts or loosen the rockers on their pivots and remove the pushrods. The pushrods must be reinstalled in their original positions.
3. Remove the valve lifters in sequence with a magnet. They must be replaced in their original positions.
4. Remove the timing gear cover and timing chain (timing gear on V8 diesel engines) and sprockets.
5. In addition to the radiator and air conditioning condenser, if so equipped, it may be necessary to remove the front grille assembly and the hook lock assembly to gain the necessary clearance to code the camshaft out of the front of the engine.

➡A camshaft removal tool, Ford part no. T65L–6250–A and adapter 14–0314 are needed to remove the diesel camshaft.

6. Coat the camshaft with engine oil liberally before installing it. Slide the camshaft into the engine very carefully so as not to scratch the bearing bores with the camshaft lobes. Install the camshaft thrust plate and tighten the attaching screws to 9–12 ft. lbs. (12–16 Nm). Measure the camshaft end-play. If the end-play is more than 0.009 in. (0.228mm), replace the thrust plate. Assemble the remaining components in the reverse order of removal.

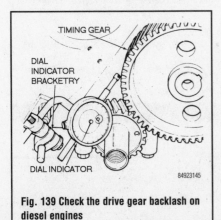

Fig. 139 Check the drive gear backlash on diesel engines

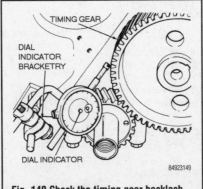

Fig. 140 Check the timing gear backlash on the diesel engines

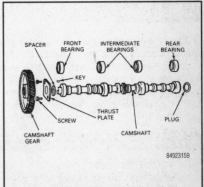

Fig. 141 Exploded view of the camshaft components—4.9L engine shown

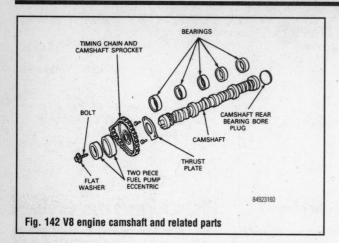

Fig. 142 V8 engine camshaft and related parts

CHECKING CAMSHAFT

Camshaft Lobe Lift

Check the lift of each lobe in consecutive order and make a note of the reading.

1. Remove the fresh air inlet tube and the air cleaner. Remove the heater hose and crankcase ventilation hoses. Remove valve cover(s).
2. Remove the rocker arm stud nut or fulcrum bolts, fulcrum seat and rocker arm.
3. Make sure the pushrod is in the valve tappet socket. Install a dial indicator D78P–4201–B or equivalent, so that the actuating point of the indicator is in the push rod socket (or the indicator ball socket adapter tool 6565–AB is on the end of the push rod) and in the same plane as the push rod movement.
4. Disconnect the I terminal and the S terminal at the starter relay. Install an auxiliary starter switch between the battery and S terminals of the start relay. Crank the engine with the ignition switch off. Turn the crankshaft over until the tappet is on the base circle of the camshaft lobe. At this position, the push rod will be in its lowest position.
5. Zero the dial indicator. Continue to rotate the crankshaft slowly until the push rod is in the fully raised position.
6. Compare the total lift recorded on the dial indicator with the specification shown on the Camshaft Specification chart.

To check the accuracy of the original indicator reading, continue to rotate the crankshaft until the indicator reads zero. If the left on any lobe is below specified wear limits listed, the camshaft and the valve tappet operating on the worn lobe(s) must be replaced.

7. Install the dial indicator and auxiliary starter switch.
8. Install the rocker arm, fulcrum seat and stud nut or fulcrum bolts. Check the valve clearance. Adjust if required (refer to procedure in this section).
9. Install the valve cover(s) and the air cleaner.

Camshaft End-Play

➡On all gasoline V8 engines, prying against the aluminum-nylon camshaft sprocket, with the valve train load on the camshaft, can break or damage the sprocket. Therefore, the rocker arm adjusting nuts must be backed off, or the rocker arm and shaft assembly must be loosened sufficiently to free the camshaft. After checking the camshaft end-play, check the valve clearance. Adjust if required (refer to procedure in this section).

1. Push the camshaft toward the rear of the engine. Install a dial indicator (Tool D78P–4201–F, –G, or equivalent, so that the indicator point is on the camshaft sprocket attaching screw.
2. Zero the dial indicator. Position a prybar between the camshaft gear and the block. Pull the camshaft forward and release it. Compare the dial indicator reading with the specifications.
3. If the end-play is excessive, check the spacer for correct installation before it is removed. If the spacer is correctly installed, replace the thrust plate.
4. Remove the dial indicator.

CAMSHAFT BEARING REPLACEMENT

▶ **See Figure 143**

1. Remove the engine following the procedures in this section and install it on a workstand.
2. Remove the camshaft, flywheel and crankshaft, following the appropriate procedures. Push the pistons to the top of the cylinder.
3. Remove the camshaft rear bearing bore plug. Remove the camshaft bearings with Tool T65L–6250–A, or equivalent.
4. Select the proper size expanding collet and back-up nut and assemble on the mandrel. With the expanding collet collapsed, install the collet assembly in the camshaft bearing and tighten the back-up nut on the expanding mandrel until the collet fits the camshaft bearing.
5. Assemble the puller screw and extension (if necessary) and install on the expanding mandrel. Wrap a cloth around the threads of the puller screw to protect the front bearing or journal. Tighten the pulling nut against the thrust bearing and pulling plate to remove the camshaft bearing. Be sure to hold a wrench on the end of the puller screw to prevent it from turning.
6. To remove the front bearing, install the puller from the rear of the cylinder block.
7. Position the new bearings at the bearing bores and press them in place with tool T65L–6250–A or equivalent. Be sure to center the pulling plate and puller screw to avoid damage to the bearing. Failure to use the correct expanding collet can cause severe bearing damage. Align the oil holes in the bearings with the oil holes in the cylinder block before pressing bearings into place.

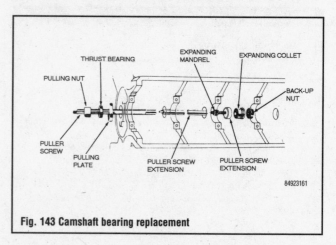

Fig. 143 Camshaft bearing replacement

➡Be sure the front bearing is installed 0.020–0.035 in. (0.508–0.889mm) for the inline six cylinder engines, 0.005–0.020 in. (0.127–0.508mm) for the gasoline V8 engines, 0.040–0.060 in. (1.016–1.524mm) for the diesel V8, below the front face of the cylinder block.

8. Install the camshaft rear bearing bore plug.
9. Install the camshaft, crankshaft, flywheel and related parts, following appropriate procedures.
10. Install the engine in the truck, following procedures described earlier in this section.

Rear Main Seal

REPLACEMENT

Early 1987 7.5L Engines With a 2-Piece Seal

▶ **See Figures 144, 145 and 146**

1. Remove the oil pan and the oil pump (if required).
2. Loosen all the main bearing cap bolts, thereby lowering the crankshaft slightly but not to exceed 1/32 in. (0.8mm).
3. Remove the rear main bearing cap and remove the oil seal from the

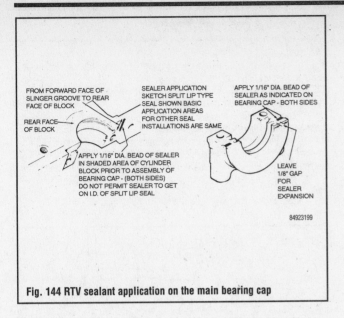

Fig. 144 RTV sealant application on the main bearing cap

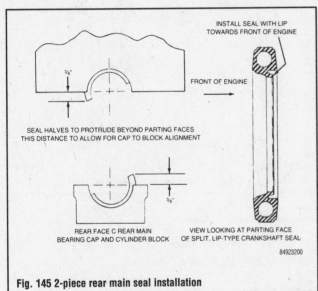

Fig. 145 2-piece rear main seal installation

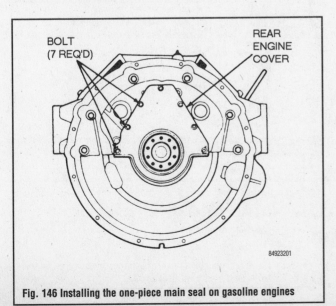

Fig. 146 Installing the one-piece main seal on gasoline engines

bearing cap and cylinder block. On the block half of the seal use a seal removal tool, or install a small metal screw in one end of the seal and pull on the screw to remove the seal. Exercise caution to prevent scratching or damaging the crankshaft seal surfaces.

4. Remove the oil seal retaining pin from the bearing cap if so equipped. The pin is not used with the split-lip seal.

5. Carefully clean the seal groove in the cap and block with a brush and solvent such as lacquer thinner, spot remover, or equivalent, or trichloroethylene. Also, clean the area thoroughly, so that no solvent touches the seal.

6. Dip the split lip-type seal halves in clean engine oil.

7. Carefully install the upper seal (cylinder block) into its groove with undercut side of the seal toward the FRONT of the engine, by rotating it on the seal journal of the crankshaft until approximately ⅜ in. (9.5mm) protrudes below the parting surface.

✸✸ WARNING

Be sure no rubber has been shaved from the outside diameter of the seal by the bottom edge of the groove. Do not allow oil to get on the sealer area.

8. Tighten the remaining bearing cap bolts to the figures listed in the Torque Specifications chart in this section.

9. Install the lower seal in the rear main bearing cap under undercut side of seal toward the FRONT of the engine, allow the seal to protrude approximately ⅜ in. (9.5mm) above the parting surface to mate with the upper seal when the cap is installed.

10. Apply an even ¹⁄₁₆ in. (1.6mm) bead of RTV silicone rubber sealer, to the areas shown, following the procedure given in the illustration.

➡ **This sealer sets up in 15 minutes.**

11. Install the rear main bearing cap. Tighten the cap bolts to specifications.

12. Install the oil pump and oil pan. Fill the crankcase with the proper amount and type of oil.

13. Operate the engine and check for oil leaks.

4.9L, 5.0L and 5.8L Engines; Most 1987 and All 1988–96 7.5L Engines

If the crankshaft rear oil seal replacement is the only operation being performed, it can be done in the vehicle as detailed in the following procedure. If the oil seal is being replaced in conjunction with a rear main bearing replacement, the engine must be removed from the vehicle and installed on a work stand.

1. Remove the starter.

2. Remove the transmission from the vehicle.

3. On manual shift transmission, remove the pressure plate and cover assembly and the clutch disc following the procedure in Section 7.

4. Remove the flywheel attaching bolts and remove the flywheel and engine rear cover plate.

5. Use an awl to punch two holes in the crankshaft rear oil seal. Punch the holes on opposite sides of the crankshaft and just above the bearing cap to cylinder block split line. Install a sheet metal screw in each hole. Use two small pry bars to pry against both screws at the same time to remove the crankshaft rear oil seal. It may be necessary to place small blocks of wood against the cylinder block to provide a fulcrum point for the pry bars. Use caution throughout this procedure to avoid scratching or otherwise damaging the crankshaft oil seal surface.

6. Clean the oil seal recess in the cylinder block and main bearing cap.

7. Clean, inspect and polish the rear oil seal rubbing surface on the crankshaft. Coat the new oil seal and the crankshaft with a light film of engine oil. Start the seal in the recess with the seal lip facing forward and install it with a seal driver. Keep the tool straight with the centerline of the crankshaft and install the seal until the tool contacts the cylinder block surface. Remove the tool and inspect the seal to be sure it was not damaged during installation.

8. Install the engine rear cover plate. Position the flywheel on the crankshaft flange. Coat the threads of the flywheel attaching bolts with oil-resistant sealer and install the bolts. Tighten the bolts in sequence across from each other to the specifications listed in the Torque chart at the beginning of this section.

9. On a manual shift transmission, install the clutch disc and the pressure plate assembly following the procedure in Section 7.

10. Install the transmission, following the procedure in Section 7.

6.9L and 7.3L Diesel Engines

♦ **See Figures 147, 148 and 149**

1. Remove the transmission, clutch and flywheel assemblies.
2. Remove the engine rear cover.
3. Using an arbor press and a 4⅛ in. (104.775mm) diameter spacer, press out the rear oil seal from the cover.

To install:

4. Clean the rear cover and engine block surfaces. Remove all traces of old RTV sealant from the oil pan and rear cover sealing surface by cleaning with a suitable solvent and drying thoroughly.
5. Coat the new rear oil seal with Lubriplate® or equivalent. Using an arbor press and spacer, install the new seal into the cover.

➡ **The seal must be installed from the engine block side of the rear** cover, flush with the seal bore inner surface.

6. Install a seal pilot, Ford part no. T83T–6701B or equivalent onto the crankshaft.
7. Apply gasket sealant to the engine block gasket surfaces and install the rear cover gasket to the engine.
8. Apply a ¼ in. (6mm) bead of RTV sealant onto the oil pan sealing surface, immediately after rear cover installation.
9. Push the rear cover into position on the engine and install the cover bolts and tighten them to 15 ft. lbs. (20 Nm).
10. Position the flywheel on the crankshaft flange. Coat the threads of the flywheel attaching bolts with sealant and install the bolts and flexplate, if equipped. Tighten the bolts to specification, alternating across from each bolt.
11. Install the clutch and transmission. Run the engine and check for oil leaks.

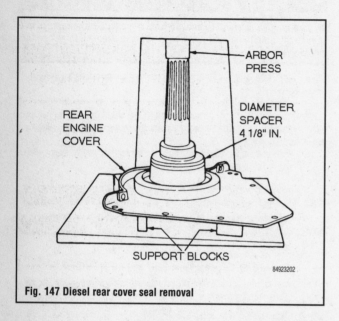

Fig. 147 Diesel rear cover seal removal

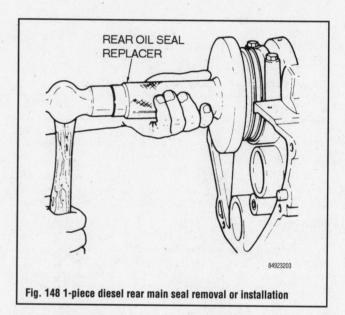

Fig. 148 1-piece diesel rear main seal removal or installation

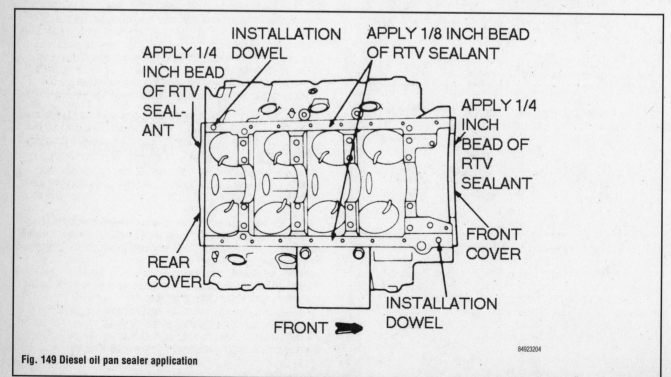

Fig. 149 Diesel oil pan sealer application

Flywheel/Flexplate and Ring Gear

➡Flexplate is the term for a flywheel mated with an automatic transmission.

REMOVAL & INSTALLATION

All Engines

▶ See Figure 150

➡The ring gear is replaceable only on engines mated with a manual transmission. Engines with automatic transmissions have ring gears which are welded to the flexplate.

1. Remove the transmission and transfer case.
2. Remove the clutch, if equipped, or torque converter from the flywheel. The flywheel bolts should be loosened a little at a time in a cross pattern to avoid warping the flywheel. On trucks with manual transmissions, replace the pilot bearing in the end of the crankshaft if removing the flywheel.
3. The flywheel should be checked for cracks and glazing. It can be resurfaced by a machine shop.
4. If the ring gear is to be replaced, drill a hole in the gear between two teeth, being careful not to contact the flywheel surface. Using a cold chisel at this point, crack the ring gear and remove it.
5. Polish the inner surface of the new ring gear and heat it in an oven to about 600°F (316°C). Quickly place the ring gear on the flywheel and tap it into place, making sure that it is fully seated.

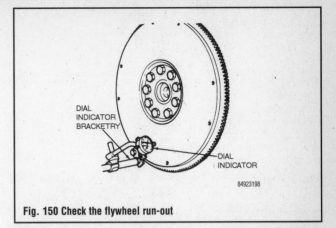

Fig. 150 Check the flywheel run-out

> ✳✳ WARNING
>
> Never heat the ring gear past 800°F (426°C), or the tempering will be destroyed.

6. Position the flywheel on the end of the crankshaft. Tighten the bolts a little at a time, in a cross pattern, to the torque figure shown in the Torque Specifications Chart.
7. Install the clutch or torque converter.
8. Install the transmission and transfer case.

EXHAUST SYSTEM

General Information

➡Safety glasses should be worn at all times when working on or near the exhaust system. Older exhaust systems will almost always be covered with loose rust particles which will shower you when disturbed. These particles are more than a nuisance and could injure your eye.

Whenever working on the exhaust system always keep the following in mind:

• Check the complete exhaust system for open seams, holes loose connections, or other deterioration which could permit exhaust fumes to seep into the passenger compartment.
• The exhaust system is usually supported by free-hanging rubber mountings which permit some movement of the exhaust system, but does not permit transfer of noise and vibration into the passenger compartment. Do not replace the rubber mounts with solid ones.
• Before removing any component of the exhaust system, ALWAYS squirt a liquid rust dissolving agent onto the fasteners for ease of removal. A lot of knuckle skin will be saved by following this rule. It may even be wise to spray the fasteners and allow them to sit overnight.

> ✳✳ CAUTION
>
> Allow the exhaust system to cool sufficiently before spraying a solvent exhaust fasteners. Some solvents are highly flammable and could ignite when sprayed on hot exhaust components.

• Annoying rattles and noise vibrations in the exhaust system are usually caused by misalignment of the parts. When aligning the system, leave all bolts and nuts loose until all parts are properly aligned, then tighten, working from front to rear.
• When installing exhaust system parts, make sure there is enough clearance between the hot exhaust parts and pipes and hoses that would be adversely affected by excessive heat. Also make sure there is adequate clearance from the floor pan to avoid possible overheating of the floor.

Muffler, Catalytic Converter, Inlet and Outlet Pipes

REMOVAL & INSTALLATION

➡The following applies to exhaust systems using clamped joints. Some models, use welded joints at the muffler. These joints will, of course, have to be cut.

1. Raise and support the truck on jackstands.
2. Remove the U-clamps securing the muffler and outlet pipe.
3. Disconnect the muffler and outlet pipe bracket and insulator assemblies.
4. Remove the muffler and outlet pipe assembly. It may be necessary to heat the joints to get the parts to come off. Special tools are available to aid in breaking loose the joints.
5. On Super Cab and Crew Cab models, remove the extension pipe.
6. Disconnect the catalytic converter bracket and insulator assembly.

➡For rod and insulator type hangers, apply a soap solution to the insulator surface and rod ends to allow easier removal of the insulator from the rod end. Don't use oil-based or silicone-based solutions since they will allow the insulator to slip back off once it's installed.

7. Remove the catalytic converter.
8. On models with Managed Thermactor® Air, disconnect the MTA tube assembly.
9. Remove the inlet pipe assembly.
10. Install the components making sure that all the components in the system are properly aligned before tightening any fasteners. Make sure all tabs are indexed and all parts are clear of surrounding body panels (see the accompanying illustrations for proper clearances and alignment).
Observe the following torque specifications:
• Inlet pipe-to-manifold: 35 ft. lbs. (47 Nm)
• MTA U-bolt: 60–96 inch lbs. (7–11 Nm)
• Inlet pipe or converter-to-muffler or extension: 45 ft. lbs. (61 Nm)
• Hanger bracket and insulator-to-frame: 24 ft. lbs. (32 Nm)
• Bracket and insulator-to-exhaust: 15 ft. lbs. (20 Nm)
• Flat flange bolts (7.5L and diesel) 30 ft. lbs. (41 Nm)

1987-96 Gasoline Engines and 1987-93 Diesel Engines
TORQUE SPECIFICATIONS

Component	U.S.	Metric
Air Conditioning Compressor		
6-4.9L		
Mounting bolts	50 ft. lbs.	68 Nm
Compressor manifold bolts	13-17 ft. lbs.	18-23 Nm
V8 Gasoline		
Mounting bolts	32 ft. lbs.	44 Nm
Compressor manifold bolts	13-17 ft. lbs.	18-23 Nm
Diesel		
Mounting bolts	32 ft. lbs.	44 Nm
Compressor manifold bolts	13-17 ft. lbs.	18-23 Nm
Alternator		
Adjusting arm-to-support		
Diesel	40-55 ft. lbs.	54-75 Nm
Adjusting arm-to-water pump		
Diesel	30-40 ft. lbs.	41-54 Nm
Adjusting bolt		
6-4.9L	25 ft. lbs.	34 Nm
8-5.0L, 8-5.8L, 8-7.5L	30-40 ft. lbs.	41-54 Nm
Diesel	40-55 ft. lbs.	54-75 Nm
Bracket-to-engine		
6-4.9L, except bottom bolt	30-40 ft. lbs.	40-55 Nm
6-4.9L, bottom bolt	39-53 ft. lbs.	53-72 Nm
8-5.0L/8-5.8L	40-50 ft. lbs.	54-68 Nm
8-7.5L	30-40 ft. lbs.	41-54 Nm
Diesel	40-55 ft. lbs.	54-75 Nm
Pivot bolt		
6-4.9L	50 ft. lbs.	68 Nm
8-5.0L/8-5.8L		
1987-91	58 ft. lbs.	79 Nm
1992-93	40-50 ft. lbs.	54-68 Nm
8-7.5L	40-53 ft. lbs.	54-71 Nm
Diesel	53-72 ft. lbs.	72-98 Nm
Support bracket-to-water pump		
Diesel	40-55 ft. lbs.	54-75 Nm
Wire terminal nuts	60-90 inch lbs.	7-10 Nm
Bellhousing attaching bolts		
6-4.9L	50 ft. lbs.	68 Nm
8-5.0L/8-5.7L	50 ft. lbs.	68 Nm
8-7.5L	50 ft. lbs.	68 Nm
Diesel	65 ft. lbs.	88 Nm
Camshaft		
Camshaft allen screw		
Diesel	18 ft. lbs.	24 Nm
Gear-to-camshaft		
8-5.0L, 8-5.8L, 8-7.5L	40-45 ft. lbs.	55-61 Nm
Diesel	15 ft. lbs.	20 Nm
Thrust plate attaching screws		
6-4.9L	12-18 ft. lbs.	16-24 Nm
8-5.0L/8-5.8L	9-12 ft. lbs.	12-16 Nm
8-7.5L	70-105 inch lbs.	8-12 Nm
Connecting rod nuts		
6-4.9L	40-45 ft. lbs.	55-61 Nm
8-5.0L	19-24 ft. lbs.	26-32 Nm
8-5.8L	40-45 ft. lbs.	55-61 Nm
8-7.5L	41-45 ft. lbs.	55-61 Nm
Diesel		
Step 1:	38 ft. lbs.	51 Nm
Step 2:	51 ft. lbs.	69 Nm

1987-96 Gasoline Engines and 1987-93 Diesel Engines
TORQUE SPECIFICATIONS

Component	U.S.	Metric
Crankshaft damper		
6-4.9L	130-150 ft. lbs.	177-203 Nm
8-5.0L/8-5.8L	70-90 ft. lbs.	95-122 Nm
8-7.5L	70-90 ft. lbs.	95-122 Nm
Diesel	90 ft. lbs.	122 Nm
Crankshaft pulley-to-damper		
6-4.9L	35-50 ft. lbs.	48-68 Nm
8-5.0L/8-5.8L	40-50 ft. lbs.	54-68 Nm
8-7.5L		
1987-91	35-50 ft. lbs.	48-68 Nm
1992-93	40-53 ft. lbs.	54-71 Nm
Cylinder Head		
6-4.9L		
Step 1:	50-55 ft. lbs.	68-75 Nm
Step 2:	60-65 ft. lbs.	82-88 Nm
Step 3:	70-85 ft. lbs.	95-116 Nm
1987 8-5.0L/8-5.8L w/4-bbl. Carburetor		
Step 1:	85 ft. lbs.	116 Nm
Step 2:	95 ft. lbs.	129 Nm
Step 3:	105-112 ft. lbs.	143-152 Nm
8-5.0L with EFI		
Step 1:	55-65 ft. lbs.	75-88 Nm
Step 2:	66-72 ft. lbs.	90-98 Nm
8-5.8L with EFI		
Step 1:	85 ft. lbs.	116 Nm
Step 2:	95 ft. lbs.	129 Nm
Step 3:	105-112 ft. lbs.	143-152 Nm
8-7.5L with 4-bbl Carburetor		
Step 1:	75 ft. lbs.	102 Nm
Step 2:	105 ft. lbs.	143 Nm
Step 3:	135 ft. lbs.	184 Nm
8-7.5L with EFI		
Step 1:	80-90 ft. lbs.	109-122 Nm
Step 2:	100-110 ft. lbs.	136-150 Nm
Step 3:	130-140 ft. lbs.	177-190 Nm
Diesel		
Step 1:	65 ft. lbs.	88 Nm
Step 2:	90 ft. lbs.	122 Nm
Step 3:	110 ft. lbs.	135 Nm
Distributor holddown bolt	25 ft. lbs.	34 Nm
Engine fan and fan clutch		
6-4.9L		
Fan-to-clutch	18 ft. lbs.	24 Nm
Clutch-to-water pump	30-100 ft. lbs.	41-135 Nm
8-5.0L/8-5.8L/8-7.5L	18 ft. lbs.	24 Nm
Diesel		
Fan-to-clutch	18 ft. lbs.	24 Nm
Hub nut	40-120 ft. lbs.	54-163 Nm
Engine mount nuts		
6-4.9L	70 ft. lbs.	95 Nm
8-5.0L/8-5.7L	80 ft. lbs.	109 Nm
8-7.5L	74 ft. lbs.	101 Nm
Diesel	80 ft. lbs.	109 Nm
Engine-to-crossmember nuts		
Diesel	70 ft. lbs.	95 Nm

84923233

84923234

1987-96 Gasoline Engines and 1987-93 Diesel Engines
TORQUE SPECIFICATIONS

Component	U.S.	Metric
Exhaust Manifold		
6-4.9L	22-32 ft. lbs.	30-43 Nm
8-5.0L/8-5.8L	18-24 ft. lbs.	25-32 Nm
8-7.5L	22-45 ft. lbs.	30-60 Nm
Diesel		
Step 1:	35 ft. lbs.	47 Nm
Step 2: retighten to	35 ft. lbs.	47 Nm
Exhaust pipe to the exhaust manifold		
6-4.9L	25-35 ft. lbs.	34 Nm
8-5.0L/8-5.7L	25-35 ft. lbs.	34-48 Nm
Flywheel-to-crankshaft		
6-4.9L	75-85 ft. lbs.	102-115 Nm
8-5.0L/8-5.8L	75-85 ft. lbs.	102-115 Nm
8-7.5L	75-85 ft. lbs.	102-115 Nm
Diesel		
To crankshaft	47 ft. lbs.	64 Nm
Secondary-to-primary	47 ft. lbs.	64 Nm
Front Cover		
6-4.9L	12-18 ft. lbs.	16-24 Nm
8-5.0L/8-5.8L	12-18 ft. lbs.	17-24 Nm
8-7.5L		
1987-91	15-20 ft. lbs.	20-27 Nm
1992-93	12-18 ft. lbs.	17-24 Nm
Diesel		
¼ in.	7 ft. lbs.	10 Nm
⁵⁄₁₆ in.	14 ft. lbs.	19 Nm
⅜ in.	24 ft. lbs.	32 Nm
Fuel pump-to-block		
6-4.9L	12-18 ft. lbs.	17-24 Nm
Fuel pump eccentric bolt		
V8 Gasoline	40-45 ft. lbs.	54-61 Nm
Glow plugs	12 ft. lbs.	16 Nm
Heater hose fitting		
Diesel	18 ft. lbs.	24 Nm
Intake manifold		
Manifold-to-cylinder head		
6-4.9L	26 ft. lbs.	35 Nm
1987 8-5.0L/8-5.8L w/4-bbl Carburetor	23-25 ft. lbs.	31-34 Nm
1987 8-7.5L w/4-bbl Carburetor	23-25 ft. lbs.	31-34 Nm
8-5.0L/8-5.8L w/EFI	23-25 ft. lbs.	31-34 Nm
8-7.5L w/EFI		
Step 1:	8-12 ft. lbs.	11-16 Nm
Step 2:	12-22 ft. lbs.	16-30 Nm
Step 3:	22-35 ft. lbs.	30-47 Nm
Diesel		
Step 1:	24 ft. lbs.	33 Nm
Step 2: Retighten to	24 ft. lbs.	33 Nm
Upper intake manifold-to-lower		
8-5.0L/8-5.8L	12-18 ft. lbs.	17-24 Nm
Main bearing cap bolts		
6-4.9L	60-70 ft. lbs.	82-94 Nm
8-5.0L	60-70 ft. lbs.	82-94 Nm
8-5.8L	95-105 ft. lbs.	129-142 Nm
8-7.5L	95-105 ft. lbs.	129-142 Nm
Diesel		
Step 1:	75 ft. lbs.	101 Nm
Step 2:	95 ft. lbs.	129 Nm

84923235

1987-96 Gasoline Engines and 1987-93 Diesel Engines
TORQUE SPECIFICATIONS

Component	U.S.	Metric
Exhaust system		
Inlet pipe-to-manifold	35 ft. lbs.	48 Nm
MTA U-bolt	60-96 inch lbs.	7-11 Nm
Inlet pipe or converter-to-muffler or extension	45 ft. lbs.	61 Nm
Hanger bracket and insulator-to-frame	24 ft. lbs.	33 Nm
Bracket and insulator-to-exhaust	15 ft. lbs.	20 Nm
Flat flange bolts		
8-7.5L	30 ft. lbs.	41 Nm
Diesel	30 ft. lbs.	41 Nm
Oil cooler-to-block		
8-7.5L	40-65 ft. lbs.	54-88 Nm
Oil Pan-to-block		
6-4.9L	10-12 ft. lbs.	14-16 Nm
8-5.0L/8-5.8L		
1987-91	10-12 ft. lbs.	14-16 Nm
1992-93	9-11 ft. lbs.	12-14 Nm
8-7.5L		
¼ in.	7-9 ft. lbs.	10-12 Nm
⁵⁄₁₆ in.	8-11 ft. lbs.	11-15 Nm
Diesel		
¼ in.-20 bolts	7 ft. lbs.	10 Nm
⁵⁄₁₆ in.-18 bolts	14 ft. lbs.	19 Nm
⅜ in.-16 bolts	24 ft. lbs.	33 Nm
Oil pan drain plug		
6-4.9L	15-25 ft. lbs.	21-33 Nm
8-5.0L/8-5.8L	15-25 ft. lbs.	21-33 Nm
8-7.5L	15-25 ft. lbs.	21-33 Nm
Diesel	28 ft. lbs.	37 Nm
Oil Pump-to-block		
6-4.9L	12-15 ft. lbs.	16-20 Nm
8-5.0L/8-5.8L		
1987-91	20-25 ft. lbs.	27-34 Nm
1992-93	22-32 ft. lbs.	30-43 Nm
8-7.5L	22-32 ft. lbs.	30-43 Nm
Diesel	14 ft. lbs.	19 Nm
Rocker arm bolts		
6-4.9L	17-23 ft. lbs.	24-31 Nm
8-5.0L/8-5.8L	18-25 ft. lbs.	24-34 Nm
8-7.5L	18-25 ft. lbs.	24-34 Nm
Diesel	20 ft.lbs.	27 Nm
Rocker arm stud-to-head		
8-5.0L/8-5.8L	18-25 ft. lbs.	25-33 Nm
8-7.5L	18-25 ft. lbs.	25-33 Nm
Rocker Covers		
6-4.9L		
1987-91	48-84 inch lbs.	5-9 Nm
1992-93	70-105 inch lbs.	8-12 Nm
8-5.0L/8-5.8L		
1987-91	10-13 ft. lbs.	14-18 Nm
1992-93	36-60 inch lbs.	4-6 Nm
8-7.5L		
1987-91	6-9 ft. lbs.	8-12 Nm
1992-93	9-11 ft. lbs.	12-15 Nm
Diesel	72 inch lbs.	8 Nm
Side cover		
6-4.9L	25-35 inch lbs.	3-4 Nm

84923236

TORQUE SPECIFICATIONS
1987-96 Gasoline Engines and 1987-93 Diesel Engines

Component	U.S.	Metric
Spark plugs		
6-4.9L	10-15 ft. lbs.	14-20 Nm
8-5.0L/8-5.8L	10-15 ft. lbs.	14-20 Nm
8-7.5L	5-10 ft. lbs.	7-13 Nm
Starter Mounting bolts		
Exc. diesel		
Starters w/3 mounting bolts	12-15 ft. lbs.	16-20 Nm
Starters w/2 mounting bolts	15-20 ft. lbs.	20-27 Nm
Diesel	20 ft. lbs.	
Thermostat housing		
6-4.9L	15 ft. lbs.	20 Nm
8-5.0L/8-5.8L		
1987-91	18 ft. lbs.	24 Nm
1992-93	9-12 ft. lbs.	13-16 Nm
8-7.5L		
1987-91	28 ft. lbs.	38 Nm
1992-93	12-18 ft. lbs.	16-24 Nm
Diesel	20 ft. lbs.	27 Nm
Torque converter-to-flywheel		
8-5.0L/8-5.7L	30 ft. lbs.	41 Nm
8-7.5L	34 ft. lbs.	46 Nm
Diesel	34 ft. lbs.	46 Nm
Torque converter inspection plate bolts		
8-5.0L/8-5.7L	60 inch lbs.	7 Nm
8-7.5L	60-90 inch lbs.	7-8 Nm
Diesel	60-90 inch lbs.	7-8 Nm
Vacuum pump		
Bracket and pump		
Diesel	14-19 ft. lbs.	19-26 Nm
Water Pump bolts		
6-4.9L	18 ft. lbs.	24 Nm
8-5.0L/8-5.8L	18 ft. lbs.	24 Nm
8-7.5L	12-18 ft. lbs.	16-24 Nm
Diesel	14 ft. lbs.	19 Nm

84923237

TORQUE SPECIFICATIONS
1994-96 7.3L DI Turbo Diesel Engines①

COMPONENT	U.S. (ft. lbs.)①	Metric (Nm)①
A/C compressor bracket to engine	30-40	40-55
A/C compressor bolt	17-22	23-31
A/C manifold lines	13-17	18-23
Crankshaft vibration damper bolt/crankshaft pulley bolt	212	287
Cylinder head bolt		
STEP 1	65	88
STEP 2	85	115
STEP 3	105	142
Connecting rod nuts		
1994 engines		
STEP 1	38	52
STEP 2	51	69
1995 engines		
STEP 1	52	71
STEP 2	80	108
1996 engines	70	95
Engine front cover bolts	15	20
Engine mount nuts	71-94	96-127
Engine rear cover bolts	15	20
Exhaust manifold to cylinder head	45	61
Fan clutch to water pump	83-113	113-153
Flywheel mounting bolt (AT)	89	121
Flywheel mounting bolt (MT)	89	121
Flywheel housing cover screws	13-17	17-23
Fuel filter housing to cylinder block	24-38	33-52
Fuel filter to cylinder block	24-38	33-52
Fuel injector hold-down clamp mounting bolt	120 inch lbs.	12
Fuel injector hold-down clamp shoulder bolt	120 inch lbs.	12
Fuel rail end plug	97 inch lbs.	11
Fuel supply tube bolt (banjo fitting)	40	55
Generator (alternator) bolt	30-40	40-55
Generator bracket to cylinder head	30-40	40-55
Glow plug	14	19
Heater hose fitting to water pump	13-18	17-24
High pressure oil pump gear bolt	95	129
Injection Control Pressure (ICP) sensor	21	29
Intake manifold cover bolts (M8)	18	24
Main bearing cap bolts		
1994 engines		
STEP 1	95	129
STEP 2	plus 45 degrees	
1995-96 engines		
STEP 1	95	129
Oil cooler plug	15	20
Oil deflector mounting bolt	120 inch lbs.	12
Oil filter to header adapter:	1 1/4-2 turns after initial seal contact	
Oil level gauge tube adapter	24	33
Oil pan drain plug	20	27
Oil pump screen cover and tube flange screws	18	24
Oil rail drain plug	53 inch lbs.	6
Oil rail end plug	60	81
Piston cooling tube bolt	97 inch lbs.	11
Power steering pump lines	22-30	30-40
Power steering pump mounting bracket to engine	30-40	40-55
Power steering pump to bracket	30-40	40-55
Radiator retainer bolts	18-25	24-34
Rocker arm post attaching bolts	20	27
Secondary flywheel to primary flywheel	47	64
Transmission to engine bolts	39-53	53-72
Turbocharger exhaust inlet pipe to inlet manifold bolts	36	49
Turbocharger exhaust inlet pipe to inlet adapter bolts	36	49
Vacuum pump to bracket	17-22	23-31
Valve cover bolts	97 inch lbs.	11
Water pump outlet mounting bolt	15	20
Water pump mounting bolts	15	20

① Unless otherwise noted in the column

88283C41

ENGINE RECONDITIONING

Determining Engine Condition

Anything that generates heat and/or friction will eventually burn or wear out (for example, a light bulb generates heat, therefore its life span is limited). With this in mind, a running engine generates tremendous amounts of both; friction is encountered by the moving and rotating parts inside the engine and heat is created by friction and combustion of the fuel. However, the engine has systems designed to help reduce the effects of heat and friction and provide added longevity. The oiling system reduces the amount of friction encountered by the moving parts inside the engine, while the cooling system reduces heat created by friction and combustion. If either system is not maintained, a break-down will be inevitable. Therefore, you can see how regular maintenance can affect the service life of your vehicle. If you do not drain, flush and refill your cooling system at the proper intervals, deposits will begin to accumulate in the radiator, thereby reducing the amount of heat it can extract from the coolant. The same applies to your oil and filter; if it is not changed often enough it becomes laden with contaminates and is unable to properly lubricate the engine. This increases friction and wear.

There are a number of methods for evaluating the condition of your engine. A compression test can reveal the condition of your pistons, piston rings, cylinder bores, head gasket(s), valves and valve seats. An oil pressure test can warn you of possible engine bearing, or oil pump failures. Excessive oil consumption, evidence of oil in the engine air intake area and/or bluish smoke from the tailpipe may indicate worn piston rings, worn valve guides and/or valve seals. As a general rule, an engine that uses no more than one quart of oil every 1000 miles is in good condition. Engines that use one quart of oil or more in less than 1000 miles should first be checked for oil leaks. If any oil leaks are present, have them fixed before determining how much oil is consumed by the engine, especially if blue smoke is not visible at the tailpipe.

COMPRESSION TEST

A noticeable lack of engine power, excessive oil consumption and/or poor fuel mileage measured over an extended period are all indicators of internal engine wear. Worn piston rings, scored or worn cylinder bores, blown head gaskets, sticking or burnt valves, and worn valve seats are all possible culprits. A check of each cylinder's compression will help locate the problem.

Gasoline Engines

▶ See Figure 151

➡A screw-in type compression gauge is more accurate than the type you simply hold against the spark plug hole. Although it takes slightly longer to use, it's worth the effort to obtain a more accurate reading.

1. Make sure that the proper amount and viscosity of engine oil is in the crankcase, then ensure the battery is fully charged.
2. Warm-up the engine to normal operating temperature, then shut the engine **OFF**.
3. Disable the ignition system.
4. Label and disconnect all of the spark plug wires from the plugs.
5. Thoroughly clean the cylinder head area around the spark plug ports, then remove the spark plugs.
6. Set the throttle plate to the fully open (wide-open throttle) position. You can block the accelerator linkage open for this, or you can have an assistant fully depress the accelerator pedal.
7. Install a screw-in type compression gauge into the No. 1 spark plug hole until the fitting is snug.

✳✳ WARNING

Be careful not to crossthread the spark plug hole.

8. According to the tool manufacturer's instructions, connect a remote starting switch to the starting circuit.
9. With the ignition switch in the **OFF** position, use the remote starting switch to crank the engine through at least five compression strokes (approximately 5 seconds of cranking) and record the highest reading on the gauge.

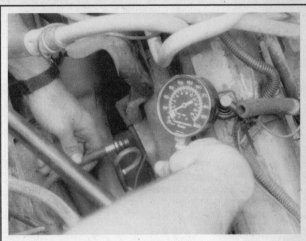

Fig. 151 A screw-in type compression gauge is more accurate and easier to use without an assistant

TCCS3801

10. Repeat the test on each cylinder, cranking the engine approximately the same number of compression strokes and/or time as the first.
11. Compare the highest readings from each cylinder to that of the others. The indicated compression pressures are considered within specifications if the lowest reading cylinder is within 75 percent of the pressure recorded for the highest reading cylinder. For example, if your highest reading cylinder pressure was 150 psi (1034 kPa), then 75 percent of that would be 113 psi (779 kPa). So the lowest reading cylinder should be no less than 113 psi (779 kPa).
12. If a cylinder exhibits an unusually low compression reading, pour a tablespoon of clean engine oil into the cylinder through the spark plug hole and repeat the compression test. If the compression rises after adding oil, it means that the cylinder's piston rings and/or cylinder bore are damaged or worn. If the pressure remains low, the valves may not be seating properly (a valve job is needed), or the head gasket may be blown near that cylinder. If compression in any two adjacent cylinders is low, and if the addition of oil doesn't help raise compression, there is leakage past the head gasket. Oil and coolant in the combustion chamber, combined with blue or constant white smoke from the tailpipe, are symptoms of this problem. However, don't be alarmed by the normal white smoke emitted from the tailpipe during engine warm-up or from cold weather driving. There may be evidence of water droplets on the engine dipstick and/or oil droplets in the cooling system if a head gasket is blown.

Diesel Engines

Checking cylinder compression on diesel engines is basically the same procedure as on gasoline engines except for the following:

1. A special compression gauge adapter suitable for diesel engines (because these engines have much greater compression pressures) must be used.
2. Remove the injector tubes and remove the injectors from each cylinder.

✳✳ WARNING

Do not forget to remove the washer underneath each injector. Otherwise, it may get lost when the engine is cranked.

3. When fitting the compression gauge adapter to the cylinder head, make sure the bleeder of the gauge (if equipped) is closed.
4. When reinstalling the injector assemblies, install new washers underneath each injector.

OIL PRESSURE TEST

Check for proper oil pressure at the sending unit passage with an externally mounted mechanical oil pressure gauge (as opposed to relying on a factory installed dash-mounted gauge). A tachometer may also be needed, as some specifications may require running the engine at a specific rpm.

1. With the engine cold, locate and remove the oil pressure sending unit.

2. Following the manufacturer's instructions, connect a mechanical oil pressure gauge and, if necessary, a tachometer to the engine.

3. Start the engine and allow it to idle.

4. Check the oil pressure reading when cold and record the number. You may need to run the engine at a specified rpm, so check the specifications.

5. Run the engine until normal operating temperature is reached (upper radiator hose will feel warm).

6. Check the oil pressure reading again with the engine hot and record the number. Turn the engine **OFF**.

7. Compare your hot oil pressure reading to specification. If the reading is low, check the cold pressure reading against the chart. If the cold pressure is well above the specification, and the hot reading was lower than the specification, you may have the wrong viscosity oil in the engine. Change the oil, making sure to use the proper grade and quantity, then repeat the test.

Low oil pressure readings could be attributed to internal component wear, pump related problems, a low oil level, or oil viscosity that is too low. High oil pressure readings could be caused by an overfilled crankcase, too high of an oil viscosity or a faulty pressure relief valve.

Buy or Rebuild?

Now if you have determined that your engine is worn out, you must make some decisions. The question of whether or not an engine is worth rebuilding is largely a subjective matter and one of personal worth. Is the engine a popular one, or is it an obsolete model? Are parts available? Will it get acceptable gas mileage once it is rebuilt? Is the car it's being put into worth keeping? Would it be less expensive to buy a new engine, have your engine rebuilt by a pro, rebuild it yourself or buy a used engine from a salvage yard? Or would it be simpler and less expensive to buy another car? If you have considered all these matters, and have still decided to rebuild the engine, then it is time to decide how you will rebuild it.

➡**The editors at Chilton feel that most engine machining should be performed by a professional machine shop. Think of it as an assurance that the job has been done right the first time. There are many expensive and specialized tools required to perform such tasks as boring and honing an engine block or having a valve job done on a cylinder head. Even inspecting the parts requires expensive micrometers and gauges to properly measure wear and clearances. A machine shop can deliver to you clean, and ready to assemble parts, saving you time and aggravation. Your maximum savings will come from performing the removal, disassembly, assembly and installation of the engine and purchasing or renting only the tools required to perform these tasks.**

A complete rebuild or overhaul of an engine involves replacing all of the moving parts (pistons, rods, crankshaft, camshaft, etc.) with new ones and machining the non-moving wearing surfaces of the block and heads. Unfortunately, this may not be cost effective. For instance, your crankshaft may have been damaged or worn, but it can be machined undersize for a minimal fee.

So although you can replace everything inside the engine, it is usually wiser to replace only those parts which are really needed, and, if possible, repair the more expensive ones. Later in this section, we will break the engine down into its two main components: the cylinder head and the engine block. We will discuss each component, and the recommended parts to replace during a rebuild on each.

Engine Overhaul Tips

Most engine overhaul procedures are fairly standard. In addition to specific parts replacement procedures and specifications for your individual engine, this section is also a guide to acceptable rebuilding procedures. Examples of standard rebuilding practice are given and should be used along with specific details concerning your particular engine.

Competent and accurate machine shop services will ensure maximum performance, reliability and engine life. In most instances it is more profitable for the do-it-yourself mechanic to remove, clean and inspect the component, buy the necessary parts and deliver these to a shop for actual machine work.

Much of the assembly work (crankshaft, bearings, piston rods, and other components) is well within the scope of the do-it-yourself mechanic's tools and abilities. You will have to decide for yourself the depth of involvement you desire in an engine repair or rebuild.

TOOLS

The tools required for an engine overhaul or parts replacement will depend on the depth of your involvement. With a few exceptions, they will be the tools found in a mechanic's tool kit (see Section 1 of this manual). More in-depth work will require some or all of the following:

- A dial indicator (reading in thousandths) mounted on a universal base
- Micrometers and telescope gauges
- Jaw and screw-type pullers
- Scraper
- Valve spring compressor
- Ring groove cleaner
- Piston ring expander and compressor
- Ridge reamer
- Cylinder hone or glaze breaker
- Plastigage®
- Engine stand

The use of most of these tools is illustrated in this section. Many can be rented for a one-time use from a local parts jobber or tool supply house specializing in automotive work.

Occasionally, the use of special tools is called for. See the information on Special Tools and the Safety Notice in the front of this book before substituting another tool.

OVERHAUL TIPS

Aluminum has become extremely popular for use in engines, due to its low weight. Observe the following precautions when handling aluminum parts:

- Never hot tank aluminum parts (the caustic hot tank solution will eat the aluminum.)
- Remove all aluminum parts (identification tag, etc.) from engine parts prior to the tanking.
- Always coat threads lightly with engine oil or anti-seize compounds before installation, to prevent seizure.
- Never overtighten bolts or spark plugs especially in aluminum threads.

When assembling the engine, any parts that will be exposed to frictional contact must be prelubed to provide lubrication at initial start-up. Any product specifically formulated for this purpose can be used, but engine oil is not recommended as a prelube in most cases.

When semi-permanent (locked, but removable) installation of bolts or nuts is desired, threads should be cleaned and coated with Loctite® or another similar, commercial non-hardening sealant.

CLEANING

▶ **See Figures 152, 153, 154 and 155**

Before the engine and its components are inspected, they must be thoroughly cleaned. You will need to remove any engine varnish, oil sludge and/or carbon deposits from all of the components to insure an accurate inspection. A crack in the engine block or cylinder head can easily become overlooked if hidden by a layer of sludge or carbon.

Most of the cleaning process can be carried out with common hand tools and readily available solvents or solutions. Carbon deposits can be chipped away using a hammer and a hard wooden chisel. Old gasket material and varnish or sludge can usually be removed using a scraper and/or cleaning solvent. Extremely stubborn deposits may require the use of a power drill with a wire brush. If using a wire brush, use extreme care around any critical machined surfaces (such as the gasket surfaces, bearing saddles, cylinder bores, etc.). USE OF A WIRE BRUSH IS NOT RECOMMENDED ON ANY ALUMINUM COMPONENTS. Always follow any safety recommendations given by the manufacturer of the tool and/or solvent.

✳✳ CAUTION

Always wear eye protection during any cleaning process involving scraping, chipping or spraying of solvents.

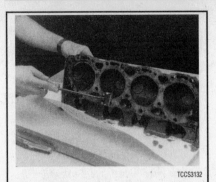

Fig. 152 Use a gasket scraper to remove the old gasket material from the mating surfaces

TCCS3132

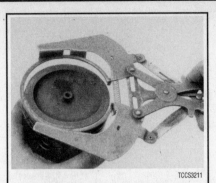

Fig. 153 Before cleaning and inspection, use a ring expander tool to remove the piston rings

TCCS3211

Fig. 154 Clean the piston ring grooves using a ring groove cleaner tool, or . . .

TCCS3208

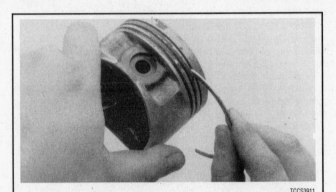

Fig. 155 . . . use a piece of an old ring to clean the grooves. Be careful, the ring can be quite sharp

TCCS3911

An alternative to the mess and hassle of cleaning the parts yourself is to drop them off at a local garage or machine shop. They should have the necessary equipment to properly clean all of the parts for a nominal fee.

Remove any oil galley plugs, freeze plugs and/or pressed-in bearings and carefully wash and degrease all of the engine components including the fasteners and bolts. Small parts such as the valves, springs, etc., should be placed in a metal basket and allowed to soak. Use pipe cleaner type brushes, and clean all passageways in the components.

Use a ring expander and remove the rings from the pistons. Clean the piston ring grooves with a special tool or a piece of broken ring. Scrape the carbon off of the top of the piston. You should never use a wire brush on the pistons. After preparing all of the piston assemblies in this manner, wash and degrease them again.

※ WARNING

Use extreme care when cleaning around the cylinder head valve seats. A mistake or slip may cost you a new seat.

When cleaning the cylinder head, remove carbon from the combustion chamber with the valves installed. This will avoid damaging the valve seats.

REPAIRING DAMAGED THREADS

▶ See Figures 156, 157, 158, 159 and 160

Several methods of repairing damaged threads are available. Heli-Coil (shown here), Keenserts® and Microdot® are among the most widely used. All involve basically the same principle—drilling out stripped threads, tapping the hole and installing a prewound insert—making welding, plugging and oversize fasteners unnecessary.

Two types of thread repair inserts are usually supplied: a standard type for most inch coarse, inch fine, metric course and metric fine thread sizes and a spark lug type to fit most spark plug port sizes. Consult the individual tool manufacturer's catalog to determine exact applications. Typical thread repair kits will contain a selection of prewound threaded inserts, a tap (corresponding to the outside diameter threads of the insert) and an installation tool. Spark plug inserts usually differ because they require a tap equipped with pilot threads and a combined reamer/tap section. Most manufacturers also supply blister-packed thread repair inserts separately in addition to a master kit containing a variety of taps and inserts plus installation tools.

Before attempting to repair a threaded hole, remove any snapped, broken or damaged bolts or studs. Penetrating oil can be used to free frozen threads. The offending item can usually be removed with locking pliers or using a screw/stud extractor. After the hole is clear, the thread can be repaired as shown in the kit manufacturer's instructions.

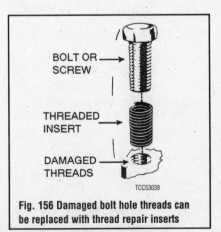

Fig. 156 Damaged bolt hole threads can be replaced with thread repair inserts

BOLT OR SCREW

THREADED INSERT

DAMAGED THREADS

TCCS3039

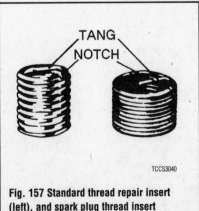

TANG
NOTCH

Fig. 157 Standard thread repair insert (left), and spark plug thread insert

TCCS3040

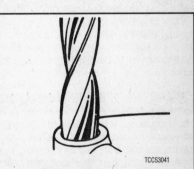

Fig. 158 Drill out the damaged threads with the specified size bit. Be sure to drill completely through the hole or to the bottom of a blind hole

TCCS3041

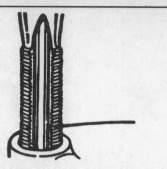

Fig. 159 Using the kit, tap the hole in order to receive the thread insert. Keep the tap well oiled and back it out frequently to avoid clogging the threads

TCCS3042

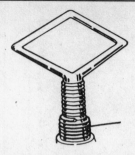

Fig. 160 Screw the insert onto the installer tool until the tang engages the slot. Thread the insert into the hole until it is ¼–½ turn below the top surface, then remove the tool and break off the tang using a punch

TCCS3043

Engine Preparation

To properly rebuild an engine, you must first remove it from the vehicle, then disassemble and diagnose it. Ideally you should place your engine on an engine stand. This affords you the best access to the engine components. Remove the flywheel or flexplate before installing the engine to the stand.

Now that you have the engine on a stand, and assuming that you have drained the oil and coolant from the engine, it's time to strip it of all but the necessary components. Before you start disassembling the engine, you may want to take a moment to draw some pictures, or fabricate some labels or containers to mark the locations of various components and the bolts and/or studs which fasten them. Modern day engines use a lot of little brackets and clips which hold wiring harnesses and such, and these holders are often mounted on studs and/or bolts that can be easily mixed up. The manufacturer spent a lot of time and money designing your vehicle, and they wouldn't have wasted any of it by haphazardly placing brackets, clips or fasteners on the vehicle. If it's present when you disassemble it, put it back when you assemble, you will regret not remembering that little bracket which holds a wire harness out of the path of a rotating part.

You should begin by unbolting any accessories still attached to the engine, such as the water pump, power steering pump, alternator, etc. Then, unfasten any manifolds (intake or exhaust) which were not removed during the engine removal procedure. Finally, remove any covers remaining on the engine such as the rocker arm, front or timing cover and oil pan. Some front covers may require the vibration damper and/or crank pulley to be removed beforehand. The idea is to reduce the engine to the bare necessities of cylinder head(s), valve train, engine block, crankshaft, pistons and connecting rods, plus any other `in block' components such as oil pumps, balance shafts and auxiliary shafts.

Finally, remove the cylinder head(s) from the engine block and carefully place on a bench. Disassembly instructions for each component follow later in this section.

Cylinder Head

There are two basic types of cylinder heads used on today's automobiles: the Overhead Valve (OHV) and the Overhead Camshaft (OHC). The latter can also be broken down into two subgroups: the Single Overhead Camshaft (SOHC) and the Dual Overhead Camshaft (DOHC). Generally, if there is only a single camshaft on a head, it is just referred to as an OHC head. Also, an engine with an OHV cylinder head is also known as a pushrod engine.

Most cylinder heads these days are made of an aluminum alloy due to its light weight, durability and heat transfer qualities. However, cast iron was the material of choice in the past, and is still used on many vehicles. Whether made from aluminum or iron, all cylinder heads have valves and seats. Some use two valves per cylinder, while the more hi-tech engines will utilize a multi-valve configuration using 3, 4 and even 5 valves per cylinder. When the valve contacts the seat, it does so on precision machined surfaces, which seals the combustion chamber. All cylinder heads have a valve guide for each valve. The guide centers the valve to the seat and allows it to move up and down within it. The clearance between the valve and guide can be critical. Too much clearance and the engine may consume oil, lose vacuum and/or damage the seat. Too little, and the valve can stick in the guide causing the engine to run poorly if at all, and possibly causing severe damage. The last component all automotive cylinder heads have are valve springs. The spring holds the valve against its seat. It also returns the valve to this position when the valve has been opened by the valve train or camshaft. The spring is fastened to the valve by a retainer and valve locks (sometimes called keepers). Aluminum heads will also have a valve spring shim to keep the spring from wearing away the aluminum.

An ideal method of rebuilding the cylinder head would involve replacing all of the valves, guides, seats, springs, etc. with new ones. However, depending on how the engine was maintained, often this is not necessary. A major cause of valve, guide and seat wear is an improperly tuned engine. An engine that is running too rich, will often wash the lubricating oil out of the guide with gasoline, causing it to wear rapidly. Conversely, an engine which is running too lean will place higher combustion temperatures on the valves and seats allowing them to wear or even burn. Springs fall victim to the driving habits of the individual. A driver who often runs the engine rpm to the redline will wear out or break the springs faster then one that stays well below it. Unfortunately, mileage takes it toll on all of the parts. Generally, the valves, guides, springs and seats in a cylinder head can be machined and re-used, saving you money. However, if a valve is burnt, it may be wise to replace all of the valves, since they were all operating in the same environment. The same goes for any other component on the cylinder head. Think of it as an insurance policy against future problems related to that component.

Unfortunately, the only way to find out which components need replacing, is to disassemble and carefully check each piece. After the cylinder head(s) are disassembled, thoroughly clean all of the components.

DISASSEMBLY

◆ See Figures 161 thru 166

Before disassembling the cylinder head, you may want to fabricate some containers to hold the various parts, as some of them can be quite small (such as keepers) and easily lost. Also keeping yourself and the components organized will aid in assembly and reduce confusion. Where possible, try to maintain a components original location; this is especially important if there is not going to be any machine work performed on the components.

1. If you haven't already removed the rocker arms and/or shafts, do so now.
2. Position the head so that the springs are easily accessed.
3. Use a valve spring compressor tool, and relieve spring tension from the retainer.

➡Due to engine varnish, the retainer may stick to the valve locks. A gentle tap with a hammer may help to break it loose.

4. Remove the valve locks from the valve tip and/or retainer. A small magnet may help in removing the locks.
5. Lift the valve spring, tool and all, off of the valve stem.
6. If equipped, remove the valve seal. If the seal is difficult to remove with the valve in place, try removing the valve first, then the seal. Follow the steps below for valve removal.
7. Position the head to allow access for withdrawing the valve.

➡Cylinder heads that have seen a lot of miles and/or abuse may have mushroomed the valve lock grove and/or tip, causing difficulty in

Fig. 161 When removing an OHV valve spring, use a compressor tool to relieve the tension from the retainer

Fig. 162 A small magnet will help in removal of the valve locks

Fig. 163 Be careful not to lose the small valve locks (keepers)

Fig. 164 Remove the valve seal from the valve stem—O-ring type seal shown

Fig. 165 Removing an umbrella/positive type seal

Fig. 166 Invert the cylinder head and withdraw the valve from the valve guide bore

removal of the valve. If this has happened, use a metal file to carefully remove the high spots around the lock grooves and/or tip. Only file it enough to allow removal.

8. Remove the valve from the cylinder head.

9. If equipped, remove the valve spring shim. A small magnetic tool or screwdriver will aid in removal.

10. Repeat Steps 3 though 9 until all of the valves have been removed.

INSPECTION

Now that all of the cylinder head components are clean, it's time to inspect them for wear and/or damage. To accurately inspect them, you will need some specialized tools:

- A 0–1 in. micrometer for the valves
- A dial indicator or inside diameter gauge for the valve guides
- A spring pressure test gauge

If you do not have access to the proper tools, you may want to bring the components to a shop that does.

Valves

▶ See Figures 167 and 168

The first thing to inspect are the valve heads. Look closely at the head, margin and face for any cracks, excessive wear or burning. The margin is the best place to look for burning. It should have a squared edge with an even width all around the diameter. When a valve burns, the margin will look melted and the edges rounded. Also inspect the valve head for any signs of tuliping. This will show as a lifting of the edges or dishing in the center of the head and will usually not occur to all of the valves. All of the heads should look the same, any that seem dished more than others are probably bad. Next, inspect the valve lock grooves and valve tips. Check for any burrs around the lock grooves, especially if you had to file them to remove the valve. Valve tips should appear flat, although slight rounding with high mileage engines is normal. Slightly worn valve tips will need to be machined flat. Last, measure the valve stem diameter

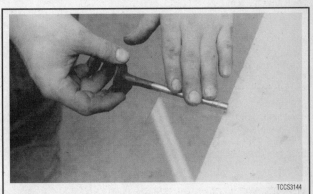

Fig. 167 Valve stems may be rolled on a flat surface to check for bends

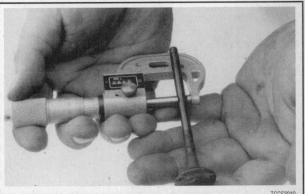

Fig. 168 Use a micrometer to check the valve stem diameter

with the micrometer. Measure the area that rides within the guide, especially towards the tip where most of the wear occurs. Take several measurements along its length and compare them to each other. Wear should be even along the length with little to no taper. If no minimum diameter is given in the specifications, then the stem should not read more than 0.001 in. (0.025mm) below the unworn portion of the stem. Any valves that fail these inspections should be replaced.

Springs, Retainers and Valve Locks

▶ See Figures 169 and 170

The first thing to check is the most obvious, broken springs. Next check the free length and squareness of each spring. If applicable, insure to distinguish between intake and exhaust springs. Use a ruler and/or carpenter's square to measure the length. A carpenter's square should be used to check the springs for squareness. If a spring pressure test gauge is available, check each springs rating and compare to the specifications chart. Check the readings against the specifications given. Any springs that fail these inspections should be replaced.

The spring retainers rarely need replacing, however they should still be checked as a precaution. Inspect the spring mating surface and the valve lock retention area for any signs of excessive wear. Also check for any signs of cracking. Replace any retainers that are questionable.

Valve locks should be inspected for excessive wear on the outside contact area as well as on the inner notched surface. Any locks which appear worn or broken and its respective valve should be replaced.

Cylinder Head

There are several things to check on the cylinder head: valve guides, seats, cylinder head surface flatness, cracks and physical damage.

VALVE GUIDES

▶ See Figure 171

Now that you know the valves are good, you can use them to check the guides, although a new valve, if available, is preferred. Before you measure any-thing, look at the guides carefully and inspect them for any cracks, chips or breakage. Also if the guide is a removable style (as in most aluminum heads), check them for any looseness or evidence of movement. All of the guides should appear to be at the same height from the spring seat. If any seem lower (or higher) from another, the guide has moved. Mount a dial indicator onto the spring side of the cylinder head. Lightly oil the valve stem and insert it into the cylinder head. Position the dial indicator against the valve stem near the tip and zero the gauge. Grasp the valve stem and wiggle towards and away from the dial indicator and observe the readings. Mount the dial indicator 90 degrees from the initial point and zero the gauge and again take a reading. Compare the two readings for an out of round condition. Check the readings against the specifications given. An Inside Diameter (I.D.) gauge designed for valve guides will give you an accurate valve guide bore measurement. If the I.D. gauge is used, compare the readings with the specifications given. Any guides that fail these inspections should be replaced or machined.

VALVE SEATS

A visual inspection of the valve seats should show a slightly worn and pitted surface where the valve face contacts the seat. Inspect the seat carefully for severe pitting or cracks. Also, a seat that is badly worn will be recessed into the cylinder head. A severely worn or recessed seat may need to be replaced. All cracked seats must be replaced. A seat concentricity gauge, if available, should be used to check the seat run-out. If run-out exceeds specifications the seat must be machined (if no specification is available given use 0.002 in. or 0.051mm).

CYLINDER HEAD SURFACE FLATNESS

▶ See Figures 172 and 173

After you have cleaned the gasket surface of the cylinder head of any old gasket material, check the head for flatness.

Place a straightedge across the gasket surface. Using feeler gauges, determine the clearance at the center of the straightedge and across the cylinder head at several points. Check along the centerline and diagonally on the head sur-

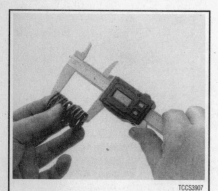

Fig. 169 Use a caliper to check the valve spring free-length

TCCS3907

Fig. 170 Check the valve spring for squareness on a flat surface; a carpenter's square can be used

TCCS3908

Fig. 171 A dial gauge may be used to check valve stem-to-guide clearance; read the gauge while moving the valve stem

TCCS3142

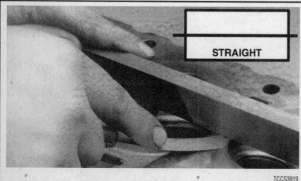

Fig. 172 Check the head for flatness across the center of the head surface using a straightedge and feeler gauge

TCCS3919

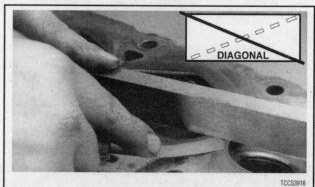

Fig. 173 Checks should also be made along both diagonals of the head surface

TCCS3918

face. If the warpage exceeds 0.003 in. (0.076mm) within a 6.0 in. (15.2cm) span, or 0.006 in. (0.152mm) over the total length of the head, the cylinder head must be resurfaced. After resurfacing the heads of a V-type engine, the intake manifold flange surface should be checked, and if necessary, milled proportionally to allow for the change in its mounting position.

CRACKS AND PHYSICAL DAMAGE

Generally, cracks are limited to the combustion chamber, however, it is not uncommon for the head to crack in a spark plug hole, port, outside of the head or in the valve spring/rocker arm area. The first area to inspect is always the hottest: the exhaust seat/port area.

A visual inspection should be performed, but just because you don't see a crack does not mean it is not there. Some more reliable methods for inspecting for cracks include Magnaflux®, a magnetic process or Zyglo®, a dye penetrant. Magnaflux® is used only on ferrous metal (cast iron) heads. Zyglo® uses a spray on fluorescent mixture along with a black light to reveal the cracks. It is strongly recommended to have your cylinder head checked professionally for cracks, especially if the engine was known to have overheated and/or leaked or consumed coolant. Contact a local shop for availability and pricing of these services.

Physical damage is usually very evident. For example, a broken mounting ear from dropping the head or a bent or broken stud and/or bolt. All of these defects should be fixed or, if unrepairable, the head should be replaced.

REFINISHING & REPAIRING

Many of the procedures given for refinishing and repairing the cylinder head components must be performed by a machine shop. Certain steps, if the inspected part is not worn, can be performed yourself inexpensively. However, you spent a lot of time and effort so far, why risk trying to save a couple bucks if you might have to do it all over again?

Valves

Any valves that were not replaced should be refaced and the tips ground flat. Unless you have access to a valve grinding machine, this should be done by a machine shop. If the valves are in extremely good condition, as well as the valve seats and guides, they may be lapped in without performing machine work.

It is a recommended practice to lap the valves even after machine work has been performed and/or new valves have been purchased. This insures a positive seal between the valve and seat.

LAPPING THE VALVES

➡Before lapping the valves to the seats, read the rest of the cylinder head section to insure that any related parts are in acceptable enough condition to continue. Also, remember that before any valve seat machining and/or lapping can be performed, the guides must be within factory recommended specifications.

1. Invert the cylinder head.
2. Lightly lubricate the valve stems and insert them into the cylinder head in their numbered order.
3. Raise the valve from the seat and apply a small amount of fine lapping compound to the seat.
4. Moisten the suction head of a hand-lapping tool and attach it to the head of the valve.
5. Rotate the tool between the palms of both hands, changing the position of the valve on the valve seat and lifting the tool often to prevent grooving.
6. Lap the valve until a smooth, polished circle is evident on the valve and seat.
7. Remove the tool and the valve. Wipe away all traces of the grinding compound and store the valve to maintain its lapped location.

⁛ WARNING

Do not get the valves out of order after they have been lapped. They must be put back with the same valve seat with which they were lapped.

Springs, Retainers and Valve Locks

There is no repair or refinishing possible with the springs, retainers and valve locks. If they are found to be worn or defective, they must be replaced with new (or known good) parts.

Cylinder Head

Most refinishing procedures dealing with the cylinder head must be performed by a machine shop. Read the sections below and review your inspection data to determine whether or not machining is necessary.

VALVE GUIDE

➡If any machining or replacements are made to the valve guides, the seats must be machined.

Unless the valve guides need machining or replacing, the only service to perform is to thoroughly clean them of any dirt or oil residue.

There are only two types of valve guides used on automobile engines: the replaceable-type (all aluminum heads) and the cast-in integral-type (most cast iron heads). There are four recommended methods for repairing worn guides.
- Knurling
- Inserts
- Reaming oversize
- Replacing

Knurling is a process in which metal is displaced and raised, thereby reducing clearance, giving a true center, and providing oil control. It is the least expensive way of repairing the valve guides. However, it is not necessarily the best, and in some cases, a knurled valve guide will not stand up for more than a short time. It requires a special knurlizer and precision reaming tools to obtain proper clearances. It would not be cost effective to purchase these tools, unless you plan on rebuilding several of the same cylinder head.

Installing a guide insert involves machining the guide to accept a bronze insert. One style is the coil-type which is installed into a threaded guide. Another is the thin-walled insert where the guide is reamed oversize to accept a split-sleeve insert. After the insert is installed, a special tool is then run through the guide to expand the insert, locking it to the guide. The insert is then reamed to the standard size for proper valve clearance.

Reaming for oversize valves restores normal clearances and provides a true valve seat. Most cast-in type guides can be reamed to accept an valve with an oversize stem. The cost factor for this can become quite high as you will need to purchase the reamer and new, oversize stem valves for all guides which were reamed. Oversizes are generally 0.003–0.030 in. (0.076–0.762mm), with 0.015 in. (0.381mm) being the most common.

To replace cast-in type valve guides, they must be drilled out, then reamed to accept replacement guides. This must be done on a fixture which will allow centering and leveling off of the original valve seat or guide, otherwise a serious guide-to-seat misalignment may occur making it impossible to properly machine the seat.

Replaceable-type guides are pressed into the cylinder head. A hammer and a stepped drift or punch may be used to install and remove the guides. Before removing the guides, measure the protrusion on the spring side of the head and record it for installation. Use the stepped drift to hammer out the old guide from the combustion chamber side of the head. When installing, determine whether or not the guide also seals a water jacket in the head, and if it does, use the recommended sealing agent. If there is no water jacket, grease the valve guide and its bore. Use the stepped drift, and hammer the new guide into the cylinder head from the spring side of the cylinder head. A stack of washers the same thickness as the measured protrusion may help the installation process.

VALVE SEATS

➡Before any valve seat machining can be performed, the guides must be within factory recommended specifications. If any machining occurred or if replacements were made to the valve guides, the seats must be machined.

If the seats are in good condition, the valves can be lapped to the seats, and the cylinder head assembled. See the valves section for instructions on lapping.

If the valve seats are worn, cracked or damaged, they must be serviced by a machine shop. The valve seat must be perfectly centered to the valve guide, which requires very accurate machining.

CYLINDER HEAD SURFACE

If the cylinder head is warped, it must be machined flat. If the warpage is extremely severe, the head may need to be replaced. In some instances, it may be possible to straighten a warped head enough to allow machining. In either case, contact a professional machine shop for service.

CRACKS AND PHYSICAL DAMAGE

Certain cracks can be repaired in both cast iron and aluminum heads. For cast iron, a tapered threaded insert is installed along the length of the crack. Aluminum can also use the tapered inserts, however welding is the preferred method. Some physical damage can be repaired through brazing or welding. Contact a machine shop to get expert advice for your particular dilemma.

ASSEMBLY

The first step for any assembly job is to have a clean area in which to work. Next, thoroughly clean all of the parts and components that are to be assembled. Finally, place all of the components onto a suitable work space and, if necessary, arrange the parts to their respective positions.

1. Lightly lubricate the valve stems and insert all of the valves into the cylinder head. If possible, maintain their original locations.
2. If equipped, install any valve spring shims which were removed.
3. If equipped, install the new valve seals, keeping the following in mind:
• If the valve seal presses over the guide, lightly lubricate the outer guide surfaces.
• If the seal is an O-ring type, it is installed just after compressing the spring but before the valve locks.
4. Place the valve spring and retainer over the stem.
5. Position the spring compressor tool and compress the spring.
6. Assemble the valve locks to the stem.
7. Relieve the spring pressure slowly and insure that neither valve lock becomes dislodged by the retainer.
8. Remove the spring compressor tool.
9. Repeat Steps 2 through 8 until all of the springs have been installed.

Engine Block

GENERAL INFORMATION

A thorough overhaul or rebuild of an engine block would include replacing the pistons, rings, bearings, timing belt/chain assembly and oil pump. For OHV engines also include a new camshaft and lifters. The block would then have the cylinders bored and honed oversize (or if using removable cylinder sleeves, new sleeves installed) and the crankshaft would be cut undersize to provide new wearing surfaces and perfect clearances. However, your particular engine may not have everything worn out. What if only the piston rings have worn out and the clearances on everything else are still within factory specifications? Well, you could just replace the rings and put it back together, but this would be a very rare example. Chances are, if one component in your engine is worn, other components are sure to follow, and soon. At the very least, you should always replace the rings, bearings and oil pump. This is what is commonly called a "freshen up".

Cylinder Ridge Removal

Because the top piston ring does not travel to the very top of the cylinder, a ridge is built up between the end of the travel and the top of the cylinder bore.

Pushing the piston and connecting rod assembly past the ridge can be difficult, and damage to the piston ring lands could occur. If the ridge is not removed before installing a new piston or not removed at all, piston ring breakage and piston damage may occur.

➡ It is always recommended that you remove any cylinder ridges before removing the piston and connecting rod assemblies. If you know that new pistons are going to be installed and the engine block will be bored oversize, you may be able to forego this step. However, some ridges may actually prevent the assemblies from being removed, necessitating its removal.

There are several different types of ridge reamers on the market, none of which are inexpensive. Unless a great deal of engine rebuilding is anticipated, borrow or rent a reamer.

1. Turn the crankshaft until the piston is at the bottom of its travel.
2. Cover the head of the piston with a rag.
3. Follow the tool manufacturers instructions and cut away the ridge, exercising extreme care to avoid cutting too deeply.

4. Remove the ridge reamer, the rag and as many of the cuttings as pssible. Continue until all of the cylinder ridges have been removed.

DISASSEMBLY

▶ **See Figures 174 and 175**

The engine disassembly instructions following assume that you have the engine mounted on an engine stand. If not, it is easiest to disassemble the engine on a bench or the floor with it resting on the bell housing or transmission mounting surface. You must be able to access the connecting rod fasteners and turn the crankshaft during disassembly. Also, all engine covers (timing, front, side, oil pan, whatever) should have already been removed. Engines which are seized or locked up may not be able to be completely disassembled, and a core (salvage yard) engine should be purchased.

Pushrod Engines

If not done during the cylinder head removal, remove the pushrods and lifters, keeping them in order for assembly. Remove the timing gears and/or timing chain assembly, then remove the oil pump drive assembly and withdraw the camshaft from the engine block. Remove the oil pick-up and pump assembly. If equipped, remove any balance or auxiliary shafts. If necessary, remove the cylinder ridge from the top of the bore. See the cylinder ridge removal procedure earlier in this section.

All Engines

Rotate the engine over so that the crankshaft is exposed. Use a number punch or scribe and mark each connecting rod with its respective cylinder number. The cylinder closest to the front of the engine is always number 1. However, depending on the engine placement, the front of the engine could either be the flywheel or damper/pulley end. Generally the front of the engine faces the front of the vehicle. Use a number punch or scribe and also mark the main bearing caps from front to rear with the front most cap being number 1 (if there are five caps, mark them 1 through 5, front to rear).

TCCS3803

Fig. 174 Place rubber hose over the connecting rod studs to protect the crankshaft and cylinder bores from damage

※ **WARNING**

Take special care when pushing the connecting rod up from the crankshaft because the sharp threads of the rod bolts/studs will score the crankshaft journal. Insure that special plastic caps are installed over them, or cut two pieces of rubber hose to do the same.

Again, rotate the engine, this time to position the number one cylinder bore (head surface) up. Turn the crankshaft until the number one piston is at the bottom of its travel, this should allow the maximum access to its connecting rod. Remove the number one connecting rods fasteners and cap and place two lengths of rubber hose over the rod bolts/studs to protect the crankshaft from damage. Using a sturdy wooden dowel and a hammer, push the connecting rod up about 1 in. (25mm) from the crankshaft and remove the upper bearing insert. Continue pushing or tapping the connecting rod up until the piston

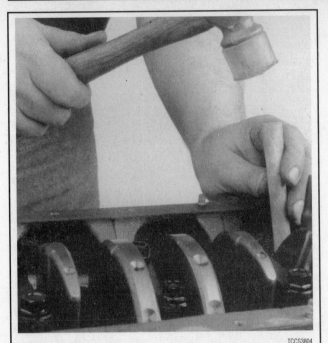

Fig. 175 Carefully tap the piston out of the bore using a wooden dowel

rings are out of the cylinder bore. Remove the piston and rod by hand, put the upper half of the bearing insert back into the rod, install the cap with its bearing insert installed, and hand-tighten the cap fasteners. If the parts are kept in order in this manner, they will not get lost and you will be able to tell which bearings came form what cylinder if any problems are discovered and diagnosis is necessary. Remove all the other piston assemblies in the same manner. On V-style engines, remove all of the pistons from one bank, then reposition the engine with the other cylinder bank head surface up, and remove that banks piston assemblies.

The only remaining component in the engine block should now be the crankshaft. Loosen the main bearing caps evenly until the fasteners can be turned by hand, then remove them and the caps. Remove the crankshaft from the engine block. Thoroughly clean all of the components.

INSPECTION

Now that the engine block and all of its components are clean, it's time to inspect them for wear and/or damage. To accurately inspect them, you will need some specialized tools:
- Two or three separate micrometers to measure the pistons and crankshaft journals
- A dial indicator
- Telescoping gauges for the cylinder bores
- A rod alignment fixture to check for bent connecting rods

If you do not have access to the proper tools, you may want to bring the components to a shop that does.

Generally, you shouldn't expect cracks in the engine block or its components unless it was known to leak, consume or mix engine fluids, it was severely overheated, or there was evidence of bad bearings and/or crankshaft damage. A visual inspection should be performed on all of the components, but just because you don't see a crack does not mean it is not there. Some more reliable methods for inspecting for cracks include Magnaflux®, a magnetic process or Zyglo®, a dye penetrant. Magnaflux® is used only on ferrous metal (cast iron). Zyglo® uses a spray on fluorescent mixture along with a black light to reveal the cracks. It is strongly recommended to have your engine block checked professionally for cracks, especially if the engine was known to have overheated and/or leaked or consumed coolant. Contact a local shop for availability and pricing of these services.

Engine Block

ENGINE BLOCK BEARING ALIGNMENT

Remove the main bearing caps and, if still installed, the main bearing inserts. Inspect all of the main bearing saddles and caps for damage, burrs or high spots. If damage is found, and it is caused from a spun main bearing, the block will need to be align-bored or, if severe enough, replacement. Any burrs or high spots should be carefully removed with a metal file.

Place a straightedge on the bearing saddles, in the engine block, along the centerline of the crankshaft. If any clearance exists between the straightedge and the saddles, the block must be align-bored.

Align-boring consists of machining the main bearing saddles and caps by means of a flycutter that runs through the bearing saddles.

DECK FLATNESS

The top of the engine block where the cylinder head mounts is called the deck. Insure that the deck surface is clean of dirt, carbon deposits and old gasket material. Place a straightedge across the surface of the deck along its centerline and, using feeler gauges, check the clearance along several points. Repeat the checking procedure with the straightedge placed along both diagonals of the deck surface. If the reading exceeds 0.003 in. (0.076mm) within a 6.0 in. (15.2cm) span, or 0.006 in. (0.152mm) over the total length of the deck, it must be machined.

CYLINDER BORES

♦ See Figure 176

The cylinder bores house the pistons and are slightly larger than the pistons themselves. A common piston-to-bore clearance is 0.0015–0.0025 in. (0.0381mm–0.0635mm). Inspect and measure the cylinder bores. The bore should be checked for out-of-roundness, taper and size. The results of this inspection will determine whether the cylinder can be used in its existing size and condition, or a rebore to the next oversize is required (or in the case of removable sleeves, have replacements installed).

The amount of cylinder wall wear is always greater at the top of the cylinder than at the bottom. This wear is known as taper. Any cylinder that has a taper of 0.0012 in. (0.305mm) or more, must be rebored. Measurements are taken at a number of positions in each cylinder: at the top, middle and bottom and at two points at each position; that is, at a point 90 degrees from the crankshaft centerline, as well as a point parallel to the crankshaft centerline. The measurements are made with either a special dial indicator or a telescopic gauge and micrometer. If the necessary precision tools to check the bore are not available, take the block to a machine shop and have them mike it. Also if you don't have the tools to check the cylinder bores, chances are you will not have the necessary devices to check the pistons, connecting rods and crankshaft. Take these components with you and save yourself an extra trip.

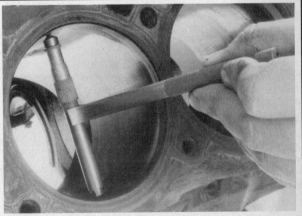

Fig. 176 Use a telescoping gauge to measure the cylinder bore diameter—take several readings within the same bore

For our procedures, we will use a telescopic gauge and a micrometer. You will need one of each, with a measuring range which covers your cylinder bore size.

1. Position the telescopic gauge in the cylinder bore, loosen the gauges lock and allow it to expand.

➡ **Your first two readings will be at the top of the cylinder bore, then proceed to the middle and finally the bottom, making a total of six measurements.**

2. Hold the gauge square in the bore, 90 degrees from the crankshaft centerline, and gently tighten the lock. Tilt the gauge back to remove it from the bore.

3. Measure the gauge with the micrometer and record the reading.

4. Again, hold the gauge square in the bore, this time parallel to the crankshaft centerline, and gently tighten the lock. Again, you will tilt the gauge back to remove it from the bore.

5. Measure the gauge with the micrometer and record this reading. The difference between these two readings is the out-of-round measurement of the cylinder.

6. Repeat steps 1 through 5, each time going to the next lower position, until you reach the bottom of the cylinder. Then go to the next cylinder, and continue until all of the cylinders have been measured.

The difference between these measurements will tell you all about the wear in your cylinders. The measurements which were taken 90 degrees from the crankshaft centerline will always reflect the most wear. That is because at this position is where the engine power presses the piston against the cylinder bore the hardest. This is known as thrust wear. Take your top, 90 degree measurement and compare it to your bottom, 90 degree measurement. The difference between them is the taper. When you measure your pistons, you will compare these readings to your piston sizes and determine piston-to-wall clearance.

Crankshaft

Inspect the crankshaft for visible signs of wear or damage. All of the journals should be perfectly round and smooth. Slight scores are normal for a used crankshaft, but you should hardly feel them with your fingernail. When measuring the crankshaft with a micrometer, you will take readings at the front and rear of each journal, then turn the micrometer 90 degrees and take two more readings, front and rear. The difference between the front-to-rear readings is the journal taper and the first-to-90 degree reading is the out-of-round measurement. Generally, there should be no taper or out-of-roundness found, however, up to 0.0005 in. (0.0127mm) for either can be overlooked. Also, the readings should fall within the factory specifications for journal diameters.

If the crankshaft journals fall within specifications, it is recommended that it be polished before being returned to service. Polishing the crankshaft insures that any minor burrs or high spots are smoothed, thereby reducing the chance of scoring the new bearings.

Pistons and Connecting Rods

PISTONS

▸ **See Figure 177**

The piston should be visually inspected for any signs of cracking or burning (caused by hot spots or detonation), and scuffing or excessive wear on the skirts. The wrist pin attaches the piston to the connecting rod. The piston should move freely on the wrist pin, both sliding and pivoting. Grasp the connecting rod securely, or mount it in a vise, and try to rock the piston back and forth along the centerline of the wrist pin. There should not be any excessive play evident between the piston and the pin. If there are C-clips retaining the pin in the piston then you have wrist pin bushings in the rods. There should not be any excessive play between the wrist pin and the rod bushing. Normal clearance for the wrist pin is approx. 0.001–0.002 in. (0.025mm–0.051mm).

Use a micrometer and measure the diameter of the piston, perpendicular to the wrist pin, on the skirt. Compare the reading to its original cylinder measurement obtained earlier. The difference between the two readings is the piston-to-wall clearance. If the clearance is within specifications, the piston may be used as is. If the piston is out of specification, but the bore is not, you will need a new piston. If both are out of specification, you will need the cylinder rebored and oversize pistons installed. Generally if two or more pistons/bores are out of specification, it is best to rebore the entire block and purchase a complete set of oversize pistons.

Fig. 177 Measure the piston's outer diameter, perpendicular to the wrist pin, with a micrometer

TCCS3210

CONNECTING ROD

You should have the connecting rod checked for straightness at a machine shop. If the connecting rod is bent, it will unevenly wear the bearing and piston, as well as place greater stress on these components. Any bent or twisted connecting rods must be replaced. If the rods are straight and the wrist pin clearance is within specifications, then only the bearing end of the rod need be checked. Place the connecting rod into a vice, with the bearing inserts in place, install the cap to the rod and torque the fasteners to specifications. Use a telescoping gauge and carefully measure the inside diameter of the bearings. Compare this reading to the rods original crankshaft journal diameter measurement. The difference is the oil clearance. If the oil clearance is not within specifications, install new bearings in the rod and take another measurement. If the clearance is still out of specifications, and the crankshaft is not, the rod will need to be reconditioned by a machine shop.

➡ **You can also use Plastigage® to check the bearing clearances. The assembling section has complete instructions on its use.**

Camshaft

Inspect the camshaft and lifters/followers as described earlier in this section.

Bearings

All of the engine bearings should be visually inspected for wear and/or damage. The bearing should look evenly worn all around with no deep scores or pits. If the bearing is severely worn, scored, pitted or heat blued, then the bearing, and the components that use it, should be brought to a machine shop for inspection. Full-circle bearings (used on most camshafts, auxiliary shafts, balance shafts, etc.) require specialized tools for removal and installation, and should be brought to a machine shop for service.

Oil Pump

➡ **The oil pump is responsible for providing constant lubrication to the whole engine and so it is recommended that a new oil pump be installed when rebuilding the engine.**

Completely disassemble the oil pump and thoroughly clean all of the components. Inspect the oil pump gears and housing for wear and/or damage. Insure that the pressure relief valve operates properly and there is no binding or sticking due to varnish or debris. If all of the parts are in proper working condition, lubricate the gears and relief valve, and assemble the pump.

REFINISHING

▸ **See Figure 178**

Almost all engine block refinishing must be performed by a machine shop. If the cylinders are not to be rebored, then the cylinder glaze can be removed with a ball hone. When removing cylinder glaze with a ball hone, use a light or penetrating type oil to lubricate the hone. Do not allow the hone to run dry as this may cause excessive scoring of the cylinder bores and wear on the hone. If new pistons are required, they will need to be installed to the connecting rods. This

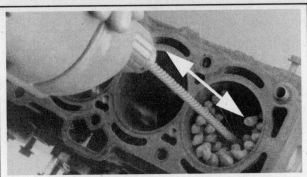

Fig. 178 Use a ball type cylinder hone to remove any glaze and provide a new surface for seating the piston rings

should be performed by a machine shop as the pistons must be installed in the correct relationship to the rod or engine damage can occur.

Pistons and Connecting Rods

▶ See Figure 179

Only pistons with the wrist pin retained by C-clips are serviceable by the home-mechanic. Press fit pistons require special presses and/or heaters to remove/install the connecting rod and should only be performed by a machine shop.

All pistons will have a mark indicating the direction to the front of the engine and the must be installed into the engine in that manner. Usually it is a notch or arrow on the top of the piston, or it may be the letter F cast or stamped into the piston.

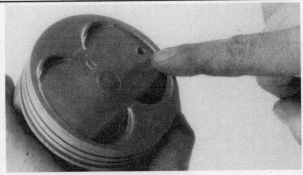

Fig. 179 Most pistons are marked to indicate positioning in the engine (usually a mark means the side facing the front)

ASSEMBLY

Before you begin assembling the engine, first give yourself a clean, dirt free work area. Next, clean every engine component again. The key to a good assembly is cleanliness.

Mount the engine block into the engine stand and wash it one last time using water and detergent (dishwashing detergent works well). While washing it, scrub the cylinder bores with a soft bristle brush and thoroughly clean all of the oil passages. Completely dry the engine and spray the entire assembly down with an anti-rust solution such as WD-40® or similar product. Take a clean lint-free rag and wipe up any excess anti-rust solution from the bores, bearing saddles, etc. Repeat the final cleaning process on the crankshaft. Replace any freeze or oil galley plugs which were removed during disassembly.

Crankshaft

▶ See Figures 180, 181, 182 and 183

1. Remove the main bearing inserts from the block and bearing caps.
2. If the crankshaft main bearing journals have been refinished to a definite undersize, install the correct undersize bearing. Be sure that the bearing inserts and bearing bores are clean. Foreign material under inserts will distort bearing and cause failure.
3. Place the upper main bearing inserts in bores with tang in slot.

➡The oil holes in the bearing inserts must be aligned with the oil holes in the cylinder block.

4. Install the lower main bearing inserts in bearing caps.
5. Clean the mating surfaces of block and rear main bearing cap.
6. Carefully lower the crankshaft into place. Be careful not to damage bearing surfaces.
7. Check the clearance of each main bearing by using the following procedure:

   a. Place a piece of Plastigage® or its equivalent, on bearing surface across full width of bearing cap and about ¼ in. off center.

   b. Install cap and tighten bolts to specifications. Do not turn crankshaft while Plastigage® is in place.

   c. Remove the cap. Using the supplied Plastigage® scale, check width of Plastigage® at widest point to get maximum clearance. Difference between readings is taper of journal.

   d. If clearance exceeds specified limits, try a 0.001 in. or 0.002 in. undersize bearing in combination with the standard bearing. Bearing clearance must be within specified limits. If standard and 0.002 in. undersize bearing does not bring clearance within desired limits, refinish crankshaft journal, then install undersize bearings.

8. Install the rear main seal.
9. After the bearings have been fitted, apply a light coat of engine oil to the journals and bearings. Install the rear main bearing cap. Install all bearing caps except the thrust bearing cap. Be sure that main bearing caps are installed in original locations. Tighten the bearing cap bolts to specifications.
10. Install the thrust bearing cap with bolts finger-tight.

Fig. 180 Apply a strip of gauging material to the bearing journal, then install and torque the cap

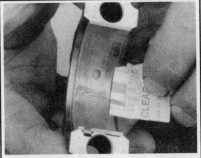

Fig. 181 After the cap is removed again, use the scale supplied with the gauging material to check the clearance

Fig. 182 A dial gauge may be used to check crankshaft end-play

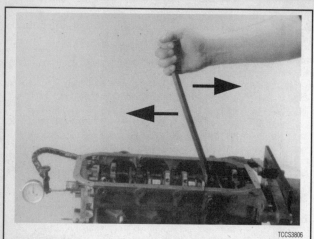
Fig. 183 Carefully pry the crankshaft back and forth while reading the dial gauge for end-play

Fig. 184 Checking the piston ring-to-ring groove side clearance using the ring and a feeler gauge

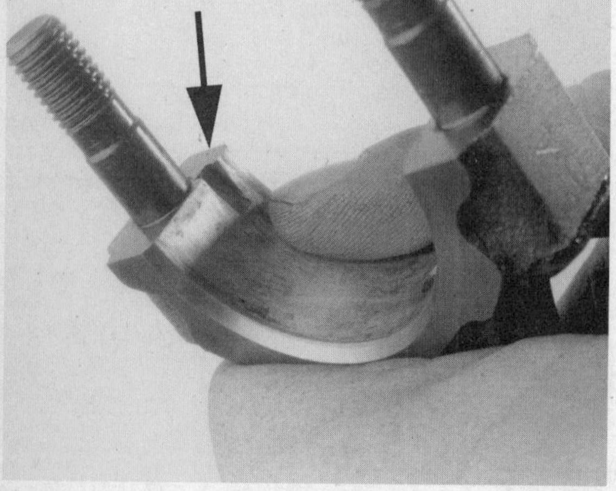

11. Pry the crankshaft forward against the thrust surface of upper half of bearing.

12. Hold the crankshaft forward and pry the thrust bearing cap to the rear. This aligns the thrust surfaces of both halves of the bearing.

13. Retain the forward pressure on the crankshaft. Tighten the cap bolts to specifications.

14. Measure the crankshaft end-play as follows:

   a. Mount a dial gauge to the engine block and position the tip of the gauge to read from the crankshaft end.

   b. Carefully pry the crankshaft toward the rear of the engine and hold it there while you zero the gauge.

   c. Carefully pry the crankshaft toward the front of the engine and read the gauge.

   d. Confirm that the reading is within specifications. If not, install a new thrust bearing and repeat the procedure. If the reading is still out of specifications with a new bearing, have a machine shop inspect the thrust surfaces of the crankshaft, and if possible, repair it.

15. Rotate the crankshaft so as to position the first rod journal to the bottom of its stroke.

Pistons and Connecting Rods

▶ See Figures 184, 185, 186 and 187

1. Before installing the piston/connecting rod assembly, oil the pistons, piston rings and the cylinder walls with light engine oil. Install connecting rod bolt protectors or rubber hose onto the connecting rod bolts/studs. Also perform the following:

   a. Select the proper ring set for the size cylinder bore.

   b. Position the ring in the bore in which it is going to be used.

   c. Push the ring down into the bore area where normal ring wear is not encountered.

   d. Use the head of the piston to position the ring in the bore so that the ring is square with the cylinder wall. Use caution to avoid damage to the ring or cylinder bore.

   e. Measure the gap between the ends of the ring with a feeler gauge. Ring gap in a worn cylinder is normally greater than specification. If the ring gap is greater than the specified limits, try an oversize ring set.

   f. Check the ring side clearance of the compression rings with a feeler gauge inserted between the ring and its lower land according to specification. The gauge should slide freely around the entire ring circumference without binding. Any wear that occurs will form a step at the inner portion of the lower land. If the lower lands have high steps, the piston should be replaced.

2. Unless new pistons are installed, be sure to install the pistons in the cylinders from which they were removed. The numbers on the connecting rod and bearing cap must be on the same side when installed in the cylinder bore. If a connecting rod is ever transposed from one engine or cylinder to another, new

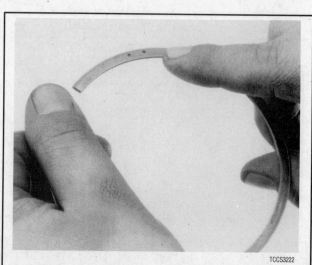
Fig. 186 Most rings are marked to show which side of the ring should face up when installed to the piston

Fig. 185 The notch on the side of the bearing cap matches the tang on the bearing insert

Fig. 187 Install the piston and rod assembly into the block using a ring compressor and the handle of a hammer

bearings should be fitted and the connecting rod should be numbered to correspond with the new cylinder number. The notch on the piston head goes toward the front of the engine.

3. Install all of the rod bearing inserts into the rods and caps.

4. Install the rings to the pistons. Install the oil control ring first, then the second compression ring and finally the top compression ring. Use a piston ring expander tool to aid in installation and to help reduce the chance of breakage.

5. Make sure the ring gaps are properly spaced around the circumference of the piston. Fit a piston ring compressor around the piston and slide the piston and connecting rod assembly down into the cylinder bore, pushing it in with the wooden hammer handle. Push the piston down until it is only slightly below the top of the cylinder bore. Guide the connecting rod onto the crankshaft bearing journal carefully, to avoid damaging the crankshaft.

6. Check the bearing clearance of all the rod bearings, fitting them to the crankshaft bearing journals. Follow the procedure in the crankshaft installation above.

7. After the bearings have been fitted, apply a light coating of assembly oil to the journals and bearings.

8. Turn the crankshaft until the appropriate bearing journal is at the bottom of its stroke, then push the piston assembly all the way down until the connecting rod bearing seats on the crankshaft journal. Be careful not to allow the bearing cap screws to strike the crankshaft bearing journals and damage them.

9. After the piston and connecting rod assemblies have been installed, check the connecting rod side clearance on each crankshaft journal.

10. Prime and install the oil pump and the oil pump intake tube.

Camshaft, Lifters And Timing Assembly

1. Install the camshaft.
2. Install the lifters/followers into their bores.
3. Install the timing gears/chain assembly.

Cylinder Head(S)

1. Install the cylinder head(s) using new gaskets.
2. Assemble the rest of the valve train (pushrods and rocker arms and/or shafts).

Engine Start-up and Break-in

STARTING THE ENGINE

Now that the engine is installed and every wire and hose is properly connected, go back and double check that all coolant and vacuum hoses are connected. Check that your oil drain plug is installed and properly tightened. If not already done, install a new oil filter onto the engine. Fill the crankcase with the proper amount and grade of engine oil. Fill the cooling system with a 50/50 mixture of coolant/water.

1. Connect the vehicle battery.

2. Start the engine. Keep your eye on your oil pressure indicator; if it does not indicate oil pressure within 10 seconds of starting, turn the vehicle **OFF**.

❊❊ WARNING

Damage to the engine can result if it is allowed to run with no oil pressure. Check the engine oil level to make sure that it is full. Check for any leaks and if found, repair the leaks before continuing. If there is still no indication of oil pressure, you may need to prime the system.

3. Confirm that there are no fluid leaks (oil or other).

4. Allow the engine to reach normal operating temperature (the upper radiator hose will be hot to the touch).

5. At this point any necessary checks or adjustments can be performed, such as ignition timing.

6. Install any remaining components or body panels which were removed.

BREAKING IT IN

Make the first miles on the new engine, easy ones. Vary the speed but do not accelerate hard. Most importantly, do not lug the engine, and avoid sustained high speeds until at least 100 miles. Check the engine oil and coolant levels frequently. Expect the engine to use a little oil until the rings seat. Change the oil and filter at 500 miles, 1500 miles, then every 3000 miles past that.

KEEP IT MAINTAINED

Now that you have just gone through all of that hard work, keep yourself from doing it all over again by thoroughly maintaining it. Not that you may not have maintained it before, heck you could have had one to two hundred thousand miles on it before doing this. However, you may have bought the vehicle used, and the previous owner did not keep up on maintenance. Which is why you just went through all of that hard work. See?

Troubleshooting Basic Charging System Problems

Problem	Cause	Solution
Noisy alternator	• Loose mountings • Loose drive pulley • Worn bearings • Brush noise • Internal circuits shorted (High pitched whine)	• Tighten mounting bolts • Tighten pulley • Replace alternator • Replace alternator • Replace alternator
Squeal when starting engine or accelerating	• Glazed or loose belt	• Replace or adjust belt
Indicator light remains on or ammeter indicates discharge (engine running)	• Broken belt • Broken or disconnected wires • Internal alternator problems • Defective voltage regulator	• Install belt • Repair or connect wiring • Replace alternator • Replace voltage regulator/alternator
Car light bulbs continually burn out—battery needs water continually	• Alternator/regulator overcharging	• Replace voltage regulator/alternator
Car lights flare on acceleration	• Battery low • Internal alternator/regulator problems	• Charge or replace battery • Replace alternator/regulator
Low voltage output (alternator light flickers continually or ammeter needle wanders)	• Loose or worn belt • Dirty or corroded connections • Internal alternator/regulator problems	• Replace or adjust belt • Clean or replace connections • Replace alternator/regulator

TCCS3C02

Troubleshooting Engine Mechanical Problems

Problem	Cause	Solution
Excessive oil consumption (cont.)	• Piston ring gaps not properly staggered	• Repair as necessary
	• Excessive main or connecting rod bearing clearance	• Measure bearing clearance, repair as necessary
No oil pressure	• Low oil level	• Add oil to correct level
	• Oil pressure gauge, warning lamp or sending unit inaccurate	• Replace oil pressure gauge or warning lamp
	• Oil pump malfunction	• Replace oil pump
	• Oil pressure relief valve sticking	• Remove and inspect oil pressure relief valve assembly
	• Oil passages on pressure side of pump obstructed	• Inspect oil passages for obstruction
	• Oil pickup screen or tube obstructed	• Inspect oil pickup for obstruction
	• Loose oil inlet tube	• Tighten or seal inlet tube
Low oil pressure	• Low oil level	• Add oil to correct level
	• Inaccurate gauge, warning lamp or sending unit	• Replace oil pressure gauge or warning lamp
	• Oil excessively thin because of dilution, poor quality, or improper grade	• Drain and refill crankcase with recommended oil
	• Excessive oil temperature	• Correct cause of overheating engine
	• Oil pressure relief spring weak or sticking	• Remove and inspect oil pressure relief valve assembly
	• Oil inlet tube and screen assembly has restriction or air leak	• Remove and inspect oil inlet tube and screen assembly. (Fill inlet tube with lacquer thinner to locate leaks.)
	• Excessive oil pump clearance	• Measure clearances
	• Excessive main, rod, or camshaft bearing clearance	• Measure bearing clearances, repair as necessary
High oil pressure	• Improper oil viscosity	• Drain and refill crankcase with correct viscosity oil
	• Oil pressure gauge or sending unit inaccurate	• Replace oil pressure gauge
	• Oil pressure relief valve sticking closed	• Remove and inspect oil pressure relief valve assembly
Main bearing noise	• Insufficient oil supply	• Inspect for low oil level and low oil pressure
	• Main bearing clearance excessive	• Measure main bearing clearance, repair as necessary
	• Bearing insert missing	• Replace missing insert
	• Crankshaft end-play excessive	• Measure end-play, repair as necessary
	• Improperly tightened main bearing cap bolts	• Tighten bolts with specified torque
	• Loose flywheel or drive plate	• Tighten flywheel or drive plate attaching bolts
	• Loose or damaged vibration damper	• Repair as necessary

TCCS3C03

Troubleshooting Engine Mechanical Problems

Problem	Cause	Solution
Connecting rod bearing noise	• Insufficient oil supply	• Inspect for low oil level and low oil pressure
	• Carbon build-up on piston	• Remove carbon from piston crown
	• Bearing clearance excessive or bearing missing	• Measure clearance, repair as necessary
	• Crankshaft connecting rod journal out-of-round	• Measure journal dimensions, repair or replace as necessary
	• Misaligned connecting rod or cap	• Repair as necessary
	• Connecting rod bolts tightened improperly	• Tighten bolts with specified torque
Piston noise	• Piston-to-cylinder wall clearance excessive (scuffed piston)	• Measure clearance and examine piston
	• Cylinder walls excessively tapered or out-of-round	• Measure cylinder wall dimensions, rebore cylinder
	• Piston ring broken	• Replace all rings on piston
	• Loose or seized piston pin	• Measure piston-to-pin clearance, repair as necessary
	• Connecting rods misaligned	• Measure rod alignment, straighten or replace
	• Piston ring side clearance excessively loose or tight	• Measure ring side clearance, repair as necessary
	• Carbon build-up on piston is excessive	• Remove carbon from piston
Valve actuating component noise	• Insufficient oil supply	• Check for: (a) Low oil level (b) Low oil pressure (c) Wrong hydraulic tappets (d) Restricted oil gallery (e) Excessive tappet to bore clearance
	• Rocker arms or pivots worn	• Replace worn rocker arms or pivots
	• Foreign objects or chips in hydraulic tappets	• Clean tappets
	• Excessive tappet leak-down	• Replace valve tappet
	• Tappet face worn	• Replace tappet; inspect corresponding cam lobe for wear
	• Broken or cocked valve springs	• Properly seat cocked springs; replace broken springs
	• Stem-to-guide clearance excessive	• Measure stem-to-guide clearance, repair as required
	• Valve bent	• Replace valve
	• Loose rocker arms	• Check and repair as necessary
	• Valve seat runout excessive	• Regrind valve seat/valves
	• Missing valve lock	• Install valve lock
	• Excessive engine oil	• Correct oil level

TCCS3C04

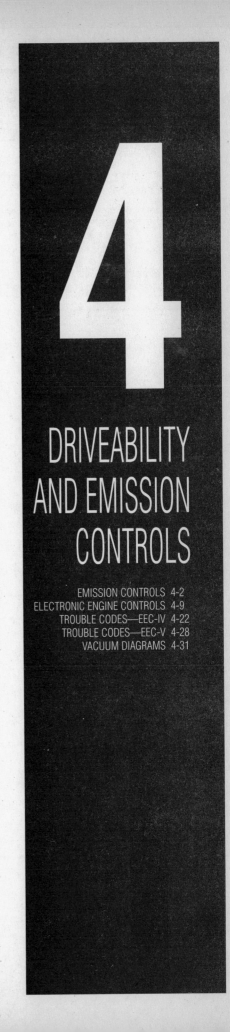

4

DRIVEABILITY AND EMISSION CONTROLS

EMISSION CONTROLS

Crankcase Ventilation System

OPERATION

▶ **See Figures 1 and 2**

The crankcase emission control equipment consists of a positive crankcase ventilation (PCV) valve, a closed oil filler cap and the hoses that connect this equipment.

When the engine is running, a small portion of the gases which are formed in the combustion chamber leak by the piston rings and enter the crankcase. Since these gases are under pressure they tend to escape from the crankcase and enter into the atmosphere. If these gases are allowed to remain in the

crankcase for any length of time, they would contaminate the engine oil and cause sludge to build up. If the gases are allowed to escape into the atmosphere, they would pollute the air, as they contain unburned hydrocarbons. The crankcase emission control equipment recycles these gases back into the engine combustion chamber, where they are burned.

Crankcase gases are recycled in the following manner: While the engine is running, clean filtered air is drawn into the crankcase through the intake air filter and then through a hose leading to the oil filler cap. As the air passes through the crankcase it picks up the combustion gases and carries them out of the crankcase, up through the PCV valve and into the intake manifold. After they enter the intake manifold they are drawn into the combustion chamber and are burned.

The most critical component of the system is the PCV valve. This vacuum-controlled valve regulates the amount of gases which are recycled into the combustion chamber. At low engine speeds the valve is partially closed, limiting the flow of gases into the intake manifold. As engine speed increases, the valve opens to admit greater quantities of the gases into the intake manifold. If the valve should become blocked or plugged, the gases will be prevented from escaping the crankcase by the normal route. Since these gases are under pressure, they will find their own way out of the crankcase. This alternate route is usually a weak oil seal or gasket in the engine. As the gas escapes by the gasket, it also creates an oil leak. Besides causing oil leaks, a clogged PCV valve also allows these gases to remain in the crankcase for an extended period of time, promoting the formation of sludge in the engine.

The above explanation and the component testing procedure which follows applies to all of the gasoline engines installed in Ford trucks, since all are equipped with PCV systems.

COMPONENT TESTING

▶ **See Figure 3**

With the engine running at idle, pull the PCV valve and hose from the valve rocker cover rubber grommet.

A hissing noise should be heard as air passes through the valve and a strong vacuum should be felt when you place a finger over the valve inlet if the valve is working properly. While you have your finger over the PCV valve inlet, check for vacuum leaks in the hose and at the connections.

When the PCV valve is removed from the engine, a metallic clicking noise should be heard when it is shaken. This indicates that the metal check ball inside the valve is still free and is not gummed up.

REMOVAL & INSTALLATION

1. Pull the PCV valve and hose from the rubber grommet in the rocker cover.
2. Remove the PCV valve from the hose. Inspect the inside of the PCV valve. If it is dirty, disconnect it from the intake manifold and replace it.
   To install:
3. If the PCV valve hose was removed, connect it to the intake manifold.
4. Connect the PCV valve to its hose.
5. Install the PCV valve into the rubber grommet in the valve rocker cover.

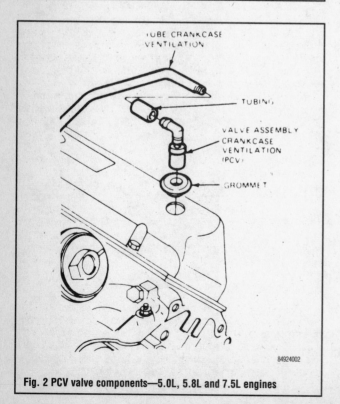

Fig. 1 A common Positive Crankcase Ventilation (PCV) system—V8 engines

84924001

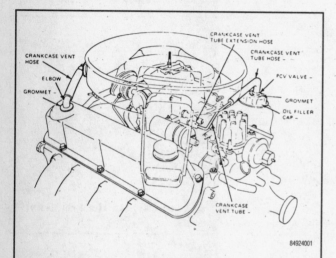

Fig. 2 PCV valve components—5.0L, 5.8L and 7.5L engines

84924002

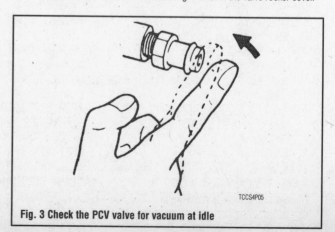

Fig. 3 Check the PCV valve for vacuum at idle

TCCS4P05

Evaporative Emission Controls

OPERATION

▶ **See Figures 4, 5, 6 and 7**

Changes in atmospheric temperature cause fuel tanks to breathe; that is, the air within the tank expands and contracts with outside temperature changes. As the temperature rises, air escapes through the tank vent tube or the vent in the tank cap. The air which escapes contains gasoline vapors. In a similar manner on carbureted engines, the gasoline which fills the carburetor float bowl expands when the engine is stopped. Engine heat causes this expansion. The vapors escape through the air cleaner.

The Evaporative Emission Control System provides a sealed fuel system with the capability to store and condense fuel vapors. The system has three parts: a fill control vent system; a vapor vent and storage system; and a pressure and vacuum relief system (special fill cap).

The fill control vent system is a modification to the fuel tank. It uses a dome air space within the tank which is 10–12 percent of the tank's volume. The air space is sufficient to provide for the thermal expansion of the fuel. The space also serves as part of the in-tank vapor vent system.

The in-tank vent system consists of the aforementioned domed air space and a vapor separator assembly. The separator assembly is mounted to the top of the fuel tank and is secured by a cam lockring, similar to the one which secures the fuel sending unit. Foam material fills the vapor separator assembly. The

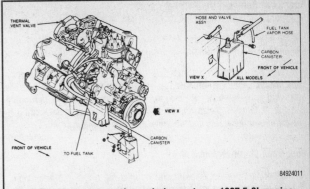

Fig. 6 A common evaporative emission system—1987 5.8L engine

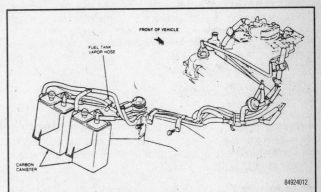

Fig. 7 A common evaporative emission system—5.8 4-bbl. Heavy Duty engine, except California

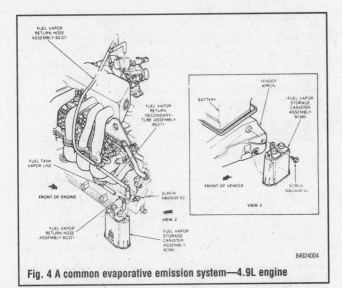

Fig. 4 A common evaporative emission system—4.9L engine

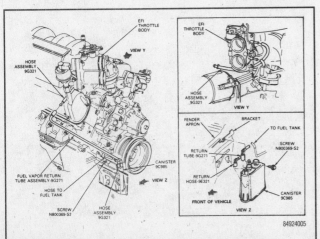

Fig. 5 A common evaporative emission system—5.0L engine

foam material separates raw fuel and vapors, thus retarding the entrance of fuel into the vapor line.

The vapor separator is an orifice valve located in the dome of the tank. The restricted size of the orifice, 0.050 in. (1.27mm) tends to allow only vapor to pass out of the tank. The orifice valve is connected to the vent line which runs forward to the carbon filled canister in the engine compartment.

The sealed filler cap has a pressure-vacuum relief valve. Under normal operating conditions, the filler cap operates as a check valve, allowing air to enter the tank to replace the fuel consumed. At the same time, it prevents vapors from escaping through the cap. In case of excessive pressure within the tank, the filler cap valve opens to relieve the pressure.

Because the filler cap is sealed, fuel vapors have only one place through which they may escape: the vapor separator assembly at the top of the fuel tank. The vapors pass through the foam material and continue through a single vapor line which leads to a canister in the engine compartment. The canister is filled with activated charcoal.

Another vapor line runs from the top of the carburetor float chamber or the intake manifold, or the throttle body, to the charcoal canister.

As the fuel vapors (hydrocarbons), enter the charcoal canister, they are absorbed by the charcoal. The air is dispelled through the open bottom of the charcoal canister, leaving the hydrocarbons trapped within the charcoal. When the engine is started, vacuum causes fresh air to be drawn into the canister from its open bottom. The fresh air passes through the charcoal picking up the hydrocarbons which are trapped there and feeding them into the engine for burning with the fuel mixture.

Fuel Tank Vapor Orifice and Rollover Valve Assembly

Fuel vapor in the fuel tank is vented to the carbon canister through the vapor valve assembly. The valve is mounted in a rubber grommet at a central location in the upper surface of the fuel tank. A vapor space between the fuel level and the tank upper surface is combined with a small orifice and float shut-off valve in the vapor valve assembly to prevent liquid fuel from passing to the carbon canister. The vapor space also allows for thermal expansion of the fuel.

Fuel Bowl Solenoid Vent Valve

The fuel bowl solenoid vent valve is located in the fuel bowl vent line on carbureted engines. The valve is open when the ignition switch is in the **OFF** position and closes when the engine is running.

➡️**If lean fuel mixture is suspected as the cause of improper engine operation, check either the solenoid vent valve or the carburetor's built-in fuel bowl vent valve to make sure they are closed when the engine is running. If the valve is open, purge vacuum will affect the fuel bowl balanced air pressure, and the carburetor will have a leaner air/fuel mixture.**

Fuel Bowl Thermal Vent Valv4e

The thermal vent valve is located in the carburetor-to-carbon canister vent line. The valve's function is to prevent fuel tank vapors from being vented through the carburetor fuel bowl when the engine is cold.

The valve is closed when the engine compartment is cold, blocking fuel vapors from entering the now-open carburetor fuel bowl vent, and instead routing them to the carbon canister. When the engine runs and the engine compartment warms up, the thermal vent valve opens. When the engine is turned off, the fuel bowl (or solenoid) vent valve opens, allowing fuel vapor to flow through the open thermal vent valve and into the carbon canister. The thermal vent valve closes as it cools, and the cycle repeats.

Auxiliary Fuel Bowl Vent Tube

On some carbureted vehicles, an auxiliary fuel bowl vent tube is connected to the fuel bowl vent tube to vent the fuel bowl when the internal fuel bowl vent or the solenoid vent valve is closed and the thermal vent valve is also closed. An air filter is installed on the air cleaner end of the tube to prevent the entrance of contaminants into the carburetor fuel bowl.

Pressure/Vacuum Relief Fuel Cap

The fuel cap contains an integral pressure and vacuum relief valve. The vacuum valve acts to allow air into the fuel tank to replace the fuel as it is used, while preventing vapors from escaping the tank through the atmosphere. The vacuum relief valve opens after a vacuum of 0.5 psi (3.45 kPa). The pressure valve acts as a backup pressure relief valve in the event the normal venting system is overcome by excessive generation of internal pressure or restriction of the normal venting system. The pressure relief range is 1.6–2.1 psi (11–14.5 kPa). Fill cap damage or contamination that stops the pressure vacuum valve from working may result in deformation of the fuel tank.

COMPONENT TESTING

▶ **See Figure 8**

Canister Purge Regulator Valve

1. Disconnect the hoses at the purge regulator valve. Disconnect the electrical lead.
2. Connect a vacuum pump to the vacuum source port.
3. Apply 5 in. Hg (16.9 kPa) to the port. The valve should hold the vacuum. If not, replace it.

Canister Purge Valve

1. Apply vacuum to port **A**. The valve should hold vacuum. If not, replace it.
2. Apply vacuum to port **B**. Valves E5VE–AA, E4VE–AA and E77E–AA should show a slight vacuum leak-down. All other valves should hold vacuum. If the valve doesn't operate properly, replace it.
3. Apply 16 in. Hg (54 kPa) to port **A** and apply vacuum to port **B**. Air should pass. On valves E5VE–AA, E4VE–AA and E77E–AA, the flow should be greater than that noted in Step 2.

➡️**Never apply vacuum to port C. Doing so will damage the valve.**

4. If the valve fails to perform properly in any of these tests, replace it.

TCCS4P04

Fig. 8 A manifold vacuum gauge can be used to check the evaporative canister components

SERVICE

System Inspection

1. Visually inspect the vapor and vacuum lines and connections for looseness, pinching, leakage, or other damage. If a fuel line, vacuum line or orifice blockage is suspected as the cause of a malfunction, correct the cause before proceeding further.
2. If applicable, check the wiring and connectors to the purge solenoid for looseness, corrosion, damage or other problems.

REMOVAL & INSTALLATION

Carbon Canister

▶ **See Figure 9**

1. Disconnect the negative battery cable.
2. Label and disconnect the vapor hoses from the carbon canister.
3. Remove the canister attaching screws and remove the canister.
4. Installation is the reverse of the removal procedure.

88284P03

Fig. 9 Remove the hoses, then unscrew the canister from its mounting

Fuel Tank Vapor Orifice and Rollover Valve Assembly

1. Disconnect the negative battery cable.
2. Remove the fuel tank as described in Section 5.
3. Remove the vapor orifice and rollover valve assembly from the fuel tank.
4. Installation is the reverse of the removal procedure.

Purge Control Valve

1. Disconnect the negative battery cable.
2. Label and disconnect the hoses from the purge control valve.
3. Remove the purge control valve.
4. Installation is the reverse of the removal procedure.

Purge Solenoid Valve

1. Disconnect the negative battery cable.
2. Label and disconnect the hoses from the purge solenoid valve.
3. Disconnect the electrical connector from the valve.
4. Remove the purge solenoid valve.
5. Installation is the reverse of the removal procedure.

Fuel Bowl Solenoid Vent Valve

1. Disconnect the negative battery cable.
2. Label and disconnect the hoses from the fuel bowl solenoid vent valve.
3. Disconnect the electrical connector from the valve.
4. Remove the fuel bowl solenoid vent valve.
5. Installation is the reverse of the removal procedure.

Fuel Bowl Thermal Vent Valve

1. Disconnect the negative battery cable.
2. Label and disconnect the hoses from the fuel bowl thermal vent valve.
3. Remove the fuel bowl thermal vent valve.
4. Installation is the reverse of the removal procedure.

Pressure/Vacuum Relief Fuel Cap

1. Unscrew the fuel filler cap. The cap has a pre-vent feature that allows the tank to vent for the first ¾ turn before unthreading.
2. Remove the screw retaining the fuel cap tether and remove the fuel cap.
3. Installation is the reverse of the removal procedure. When installing the cap, continue to turn clockwise until the ratchet mechanism gives off 3 or more loud clicks.

Exhaust Gas Recirculation (EGR) System

OPERATION

▶ See Figure 10

All models are equipped with an exhaust gas recirculation (EGR) system which reintroduces the exhaust gas into the combustion cycle. This process lowers the combustion temperatures and reduces the formation of oxides of nitrogen. There are several systems that are utilized on the Ford trucks covered by this manual.

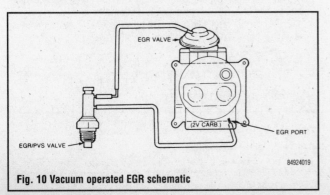

Fig. 10 Vacuum operated EGR schematic

84924019

Electronic EGR (EEGR) System

The Electronic EGR system (EEGR) is found in all systems in which EGR flow is controlled according to computer commands by means of an EGR valve position sensor (EVP) attached to the valve.

The EEGR valve is operated by a vacuum signal from the dual EGR Solenoid Valves, or the electronic vacuum regulator which actuates the valve diaphragm.

As supply vacuum overcomes the spring load, the diaphragm is actuated lifting the pintle off of its seat allowing the exhaust gas to flow. The amount of flow is directly proportional to the pintle position. The EVP sensor sends an electrical signal to notify the EEC of its position.

The EEGR valve is not serviceable. The EVP sensor must be serviced separately.

Integral Backpressure (IBP) EGR System

The Integral Backpressure (IBP) EGR system combines inputs of EGR port vacuum and backpressure into one unit. The valve requires both inputs for proper operation. The valve won't operate on vacuum alone.

There are two types of backpressure valves: the poppet type and the tapered pintle type.

Ported EGR Valve

The ported EGR valve is operated by engine vacuum alone. A vacuum signal from the carburetor activates the EGR valve diaphragm. As the vacuum signal increase it gradually opens the valve pintle allowing exhaust gases to flow. The amount of flow is directly proportional to the pintle position.

COMPONENT TESTING

▶ See Figures 11 and 12

Electronic EGR (EEGR) System

SYSTEM INTEGRITY

1. Inspect vacuum hoses and connections for looseness, pinching, leakage, splitting or blockage.
2. If the lines look good, check routing against the vacuum routing schematic for the vehicle you are working on.
3. Inspect the EGR valve for loose attaching bolts or damaged flange gasket. Repair or replace as necessary.

VACUUM AT IDLE

1. Start the engine and run until normal operating temperature is reached.
2. With the engine idling, disconnect the EGR vacuum supply at the valve and check for a vacuum signal. The signal should be less than 1.0 in. Hg (3.4 kPa) at idle. If not check the EVR solenoid for leakage.

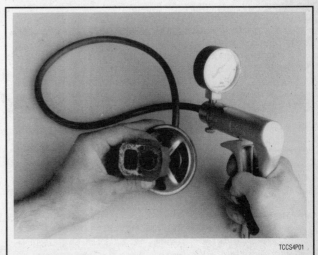

TCCS4P01

Fig. 11 Some EGR valves may be tested using a vacuum pump by watching for diaphragm movement

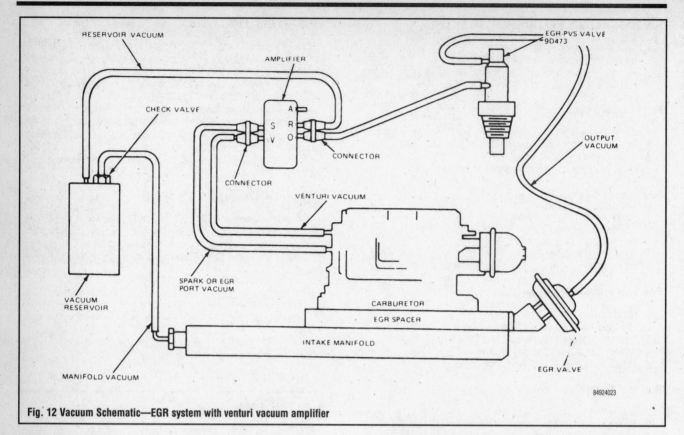

Fig. 12 Vacuum Schematic—EGR system with venturi vacuum amplifier

EGR VALVE FUNCTION

1. Install a suitable tachometer.
2. Disconnect the wiring to the IAC solenoid.
3. Remove and plug the vacuum supply hose from the EGR valve nipple.
4. Start the engine. Let it idle with the transmission in NEUTRAL.
5. Observe the idle speed. If the engine idles, the EGR valve is functioning normally.
6. If the engine will not idle with the IAC solenoid disconnected, provide an air bypass to the engine by slightly opening the throttle plate, or by creating an intake vacuum leak. Do not exceed a typical idle rpm.
7. Slowly apply 5–10 in. Hg (16.9–33.8 kPa) of vacuum to the EGR valve nipple using a hand vacuum pump. If the idle speed drops more than 100 rpm, inspect the EGR valve for blockage. Clean, inspect again for vacuum leakage, or replace as necessary.

Integral Backpressure (IBP) EGR System

1. Inspect vacuum hoses and connections for looseness, pinching, leakage, splitting or blockage.
2. Start the engine and let it idle until normal operating temperature is reached. Make certain there is no vacuum to the EGR valve.
3. Install a suitable tachometer.

✷✷ CAUTION

The exhaust system is HOT! Take care not to burn yourself when working on the tailpipe.

4. Shut off the engine and let the exhaust system cool. When the tailpipe is cool to the touch, fashion a restrictor to reduce the effective exhaust outlet to about ½ in. (13mm). This will increase the exhaust system backpressure.
5. Remove the vacuum supply hose from the EGR valve nipple, then plug the hose.
6. Place the transmission in NEUTRAL, then start the engine.
7. Observe the idle speed. If the engine idles, the EGR valve is functioning normally.
8. Slowly apply 5–10 in. Hg (16.9–33.8 kPa) of vacuum to the EGR valve nipple using a hand vacuum pump. Replace the EGR valve is:

a. The engine does not stall.
b. The idle speed does not drop more than 100 rpm.
c. The idle speed does not return to approximately normal after the vacuum is removed.
9. If the EGR is not replaced, connect the idle air bypass valve wiring.
10. Unplug and connect the EGR vacuum hose.
11. The EGR system is functioning normally.

Ported EGR Valve

1. Inspect vacuum hoses and connections for looseness, pinching, leakage, splitting or blockage.
2. Start the engine and let it idle until normal operating temperature is reached. Make certain there is no vacuum to the EGR valve.
3. Install a suitable tachometer.
4. Disconnect the idle air bypass valve wiring (EFI engines only).
5. Remove the vacuum supply hose from the EGR valve nipple, then plug the hose.
6. Place the transmission in NEUTRAL, then start the engine.
7. Observe the idle speed. If the engine idles, the EGR valve is functioning normally.
8. Slowly apply 5–10 in. Hg (16.9–33.8 kPa) of vacuum to the EGR valve nipple using a hand vacuum pump. Perform the following:
a. If the idle speed drops more than 100 rpm, or if the engine stalls, perform the next step. Otherwise replace the EGR valve.
b. Remove the vacuum from the EGR valve. If the idle speed does not return to approximately normal, replace the EGR valve.
9. Connect the idle air bypass valve wiring.
10. Unplug and connect the EGR vacuum hose.
11. The EGR system is functioning normally.

REMOVAL & INSTALLATION

Electronic EGR

▶ See Figures 13, 14, 15 and 16

1. Disconnect the negative battery cable.
2. Disconnect the EVP sensor wiring.

Fig. 13 Disconnect the EVP sensor wiring

Fig. 14 Disconnect the exhaust gas inlet tube

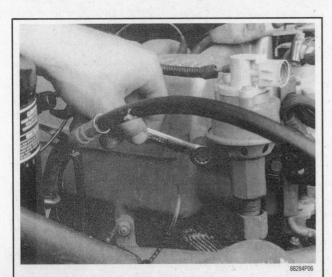

Fig. 15 Unbolt the EGR from the engine

Fig. 16 Scrape the gasket surfaces clean without scuffing them

3. Disconnect the vacuum line from the EGR valve.
4. Disconnect the exhaust gas inlet tube.
5. Remove the mounting bolts and remove the EGR valve.
6. Remove the EVP sensor from the EGR valve.
7. Remove any old gasket material from the engine mating area.

To install:
8. Attach the EVP sensor to the EGR valve.
9. Install the EGR valve to the engine with a new gasket and tighten.
10. Attach the vacuum line to the valve.
11. Connect the EVP sensor wiring.
12. Disconnect the exhaust gas inlet tube.
13. Connect the negative battery cable.

Ported EGR

1. Disconnect the negative battery cable.
2. Tag and disconnect the vacuum line from the EGR valve.
3. Remove the mounting bolts and remove the EGR valve.
4. Scrape the old gasket off of the engine mating area.

To install:
5. Attach the EGR valve with a new gasket and tighten.
6. Attach the vacuum lines to the valve.
7. Connect the negative battery cable.

Pressure Feedback Electronic (PFE) Transducer

The PFE EGR transducer converts exhaust pressure into proportional voltage which is digitized by the PCM. The PCM utilizes the signal from the PFE to maintain optimum EGR flow.
1. Disconnect the negative battery cable.
2. Detach the electrical connector and exhaust pressure line from the transducer.
3. Remove the transducer from the vehicle.

To install:
4. Attach the transducer to the engine and tighten the mounting bolt.
5. Attach the electrical connector and exhaust pressure line to the transducer.

EGR VALVE CLEANING

If the EGR valve is serviceable, remove the EGR valve for cleaning. Do not strike or pry on the valve diaphragm housing or supports, as this may damage the valve operating mechanism and/or change the valve calibration. Check orifice hole in the EGR valve body for deposits. A small hand drill of no more than 0.060 in. (1.5mm) diameter may be used to clean the hole if plugged. Extreme care must be taken to avoid enlarging the hole or damaging the surface of the orifice plate.

Managed Thermactor Air (MTA) System

OPERATION

The MTA system is used to inject fresh air into the exhaust manifolds or catalytic converters via an air control valve. Under some operating conditions, the air can be dumped back into the atmosphere via an air bypass valve. On some applications the two valves are combined into one unit. The air bypass valve can be either the normally closed type, when the valves are separate, or the normally open type, when the valves are combined.

TESTING

Normally Closed Air Bypass Valve Functional Test

1. Disconnect the air supply hose at the valve.
2. Run the engine to normal operating temperature.
3. Disconnect the vacuum line and make sure vacuum is present. If no vacuum is present, remove or bypass any restrictors or delay valves in the vacuum line.
4. Run the engine at 1500 rpm with the vacuum line connected. Air pump supply air should be heard and felt at the valve outlet.
5. With the engine still at 1500 rpm, disconnect the vacuum line. Air at the outlet should shut off or dramatically decrease. Air pump supply air should now be felt or heard at the silencer ports.
6. If the valve doesn't pass each of these tests, replace it.

Normally Open Air Bypass Valve Functional Test

1. Disconnect the air supply hose at the valve.
2. Run the engine to normal operating temperature.
3. Disconnect the vacuum lines from the valve.
4. Run the engine at 1500 rpm with the vacuum lines disconnected. Air pump supply air should be heard and felt at the valve outlet.
5. Shut off the engine. Using a spare length of vacuum hose, connect the vacuum nipple of the valve to direct manifold vacuum.
6. Run the engine at 1500 rpm. Air at the outlet should shut off or dramatically decrease. Air pump supply air should now be felt or heard at the silencer ports.
7. With the engine still in this mode, cap the vacuum vent. Accelerate the engine to 2,000 rpm and suddenly release the throttle. A momentary interruption of air pump supply air should be felt at the valve outlet.
8. If the valve doesn't pass each of these tests, replace it. Reconnect all lines.

Air Control Valve Functional Test

1. Run the engine to normal operating temperature, then increase the speed to 1500 rpm.
2. Disconnect the air supply hose at the valve inlet and verify that there is airflow present.
3. Reconnect the air supply hose.
4. Disconnect both air supply hoses.
5. Disconnect the vacuum hose from the valve.
6. With the engine running at 1,500 rpm, airflow should be felt and heard at the outlet on the side of the valve, with no airflow heard or felt at the outlet opposite the vacuum nipple.
7. Shut off the engine.
8. Using a spare piece of vacuum hose, connect direct manifold vacuum to the valve's vacuum fitting. Airflow should be heard and felt at the outlet opposite the vacuum nipple, and no airflow should be present at the other outlet.
9. If the valve is not functioning properly, replace it.

Air Supply Pump Functional Check

▶ See Figures 17, 18, 19 and 20

1. Check and, if necessary, adjust the belt tension. Press at the mid-point of the belt's longest straight run. You should be able to depress the belt about ½ in. (13mm) at most.
2. Run the engine to normal operating temperature and let it idle.

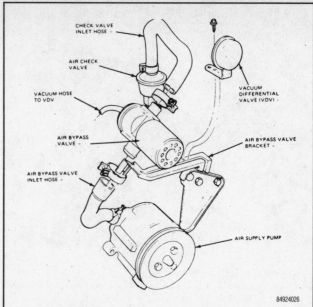

Fig. 17 Thermactor® air pump system components. Locations vary slightly among engines

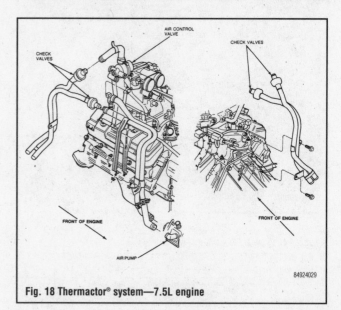

Fig. 18 Thermactor® system—7.5L engine

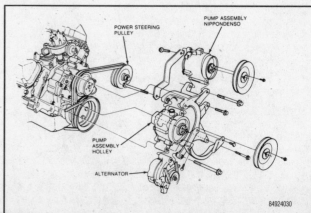

Fig. 19 Dual air pump system on 5.8L 4-bbl. and 7.5L 4-bbl. engines, except California

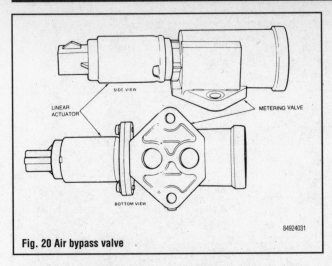

LINEAR
ACTUATOR

SIDE VIEW

METERING VALVE

BOTTOM VIEW

84924031

Fig. 20 Air bypass valve

3. Disconnect the air supply hose from the bypass control valve. If the pump is operating properly, airflow should be felt at the pump outlet. The flow should increase as you increase the engine speed. The pump is not serviceable and should be replaced if it is not functioning properly.

Bypass Air Idle Speed Control

The air bypass solenoid is used to control the engine idle speed and is operated by the EEC module.

The valve allows air to pass around the throttle plates to control:
- Cold engine fast idle
- Cold starting
- Dashpot operation
- Over-temperature idle boost
- Engine load correction

The valve is not serviceable and correction is by replacement only.

ELECTRONIC ENGINE CONTROLS

Powertrain Control Module

OPERATION

➡**The 1988–95 gasoline powered Ford vehicles covered by this manual employ the fourth generation Electronic Engine Control system, commonly designated EEC-IV, to manage fuel, ignition and emissions on vehicle engines. All 1995–1996 diesel engines and some 1996 gasoline engines (depending on engine application), will be equipped with EEC-V.**

The Powertrain Control Module (PCM) is responsible for the operation of the emission control devices, cooling fans, ignition and advance, and in some cases, automatic transmission functions. Because the EEC system oversees both the ignition timing and the fuel injector operation, a precise air/fuel ratio will be maintained under all operating conditions. The PCM is a microprocessor or small computer which receives electrical inputs from several sensors, switches and relays on and around the engine.

➡**PCM's for EEC-IV systems use a 60-pin connector. For the EEC-V PCM, a 104-pin connector is used.**

Based on combinations of these inputs, the PCM controls outputs to various devices concerned with engine operation and emissions. The engine control assembly relies on the signals to form a correct picture of current vehicle operation. If any of the input signals is incorrect, the PCM reacts to what ever picture is painted for it. For example, if the coolant temperature sensor is inaccurate and reads too low, the PCM may see a picture of the engine never warming up. Consequently, the engine settings will be maintained as if the engine were cold. Because so many inputs can affect one output, correct diagnostic procedures are essential on these systems.

The EEC system employs adaptive fuel logic. This process is used to compensate for normal wear and variability within the fuel system. Once the engine

Emissions Maintenance Warning (EMW) Light

DESCRIPTION

All gasoline engine equipped light trucks built for sale outside of California employ this device.

The EMW consists of an instrument panel mounted amber light imprinted with the word EGR, EMISS, or EMISSIONS. The light is connected to a sensor module located under the instrument panel. The purpose is to warn the driver that the 60,000 mile (96,618 km) emission system maintenance is required on the vehicle. Specific emission system maintenance requirements are listed in the truck's owner's manual maintenance schedule.

RESETTING THE LIGHT

1. Turn the key to the **OFF** position.
2. Lightly push a Phillips screwdriver through the 0.2 in. (5mm) diameter hole labeled RESET, and lightly press down and hold it.
3. While maintaining pressure with the screwdriver, turn the key to the **RUN** position. The EMW lamp will light and stay lit as long as you keep pressure on the screwdriver. Hold the screwdriver down for about 5 seconds.
4. Remove the screwdriver. The lamp should go out within 2–5 seconds. If not, repeat Steps 1–3.
5. Turn the key **OFF**.
6. Turn the key to the **RUN** position. The lamp will light for 2–5 seconds and then go out. If not, repeat the rest procedure.

➡**If the light comes on between 15,000 and 45,000 miles (24,155–72,464 km) or between 75,000 and 105,000 miles (120,773–169,082 km), you'll have to replace the 1000 hour pre-timed module.**

enters steady-state operation, the engine control assembly watches the oxygen sensor signal for a bias or tendency to run slightly rich or lean. If such a bias is detected, the adaptive logic corrects the fuel delivery to bring the air/fuel mixture towards a centered or 14.7:1 ratio. This compensating shift is stored in a non-volatile memory which is retained by battery power even with the ignition switched off. The correction factor is then available the next time the vehicle is operated.

The Powertrain Control Module (PCM) is usually located under the instrument panel or passenger's seat and is usually covered by a kick panel. A multi-pin connector links the PCM with all system components. The processor provides a continuous reference voltage to the B/MAP, EVP and TP sensors. EEC systems use a 5 volt reference signal. Different calibration information is used in different vehicle applications, such as California or Federal models. For this reason, careful identification of the engine, year, model and type of electronic control system is essential to ensure correct component replacement.

➡**If the battery cable(s) is disconnected for longer than 5 minutes, the adaptive fuel factor will be lost. After repair it will be necessary to drive the truck at least 10 miles to allow the processor to relearn the correct factors. The driving period should include steady-throttle open road driving if possible. During the drive, the vehicle may exhibit driveability symptoms not noticed before. These symptoms should clear as the PCM computes the correction factor. The PCM will also store Code 19 indicating loss of power to the controller.**

Electronic Engine Control

The electronic engine control subsystem consists of the PCM and various sensors and actuators. The PCM reads inputs from engine sensors, then outputs a voltage signal to various components (actuators) to control engine functions. The period of time that the injectors are energized ("ON" time or "pulse width") determines the amount of fuel delivered to each cylinder. The longer the pulse width, the richer the fuel mixture.

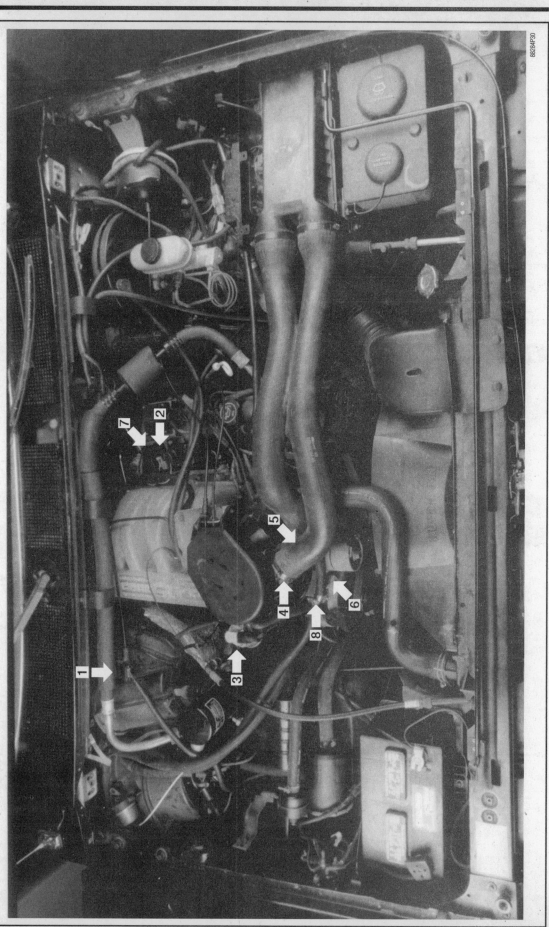

EMISSIONS AND ELECTRONIC ENGINE CONTROLS - 1990 5.0L ENGINE SHOWN

1. Manifold Absolute Pressure (MAP) sensor
2. Thermactor Air Bypass (TAB) solenoid
3. EGR Valve Position (EVP) sensor
4. Throttle Position Sensor (TPS)
5. Idle air bypass valve
6. Engine Coolant Temperature (ECT) sensor
7. Thermactor Air Diverter (TAD) solenoid
8. Canister purge solenoid

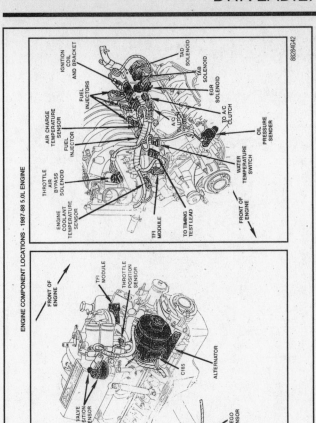

ENGINE COMPONENT LOCATIONS - 1987-88 5.0L ENGINE

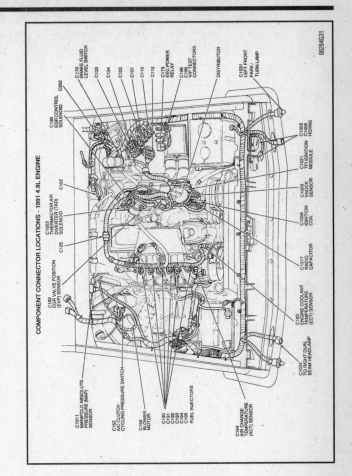

COMPONENT CONNECTOR LOCATIONS - 1991 4.9L ENGINE

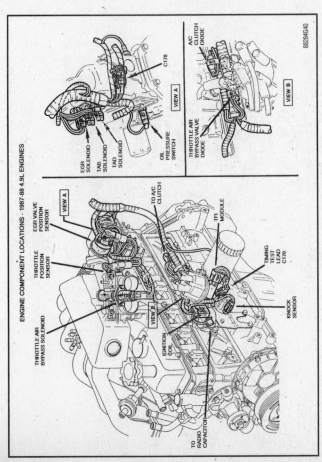

ENGINE COMPONENT LOCATIONS - 1987-88 4.9L ENGINES

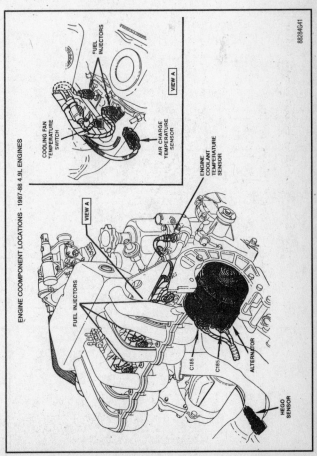

ENGINE COMPONENT LOCATIONS - 1987-88 4.9L ENGINES

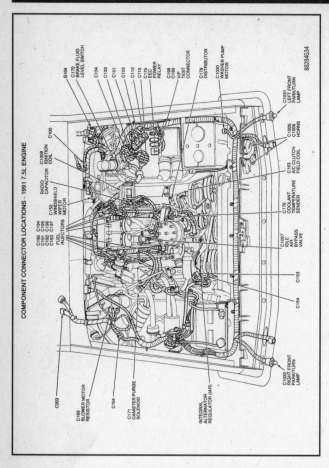

COMPONENT CONNECTOR LOCATIONS - 1991 7.5L ENGINE

88284G34

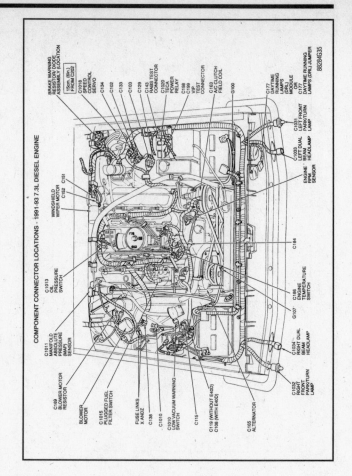

COMPONENT CONNECTOR LOCATIONS - 1991-93 7.3L DIESEL ENGINE

88284G35

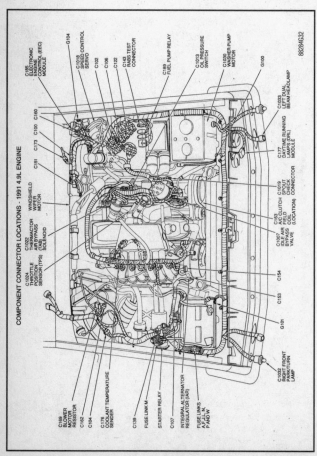

COMPONENT CONNECTOR LOCATIONS - 1991 4.9L ENGINE

88284G32

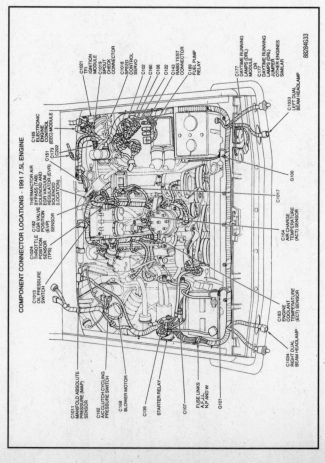

COMPONENT CONNECTOR LOCATIONS - 1991 7.5L ENGINE

88284G33

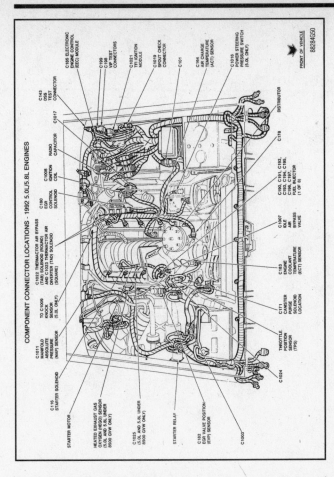

COMPONENT CONNECTOR LOCATIONS - 1992 5.0L/5.8L ENGINES

88284G50

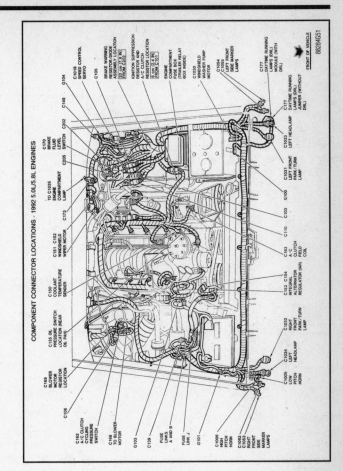

COMPONENT CONNECTOR LOCATIONS - 1992 5.0L/5.8L ENGINES

88284G51

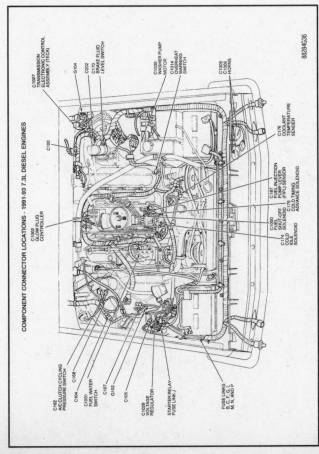

COMPONENT CONNECTOR LOCATIONS - 1991-93 7.3L DIESEL ENGINES

88284G36

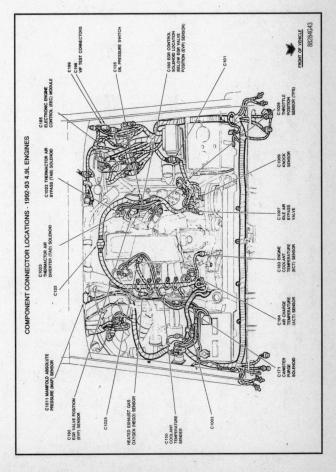

COMPONENT CONNECTOR LOCATIONS - 1992-93 4.9L ENGINES

88284G43

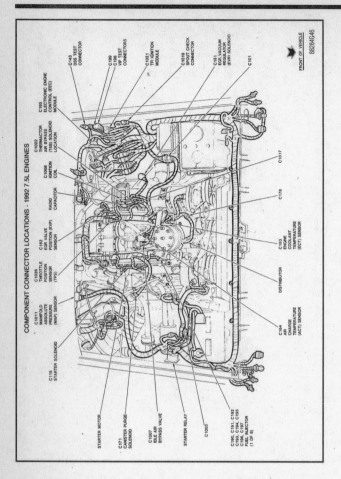

COMPONENT CONNECTOR LOCATIONS - 1992 7.5L ENGINES

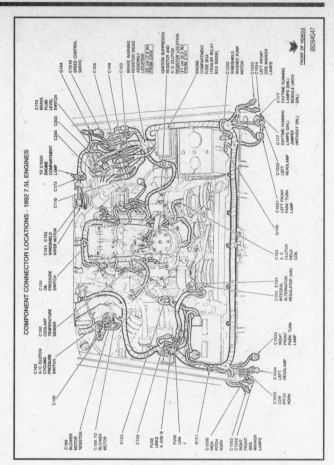

COMPONENT CONNECTOR LOCATIONS - 1992 7.5L ENGINES

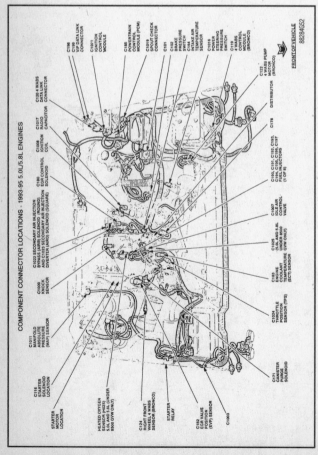

COMPONENT CONNECTOR LOCATIONS - 1993-95 5.0L/5.8L ENGINES

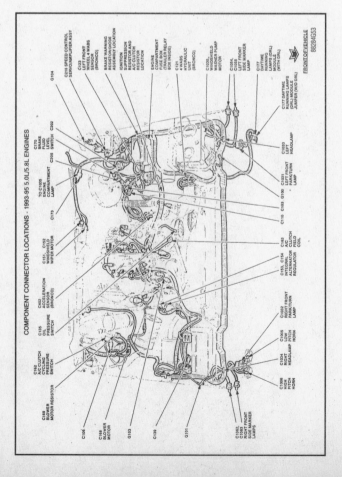

COMPONENT CONNECTOR LOCATIONS - 1993-95 5.0L/5.8L ENGINES

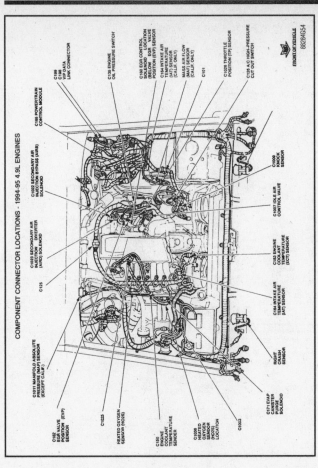

COMPONENT CONNECTOR LOCATIONS - 1994-95 4.9L ENGINES

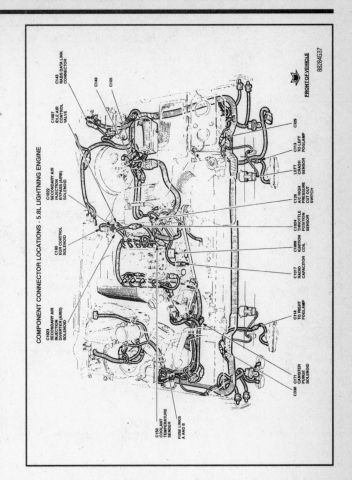

COMPONENT CONNECTOR LOCATIONS - 5.8L LIGHTNING ENGINE

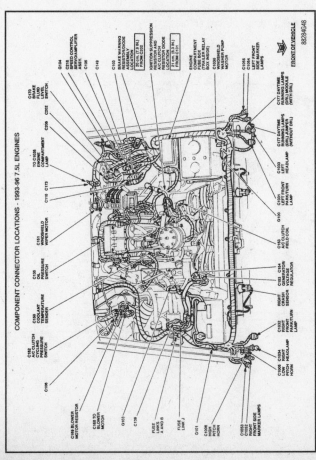

COMPONENT CONNECTOR LOCATIONS - 1993-96 7.5L ENGINES

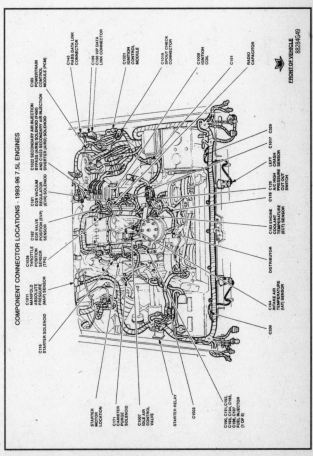

COMPONENT CONNECTOR LOCATIONS - 1993-96 7.5L ENGINES

COMPONENT CONNECTOR LOCATIONS - 1994-96 D1 TURBO DIESEL ENGINES

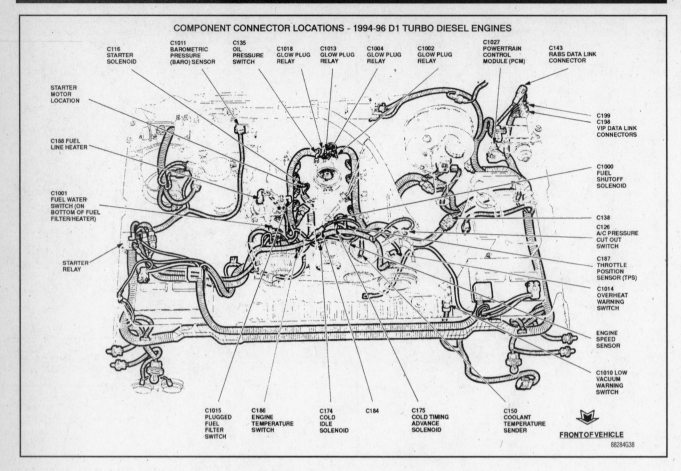

COMPONENT CONNECTOR LOCATIONS - 1994-96 D1 TURBO DIESEL ENGINES

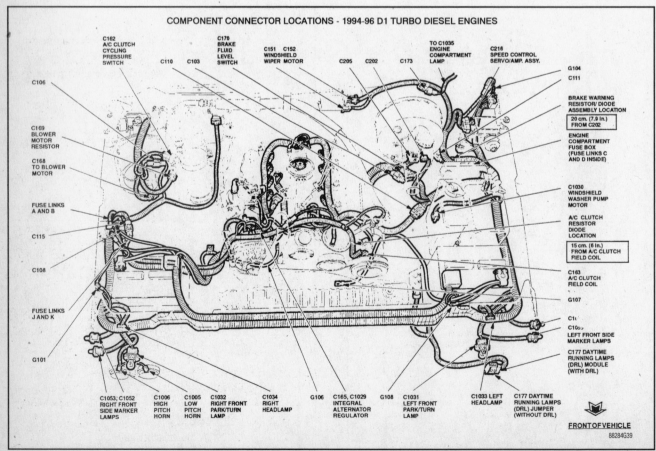

➡The operating reference voltage (Vref) between the PCM and its sensors and actuators is 5 volts. This allows these components to work during the crank operation even though the battery voltage drops.

In order for the PCM to properly control engine operation, it must first receive current status reports on various operating conditions. The control unit constantly monitors crankshaft position, throttle plate position, engine coolant temperature, exhaust gas oxygen level, air intake volume and temperature, air conditioning (On/Off), spark knock and barometric pressure.

REMOVAL & INSTALLATION

1. Disconnect the negative battery cable.
2. Disconnect the module wiring leading to the unit.
3. Unscrew, then remove the control unit from the vehicle.

To install:
4. Attach the module to the bracket, then screw in place.
5. Attach the wiring to the module.
6. Connect the negative battery cable.

Oxygen Sensor

OPERATION

An Oxygen Sensor (O_2S) or heated Oxygen Sensor (HO_2S) is used on all engines. The sensor is mounted in the right side exhaust manifold on some V8 engines, while other V8 engines use a sensor in both right and left manifolds. The sensor protrudes into the exhaust stream and monitors the oxygen content of the exhaust hoses. The difference between the oxygen content of the exhaust gases and that of the outside air generates a voltage signal to the PCM. The PCM monitors this voltage and, depending upon the value of the signal received, issues a command to adjust for a rich or a lean condition.

TESTING

No attempt should ever be made to measure the voltage output of the sensor. The current drain of any conventional voltmeter would be such that it would permanently damage the sensor. No jumpers, test leads or any other electrical connections should ever be made to the sensor. Use these tools ONLY on the PCM side of the wiring harness connector AFTER disconnecting it from the sensor.

REMOVAL & INSTALLATION

◆ **See Figures 21, 22 and 23**

The oxygen sensor must be replaced every 30,000 miles (48,000 km). The sensor may be difficult to remove when the engine temperature is below 120°F (48°C). Excessive removal force may damage the threads in the exhaust manifold or pipe; follow the removal procedure carefully.

1. Locate the oxygen sensor. It protrudes from the center of the exhaust manifold and looks somewhat like a spark plug.

2. Disconnect the electrical connector from the oxygen sensor.
3. Spray a commercial solvent onto the sensor threads and allow it to soak in for at least five minutes.
4. Carefully unscrew and remove the sensor.

To install:
5. Coat the new sensor's threads with anti-seize compound made for oxygen sensors. This is NOT a conventional anti-seize paste. The use of a regular compound may electrically insulate the sensor, rendering it inoperative. You must coat the threads with an electrically conductive anti-seize compound.
6. Installation torque is 30 ft. lbs. (42 Nm). Do not overtighten.
7. Reconnect the electrical connector. Be careful not to damage the connector.

Heated Oxygen Sensor

OPERATION

Heated oxygen sensors are located in the exhaust pipes below the exhaust manifolds. The sensors react with the oxygen in the exhaust gasses and generates a voltage based on this reaction. A low voltage indicates too much oxygen or a lean condition. Where as a high voltage indicates not enough oxygen or a rich condition.

TESTING

1. Disconnect the Oxygen Sensor (O_2S). Measure resistance between PWR and GND (heater) terminals of the sensor. If the reading is about 6 ohms at 68°F (20°C). the sensor's heater element is okay.
2. With the O_2S connected and engine running, measure voltage with DVOM between terminals HO_2S and **SIG RTN** (GND) of the oxygen sensor connector. If the voltage readings are about equal to those in the table, the sensor is okay.

REMOVAL & INSTALLATION

1. Disconnect the negative battery cable.
2. Raise and safely support the vehicle.
3. Disconnect the heated oxygen sensor from the engine control sensor wiring.

➡If excessive force is needed to remove the sensors, lubricate the sensors with penetrating oil prior to removal.

4. Remove the sensors from the Y pipe or left manifold with a sensor removal tool T94P-9472-A or equivalent.

To install:
5. Install the sensor in its correct location, tighten to 26–34 ft. lbs. (36–46 Nm).
6. Connect the sensor electrical wiring.
7. Lower the vehicle.
8. Connect the negative battery cable.

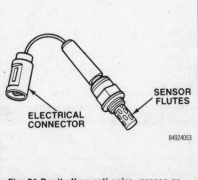

Fig. 21 Don't allow anti-seize, grease or oil to contaminate the oxygen sensor prior to installation

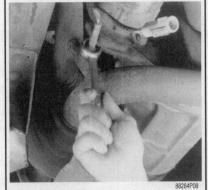

Fig. 22 Use a flare wrench to avoid rounding off the hex head

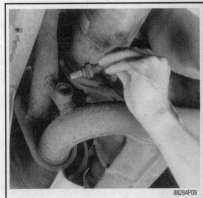

Fig. 23 Remove the oxygen sensor from the exhaust system

Idle Air Control Valve (IAC)

OPERATION

The idle air control valve (IAC) control the engine idle speed and dashpot functions. The valve is located on the throttle body on. This valve allows air to bypass the throttle plate. The amount of air is determined by the Powertrain Control Module (PCM) and controlled by a duty cycle signal.

TESTING

1. Make sure the ignition key is **OFF**.
2. Disconnect the air control valve.
3. Use an ohmmeter to measure the resistance between the terminals of the valve solenoid.

➡**Due to the diode in the solenoid, place the ohmmeter positive lead on the VPWR pin and the negative lead on the ISC pin.**

4. If the resistance is not 7–13 ohms replace the air control valve.

REMOVAL & INSTALLATION

▶ **See Figures 24, 25 and 26**

1. Disconnect the negative battery cable.
2. Disconnect the engine wiring to the IAC sensor.
3. Remove the two retaining screws for the valve.
4. Remove the IAC valve and discard of the old gasket.
To install:
5. Clean the area of old gasket material.

Fig. 24 Remove the two screws retaining the IAC valve   88284P11

Fig. 25 Remove the detached IAC valve from the throttle body   88284P12

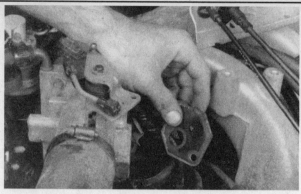

Fig. 26 Remove the gasket from the throttle body   88284P13

6. Using a new gasket, attach the IAC valve to the engine. Tighten the retaining screws to 71–102 inch lbs. (8–12 Nm).
7. Connect the IAC valve wiring to the unit.
8. Connect the negative battery cable.

Engine Coolant Temperature (ECT) Sensor

OPERATION

The ECT sensor is located either in the heater supply tube at the rear of the engine, or in the lower intake manifold. The ECT sensor is a thermistor (changes resistance as temperature changes). The sensor detects the temperature of engine coolant and provides a corresponding signal to the PCM. From this signal, the PCM will modify the air/fuel ratio (mixture), idle speed, spark advance, EGR and Canister purge control. When the engine coolant is cold, the ECT sensor signal causes the PCM to provide enrichment to the air/fuel ratio for good cold drive away as engine coolant warms up, the voltage will drop.

TESTING

▶ **See Figure 27 and 27a**

1. Disconnect the temperature sensor.
2. Connect an ohmmeter between the sensor terminals and set the ohmmeter scale on 200,000 ohms.
3. Measure the resistance with the engine off and cool and with the engine running and warmed up. Compare the resistance values obtained with the chart.
4. Replace the sensor if the readings are incorrect.

REMOVAL & INSTALLATION

1. Drain the engine cooling system slightly.
2. Disconnect the negative battery cable.
3. Detach the wiring connection from the sensor.
4. Remove the coolant temperature sensor.
5. Clean the sensor area of any debris.
To install:
6. Install a new sensor. Tighten the 6–14 ft. lbs. (8–19 Nm).
7. Attach the sensor wiring to the unit.
8. Connect the negative battery cable.
9. Fill the engine cooling system with a 50/50 coolant water mixture.
10. Start the engine and top off the cooling system.

Intake Air Temperature (IAT) Sensor

OPERATION

The intake air temperature sensor (IAT) changes the resistance in response to the intake air temperature. The sensor resistance decreases as the surrounding air temperature increases. This provides a signal to the PCM indicating the temperature of the incoming air intake.

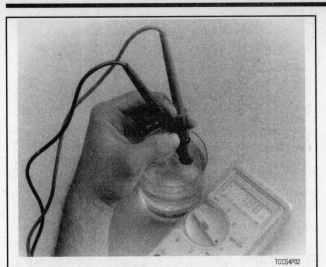

TCCS4P02

Fig. 27 Submerge the end of the temperature sensor in cold or hot water and check resistance

TESTING

▶ **See Figures 27 and 27a**

With ignition **OFF**, disconnect the IAT sensor. Measure the resistance across the sensor connector terminals. If the reading for a given temperature is about that shown in the table, the IAT sensor is okay.

REMOVAL & INSTALLATION

1. Disconnect the negative battery cable.
2. Disconnect the wiring to the IAT.
3. Remove the sensor from the intake manifold (MFI engines) or air cleaner/tube (SFI engines).
To install:
4. Clean the sensor area. Install the sensor into the intake manifold and tighten to 12–15 ft. lbs. (16–24 Nm) on MFI engines. Fasten the twist-lock part on SFI engines.
5. Attach the wiring to the unit.
6. Connect the negative battery cable.

Mass Air Flow (MAF) Sensor

OPERATION

The Mass Air Flow (MAF) sensor directly measures the mass of the air flow-ing into the engine. The sensor output is an analog signal ranging from about 0.5–5.0 volts. The signal is used by the PCM to calculate the injector pulse width. The sensing element is a thin platinum wire wound on a ceramic bobbin and coated with glass. This "hot wire" is maintained at 200°C above the ambient temperature as measured by a constant "cold wire". The MAF sensor is located in the outlet side of the air cleaner lid assembly.

TESTING

1. Make sure the ignition key is **OFF**.
2. Connect Breakout Box T83L–50–EEC-IV or equivalent, to the PCM harness and connect the PCM.
3. Start the engine and let it idle.
4. Use a voltmeter to measure the voltage between test pin **50** of the Breakout Box and the battery negative post.
5. Replace the MAF sensor if the voltage is not 0.36–1.50 volts.

REMOVAL & INSTALLATION

> ✷✷ **CAUTION**

The mass air flow sensor hot wire sensing element and housing are calibrated as a unit and must be serviced as a complete assembly. Do not damage the sensing element or possible failure of the sensor may occur.

1. Disconnect the negative battery cable.
2. Disconnect the air tube at the sensor.
3. Disconnect the engine control sensor wiring from the MAF sensor.
4. Disconnect the mass air flow sensor.
5. Remove the gasket.
To install:
6. Install the MAF sensor to the vehicle.
7. Install the air cleaner cover and tighten the outlet tube clamps to 12–22 inch lbs. (1–3 Nm).
8. Attach the engine control sensor wiring to the sensor.
9. Connect the negative battery cable.

Barometric/Manifold Absolute Pressure Sensors (B/MAP)

OPERATION

The B/MAP sensor used on some engines is separate from the barometric sensor and is located on the left fender panel in the engine compartment. The barometric sensor signals the PCM of changes in atmospheric pressure and density to regulate calculated air flow into the engine. The MAP sensor monitors and signals the PCM of changes in intake manifold pressure which result from engine load, speed and atmospheric pressure changes.

ENGINE COOLANT/INTAKE AIR TEMPERATURE SENSORS PARAMETER CHART

Temperature		Engine Coolant/Intake Air Temperature Sensor Values	
°F	°C	Voltage (volts)	Resistance (K ohms)
248	120	.27	1.18
230	110	.35	1.55
212	100	.46	2.07
194	90	.60	2.80
176	80	.78	3.84
158	70	1.02	5.37
140	60	1.33	7.70
122	50	1.70	10.97
104	40	2.13	16.15
86	30	2.60	24.27
68	20	3.07	27.30
50	10	3.51	58.75

88284GT1

Fig. 27a The ECT and IAT sensors are tested using an ohmmeter and a thermometer.

The Manifold Absolute Pressure (MAP) sensor measures the pressure in the intake manifold and sends a variable frequency signal to the PCM. When the ignition is **ON** and the engine **OFF**, the MAP sensor will indicate the barometric pressure in the intake manifold.

TESTING

1. Connect **MAP/BARO** tester to sensor connector and sensor harness connector. With ignition **ON** and engine **OFF**, use a DVOM to measure voltage across tester terminals. If the tester's 4-6V indicator is ON, the reference voltage input to the sensor is okay.
2. If the DVOM voltage reading is as indicated in the table, the sensor is okay.

REMOVAL & INSTALLATION

▶ **See Figure 28**

1. Disconnect the negative battery cable.
2. Disengage the electrical connector and the vacuum line from the sensor.
3. Unfasten the sensor mounting bolts and remove the sensor.
To install:
4. Install the sensor with the mounting bolts and tighten.
5. Attach the electrical wiring lead to the sensor.
6. Attach the vacuum line to the sensor.
7. Connect the negative battery cable.

88284P02

Fig. 28 Disengage the MAP sensor connector, then unbolt the sensor from the vehicle

Throttle Position (TP) Sensor

OPERATION

The Throttle Position (TP) sensor is a potentiometer that provides a signal to the PCM that is directly proportional to the throttle plate position. The TP sensor is mounted on the side of the throttle body and is connected to the throttle plate shaft.

The TP senses the throttle movement and position and transmits an appropriate electrical signal to the PCM. These signals are used by the PCM to adjust the air/fuel mixture, spark timing and EGR operation according to engine load at idle, part throttle, or full throttle. The TP sensor has 2 versions, an adjustable and a non-adjustable; the difference being elongated mounting holes that allow the rotary sensor to be turned slightly to adjust the output voltage. The rotary TP sensor with round mounting holes are not adjustable.

TESTING

▶ **See Figures 29a and 29b**

With ignition **F**, disconnect the TP sensor connector. Measure resistance between sensor connector terminals **SIG RTN** and TP. If resistance readings are about equal to the values in the tables, the sensor is okay.

REMOVAL & INSTALLATION

▶ **See Figure 29c**

1. Disconnect the TP sensor wiring harness.
2. On 5.0L and 5.8L engines, it may be necessary to remove the throttle body. On all other engines proceed to the next step.
3. Disconnect the wiring from the sensor.
4. Matchmark the TP sensor and throttle body. Remove the 2 retaining screws and the sensor.
To install:

※ WARNING

Slide the rotary tangs into position over the throttle shaft blade, then rotate the TP sensor CLOCKWISE only to the installed position. Failure to follow this step may result in high idle speeds for 5.0L and 5.8L engines.

5. On 5.0L and 5.8L engines, position the TP sensor so that the pigtail points toward the IAC valve.
6. Secure the TP sensor to the throttle body with the retaining screws. Tighten to 18–27 inch lbs. (2–3 Nm) on 4.9L engines or 11–16 inch lbs. (1.2–1.8 Nm) on 5.0L/5.8L engines.
7. If applicable, install the throttle body.
8. Connect the wiring.
9. Connect the negative battery cable.

Camshaft Position (CMP) Sensor

OPERATION

The Camshaft Position Sensor, is a Hall-effect sensor that generates a digital frequency while windows in a target wheel pass through its magnetic field. The frequency of the windows passing by the sensor, as well as the width of selected windows, allows the PCM to detect engine speed and position.

TESTING

Two-Wire Sensors

1. With the ignition **OFF**, install a Breakout Box.
2. Connect CMP sensor and ECM.
3. Using DVOM on AC scale and set to monitor less than 5V, measure voltage between Breakout Box terminals 24 and 46 with the engine running at varying RPM. If the voltage reading varies more than 0.1V AC, the sensor is okay.

Three-Wire Sensors

1. With the ignition **OFF**, disconnect the CMP sensor. With the ignition **ON** and the engine **OFF**, measure the voltage between sensor harness connector VPWR and PWR GND terminals (refer to the figure). If the reading is greater than 10.5V, the power circuit to the sensor is okay.
2. With the ignition **OFF**, install a Breakout Box. Connect CMP sensor and PCM. Using DVOM on AC and scale set to monitor less than 5V, measure voltage between Breakout Box terminals 24 and 40 with the engine running at varying RPM. If the voltage reading varies more than 0.1V AC, the sensor is okay.

REMOVAL & INSTALLATION

Diesel Engine

1. Disconnect the camshaft position sensor wiring.

THROTTLE POSITION (TP) SENSOR SPECIFICATIONS

Throttle Position Sensor Setting (K.O.E.O. and K.O.E.R.)			TP Circuit (Signal) Operating Voltage Range (K.O.E.O.)	
Engine Application	Rotational Degree Range	Voltage Range	Minimum	Maximum
4.9L EFI ①	1°–13°	0.66–1.22	0.34	4.84
5.0L EFI ①	1°–13°	0.66–1.22	0.34	4.84
5.8L EFI ①	1°–13°	0.66–1.22	0.34	4.84
7.0L EFI ①	1°–13°	0.66–1.22	0.34	4.84
7.5L EFI ①	1°–13°	0.66–1.22	0.34	4.84
4.9L, 5.0L, 5.8L, 7.5L EFI with E4OD	1°–13°	0.66–1.22	0.34	4.84

① Except E4OD transmissions

88284GA2

Fig. 29a Throttle Position (TP) sensor throttle angle vs voltage specification.

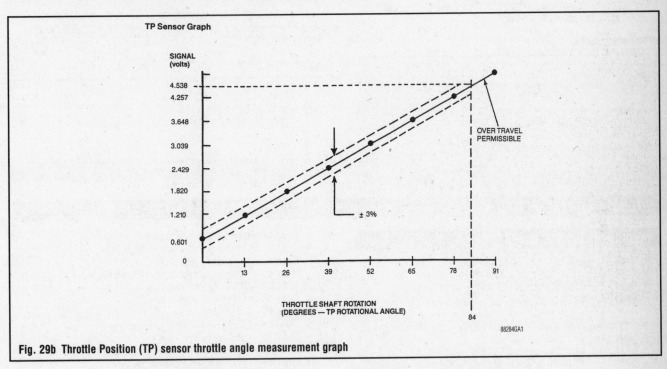

Fig. 29b Throttle Position (TP) sensor throttle angle measurement graph

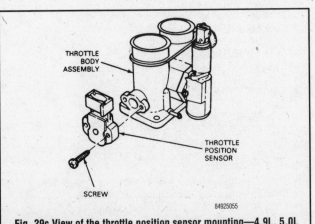

Fig. 29c View of the throttle position sensor mounting—4.9L, 5.0L and 5.8L MFI engines shown, others similar

2. Remove the bolt, then the camshaft position sensor.
To install:
3. Install the CMP sensor and bolt in place.
4. Engage the wiring connector.

Crankshaft Position (CP) Sensor

OPERATION

The CP sensor is mounted on the right front of some V8 engines, is a variable reluctance sensor triggered by a trigger pulse wheel (36 minus 1 tooth). Its purpose is to provide the PCM with an accurate ignition timing reference (when the piston reaches 10 degrees BTDC) and injector operation information (twice each crankshaft revolution). The crankshaft vibration damper is fitted with a 4 lobe pulse ring. As the crankshaft rotates, the pulse ring lobes interrupt the magnetic field at the tip of the CP sensor.

TESTING

Using DVOM on the AC scale and set to monitor less than 5V, measure voltage between the sensor Cylinder Identification (CID) terminal and ground. The sensor is okay if the voltage reading varies more than 0.1V AC with the engine running at varying RPM.

Knock Sensor (KS)

OPERATION

This sensor is used on some 4.9L engines. The KS detects engine vibrations caused by preignition or detonation and provides information to the PCM, which then retards the timing to eliminate detonation.

TESTING

1. With ignition **ON** and engine **OFF**, measure voltage between KS connector terminals. If voltage reading is 2.4–2.6V, the circuit between the ECM and KS is okay.
2. With engine running at idle and 3000 rpm, measure voltage using a DVOM on the AC setting between the KS terminals. If the AC voltage reading increases as the rpm increases, the sensor is okay.

REMOVAL & INSTALLATION

1. Disconnect the negative battery cable.
2. Disconnect the wiring from the sensor.
3. Remove the sensor from the cylinder block.
To install:
4. Attach the KS to the cylinder block.
5. Attach the electrical connector to the sensor.
6. Connect the negative battery cable.

EGR Valve Position (EVP) Sensor EEC-IV Management System

OPERATION

The Exhaust Gas Recirculation (EGR) Valve Position (EVP) system uses an electronic EGR valve to control the flow of exhaust gases. The Engine Control Module (ECM) monitors the flow by means of an EVP sensor and regulates the electronic EGR valve accordingly. The valve is operated by a vacuum signal from the EGR Vacuum Regulator (EVR) solenoid which actuates the valve diaphragm.

As the supply vacuum overcomes the spring load, the diaphragm is actuated. This lifts the pintle off its seat and allows exhaust gases to flow. The amount of flow is proportional to the pintle position. The EVP sensor, mounted on the valve, sends an electronic signal representing pintle position to the ECM.

TESTING

1. Disconnect the EVP sensor connector. With the ignition **ON** and the engine **OFF**, measure the voltage between **VREF** and **SIG RTN** terminals of EVP sensor harness connector. If the voltage is 4.0–6.0V, the power circuits to the sensor are okay.
2. Reconnect the EVP sensor. With the ignition **ON** and the engine **OFF**, measure the voltage between EVP sensor terminals EVP and **SIG RTN**. If the voltage reading is 0.67V or less, the sensor is okay.

REMOVAL & INSTALLATION

1. Disconnect the negative battery cable.
2. Disconnect the wiring from the sensor.
3. Remove the sensor mounting nuts and remove the sensor from the EGR valve.
To install:
4. Attach the sensor to the EGR valve and tighten the mounting nuts.
5. Connect the sensor electrical lead to the sensor.
6. Connect the negative battery cable.

TROUBLE CODES—EEC-IV

Diagnostic Trouble Codes (DTC)

- **Code 11**—System pass
- **Code 12**—RPM unable to reach upper test limit
- **Code 13**—RPM unable to reach lower test limit
- **Code 14**—Pip circuit failure
- **Code 15**—PCM read only memory test failed
- **Code 15**—PCM keep alive memory test failed
- **Code 16**—IDM signal not received
- **Code 18**—SPOUT circuit open or spark angle word failure
- **Code 18**—IDM circuit failure or SPOUT circuit grounded
- **Code 19**—Failure in PCM internal voltage
- **Code 21**—ECT out of self-test range
- **Code 22**—BP sensor out of self-test range
- **Code 22**—BP sensor or MAP out of range
- **Code 23**—TP sensor out of self-test range
- **Code 24**—ACT sensor out of self-test range
- **Code 25**—Knock not sensed during dynamic test
- **Code 26**—VAF/MAF out of self-test range
- **Code 26**—TOT out of self-test range
- **Code 26**—TOT sensor out of self-test range (E-400)
- **Code 28**—Loss of IDM, right side
- **Code 29**—Insufficient input from vehicle speed sensor
- **Code 31**—PFE, EVP or EVR circuit below minimum voltage
- **Code 32**—EVP voltage below closed limit
- **Code 33**—EGR valve opening not detected
- **Code 34**—EVP voltage above closed limit
- **Code 35**—PFE or EVP circuit above closed limit
- **Code 41**—HEGO sensor circuit indicates system lean
- **Code 41**—No HEGO switching detected
- **Code 42**—HEGO sensor circuit indicates system rich

- **Code 44**—Thermactor air system inoperative–right side
- **Code 45**—Thermactor air upstream during self-test
- **Code 45**—Coil 1, 2 or 3 failure
- **Code 46**—Thermactor air not bypassed during self-test
- **Code 47**—4WD switch closed (E40D)
- **Code 48**—Loss of IDM, left side
- **Code 49**—1–2 shift error (E40D)
- **Code 51**—ECT/ACT reads –40°F or circuit open
- **Code 52**—Power steering pressure switch circuit open
- **Code 52**—Power steering pressure switch always open or closed
- **Code 53**—TP circuit above maximum voltage
- **Code 54**—ACT sensor circuit open
- **Code 56**—VAF or MAF circuit above maximum voltage
- **Code 56**—TOT reads –40°F or circuit open (E40D)
- **Code 59**—2–3 shift error (E40D)
- **Code 61**—ECT reads 254°F or circuit grounded
- **Code 63**—TP circuit below minimum voltage
- **Code 64**—ACT sensor grounded or input reads 254°F
- **Code 65**—Overdrive cancel switch open, no change seen (E40D)
- **Code 66**—MAF sensor input below minimum voltage
- **Code 66**—TOT grounded or reads 290°F (E40D)
- **Code 67**—Neutral/drive switch open or A/C on
- **Code 67**—Clutch switch circuit failure
- **Code 67**—MLP sensor out of range or A/C on (E40D)
- **Code 69**—3–4 shift error
- **Code 72**—Insufficient MAF/MAP change during dynamic test
- **Code 73**—Insufficient TP change during dynamic test
- **Code 74**—Brake on/off switch failure or not actuated
- **Code 77**—Operator error
- **Code 79**—A/C on during self-test
- **Code 79**—A/C or defrost on during self-test

- **Code 81**—Air management 2 circuit failure
- **Code 82**—Air management 1 circuit failure
- **Code 84**—EGR vacuum solenoid circuit failure
- **Code 85**—Canister purge solenoid circuit failure
- **Code 86**—Shift solenoid circuit failure
- **Code 87**—Fuel pump primary circuit failure
- **Code 88**—Loss of dual plug input control
- **Code 89**—Converter clutch solenoid circuit failure
- **Code 91**—Shift solenoid 1 circuit failure (E40D)
- **Code 92**—Shift solenoid 2 circuit failure (E40D)
- **Code 93**—Coast clutch solenoid circuit failure (E40D)
- **Code 94**—Converter clutch solenoid circuit failure (E40D)
- **Code 95**—Fuel pump secondary circuit failure— PCM to ground
- **Code 96**—Fuel pump secondary circuit failure—battery to PCM
- **Code 97**—Overdrive cancel indicator light—circuit failure(E40D)
- **Code 98**—Electronic pressure control driver open in PCM (E40D)
- **Code 98**—Hard fault present
- **Code 99**—Electronic pressure control circuit failure (E40D)
- **Code 111**—System pass
- **Code 112**—ACT sensor circuit grounded or reads 254° F
- **Code 113**—ACT sensor circuit open or reads –40° F
- **Code 114**—ACT outside test limits during KOEO or KOER tests
- **Code 116**—ECT outside test limits during KOEO or KOER tests
- **Code 117**—ECT sensor circuit grounded
- **Code 117**—ECT sensor circuit below minimum voltage or reads 254°F
- **Code 118**—ECT sensor circuit open
- **Code 118**—ECT sensor circuit below maximum voltage or reads –40°F
- **Code 121**—Closed throttle voltage higher or
- **Code 122**—TP sensor circuit below minimum voltage
- **Code 123**—TP sensor circuit below maximum voltage
- **Code 126**—BP or MAP sensor higher or lower than expected
- **Code 128**—MAP vacuum circuit failure
- **Code 129**—Insufficient MAF or MAP change during dynamic responded test
- **Code 144**—No HEGO switching detected
- **Code 167**—Insufficient TP change during dynamic response test
- **Code 171**—Fuel system at adaptive limit, HEGO unable to switch
- **Code 172**—HEGO shows system always lean
- **Code 173**—HEGO shows system always rich
- **Code 174**—HEGO switching time is slow
- **Code 179**—Fuel at lean adaptive limit at part throttle: system rich
- **Code 181**—Fuel at rich adaptive limit at part throttle; system lean
- **Code 182**—Fuel at lean adaptive limit at idle; system rich
- **Code 183**—Fuel at rich adaptive limit at idle; system lean
- **Code 211**—PIP circuit fault
- **Code 212**—Loss of IDM input to PCM or SPOUT circuit grounded
- **Code 213**—Spout circuit open
- **Code 224**—Erratic IDM input to processor
- **Code 225**—Knocked not sensed during dynamic response test
- **Code 311**—Thermactor air system inoperative
- **Code 312**—Thermactor air upstream during self-test
- **Code 313**—Thermactor air not bypassed during self-test
- **Code 327**—EVP or DPFE circuit below minimum voltage
- **Code 328**—EGR closed voltage lower than expected
- **Code 332**—Insufficient EGR flow detected
- **Code 334**—EGR closed voltage higher than expected
- **Code 337**—EVP or DPFE circuit above maximum voltage
- **Code 411**—Cannot control rpm during KOER low rpm check
- **Code 412**—Cannot control rpm during KOER high rpm check
- **Code 452**—Insufficient input from vehicle speed sensor
- **Code 511**—EEC processor ROM test failed
- **Code 512**—EEC processor Keep Alive Memory test failed
- **Code 513**—Failure in EEC processor internal voltage
- **Code 519**—Power steering pressure switch circuit open
- **Code 521**—Power steering pressure switch did not change state
- **Code 525**—Vehicle in gear or A/C on during self-test
- **Code 536**—Brake on/off circuit failure, switch not actuated during KOER test
- **Code 538**—Insufficient RPM change during KOER dynamic response test
- **Code 538**—Operator error
- **Code 542**—Fuel pump secondary circuit failure: PCM to ground

- **Code 543**—Fuel pump secondary circuit failure: Battery to PCM
- **Code 552**—Air management 1 circuit failure
- **Code 553**—Air management 2 circuit failure
- **Code 556**—Fuel pump primary circuit failure
- **Code 558**—EGR vacuum regulator circuit failure
- **Code 565**—Canister purge circuit failure
- **Code 569**—Canister purge 2 circuit failure
- **Code 617**—1–2 shift error (E40D)
- **Code 618**—2–3 shift error (E40D)
- **Code 619**—3–4 shift error (E40D)
- **Code 621**—Shift solenoid 1 circuit failure
- **Code 622**—Shift solenoid 2 circuit failure
- **Code 624**—EPC solenoid or driver circuit failure
- **Code 625**—EPC driver open in PCM
- **Code 626**—Coast clutch solenoid circuit failure (E40D)
- **Code 627**—Converter clutch solenoid circuit failure (E40D)
- **Code 628**—Converter clutch error (E40D)
- **Code 629**—Converter clutch control circuit failure
- **Code 631**—Overdrive cancel indicator light circuit failure
- **Code 632**—Overdrive cancel switch not changing states (E40D)
- **Code 633**—4WD switch is closed
- **Code 634**—MLP sensor voltage out of self-test range. A/C on
- **Code 636**—TOT sensor voltage out of self-test range
- **Code 637**—TOT sensor circuit above maximum voltage
- **Code 638**—TOT sensor circuit below minimum voltage
- **Code 654**—MLP sensor not in park position
- **Code 998**—Hard fault present

General Information

POWERTRAIN CONTROL MODULE

One part of the PCM is devoted to monitoring both input and output functions within the system. This ability forms the core of the self-diagnostic system. If a problem is detected within a circuit, the controller will recognize the fault, assign it an identification code, and store the code in a memory section. Depending on the year and model, the fault code(s) may be represented by two or three-digit numbers. The stored code(s) may be retrieved during diagnosis.

While the EEC-IV system is capable of recognizing many internal faults, certain faults will not be recognized. Because the computer system sees only electrical signals, it cannot sense or react to mechanical or vacuum faults affecting engine operation. Some of these faults may affect another component which will set a code. For example, the PCM monitors the output signal to the fuel injectors, but cannot detect a partially clogged injector. As long as the output driver responds correctly, the computer will read the system as functioning correctly. However, the improper flow of fuel may result in a lean mixture. This would, in turn, be detected by the oxygen sensor and noticed as a constantly lean signal by the PCM. Once the signal falls outside the pre-programmed limits, the engine control assembly would notice the fault and set an identification code.

Failure Mode Effects Management (FMEM)

The PCM contains back-up programs which allow the engine to operate if a sensor signal is lost. If a sensor input is seen to be out of range—either high or low—the FMEM program is used. The processor substitutes a fixed value for the missing sensor signal. The engine will continue to operate, although performance and driveability may be noticeably reduced. This function of the controller is sometimes referred to as the limp-in or fail-safe mode. If the missing sensor signal is restored, the FMEM system immediately returns the system to normal operation. The dashboard warning lamp will be lit when FMEM is in effect.

Hardware Limited Operation Strategy (HLOS)

This mode is only used if the fault is too extreme for the FMEM circuit to handle. In this mode, the processor has ceased all computation and control; the entire system is run on fixed values. The vehicle may be operated but performance and driveability will be greatly reduced. The fixed or default settings provide minimal calibration, allowing the vehicle to be carefully driven in for service. The dashboard warning lamp will be lit when HLOS is engaged. Codes cannot be read while the system is operating in this mode.

MALFUNCTION INDICATOR LAMP (MIL)

The CHECK ENGINE or SERVICE ENGINE SOON dashboard warning lamp is referred to as the Malfunction Indicator Lamp (MIL). The lamp is connected to the engine control assembly and will alert the driver to certain malfunctions within the EEC-IV system. When the lamp is lit, the PCM has detected a fault and stored an identity code in memory. The engine control system will usually enter either FMEM or HLOS mode and driveability will be impaired.

The light will stay on as long as the fault causing it is present. Should the fault self-correct, the MIL will extinguish but the stored code will remain in memory.

Under normal operating conditions, the MIL should light briefly when the ignition key is turned **ON**. As soon as the PCM receives a signal that the engine is cranking, the lamp will be extinguished. The dash warning lamp should remain out during the entire operating cycle.

HAND-HELD SCAN TOOLS

Although stored codes may be read through the flashing of the CHECK ENGINE or SERVICE ENGINE SOON lamp, the use of hand-held scan tools such as Ford's Self-Test Automatic Readout (STAR) tester or the second generation SUPER STAR II tester or their equivalent is highly recommended. There are many manufacturers of these tools; the purchaser must be certain that the tool is proper for the intended use.

The scan tool allows any stored faults to be read from the engine controller memory. Use of the scan tool provides additional data during troubleshooting, but does not eliminate the use of the charts. The scan tool makes collecting information easier, but the data must be correctly interpreted by an operator familiar with the system.

ELECTRICAL TOOLS

The most commonly required electrical diagnostic tool is the Digital Multimeter, allowing voltage, ohms (resistance) and amperage to be read by one instrument. Many of the diagnostic charts require the use of a volt or ohmmeter during diagnosis.

The multimeter must be a high impedance unit, with 10 megohms of impedance in the voltmeter. This type of meter will not place an additional load on the circuit it is testing; this is extremely important in low voltage circuits. The multimeter must be of high quality in all respects. It should be handled carefully and protected from impact or damage. Replace the batteries frequently in the unit.

Additionally, an analog (needle type) voltmeter may be used to read stored fault codes if the STAR tester is not available. The codes are transmitted as visible needle sweeps on the face of the instrument.

Almost all diagnostic procedures will require the use of a Breakout Box, a device which connects into the EEC-IV harness and provides testing ports for the 60 wires in the harness. Direct testing of the harness connectors at the terminals or by backprobing is not recommended; damage to the wiring and terminals is almost certain to occur.

Other necessary tools include a quality tachometer with inductive (clip-on) pickup, a fuel pressure gauge with system adapters and a vacuum gauge with an auxiliary source of vacuum.

Reading Codes

Diagnosis of a driveability problem requires attention to detail and following the diagnostic procedures in the correct order. Resist the temptation to begin extensive testing before completing the preliminary diagnostic steps. The preliminary or visual inspection must be completed in detail before diagnosis begins. In many cases this will shorten diagnostic time and often cure the problem without electronic testing.

VISUAL INSPECTION

This is possibly the most critical step of diagnosis. A detailed examination of all connectors, wiring and vacuum hoses can often lead to a repair without further diagnosis. Performance of this step relies on the skill of the technician performing it; a careful inspector will check the undersides of hoses as well as the integrity of hard-to-reach hoses blocked by the air cleaner or other components. Wiring should be checked carefully for any sign of strain, burning, crimping or terminal pull-out from a connector.

Checking connectors at components or in harnesses is required; usually, pushing them together will reveal a loose fit. Pay particular attention to ground circuits, making sure they are not loose or corroded. Remember to inspect connectors and hose fittings at components not mounted on the engine, such as the evaporative canister or relays mounted on the fender aprons. Any component or wiring in the vicinity of a fluid leak or spillage should be given extra attention during inspection.

Additionally, inspect maintenance items such as belt condition and tension, battery charge and condition and the radiator cap carefully. Any of these very simple items may affect the system enough to set a fault.

ELECTRONIC TESTING

If a code was set before a problem self-corrected (such as a momentarily loose connector), the code will be erased if the problem does not reoccur within 80 warm-up cycles. Codes will be output and displayed as numbers on the hand-held scan tool, such as 23. If the codes are being read through the dashboard warning lamp, the codes will be displayed as groups of flashes separated by pauses. Code 23 would be shown as two flashes, a pause and three more flashes. A longer pause will occur between codes. If the codes are being read on an analog voltmeter, the needle sweeps indicate the code digits in the same manner as the lamp flashes.

In all cases, the codes 11 or 111 are used to indicate PASS during testing. Note that the PASS code may appear, followed by other stored codes. These are codes from the continuous memory and may indicate intermittent faults, even though the system does not presently contain the fault. The PASS designation only indicates the system passes all internal tests at the moment.

Key On Engine Off (KOEO) Test

▶ **See Figures 30 and 31**

1. Connect the scan tool to the self-test connectors. Make certain the test button is unlatched or up.
2. Start the engine and run it until normal operating temperature is reached.
3. Turn the engine **OFF** for 10 seconds.
4. Activate the test button on the STAR tester.

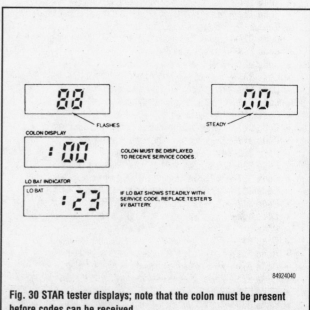

Fig. 30 STAR tester displays; note that the colon must be present before codes can be received

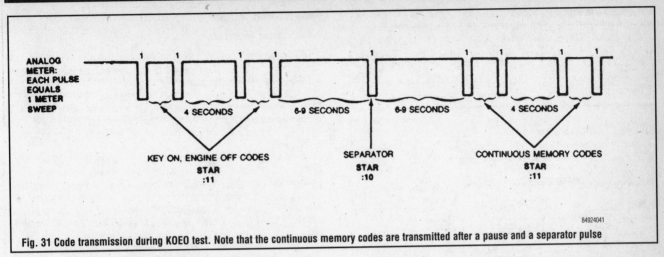

Fig. 31 Code transmission during KOEO test. Note that the continuous memory codes are transmitted after a pause and a separator pulse

5. Turn the ignition switch **ON** but do not start the engine. For vehicles with 4.9L engines, depress the clutch during the entire test. For vehicles with the 7.3L diesel engine, hold the accelerator to the floor during the test.

6. The KOEO codes will be transmitted. Six to nine seconds after the last KOEO code, a single separator pulse will be transmitted. Six to nine seconds after this pulse, the codes from the Continuous Memory will be transmitted.

7. Record all service codes displayed. Do not depress the throttle on gasoline engines during the test.

Key On Engine Running (KOER) Test

▶ **See Figures 30 and 32**

1. Make certain the self-test button is released or de-activated on the STAR tester.

2. Start the engine and run it at 2000 rpm for two minutes. This action warms up the oxygen sensor.

3. Turn the ignition switch **OFF** for 10 seconds.

4. Activate or latch the self-test button on the scan tool.

5. Start the engine. The engine identification code will be transmitted. This is a single digit number representing ½ the number of cylinders in a gasoline engine. On the STAR tester, this number may appear with a zero, such as 20 = 2. For 7.3L diesel engines, the ID code is 5. The code is used to confirm that the correct processor is installed and that the self-test has begun.

6. If the vehicle is equipped with a Brake On/Off (BOO) switch, the brake pedal must be depressed and released after the ID code is transmitted.

7. If the vehicle is equipped with a Power Steering Pressure Switch (PSPS), the steering wheel must be turned at least ½ turn and released within 2 seconds after the engine ID code is transmitted.

8. If the vehicle is equipped with the E4OD transmission, the Overdrive Cancel Switch (OCS) must be cycled after the engine ID code is transmitted.

9. Certain Ford vehicles will display a Dynamic Response code 6–20 seconds after the engine ID code. This will appear as one pulse on a meter or as a 10 on the STAR tester. When this code appears, briefly take the engine to wide open throttle. This allows the system to test the throttle position, MAF and MAP sensors.

10. All relevant codes will be displayed and should be recorded. Remember that the codes refer only to faults present during this test cycle. Codes stored in Continuous Memory are not displayed in this test mode.

11. Do not depress the throttle during testing unless a dynamic response code is displayed.

Reading Codes With Analog Voltmeter

▶ **See Figures 33 and 34**

In the absence of a scan tool, an analog voltmeter may be used to retrieve stored fault codes. Set the meter range to read DC 0–15 volts. Connect the + lead of the meter to the battery positive terminal and connect the − lead of the meter to the self-test output pin of the diagnostic connector.

Follow the directions given previously for performing the KOEO and KOER tests. To activate the tests, use a jumper wire to connect the signal return pin on

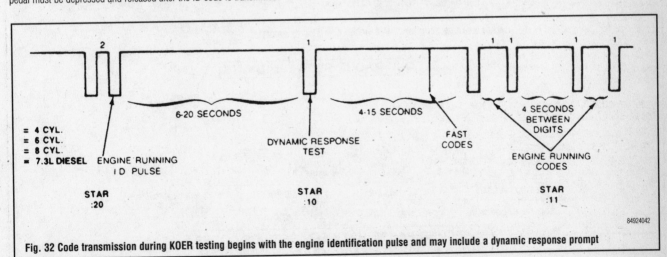

Fig. 32 Code transmission during KOER testing begins with the engine identification pulse and may include a dynamic response prompt

the diagnostic connector to the self-test input connector. The self-test input line is the separate wire and connector with or near the diagnostic connector.

The codes will be transmitted as groups of needle sweeps. This method may be used to read either 2 or 3-digit codes. The Continuous Memory codes are separated from the KOEO codes by 6 seconds, a single sweep and another 6 second delay.

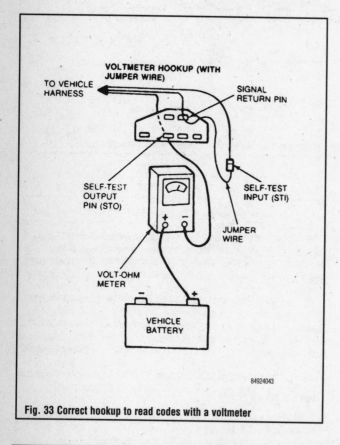

Fig. 33 Correct hookup to read codes with a voltmeter

Reading Codes With MIL

▸ **See Figures 35 and 36**

The Malfunction Indicator Lamp on the dashboard may also be used to retrieve the stored codes. This method displays only the stored codes and does not allow for any system investigation.

Follow the directions given previously for performing the KOEO and KOER tests. To activate the tests, use a jumper wire to connect the signal return pin on the diagnostic connector to the self-test input connector. The self-test input line is the separate wire and connector with or near the diagnostic connector.

Codes are transmitted by place value with a pause between the digits; Code 32 would be sent as 3 flashes, a pause and 2 flashes. A slightly longer pause divides codes from each other. Be ready to count and record codes; the only way to repeat a code is to re-cycle the system. This method may be used to read either 2 or 3-digit codes. The Continuous Memory codes are separated from the KOEO codes by 6 seconds, a single flash and another 6 second delay.

To perform the KOER test:
1. Hold in all 3 buttons, start the engine and release the buttons.
2. Press the SELECT or GAUGE SELECT button 3 times. The message **dealer 4** should appear at the bottom of the message panel.
3. Initiate the test by using a jumper wire to connect the signal return pin on the diagnostic connector to the self-test input connector. The self-test input line is the separate wire and connector with or near the diagnostic connector.
4. The stored codes will be output to the vehicle display.
5. To exit the test, turn the ignition switch **OFF** and disconnect the jumper wire.

Other Test Modes

CONTINUOUS MONITOR OR WIGGLE TEST

Once entered, this mode allows the operator to attempt to recreate intermittent faults by wiggling or tapping components, wiring or connectors. The test may be performed during either KOEO or KOER procedures. The test requires the use of either an analog voltmeter or a hand-held scan tool.

To enter the continuous monitor mode during KOEO testing, turn the ignition switch **ON**. Activate the test, wait 10 seconds, then deactivate and reactivate the test; the system will enter the continuous monitor mode. Tap, move or wiggle the harness, component or connector suspected of causing the problem; if a

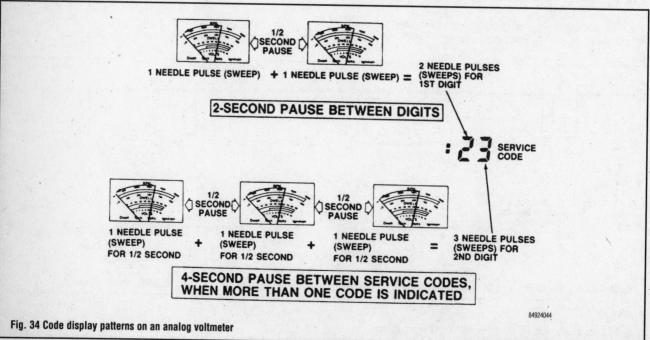

Fig. 34 Code display patterns on an analog voltmeter

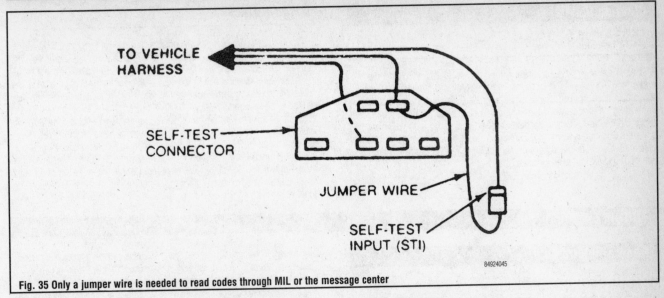

Fig. 35 Only a jumper wire is needed to read codes through MIL or the message center

fault is detected, the code will store in the memory. When the fault occurs, the dash warning lamp will illuminate, the STAR tester will light a red indicator (and possibly beep) and the analog meter needle will sweep once.

To enter this mode in the KOER test:

1. Start the engine and run it at 2000 rpm for two minutes. This action warms up the oxygen sensor.

2. Turn the ignition switch **OFF** for 10 seconds.

3. Start the engine.

4. Activate the test, wait 10 seconds, then deactivate and reactivate the test; the system will enter the continuous monitor mode.

5. Tap, move or wiggle the harness, component or connector suspected of causing the problem; if a fault is detected, the code will store in the memory.

6. When the fault occurs, the dash warning lamp will illuminate, the STAR tester will light a red indicator (and possibly beep) and the analog meter needle will sweep once.

OUTPUT STATE CHECK

This testing mode allows the operator to energize and de-energize most of the outputs controlled by the EEC-IV system. Many of the outputs may be checked at the component by listening for a click or feeling the item move or engage by a hand placed on the case. To enter this check:

1. Enter the KOEO test mode.

2. When all codes have been transmitted, depress the accelerator all the way to the floor and release it.

3. The output actuators are now all ON. Depressing the throttle pedal to the floor again switches the all the actuator outputs OFF.

4. This test may be performed as often as necessary, switching between ON and OFF by depressing the throttle.

5. Exit the test by turning the ignition switch **OFF**, disconnecting the jumper at the diagnostic connector or releasing the test button on the scan tool.

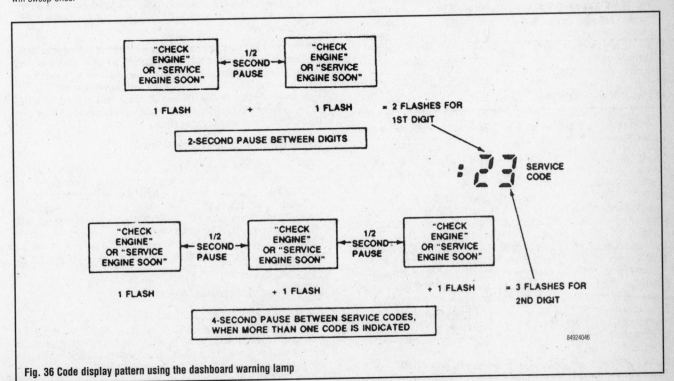

Fig. 36 Code display pattern using the dashboard warning lamp

Clearing Codes

CONTINUOUS MEMORY CODES

These codes are retained in memory for 80 warm-up cycles. To clear the codes for the purposes of testing or confirming repair, perform the KOEO test. When the fault codes begin to be displayed, de-activate the test by either disconnecting the jumper wire (meter, MIL or message center) or releasing the test button on the hand scanner. Stopping the test during code transmission will erase the Continuous Memory. Do not disconnect the negative battery cable to clear these codes; the Keep Alive memory will be cleared and a new code, 19, will be stored for loss of PCM power.

TROUBLE CODES—EEC-V

General Information

ON BOARD DIAGNOSTICS (OBD) II

➡ **The 1988–95 gasoline powered Ford vehicles covered by this manual employ the fourth generation Electronic Engine Control system, commonly designated EEC-IV, to manage fuel, ignition and emissions on vehicle engines. All 1995–96 diesel engines and some 1996 gasoline engines (depending on engine application), will be equipped with EEC-V.**

Ford developed the EEC-V system in response to the increased diagnostic requirements for the California Air Resource Board. The regulations developed by the Environmental Protection Agency are designated as the OBD II system.

The On Board Diagnostics (OBD) II system is similar to the OBD I system, but not identical. The OBD I requires that the Malfunction Indicator Lamp (MIL) illuminates to inform the driver when an emissions component or monitored system fails. The MIL also lights up to indicate when the Powertrain Control Module (PCM) is operating in Hardware Limited Operation Strategy (HLOS).

The EEC-V is an evolutionary development from the EEC-IV. None of the components involved are actually new, only the applications have changed.

The only component that has been added is another heated Oxygen sensor (HO2S located behind the catalyst. These downstream sensors are called the Catalyst Monitor Sensors (CMS). This means that there are four sensors on models so equipped, instead of two.

POWERTRAIN CONTROL MODULE (PCM)

➡ **PCM's for EEC-IV systems use a 60-pin connector. For the EEC-V PCM, a 104-pin connector is used.**

As with the EEC-IV system, the PCM is given responsibility for the operation of the emission control devices, cooling fans, ignition and advance and in some cases, automatic transmission functions. Because the EEC system oversees both the ignition timing and the fuel injector operation, a precise air/fuel ratio will be maintained under all operating conditions. The PCM is a microprocessor or small computer which receives electrical inputs from several sensors, switches and relays on and around the engine.

Based on combinations of these inputs, the PCM controls outputs to various devices concerned with engine operation and emissions. The engine control assembly relies on the signals to form a correct picture of current vehicle operation. If any of the input signals is incorrect, the PCM reacts to what ever picture is painted for it. For example, if the coolant temperature sensor is inaccurate and reads too low, the PCM may see a picture of the engine never warming up. Consequently, the engine settings will be maintained as if the engine were cold. Because so many inputs can affect one output, correct diagnostic procedures are essential on these systems.

One part of the PCM is devoted to monitoring both input and output functions within the system. This ability forms the core of the self-diagnostic system. If a problem is detected within a circuit, the controller will recognize the

KEEP ALIVE MEMORY

The Keep Alive Memory (KAM) contains the adaptive factors used by the processor to compensate for component tolerances and wear. It should not be routinely cleared during diagnosis. If an emissions related part is replaced during repair, the KAM must be cleared. Failure to clear the KAM may cause severe driveability problems since the correction factor for the old component will be applied to the new component.

To clear the Keep Alive Memory, disconnect the negative battery cable for at least 5 minutes. After the memory is cleared and the battery reconnected, the vehicle must be driven at least 10 miles (16 km) so that the processor may relearn the needed correction factors. The distance to be driven depends on the engine and vehicle, but all drives should include steady-throttle cruise on open roads. Certain driveability problems may be noted during the drive because the adaptive factors are not yet functioning.

fault, assign it an identification code, and store the code in a memory section. The fault codes may be retrieved during diagnosis.

While the EEC system is capable of recognizing many internal faults, certain faults will not be recognized. Because the computer system sees only electrical signals, it cannot sense or react to mechanical or vacuum faults affecting engine operation. Some of these faults may affect another component which will set a code. For example, the PCM monitors the output signal to the fuel injectors, but cannot detect a partially clogged injector. As long as the output driver responds correctly, the computer will read the system as functioning correctly. However, the improper flow of fuel may result in a lean mixture. This would, in turn, be detected by the oxygen sensor and noticed as a constantly lean signal by the PCM. Once the signal falls outside the pre-programmed limits, the engine control assembly would notice the fault and set an identification code.

Additionally, the EEC system employs adaptive fuel logic. This process is used to compensate for normal wear and variability within the fuel system. Once the engine enters steady-state operation, the engine control assembly watches the oxygen sensor signal for a bias or tendency to run slightly rich or lean. If such a bias is detected, the adaptive logic corrects the fuel delivery to bring the air/fuel mixture towards a centered or 14.7:1 ratio. This compensating shift is stored in a non-volatile memory which is retained by battery power even with the ignition switched off. The correction factor is then available the next time the vehicle is operated.

➡ **If the battery cable(s) is disconnected for longer than 5 minutes, the adaptive fuel factor will be lost. After repair it will be necessary to drive the car at least 10 miles (16 km) to allow the processor to relearn the correct factors. The driving period should include steady-throttle open road driving if possible. During the drive, the vehicle may exhibit driveability symptoms not noticed before. These symptoms should clear as the PCM computes the correction factor.**

Failure Mode Effects Management (FMEM)

The engine controller assembly contains back-up programs which allow the engine to operate if a sensor signal is lost. If a sensor input is seen to be out of range—either high or low—the FMEM program is used. The processor substitutes a fixed value for the missing sensor signal. The engine will continue to operate, although performance and driveability may be noticeably reduced. This function of the controller is sometimes referred to as the limp-in or fail-safe mode. If the missing sensor signal is restored, the FMEM system immediately returns the system to normal operation. The dashboard warning lamp will be lit when FMEM is in effect.

Hardware Limited Operation Strategy (HLOS)

This mode is only used if the fault is too extreme for the FMEM circuit to handle. In this mode, the processor has ceased all computation and control; the entire system is run on fixed values. The vehicle may be operated but performance and driveability will be greatly reduced. The fixed or default settings provide minimal calibration, allowing the vehicle to be carefully driven in for service. The dashboard warning lamp will be lit when HLOS is engaged. Codes cannot be read while the system is operating in this mode.

Data Link Connector (DLC)

The DLC for the EEC-V system is located in the passenger's compartment of the vehicle, attached to the instrument panel, and is accessible from the driver's seat.

The DLC is rectangular in design and capable of allowing access to 16 terminals. The connector has keying features that allow easy connection. The test equipment and the DLC have a latching feature to ensure a good mated connection.

Reading Codes

The EEC-V (OBD II) codes differ from the 2 or 3-digit codes of the (former) EEC-IV system in that they are accompanied by a letter prefix before a 4-digit number. Example: P0102 would indicate a Mass Air Flow (MAF) Sensor circuit (low input).

➡The number of digits used in the OBD II codes, along with the letter prefix makes flash diagnosis all but impossible, so no provision has been made in OBD II systems to read codes in any other way than with a scan tool.

When diagnosing the OBD II EEC-V system, the New Generation Star (NGS) tester or generic scan tool may be used to retrieve codes, view the system operating specifications or test the system components. There are also several other pieces of equipment which may be used for diagnosis purposes.
- Vacuum pressure gauge and pump
- Tach/Dwell Volt/Ohmmeter tester
- 104-pin Breakout Box
- Multimeter with a 10 megaohm impedance
- Distributorless ignition system tester
- Constant control relay modular tester
- Tachometer adapter
- Fuel pressure gauge
- Timing light
- Test light (non-powered)

Clearing Codes

PCM RESET

The PCM reset mode allows the scan tool to clear any emission related diagnostic information from the PCM. When resetting the PCM, a DTC P1000 will be stored until all OBD II system monitors or components have been tested to satisfy a trip without any other faults occurring.

The following items occur when the PCM Reset is performed:
- The DTC is cleared
- The freeze frame data is cleared
- The oxygen sensor test data is cleared
- The status of the OBD II system monitors is reset
- A DTC P1000 code is set

PCM fault codes may be cleared by using the scan tool or disconnecting the negative battery cable for a minimum of 15 seconds.

KEEP ALIVE MEMORY (KAM) RESET

The Keep Alive Memory (KAM) contains the adaptive factors used by the processor to compensate for component tolerances and wear. It should not be routinely cleared during diagnosis. If and emissions related part is replaced during repair, the KAM must be cleared. Failure to clear the KAM may cause severe driveability problems, since the correction factor for the old component will be applied to the new component.

To clear the KAM disconnect the negative battery cable for at least 5 minuets. After the memory is cleared and the battery is reconnected, the vehicle must be driven a couple of miles so that the PCM may relearn the needed correction factors. The distance to be driven depends on the engine and vehicle, but all drives should include steady throttle cruise on the open roads. Certain driveability problems may be noted during the drive because the adaptive factors are not yet functioning.

Test Equipment

The Ford EEC-V system will requires the use of a 104-pin Brake Out Box (BOB) to be used for diagnosis. The 104-pin BOB is used to test circuits exactly as the 60-pin BOB is used on the EEC-IV. Another piece of test equipment is the STAR (NSG) tester. This tester may be used on OBD I also.

TESTING

These test procedures listed below are for a generic scan tool in the enhanced diagnostic test mode. Only the manufacturer has the STAR tool. Your local jobber should have a generic tool available.

When performing these tests, always do a visual check and preparation of the vehicle first.
- Inspect the air cleaner and inlet ducting.
- Check all of the engine hoses for damages, leaks, cracks, proper routing etc.
- Check the EEC system wiring harness for good connections, bent or broken pins, corrosion, loose wiring etc.
- Check the engine coolant for proper levels and mixture.
- Check the PCM, sensors and actuators for any damages.
- Check the transmission fluid level and quality.
- Make any necessary repairs before proceeding with testing.
- Check the vehicle for safety such as the parking brake must be on. Wheels blocked, etc.
- Turn off all lights, radios, blower switches etc.
- Bring the engine up to operating temperature before running a quick test.

Key On Engine Off (KOEO)

A series of characters must be entered into the scan tool to perform this test. The codes are listed below and must be entered as such to perform the test correctly. See the manufacture of the scan tool for any additional instructions.
1. Perform the necessary vehicle preparation and visual inspection.
2. Connect the scan tool to the DLC.
3. Turn the ignition to the **ON** position but DO NOT start the engine.
4. Verify that the scan tool is connected and communicating correctly by entering the OBD II system readiness test. All scan tools are required to automatically enter this test once communication is established between the tool and the PCM.
5. Enter the following strings of information to initiate the KOEO self-test.
6. Enter the four strings separately and in the order shown. All of the string ID numbers must match in the order shown:
   a. 04, 31, 21, C4 103381, 9E 00 445443287329 20 8042 20 8062 20 8082 A851 FF, 2E
   b. 03, 32, 22FF, C4 10220202, 9E 00 434E54 20 8061 A961 00 04, EA
   c. 02, 32, 21, C4 10328100, 9E 00 574149 54 20 8081 A181 61 03, 5E
   d. 01, 32, 21, C4 103181, 9E 00 53544155254 20 8081 A 181 00 02, 54
7. Turn the ignition **OFF** to end the test cycle.

Key On Engine Running (KOER)

A series of characters must be entered into the scan tool to perform this test. The codes are listed below and must be entered as such to perform the test correctly. See the manufacture of the scan tool for any additional instructions.
1. Perform the necessary vehicle preparation and visual inspection.
2. Connect the scan tool to the DLC.
3. Turn the ignition to the **ON** position and start the engine.
4. Verify that the scan tool is connected and communicating correctly by entering the OBD II system readiness test. All scan tools are required to automatically enter this test once communication is established between the tool and the PCM.
5. Enter the following strings of information to initiate the KOEO self-test.

➡After the test begins, cycle BOO, 4X4 and Transmission Control (TCS) switches, if equipped.

6. Enter the four strings separately and in the order shown. All of the string ID numbers must match in the order shown:
   a. 08, 31, 21, C4103382, 9E 00 445443287329 20 8042 20 8062 20 8082 A851 FF, 33

b. 07, 32, 22FF, C410220202, 9E 00 434E54 20 8061 A961 00 08, F2
c. 06, 32, 21, C4 10328200, 9E 00 574149 54 20 8081 A181 61 07, 67
d. 05, 32, 21, C4 103182, 9E 00 5354415254 20 8081 A181 00 06, 5D
7. Turn the ignition **OFF** to end the test cycle.

Continuous Memory Self-Test

1. Perform the necessary vehicle preparation and visual inspection.
2. Connect the scan tool to the DLC.
3. Turn the key to the **ON** position or start the vehicle.
4. See the manufacture's instructions to retrieve the DTC's.
5. When finished, turn the ignition **OFF**.
6. Disconnect the scan tool from the vehicle.

Accessing All Continuous Memory DTC's

1. Perform the necessary vehicle preparation and visual inspection.
2. Connect the scan tool to the DLC.
3. Turn the key to the **ON** position or start the vehicle. This may depend on the pinpoint manual instructions for the type of data requested.
4. Verify the tool is connected properly and communicating.
5. Enter the following string of characters to retrieve all the continuous DTC's (DTC CNT):
   - 09, 2C, 21, C4 10 13,, 9E 00 44 54 43 20 43 4E 54 20 8B 44, B2
6. The scan tool will display all the continuous DTC's.

FORD EEC-V (OBD II) CODES

1995–96 Vehicles

- DTC **P0102**—Mass Air Flow (MAF) Sensor circuit low input
- DTC **P0103**—Mass Air Flow (MAF) Sensor circuit high input
- DTC **P0112**—Intake Air Temperature (IAT) Sensor circuit low input
- DTC **P0113**—Intake Air Temperature (IAT) Sensor high input
- DTC **P0117**—Engine Coolant Temperature (ECT) low input
- DTC **P0118**—Engine Coolant Temperature (ECT) Sensor circuit high input
- DTC **P0122**—Throttle Position (TP) Sensor circuit low input
- DTC **P0123**—Throttle Position (TP) Sensor high input
- DTC **P0125**—Insufficient coolant temperature to enter closed loop fuel control
- DTC **P0132**—Upstream Heated Oxygen Sensor (HO2S 11) circuit high voltage (Bank #1)
- DTC **P0135**—Heated Oxygen Sensor Heater (HTR 11) circuit malfunction
- DTC **P0138**—Downstream Heated Oxygen Sensor (HO2S 12) circuit high voltage (Bank #1)
- DTC **P0140**—Heated Oxygen Sensor (HO2S 12) circuit no activity detected (Bank #1)
- DTC **P0141**—Heated Oxygen Sensor Heater (HTR 12) circuit malfunction
- DTC **P0152**—Upstream Heated Oxygen Sensor (HO2S 21) circuit high voltage (Bank #2)
- DTC **P0155**—Heated Oxygen Sensor Heater (HTR 21) circuit malfunction
- DTC **P0158**—Downstream Heated Oxygen Sensor (HO2S 22) circuit high voltage (Bank #2)
- DTC **P0160**—Heated Oxygen Sensor (HO2S 12) circuit no activity detected (Bank #2)
- DTC **P0161**—Heated Oxygen Sensor Heater (HTR 22) circuit malfunction
- DTC **P0171**—System (adaptive fuel) too lean (Bank #1)
- DTC **P0172**—System (adaptive fuel) too lean (Bank #1)
- DTC **P0174**—System (adaptive fuel) too lean (Bank #1)
- DTC **P0175**—System (adaptive fuel) too lean (Bank #1)
- DTC **P0300**—Random misfire detected
- DTC **P0301**—Cylinder #1 misfire detected
- DTC **P0302**—Cylinder #2 misfire detected
- DTC **P0303**—Cylinder #3 misfire detected
- DTC **P0304**—Cylinder #4 misfire detected
- DTC **P0305**—Cylinder #5 misfire detected

- DTC **P0306**—Cylinder #6 misfire detected
- DTC **P0307**—Cylinder #7 misfire detected
- DTC **P0308**—Cylinder #8 misfire detected
- DTC **P0320**—Ignition engine speed (Profile Ignition Pickup or PIP) input circuit malfunction
- DTC **P0340**—Camshaft Position (CMP) sensor circuit malfunction (CID)
- DTC **P0402**—Exhaust Gas Recirculation (EGR) excess flow detected (valve open at idle)
- DTC **P0420**—Catalyst system efficiency below threshold (Bank #1)
- DTC **P0430**—Catalyst system efficiency below threshold (Bank #2)
- DTC **P0443**—Evaporative emission control system Canister Purge (CANP) Control Valve circuit malfunction
- DTC **P0500**—Vehicle Speed Sensor (VSS) malfunction
- DTC **P0505**—Idle Air Control (IAC) system malfunction
- DTC **P0605**—Powertrain Control Module (PCM)—Read Only Memory (ROM) test error
- DTC **P0703**—Brake On/Off (BOO) switch input malfunction
- DTC **P0707**—Manual Lever Position (MLP) sensor circuit low input
- DTC **P0708**—Manual Lever Position (MLP) sensor circuit high input
- DTC **P0720**—Output Shaft Speed (OSS) sensor circuit malfunction
- DTC **P0741**—Torque Converter Clutch (TCC) system incorrect mechanical performance
- DTC **P0743**—Torque Converter Clutch (TCC) system electrical failure
- DTC **P0750**—Shift Solenoid #1 (SS1) circuit malfunction
- DTC **P0751**—Shift Solenoid #1 (SS1) performance
- DTC **P0755**—Shift Solenoid #2 (SS2) circuit malfunction
- DTC **P0756**—Shift Solenoid #2 (SS2) performance
- DTC **P1000**—OBD II Monitor Testing not complete
- DTC **P1100**—Mass Air Flow (MAF) sensor intermittent
- DTC **P1101**—Mass Air Flow (MAF) sensor out of Self-Test range
- DTC **P1112**—Intake Air Temperature (IAT) sensor intermittent
- DTC **P1116**—Engine Coolant Temperature (ECT) sensor out of Self-Test range
- DTC **P1117**—Engine Coolant Temperature (ECT) sensor intermittent
- DTC **P1120**—Throttle Position (TP) sensor out of range low
- DTC **P1121**—Throttle Position (TP) sensor inconsistent with MAF sensor
- DTC **P1124**—Throttle Position (TP) sensor out of Self-Test range
- DTC **P1125**—Throttle Position (TP) sensor circuit intermittent
- DTC **P1130**—Lack of HO2S 11 switch, adaptive fuel at limit
- DTC **P1131**—Lack of HO2S 11 switch, sensor indicates lean (Bank #1)
- DTC **P1132**—Lack of HO2S 11 switch, sensor indicates rich (Bank #1)
- DTC **P1137**—Lack of HO2S 12 switch, sensor indicates lean (Bank #1)
- DTC **P1138**—Lack of HO2S 12 switch, sensor indicates rich (Bank #1)
- DTC **P1150**—Lack of HO2S 21 switch, adaptive fuel at limit
- DTC **P1151**—Lack of HO2S 21 switch, sensor indicates lean (Bank #2)
- DTC **P1152**—Lack of HO2S 21 switch, sensor indicates rich (Bank #2)
- DTC **P1157**—Lack of HO2S 22 switch, sensor indicates lean (Bank #2)
- DTC **P1158**—Lack of HO2S 22 switch, sensor indicates rich (Bank #2)
- DTC **P1351**—Ignition Diagnostic Monitor (IDM) circuit input malfunction
- DTC **P1352**—Ignition coil A primary circuit malfunction
- DTC **P1353**—Ignition coil B primary circuit malfunction
- DTC **P1354**—Ignition coil C primary circuit malfunction
- DTC **P1355**—Ignition coil D primary circuit malfunction
- DTC **P1364**—Ignition coil primary circuit malfunction
- DTC **P1390**—Octane Adjust (OCT ADJ) out of Self-Test range
- DTC **P1400**—Differential Pressure Feedback Electronic (DPFE) sensor circuit low voltage detected
- DTC **P1401**—Differential Pressure Feedback Electronic (DPFE) sensor circuit high voltage detected
- DTC **P1403**—Differential Pressure Feedback Electronic (DPFE) sensor hoses reversed
- DTC **P1405**—Differential Pressure Feedback Electronic (DPFE) sensor upstream hose off or plugged
- DTC **P1406**—Differential Pressure Feedback Electronic (DPFE) sensor downstream hose off or plugged
- DTC **P1407**—Exhaust Gas Recirculation (EGR) no flow detected (valve stuck closed or inoperative)
- DTC **P1408**—Exhaust Gas Recirculation (EGR) flow out of Self-Test range

- DTC **P1473**—Fan Secondary High with fan(s) off
- DTC **P1474**—Low Fan Control primary circuit malfunction
- DTC **P1479**—High Fan Control primary circuit malfunction
- DTC **P1480**—Fan Secondary low with low fan on
- DTC **P1481**—Fan Secondary low with high fan on
- DTC **P1500**—Vehicle Speed Sensor (VSS) circuit intermittent
- DTC **P1505**—Idle Air Control (IAC) system at adaptive clip
- DTC **P1605**—Powertrain Control Module (PCM)—Keep Alive Memory (KAM) test error
- DTC **P1703**—Brake On/Off (BOO) switch out of Self-Test range
- DTC **P1705**—Manual Lever Position (MLP) sensor out of Self-Test range
- DTC **P1711**—Transmission Fluid Temperature (TFT) sensor out of Self-Test range

- DTC **P1742**—Torque Converter Clutch (TCC) solenoid mechanically failed (turns MIL on)
- DTC **P1743**—Torque Converter Clutch (TCC) solenoid mechanically failed (turns TCIL on)
- DTC **P1744**—Torque Converter Clutch (TCC) system mechanically stuck in off position
- DTC **P1746**—Electronic Pressure Control (EPC) solenoid circuit low input (open circuit)
- DTC **P1747**—Electronic Pressure Control (EPC) solenoid circuit high input (short circuit)
- DTC **P1751**—Shift Solenoid #1 (SS1) performance
- DTC **P1756**—Shift Solenoid #2 (SS2) performance
- DTC **P1780**—Transmission Control Switch (TCS) circuit out of Self-Test range

VACUUM DIAGRAMS

▶ **See Figures 37 thru 47**

Following are vacuum diagrams for most of the engine and emissions package combinations covered by this manual. Because vacuum circuits will vary based on various engine and vehicle options, always refer first to the vehicle emission control information label, if present. Should the label be missing, or should vehicle be equipped with a different engine from the vehicle's original equipment, refer to the following diagrams for the same or similar configuration.

If you wish to obtain a replacement emissions label, most manufacturers make the labels available for purchase. The labels can usually be ordered from a local dealer.

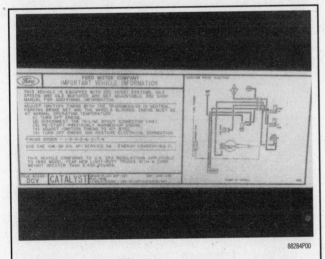

Fig. 37 Always refer first to the factory vacuum diagram sticker affixed under the hood

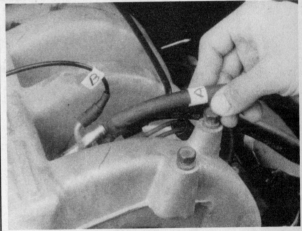

Fig. 38 To avoid a mixup, label vacuum lines prior to removing them

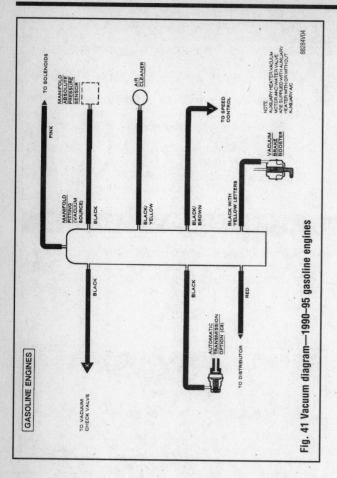

Fig. 41 Vacuum diagram—1990–95 gasoline engines

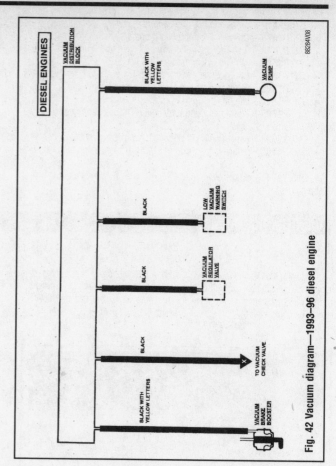

Fig. 42 Vacuum diagram—1993–96 diesel engine

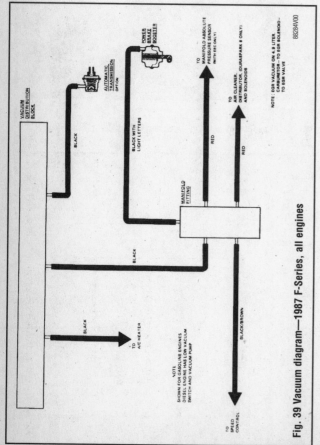

Fig. 39 Vacuum diagram—1987 F-Series, all engines

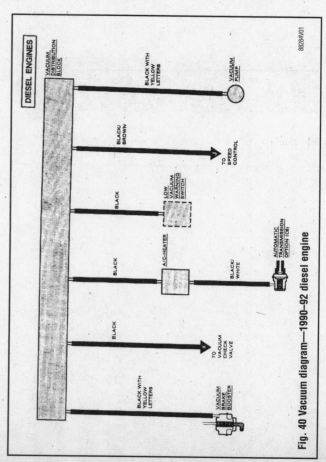

Fig. 40 Vacuum diagram—1990–92 diesel engine

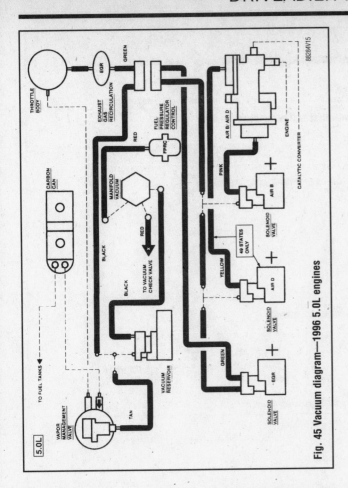

Fig. 45 Vacuum diagram—1996 5.0L engines

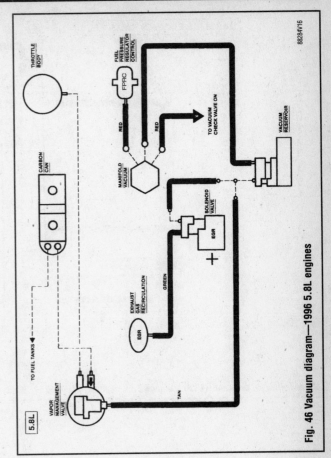

Fig. 46 Vacuum diagram—1996 5.8L engines

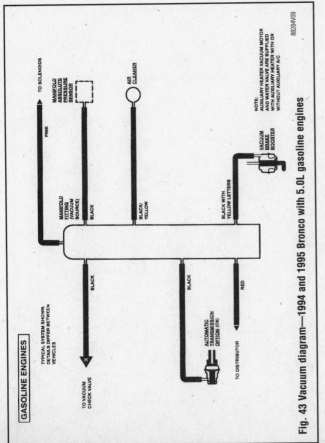

Fig. 43 Vacuum diagram—1994 and 1995 Bronco with 5.0L gasoline engines

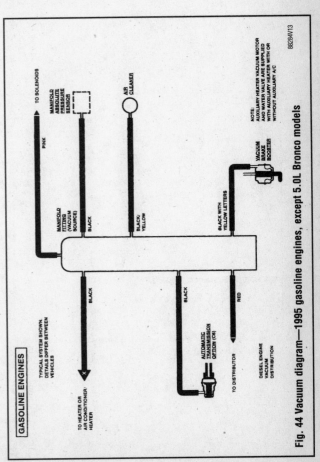

Fig. 44 Vacuum diagram—1995 gasoline engines, except 5.0L Bronco models

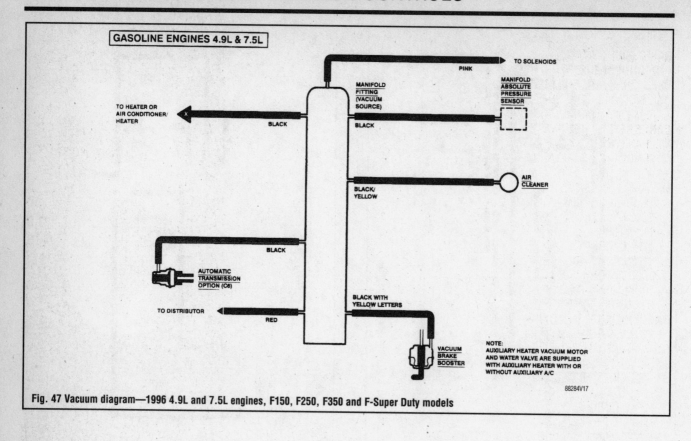

Fig. 47 Vacuum diagram—1996 4.9L and 7.5L engines, F150, F250, F350 and F-Super Duty models

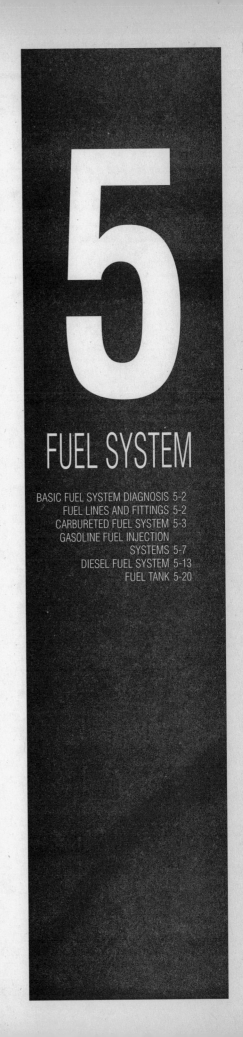

5

FUEL SYSTEM

BASIC FUEL SYSTEM DIAGNOSIS

When there is a problem starting or driving a vehicle, two of the most important checks involve the ignition and the fuel systems. The questions most mechanics attempt to answer first, "is there spark?" and "is there fuel?" will often lead to solving most basic problems. For ignition system diagnosis and testing, please refer to the information on engine electrical components and ignition systems found earlier in this manual. If the ignition system checks out (there is spark), then you must determine if the fuel system is operating properly (is there fuel?).

FUEL LINES AND FITTINGS

Quick-Connect Line Fittings

REMOVAL & INSTALLATION

♦ See Figures 1 and 2

The fuel system, depending on model year of the vehicle, may be equipped with push type connectors or spring lock couplings. When removing the fuel lines on these vehicles, it will be necessary to use Fuel Line Coupling Disconnect Tool D87L–9280–A or–B, or equivalent.

➡ Quick-Connect (push) type fittings must be disconnected using proper procedures or the fitting may be damaged. Two types of retainers are used on the push connect fittings. Line sizes of ⅜ in. and ⁵⁄₁₆ in. use a hairpin clip retainer. ¼ in. line connectors use a Duck bill clip retainer.

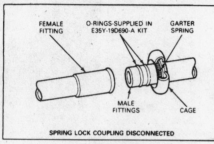

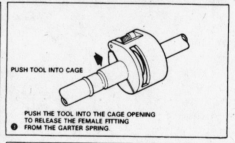

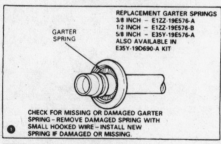

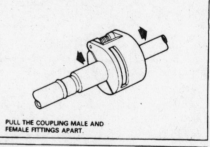

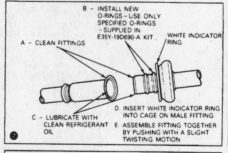

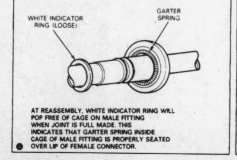

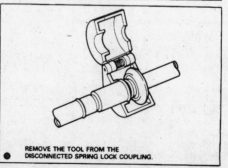

Fig. 1 MFI fuel line connectors

84925010

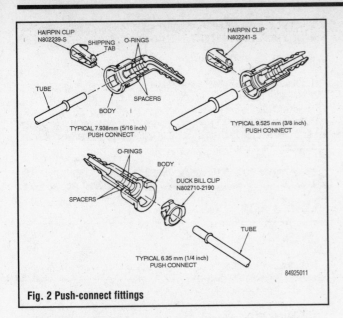

Fig. 2 Push-connect fittings

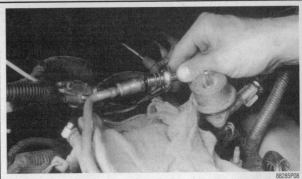

Fig. 3 Disengage the push connect fittings, taking care not to bend the lines

Push Connectors and Spring Lock Couplings

▶ See Figures 3 and 4

If the fuel system is equipped with spring lock couplings, remove the retaining clip from the spring lock coupling by hand only. Do not use any sharp tool or screwdriver as it may damage the spring lock coupling.

1. Twist the fitting to free it from any adhesion at the O-ring seals.

→Inspect the condition of the O-ring seals and replace them with the correct parts if necessary.

2. Fit Spring Lock Coupling Tool D87L–9280–A/B or equivalent to the coupling.
3. Close the tool and push it into the open side of the cage to expand garter spring and release the female fitting.
4. After the garter spring is expanded, pull the fittings apart.
5. Remove the tool from the disconnected coupling.

Hairpin Clip

1. Clean all dirt and/or grease from the fittings. Spread the two clip legs about an ⅛ in. each to disengage from the fitting and pull the clip outward from the fitting. Use finger pressure only, do not use any tools.

✳✳ CAUTION

Never smoke when working around gasoline! Avoid all sources of sparks or ignition. Gasoline vapors are EXTREMELY volatile!

2. Grasp the fittings and hose assembly and pull away from the steel line. Twist the fitting and hose assembly slightly while pulling, if necessary, when a sticking condition exists.
3. Inspect the hairpin clip for damage, replace the clip if necessary. Reinstall the clip in position on the fitting.
4. Inspect the fitting and inside of the connector to ensure freedom of dirt or obstruction. Install fitting into the connector and push together. A click will be heard when the hairpin snaps into proper connection. Pull on the line to insure full engagement.

CARBURETED FUEL SYSTEM

Mechanical Fuel Pump

The mechanical fuel pump is camshaft eccentric-actuated and located on the left side of the front cover on V8 engines.

A mechanical pump is used on all carbureted engines, except, in some cases on the 7.5L engine. On some of these engines an electric in-tank fuel pump is used.

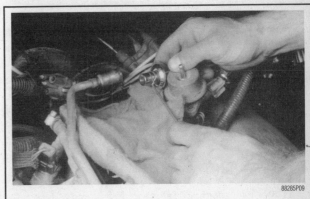

Fig. 4 Inspect the O-rings for cracks or deterioration

Duck Bill Clip

1. A special tool is available for Ford for removing the retaining clip (Ford Tool No. T82L–9500–AH). If the tool is not on hand see Step 2. Align the slot on the push connector disconnect tool with either tab on the retaining clip. Pull the line from the connector.

✳✳ CAUTION

Never smoke when working around gasoline! Avoid all sources of sparks or ignition. Gasoline vapors are EXTREMELY volatile!

2. If the special clip tool is not available, use a pair of narrow 6 in. (152mm) locking pliers with a jaw width of 0.2 in. (5mm) or less. Align the jaws of the pliers with the openings of the fitting case and compress the part of the retaining clip that engages the case. Compressing the retaining clip will release the fitting which may be pulled from the connector. Both sides of the clip must be compressed at the same time to disengage.
3. Inspect the retaining clip, fitting end and connector. Replace the clip if any damage is apparent.
4. Push the line into the steel connector until a click is heard, indicating the clip is in place. Pull on the line to check engagement.

REMOVAL & INSTALLATION

▶ See Figure 5

✳✳ CAUTION

Never smoke when working around gasoline! Avoid all sources of sparks or ignition. Gasoline vapors are EXTREMELY volatile!

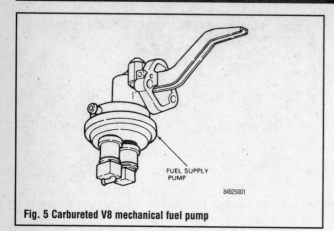

FUEL SUPPLY
PUMP

84925001

Fig. 5 Carbureted V8 mechanical fuel pump

1. Disconnect the fuel inlet and outlet lines at the fuel pump. Discard the fuel inlet retaining clamp.
2. Remove the pump retaining bolts. Remove the pump assembly and gasket from the engine. Discard the gasket.

To install:

3. If a new pump is to be installed, remove the fuel line connector fitting from the old pump and install it in the new pump.
4. Remove all gasket material from the mounting pad and pump flange. Apply oil resistant sealer to both sides of a new gasket.
5. Position the new gasket on the pump flange and hold the pump in position against the mounting pad. Make sure that the rocker arm is riding on the camshaft eccentric.
6. Press the pump tight against the pad, install the retaining bolts and alternately torque them to 19–27 ft. lbs. (26–37 Nm). Connect the fuel lines, tightening them to 15–18 ft. lbs. (20–24 Nm). Use a new clamp on the fuel inlet lines.
7. Operate the engine and check for leaks.

TESTING

Incorrect fuel pump pressure and low volume (flow rate) are the two most likely fuel pump troubles that will affect engine performance. Low pressure will cause a lean mixture and fuel starvation at high speeds and excessive pressure will cause high fuel consumption and carburetor flooding.

To determine that the fuel pump is in satisfactory operating condition, tests for both fuel pump pressure and volume should be performed.

The test are performed with the fuel pump installed on the engine and the engine at normal operating temperature and at idle speed.

Before the test, make sure that the replaceable fuel filter has been changed at the proper mileage interval. If in doubt, install a new filter.

Pressure Test

1. Remove the air cleaner assembly. Disconnect the fuel inlet line of the fuel filter at the carburetor. Use care to prevent fire, due to fuel spillage. Place an absorbent cloth under the connection before removing the line to catch any fuel that might flow out of the line.
2. Connect a pressure gauge, a restrictor and a flexible hose between the fuel filter and the carburetor.
3. Position the flexible hose and the restrictor so that the fuel can be discharged into a suitable, graduated container.
4. Before taking a pressure reading, operate the engine at the specified idle rpm and vent the system into the container by opening the hose restrictor momentarily.
5. Close the hose restrictor, allow the pressure to stabilize and note the reading. The pressure should be 5 psi. (34.5 kPa).

If the pump pressure is not within 4–6 psi (27.6–41.4 kPa) and the fuel lines and filter are in satisfactory condition, the pump is defective and should be replaced.

If the pump pressure is within the proper range, perform the test for fuel volume.

Volume Test

1. Operate the engine at the specified idle rpm.
2. Open the hose restrictor and catch the fuel in the container while observing the time it takes to pump 1 pint. 1 pint should be pumped in 20 seconds. If the pump does not pump to specifications, check for proper fuel tank venting or a restriction in the fuel line leading from the fuel tank to the carburetor before replacing the fuel pump.

Electric Fuel Pump

REMOVAL & INSTALLATION

7.5L Engine

Models equipped with the 7.5L carbureted engine use a single low pressure pump mounted in the fuel tank.

1. Disconnect the negative battery cable.
2. Remove the fuel tank as described below.
3. On steel tanks:
   a. Disconnect the wiring at the connector.
   b. Remove all dirt from the area of the sender.
   c. Disconnect the fuel lines.
   d. Turn the locking ring counterclockwise to remove it. There is a wrench designed for this purpose. If the wrench is not available, you can loosen the locking ring by placing a WOOD dowel against on the tabs on the locking ring and hammering it loose. NEVER USE A METAL DRIFT!

4. Lift out the fuel pump and sending unit. Discard the gasket.
5. On plastic tanks:
   a. Disconnect the wiring at the connector.
   b. Remove all dirt from the area of the sender.
   c. Disconnect the fuel lines.
   d. Turn the locking ring counterclockwise to remove it. A band-type oil filter wrench is ideal for this purpose. Lift out the fuel pump and sending unit. Discard the gasket.

To install:

6. Place a new gasket in position in the groove in the tank.
7. Place the sending unit/fuel pump assembly in the tank, indexing the tabs with the slots in the tank. Make sure the gasket stays in place.
8. Hold the assembly in place and position the locking ring.
   • On steel tanks, turn the locking ring clockwise until the stop is against the retainer ring tab.
   • On plastic tanks, turn the retaining ring clockwise until hand-tight. There is a special tool available to set the tightening torque for the locking ring. If you have this tool, torque the ring to 40–55 ft. lbs. (54–75 Nm). If you don't have the tool, just tighten the ring securely with the oil filter wrench.
9. Make sure the gasket is still in place.
10. Connect the fuel lines and wiring.
11. Install the tank.
12. Connect the negative battery cable.

VOLUME TEST

7.5L Engine

1. Operate the engine at the specified idle rpm.

2. Open the hose restrictor and catch the fuel in the container while observing the time it takes to pump 16 fl. oz. (473 ml). The amount of time to pump 16 fl. oz. (473 ml) should be at most 10 seconds. If the pump does not pump to specifications, check for proper fuel tank venting or a restriction in the fuel line leading from the fuel tank to the carburetor before replacing the fuel pump.

Carburetor

APPLICATION

The Holley 4180-C 4bbl. carburetor is used on 1987 5.8L engines found in trucks with a GVW over 8500 lbs., except in California.

The carburetor is also found on 7.5L engines made for sale in California and Canada.

REMOVAL & INSTALLATION

1. Remove the air cleaner.

✳✳ CAUTION

Never smoke when working around gasoline! Avoid all sources of sparks or ignition. Gasoline vapors are EXTREMELY volatile!

2. Remove the throttle cable or rod from the throttle lever. Disconnect the distributor vacuum line, EGR vacuum line, if so equipped, the inline fuel filter and the choke heat tube at the carburetor.

3. Disconnect the choke clean air tube from the air horn. Disconnect the choke actuating cable, if so equipped.

4. Remove the carburetor retaining nuts then remove the carburetor. Remove the carburetor mounting gasket, spacer (if so equipped), and the lower gasket from the intake manifold.

5. Before installing the carburetor, clean the gasket mounting surfaces of the spacer and carburetor. Place the spacer between two new gaskets and position the spacer and gaskets on the intake manifold. Position the carburetor body flange, snug the nuts, then alternately tighten each nut in a criss-cross pattern.

6. Connect the inline fuel filter, throttle cable, choke heat tube, distributor vacuum line, EGR vacuum line, and choke cable.

7. Connect the choke clean air line to the air horn.

8. Adjust the engine idle speed, the idle fuel mixture and anti-stall dashpot (if so equipped). Install the air cleaner.

ADJUSTMENTS

Float and Fuel Level

▶ See Figure 6

✳✳ CAUTION

Never smoke when working around gasoline! Avoid all sources of sparks or ignition. Gasoline vapors are EXTREMELY volatile!

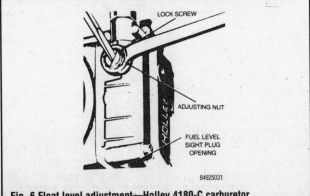

LOCK SCREW

HOLLEY

ADJUSTING NUT

FUEL LEVEL SIGHT PLUG OPENING

84925031

Fig. 6 Float level adjustment—Holley 4180-C carburetor

DRY FLOAT

To perform a preliminary dry float adjustment on both the primary and secondary fuel bowl float assemblies, remove the fuel bowls and invert them allowing the float to rest on the fuel inlet valve and set assembly. The fuel inlet valve and seat can be rotated until the float is parallel with the fuel bowl floor (actually the top of the fuel bowl chamber inverted). Note that this is an initial dry float setting which must be rechecked with the carburetor assembled and on the engine to obtain the proper wet fuel level.

WET FLOAT

This carburetor has an externally adjustable needle and seat assembly which allows the fuel level to be checked and adjust without removing the carburetor from the engine.

1. Run the engine with the vehicle resting on a level surface until the engine temperature has normalized.

2. Remove the air cleaner assembly.

3. Place a suitable container or an absorbent cloth below the fuel level sight plug in the fuel bowl.

4. Stop the engine and remove the sight plug and gasket from the primary float bowl. The fuel level in the bowl should be at the lower edge of the sight plug hole. If fuel spills out when the plug is removed, lower the level; if the fuel is below the hole, raise the level.

✳✳ CAUTION

Never loosen the lockscrew or nut, or attempt to adjust the fuel level with the sight plug removed or the engine running, since fuel will spray out creating a fire hazard!

5. To adjust the fuel level, install the sight plug and gasket. Loosen the lockscrew on top of the fuel bowl just enough to allow the adjusting nut to be turned. Turn the adjusting nut about ½ of a turn in to lower the fuel level and out to raise the fuel level. By turning the adjusting nut 5⁄32 of a turn, the fuel level will change 1⁄32 in. (0.8mm) at the sight plug.

6. Start the engine and allow the fuel level to stabilize. Check the fuel level as outlined in Step 4.

7. Repeat the procedure for the secondary float bowl adjustment.

8. Install the air cleaner assembly if no further adjustments are necessary.

Secondary Throttle Plate

1. Remove the carburetor.

✳✳ CAUTION

Never smoke when working around gasoline! Avoid all sources of sparks or ignition. Gasoline vapors are EXTREMELY volatile!

2. Hold the secondary throttle plates closed.

3. Turn the secondary throttle shaft lever stop screw out until the secondary throttle plates seat in the throttle bores.

4. Turn the screw back in until it just touches the lever, then ⅜ additional turn.

Fast Idle

▶ See Figure 7

1. Remove the spark delay valve, if so equipped, from the distributor vacuum advance line, and route the vacuum line directly to the advance side of the distributor.

✳✳ CAUTION

Never smoke when working around gasoline! Avoid all sources of sparks or ignition. Gasoline vapors are EXTREMELY volatile!

2. Trace the EGR signal vacuum line from the EGR valve to the carburetor and if there is EGR/PVS valve or temperature vacuum switch located in the vacuum line routing, disconnect the EGR vacuum line at the EGR valve and plug the line.

3. If not equipped with an EGR/PVS valve or temperature vacuum switch do not detach the EGR vacuum line.

4. Trace the purge valve vacuum line from the purge valve located on the

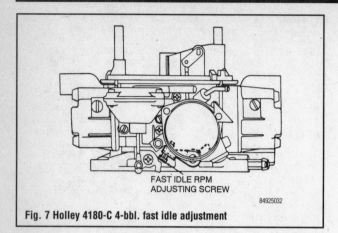

Fig. 7 Holley 4180-C 4-bbl. fast idle adjustment

canister, to the first point where the vacuum line can be detached from the underhood hose routing. Disconnect the vacuum line at that point, cap the open port, and plug the vacuum line.

❋❋ WARNING

To prevent damage to the purge valve do not disconnect the vacuum line at the purge valve.

5. With the engine running at normal operating temperature, the choke plate fully opened and the manual transmission in Neutral and the automatic transmission in Park, place the fast idle level on the 2nd or kickdown step of the fast idle cam.

6. Adjust the fast idle screw to within 100 rpm of the specified speed given on the Vehicle Emission Control Decal.

7. Reconnect all vacuum lines.

Vacuum Operated Throttle Modulator

▶ See Figure 8

1. Set the parking brake, put the transmission in Park or Neutral and run the engine up to operating temperature.

❋❋ CAUTION

Never smoke when working around gasoline! Avoid all sources of sparks or ignition. Gasoline vapors are EXTREMELY volatile!

2. Turn off the air conditioning and heater controls.

3. Disconnect and plug the vacuum hoses at the air control valve and EGR valve and purge control valve.

4. Place the transmission in the position specified on the underhood decal.

5. If necessary, check and adjust the curb idle rpm.

6. Place the transmission in Neutral or Park and rev the engine. Place the transmission in the specified position according to the underhood decal and recheck the curb idle rpm. Readjust if necessary.

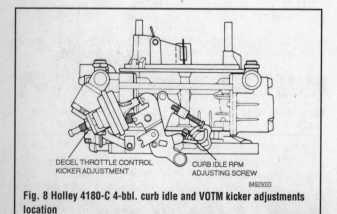

Fig. 8 Holley 4180-C 4-bbl. curb idle and VOTM kicker adjustments location

7. Connect an external vacuum source which provides a minimum of 10 in. Hg of vacuum to the VOTM (Vacuum Operated Throttle Modulator) kicker.

8. Place the transmission in the specified position.

9. Adjust the VOTM (throttle kicker) locknut if necessary to obtain the proper idle rpm.

10. Reconnect all vacuum hoses.

Choke Plate Pulldown Clearance

▶ See Figure 9

1. Remove the choke thermostat housing, gasket and retainer.

2. Insert a piece of wire into the choke piston bore to move the piston down against the stop screw.

❋❋ CAUTION

Never smoke when working around gasoline! Avoid all sources of sparks or ignition. Gasoline vapors are EXTREMELY volatile!

3. Measure the gap between the lower edge of the choke plate and the air horn wall.

4. Turn the adjustment screw to specifications.

5. Reinstall the choke thermostat housing, gasket and retainer.

Automatic Choke Housing

This adjustment is present and should not be changed.

Accelerator Pump Lever

1. Hold the primary throttle plates in the wide open position.

❋❋ CAUTION

Never smoke when working around gasoline! Avoid all sources of sparks or ignition. Gasoline vapors are EXTREMELY volatile!

2. Using a feeler gauge, check the clearance at the accelerator pump operating lever adjustment screw head and the pump arm while depressing the pump arm with your finger. The clearance should be 1/64 in. (0.39mm).

3. To make an adjustment, hold the adjusting screw locknut and turn the adjusting screw inward to increase, or outward to decrease, the adjustment. 1/2 turn will change the clearance by 1/64 in. (0.39mm).

Accelerator Pump Stroke

This adjustment is preset and should not be changed.

TROUBLESHOOTING

The best way to diagnose a bad carburetor is to eliminate all other possible sources of the problem. If the carburetor is suspected to be the problem, first perform all of the adjustments given in this section. If this doesn't correct the difficulty, then check the following. Check the ignition system to make sure that the spark plugs are in good condition and adjusted to the proper specifications.

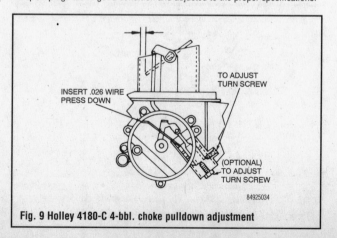

Fig. 9 Holley 4180-C 4-bbl. choke pulldown adjustment

Examine the emission control equipment to make sure that all the vacuum lines are connected and none are blocked or clogged. See the first half of this section. Check the ignition timing adjustment. Check all of the vacuum lines on the engine for loose connections, slips or breaks. Torque the carburetor and intake manifold attaching bolts to the proper specifications. If, after performing all of these checks and adjustments, the problem is still not solved, then you can safely assume that the carburetor is the source of the problem.

OVERHAUL

> ✳✳ **CAUTION**
>
> **Never smoke when working around gasoline! Avoid all sources of sparks or ignition. Gasoline vapors are EXTREMELY volatile!**

Overhaul Kits

Carburetor overhaul kits are recommended for each overhaul. These kits contain all gaskets and new parts to replace those which deteriorate most rapidly. Failure to replace all of the parts supplied with the kit (especially gaskets) can result in poor performance later.

Most carburetor manufacturers supply overhaul kits of three basic types:

Minor Repair Kits:
- All gaskets
- Float needle valve
- Volume control screw
- All diaphragms
- Spring for the pump diaphragm

Major Repair Kits:
- All jets and gaskets
- All diaphragms
- Float needle valve
- Volume control screw
- Pump ball valve
- Main jet carrier
- Float
- Other necessary items
- Some cover hold-down screws and washers

Gasket Kits:
- All gaskets

Preliminary Instructions

Efficient carburetion depends greatly on careful cleaning and inspection during overhaul since dirt, gum, water or varnish in or on the carburetor parts are often responsible for poor performance.

Overhaul the carburetor in a clean, dust free area. Carefully disassemble the carburetor, referring often to the exploded views. Keep all similar and look-alike parts segregated during disassembly and cleaning to avoid accidental interchange during assembly. Make a note of all jet sizes.

When the carburetor is disassembled, wash all parts (except diaphragms, electric choke units, pump plunger and any other plastic, leather, fiber, or rubber parts) in clean carburetor solvent. Do not leave the parts in the solvent any longer than is necessary to sufficiently loosen the dirt and deposits. Excessive cleaning may remove the special finish from the float bowl and choke valve bodies, leaving these parts unfit for service. Rinse all parts in clean solvent and blow them dry with compressed air or allow them to air dry, while resting on clean, lintless paper. Wipe clean all cork, plastic, leather and fiber parts with clean, lint free cloth.

Blow out all passages and jets with compressed air and be sure that there are no restrictions or blockages. Never use wire or similar tools to clean jets, fuel passages or air bleeds. Clean all jets and valves separately to avoid accidental interchange.

Examine all parts for wear or damage. If wear or damage is found, replace the defective parts. Especially, inspect the following:

1. Check the float needle and seat for wear. If wear is found, replace the complete assembly.

2. Check the float hinge pin for wear and the float(s) for dents or distortion. Replace the float if fuel has leaked into it.

3. Check the throttle and choke shaft bores for wear or an out-of-round condition. Damage or wear to the throttle arm, shaft or shaft bore will often require replacement of the throttle body. These parts require a close tolerance of fit; wear may allow air leakage, which could affect starting and idling.

➡**Throttle shaft and bushings are not normally included in overhaul kits. They can be purchased separately.**

4. Inspect the idle mixture adjusting needles for burrs and grooves. Any such condition requires replacement of the needle, since you will not be able to obtain a satisfactory idle.

5. Test the accelerator pump check valves. They should pass air one way, but not the other. Test for proper seating by blowing and sucking on the valve. Replace the valve as necessary. If the valve is satisfactory, wash the valve again to remove moisture.

6. Check the bowl cover for warped surfaces with a straightedge.

7. Closely inspect the valves and seats for wear and damage, replacing as necessary.

8. After the carburetor is assembled, check the choke valve for freedom of operation.

After cleaning and checking all components, reassemble the carburetor, using new parts and referring to the exploded view. When reassembling, make sure that all screws and jets are right in their seat, but do not overtighten, as the tip will be distorted. Tighten all screws gradually, in rotation. Do not tighten needle valves into their seats; uneven jetting will result. Always use new gaskets. Be sure to adjust the float level.

GASOLINE FUEL INJECTION SYSTEMS

General Information

MULTI-PORT AND SEQUENTIAL FUEL INJECTION SYSTEMS

➡**Both the Multi-port Fuel Injection (MFI) and Sequential Fuel Injection (SFI) systems are types of "multi-point" fuel injection. While Ford Motor Co. has changed terminology for many of its fuel system components, in many cases the technology has remained the same. For purposes of uniformity, the latest names of components will generally be used in this manual.**

The Multi-port Fuel Injection (MFI) and Sequential Fuel Injection (SFI) subsystems include a high pressure inline electric fuel pump, a low-pressure tank-mounted fuel pump, fuel charging manifold, pressure regulator, fuel filter, and both solid and flexible fuel lines. The fuel charging manifold includes 6 or 8 electronically controlled fuel injectors, each mounted directly above an intake port in the lower intake manifold. On the 6-cylinder MFI system, all injectors are energized simultaneously and spray once every crankshaft revolution, delivering a predetermined quantity of fuel into the intake air stream. On the V8 MFI engines, the injectors are energized in 2 banks of 4, once each crankshaft revolution. On the SFI engines, each fuel injector is energized once every other crankshaft revolution in sequence with the engine firing order.

The fuel pressure regulator maintains a constant pressure drop across the injector nozzles. The regulator is referenced to intake manifold vacuum and is connected parallel to the fuel injectors and positioned on the far end of the fuel rail. Any excess fuel supplied by the pump passes through the regulator and is returned to the fuel tank via a return line.

➡**The pressure regulator reduces fuel pressure to 39–40 psi (269–276 kPa) under normal operating conditions. At idle or high manifold vacuum condition, fuel pressure is reduced to approximately 30 psi (207 kPa).**

The fuel pressure regulator is a diaphragm operated relief valve in which the inside of the diaphragm senses fuel pressure and the other side senses manifold vacuum. Normal fuel pressure is established by a spring preload applied to the diaphragm. Control of the fuel system is maintained through the EEC power relay and the EEC-IV or EEC-V control unit, although electrical power is routed through the fuel pump relay and an inertia switch. The fuel pump relay is normally located on a bracket somewhere above the Powertrain Control Module

(PCM) and the inertia switch is located in the cab. The in-line fuel pump is usually mounted on a bracket at the fuel tank, or on a frame rail. Tank-mounted pumps can be either high or low-pressure, depending on the model.

The inertia switch opens the power circuit to the fuel pump in the event of a collision. Once tripped, the switch must be reset manually by pushing the reset button on the assembly. Check that the inertia switch is reset before diagnosing power supply problems to the fuel pump circuit.

Fuel Pump

The fuel delivery system uses either a high or low-pressure in-line or in-tank electric fuel pump, with some models equipped with both. It is a recirculating system that delivers fuel to a pressure regulating valve in the throttle body and returns excess fuel from the throttle body regulator back to the fuel tank. The electrical system uses two types of control relays, one controlled by a vacuum switch and the other controlled by the powertrain control module (PCM) to provide power to the fuel pump under various operating conditions.

✳✳ CAUTION

Fuel supply lines on vehicles equipped with a high pressure fuel system will remain pressurized for long periods of time after engine shutdown. The fuel pressure must be relieved before servicing the fuel system.

An inertia switch is used as a safety device in the fuel system. The inertia switch is located in the cab, generally under the dashboard on the right side. It is designed to open the fuel pump power circuit in the event of a collision. The switch is reset by pushing each of 2 buttons on the switch simultaneously (some models use switches with only one reset button). The inertia switch should not be reset until the fuel system has been inspected for damage or leaks.

When the ignition switch is **ON**, it turns the EEC power relay **ON**. The EEC power relay provides power to the powertrain control module (PCM) and the control side of the fuel pump relay. Power for the fuel pump(s) is supplied through a fuse link or high current fuse attached to the starter solenoid (battery side). From the fuse link or high current fuse, current flows through the fuel pump relay and inertia switch to the fuel pump(s). The fuel pump relay is controlled by the PCM.

When the ignition switch is turned **ON**, the fuel pump(s) will operate. If the ignition switch is not turned to the **START** position the PCM will shut the fuel pump(s) **OFF** after 1 second. The PCM will operate the fuel pump(s) operate the fuel pump(s) when the ignition switch is turn to **START** position to provide fuel while cranking.

After the engine starts, the PCM will continue to operate the fuel pump(s) unless the engine stops, drops below 120 rpm or the inertia switch is tripped.

Fuel Charging Assembly

The fuel charging assembly controls air/fuel ratio. It consists of a butterfly valve throttle body. It has bore(s) without venturis. The throttle shaft and valves control engine air flow based on driver demand. The throttle body attaches to the intake manifold mounting pad.

A throttle position sensor is attached to the throttle shaft. It includes a potentiometer that electrically senses throttle opening. Some vehicles incorporate a throttle kicker solenoid fastens opposite the throttle position sensor. During air conditioning operation, the solenoid extends to slightly increase engine idle speed.

Fuel Pressure Regulator

The fuel pressure regulator controls critical injector fuel pressure. The regulator receives fuel from the electric fuel pump and then adjusts the fuel pressure for uniform pressure differential between the intake plenum and the fuel injector pressure. The regulator sets fuel pressure at 13–17 psi (90–120 kPa).

Fuel Manifold

The fuel manifold (or fuel rail) distributes fuel to each injector. The end of the fuel rail contains a relief valve for testing fuel pressure during engine operation and relieving fuel system pressure before work is performed on the system.

Fuel Pressure Testing

✳✳ CAUTION

Fuel pressure must be relieved before attempting to disconnect any fuel lines.

The diagnostic pressure valve (Schrader type) is located on the fuel rail on multi-port systems. This valve provides a convenient point to monitor fuel pressure, release the system pressure prior to maintenance, and to bleed out air which may become trapped in the system during filter replacement. A pressure gauge with an adapter is required to perform pressure tests.

If the pressure tap is not installed or an adapter is not available, use a T-fitting to install the pressure gauge between the fuel filter line and the throttle body fuel inlet or fuel rail.

Testing fuel pressure requires the use of a special pressure gauge (T80L–9974–A or equivalent) that attaches to the diagnostic pressure tap fitting. Depressurize the fuel system before disconnecting any lines.

Fuel Injectors

The fuel injectors are electromechanical (solenoid) type designed to meter and atomize fuel delivered to the intake ports of the engine. The injectors are mounted in the lower intake manifold and positioned so that their spray nozzles direct the fuel charge in front of the intake valves. The injector body consists of a solenoid actuated pintle and needle valve assembly. The control unit sends an electrical impulse that activates the solenoid, causing the pintle to move inward off the seat and allow the fuel to flow. The amount of fuel delivered is controlled by the length of time the injector is energized (pulse width), since the fuel flow orifice is fixed and the fuel pressure drop across the injector tip is constant. Correct atomization is achieved by contouring the pintle at the point where the fuel enters the pintle chamber.

The computer, based on voltage inputs from the crankshaft position sensor, operates each injector solenoid 2 times per engine revolution. When the injector metering valve unseats, fuel is sprayed in a fine mist into the intake manifold. The computer varies fuel enrichment based on voltage inputs from the exhaust gas oxygen sensor, barometric pressure sensor, manifold absolute pressure sensor, etc., by calculating how long to hold the injectors open. The longer the injectors remain open, the richer the mixture. This injector "on" time is called pulse duration.

➡ **Exercise care when handling fuel injectors during service. Be careful not to lose the pintle cap and replace O-rings to assure a tight seal. Never apply direct battery voltage to test a fuel injector.**

The injectors receive high pressure fuel from the fuel manifold (fuel rail) assembly. The complete assembly includes a single, preformed tube with 4, 6, or 8 injector connectors, mounting flange for the pressure regulator, mounting attachments to locate the manifold and provide the fuel injector retainers and a Schrader® quick-disconnect fitting used to perform fuel pressure tests.

The fuel manifold is normally removed with fuel injectors and pressure regulator attached. Fuel injector electrical connectors are plastic and have locking tabs that must be released when disconnecting when disconnecting the wiring harness.

Throttle Air Bypass Valve

The throttle air bypass valve is an electro-mechanical (solenoid) device whose operation is controlled by the EEC-IV or EEC-V control unit. A variable air metering valve controls both cold and warm idle air flow in response to commands from the control unit. The valve operates by bypassing a regulated amount of air around the throttle plate; the higher the voltage signal from the control unit, the more air is bypassed through the valve. In this manner, additional air can be added to the fuel mixture without moving the throttle plate. At curb idle, the valve provides smooth idle for various engine coolant temperatures, compensates for air conditioning load and compensates for transmission load and no-load conditions. The valve also provides fast idle for start-up, replacing the fast idle cam, throttle kicker and anti-dieseling solenoid common to previous models.

There are no curb idle or fast idle adjustments. As in curb idle operation, the fast idle speed is proportional to engine coolant temperature. Fast idle kickdown will occur when the throttle is kicked. A time-out feature in the PCM will also automatically kick-down fast idle to curb idle after a time period of approximately 15–25 seconds; after coolant has reached approximately 71°C (160°F). The signal duty cycle from the PCM to the valve will be at 100% (maximum current) during the crank to provide maximum air flow to allow no touch starting at any time (engine cold or hot).

Relieving Fuel System Pressure

➡ **A special tool is necessary for this procedure.**

1. Make sure the ignition switch is in the **OFF** position.

✳✳ CAUTION

Never smoke when working around gasoline! Avoid all sources of sparks or ignition. Gasoline vapors are EXTREMELY volatile!

2. Disconnect the battery ground.
3. Remove the fuel filler cap.
4. Using MFI Pressure Gauge T80L–9974–A, or equivalent, at the fuel pressure relief valve (located in the fuel line in the upper right corner of the engine compartment) relieve the fuel system pressure. A valve cap must first be removed to gain access to the pressure relief valve.

Electric Fuel Pump

GENERAL INFORMATION

1987–89 Fuel Injected Engines

Two electric pumps are used on fuel injected models; a low pressure boost pump mounted in the fuel tank and a high pressure pump mounted on the vehicle frame.

The low pressure pump is used to provide pressurized fuel to the inlet of the high pressure pump and helps prevent noise and heating problems. The externally mounted high pressure pump is capable of supplying 15.9 gallons of fuel an hour. System pressure is controlled by a pressure regulator mounted on the engine.

1990–96 Engines

♦ **See Figure 10**

These trucks employ a single, high pressure pump which is part of the modular, In-Tank Reservoir (ITR) assembly. Besides the pump, the ITR consists of a venturi jet pump, a supply check valve and a shuttle selector valve. All this is mounted on the fuel gauge sender flange. The sending unit is separate from the ITR module.

REMOVAL & INSTALLATION

➡ **On internally mounted pumps, tank removal is required. Frame mounted models can be accessed from under the vehicle. Prior to ser-**

vicing, release the fuel system pressure. Refer to the applicable Fuel Injection System procedures listed in this section for details. Disconnect the negative battery cable prior to pump removal.

In-Tank Pump

♦ **See Figures 11 and 12**

1. Release the fuel system pressure. Disconnect the negative battery cable.
2. Remove the fuel tank as described below.
3. On steel tanks:
   a. Disconnect the wiring at the connector.
   b. Remove all dirt from the area of the sender.
   c. Disconnect the fuel lines.
   d. Turn the locking ring counterclockwise to remove it. There is a wrench designed for this purpose. If the wrench is not available, you can loosen the locking ring by placing a WOOD dowel against on the tabs on the locking ring and hammering it loose. NEVER USE A METAL DRIFT!

✳✳ CAUTION

Use of metal will result in sparks which could cause an explosion!

4. Lift out the fuel pump and sending unit. Discard the gasket.
5. On plastic tanks:
   a. Disconnect the wiring at the connector.
   b. Remove all dirt from the area of the sender.
   c. Disconnect the fuel lines.
   d. Turn the locking ring counterclockwise to remove it. A band-type oil filter wrench is ideal for this purpose. Lift out the fuel pump and sending unit. Discard the gasket.

To install:

6. Place a new gasket in position in the groove in the tank.
7. Place the sending unit/fuel pump assembly in the tank, indexing the tabs with the slots in the tank. Make sure the gasket stays in place.
8. Hold the assembly in place and position the locking ring.

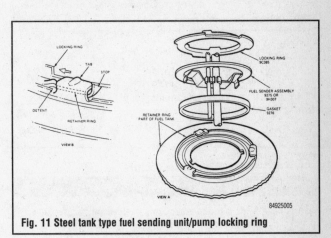

Fig. 11 Steel tank type fuel sending unit/pump locking ring

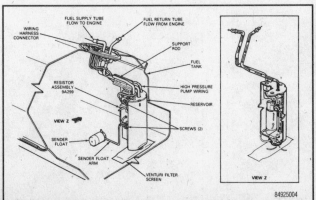

Fig. 10 Electric fuel pump assembly—1990–96 engines

Fig. 12 Plastic tank type fuel sending unit/pump locking ring

- On steel tanks, turn the locking ring clockwise until the stop is against the retainer ring tab.
- On plastic tanks, turn the retaining ring clockwise until hand-tight. There is a special too available to set the tightening torque for the locking ring. If you have this tool, torque the ring to 40–55 ft. lbs. (54–75 Nm). If you don't have the tool, just tighten the ring securely with the oil filter wrench.

9. Make sure the gasket is still in place.
10. Connect the fuel lines and wiring.
11. Install the tank.

External Pump

▶ See Figure 13

1. Disconnect the negative battery cable.

✳✳ CAUTION

Never smoke when working around gasoline! Avoid all sources of sparks or ignition. Gasoline vapors are EXTREMELY volatile!

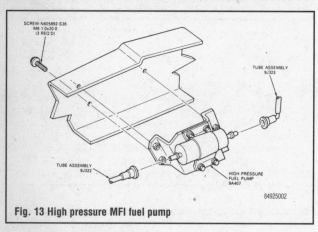

Fig. 13 High pressure MFI fuel pump

2. Depressurize the fuel system.
3. Raise and support the rear of the vehicle on jackstands.
4. Disconnect the inlet and outlet fuel lines.
5. Remove the pump from the mounting bracket.
6. Install in reverse order, make sure the pump is indexed correctly in the mounting bracket insulator.

VOLUME TEST

1. Operate the engine at the specified idle rpm.

✳✳ CAUTION

Never smoke when working around gasoline! Avoid all sources of sparks or ignition. Gasoline vapors are EXTREMELY volatile!

2. Open the hose restrictor and catch the fuel in the container while observing the time it takes to pump 1 pint. 1 pint should be pumped in 20 seconds. If the pump does not pump to specifications, check for proper fuel tank venting or a restriction in the fuel line leading from the fuel tank to the carburetor before replacing the fuel pump.

Throttle Body

REMOVAL & INSTALLATION

4.9L, 5.0L and 5.8L Engines

EXCEPT LIGHTNING ENGINE

▶ See Figures 14, 15, 16 and 17

1. Remove the throttle body cover, if equipped.
2. Disconnect the air intake hose.

✳✳ CAUTION

Never smoke when working around gasoline! Avoid all sources of sparks or ignition. Gasoline vapors are EXTREMELY volatile!

3. Disconnect the throttle cable from the pivot ball on top of the throttle body.
4. Disconnect the air bypass hose, if equipped.
5. Disconnect the throttle position sensor and air by-pass valve connectors.
6. Remove the four throttle body mounting nuts and carefully separate the air throttle body from the upper intake manifold.
7. Remove and discard the mounting gasket. Clean all mounting surfaces using care not to damage the gasket surfaces of the throttle body and manifold. Do not allow any material to drop into the intake manifold.
8. Install the throttle body in the reverse order of removal. The mounting nuts are tightened to 12–15 ft. lbs. (16–20 Nm).

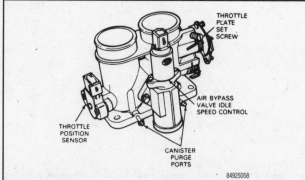

Fig. 14 Throttle body assembly, including throttle position sensor and air bypass valve—4.9L, 5.0L and 5.8L engines

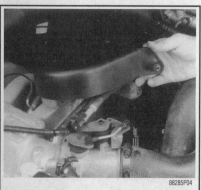

Fig. 15 Remove the shroud (cover) from the throttle body

Fig. 16 Disconnect the throttle cable linkage

Fig. 17 Disconnect the air bypass hose

LIGHTNING ENGINE

▶ See Figure 18

1. Disconnect the battery ground cable.

➡ On EEC equipped vehicles, disconnecting and reconnecting the battery may cause abnormal drive symptoms as the powertrain control module relearns its codes. The truck may need to be driven 10 miles or more until normal driveability is restored.

2. Remove the snow/ice shield.
3. Disconnect the air intake hose.

✳✳ CAUTION

Never smoke when working around gasoline! Avoid all sources of sparks or ignition. Gasoline vapors are EXTREMELY volatile!

4. Remove the PCV fresh air tube from the throttle body.
5. Disconnect the throttle position sensor and air by-pass valve connectors.
6. With the engine cool, remove the radiator cap and remove the plug the coolant hoses at the EGR spacer.
7. Remove the AIRB/AIRD bracket nuts and position the bracket out of the way.
8. Remove the throttle body mounting nuts and carefully separate the air throttle body from the EGR spacer.
9. Disconnect the throttle cable from the ball stud by prying it off. DO NOT pull it off!
10. Remove and discard the mounting gasket. Clean all mounting surfaces using care not to damage the gasket surfaces of the throttle body and manifold. Do not allow any material to drop into the intake manifold.
11. Install the throttle body in the reverse order of removal. The mounting nuts are tightened to 12–18 ft. lbs. (16–24 Nm).

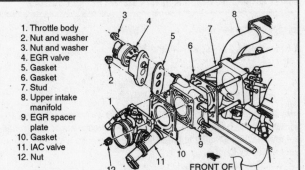

1. Throttle body
2. Nut and washer
3. Nut and washer
4. EGR valve
5. Gasket
6. Gasket
7. Stud
8. Upper intake manifold
9. EGR spacer plate
10. Gasket
11. IAC valve
12. Nut

FRONT OF ENGINE

84925066

Fig. 18 Exploded view of Lightning engine's throttle body assembly

7.5L Engine

▶ See Figure 19

1. Relieve the fuel system pressure.

✳✳ CAUTION

Never smoke when working around gasoline! Avoid all sources of sparks or ignition. Gasoline vapors are EXTREMELY volatile!

2. Disconnect the throttle position sensor wire.
3. Disconnect the water lines at the throttle body.
4. Remove the 4 throttle body bolts and carefully lift off the throttle body. Discard the gasket.
5. Installation is the reverse of removal. Torque the bolts to 18 ft. lbs. (24 Nm).

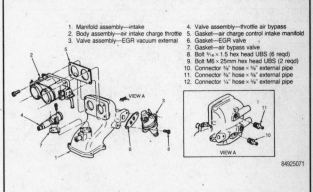

1. Manifold assembly—intake
2. Body assembly—air intake charge throttle
3. Valve assembly—EGR vacuum external
4. Valve assembly—throttle air bypass
5. Gasket—air charge control intake manifold
6. Gasket—EGR valve
7. Gasket—air bypass valve
8. Bolt 5⁄16 × 1.5 hex head UBS (6 reqd)
9. Bolt M6 × 25mm hex head UBS (2 reqd)
10. Connector 3⁄8" hose × 3⁄8" external pipe
11. Connector 3⁄8" hose × 3⁄8" external pipe
12. Connector 1⁄4" hose × 3⁄8" external pipe

VIEW A

VIEW A

84925071

Fig. 19 Throttle body and upper intake manifold—7.5L engine

Fuel Injectors

REMOVAL & INSTALLATION

▶ See Figures 20 thru 26

1. Relieve the fuel system pressure.

✳✳ CAUTION

Never smoke when working around gasoline! Avoid all sources of sparks or ignition. Gasoline vapors are EXTREMELY volatile!

2. For all except 7.5L engines, remove the upper intake manifold assembly.
3. Remove the fuel rail.
4. Disconnect the wiring at each injector.

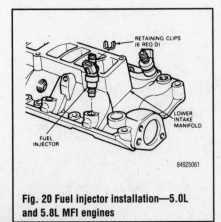

RETAINING CLIPS (6 REQ'D)

LOWER INTAKE MANIFOLD

FUEL INJECTOR

84925061

Fig. 20 Fuel injector installation—5.0L and 5.8L MFI engines

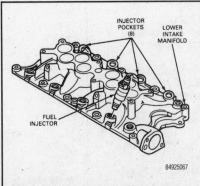

INJECTOR POCKETS (8)

LOWER INTAKE MANIFOLD

FUEL INJECTOR

84925067

Fig. 21 Lower intake manifold showing injector positions—Lightning

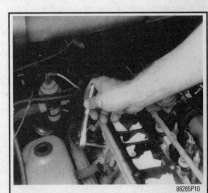

88285P10

Fig. 22 Remove the fuel rail retaining screws

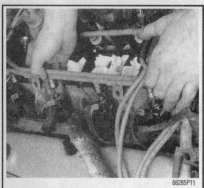

Fig. 23 Carefully lift the fuel rail away from the injectors

Fig. 24 Unplug the harness connectors from the individual injectors

Fig. 25 Pull out the injector from the engine

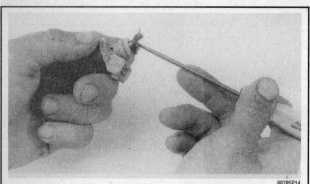

Fig. 26 Inspect the O-ring carefully. Do not hesitate to replace any that show wear

5. Pull upward on the injector body while gently rocking it from side-to-side.

6. Inspect the O-rings on the injector for any sign of leakage or damage. Replace any suspected O-rings.

7. Inspect the plastic cap at the top of each injector and replace it if any sign of deterioration is noticed.

To install:

8. Lubricate the O-rings with clean engine oil ONLY!

9. Install the injectors by pushing them in with a gentle rocking motion.

10. Connect the electrical wiring.

11. Install the fuel rail.

12. If applicable, install the upper intake manifold.

TESTING

Fuel Injector Pressure Test

1. Connect pressure gauge T80L–9974–A, or equivalent, to the fuel pressure test fitting. Disconnect the coil connector from the coil. Disconnect the electrical lead from one injector and pressurize the fuel system. Disable the fuel pump by disconnecting the inertia switch or the fuel pump relay and observe the pressure gauge reading.

2. Crank the engine for 2 seconds. Turn the ignition **OFF** and wait 5 seconds, then observe the pressure drop. If the pressure drop is 2–16 psi (14–110 kPa), the injector is operating properly. Reconnect the injector, activate the fuel pump, then repeat the procedure for other injector.

3. If the pressure drop is less than 2 psi (14 kPa) or more than 16 psi (110 kPa), switch the electrical connectors on injectors and repeat the test. If the pressure drop is still incorrect, replace the disconnected injector with one of the same color code, then reconnect both injectors properly and repeat the test.

4. Disconnect and plug the vacuum hose at EGR valve. It may be necessary to disconnect the idle air control valve and use the throttle body stop screw to set the engine speed. Start and run the engine at 1,800 rpm (2,000 rpm on 1984

and later models). Disconnect the left injector electrical connector. Note the rpm after the engine stabilizes (around 1,200 rpm). Reconnect the injector and allow the engine to return to high idle.

5. Perform the same procedure for the right injector. Note the difference between the rpm readings of the left and right injectors. If the difference is 100 rpm or less, check the oxygen sensor. If the difference is more than 100 rpm, replace both injectors.

Fuel Pressure Regulator

REMOVAL & INSTALLATION

✳✳✳ CAUTION

Never smoke when working around gasoline! Avoid all sources of sparks or ignition. Gasoline vapors are EXTREMELY volatile!

Except Lightning Engine

▶ See Figures 27, 28, 29, 30 and 31

1. Relieve the fuel system pressure.
2. Disconnect the vacuum line at the regulator.
3. Remove the 3 Allen screws from the regulator housing.

➡In some cases the factory bent the fuel line over one of the 3 Allen screws making it difficult to remove with an Allen wrench. A pair of pliers may have to be used to break the screw loose so it can be unthreaded by hand.

4. Remove the regulator.
5. Inspect the regulator O-ring for signs of deterioration or damage. Discard the gasket.

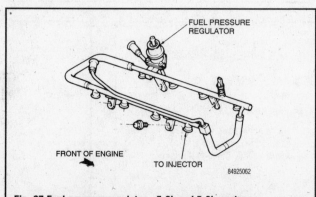

Fig. 27 Fuel pressure regulator—5.0L and 5.8L engines

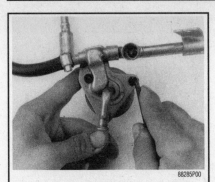

Fig. 28 Remove the Allen screws—note the fuel line fitting blocking access to the screw

Fig. 29 Once the screws are removed, disengage the fuel pressure regulator from the fuel rail

Fig. 30 Check the condition of the O-ring and replace if it is deteriorated or cracked

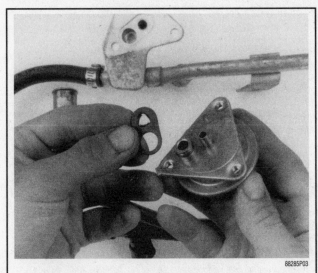

Fig. 31 Discard the gasket and replace it with a new one

To install:

6. Lubricate the O-ring with clean engine oil ONLY!
7. Make sure that the mounting surfaces are clean.
8. Using a new gasket, install the regulator. Tighten the retaining screws to 40 inch lbs. (4.5 Nm).
9. Connect the vacuum line.

Lightning Engine

1. Relieve the fuel system pressure.

⚞⚟ CAUTION

Never smoke when working around gasoline! Avoid all sources of sparks or ignition. Gasoline vapors are EXTREMELY volatile!

2. Remove the fuel supply manifold.
3. Remove the 3 Allen screws from the regulator housing.
4. Remove the regulator.
5. Inspect the regulator O-ring for signs of deterioration or damage. Discard the gasket.
6. Lubricate the O-ring with clean engine oil ONLY!
7. Make sure that the mounting surfaces are clean.
8. Using a new gasket, install the regulator. Tighten the retaining screws to 40 inch lbs. (4.5 Nm).
9. Install the fuel supply manifold.

Pressure Relief Valve

REMOVAL & INSTALLATION

⚞⚟ CAUTION

Never smoke when working around gasoline! Avoid all sources of sparks or ignition. Gasoline vapors are EXTREMELY volatile!

4.9L Engine

1. Relieve the fuel system pressure.
2. Unscrew the valve from the fuel line.
3. When installing the valve, tighten it to 80 inch lbs. (9 Nm)
4. Tighten the cap to 5 inch lbs. (0.56 Nm).

DIESEL FUEL SYSTEM

Injection Lines

REMOVAL & INSTALLATION

♦ **See Figures 32 and 33**

➡ **Before removing any fuel lines, clean the exterior with clean fuel oil, or solvent to prevent entry of dirt into the fuel system when the fuel lines are removed. If available, blow dry with compressed air.**

1. Disconnect the battery ground cables from both batteries.
2. Remove the air cleaner and cap intake manifold opening with clean rags.
3. Disconnect the accelerator cable and speed control cable, if so equipped, from the injection pump.
4. Remove the accelerator cable bracket from the intake manifold and position out of the way with cable(s) attached.

⚞⚟ WARNING

To prevent fuel system contamination, cap all fuel lines and fittings.

5. Disconnect the fuel line from the fuel filter to injection pump and cap all fittings.
6. Disconnect and cap the nozzle fuel lines at nozzles.
7. Remove the fuel line clamps from the fuel lines to be removed.
8. Remove and cap the injection pump inlet elbow.
9. Remove and cap the inlet fitting adapter.
10. Remove the injection nozzle lines, one at a time, from the injection pump using Tool T83T–9396–A, or equivalent.

➡ **Fuel lines must be removed following this sequence: 5–6–4–8–3–1–7–2. Install caps on the end of each fuel line and pump fitting as the line is disconnected and identify each fuel line accordingly.**

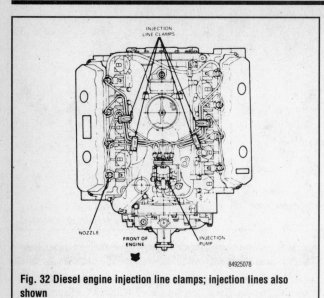

Fig. 32 Diesel engine injection line clamps; injection lines also shown

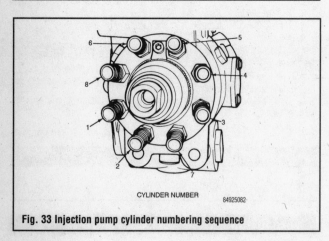

Fig. 33 Injection pump cylinder numbering sequence

To install:

11. Install fuel lines on injection pump, one at a time, and tighten to 22 ft. lbs. (30 Nm).

➡Fuel lines must be installed in the following sequence: 2–7–1–3–8–4–6–5.

12. Clean the old sealant from the injection pump elbow, using clean solvent, and dry thoroughly.

13. Apply a light coating of pipe sealant on the elbow threads.

Injectors

REMOVAL & INSTALLATION

1987–93 Engines

◗ **See Figures 34 and 35**

➡Before removing the nozzle assemblies, clean the exterior of each nozzle assembly and the surrounding area with clean fuel oil or solvent to prevent entry of dirt into the engine when nozzle assemblies are removed. Also, clean the fuel inlet and fuel leak-off piping connections. Blow dry with compressed air.

1. Remove the fuel line retaining clamp(s) from the injection lines.
2. Disconnect the fuel injection lines and fuel leak-off tees from each injector and position out of the way. Cap the open ends of the fuel injectors with protective caps to prevent dirt from entering.
3. Remove the injectors by turning them counterclockwise. Pull the assembly with the copper washer attached from the engine. Cover the nozzle spray tips with plastic caps.

➡Remove the copper injector nozzle gasket from the nozzle bore with special tool, T71P–19703–C, or equivalent, whenever the gasket does not come out with the injector.

4. Place the injector assemblies in a fabricated holder as they are removed from the heads. The holder should be marked with numbers corresponding to the cylinder numbering of the engine.

To install:

5. Thoroughly clean the injector bore in cylinder head with nozzle special tool T83T–9527–A or an equivalent nozzle seat cleaner. Make certain that no small particles of metal or carbon remain on the seating surface. Blow out the particles with compressed air.
6. Remove the protective cap and install a new copper gasket on the nozzle tip with a small dab of grease.

➡Anti-seize compound or equivalent should be used on injectors threads to aid in installation and future removal.

7. Install the injector assembly into the cylinder head and tighten to 33 ft. lbs. (45 Nm).
8. Remove the protective caps from injectors and fuel lines.
9. Connect the high pressure fuel lines and tighten them with a flare nut wrench.
10. Install the leak-off tees to the nozzle assemblies.

➡Install two new O-ring seals for each fuel return tee.

11. Install the fuel line retainer clamps.
12. Start the engine and check for leaks.

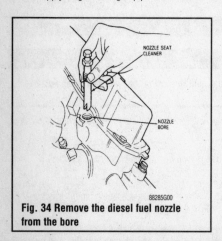

Fig. 34 Remove the diesel fuel nozzle from the bore

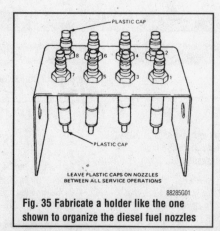

Fig. 35 Fabricate a holder like the one shown to organize the diesel fuel nozzles

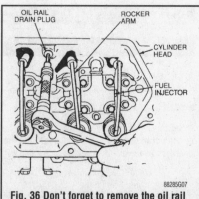

Fig. 36 Don't forget to remove the oil rail drain plug—1994-96 engines

1994–96 Engines

♦ See Figures 36, 37 and 38

※※ CAUTION

The red-striped wires on the DI Turbo carry 115 volts DC. A severe electrical shock may be given. Do not pierce the wires.

※※ WARNING

Do not pierce the wires or damage to the harness could occur.

Special tools required:
- Slide Hammer, No. T50T–100–A, or equivalent
- Injector Remover, No. T94T–9000–AH1, or equivalent
- Injector Replacer, No. T94T–9000–AH2, or equivalent
1. Remove the valve cover.
2. Disengage the fuel injector electrical connector.

※※ WARNING

Remove the oil drain plugs prior to removing the injectors or oil could enter the combustion chamber which could result in hydrostatic lock and severe engine damage.

3. Remove the oil rail drain plugs.
4. Remove the retaining screw and oil deflector. The shoulder bolt on the inboard side of the fuel injector does not require removal.
5. Remove the outboard fuel injector retaining bolt.
6. Remove the heater distribution box screws, nuts and clip. Remove the outer half of the case (to service No. 4 fuel injector only).
7. Remove the fuel injector using Injector Remover No. T94T–9000–AH1, or equivalent. Position the tool's fulcrum beneath the fuel injector hold-down plate and over the edge of the cylinder head. Install the remover screw in the

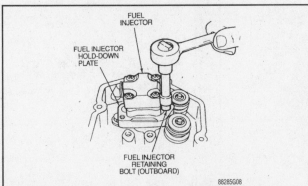

Fig. 37 Remove the outboard fuel injector retaining bolt as shown— 1994–96 engines

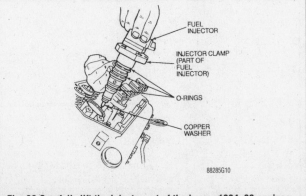

Fig. 38 Carefully lift the injector out of the bore—1994–96 engines

threaded hole of the fuel injector plate (see illustration). Tighten the screw to lift out the injector from its bore. Place the injector in a suitable protective sleeve such as Rotunda Injector Protective Sleeve, No. 014–00933–2, and set the injector in a suitable holding rack.

8. Remove the fuel injector sleeves, if required. Insert the Injector Sleeve Tap Plug, 014–00934–3 into the injector sleeve to prevent debris from entering the combustion chamber. Insert Injector Sleeve Tap Pilot into the fuel injector sleeve and tighten 1–1 ½ turns. Attach Slide Hammer T50T–100–A to the Injector Sleeve Tap 014–00934–1 and 014–00934–2 Injector Sleeve Tap Pilot and remove the fuel injector sleeve from the bore.

9. Use Rotunda Injector Sleeve Brush 104–00934–A, or equivalent to clean the injector bore of any sealant residue. Make sure to remove any debris.

To install:

10. If removed, install the fuel injector sleeves using Rotunda Sleeve Replacer, No. 014–00934–4, or equivalent. Apply Threadlock, No. 262–E2FZ–19554–B, or equivalent to the fuel injector sleeves as shown (see illustration). Using a rubber mallet, tap on the tool to seat the injector bore. Remove the tool and remove any residue sealant.

11. Clean the fuel injector sleeve using a suitable sleeve brush set. Clean any debris from the sleeve.

12. Clean the injector bore with a lint-free shop towel.

13. Install the fuel injectors using special tools as follows:

   a. Lubricate the injectors with clean engine oil. Using new copper washers, carefully push the injectors square into the bore using hand pressure only to seat the O-rings.

   b. Position the open end of Injector Replacer, No. T94T–9000–AH2, or equivalent between the fuel injector body and injector hold-down plate, while positioning the opposite end of the tool over the edge of the cylinder head.

   c. Align the hole in the tool with the threaded hole in the cylinder head and install the bolt from the tool kit. Tighten the bolt to fully seat the injector, then remove the bolt and tool.

14. Install the outer half of the heater distribution box and retaining hardware (for No. 4 injector only).

15. Install the oil deflector and bolt. Tighten the bolt to 108 inch lbs. (12 Nm).

16. Install the fuel rail drain plug, tightening it to 96 inch lbs. (11 Nm).

17. Install the oil rail drain plug, tightening it to 53 inch lbs. (6 Nm).

18. Install the heater distribution box.

19. Connect the fuel injector wiring harness.

20. Install the valve cover.

Fuel Supply Pump

REMOVAL & INSTALLATION

1987–93 Engines

♦ See Figure 39

1. Loosen the threaded connections with the proper size wrench (a flare nut wrench is preferred) and retighten snugly. Do not remove the lines at this time.

2. Loosen the mounting bolts, one to two turns. Apply force with your hand to loosen the fuel pump if the gasket is stuck. Rotate the engine by nudging the starter, until the fuel pump cam lobe is at the low position. At this position, spring tension against the fuel pump bolts will be greatly reduced.

3. Disconnect the fuel supply pump inlet, outlet and fuel return line.

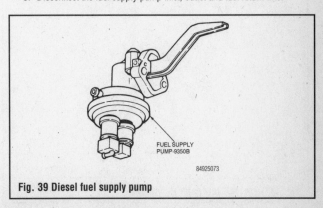

Fig. 39 Diesel fuel supply pump

※ CAUTION

Use care to prevent combustion of the spilled fuel.

4. Remove the fuel pump attaching bolts and remove the pump and gasket. Discard the old gasket.

5. Remove the remaining fuel pump gasket material from the engine and from the fuel pump if you are reinstalling the old pump. Make sure both mounting surfaces are clean.

To install:

6. Install the attaching bolts into the fuel supply pump and install a new gasket on the bolts. Position the fuel pump onto the mounting pad. Turn the attaching bolts alternately and evenly and tighten the bolts to the specifications according to the size bolts used on the pump. See the accompanying standard torque chart for reference.

➡The cam must be at its low position before attempting to install the fuel supply pump. If it is difficult to start the mounting bolts, remove the pump and reinstall with a lever on the bottom side of the cam.

7. Install the fuel outlet line. Start the fitting by hand to avoid crossthreading.

8. Install the inlet line and the fuel return line.

9. Start the engine and observe all connections for fuel leaks for two minutes.

10. Stop the engine and check all fuel supply pump fuel line connections. Check for oil leaks at the pump mounting pad.

1994–96 Engines

▶ **See Figures 40 and 41**

1. Remove the turbocharger assembly.
2. Remove the fuel line banjo bolt at the pump.
3. Remove the fuel line fittings at the rear of the cylinder heads.
4. Remove the fuel lines assembly.
5. Loosen the two hose clamps at the fuel pump fittings.
6. Disconnect the water drain hose at the fuel filter.

7. Disconnect the filter and position it forward.

8. Remove the fuel pump retaining bolts, then lift the pump out of the crankcase bore.

9. Remove the fuel pump tappet from the crankcase bore.

To install:

10. Rotate the engine so the fuel pump eccentric is on the base circle.

11. Install the fuel pump tappet in the base of the fuel pump.

12. Replace the O-ring on the fuel pump base.

13. Install the fuel pump and bolt it in place.

14. Install the fuel filter and connect the water drain hose.

15. Connect the two fuel hoses at the front of the fuel pump.

16. Tighten the fuel line clamps and install the fuel filter retaining bolts.

17. Install the fuel line assembly and new seal rings at the rear of the pump.

18. Loosely install the fuel line fittings at the rear of the cylinder heads.

19. Install the fuel line banjo fitting at the pump. Tighten the fitting to 40 ft. lbs. (54 Nm).

20. Tighten the fuel line fittings.

21. Install the turbocharger assembly.

Injection Pump

REMOVAL & INSTALLATION

▶ **See Figures 42, 43, 44, 45 and 46**

1. Remove the engine oil filler neck.
2. Remove the bolts attaching injection pump to drive gear.

※ WARNING

Before removing the fuel lines, clean the exterior with clean fuel oil or solvent to prevent entry of dirt into the engine when the fuel lines are removed. Also, do not wash or steam clean engine while engine is running. Serious damage to injection pump could occur.

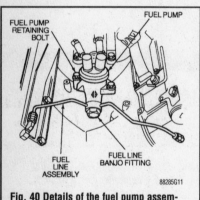

Fig. 40 Details of the fuel pump assembly—1994–96 diesel engine

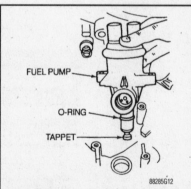

Fig. 41 View of the fuel pump—1994–96 diesel engine

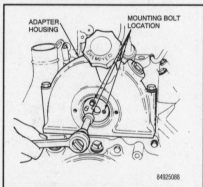

Fig. 42 Diesel injection pump drive gear attaching bolts

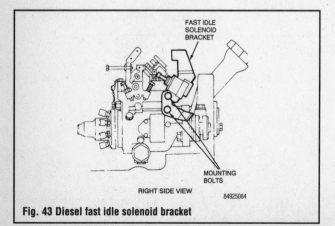

Fig. 43 Diesel fast idle solenoid bracket

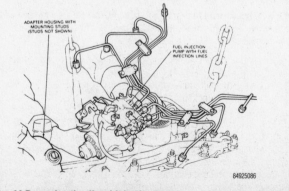

Fig. 44 Removing the diesel injection pump

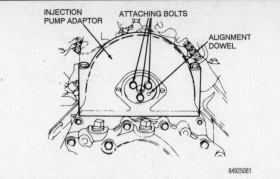

Fig. 45 Be sure to fit the alignment dowel on the pump into the hole in the drive gear

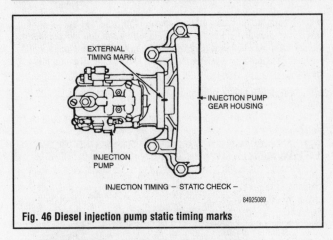

Fig. 46 Diesel injection pump static timing marks

3. Disconnect battery ground cables from both batteries.

4. Disengage the electrical connectors to the injection pump.

5. Remove the fast idle solenoid bracket assembly to provide access to the injection pump mounting nuts.

6. Disconnect the accelerator cable and speed control cable from throttle lever, if so equipped.

7. Remove the air cleaner and install clean rags to prevent dirt from entering the intake manifold.

8. Remove the accelerator cable bracket, with cables attached, from the intake manifold and position out of the way.

➡ **All fuel lines and fittings must be capped using Fuel System Protective Cap Set T83T–9395–A or equivalent, to prevent fuel contamination.**

9. Remove the fuel filter-to-injection pump fuel line and cap the fittings.

10. Remove and cap the injection pump inlet elbow and the injection pump fitting adapter.

11. Remove the fuel return line on the injection pump, then rotate out of the way, and cap all fittings.

➡ **It is not necessary to remove injection lines from the injection pump. If lines are to be removed, loosen the injection line fittings at the injection pump before removing it from engine.**

12. Remove the fuel injection lines from the nozzles, and cap the lines and nozzles.

13. Remove the three nuts attaching the injection pump to the injection pump adapter using Tool T83T–9000–B.

14. If the injection pump is to be replaced, loosen the injection line retaining clips and the injection nozzle fuel lines with Tool T83T–9396–A and cap all fittings at this time with protective cap set T83T–9395–A or equivalent. Do not install the injection nozzle fuel lines until the new pump is installed in the engine.

15. Lift the injection pump, with the nozzle lines attached, up and out of the engine compartment.

Do not carry injection pump by injection nozzle fuel lines as this could cause lines to bend or crimp.

To install:

16. Install a new O-ring on the drive gear end of the injection pump.

17. Move the injection pump down and into position.

18. Position the alignment dowel on injection pump into the alignment hole on drive gear.

19. Install the bolts attaching the injection pump to drive gear and tighten.

20. Install the nuts attaching injection pump to adapter. Align scribe lines on the injection pump flange and the injection pump adapter and tighten to 14 ft. lbs. (19 Nm).

21. If the injection nozzle fuel lines were removed from the injection pump install at this time, refer to the Injection Lines installation procedure in this section.

22. Remove the caps from nozzles and the fuel lines and install the fuel line nuts on the nozzles and tighten to 22 ft. lbs. (30 Nm).

23. Connect the fuel return line to injection pump and tighten the nuts.

24. Install the injection pump fitting adapter with a new O-ring.

25. Clean the old sealant from the injection pump elbow threads, using clean solvent, and dry thoroughly. Apply a light coating of pipe sealant to the elbow threads.

26. Install the elbow in the injection pump adapter and tighten to a minimum of 72 inch lbs. (8 Nm). Then tighten further, if necessary, to align the elbow with the injection pump fuel inlet line, but do not exceed 360 degrees of rotation or 10 ft. lbs. (13 Nm).

27. Remove the caps and connect the fuel filter-to-injection pump fuel line.

28. Install the accelerator cable bracket on the intake manifold.

29. Remove the rags from the intake manifold and install the air cleaner.

30. Connect the accelerator and speed control cable, if so equipped, to the throttle lever.

31. Install the fast idle solenoid bracket assembly.

32. Install the electrical connectors on injection pump.

33. Clean the injection pump adapter and oil filler neck sealing surfaces.

34. Apply a ⅛ in. (3mm) bead of RTV sealant on the adapter housing.

35. Install the oil filler neck and tighten the bolts.

36. Connect the battery ground cables to both batteries.

37. Run the engine and check for fuel leaks.

38. If necessary, purge high pressure fuel lines of air by loosening connector one half to one turn and cranking engine until solid fuel, free from bubbles flows from connection.

Keep eyes and hands away from nozzle spray. Fuel spraying from the nozzle under high pressure can penetrate the skin.

39. Check and adjust injection pump timing as described in this section.

INJECTION TIMING

◗ **See Figures 47, 48 and 49**

Static Timing

1. Break the torque of the injection pump mounting nuts (keeping the nuts snug).

2. Rotate the injection pump using Tool T83–9000–C or equivalent to bring the mark on the pump into alignment with the mark on the pump mounting adapter.

3. Visually recheck the alignment of the timing marks and tighten the injection pump mounting nuts.

Dynamic Timing

1. Start the engine and bring it up to normal operating temperature.

2. Stop the engine and install a dynamic timing meter, Rotunda 78–0100 or equivalent, by placing the magnetic probe pick-up into the probe hole.

3. Remove the No. 1 glow plug wire and remove the glow plug, install the

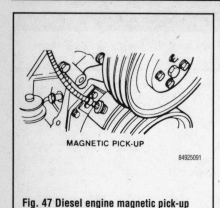

Fig. 47 Diesel engine magnetic pick-up probe hole location

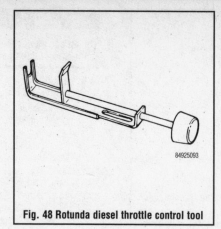

Fig. 48 Rotunda diesel throttle control tool

Dynamic Timing Specifications

		Altitude	
Fuel Cetane Value	0-3000 Ft ①	0-3000 Ft ①	Above 3000 Ft ①
38–42		6° ATDC	7° ATDC
43–46		5° ATDC	6° ATDC
47–50		4° ATDC	5° ATDC

① Installation of resetting tolerance for dynamic timing is ± 1°. Service limit is ± 2°.

Fig. 49 Diesel engine dynamic timing specifications

luminosity probe and tighten to 12 ft. lbs. (16 Nm). Install the photocell over the probe.

4. Connect the dynamic timing meter to the battery and adjust the offset of the meter.

5. Set the transmission in neutral and raise the rear wheels off the ground. Using Rotunda 14–0302, throttle control, set the engine speed to 1,400 rpm with no accessory load. Observe the injection timing on the dynamic timing meter.

➡ Obtain the fuel sample from the vehicle and check the cetane value using the tester supplied with the Ford special tools 78–0100 or equivalent. Refer to the dynamic timing chart to find the correct timing in degrees.

6. If the dynamic timing is not within plug or minus 2 degrees of specification, then the injection pump timing will require adjustment.

7. Turn the engine **OFF**. Note the timing mark alignment. Loosen the injection pump-to-adapter nuts.

8. Rotate the injection pump clockwise (when viewed from the front of the engine) to retard or counterclockwise to advance the timing. Two degrees of dynamic timing equals approximately 0.030 in. (0.76mm) of timing mark movement.

9. Start the engine and recheck the timing. If the timing is not within plus or minus 1 degree of specification, repeat steps 7 through 9.

10. Turn the engine **OFF**. Remove the dynamic timing equipment. Lightly coat the glow plug thread with anti-seize compound, install the glow plugs and tighten to 12 ft. lbs. (16 Nm). Connect the glow plug wires.

High Pressure Oil Pump

REMOVAL & INSTALLATION

1994–96 DI Turbo Engine Only

▶ See Figures 50, 51, 52 and 53

1. Loosen the compressor manifold hose clamps and remove the compressor manifold.

2. Remove the oil from the high pressure oil pump using a suitable vacuum pump.

3. Remove the fuel filter.

4. Remove the high pressure manifold supply hoses from the pump.

5. Disengage the wire connector from the injector control pressure solenoid.

6. Remove the nut securing the injection control pressure solenoid if you are replacing the high pressure oil pump. Remove the solenoid and injection pressure regulator.

7. Remove the cover plate and bolts at the crankcase front cover.

8. Remove the oil pump drive sprocket bolt and washer.

9. Remove the retaining bolts from the oil reservoir and remove the high pressure oil pump.

To install:

10. Install the high pressure oil pump and gasket.

11. Install the retaining bolts to the oil reservoir.

➡ Make sure the oil pump drive sprocket is fully seated on the shaft of the high pressure oil pump before installing the bolt and washer or the sprocket may not seat properly. The end of the high pressure oil pump shaft should be flush with the front face of the oil pump drive sprocket.

12. Install the oil pump drive sprocket, bolt and washer. tighten the bolt to 95 ft. lbs. (129 Nm).

13. Apply RTV sealer to the crankcase front cover and install the cover plate and retaining bolts.

14. If removed, install the injection pressure regulator. Tighten the regulator to 35 ft. lbs. (47 Nm).

15. Install the injection control pressure solenoid and retaining nut. Tighten the nut to 55 inch lbs. (6 Nm).

16. Engage the wire connector to the injection control pressure solenoid.

17. Install the high pressure manifold supply hoses to the high pressure oil pump. Tighten the hose fittings to 19.5 ft. lbs. (26 Nm).

18. Install the fuel filter.

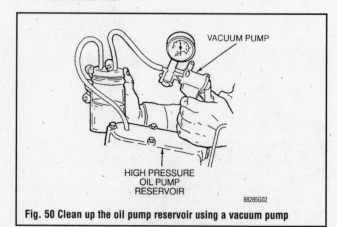

Fig. 50 Clean up the oil pump reservoir using a vacuum pump

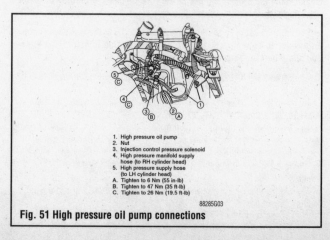

1. High pressure oil pump
2. Nut
3. Injection control pressure solenoid
4. High pressure manifold supply hose (to RH cylinder head)
5. High pressure supply hose (to LH cylinder head)
A. Tighten to 6 Nm (55 in-lb)
B. Tighten to 47 Nm (35 ft-lb)
C. Tighten to 26 Nm (19.5 ft-lb)

Fig. 51 High pressure oil pump connections

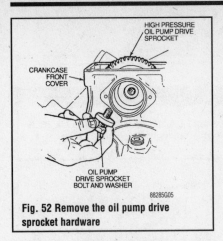

Fig. 52 Remove the oil pump drive sprocket hardware

Fig. 53 Remove the high pressure oil pump

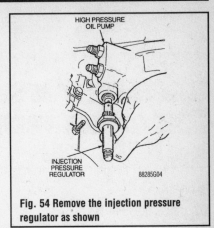

Fig. 54 Remove the injection pressure regulator as shown

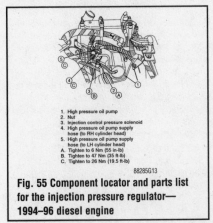

1. High pressure oil pump
2. Nut
3. Injection control pressure solenoid
4. High pressure oil pump supply hose (to RH cylinder head)
5. High pressure oil pump supply hose (to LH cylinder head)
A. Tighten to 6 Nm (55 in-lb)
B. Tighten to 47 Nm (35 ft-lb)
C. Tighten to 26 Nm (19.5 ft-lb)

Fig. 55 Component locator and parts list for the injection pressure regulator—1994–96 diesel engine

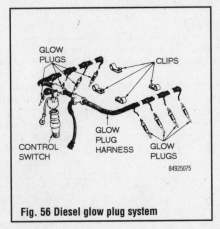

Fig. 56 Diesel glow plug system

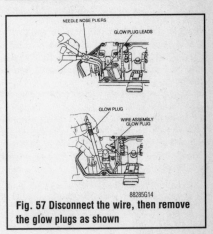

Fig. 57 Disconnect the wire, then remove the glow plugs as shown

19. Install the compressor manifold hose clamps and tighten them securely.
20. Refill the oil reservoir with clean engine oil.

Injection Pressure Regulator

REMOVAL & INSTALLATION

1994–96 DI Turbo

▶ See Figures 54 and 55

1. Disengage the wire connector from the injection control pressure solenoid.
2. Remove the nut securing the injection control pressure solenoid to the injection pressure regulator.
3. Remove the injection control pressure solenoid.
4. Remove the injection pressure regulator from the high pressure oil pump.
5. To install, reverse the removal procedure. Tighten the injection pressure regulator to 35 ft. lbs. (47 Nm). Tighten the injection control pressure solenoid nut to 55 inch lbs. (6 Nm).

Glow Plugs

GENERAL INFORMATION

▶ See Figure 56

The diesel engine utilizes an electric glow plug system to aid in the start of the engine. The function of this stem is to pre-heat the combustion chamber to aid ignition of the fuel.

The system consists of eight glow plugs (one for each cylinder), control switch, power relay, after glow relay, wait lamp latching relay, wait lamp and the eight fusible links located between the harness and the glow plug terminal.

On initial start with cold engine, the glow plug system operates as follows:

The glow plug control switch energizes the power relay (which is a magnetic switch) and the power relay contacts close. Battery current energizes the glow plugs. Current to the glow plugs and a wait lamp will be shut off when the glow plugs are hot enough. This takes from 2 to 10 second after the key is first turned on. When the wait lamp goes off, the engine is ready to start. After the engine is started, the glow plugs begin an on-off cycle for about 40 to 90 seconds. This cycle helps to clear start-up smoke. The control switch (the brain of the operation) is threaded into the left cylinder head coolant jacket; this control unit senses engine coolant temperature. Since the control unit senses temperature and glow plug operation, the glow plug system will not be activated unless needed. On a restart (warm engine) the glow plug system will not be activated unless the coolant temperature drops before 165°F (91°C).

Since the fast start system utilizes 6 volt glow plugs in a 12 volt system to achieve rapid heating of the glow plug, a cycling device is required in the circuit.

✳✳ CAUTION

Never bypass the power relay of the glow plug system. Constant battery current (12 volts) to glow plugs will cause them to overheat and fail.

REMOVAL & INSTALLATION

▶ See Figure 57

✳✳ CAUTION

The red-striped wires on the 1994–96 DI Turbo engine carry 115 volts DC. A severe electrical shock may be given. Do not pierce the wires.

1. Make sure the ignition switch is **OFF**.
2. For 1994–96 engines, remove the valve cover.
3. Disconnect the wire connector from the glow plug.
4. Using a 10mm deep socket, with enough clearance as to not break or bend the wiring connector, unscrew the glow plug from the manifold.

To install:

5. Place anti-seize on the threads of the glow plug and screw it into the manifold.

6. Tighten the glow plug to 12 ft. lbs. (16 Nm).

FUEL TANK

Tank Assembly

REMOVAL & INSTALLATION

Except Bronco

STEEL MID-SHIP TANK(S)

> ※ **CAUTION**
>
> **Never smoke when working around gasoline! Avoid all sources of sparks or ignition. Gasoline vapors are EXTREMELY volatile! On fuel injected engines, depressurize the fuel system. Refer to the applicable Fuel Injection System procedures listed in this section for details.**

1. On vehicles with a single fuel tank, disconnect the battery ground cable, then, drain the fuel from the tank into a suitable container by either removing the drain plug, if so equipped, or siphoning through the filler cap opening.

2. On vehicles with dual tanks, drain the fuel tanks by disconnecting the connector hoses, then disconnect the battery ground cable.

3. Disconnect the fuel gauge sending unit wire and fuel outlet line.

4. Disconnect the air relief tube from the filler neck and fuel tank.

5. Loosen the filler neck hose clamp at the fuel tank and pull the filler neck away from the tank.

6. Remove the retaining strap mounting nuts and/or bolts and lower the tank(s) to the floor.

7. If a new tank is being installed, change over the fuel gauge sending unit to the new tank.

8. Install the fuel tank(s) in the reverse order of removal. Torque the strap nuts to 30 ft. lbs. (41 Nm).

PLASTIC MID-SHIP TANK

> ※ **CAUTION**
>
> **Never smoke when working around gasoline! Avoid all sources of sparks or ignition. Gasoline vapors are EXTREMELY volatile! On fuel injected engines, depressurize the fuel system. Refer to the applicable Fuel Injection System procedures listed in this section for details.**

1. Drain the fuel from the tank into a suitable container by either removing the drain plug, if so equipped, or siphoning through the filler cap opening.

2. Disconnect the battery ground cable(s).

3. Remove the skid plate and heat shields.

4. Disconnect the fuel gauge sending unit wire at the tank.

5. Loosen the filler neck hose clamp at the fuel tank and pull the filler neck away from the tank.

6. Disconnect the fuel line push-connect fittings at the fuel gauge sending unit.

7. Support the tank. Remove the retaining strap mounting bolts and lower the tank to the floor.

8. If a new tank is being installed, change over the fuel gauge sending unit to the new tank.

9. Install the fuel tank(s) in the reverse order of removal. Torque the strap bolts to 12–18 ft. lbs. (16–24 Nm).

PLASTIC OR STEEL BEHIND-THE-AXLE TANK

> ※ **CAUTION**
>
> **Never smoke when working around gasoline! Avoid all sources of sparks or ignition. Gasoline vapors are EXTREMELY volatile! On fuel**

7. Plug the wiring connector.

8. Connect the negative battery cable.

9. For 1994–96 engines, install the valve cover.

injected engines, depressurize the fuel system. Refer to the appropriate Fuel Injection System procedures listed in this section for details.

1. Raise the rear of the truck.

2. Disconnect the negative battery cable.

3. On trucks with a single tank, disconnect the fuel gauge sending unit wire at the fuel tank. Remove the fuel drain plug or siphon the fuel from the tank into a suitable container.

4. On vehicles with dual tanks, drain the fuel tanks by disconnecting the connector hoses.

5. Disconnect the fuel line push-connect fittings at the fuel gauge sending unit.

6. Loosen the clamps on the fuel filler pipe and vent hose as necessary and disconnect the filler pipe hose and vent hose from the tank.

7. If the tank is the metal type, support the tank and remove the bolts attaching the tank support or skid plate to the frame. Carefully lower the tank or tank/skid plate assembly and disconnect the vent tube from the vapor emission control valve in the top of the tank. Finish removing the filler pipe and filler pipe vent hose if not possible previously. Remove the tank from under the vehicle.

8. If the tank is the plastic type, support the tank and remove the bolts attaching the combination skid plate and tank support to the frame. Carefully lower the tank and disconnect the vent tube from the vapor emission control valve in the top of the tank. Finish removing the filler pipe and filler pipe vent hose if it was not possible previously. Remove the skid plate and tank from under the vehicle. Remove the skid plate from the tank.

9. If the sending unit is to be removed, turn the unit retaining ring counterclockwise and remove the sending unit, retaining ring and gasket. Discard the gasket.

10. Install the tank in the reverse order of removal. With metal tanks, use thread adhesive such as Loctite® on the bolt threads, and torque these bolts to 27–37 ft. lbs. (37–50 Nm). With plastic tanks, DO NOT use thread adhesive. Torque the bolts to 25–35 ft. lbs. (34–47 Nm).

Bronco

> ※ **CAUTION**
>
> **Never smoke when working around gasoline! Avoid all sources of sparks or ignition. Gasoline vapors are EXTREMELY volatile!**

1. Raise and support the rear end on jackstands.

2. Disconnect the negative battery cable.

3. Disconnect fuel gauge sending unit wire at fuel tank.

4. Remove the fuel drain plug or siphon the fuel from the tank into a suitable container.

5. Loosen the fuel line hose clamps, slide them forward and disconnect fuel line at the fuel gauge sending unit.

6. Loosen the clamps on the fuel filler pipe and vent hose as necessary and disconnect the filler pipe hose and vent hose from the tank.

7. Support the tank and remove the lower attaching bolts or skid plate bolts supporting the tank to the frame. Carefully lower the tank or tank/skid plate assembly and disconnect the vent tube from the vapor emission control valve in the top of the tank. Finish removing the filler pipe and filler pipe vent hose if not possible previously. Remove the tank from under the vehicle.

8. If the sending unit is being removed, turn the unit's retaining ring counterclockwise and remove the sending unit, retaining ring and gasket. Discard the gasket.

9. Install the tank in the reverse order of removal. Use threadlocking compound on the bolt threads and torque the bolts to 27–37 ft. lbs. (37–50 Nm).

6

CHASSIS
ELECTRICAL

UNDERSTANDING AND TROUBLESHOOTING ELECTRICAL SYSTEMS

Basic Electrical Theory

♦ **See Figure 1**

For any 12 volt, negative ground, electrical system to operate, the electricity must travel in a complete circuit. This simply means that current (power) from the positive (+) terminal of the battery must eventually return to the negative (-) terminal of the battery. Along the way, this current will travel through wires, fuses, switches and components. If, for any reason, the flow of current through the circuit is interrupted, the component fed by that circuit will cease to function properly.

Perhaps the easiest way to visualize a circuit is to think of connecting a light bulb (with two wires attached to it) to the battery—one wire attached to the negative (-) terminal of the battery and the other wire to the positive (+) terminal. With the two wires touching the battery terminals, the circuit would be complete and the light bulb would illuminate. Electricity would follow a path from the battery to the bulb and back to the battery. It's easy to see that with longer wires on our light bulb, it could be mounted anywhere. Further, one wire could be fitted with a switch so that the light could be turned on and off.

The normal automotive circuit differs from this simple example in two ways. First, instead of having a return wire from the bulb to the battery, the current travels through the frame of the vehicle. Since the negative (-) battery cable is attached to the frame (made of electrically conductive metal), the frame of the vehicle can serve as a ground wire to complete the circuit. Secondly, most automotive circuits contain multiple components which receive power from a single circuit. This lessens the amount of wire needed to power components on the vehicle.

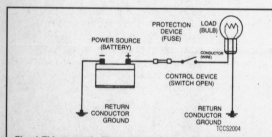

Fig. 1 This example illustrates a simple circuit. When the switch is closed, power from the positive (+) battery terminal flows through the fuse and the switch, and then to the light bulb. The light illuminates and the circuit is completed through the ground wire back to the negative (-) battery terminal. In reality, the two ground points shown in the illustration are attached to the metal frame of the vehicle, which completes the circuit back to the battery

HOW DOES ELECTRICITY WORK: THE WATER ANALOGY

Electricity is the flow of electrons—the subatomic particles that constitute the outer shell of an atom. Electrons spin in an orbit around the center core of an atom. The center core is comprised of protons (positive charge) and neutrons (neutral charge). Electrons have a negative charge and balance out the positive charge of the protons. When an outside force causes the number of electrons to unbalance the charge of the protons, the electrons will split off the atom and look for another atom to balance out. If this imbalance is kept up, electrons will continue to move and an electrical flow will exist.

Many people have been taught electrical theory using an analogy with water. In a comparison with water flowing through a pipe, the electrons would be the water and the wire would be the pipe.

The flow of electricity can be measured much like the flow of water through a pipe. The unit of measurement used is amperes, frequently abbreviated as amps (a). You can compare amperage to the volume of water flowing through a pipe. When connected to a circuit, an ammeter will measure the actual amount of current flowing through the circuit. When relatively few electrons flow through a circuit, the amperage is low. When many electrons flow, the amperage is high.

Water pressure is measured in units such as pounds per square inch (psi); The electrical pressure is measured in units called volts (v). When a voltmeter is

connected to a circuit; it is measuring the electrical pressure.

The actual flow of electricity depends not only on voltage and amperage, but also on the resistance of the circuit. The higher the resistance, the higher the force necessary to push the current through the circuit. The standard unit for measuring resistance is an ohm. Resistance in a circuit varies depending on the amount and type of components used in the circuit. The main factors which determine resistance are:

- Material—some materials have more resistance than others. Those with high resistance are said to be insulators. Rubber materials (or rubber-like plastics) are some of the most common insulators used in vehicles as they have a very high resistance to electricity. Very low resistance materials are said to be conductors. Copper wire is among the best conductors. Silver is actually a superior conductor to copper and is used in some relay contacts, but its high cost prohibits its use as common wiring. Most automotive wiring is made of copper.
- Size—the larger the wire size being used, the less resistance the wire will have. This is why components which use large amounts of electricity usually have large wires supplying current to them.
- Length—for a given thickness of wire, the longer the wire, the greater the resistance. The shorter the wire, the less the resistance. When determining the proper wire for a circuit, both size and length must be considered to design a circuit that can handle the current needs of the component.
- Temperature—with many materials, the higher the temperature, the greater the resistance (positive temperature coefficient). Some materials exhibit the opposite trait of lower resistance with higher temperatures (negative temperature coefficient). These principles are used in many of the sensors on the engine.

OHM'S LAW

There is a direct relationship between current, voltage and resistance. The relationship between current, voltage and resistance can be summed up by a statement known as Ohm's law.

Voltage (E) is equal to amperage (I) times resistance (R): $E = I \times R$

Other forms of the formula are $R = E/I$ and $I = E/R$

In each of these formulas, E is the voltage in volts, I is the current in amps and R is the resistance in ohms. The basic point to remember is that as the resistance of a circuit goes up, the amount of current that flows in the circuit will go down, if voltage remains the same.

The amount of work that the electricity can perform is expressed as power. The unit of power is the watt (w). The relationship between power, voltage and current is expressed as:

Power (w) is equal to amperage (I) times voltage (E): $W = I \times E$

This is only true for direct current (DC) circuits; The alternating current formula is a tad different, but since the electrical circuits in most vehicles are DC type, we need not get into AC circuit theory.

Electrical Components

POWER SOURCE

Power is supplied to the vehicle by two devices: The battery and the alternator. The battery supplies electrical power during starting or during periods when the current demand of the vehicle's electrical system exceeds the output capacity of the alternator. The alternator supplies electrical current when the engine is running. Just not does the alternator supply the current needs of the vehicle, but it recharges the battery.

The Battery

In most modern vehicles, the battery is a lead/acid electrochemical device consisting of six 2 volt subsections (cells) connected in series, so that the unit is capable of producing approximately 12 volts of electrical pressure. Each subsection consists of a series of positive and negative plates held a short distance apart in a solution of sulfuric acid and water.

The two types of plates are of dissimilar metals. This sets up a chemical reaction, and it is this reaction which produces current flow from the battery when its positive and negative terminals are connected to an electrical load . The power removed from the battery is replaced by the alternator, restoring the battery to its original chemical state.

The Alternator

On some vehicles there isn't an alternator, but a generator. The difference is that an alternator supplies alternating current which is then changed to direct current for use on the vehicle, while a generator produces direct current. Alternators tend to be more efficient and that is why they are used.

Alternators and generators are devices that consist of coils of wires wound together making big electromagnets. One group of coils spins within another set and the interaction of the magnetic fields causes a current to flow. This current is then drawn off the coils and fed into the vehicles electrical system.

GROUND

Two types of grounds are used in automotive electric circuits. Direct ground components are grounded to the frame through their mounting points. All other components use some sort of ground wire which is attached to the frame or chassis of the vehicle. The electrical current runs through the chassis of the vehicle and returns to the battery through the ground (-) cable; if you look, you'll see that the battery ground cable connects between the battery and the frame or chassis of the vehicle.

➡**It should be noted that a good percentage of electrical problems can be traced to bad grounds.**

PROTECTIVE DEVICES

▶ See Figure 2

It is possible for large surges of current to pass through the electrical system of your vehicle. If this surge of current were to reach the load in the circuit, the surge could burn it out or severely damage it. It can also overload the wiring, causing the harness to get hot and melt the insulation. To prevent this, fuses, circuit breakers and/or fusible links are connected into the supply wires of the electrical system. These items are nothing more than a built-in weak spot in the system. When an abnormal amount of current flows through the system, these protective devices work as follows to protect the circuit:

• Fuse—when an excessive electrical current passes through a fuse, the fuse "blows" (the conductor melts) and opens the circuit, preventing the passage of current.

• Circuit Breaker—a circuit breaker is basically a self-repairing fuse. It will open the circuit in the same fashion as a fuse, but when the surge subsides, the circuit breaker can be reset and does not need replacement.

• Fusible Link—a fusible link (fuse link or main link) is a short length of special, high temperature insulated wire that acts as a fuse. When an excessive electrical current passes through a fusible link, the thin gauge wire inside the link melts, creating an intentional open to protect the circuit. To repair the cir-

cuit, the link must be replaced. Some newer type fusible links are housed in plug-in modules, which are simply replaced like a fuse, while older type fusible links must be cut and spliced if they melt. Since this link is very early in the electrical path, it's the first place to look if nothing on the vehicle works, yet the battery seems to be charged and is properly connected.

❋❋ CAUTION

Always replace fuses, circuit breakers and fusible links with identically rated components. Under no circumstances should a component of higher or lower amperage rating be substituted.

SWITCHES & RELAYS

▶ See Figures 3 and 4

Switches are used in electrical circuits to control the passage of current. The most common use is to open and close circuits between the battery and the various electric devices in the system. Switches are rated according to the amount of amperage they can handle. If a sufficient amperage rated switch is not used in a circuit, the switch could overload and cause damage.

Some electrical components which require a large amount of current to operate use a special switch called a relay. Since these circuits carry a large amount of current, the thickness of the wire in the circuit is also greater. If this large wire were connected from the load to the control switch, the switch would have to carry the high amperage load and the fairing or dash would be twice as large to accommodate the increased size of the wiring harness. To prevent these problems, a relay is used.

Relays are composed of a coil and a set of contacts. When the coil has a current passed though it, a magnetic field is formed and this field causes the contacts to move together, completing the circuit. Most relays are normally open, preventing current from passing through the circuit, but they can take any electrical form depending on the job they are intended to do. Relays can be considered "remote control switches." They allow a smaller current to operate devices that require higher amperages. When a small current operates the coil, a larger current is allowed to pass by the contacts. Some common circuits which may use relays are the horn, headlights, starter, electric fuel pump and other high draw circuits.

LOAD

Every electrical circuit must include a "load" (something to use the electricity coming from the source). Without this load, the battery would attempt to deliver its entire power supply from one pole to another. This is called a "short circuit." All this electricity would take a short cut to ground and cause a great amount of damage to other components in the circuit by developing a tremendous amount of heat. This condition could develop sufficient heat to melt the insulation on all the surrounding wires and reduce a multiple wire cable to a lump of plastic and copper.

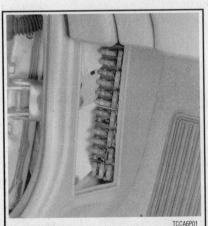

Fig. 2 Most vehicles use one or more fuse panels. This one is located on the driver's side kick panel

TCCA6P01

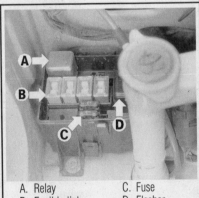

A. Relay   C. Fuse
B. Fusible link   D. Flasher

TCCA6P02

Fig. 3 The underhood fuse and relay panel usually contains fuses, relays, flashers and fusible links

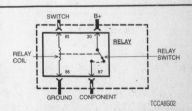

TCCA6G02

Fig. 4 Relays are composed of a coil and a switch. These two components are linked together so that when one operates, the other operates at the same time. The large wires in the circuit are connected from the battery to one side of the relay switch (B+) and from the opposite side of the relay switch to the load (component). Smaller wires are connected from the relay coil to the control switch for the circuit and from the opposite side of the relay coil to ground

WIRING & HARNESSES

The average vehicle contains meters and meters of wiring, with hundreds of individual connections. To protect the many wires from damage and to keep them from becoming a confusing tangle, they are organized into bundles, enclosed in plastic or taped together and called wiring harnesses. Different harnesses serve different parts of the vehicle. Individual wires are color coded to help trace them through a harness where sections are hidden from view.

Automotive wiring or circuit conductors can be either single strand wire, multi-strand wire or printed circuitry. Single strand wire has a solid metal core and is usually used inside such components as alternators, motors, relays and other devices. Multi-strand wire has a core made of many small strands of wire twisted together into a single conductor. Most of the wiring in an automotive electrical system is made up of multi-strand wire, either as a single conductor or grouped together in a harness. All wiring is color coded on the insulator, either as a solid color or as a colored wire with an identification stripe. A printed circuit is a thin film of copper or other conductor that is printed on an insulator backing. Occasionally, a printed circuit is sandwiched between two sheets of plastic for more protection and flexibility. A complete printed circuit, consisting of conductors, insulating material and connectors for lamps or other components is called a printed circuit board. Printed circuitry is used in place of individual wires or harnesses in places where space is limited, such as behind instrument panels.

Since automotive electrical systems are very sensitive to changes in resistance, the selection of properly sized wires is critical when systems are repaired. A loose or corroded connection or a replacement wire that is too small for the circuit will add extra resistance and an additional voltage drop to the circuit.

The wire gauge number is an expression of the cross-section area of the conductor. Vehicles from countries that use the metric system will typically describe the wire size as its cross-sectional area in square millimeters. In this method, the larger the wire, the greater the number. Another common system for expressing wire size is the American Wire Gauge (AWG) system. As gauge number increases, area decreases and the wire becomes smaller. An 18 gauge wire is smaller than a 4 gauge wire. A wire with a higher gauge number will carry less current than a wire with a lower gauge number. Gauge wire size refers to the size of the strands of the conductor, not the size of the complete wire with insulator. It is possible, therefore, to have two wires of the same gauge with different diameters because one may have thicker insulation than the other.

It is essential to understand how a circuit works before trying to figure out why it doesn't. An electrical schematic shows the electrical current paths when a circuit is operating properly. Schematics break the entire electrical system down into individual circuits. In a schematic, usually no attempt is made to represent wiring and components as they physically appear on the vehicle; switches and other components are shown as simply as possible. Face views of harness connectors show the cavity or terminal locations in all multi-pin connectors to help locate test points.

CONNECTORS

▶ **See Figures 5 and 6**

Three types of connectors are commonly used in automotive applications—weatherproof, molded and hard shell.

Fig. 5 Hard shell (left) and weatherproof (right) connectors have replaceable terminals

TCCA6P03

Fig. 6 Weatherproof connectors are most commonly used in the engine compartment or where the connector is exposed to the elements

TCCA6P04

• Weatherproof—these connectors are most commonly used where the connector is exposed to the elements. Terminals are protected against moisture and dirt by sealing rings which provide a weathertight seal. All repairs require the use of a special terminal and the tool required to service it. Unlike standard blade type terminals, these weatherproof terminals cannot be straightened once they are bent. Make certain that the connectors are properly seated and all of the sealing rings are in place when connecting leads.

• Molded—these connectors require complete replacement of the connector if found to be defective. This means splicing a new connector assembly into the harness. All splices should be soldered to insure proper contact. Use care when probing the connections or replacing terminals in them, as it is possible to create a short circuit between opposite terminals. If this happens to the wrong terminal pair, it is possible to damage certain components. Always use jumper wires between connectors for circuit checking and NEVER probe through weatherproof seals.

• Hard Shell—unlike molded connectors, the terminal contacts in hardshell connectors can be replaced. Replacement usually involves the use of a special terminal removal tool that depresses the locking tangs (barbs) on the connector terminal and allows the connector to be removed from the rear of the shell. The connector shell should be replaced if it shows any evidence of burning, melting, cracks, or breaks. Replace individual terminals that are burnt, corroded, distorted or loose.

Test Equipment

Pinpointing the exact cause of trouble in an electrical circuit is most times accomplished by the use of special test equipment. The following describes different types of commonly used test equipment and briefly explains how to use them in diagnosis. In addition to the information covered below, the tool manufacturer's instructions booklet (provided with the tester) should be read and clearly understood before attempting any test procedures.

JUMPER WIRES

✳✳ CAUTION

Never use jumper wires made from a thinner gauge wire than the circuit being tested. If the jumper wire is of too small a gauge, it may overheat and possibly melt. Never use jumpers to bypass high resistance loads in a circuit. Bypassing resistances, in effect, creates a short circuit. This may, in turn, cause damage and fire. Jumper wires should only be used to bypass lengths of wire or to simulate switches.

Jumper wires are simple, yet extremely valuable, pieces of test equipment. They are basically test wires which are used to bypass sections of a circuit. Although jumper wires can be purchased, they are usually fabricated from lengths of standard automotive wire and whatever type of connector (alligator clip, spade connector or pin connector) that is required for the particular application being tested. In cramped, hard-to-reach areas, it is advisable to have insulated boots over the jumper wire terminals in order to prevent accidental grounding. It is also advisable to include a standard automotive fuse in any jumper wire. This is commonly referred to as a "fused jumper". By inserting an in-line fuse holder between a set of test leads, a fused jumper wire can be used for bypassing open circuits. Use a 5 amp fuse to provide protection against voltage spikes.

Jumper wires are used primarily to locate open electrical circuits, on either the ground (-) side of the circuit or on the power (+) side. If an electrical component fails to operate, connect the jumper wire between the component and a good ground. If the component operates only with the jumper installed, the ground circuit is open. If the ground circuit is good, but the component does not operate, the circuit between the power feed and component may be open. By moving the jumper wire successively back from the component toward the power source, you can isolate the area of the circuit where the open is located. When the component stops functioning, or the power is cut off, the open is in the segment of wire between the jumper and the point previously tested.

You can sometimes connect the jumper wire directly from the battery to the "hot" terminal of the component, but first make sure the component uses 12 volts in operation. Some electrical components, such as fuel injectors or sensors, are designed to operate on about 4 to 5 volts, and running 12 volts directly to these components will cause damage.

TEST LIGHTS

▶ **See Figure 7**

The test light is used to check circuits and components while electrical current is flowing through them. It is used for voltage and ground tests. To use a 12 volt test light, connect the ground clip to a good ground and probe wherever necessary with the pick. The test light will illuminate when voltage is detected. This does not necessarily mean that 12 volts (or any particular amount of voltage) is present; it only means that some voltage is present. It is advisable before using the test light to touch its ground clip and probe across the battery posts or terminals to make sure the light is operating properly.

✳✳ WARNING

Do not use a test light to probe electronic ignition, spark plug or coil wires. Never use a pick-type test light to probe wiring on computer controlled systems unless specifically instructed to do so. Any wire insulation that is pierced by the test light probe should be taped and sealed with silicone after testing.

Like the jumper wire, the 12 volt test light is used to isolate opens in circuits. But, whereas the jumper wire is used to bypass the open to operate the load, the 12 volt test light is used to locate the presence of voltage in a circuit. If the test light illuminates, there is power up to that point in the circuit; if the test light does not illuminate, there is an open circuit (no power). Move the test light in successive steps back toward the power source until the light in the handle illuminates. The open is between the probe and a point which was previously probed.

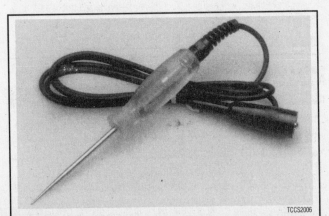
TCCS2006
Fig. 7 A 12 volt test light is used to detect the presence of voltage in a circuit

The self-powered test light is similar in design to the 12 volt test light, but contains a 1.5 volt penlight battery in the handle. It is most often used in place of a multimeter to check for open or short circuits when power is isolated from the circuit (continuity test).

The battery in a self-powered test light does not provide much current. A weak battery may not provide enough power to illuminate the test light even when a complete circuit is made (especially if there is high resistance in the circuit). Always make sure that the test battery is strong. To check the battery, briefly touch the ground clip to the probe; if the light glows brightly, the battery is strong enough for testing.

➡**A self-powered test light should not be used on any computer controlled system or component. The small amount of electricity transmitted by the test light is enough to damage many electronic automotive components.**

MULTIMETERS

Multimeters are an extremely useful tool for troubleshooting electrical problems. They can be purchased in either analog or digital form and have a price range to suit any budget. A multimeter is a voltmeter, ammeter and ohmmeter (along with other features) combined into one instrument. It is often used when testing solid state circuits because of its high input impedance (usually 10 megaohms or more). A brief description of the multimeter main test functions follows:

• Voltmeter—the voltmeter is used to measure voltage at any point in a circuit, or to measure the voltage drop across any part of a circuit. Voltmeters usually have various scales and a selector switch to allow the reading of different voltage ranges. The voltmeter has a positive and a negative lead. To avoid damage to the meter, always connect the negative lead to the negative (-) side of the circuit (to ground or nearest the ground side of the circuit) and connect the positive lead to the positive (+) side of the circuit (to the power source or the nearest power source). Note that the negative voltmeter lead will always be black and that the positive voltmeter will always be some color other than black (usually red).

• Ohmmeter—the ohmmeter is designed to read resistance (measured in ohms) in a circuit or component. Most ohmmeters will have a selector switch which permits the measurement of different ranges of resistance (usually the selector switch allows the multiplication of the meter reading by 10, 100, 1,000 and 10,000). Some ohmmeters are "auto-ranging" which means the meter itself will determine which scale to use. Since the meters are powered by an internal battery, the ohmmeter can be used like a self-powered test light. When the ohmmeter is connected, current from the ohmmeter flows through the circuit or component being tested. Since the ohmmeter's internal resistance and voltage are known values, the amount of current flow through the meter depends on the resistance of the circuit or component being tested. The ohmmeter can also be used to perform a continuity test for suspected open circuits. In using the meter for making continuity checks, do not be concerned with the actual resistance readings. Zero resistance, or any ohm reading, indicates continuity in the circuit. Infinite resistance indicates an opening in the circuit. A high resistance reading where there should be none indicates a problem in the circuit. Checks for short circuits are made in the same manner as checks for open circuits, except that the circuit must be isolated from both power and normal ground. Infinite resistance indicates no continuity, while zero resistance indicates a dead short.

✳✳ WARNING

Never use an ohmmeter to check the resistance of a component or wire while there is voltage applied to the circuit.

• Ammeter—an ammeter measures the amount of current flowing through a circuit in units called amperes or amps. At normal operating voltage, most circuits have a characteristic amount of amperes, called "current draw" which can be measured using an ammeter. By referring to a specified current draw rating, then measuring the amperes and comparing the two values, one can determine what is happening within the circuit to aid in diagnosis. An open circuit, for example, will not allow any current to flow, so the ammeter reading will be zero. A damaged component or circuit will have an increased current draw, so the reading will be high. The ammeter is always connected in series with the circuit being tested. All of the current that normally flows through the circuit must also flow through the ammeter; if there is any other path for the current to follow, the ammeter reading will not be accurate. The ammeter itself has very little resistance to current flow and, therefore, will not affect the circuit, but it will measure current draw only when the circuit is closed and electricity is flowing. Excessive current draw can blow fuses and drain the battery, while a reduced current draw can cause motors to run slowly, lights to dim and other components to not operate properly.

Troubleshooting Electrical Systems

When diagnosing a specific problem, organized troubleshooting is a must. The complexity of a modern automotive vehicle demands that you approach any problem in a logical, organized manner. There are certain troubleshooting techniques, however, which are standard:

• Establish when the problem occurs. Does the problem appear only under certain conditions? Were there any noises, odors or other unusual symptoms? Isolate the problem area. To do this, make some simple tests and observations, then eliminate the systems that are working properly. Check for obvious problems, such as broken wires and loose or dirty connections. Always check the obvious before assuming something complicated is the cause.

• Test for problems systematically to determine the cause once the problem area is isolated. Are all the components functioning properly? Is there power going to electrical switches and motors. Performing careful, systematic checks will often turn up most causes on the first inspection, without wasting time checking components that have little or no relationship to the problem.

• Test all repairs after the work is done to make sure that the problem is fixed. Some causes can be traced to more than one component, so a careful verification of repair work is important in order to pick up additional malfunctions that may cause a problem to reappear or a different problem to arise. A blown fuse, for example, is a simple problem that may require more than another fuse to repair. If you don't look for a problem that caused a fuse to blow, a shorted wire (for example) may go undetected.

Experience has shown that most problems tend to be the result of a fairly simple and obvious cause, such as loose or corroded connectors, bad grounds or damaged wire insulation which causes a short. This makes careful visual inspection of components during testing essential to quick and accurate troubleshooting.

Testing

OPEN CIRCUITS

▶ See Figure 8

This test already assumes the existence of an open in the circuit and it is used to help locate the open portion.

1. Isolate the circuit from power and ground.
2. Connect the self-powered test light or ohmmeter ground clip to the ground side of the circuit and probe sections of the circuit sequentially.
3. If the light is out or there is infinite resistance, the open is between the probe and the circuit ground.
4. If the light is on or the meter shows continuity, the open is between the probe and the end of the circuit toward the power source.

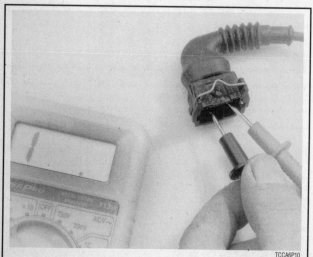

Fig. 8 The infinite reading on this multimeter indicates that the circuit is open

TCCA6P10

SHORT CIRCUITS

➡**Never use a self-powered test light to perform checks for opens or shorts when power is applied to the circuit under test. The test light can be damaged by outside power.**

1. Isolate the circuit from power and ground.
2. Connect the self-powered test light or ohmmeter ground clip to a good ground and probe any easy-to-reach point in the circuit.
3. If the light comes on or there is continuity, there is a short somewhere in the circuit.
4. To isolate the short, probe a test point at either end of the isolated circuit (the light should be on or the meter should indicate continuity).
5. Leave the test light probe engaged and sequentially open connectors or switches, remove parts, etc. until the light goes out or continuity is broken.
6. When the light goes out, the short is between the last two circuit components which were opened.

VOLTAGE

This test determines voltage available from the battery and should be the first step in any electrical troubleshooting procedure after visual inspection. Many electrical problems, especially on computer controlled systems, can be caused by a low state of charge in the battery. Excessive corrosion at the battery cable terminals can cause poor contact that will prevent proper charging and full battery current flow.

1. Set the voltmeter selector switch to the 20V position.
2. Connect the multimeter negative lead to the battery's negative (-) post or terminal and the positive lead to the battery's positive (+) post or terminal.
3. Turn the ignition switch **ON** to provide a load.
4. A well charged battery should register over 12 volts. If the meter reads below 11.5 volts, the battery power may be insufficient to operate the electrical system properly.

VOLTAGE DROP

▶ See Figure 9

When current flows through a load, the voltage beyond the load drops. This voltage drop is due to the resistance created by the load and also by small resistances created by corrosion at the connectors and damaged insulation on the wires. The maximum allowable voltage drop under load is critical, especially if there is more than one load in the circuit, since all voltage drops are cumulative.

1. Set the voltmeter selector switch to the 20 volt position.
2. Connect the multimeter negative lead to a good ground.
3. Operate the circuit and check the voltage prior to the first component (load).
4. There should be little or no voltage drop in the circuit prior to the first component. If a voltage drop exists, the wire or connectors in the circuit are suspect.
5. While operating the first component in the circuit, probe the ground side of the component with the positive meter lead and observe the voltage readings. A small voltage drop should be noticed. This voltage drop is caused by the resistance of the component.
6. Repeat the test for each component (load) down the circuit.
7. If a large voltage drop is noticed, the preceding component, wire or connector is suspect.

RESISTANCE

▶ See Figures 10 and 11

✳✳ WARNING

Never use an ohmmeter with power applied to the circuit. The ohmmeter is designed to operate on its own power supply. The normal 12 volt electrical system voltage could damage the meter!

1. Isolate the circuit from the vehicle's power source.
2. Ensure that the ignition key is **OFF** when disconnecting any components or the battery.
3. Where necessary, also isolate at least one side of the circuit to be checked, in order to avoid reading parallel resistances. Parallel circuit resistances will always give a lower reading than the actual resistance of either of the branches.

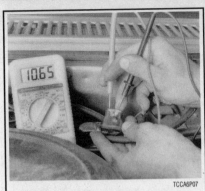

Fig. 9 This voltage drop test revealed high resistance (low voltage) in the circuit

Fig. 10 Checking the resistance of a coolant temperature sensor with an ohm-meter. Reading is 1.04 kilohms

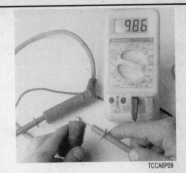

Fig. 11 Spark plug wires can be checked for excessive resistance using an ohmmeter

4. Connect the meter leads to both sides of the circuit (wire or component) and read the actual measured ohms on the meter scale. Make sure the selector switch is set to the proper ohm scale for the circuit being tested, to avoid mis-reading the ohmmeter test value.

Wire and Connector Repair

Almost anyone can replace damaged wires, as long as the proper tools and parts are available. Wire and terminals are available to fit almost any need. Even the specialized weatherproof, molded and hard shell connectors are now available from aftermarket suppliers.

Be sure the ends of all the wires are fitted with the proper terminal hardware and connectors. Wrapping a wire around a stud is never a permanent solution and will only cause trouble later. Replace wires one at a time to avoid confusion. Always route wires exactly the same as the factory.

➡If connector repair is necessary, only attempt it if you have the proper tools. Weatherproof and hard shell connectors require special tools to release the pins inside the connector. Attempting to repair these connectors with conventional hand tools will damage them.

BATTERY CABLES

Disconnecting the Cables

✳✳ WARNING

Make sure the battery cables are connected to the correct battery terminals. Reverse polarity may damage electrical components, particularly the (expensive) PCM.

Before performing work on the vehicle, it is usually required to disconnect the battery from the electrical system. Whether this is to prevent a mistaken start-up or electrical power from being supplied to the system components, the certain measure is to shut off the power at the source.

To disconnect the battery cable(s), perform the following:
1. Make sure the ignition switch is **OFF**.

➡Disconnecting the negative battery cable FIRST with the ignition turned OFF is required to prevent unwanted surges through the electrical system. If a voltage spike is fed through the system, delicate and expensive components (like the PCM) could be destroyed in fractions of a second.

2. Use the appropriate size wrench(es) to loosen the hardware on the cable clamps. ALWAYS begin with the negative battery cable.

✳✳ WARNING

Diesel engine models have two 12 volt batteries connected in parallel (positive-positive/negative-negative). The secondary on the passenger's side is dedicated to providing current to the intake manifold air heater. The primary battery on the driver's side is dedicated to all other vehicle electrical requirements. In order to ensure accurate diagnostic results, these batteries must be disconnected from each other and from the vehicle electrical system when being tested.

3. If necessary, use a puller tool designed for battery cable clamps and remove the clamp, then isolate it from the battery terminal.
4. Remove the positive battery cable, if required, once the negative battery cable has been removed.

SUPPLEMENTAL RESTRAINT SYSTEM (SRS OR AIR BAG)

General Information

The Supplemental Restraint System (SRS or Air Bag), is designed to provide additional protection for the driver in addition to that which is provided by the use of a seat belt.

The system is made up of two basic systems. They are the air bag(s) and the electrical components made up of the impact sensors, backup power supply and electronic air bag diagnostic monitor assembly.

Special attention should always be applied when working on a vehicle equipped with an air bag. If for any reason the indicator light in the dash should come on, consult an authorized dealer immediately for complete diagnostic service.

SYSTEM OPERATION

The Supplemental Restraint System (SRS or Air Bag) provides increased protection for the driver and/or passenger in the event of an accident. The word "supplemental is key, as the air bag is designed to be used in addition to the seat belts. In the event of an accident, the air bag will be the most effective if the vehicle's occupants are held in position by the seat belts.

SYSTEM COMPONENTS

The air bag system consists of two subsystems: the air bag(s), and the electrical system, which includes the impact sensors and electronic diagnostic monitor.

➡For removal and installation procedures, refer to the Steering Wheel coverage in Section 8.

Air Bag Module

▶ See Figure 12

The air bag module consists of the inflator, bag assembly, a mounting plate or housing, and a trim cover.

➡The air bag module components cannot be serviced. The air bag module is only serviced as a complete assembly.

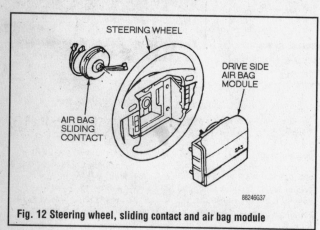

Fig. 12 Steering wheel, sliding contact and air bag module

INFLATOR

Inside the inflator is an igniter. When two or more impact sensors detects a crash and the sensor contacts close, battery power flows to the igniter, which then converts the electrical energy to thermal (heat) energy, igniting the sodium azide/copper oxide gas inside the air bag. The combustion process produces nitrogen gas, which inflates the air bag.

AIR BAG

The air bag itself is constructed of neoprene coated nylon. Fill volume of the air bag is 2.3 cubic feet.

MOUNTING PLATE/HOUSING

A mounting plate and retainer attach and seal the air bag to the inflator. The mounting plate is used to attach the trim cover and to mount the entire module to the steering wheel or dash panel, depending on which side of the vehicle the air bag is mounted.

TRIM COVER

When the air bag is activated, tear seams molded into the trim cover separate to allow the air bag to inflate.

Diagnostic Monitor

The diagnostic monitor continually monitors all air bag system components and wiring connections for possible faults. If a fault is detected, a code will be displayed on the air bag warning light, located on the instrument cluster.

The diagnostic monitor illuminates the air bag light for approximately 6 seconds when the ignition switch is turned **ON**, then turns it off. This indicates that the air bag light is operational. If the air bag light does not illuminate, or if it stays on or flashes at any time, a fault has been detected by the diagnostic monitor.

Performing system diagnostics is the main purpose of the diagnostic monitor. The diagnostic monitor does not deploy the air bags in the event of a crash.

Sensors

▶ See Figure 13

The sensor is an electrical switch that reacts to impacts according to direction and force. It can discriminate between impacts that do or do not require air bag deployment. When an impact occurs that requires air bag deployment, the sensor contacts close and complete the electrical circuit necessary for system operation.

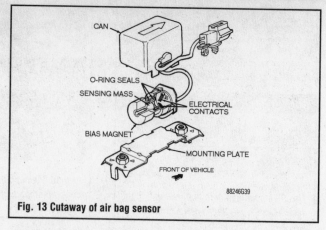

Fig. 13 Cutaway of air bag sensor

Four crash sensors are used on air bag equipped vehicles: a dual crash and safing sensor located at the hood latch support, a crash sensor at each of the right and left fender aprons, and a safing sensor at the left-hand cowl side in the passenger compartment.

At least 2 crash sensors, one safing and one front, must be activated to inflate the air bag.

SERVICE PRECAUTIONS

• Always wear safety glasses when servicing an air bag vehicle, and when handling an air bag.

• Never attempt to service the steering wheel or steering column on an air bag equipped vehicle without first properly disarming the air bag system. The air bag system should be properly disarmed whenever ANY service procedure in this manual indicates that you should do so.

• When carrying a live air bag module, always make sure the bag and trim cover are pointed away from your body. In the unlikely event of an accidental deployment, the bag will then deploy with minimal chance of injury.

• When placing a live air bag on a bench or other surface, always face the bag and trim cover up, away from the surface. This will reduce the motion of the air bag if it is accidentally deployed.

• If you should come in contact with a deployed air bag, be advised that the air bag surface may contain deposits of sodium hydroxide, which is a product of the gas combustion and is irritating to the skin. Always wear gloves and safety glasses when handling a deployed air bag, and wash your hands with mild soap and water afterwards.

➡For removal and installation procedures, refer to the Steering Wheel coverage in Section 8.

DISARMING THE SYSTEM

1. Disconnect the negative battery cable.
2. Disengage the electrical connector from the backup power supply.

➡The backup power supply allows air bag deployment if the battery or battery cables are damaged in an accident before the crash sensors close. The power supply is a capacitor that will leak down in approximately 15 minutes after the battery is disconnected, or in 1 minute if the battery positive cable is grounded. It is located in the instrument panel and is combined with the diagnostic monitor. The backup power supply must be disconnected before any air bag related service is performed.

3. Remove the nut and washer assemblies retaining the driver air bag module to the steering wheel.
4. Disconnect the driver air bag module connector and attach a jumper wire to the air bag terminals on the clockspring.
5. Connect the backup power supply and negative battery cable.

REACTIVATING THE SYSTEM

➡For removal and installation procedures, refer to the Steering Wheel coverage in Section 8.

1. Disconnect the negative battery cable and then the backup power supply.
2. Remove the jumper wire from the air bag terminals on the clockspring assembly and reconnect the air bag connector.

3. Position the air bag assembly.
4. Connect the backup power supply and negative battery cable. Verify that the air bag light illuminates when the ignition switch first is turned **ON**.

HEATER

Blower Motor

REMOVAL & INSTALLATION

♦ **See Figures 14 and 15**

Without Air Conditioning

1. Disconnect the negative battery cable.
2. On trucks built for sale in California, remove the emission module located in front of the blower.
3. Disconnect the wiring harness at the blower.
4. Disconnect the blower motor cooling tube at the blower.
5. Remove the 3 blower motor mounting screws.
6. Hold the cooling tube to one side and pull the blower motor from the housing.
7. Installation is the reverse of removal.

With Air Conditioning

♦ **See Figures 16 and 17**

1. Disconnect the negative battery cable(s).
2. On some California models, remove the emission module forward of the blower motor, if necessary.
3. Disconnect the blower motor wiring at the blower.
4. Disconnect the cooling tube at the blower.
5. Remove the 4 mounting screws and pull the motor from the housing.

6. Installation is the reverse of removal. Cement the cooling tube on the nipple at the housing using Liquid Butyl Sealer D9AZ–19554–A, or equivalent.

Heater Core

REMOVAL & INSTALLATION

♦ **See Figures 18 and 19**

Without Air Conditioning

1. Drain the cooling system to a level below the heater core.

✢✢ CAUTION

When draining the coolant, keep in mind that cats and dogs are attracted by ethylene glycol antifreeze, and are quite likely to drink any that is left in an uncovered container or in puddles on the ground. This will prove fatal in sufficient quantity. Always drain the coolant into a sealable container. Coolant should be reused unless it is contaminated or several years old.

2. Disconnect the coolant hoses at the heater core tubes.
3. From inside the passenger's compartment, remove the 7 screws that secure the heater core access cover to the plenum chamber. Remove the cover. On some models, it might be easier to first remove the glove compartment.
4. Remove the heater core.
5. Installation is the reverse of removal. Replace any damaged sealer.

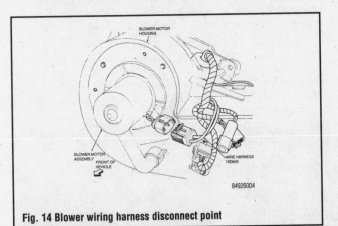

Fig. 14 Blower wiring harness disconnect point

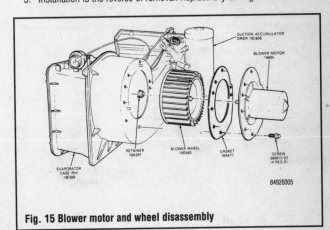

Fig. 15 Blower motor and wheel disassembly

Fig. 16 Unplug the harness connection from the back of the blower motor

Fig. 17 Unbolt, then remove the motor and blower fan assembly

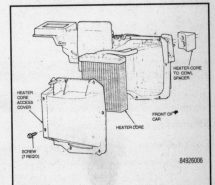

Fig. 18 Heater core removal for 1987–88 models

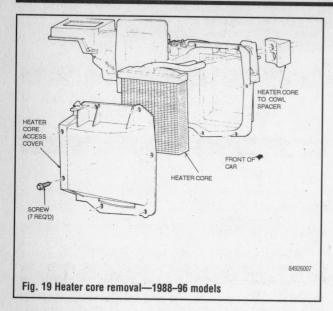

Fig. 19 Heater core removal—1988–96 models

With Air Conditioning

▶ See Figures 20, 21, 22 and 23

1. Drain the cooling system to a level below the heater core.

✳✳ CAUTION

When draining the coolant, keep in mind that cats and dogs are attracted by ethylene glycol antifreeze, and are quite likely to drink any that is left in an uncovered container or in puddles on the ground. This will prove fatal in sufficient quantity. Always drain the coolant into a sealable container. Coolant should be reused unless it is contaminated or several years old.

2. Disconnect the coolant hoses at the heater core tubes.
3. Remove the glove compartment.
4. Disconnect the temperature and function cables.
5. From inside the passenger's compartment, remove the 7 screws that secure the heater core access cover to the plenum chamber. Remove the cover.

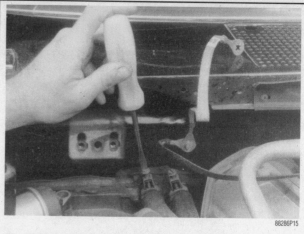

Fig. 20 Disconnect the heater hoses at the firewall

6. Remove the heater core.
7. Installation is the reverse of removal. Replace any damaged sealer.

Air Conditioning Components

REMOVAL & INSTALLATION

Repair or service of air conditioning components is not covered by this manual, because of the risk of personal injury or death, and because of the legal ramifications of servicing these components without the proper EPA certification and experience. Cost, personal injury or death, environmental damage, and legal considerations (such as the fact that it is a federal crime to vent refrigerant into the atmosphere), dictate that the A/C components on your vehicle should be serviced only by a Motor Vehicle Air Conditioning (MVAC) trained, and EPA certified automotive technician.

➡ If your vehicle's A/C system uses R-12 refrigerant and is in need of recharging, the A/C system can be converted over to R-134a refrigerant (less environmentally harmful and expensive). Refer to Section 1 for additional information on R-12 to R-134a conversions, and for additional considerations dealing with your vehicle's A/C system.

Fig. 21 Remove the glovebox

Fig. 22 Remove the heater core access cover from the plenum chamber

Fig. 23 Remove the heater core from the vehicle

CRUISE CONTROL SYSTEM

Control Switches

Please refer to Section 8, under Steering Wheel Removal and Installation.

Speed Sensor

REMOVAL & INSTALLATION

1. Unplug the wiring at the sensor on the transmission.

2. Disconnect the speedometer cable from the speed sensor.
3. Remove the retaining bolt and remove the sensor. Remove the drive gear.
4. Installation is the reverse of removal.

Amplifier

REMOVAL & INSTALLATION

1. Disconnect the wiring at the amplifier, located behind the instrument panel.

2. Remove the amplifier mounting bracket attaching screws or nuts and remove the amplifier and bracket.
3. Remove the amplifier from the bracket.
4. Installation is the reverse of removal.

Servo

The servo is the throttle actuator and is located under the hood.

REMOVAL & INSTALLATION

▶ See Figures 24 and 25

1. Disconnect the wiring at the servo.
2. Disconnect the adjuster from the accelerator cable.
3. Disconnect the vacuum line at the servo.
4. Remove the actuator cable-to-bracket screw.
5. Remove the pins and nuts retaining the servo to its mounting bracket and lift it out.
6. Installation is the reverse of removal.

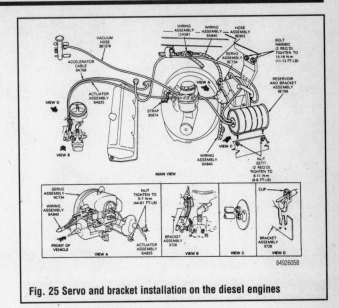

Fig. 25 Servo and bracket installation on the diesel engines

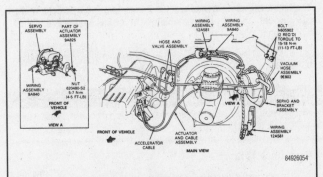

Fig. 24 Servo and bracket installation on the 4.9L engine

LINKAGE ADJUSTMENT

1. Snap the molded cable retainer over the accelerator cable end fitting attached, to the throttle ball stud.
2. Remove the adjuster retainer clip, if installed, from the adjuster mounting tab.
3. Insert the speed control actuator cable adjuster mounting tab in the slot provided in the accelerator cable support bracket.
4. Pull the cable through the adjuster until a slight tension is felt **without** opening the throttle plate.
5. Insert the adjuster cable retainer clip slowly, until engagement is felt, then, push it downwards until it locks in position.

ENTERTAINMENT SYSTEM

Radio

REMOVAL & INSTALLATION

▶ See Figures 26, 27, 28, 29 and 30

1. Remove the bezel retaining screws.
2. Disconnect the negative battery cable.
3. Remove the screws securing the radio mounting plate to the instrument panel and pull out the radio.
4. Disconnect the antenna cable, speaker wires and power wire.
5. Installation is the reverse of removal.

Fig. 26 Remove the radio trim cover—1990 F-150 shown

Fig. 27 Remove the radio retaining screws

Fig. 28 Carefully pull the radio out of the cavity

Fig. 29 Unplug the antenna connector

Fig. 30 Disengage the harness connector from the radio

WINDSHIELD WIPERS AND WASHERS

Wiper Arm

REMOVAL & INSTALLATION

▶ **See Figures 31 and 32**

Raise the blade end of the arm off of the windshield and move the slide latch away from the pivot shaft. This will unlock the wiper arm from the pivot shaft and hold the blade end of the arm off of the glass at the same time. The wiper arm can now be pulled off of the pivot shaft without the aid of any tools.

When installing the wiper arm, the arm must be positioned properly. There is a measurement which can be made to determine the proper blade positioning. With the wiper motor in the **PARK** position, install the arm so that the distance between the blade-to-arm saddle and the lower windshield molding is:

- 1987: 62–93mm (2.4–3.7 in.) on both sides
- 1988–96: 44–76mm (1.7–3.0 in.) on the passenger's side, and 48–80mm (1.9–3.1 in.) on the driver's side.

Blade Assembly

REMOVAL & INSTALLATION

1. Cycle arm and blade assembly to a position on the windshield where removal of blade assembly can be performed without difficulty. Turn ignition key off at desired position.
2. With the blade assembly resting on windshield, grasp either end of the wiper blade frame and pull away from windshield, then pull blade assembly from pin.

➡The rubber element extends past the frame. To prevent damage to the blade element, be sure to grasp the blade frame and not the end of the blade element.

3. To install, push the blade assembly onto the pin until fully seated. Be sure the blade is securely attached to the wiper arm.

Windshield Wiper Motor

REMOVAL & INSTALLATION

▶ **See Figures 33 thru 38**

1. Disconnect the negative battery cable.
2. Remove both wiper arm and blade assemblies.
3. Remove the cowl grille attaching screws and lift the cowl grille slightly.
4. Disconnect the washer nozzle hose and remove the cowl grille assembly.
5. Remove the wiper linkage clip from the motor output arm.
6. Disconnect the wiper motor's wiring connector.
7. Remove the wiper motor's three attaching screws and remove the motor.
To install:
8. Install the motor and attach the three attaching screws. Tighten to 60–85 inch lbs.
9. Connect wiper motor's wiring connector.
10. Install wiper linkage clip to the motor's output arm.
11. Connect the washer nozzle hose and install the cowl assembly and attaching screws.
12. Install both wiper arm assemblies.
13. Connect the negative battery cable.

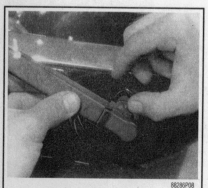

Fig. 31 Slide the latch to disengage the wiper arm—1990 F-150 shown

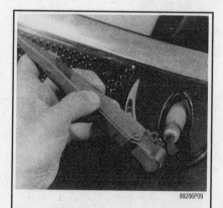

Fig. 32 Pull the wiper arm from the shaft

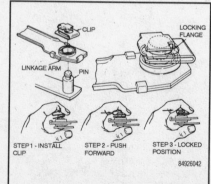

Fig. 33 Installing the wiper arm connecting clip

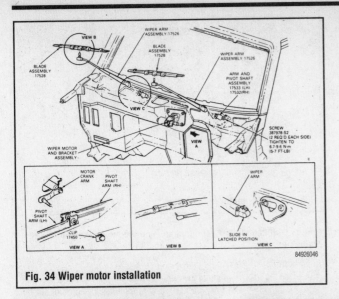

Fig. 34 Wiper motor installation

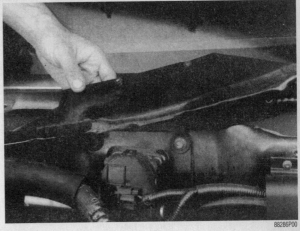

Fig. 35 Remove the trim piece if it interferes with the removal of the wiper motor

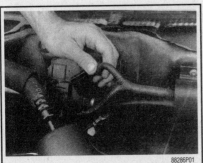

Fig. 36 Disengage the harness connections from the motor

Fig. 37 Remove the motor retaining bolts

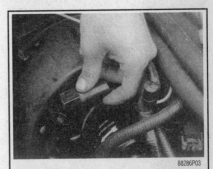

Fig. 38 Remove the wiper motor from the cowl along with the linkage

Interval Governor

REMOVAL & INSTALLATION

▶ See Figure 39

1. Reach up under the instrument panel, behind the wiper switch, and locate the governor. Unplug the wiring connector and remove the wiring clip from the panel reinforcement.
2. Remove the governor attaching screw and remove the governor.
3. Installation is the reverse of removal.

Wiper Linkage

REMOVAL & INSTALLATION

▶ See Figure 40

1. Disconnect the negative battery cable.
2. Remove both wiper arm assemblies.
3. Remove the cowl grille attaching screws and lift the cowl grille slightly.
4. Disconnect the washer nozzle hose and remove the cowl grille assembly.
5. Remove the wiper linkage clip from the motor output arm and pull the linkage from the output arm.
6. Remove the pivot body to cowl screws and remove the linkage and pivot shaft assembly (three screws on each side). The left and right pivots and linkage are independent and can be serviced separately.

To install:

7. Attach the linkage and pivot shaft assembly to cowl with attaching screws.
8. Replace the linkage to the output arm and attach the linkage clip.

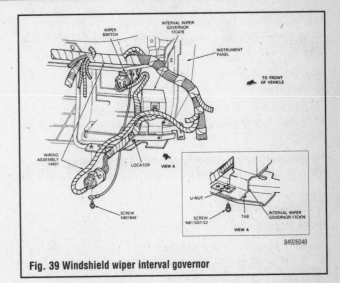

Fig. 39 Windshield wiper interval governor

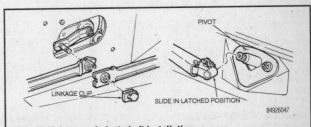

Fig. 40 Linkage and pivot shaft installation

9. Connect the washer nozzle hose and cowl grills assembly.
10. Attach cowl grille attaching screws.
11. Replace both wiper arm assemblies.
12. Connect the negative battery cable.

Windshield Washer Fluid Reservoir

REMOVAL & INSTALLATION

1. Disconnect the wiring at the pump motor. Use a small prytool to unlock the connector tabs.
2. Remove the washer hose.
3. Remove the reservoir attaching screws or nuts and lift the assembly from the truck. Depending on the year, model and optional equipment, the reservoir could be on the fender apron, radiator support, or air cleaner bracket.

➡The cover is not removable from the reservoir.

Windshield Washer Motor

REMOVAL & INSTALLATION

▶ **See Figure 41**

1. Remove the reservoir.
2. Using a small prytool, pry out the motor retaining ring.
3. Using pliers, grip one edge of the electrical connector ring and pull the motor, seal and impeller from the reservoir.

INSTRUMENTS AND SWITCHES

Precautions

Electronic modules, such as instrument clusters, powertrain controls and sound systems are sensitive to static electricity and can be damaged by static discharges which are below the levels that you can hear "snap" or detect on your skin. A detectable snap or shock of static electricity is in the 3,000 volt range. Some of these modules can be damaged by a charge of as little as 100 volts.

The following are some basic safeguards to avoid static electrical damage:
• Leave the replacement module in its original packing until you are ready to install it.
• Avoid touching the module connector pins
• Avoid placing the module on a non-conductive surface
• Use a commercially available static protection kit. These kits contain such things as grounding cords and conductive mats.

Instrument Cluster

REMOVAL & INSTALLATION

▶ **See Figure 42**

1. Disconnect the negative battery cable.
2. Remove the wiper-washer knob. Use a hook tool to release each knob lock tab.
3. Remove the knob from the headlamp switch. Remove the fog lamp switch knob, if so equipped.
4. Remove the steering column shroud. Care must be taken not to damage the transmission control selector indicator (PRNDL) cable on vehicles equipped with an automatic transmission.
5. On vehicles equipped with an automatic transmission, remove the loop on the indicator cable assembly from the retainer pin. Remove the bracket screw from the cable bracket and slide the bracket out of the slot in the tube.
6. Remove the cluster trim cover. Remove the 4 cluster attaching screws, disconnect the speedometer cable wire connector from the printed circuit, 4x4 indicator light and remove the cluster.

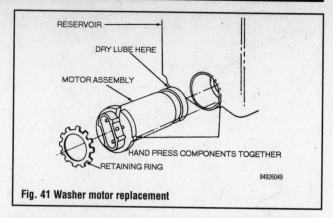

Fig. 41 Washer motor replacement

➡If the seal and impeller come apart from the motor, it can all be re-assembled.

To install:
4. Take the time to clean out the reservoir before installing the motor.
5. Coat the seal with a dry lubricant, such as powdered graphite or spray Teflon®. This will aid assembly.
6. Align the small projection on the motor end cap with the slot in the reservoir and install the motor so that the seal seats against the bottom of the motor cavity.
7. Press the retaining ring into position. A 1 in., 12-point socket or length of 1 in. tubing, will do nicely as an installation tool.
8. Install the reservoir and connect the wiring.

➡It's not a good idea to run a new motor without filling the reservoir first. Dry-running will damage a new motor.

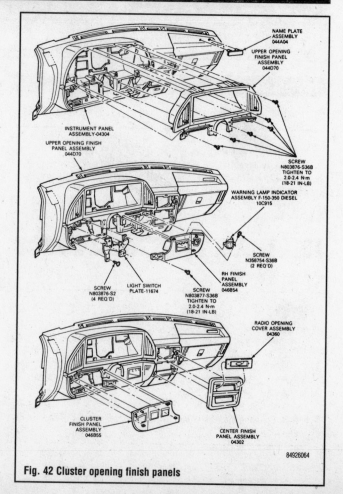

Fig. 42 Cluster opening finish panels

7. Position the cluster at the opening and connect the multiple connector, the speedometer cable and 4x4 indicator light. Install the 4 cluster retaining screws.

8. If so equipped, place the loop on the transmission indicator cable assembly over the retainer on the column.

9. Position the tab on the steering column bracket into the slot on the column. Align and attach the screw.

10. Place the transmission selector lever on the steering column into the **DRIVE** position.

11. Adjust the slotted bracket so the pin is within the letter band.

12. Install the trim cover.

13. Install the headlamp switch knob. If so equipped, install the fog lamp switch.

14. Install the wiper washer control knobs.

15. Connect the battery cable, and check the operation of all gauges, lights and signals.

Tachometer

REMOVAL & INSTALLATION

1. Disconnect the negative battery cable.
2. Remove the instrument cluster.
3. Remove the cluster mask and lens.
4. Remove the tachometer by prying the dial away from the cluster back plate. The tachometer is retained by clips.
5. Installation is the reverse of removal. Make sure the clips are properly seated.

Speedometer Cable Core

REMOVAL & INSTALLATION

♦ **See Figures 43 and 44**

➡**1988–96 models equipped with the 4.9L MFI, 5.0L MFI and 5.8L MFI engines have a speed sensor attached to the transmission. This device sends information on vehicle speed to the Engine Management System and Cruise Control System. For replacement of this unit, see the Cruise Control procedures in this section.**

1. Reach up behind the cluster and disconnect the cable by depressing the quick disconnect tab and pulling the cable away.
2. Remove the cable from the casing. If the cable is broken, raise the vehicle on a hoist and disconnect the cable from the transmission.
3. Remove the cable from the casing.
4. To remove the casing from the vehicle pull it through the floor pan.

To install:

5. To replace the cable, slide the new cable into the casing and connect it at the transmission.

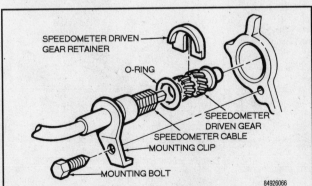

Fig. 43 Speedometer driven gear-to-transmission installation — all models

84926066

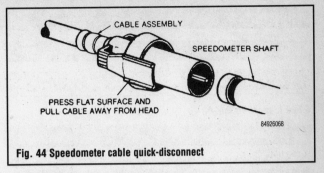

Fig. 44 Speedometer cable quick-disconnect

84926068

6. Route the cable through the floor pan and position the grommet in its groove in the floor.

7. Push the cable onto the speedometer head.

Speedometer Head

REMOVAL & INSTALLATION

1. Remove the instrument cluster.
2. Disconnect the cable from the head.
3. Remove the lens and any surrounding trim.
4. Remove the 2 attaching screws.
5. Installation is the reverse of removal. Place a glob of silicone grease on the end of the cable core prior to connection.

Fuel Gauge

REMOVAL & INSTALLATION

1. Disconnect the negative battery cable.
2. Remove the instrument cluster.
3. Remove the cluster mask and lens.
4. Remove the 2 nuts attaching the gauge to the cluster back plate.
5. Installation is the reverse of removal.

Windshield Wiper Switch

REMOVAL & INSTALLATION

1. Disconnect the negative battery cable.
2. Remove the switch knob, bezel nut and bezel.
3. Pull the switch out from under the panel and unplug the wiring.
4. Installation is the reverse of removal.

Headlight Switch

REMOVAL & INSTALLATION

1. Disconnect the negative battery cable.
2. Depending on the year and model remove the wiper-washer and fog lamp switch knob if they will interfere with the headlight switch knob removal. Check the switch body (behind dash, see Step 3) for a release button. Press in on the button and remove the knob and shaft assembly. If not equipped with a release button, a hook tool may be necessary for knob removal.
3. Remove the steering column shrouds and cluster panel finish panel if they interfere with the required clearance for working behind the dash.
4. Unscrew the switch mounting nut from the front of the dash. Remove the switch from the back of the dash and disconnect the wiring harness.
5. Install in reverse order.

LIGHTING

Headlights

REMOVAL & INSTALLATION

▶ See Figures 45 and 46

> ✳✳ **CAUTION**
>
> The headlamp bulb contains high pressure halogen gas. The bulb may shatter if scratched or dropped! Hold the bulb by its plastic base only. If you touch the glass portion with your fingers, or if any dirt or oily deposits are found on the glass, it must be wiped clean with an alcohol soaked paper towel. Even the oil from your skin will cause the bulb to burn out prematurely due to hot-spotting.

1. Make sure that the headlight switch is OFF.
2. Raise the hood and find the bulb base protruding from the back of the headlamp assembly
3. Disconnect the wiring by grasping the connector and snapping it rearward firmly.
4. Rotate the bulb retaining ring counterclockwise (rear view) about ⅛ turn and slide it off the bulb base. Don't lose it; it's re-usable.
5. Carefully pull the bulb straight out of the headlamp assembly. Don't rotate it during removal.

> ✳✳ **WARNING**
>
> Don't remove the old bulb until you are ready to immediately replace it! Leaving the headlamp assembly open, without a bulb, will allow foreign matter such as water, dirt, leaves, oil, etc. to enter the housing. This type of contamination will cut down on the amount and direction of light emitted, and eventually cause premature blow-out of the bulb.

To install:

6. With the flat side of the bulb base facing upward, insert it into the headlamp assembly. You may have to turn the bulb slightly to align the locating tabs. Once aligned, push the bulb firmly into place until the bulb base contacts the mounting flange in the socket.
7. Place the retaining ring over the bulb base, against the mounting flange and rotate it clockwise to lock it. It should lock against a definite stop when fully engaged.
8. Snap the electrical connector into place. A definite snap will be felt.
9. Turn the headlights on and check that everything works properly.

AIMING

▶ See Figure 47

The headlights must be properly aimed to provide the best, safest road illumination. The lights should be checked for proper aim and adjusted as necessary. Certain state and local authorities have requirements for headlight aiming; these should be checked before adjustment is made.

Each headlight is adjusted by means of 2 screws located at the 10 o'clock and 3 o'clock positions on the headlight underneath the trim ring. Always bring each beam into final position by turning the adjusting screws clockwise so that the headlight will be held against the tension springs when the operation is completed.

Headlight adjustment may be temporarily made using a wall, as described below, or on the rear of another vehicle. When adjusted, the lights should not glare in oncoming car or truck windshields, nor should they illuminate the passenger's compartment of vehicles driving in front of you. These adjustments are rough and should always be fine-tuned by a repair shop which is equipped with headlight aiming tools. Improper adjustments may be both dangerous and illegal.

Before making any headlight adjustments, perform the following preparatory steps:

1. Make sure all tires are properly inflated.
2. Take into consideration any faulty wheel alignment or improper rear axle tracking.
3. Make sure there is no load in the truck other than the driver.
4. The truck's fuel tank should be about half full.
5. Make sure all lenses are clean.

To adjust:

6. Park the truck on a level surface, with the fuel tank no more than ½ full and with the vehicle empty of all extra cargo (unless normally carried). The vehicle should be facing a wall which is no less than 6 feet (1.8m) high and 12 feet (3.7m) wide. The front of the vehicle should be about 25 feet (7.6m) from the wall.
7. If this is be performed outdoors, it is advisable to wait until dusk in order to properly see the headlight beams on the wall. If done in a garage, darken the area around the wall as much as possible by closing shades or hanging cloth over the windows.
8. Turn the headlights ON and mark the wall at the center of each light's low beam, then switch on the "brights" and mark the center of each light's high beam. A short length of masking tape which is visible from the front of the truck may be used. Although marking all 4 positions is advisable, marking 1 position from each light should be sufficient.
9. If neither beam on one side of the vehicle is working, park another like-sized truck in the exact spot where the truck was and mark the beams using the same side light on that truck. Then switch the trucks so the truck being worked on is back in the original spot. The truck must be parked no closer to or farther away from the wall than the second vehicle.

Fig. 45 Twist it counterclockwise

Fig. 46 DO NOT touch the headlight bulb glass—if you do, wipe it clean with an alcohol soaked paper towel

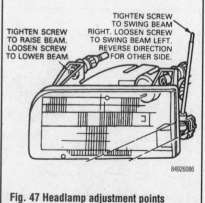

TIGHTEN SCREW TO RAISE BEAM. LOOSEN SCREW TO LOWER BEAM.

TIGHTEN SCREW TO SWING BEAM RIGHT. LOOSEN SCREW TO SWING BEAM LEFT. REVERSE DIRECTION FOR OTHER SIDE.

Fig. 47 Headlamp adjustment points

10. Perform the necessary repairs, but make sure the truck is not moved or is returned to the exact spot from which the lights were marked. Turn the headlights ON and adjust the beams to match the marks on the wall.

11. Have the headlight adjustment checked as soon as possible by a reputable repair shop.

Signal and Marker Lights

REMOVAL & INSTALLATION

Front Turn Signal and Parking Lights

1. Remove the headlamp assembly attaching screws.
2. Pull the headlamp assembly out and disconnect the parking lamp socket from the headlamp body.
3. Replace the bulb.
4. Installation is the reverse of removal.

Rear Turn Signal, Brake and Parking Lights

STYLE SIDE PICK-UPS AND BRONCO

▶ See Figures 48, 49, 50 and 51

1. Remove the screws that attach the combination light lens assembly and remove the lens.
2. Turn the affected bulb socket counterclockwise to remove the bulb; clockwise to install a new bulb.

FLARE SIDE PICK-UPS

▶ See Figure 52

The bulbs can be replaced by removing the lens (4 screws). To replace the lamp assembly, remove the 3 nuts from the mounting studs, disconnect the wiring inside the frame rail, unhook the wiring from the retaining clip, pull out the wires and remove the lamp assembly.

High-mount Brake Light

▶ See Figures 53, 54 and 55

1. Remove the 2 screws that retain the hi-mount light.
2. Pull the rear hi-mount light away from the top.
3. To remove the bulb, disconnect the socket from the light assembly, then pull out the bulb.
4. To remove the light assembly, disconnect the wiring from the light, then remove the light.
5. Reverse the removal procedure to install.

Dome/ Map Light

BRONCO MODELS

1. Carefully pry the dome lamp lens, at the corners, from the housing.
2. Remove the 2 screws attaching the map lamp lens housing to the lamp base and remove the bulbs. The lamp base is retained to the roof by 4 screws.
3. Installation is the reverse of removal.

F-150, F-250, F-350 AND F-SUPER DUTY MODELS

▶ See Figures 56 and 57

1. To replace the bulb, snap the lens out of the lamp body and remove the bulb.
2. To remove the lamp body, remove the 4 retaining screws.
3. Installation is the reverse of removal.

Cargo Lamp

F-150/250/350 AND SUPER-DUTY MODELS

Remove the 2 lamp retaining screws and remove the lamp. Remove the bulb from the lamp. Installation is the reverse of removal.

BRONCO MODELS

Carefully unsnap the lamp from the side of the truck, disconnect the wiring and remove the bulb. Installation is the reverse of removal.

Fig. 48 Remove the screws from the rear of the rear light lens

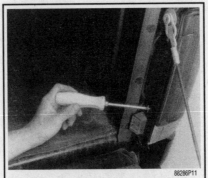

Fig. 49 Lower the tailgate, then remove the retaining screw from the rear lens

Fig. 50 Twist the bulb socket counterclockwise, then pull it from the light assembly

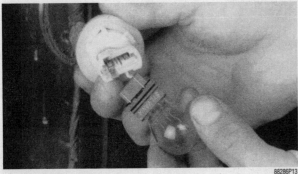

Fig. 51 Pull the affected bulb from the socket and replace it with the correct type bulb

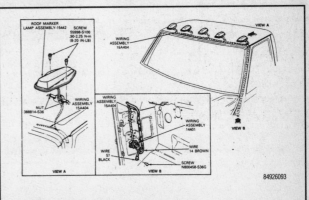

Fig. 52 Roof marker lamps for all models

Fig. 53 Remove the retaining screws from the hi-mount brake light

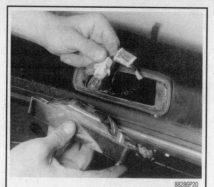

Fig. 54 Turn the light bulb socket to disengage it from the light assembly

Fig. 55 Pull out the bulb from the socket—always replace it with the specified bulb

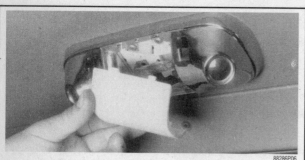

Fig. 56 Remove the lens to access the dome light mounting screws—F-150 shown, others similar

Fig. 57 Simply pull the bulb from its connections as demonstrated

TRAILER WIRING

Wiring the vehicle for towing is fairly easy. There are a number of good wiring kits available and these should be used, rather than trying to design your own.

All trailers will need brake lights and turn signals as well as tail lights and side marker lights. Most areas require extra marker lights for overly wide trailers. Also, most areas have recently required back-up lights for trailers, and most trailer manufacturers have been building trailers with back-up lights for several years.

Additionally, some Class I, most Class II and just about all Class III trailers will have electric brakes. Add to this number an accessories wire, to operate trailer internal equipment or to charge the trailer's battery, and you can have as many as seven wires in the harness.

Determine the equipment on your trailer and buy the wiring kit necessary. The kit will contain all the wires needed, plus a plug adapter set which includes the female plug, mounted on the bumper or hitch, and the male plug, wired into, or plugged into the trailer harness.

When installing the kit, follow the manufacturer's instructions. The color coding of the wires is usually standard throughout the industry. One point to note: some domestic vehicles, and most imported vehicles, have separate turn signals. On most domestic vehicles, the brake lights and rear turn signals operate with the same bulb. For those vehicles with separate turn signals, you can purchase an isolation unit so that the brake lights won't blink whenever the turn signals are operated, or, you can go to your local electronics supply house and buy 4 diodes to wire in series with the brake and turn signal bulbs. Diodes will isolate the brake and turn signals. The choice is yours. The isolation units are simple and quick to install, but far more expensive than the diodes. The diodes, however, require more work to install properly, since they require the cutting of each bulb's wire and soldering in place of the diode.

One, final point, the best kits are those with a spring loaded cover on the vehicle mounted socket. This cover prevents dirt and moisture from corroding the terminals. Never let the vehicle socket hang loosely; always mount it securely to the bumper or hitch.

CIRCUIT PROTECTION

Fuses

▶ See Figures 58, 59, 60 and 61

On earlier models, the fuse panel is located on the firewall above the driver's left foot.

On later models, the fuse panel is located on the underside of the instrument panel, covered with an access door.

Circuit Breakers

▶ See Figures 60 and 61

Two circuits are protected by circuit breakers located in the fuse panel: the power windows (20 amp) or power windows and Shift-On-The-Fly (30 amp) and the power door locks (30 amp). The breakers are self-resetting.

Turn Signal and Hazard Flasher Locations

▶ See Figures 60 and 61

Both the turn signal flasher and the hazard warning flasher are mounted on the fuse panel. The turn signal flasher is mounted on the front of the fuse panel, and the hazard warning flasher is mounted on the rear of the fuse panel.

Fuse Link

The fuse link is a short length of special, Hypalon (high temperature) insulated wire, integral with the engine compartment wiring harness and should not be confused with standard wire. It is several wire gauges smaller than the circuit which it protects. Under no circumstances should a fuse link replacement repair be made using a length of standard wire cut from bulk stock or from another wiring harness.

Fig. 58 Remove the cover from the fuse panel

Fig. 59 Use only the fuses specified for the circuit

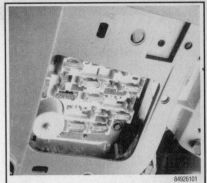

Fig. 60 Instrument panel-mounted fuse box

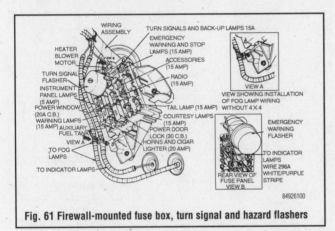

Fig. 61 Firewall-mounted fuse box, turn signal and hazard flashers

To repair any blown fuse link use the following procedure:

1. Determine which circuit is damaged, its location and the cause of the open fuse link. If the damaged fuse link is one of three fed by a common No. 10 or 12 gauge feed wire, determine the specific affected circuit.

2. Disconnect the negative battery cable.

3. Cut the damaged fuse link from the wiring harness and discard it. If the fuse link is one of 3 circuits fed by a single feed wire, cut it out of the harness at each splice end and discard it.

4. Identify and procure the proper fuse link and butt connectors for attaching the fuse link to the harness.

5. To repair any fuse link in a 3-link group with one feed:

    a. After cutting the open link out of the harness, cut each of the remaining undamaged fuse links close to the feed wire weld.

    b. Strip approximately ½ in. (13mm) of insulation from the detached ends of the 2 good fuse links. Then insert 2 wire ends into one end of a butt connector and carefully push one stripped end of the replacement fuse link into the same end of the butt connector and crimp all three firmly together.

➡ **Care must be taken when fitting the 3 fuse links into the butt connector as the internal diameter is a snug it for 3 wires. Make sure to use a proper crimping tool. Pliers, side cutters, etc. will not apply the proper crimp to retain the wires and withstand a pull test.**

    c. After crimping the butt connector to the 3 fuse links, cut the weld portion from the feed wire and strip approximately ½ in. (13mm) of insulation from the cut end. Insert the stripped end into the open end of the butt connector and crimp very firmly.

    d. To attach the remaining end of the replacement fuse link, strip approximately ½ in. (13mm) of insulation from the wire end of the circuit from which the blown fuse link was removed, and firmly crimp a butt connector or equivalent to the stripped wire. Then, insert the end of the replacement link into the other end of the butt connector and crimp firmly.

    e. Using rosin core solder with a consistency of 60 percent tin and 40 percent lead, solder the connectors and the wires at the repairs and insulate with electrical tape.

6. To replace any fuse link on a single circuit in a harness, cut out the damaged portion, strip approximately ½ in. (13mm) of insulation from the 2 wire ends and attach the appropriate replacement fuse link to the stripped wire ends with 2 proper size butt connectors. Solder the connectors and wires and insulate the tape.

7. To repair any fuse link which has an eyelet terminal on one end such as the charging circuit, cut off the open fuse link behind the weld, strip approximately ½ in. (13mm) of insulation from the cut end and attach the appropriate new eyelet fuse link to the cut stripped wire with an appropriate size butt connector. Solder the connectors and wires at the repair and insulate with tape.

8. Connect the negative battery cable to the battery and test the system for proper operation.

➡ **Do not mistake a resistor wire for a fuse link. The resistor wire is generally longer and has print stating, "Resistor: don't cut or splice."**

WIRING DIAGRAMS

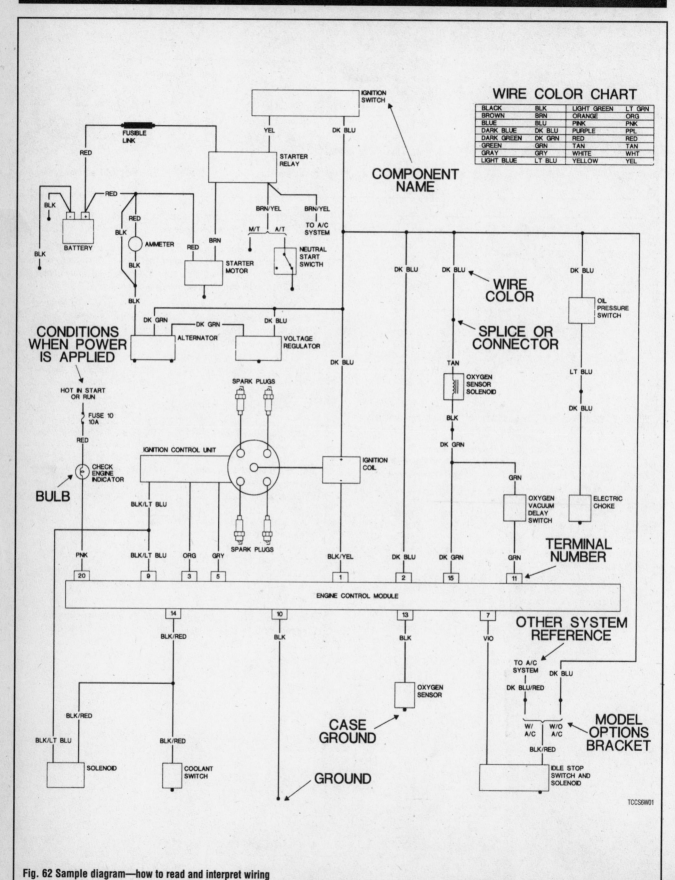

WIRE COLOR CHART

BLACK	BLK	LIGHT GREEN	LT GRN
BROWN	BRN	ORANGE	ORG
BLUE	BLU	PINK	PNK
DARK BLUE	DK BLU	PURPLE	PPL
DARK GREEN	DK GRN	RED	RED
GREEN	GRN	TAN	TAN
GRAY	GRY	WHITE	WHT
LIGHT BLUE	LT BLU	YELLOW	YEL

Fig. 62 Sample diagram—how to read and interpret wiring

TCCS6W01

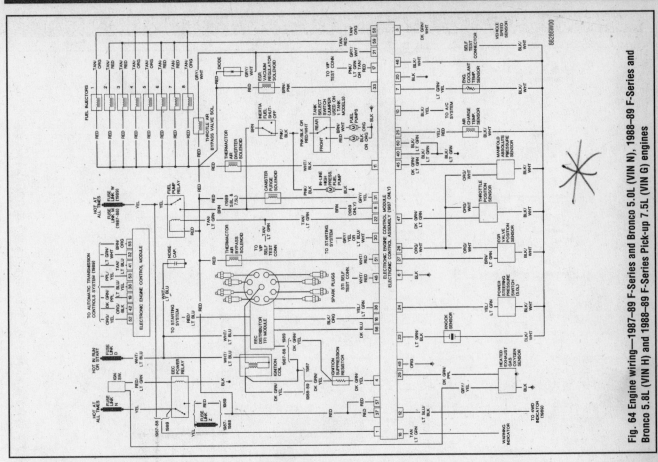

Fig. 64 Engine wiring—1987–89 F-Series and Bronco 5.0L (VIN N), 1988–89 F-Series and Bronco 5.8L (VIN H) and 1988–89 F-Series Pick-up 7.5L (VIN G) engines

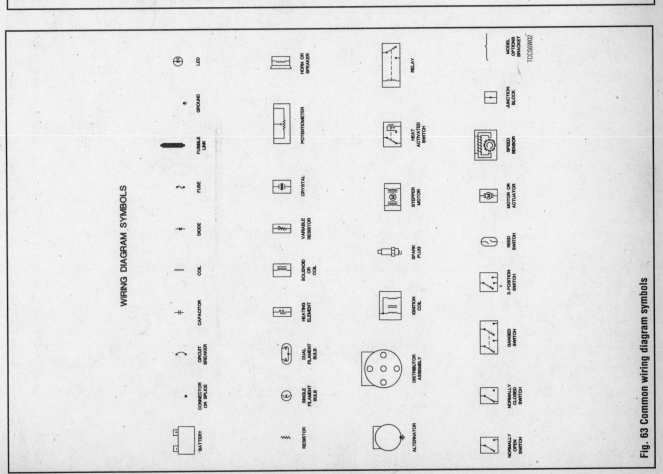

Fig. 63 Common wiring diagram symbols

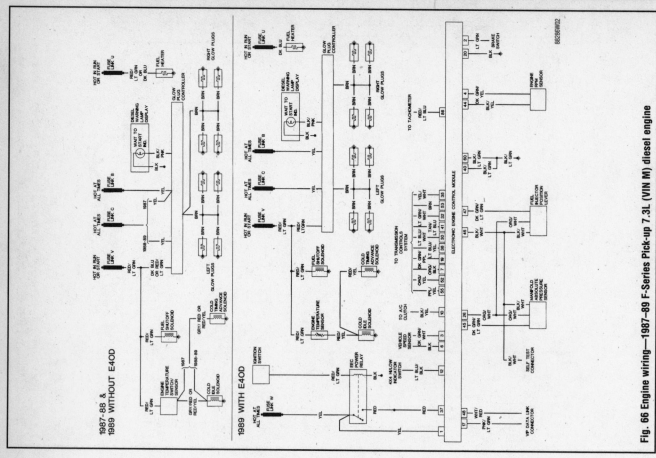

Fig. 66 Engine wiring—1987-89 F-Series Pick-up 7.3L (VIN M) diesel engine

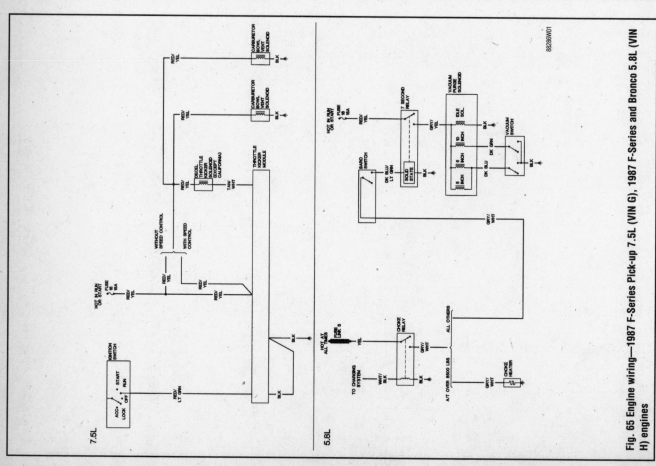

Fig. 65 Engine wiring—1987 F-Series Pick-up 7.5L (VIN G), 1987 F-Series and Bronco 5.8L (VIN H) engines

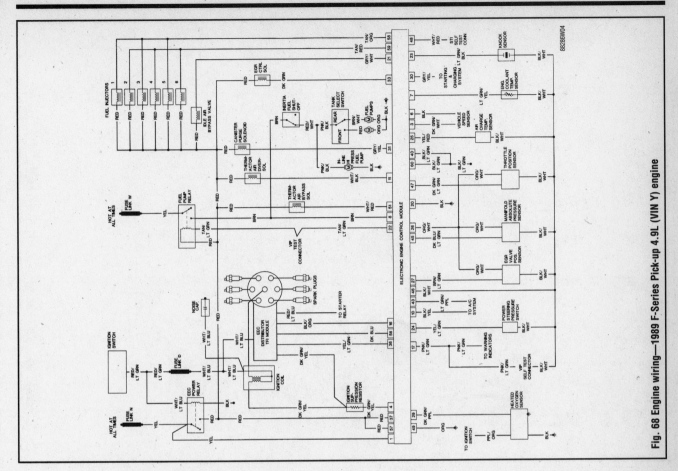

Fig. 68 Engine wiring—1989 F-Series Pick-up 4.9L (VIN Y) engine

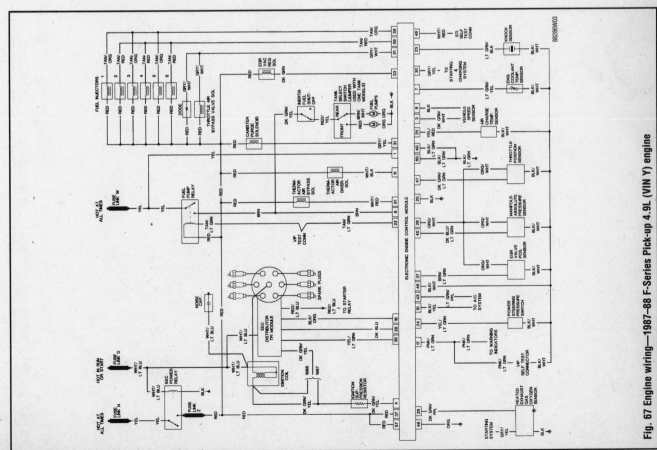

Fig. 67 Engine wiring—1987-88 F-Series Pick-up 4.9L (VIN Y) engine

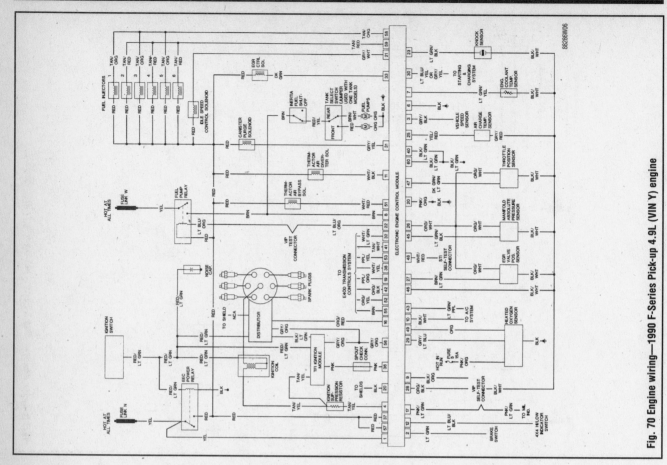

Fig. 70 Engine wiring—1990 F-Series Pick-up 4.9L (VIN Y) engine

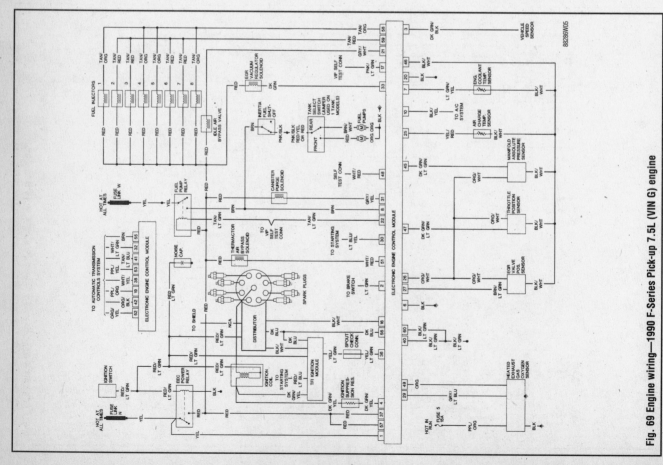

Fig. 69 Engine wiring—1990 F-Series Pick-up 7.5L (VIN G) engine

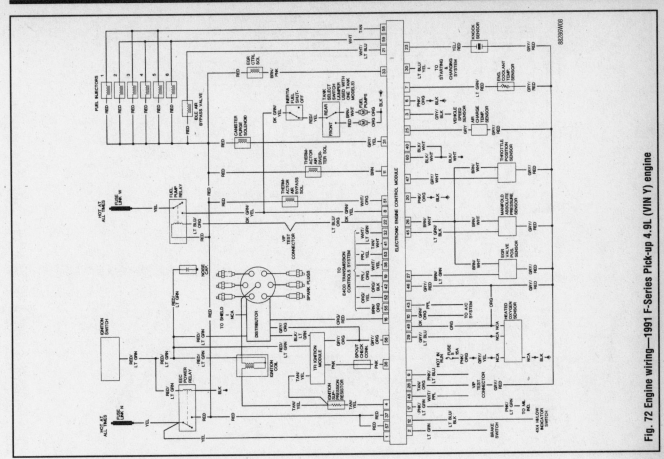

Fig. 72 Engine wiring—1991 F-Series Pick-up 4.9L (VIN Y) engine

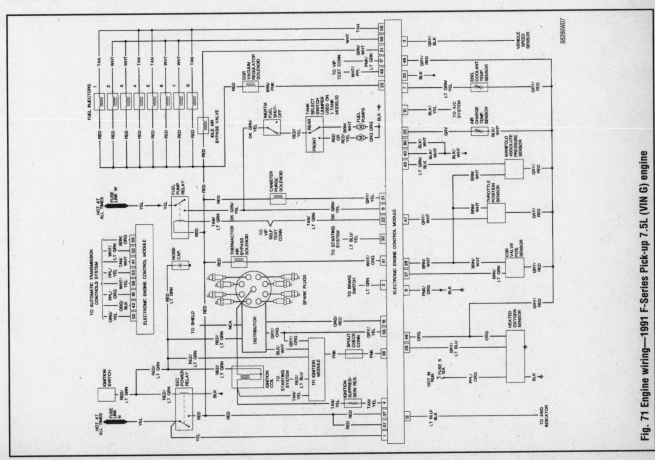

Fig. 71 Engine wiring—1991 F-Series Pick-up 7.5L (VIN G) engine

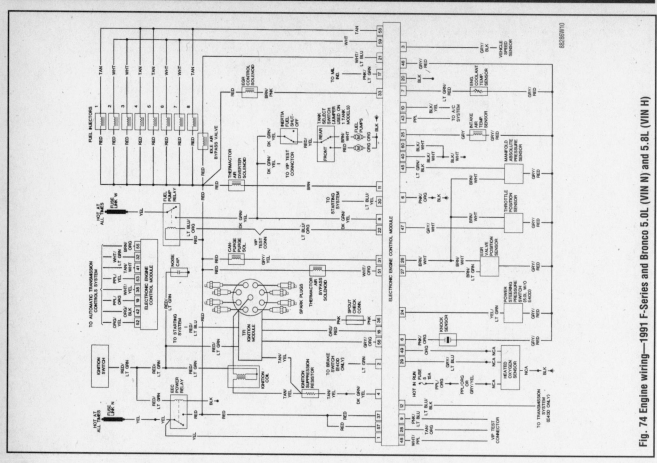

Fig. 74 Engine wiring—1991 F-Series and Bronco 5.0L (VIN N) and 5.8L (VIN H)

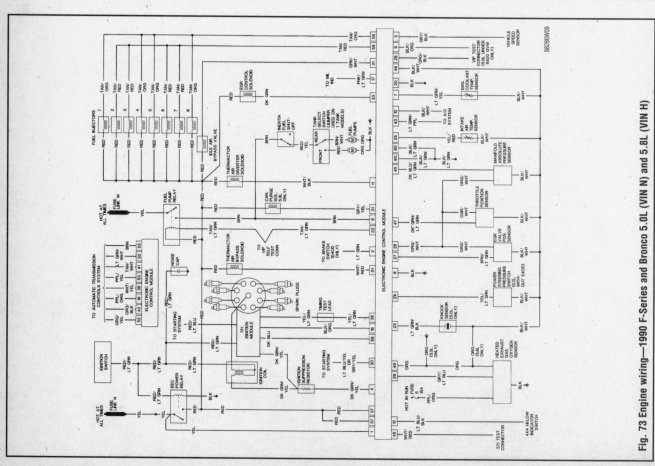

Fig. 73 Engine wiring—1990 F-Series and Bronco 5.0L (VIN N) and 5.8L (VIN H)

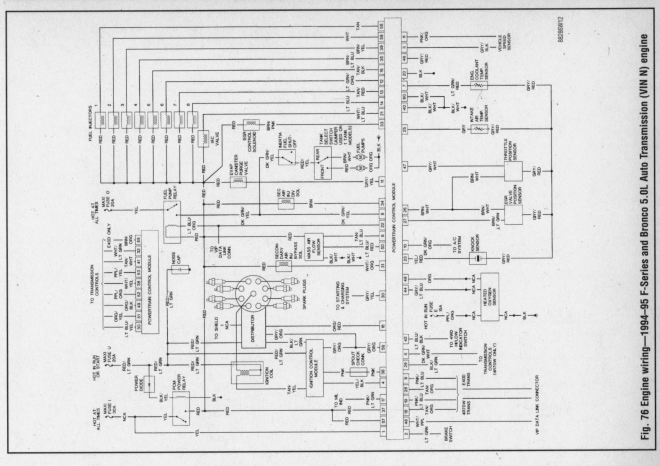

Fig. 76 Engine wiring—1994-95 F-Series and Bronco 5.0L Auto Transmission (VIN N) engine

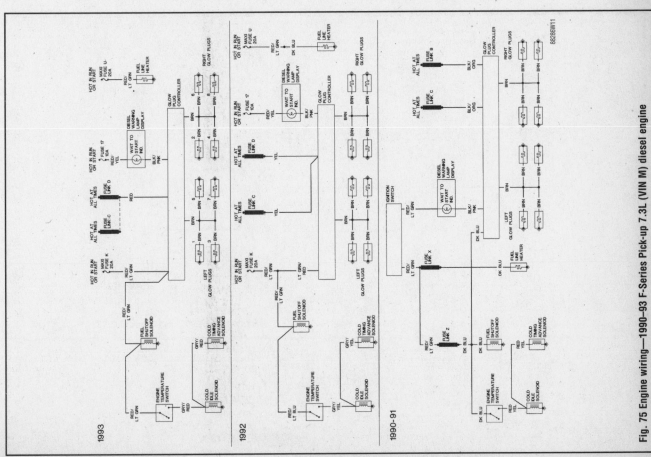

Fig. 75 Engine wiring—1990-93 F-Series Pick-up 7.3L (VIN M) diesel engine

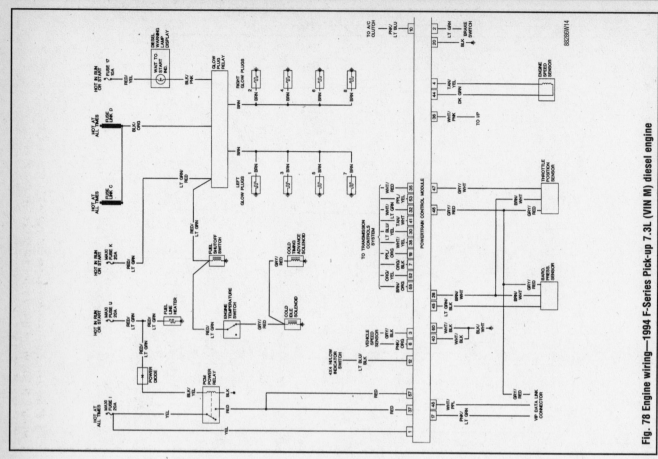

Fig. 78 Engine wiring—1994 F-Series Pick-up 7.3L (VIN M) diesel engine

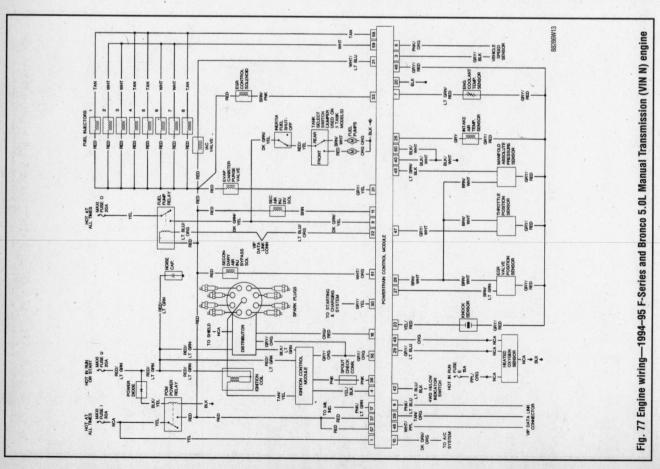

Fig. 77 Engine wiring—1994-95 F-Series and Bronco 5.0L Manual Transmission (VIN N) engine

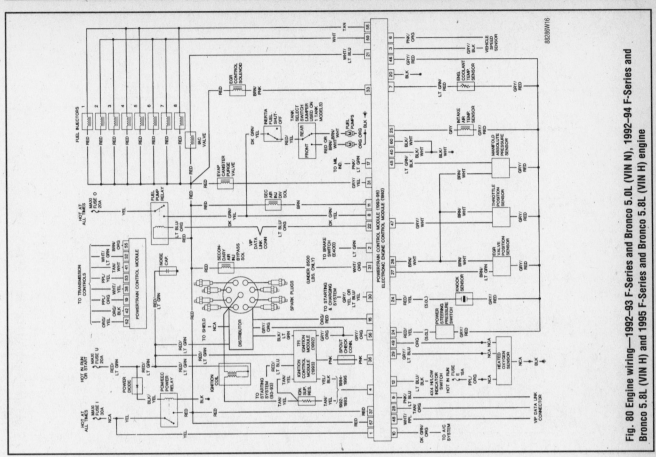

Fig. 80 Engine wiring—1992-93 F-Series and Bronco 5.0L (VIN N), 1992-94 F-Series and Bronco 5.8L (VIN H) and 1995 F-Series and Bronco 5.8L (VIN H) engine

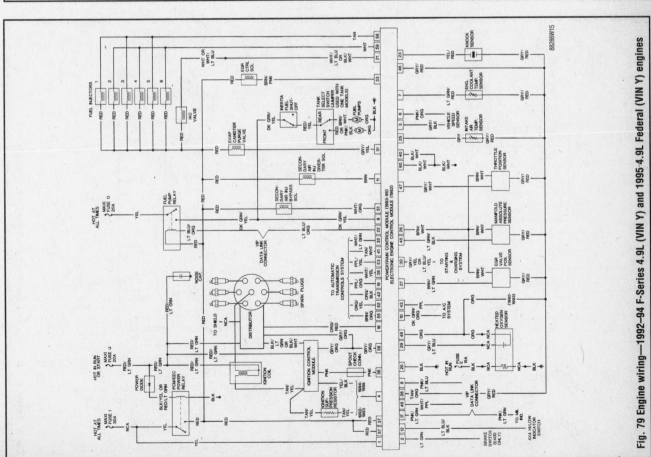

Fig. 79 Engine wiring—1992-94 F-Series 4.9L (VIN Y) and 1995 4.9L Federal (VIN Y) engines

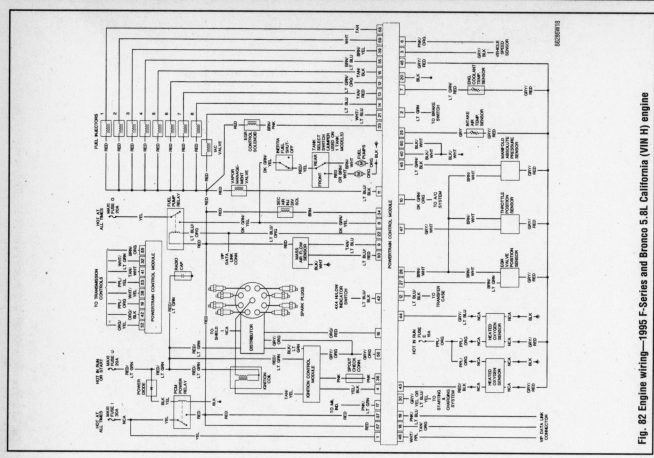

Fig. 82 Engine wiring—1995 F-Series and Bronco 5.8L California (VIN H) engine

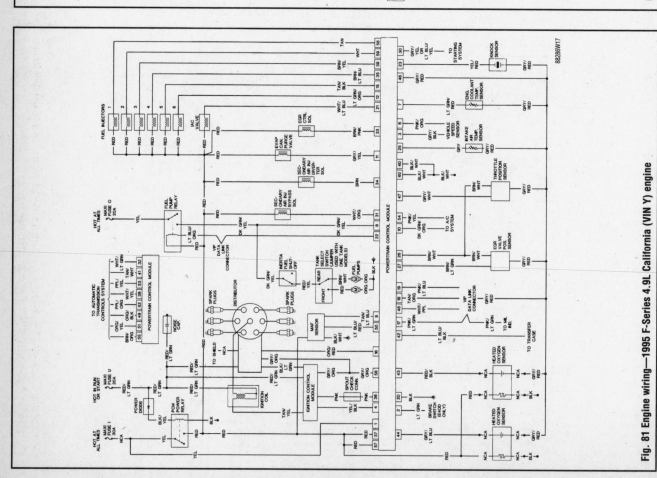

Fig. 81 Engine wiring—1995 F-Series 4.9L California (VIN Y) engine

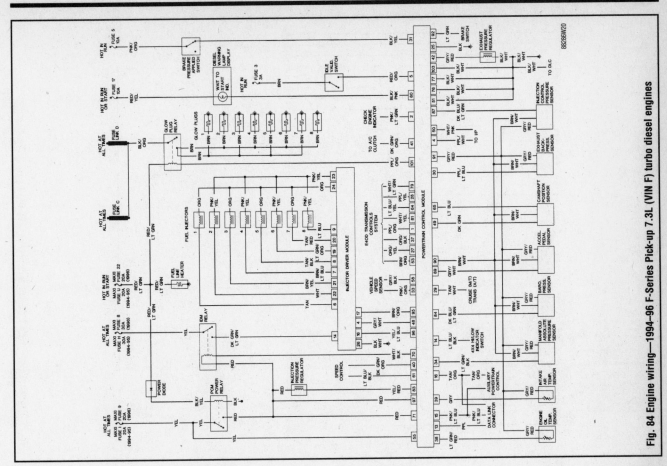

Fig. 84 Engine wiring—1994-96 F-Series Pick-up 7.3L (VIN F) turbo diesel engines

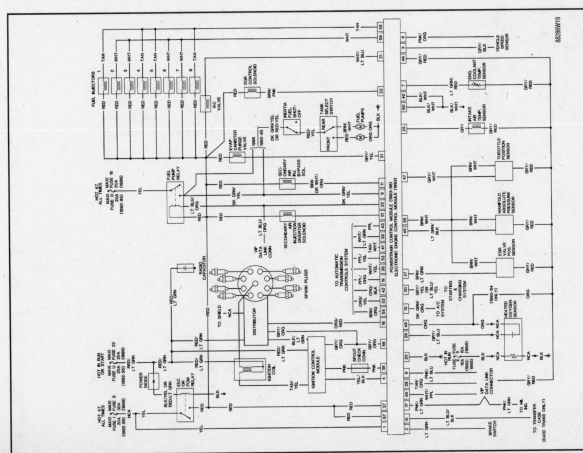

Fig. 83 Engine wiring—1992-95 F-Series 7.5L (VIN G), 1996 F-Series 7.5L Federal (VIN G) and 1996 F-Series Pick-up 5.8L (VIN H over 8500 GVW) engines

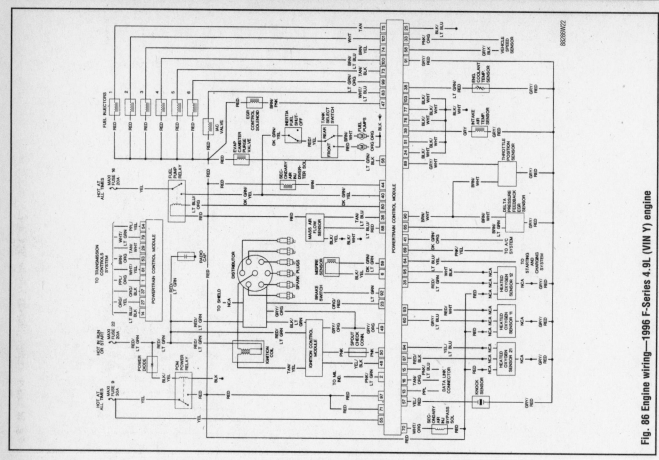

Fig. 86 Engine wiring—1996 F-Series 4.9L (VIN Y) engine

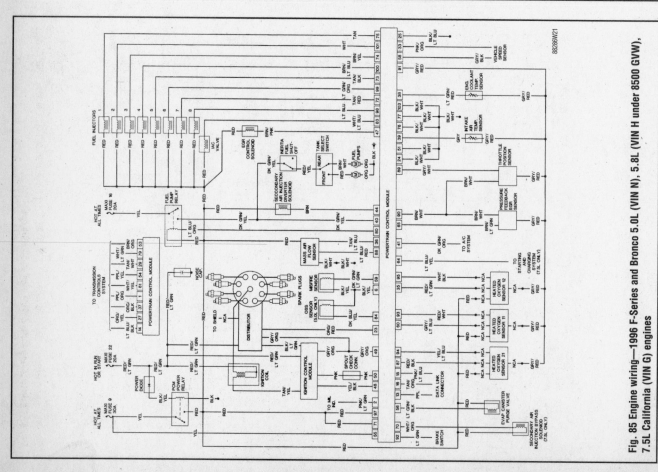

Fig. 85 Engine wiring—1996 F-Series and Bronco 5.0L (VIN N), 5.8L (VIN H under 8500 GVW), 7.5L California (VIN G) engines

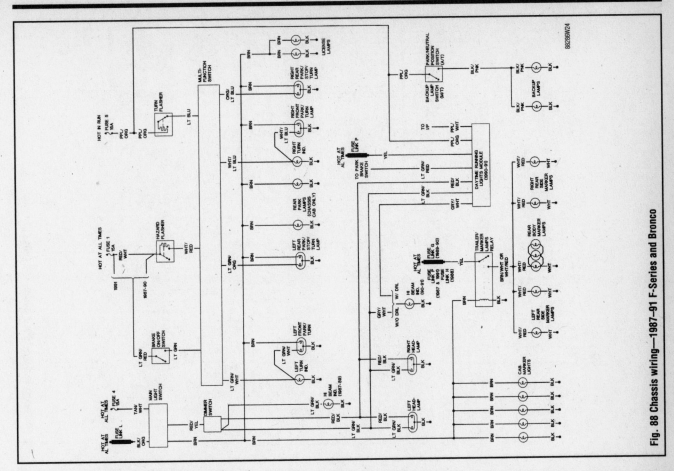

Fig. 88 Chassis wiring—1987-91 F-Series and Bronco

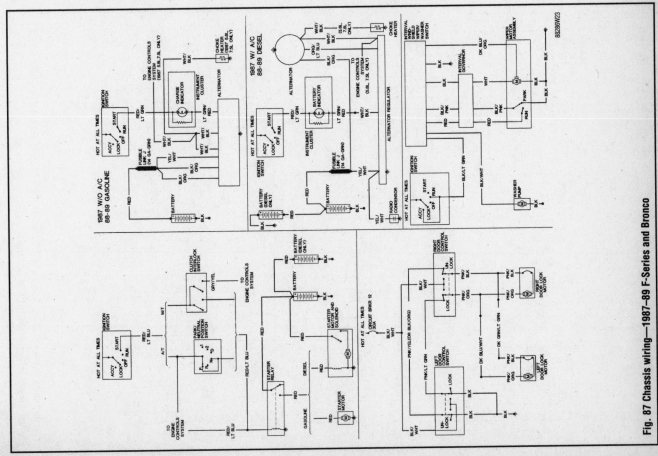

Fig. 87 Chassis wiring—1987-89 F-Series and Bronco

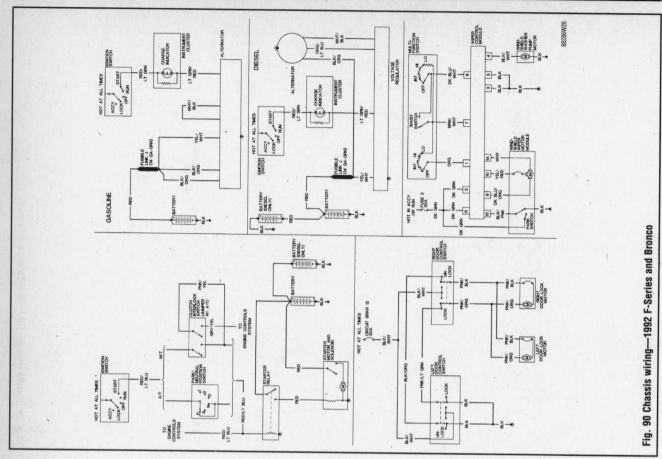

Fig. 90 Chassis wiring—1992 F-Series and Bronco

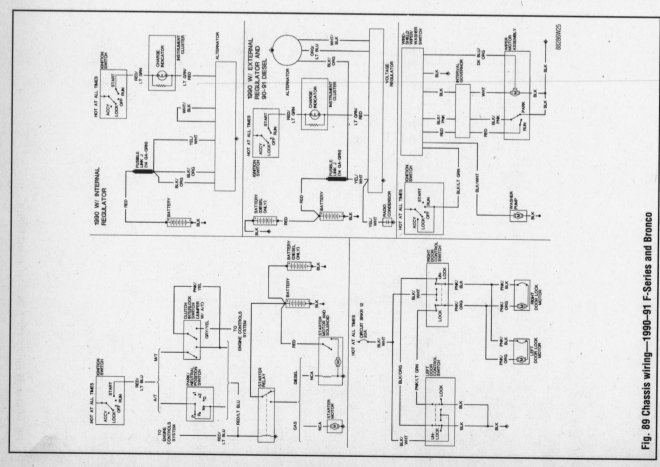

Fig. 89 Chassis wiring—1990-91 F-Series and Bronco

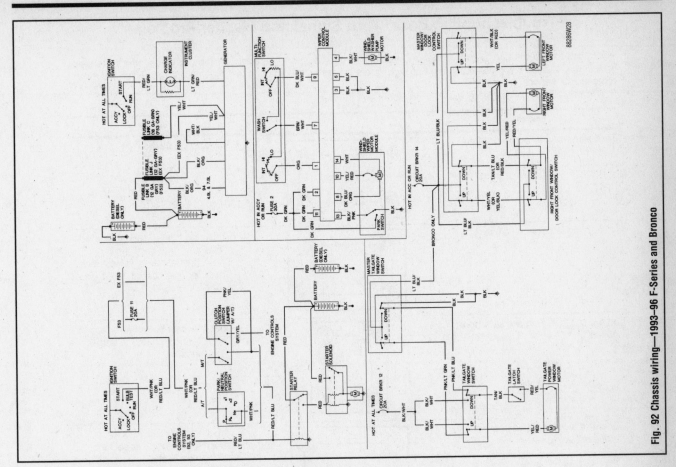

Fig. 92 Chassis wiring—1993-96 F-Series and Bronco

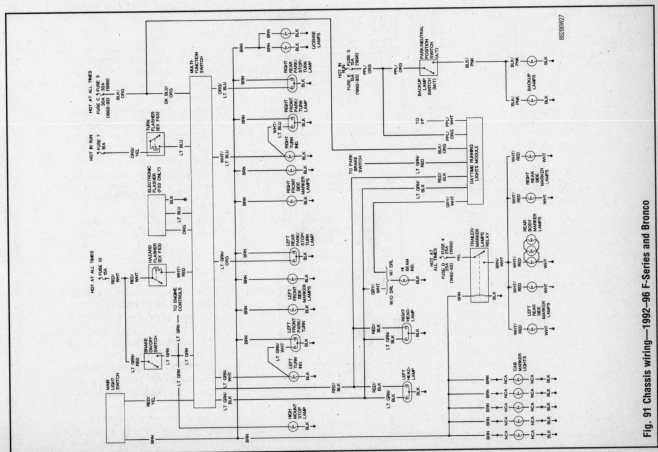

Fig. 91 Chassis wiring—1992-96 F-Series and Bronco

Troubleshooting Basic Turn Signal and Flasher Problems

Most problems in the turn signals or flasher system can be reduced to defective flashers or bulbs, which are easily replaced. Occasionally, problems in the turn signals are traced to the switch in the steering column, which will require professional service.

F = Front   R = Rear   • = Lights off   o = Lights on

Problem		Solution
Turn signals light, but do not flash		• Replace the flasher
No turn signals light on either side		• Check the fuse. Replace if defective. • Check the flasher by substitution • Check for open circuit, short circuit or poor ground
Both turn signals on one side don't work		• Check for bad bulbs • Check for bad ground in both housings
One turn signal light on one side doesn't work		• Check and/or replace bulb • Check for corrosion in socket. Clean contacts. • Check for poor ground at socket
Turn signal flashes too fast or too slow		• Check any bulb on the side flashing too fast. A heavy-duty bulb is probably installed in place of a regular bulb. • Check the bulb flashing too slow. A standard bulb was probably installed in place of a heavy-duty bulb. • Check for loose connections or corrosion at the bulb socket
Indicator lights don't work in either direction		• Check if the turn signals are working • Check the dash indicator lights • Check the flasher by substitution
One indicator light doesn't light		• On systems with 1 dash indicator: See if the lights work on the same side. Often the filaments have been reversed in systems combining stoplights with taillights and turn signals. Check the flasher by substitution • On systems with 2 indicators: Check the bulbs on the same side Check the indicator light bulb Check the flasher by substitution

7

DRIVE TRAIN

MANUAL TRANSMISSION

Adjustments

LINKAGE

3.03 Three Speed

♦ See Figures 1 and 2

A column shift is used with this transmission.
1. Install a 3/16 (4.76mm) diameter gauge pin, through the locating hole in the steering column shift levers and the plastic spacer.
2. Locate the levers in the center of the steering column window.
3. Loosen nuts **A** and **B** and position the transmission shift levers in the **Neutral** detents.
4. Tighten nuts **A** and **B** to 12–18 ft. lbs. (17–24 Nm), using care to prevent motion between the stud and rod.
5. Remove the gauge pin.
6. Check the linkage operation. Make sure there is no interference between the steering column levers and window when shifting into gear.

➡**Always use new retaining rings and new insulators when making transmission control adjustments. New retaining rings should also be used whenever the existing retaining rings are removed. The rings as well as the plastic grommets where the shift rods are attached, should be replaced whenever excessive wear or looseness is noted during normal vehicle inspections.**

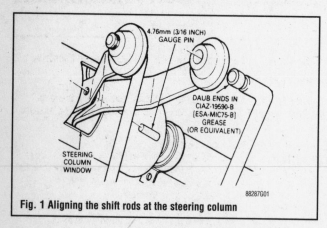

Fig. 1 Aligning the shift rods at the steering column

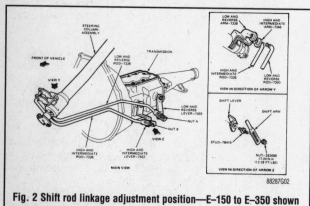

Fig. 2 Shift rod linkage adjustment position—E–150 to E–350 shown

Ford TOD 4-Speed Overdrive

♦ See Figure 3

A floor mounted shift is used with this transmission.
1. Attach the shift rods in the levers.
2. Rotate the output shaft to determine that the transmission is in **Neutral**.

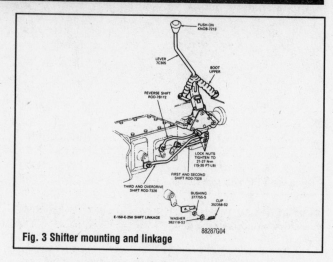

Fig. 3 Shifter mounting and linkage

3. Insert a alignment pin into the shift control assembly alignment hole.
4. Attach the slotted end of the shift rods over the flats of the studs in the shift control assembly.
5. Install the locknuts and tighten the locknuts to 15–20 ft. lbs. (21–27 Nm). Remove the alignment pin.

CLUTCH SWITCH

♦ See Figures 4 and 5

The clutch interlock switch is used on all truck models, however this switch is adjustable in some models up to 1991. On vehicles after 1991 the switch in non-adjustable. If the switch does not function it must be replaced.
1. Disconnect the negative battery cable.
2. If the adjusting clip is out of position on the rod, remove both halves of the clip.
3. Position both halves of the clip closer to the switch and snap the clips together on the rod.
4. Depress the clutch pedal to the floor to adjust the switch.
5. Connect the negative battery cable.
6. Check switch function by attempting to start the engine without depressing the clutch pedal, the engine should not start. The engine should start when the clutch pedal is depress.

✳✳ CAUTION

Make sure the transmission is in NEUTRAL and the hand brake is applied when attempting to start the vehicle without the clutch pedal depressed.

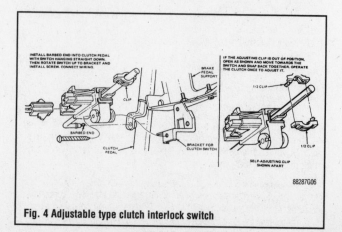

Fig. 4 Adjustable type clutch interlock switch

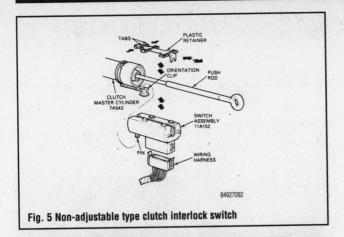

Fig. 5 Non-adjustable type clutch interlock switch

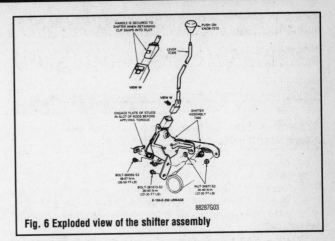

Fig. 6 Exploded view of the shifter assembly

Shift Linkage

REMOVAL & INSTALLATION

3.03 Three Speed Transmission

➡Most column mounted shift lever assemblies incorporate a plastic grommet in each lever arm. A special tool T67P–7341 or equivalent is required to install the grommet in the shaft lever and to install the shaft linkage rod into the grommet.

1. To remove the rod end connected to the shift column, place the lower jaw of the tool between the shift lever and the shift rod. If working in limited space use tool T84P-341-A or equivalent.

2. Position the stop pin against the end of the shift rod and force the rod out of the grommet.

3. The grommet is removed from the lever by cutting off the large shoulder of the grommet.

4. Remove the grommet from the lever by pushing it out of the lever.

5. Disconnect the rod at the transmission manual shift lever by removing the attaching nut and remove the linkage.

To install:

6. Prior to installing a new grommet, adjust the stop pin if necessary to properly install the grommet. Coat the outside of the grommet with a Multipurpose Long Life lubricant. Then place the grommet on the stop pin and force it into the shift lever hole. Turn the grommet several times to be sure it is properly seated.

7. Re-adjust the stop pin to a length which is sufficient to install the shift rod into the grommet. If the pin height is not adjusted, the shaft rod may be pushed too far through the grommet, causing damage to the grommet retaining lip.

8. With the pin height properly adjusted, position the shift rod on the tool and force the rod into the grommet until the groove in the rod seats on the inner retaining lip of the grommet.

9. Install the shift rods to the correct shift lever and install the retaining nuts. Do not tighten.

10. Adjust the shift linkage as described in this section.

4-Speed Overdrive Transmission

▶ See Figure 6

1. Raise the vehicle and safely support it with jackstands.

➡The shift linkage consist of 3 shift rods connected between the shifter and transmission. If all shift rods are being removed, matchmark each rod to the lever it is being removed from. This will insure proper installation location of each rod.

2. Disconnect the 3 shift rods at the transmission end by removing the retainer clip and washer then pull each rod free from the shift lever. A bushing should be inside the eye of the shift linkage. Replace this bushing if required.

3. Disconnect the shift linkage at the shifter end by removing the locknuts and remove the shift linkage from the vehicle.

To install:

4. Install the shift rods one at a time to the correct locations marked.

5. Replace the bushing at the end of the rod (transmission side) as required.

6. Connect the rod to the transmission shift lever and install the washer and retainer clip.

7. Connect the rod to the shifter and install the locknut, but do not tighten. Adjust the shift linkage. See the above procedure.

8. Remove the jackstands and lower the vehicle.

Shift Handle

REMOVAL & INSTALLATION

Borg Warner T-18 and T-19; New Process 435 4-Speed Overdrive

▶ See Figure 6

➡Remove the shift ball only if the shift ball, boot or lever is the be replaced. If either the ball, boot or lever is not being replaced, remove the ball, boot and lever as an assembly.

1. Disconnect the negative battery cable.

2. Remove the plastic insert from the shift ball. Warm the ball with a heat gun to 140–180°F (60–82°C) knock the ball off the lever with a block of wood and a hammer taking care not damage the finish on the shift lever.

3. Remove the rubber boot and floor pan cover.

4. Except 4 speed overdrive transmission, shift the unit into second gear, remove the lockpin and remove the shift lever from the shifter housing.

5. Vehicles with 4 speed overdrive transmission, shift the unit into second gear. Depress the retainer clip on the end of the shift lever and remove the shift lever from the housing.

To install:

6. Except 4 speed overdrive transmission, install the shift lever in the shifter housing, making sure that the slot in the lever aligns with the tab in the housing. Install the lockpin.

7. Vehicles with 4 speed overdrive transmission, install the shift lever in the shifter housing, making sure that the retaining clip on the lever aligns with the slot in the housing and snaps into place. Install the lockpin.

8. Install the rubber boot and floor pan cover.

9. Warm the ball with a heat gun to 140–180°F (60–82°C) and tap the ball on the lever with a 7/16 inch socket and mallet. Install the plastic shift pattern insert.

10. Vehicles with 4 speed overdrive transmission, the shifter is removed by depressing the retainer clip on the end of the shift lever.

11. Connect the negative battery cable.

Ford TOD 4-Speed Overdrive

➡Remove the shift ball only if the shift ball, boot or lever is to be replaced. If neither the ball, boot nor lever is not being replaced, remove the ball, boot and lever as an assembly.

1. Disconnect the negative battery cable.

2. Remove the plastic insert from the shift ball. Warm the ball with a heat

gun to 140–180°F (60–82°C) knock the ball off the lever with a block of wood and a hammer taking care not damage the finish on the shift lever.

3. Remove the screws retaining the boot and pad to the floor plate.

4. Shift the transmission into **Neutral**.

5. Remove the boot from the cap. Place an oil filter wrench around the gearshift housing cap and twist off the cap.

✳✳ WARNING

Do not twist the gearshift housing cap by hand. Due to the clearance between the floor plate and cap, the hands may be cut.

6. Remove the shift lever from the transmission.

To install:

7. Install the shift lever in the gearshift housing, making sure that the slots in the lever aligns with the pins in the housing.

8. Install the rubber boot and pad. Install the screws retaining the boot and pad to the floor plate.

9. Warm the ball with a heat gun to 140–180°F (60–82°C) and tap the ball on the lever with a ⁷⁄₁₆ inch socket and mallet. Install the plastic shift pattern insert.

10. Connect the negative battery cable.

ZF S5–42 and ZF S5–47

1. Disconnect the negative battery cable.

2. Remove the shifter boot and bezel assembly from the transmission opening cover.

3. Remove the 2 bolts retaining the upper shift lever to the lower shift lever and remove the upper shift lever.

To install:

4. Install the upper shift lever to the lower lever and install the retaining bolts. Tighten 16–24 ft. lbs. (22–33 Nm).

5. Install shifter boot and bezel assembly to the transmission opening cover.

6. Install the shift ball on the upper shifter if removed.

7. Connect the negative battery cable.

Mazda M50D 5-Speed

◆ See Figures 7 thru 13

1. Disconnect the negative battery cable.

2. Shift the transmission into **Neutral**

3. Remove the carpet or floor mats.

4. Remove the shifter boot retainer screws and slide the boot up the shift lever shaft.

5. Remove the shift lever retaining bolt locknut.

6. Remove the shift lever retaining bolt by placing the locknut on the opposite end of the bolt and tightening to loosen the bolt.

Fig. 7 Removing the shifter boot retaining screws

Fig. 8 Pull the boot up over the shift lever, exposing the sound deadening material

Fig. 9 Examine the condition of the boot and sound deadening material

Fig. 10 If removing the shift lever from the stub shaft, install and tighten the locknut from the opposite side

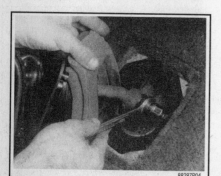

Fig. 11 The shift lever can be removed from the stub shaft by removing the shift lever-to-stub shaft bolt

Fig. 12 To remove the shift lever and stub shaft together, remove the shift dust cover retaining screws

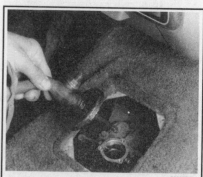

Fig. 13 Removing the shift lever assembly with the stub shaft

7. The shifter may be removed either by removing the bolt retaining the shifter to the shifter stub and then pulling the shifter off or by removing the screws retaining the shifter to the shift housing and remove the shifter and boot assembly.

To install:

8. If shifter was removed from the shifter stub shaft, install the retaining bolt in the shift lever hole so that the flat aligns with the mating flat on the transmission stub shaft. Push the bolt fully into position. Install the nut and tighten to 12–18 ft. lbs. (16–24 Nm).

9. If the shifter and stub shaft were removed together, position the shifter lever into the shift housing aligning the end of the shifter with the slot in the transmission. Install the retaining screws and tighten to 6–8 ft. lbs. (8–11 Nm).

10. Slide the gearshift boot and sound deadening material into position on the gearshift lever and housing, then install the retaining screws.

11. Install the Isolator pan assembly. Install the floor pan cover and floor carpet it removed.

12. Connect the negative battery cable.

Back-up Light Switch

REMOVAL & INSTALLATION

♦ **See Figure 14**

3.03 3-Speed

The back-up light switch is located on the transmission assembly.
1. Disconnect the negative battery cable.
2. Raise and support the vehicle safely with jackstands.
3. Disengage the harness from the back-up light switch.
4. Using a suitable wrench or ratchet/socket, remove the switch from the transmission.

To install:

5. Tread the back-up light switch into the transmission. Tighten the switch 8–12 ft. lbs. (11–16 Nm).

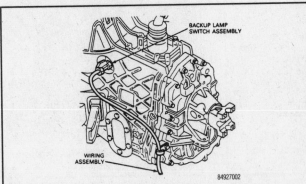

Fig. 14 Typical back-up lamp switch located—mounted on the transmission

---

6. Engage the harness to the switch.
7. Remove the jackstands and lower the vehicle
8. Connect the negative battery cable. Check switch operation.

4-Speed Overdrive Transmission

The Back-up light switch is mounted on to the floor shift assembly on the transmission extension housing on F150–F250 or on a bracket attached to the transmission case for E150–E350 vehicles.
1. Disconnect the negative battery cable.
2. Place the transmission shift lever in any gear except **Reverse**.
3. Raise and support the vehicle safely with jackstands.
4. Disengage the electrical connector from the switch.
5. Using a suitable wrench or ratchet/socket, remove the switch from the shifter housing.

To install:

6. Install the back-up light switch into the floor shift assembly or to the transmission case.
7. Engage the harness to the switch.
8. Remove the jackstands and lower the vehicle
9. Connect the negative battery cable. Check switch operation.

Borg Warner T-18 and T-19; New Process 435; TOD 4 Speed Overdrive

♦ **See Figure 15**

The back-up light switch is located at the rear of the gear shift housing cover.
1. Disconnect the negative battery cable.
2. Raise and support the vehicle safely with jackstands.
3. Disengage the harness from the back-up light switch.
4. Using a suitable wrench or ratchet/socket, remove the switch from the transmission.

To install:

5. Tread the back-up light switch into the transmission. Tighten the switch 15–25 ft. lbs. (20–47 Nm) for T–18 and T–19 or 20–30 ft. lbs. (28–54 Nm) for NP 435 transmission.
6. Engage the harness to the switch.
7. Remove the jackstands and lower the vehicle
8. Connect the negative battery cable. Check switch operation.

Extension Housing Seal

REMOVAL & INSTALLATION

2WD Models

♦ **See Figures 16, 17 and 18**

The extension seal on 2WD drive vehicles is located at the rear of the transmission case.
1. Raise and support the vehicle safely.
2. Drain the transmission of lubricant.

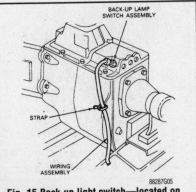

Fig. 15 Back-up light switch—located on the shifter housing

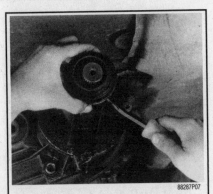

Fig. 16 Removing the extension housing seal

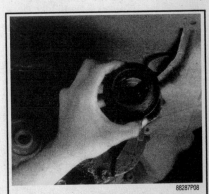

Fig. 17 Always replace the old seal with a new one

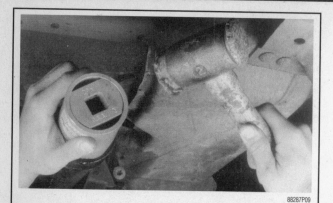

Fig. 18 Using a special tool and mallet, install the new seal

3. Matchmark the driveshaft to the yoke for reassembly and remove the driveshaft.

4. Remove the old seal using a seal puller or appropriate prytool.

To install:

5. Install a new seal, coated with sealing compound, using an appropriate seal installation tool.

➡Tool J-35582 or equivalent is recommended for AX4/5/15 transmissions. Tool J-21426 or equivalent is recommended for Warner T4/5 transmissions.

6. Install the driveshaft, making certain to align the matchmark.

7. Fill the transmission to the level of the fill plug hole. Install the plug and lower the vehicle.

4WD Models

The extension seal on 4WD drive vehicles is located at the rear of the transfer case.

Transmission Assembly

REMOVAL & INSTALLATION

◆ **See Figures 19 thru 25**

☀ CAUTION

The clutch driven disc may contain asbestos, which has been determined to be a cancer causing agent. Never clean clutch surfaces with compressed air! Avoid inhaling any dust from any clutch surface! When cleaning clutch surfaces, use a commercially available brake cleaning fluid.

3.03 3-Speed

1. Disconnect the negative battery cable.
2. Raise the vehicle and safely support it with jackstands.
3. Support the engine with a jack and wood under the oil pan.
4. Drain the transmission.
5. Disconnect the gear shift linkage at the transmission.
6. Disconnect the speedometer cable. Disengage the harness from the back-up light switch.
7. Remove the driveshaft.
8. Raise the transmission just enough to remove the rear support, insulator and retainer assembly.

Fig. 19 Before removing the crossmember bolt, always have the transmission supported

Fig. 20 With the transmission jack in place, remove the frame-to-crossmember bolts

Fig. 21 Removing the frame-to-crossmember bolts on the opposite side

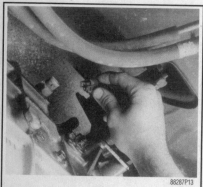

Fig. 22 Disengage any connectors at the transmission

Fig. 23 With the transmission jack in place, remove the transmission mount bolts

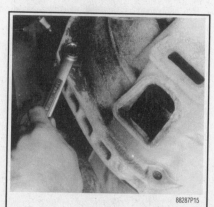

Fig. 24 Remove the bell housing bolts

Fig. 25 Carefully pull the transmission away from the clutch assembly until the input shaft is completely clear

9. Position a transmission jack under the transmission and secure it to the jack.

10. Remove the transmission-to-flywheel housing attaching bolts.

11. Move the transmission to the rear until the input shaft clears the clutch housing.

12. Carefully lower the transmission from the vehicle.

To install:

➡ Prior to installing the transmission, apply a light film of a Multi-Purpose Long-life lubricant to the release bearing inner hub surfaces, release lever fulcrum, fork and transmission front bearing retainer. Be sure to exercise care to avoid contaminating the clutch disc with grease.

13. Secure the transmission on the transmission jack.

14. Raise the transmission until the input shaft splines are in-line with the clutch disc splines. The clutch release bearing and hub must be properly positioned in the release lever fork.

15. Install a guide stud in each lower flywheel housing-to-transmission case mounting bolt holes and align the splines on the input shaft with the spines on the clutch disc.

16. Slide the transmission forward on the guide studs until it contacts the clutch housing.

17. Install the 2 transmission-to-flywheel housing upper mounting bolts. Remove the 2 guide studs and install the lower mounting bolts. Tighten the 4 mounting bolts to 42–50 ft. lbs. (57–67 Nm).

18. Install the rear support, insulator and retainer assembly and tighten the attaching bolts and nuts to 48–65 ft. lbs. (65–88 Nm).

19. Remove the transmission jack and engine jack.

20. Connect the speedometer cable and the driven gear.

21. Install the driveshaft.

22. Connect each shift rod to its respective lever on the transmission.

23. Install the lower extension housing-to-rear mount bolts and tighten to 60–80 ft. lbs. (82–108 Nm). Install the rear mount-to-frame nuts to 50–70 ft. lbs. (68–94 Nm).

24. Adjust the shift linkage as required.

25. Connect the wiring to the back-up light switch.

Warner T-18, T-19A, T-19C 4-Speed

2-WHEEL DRIVE

1. Remove the rubber boot, floor mat, and the body floor pan cover.
2. Remove the gearshift lever, shift ball and boot as an assembly.
3. Raise the vehicle and support it with jackstands.
4. Drain the transmission.
5. Remove the driveshaft.
6. Disconnect the speedometer cable.
7. Remove the crossmember-to-transmission bolts.
8. Secure the transmission to a transmission jack.

9. Remove the crossmember.

10. Remove the 4 transmission-to-bell housing bolts, roll the transmission rearward and remove it.

To install:

➡ You can make installation a lot easier if you fabricate 2 guide pins, made by cutting the heads off of 2 long bolts. These guide pins are inserted into the upper bolt holes in the back of the bell housing and serve to align the bolt holes.

11. Raise the transmission and roll it forward using the guide pins to align the bolt holes. Turn the output shaft by hand to align the input shaft splines with the clutch.

12. Install the 2 lower bolts and snug them down.

13. Remove the guide pins and install the 2 remaining bolts. Torque all 4 bolts to 50 ft. lbs. (68 Nm).

14. Install the crossmember. Crossmember-to-frame bolt torque is 55 ft. lbs. (75 Nm).

15. Remove the transmission jack.

16. Install the Crossmember-to-transmission bolts. Tighten the bolts to 50 ft. lbs. (68 Nm).

17. Connect the speedometer cable.

18. Install the driveshaft.

19. Install the drain plug and fill the transmission. Drain plug torque is 50 ft. lbs. (68 Nm).

20. Lower the vehicle.

21. Install the gearshift lever, shift ball and boot as an assembly.

22. Install the body floor pan cover, floor mat, and the rubber boot.

4-WHEEL DRIVE

1. Remove the rubber boot, floor mat, and the body floor pan cover. Remove the gearshift lever. Remove the weather pad.

2. Remove the transfer case shift lever, shift ball and boot as an assembly.

3. Disconnect the back-up light switch at the rear of the gearshift housing cover.

4. Raise the vehicle and support it with jackstands. Remove the drain and fill plugs and drain the lubricant.

5. Position a transmission jack under the transfer case and disconnect the speedometer cable.

6. Matchmark the flanges and disconnect the rear driveshaft from the transfer case. Wire it up and out of the way.

7. Matchmark and disconnect the front driveshaft at the transfer case. Wire it up and out of the way.

8. Remove the shift link from the transfer case.

9. Unbolt the transfer case from the transmission (6 bolts) and lower the transfer case from the vehicle.

10. Position the transmission jack under the transmission.

11. Remove the 8 rear transmission support-to-transmission bolts.

12. Remove the rear transmission support.

13. Remove the 4 transmission-to-clutch housing attaching bolts.

14. Move the transmission to the rear until the input shaft clears the flywheel housing and lower the transmission.

To install:

➡ You can make installation a lot easier if you fabricate 2 guide pins, made by cutting the heads off of 2 long bolts. These guide pins are inserted into the upper bolt holes in the back of the bell housing and serve to align the bolt holes.

15. Before installing the transmission, apply a light film of grease to the inner hub surface of the clutch release bearing, the release lever fulcrum and the front bearing retainer of the transmission. Do not apply excessive grease because it will fly off onto the clutch disc.

16. Install the transmission in the reverse order of removal. It may be necessary to turn the output shaft with the transmission in gear to align the input shaft splines with the splines in the clutch disc. Fill the transmission with SAE 80W/90 lubricant if it was drained. The transfer case is filled with Dexron®II ATF. Observe the following torque specifications:

- Back-up light switch: 25 ft. lbs. (34 Nm)
- Transmission-to-clutch housing bolts: 65 ft. lbs. (88 Nm)
- Transfer case-to-transmission: 40 ft. lbs. (54 Nm)
- Drain plug: 50 ft. lbs. (68 Nm)
- Fill plug: 50 ft. lbs. (68 Nm)

- Transmission to rear support: 80 ft. lbs. (108 Nm)
- Rear support-to-frame: 55 ft. lbs. (75 Nm)

New Process 435 4-Speed

2-WHEEL DRIVE

1. Remove the floor mat.
2. Remove the shift lever boot.
3. Remove the floor pan, transmission cover plate, and weather pad. It may be necessary to remove the seat assembly.
4. Remove the shift lever and knob by first removing the inner cap using tool T73T–7220–A, or equivalent. Then, remove the spring seat and spring. Remove the shift lever from the housing.
5. Disconnect the back-up light switch located in the left side of the gearshift housing cover.
6. Raise the vehicle and place jackstands under the frame to support it. Place a transmission jack under the transmission and disconnect the speedometer cable.
7. Matchmark and disconnect the driveshaft.
8. Remove the transmission rear support.
9. Remove the transmission-to-flywheel housing attaching bolts, slide the transmission rearward until the input shaft clears the flywheel housing and lower it out from under the truck.
10. Before installing the transmission, apply a light film of grease of the inner hub surface of the clutch release bearing, release lever fulcrum and fork, and the front bearing retainer of the transmission. Do not apply excessive grease because if will fly off and contaminate the clutch disc.
11. Install the transmission in the reverse order of removal. It may be necessary to turn the output shaft with the transmission in gear to align the input shaft splines with the splines in the clutch disc. The front bearing retainer is installed through the clutch release bearing. Observe the following torques:
- Transmission-to-clutch housing bolts: 65 ft. lbs. (88 Nm)
- Back-up light switch: 25 ft. lbs. (34 Nm)
- Drain and fill plugs: 30 ft. lbs. (41 Nm)
- Transmission-to-support: 80 ft. lbs. (108 Nm)
- Support-to-frame: 55 ft. lbs. (75 Nm)

4-WHEEL DRIVE

1. Remove the transmission lever rubber boot and floor mat.
2. Remove the transfer case shift lever, boot and ball as an assembly.
3. Remove the floor pan, transmission cover plate, and weather pad. It may be necessary to remove the seat assembly.
4. Remove the shift lever and knob by first removing the inner cap using tool T73T–7220–A, or equivalent. Then, remove the spring seat and spring. Remove the shift lever from the housing.
5. Disconnect the back-up light switch located in the left side of the gearshift housing cover.
6. Raise the vehicle and place jackstands under the frame to support it. Place a transmission jack under the transfer case and disconnect the speedometer cable.
7. Drain the transfer case.
8. Matchmark and disconnect the front driveshaft from the transfer case. Wire is up out of the way.
9. Matchmark and disconnect the rear driveshaft from the transfer case. Wire it up out of the way.
10. Disconnect the shift link from the transfer case.
11. Remove the 3 bolts securing the transfer case to the support bracket.
12. Remove the 6 bolts securing the transfer case to the transmission.
13. Lower the transfer case from the truck.
14. Place the transmission jack under the transmission.
15. Remove the transmission rear support.
16. Remove the transmission-to-flywheel housing attaching bolts, slide the transmission rearward until the input shaft clears the flywheel housing and lower it out from under the truck.

To install:

17. Before installing the transmission, apply a light film of grease of the inner hub surface of the clutch release bearing, release lever fulcrum and fork, and the front bearing retainer of the transmission. Do not apply excessive grease because if will fly off and contaminate the clutch disc.
18. Install the transmission in the reverse order of removal. It may be neces-

sary to turn the output shaft with the transmission in gear to align the input shaft splines with the splines in the clutch disc. The front bearing retainer is installed through the clutch release bearing. Observe the following torques:
- Back-up light switch: 25 ft. lbs. (34 Nm)
- Transmission-to-clutch housing bolts: 65 ft. lbs. (88 Nm)
- Drain and fill plugs: 30 ft. lbs. (41 Nm)
- Transmission-to-support: 80 ft. lbs. (108 Nm)
- Support-to-frame: 55 ft. lbs. (75 Nm)
- Transfer case-to-transmission: 40 ft. lbs. (54 Nm)

Ford TOD 4-Speed Overdrive

2-WHEEL DRIVE

1. Raise the truck and support it on jackstands. Drain the transmission.
2. Mark the driveshaft so that it can be installed in the same position.
3. Disconnect the driveshaft at the rear U-joint and slide it off the transmission output shaft.
4. Disconnect the speedometer cable, back-up light switch and high gear switch from the transmission.
5. Remove the shift rods from the levers and the shift control from the extension housing.
6. Support the engine on a jack and remove the extension housing-to-crossmember bolts. Raise the engine just high enough to take the weight off the rear crossmember. Remove the crossmember.
7. Support the transmission on a jack and unbolt it from the clutch housing.
8. Move the transmission and jack rearward until clear. If necessary, lower the engine enough for clearance.

To install:

9. Installation is the reverse of removal. It is a good idea to install and snug down the upper transmission-to-engine bolts first, then the lower. For linkage adjustment, see the beginning of this Section. check the fluid level. Observe the following torques:
- Back-up light switch: 25 ft. lbs. (34 Nm)
- Transmission-to-clutch housing bolts: 65 ft. lbs. (88 Nm)
- Drain and fill plugs: 30 ft. lbs. (41 Nm)
- Transmission-to-support: 80 ft. lbs. (108 Nm)
- Support-to-frame: 55 ft. lbs. (75 Nm)

4-WHEEL DRIVE

1. Raise the truck and support it on jackstands. Drain the transmission and transfer case.
2. Mark the driveshaft so that it can be installed in the same position.
3. Matchmark and disconnect the front and rear driveshafts at the transfer case.
4. Disconnect the speedometer cable and 4WD drive indicator switch from the transfer case; the back-up light switch and high gear switch from the transmission.
5. Remove the skid plate.
6. Disconnect the shift link from the transfer case.
7. Remove the shift lever from the transmission.
8. Support the transmission on a jack and remove the transmission housing rear support bracket.
9. Raise the transmission just high enough to take the weight off the rear crossmember.
10. Remove the 2 nuts securing the upper gusset to the frame on both sides of the frame.
11. Remove the nut and bolt connecting the gusset to the support. Remove the gusset on the left side.
12. Remove the transmission-to-support plate bolts.
13. Remove the support plate and right gusset.
14. Remove the crossmember.
15. Remove the transfer case heat shield. Be very careful if the catalytic converter is hot!
16. Support the transfer case on a jack and unbolt it from the transmission.
17. Move the transfer case and jack rearward until clear and lower it. Discard the adapter gasket.
18. Support the transmission on a jack and unbolt it from the clutch housing.
19. Move the transmission and jack rearward until clear. If necessary, lower the engine for clearance.

To install:

20. Installation is the reverse of removal. It is a good idea to install and snug down the upper transmission-to-clutch housing bolts first, then the lower. For linkage adjustment, see the beginning of this Section. Check the fluid level. Observe the following torques:

- Back-up light switch: 25 ft. lbs. (34 Nm)
- Transmission-to-clutch housing bolts: 65 ft. lbs. (88 Nm)
- Transfer case-to-transmission: 40 ft. lbs. (54 Nm)
- Rear driveshaft-to-yoke: 25 ft. lbs. (34)
- Front driveshaft-to-yoke: 15 ft. lbs. (20 Nm)
- Drain and fill plugs: 30 ft. lbs. (41 Nm)
- Transmission-to-support: 80 ft. lbs. (108 Nm)
- Support-to-frame: 55 ft. lbs. (75 Nm)

Mazda M5OD 5-Speed

1. Raise and support the truck on jackstands. Prop the clutch pedal in the full up position with a block of wood.
2. Matchmark the driveshaft-to-flange relation.
3. Disconnect the driveshaft at the rear axle and slide it off of the transmission output shaft. Lubricant will leak out of the transmission so be prepared to catch it, or plug the opening with rags or a seal installation tool.
4. Disconnect the speedometer cable at the transmission.
5. Disconnect the shift rods from the shift levers.
6. Remove the shift control from the extension housing and transmission case.
7. On 4WD drive models, remove the transfer case.
8. Remove the extension housing-to-rear support bolts.
9. Take up the weight of the transmission with a transmission jack. Chain the transmission to the jack.
10. Raise the transmission just enough to take the weight off of the No.3 crossmember.
11. Unbolt the crossmember from the frame rails and remove it.
12. Place a jackstand under the rear of the engine at the bell housing.
13. Lower the jack and allow the jackstand to take the weight of the engine. The engine should be angled slightly downward to allow the transmission to roll backward.
14. Remove the transmission-to bell housing bolts.
15. Roll the jack rearward until the input shaft clears the bell housing. Lower the jack and remove the transmission.

❊❊ WARNING

Do not depress the clutch pedal with the transmission removed.

To install:

16. Clean all machined mating surfaces thoroughly.
17. Install a guide pin in each lower bolt hole. Position the spacer plate on the guide pins.
18. Raise the transmission and start the input shaft through the clutch release bearing.
19. Align the input shaft splines with the clutch disc splines. Roll the trans-

mission forward so that the input shaft will enter the clutch disc. If the shaft binds in the release bearing, work the release arm back and forth.

20. Once the transmission is all the way in, install the 2 upper retaining bolts and washers and remove the lower guide pins. Install the lower bolts. Tighten the bolts to 50 ft. lbs. (68 Nm).
21. Raise the transmission just enough to allow installation of the No. 3 crossmember.
22. Install the crossmember on the frame rails. Tighten the bolts to 80 ft. lbs. (108 Nm).
23. Lower the transmission onto the crossmember and install the nuts. Tighten the nuts to 70 ft. lbs. (95 Nm).
24. Remove the transmission jack.
25. The balance of installation is the reverse of removal.

ZF S5-42 and ZF S5-47 5-Speed

1. Place the transmission in **Neutral**.
2. Remove the carpet or floor mat.
3. Remove the ball from the shift lever.
4. Remove the boot and bezel assembly from the floor.
5. Remove the 2 bolts and disengage the upper shift lever from the lower shift lever.
6. Raise and support the tuck on jackstands.
7. Disconnect the speedometer cable.
8. Disconnect the back-up switch wire.
9. Place a drain pan under the case and drain the case through the drain plug.
10. Position a transmission jack under the case and safety-chain the case to the jack.
11. Remove the driveshaft.
12. Disconnect the clutch linkage.
13. On F-Super Duty models, remove the transmission-mounted parking brake. See Section 9.
14. On 4WD drive models, remove the transfer case.
15. Remove the transmission rear insulator and lower retainer.
16. Unbolt and remove the crossmember.
17. Remove the transmission-to-engine block bolts.
18. Roll the transmission rearward until the input shaft clears, lower the jack and remove the transmission.

To install:

19. Install 2 guide studs into the lower bolt holes.
20. Raise the transmission until the input shaft splines are aligned with the clutch disc splines. The clutch release bearing and hub must be properly positioned in the release lever fork.
21. Position the transmission forward into the front case.
22. Install and tighten the bolts to 50 ft. lbs. (68 Nm), then remove the guide studs and install the 2 remaining bolts.
23. Install the crossmember, tighten the bolts to 55 ft. lbs. (68 Nm).
24. Install the transmission rear insulator and lower retainer. Tighten the bolts to 60 ft. lbs. (81 Nm).
25. On 4WD drive models, install the transfer case.
26. The balance of installation is the reverse of removal.

CLUTCH

Clutch Disc and Pressure Plate

REMOVAL & INSTALLATION

♦ **See Figures 26 thru 36**

❊❊ CAUTION

The clutch driven disc contains asbestos, which has been determined to be a cancer causing agent. Never clean clutch surfaces with compressed air! Avoid inhaling any dust from any clutch surface! When cleaning clutch surfaces, use a commercially available brake cleaning fluid.

1987 Models

1. Raise and support the truck end on jackstands.
2. Remove the clutch slave cylinder.
3. Remove the transmission.
4. If the clutch housing does not have a dust cover, remove the starter. Remove the flywheel housing attaching bolts and remove the housing.
5. If the flywheel housing does have a dust cover, remove the cover and then remove the release lever and bearing from the clutch housing: To remove the release lever:
   a. Remove the dust boot.
   b. Push the release lever forward to compress the slave cylinder.
   c. On all engines except the diesel and the 7.5L gasoline engines, remove the plastic clip that retains the slave cylinder to the bracket. Remove the slave cylinder.

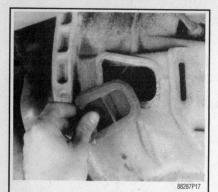

Fig. 26 Remove the inspection plug to view the clutch assembly components

Fig. 27 View of the clutch assembly with the transmission removed

Fig. 28 Always use a clutch pilot tool during removal or installation of the clutch assembly

Fig. 29 Using a holding tool, hold the driveplate and remove the clutch pressure plate-to-driveplate bolts

Fig. 30 When removing the pressure plate be careful not to allow the fiction disc to drop

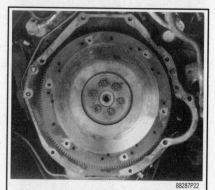

Fig. 31 Examine the driveplate for cracks, heat spots and scoring

Fig. 32 Using a holding tool, hold the drive plate and remove the driveplate bolts

Fig. 33 Exercise extreme care when removing the driveplate, it is heavy

Fig. 34 View of the rear engine section with the driveplate removed

Fig. 35 Use a torque wrench to tighten the driveplate bolts and a crisscross pattern

Fig. 36 With the clutch pilot tool in place, use a torque wrench to tighten the pressure plate-to-driveplate bolts

d. On the diesel and the 7.5L, the steel retaining clip is permanently attached to the slave cylinder. Remove the slave cylinder by prying on the clip to free the tangs while pulling the cylinder clear.

e. Remove the release lever by pulling it outward.

6. Mark the pressure plate and cover assembly and the flywheel so that they can be reinstalled in the same relative position.

7. Loosen the pressure plate and cover attaching bolts evenly in a staggered sequence a turn at time until the pressure plate springs are relieved of their tension. Remove the attaching bolts.

8. Remove the pressure plate and cover assembly and the clutch disc from the flywheel.

To install:

9. Position the clutch disc on the flywheel so that an aligning tool or spare transmission mainshaft can enter the clutch pilot bearing and align the disc.

10. When reinstalling the original pressure plate and cover assembly, align the assembly and flywheel according to the marks made during removal. Position the pressure plate and cover assembly on the flywheel, align the pressure plate and disc, and install the retaining bolts. Tighten the bolts in an alternating sequence a few turns at a time until the proper torque is reached:

• 10 in. and 12 in. clutch: 15–20 ft. lbs. (20–27 Nm)
• 11 in. clutch: 20–29 ft. lbs. (27–39 Nm)

11. Remove the tool used to align the clutch disc.

12. With the clutch fully released, apply a light coat of grease on the sides of the driving lugs.

13. Position the clutch release bearing and the bearing hub on the release lever. Install the release lever on the fulcrum in the flywheel housing. Apply a light coating of grease to the release lever fingers and the fulcrum. Fill the groove of the release bearing hub with grease.

14. If the flywheel housing has been removed, position it against the rear engine cover plate and install the attaching bolts and tighten them to 40–50 ft. lbs. (54–68 Nm).

15. Install the starter motor.

16. Install the transmission.

17. Install the salve cylinder and bleed the system.

1988–89 Models

1. Raise and support the truck end on jackstands.

2. On trucks with the externally mounted slave cylinder, remove the clutch slave cylinder. On trucks with an internally mounted slave cylinder, disconnect the quick-disconnect coupling with a spring coupling tool such as T88T-70522-A.

3. Remove the transmission.

4. On gasoline engine models, except the 7.5L engine, remove the starter. Remove the flywheel housing attaching bolts and remove the housing. On diesel engine models and the 7.5L gasoline engine, remove the cover and then remove the release lever and bearing from the clutch housing. To remove the release lever:

a. Remove the dust boot.

b. Push the release lever forward to compress the slave cylinder.

c. Remove the slave cylinder by prying on the steel clip to free the tangs while pulling the cylinder clear.

d. Remove the release lever by pulling it outward.

5. Mark the pressure plate and cover assembly and the flywheel so that they can be reinstalled in the same relative position.

6. Loosen the pressure plate and cover attaching bolts evenly in a staggered sequence a turn at time until the pressure plate springs are relieved of their tension. Remove the attaching bolts.

7. Remove the pressure plate and cover assembly and the clutch disc from the flywheel.

To install:

8. Position the clutch disc on the flywheel so that an aligning tool or spare transmission mainshaft can enter the clutch pilot bearing and align the disc.

9. When reinstalling the original pressure plate and cover assembly, align the assembly and flywheel according to the marks made during removal. Position the pressure plate and cover assembly on the flywheel, align the pressure plate and disc, and install the retaining bolts. Tighten the bolts in an alternating sequence a few turns at a time until the proper torque is reached:

• 10 in. and 12 in. clutch: 15–20 ft. lbs. (20–27 Nm)
• 11 in. clutch: 20–29 ft. lbs. (27–39 Nm)

10. Remove the tool used to align the clutch disc.

11. With the clutch fully released, apply a light coat of grease on the sides of the driving lugs.

12. Position the clutch release bearing and the bearing hub on the release lever. Install the release lever on the fulcrum in the flywheel housing. Apply a light coating of grease to the release lever fingers and the fulcrum. Fill the groove of the release bearing hub with grease.

13. If the flywheel housing has been removed, position it against the rear engine cover plate and install the attaching bolts and tighten them to 40–50 ft. lbs. (54–68 Nm).

14. Install the starter motor, if removed.

15. Install the transmission.

16. Install the salve cylinder and bleed the system.

1990–96

▶ See Figures 37 and 38

1. Raise and support the truck end on jackstands.

2. On trucks with the externally mounted slave cylinder, remove the clutch slave cylinder. On trucks with an internally mounted slave cylinder, disconnect the quick-disconnect coupling with a spring coupling tool such as T88T-70522-A.

3. Remove the transmission.

4. On models with the internally mounted slave cylinder, remove the starter. Remove the flywheel housing attaching bolts and remove the housing. On models with the externally mounted slave cylinder, remove the cover and then remove the release lever and bearing from the clutch housing. To remove the release lever:

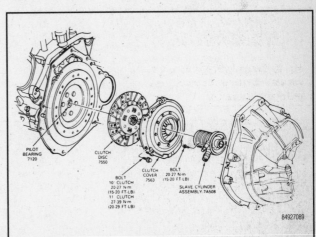

Fig. 37 Clutch assembly for 1990–96 F-150, F-250, and Bronco with the 4.9L, 5.0L and 5.8L engines, except with the Borg-Warner T-18 transmission

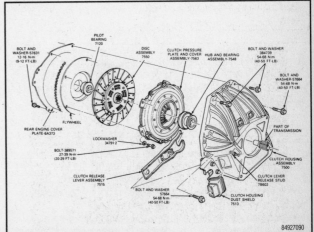

Fig. 38 Clutch assembly for 1990–93 F-150, F-250, and Bronco with 4.9L, and 5.0L engines, with the Borg-Warner T-18 transmission

a. Remove the dust boot.

b. Push the release lever forward to compress the slave cylinder.

c. Remove the slave cylinder by prying on the steel clip to free the tangs while pulling the cylinder clear.

d. Remove the release lever by pulling it outward.

5. Mark the pressure plate and cover assembly and the flywheel so that they can be reinstalled in the same relative position.

6. Loosen the pressure plate and cover attaching bolts evenly in a staggered sequence a turn at time until the pressure plate springs are relieved of their tension. Remove the attaching bolts.

7. Remove the pressure plate and cover assembly and the clutch disc from the flywheel.

To install:

8. Position the clutch disc on the flywheel so that an aligning tool or spare transmission mainshaft can enter the clutch pilot bearing and align the disc.

✲✲ WARNING

New pressure plate/cover bolts have been issued for use on the diesel and the 7.5L gasoline engine. The bolts for the diesel are 5/16 in. X 18 X 3/4 in. The bolts for the 7.5L are 5/16 in. X 18 X 59/64 in. The 59/64 in. bolts cannot be used with the dual mass flywheel used on the diesel, since they would interfere with the operation of the primary flywheel.

9. When reinstalling the original pressure plate and cover assembly, align the assembly and flywheel according to the marks made during removal. Position the pressure plate and cover assembly on the flywheel, align the pressure plate and disc, and install the retaining bolts. Tighten the bolts in an alternating sequence a few turns at a time until the proper torque is reached:

- 10 in. and 12 in. clutch: 15–20 ft. lbs. (20–27 Nm)
- 11 in. clutch: 20–29 ft. lbs. (27–39 Nm)

10. Remove the tool used to align the clutch disc.

11. With the clutch fully released, apply a light coat of grease on the sides of the driving lugs.

12. Position the clutch release bearing and the bearing hub on the release lever. On the diesel and the 7.5L engine, clean and lubricate the transmission bearing retainer. Install the release lever on the fulcrum in the flywheel housing. Apply a light coating of grease to the release lever fingers and the fulcrum. Fill the groove of the release bearing hub with grease.

13. If the flywheel housing has been removed, position it against the rear engine cover plate and install the attaching bolts and tighten them to 40–50 ft. lbs. (54–68 Nm).

14. Install the starter motor, if removed.

15. Install the transmission.

16. Install the salve cylinder and bleed the system.

Master Cylinder and Slave Cylinder

The hydraulic clutch system operates much like a hydraulic brake system. When you push down (disengage) the clutch pedal, the mechanical clutch pedal movement is converted into hydraulic fluid movement, which is then converted back into mechanical movement by the slave cylinder to actuate the clutch release lever.

The system consists of a combination clutch fluid reservoir/master cylinder assembly, a slave cylinder mounted on the bell housing, and connecting tubing.

Fluid level is checked at the master cylinder reservoir. The hydraulic clutch system continually remains in adjustment, like a hydraulic disc brake system, so not clutch linkage or pedal adjustment is necessary.

REMOVAL & INSTALLATION

There are 2 types of slave cylinders used: an internally mounted (in the bell housing) and an externally mounted type.

- 1987 models use the externally mounted type
- 1988–89 diesel engines and the 7.5L gasoline engine use the externally mounted type; all others use the internally mounted type
- 1990–96 diesel engines, 7.5L gasoline engines and V8 gasoline engines equipped with the M50DHD transmission use the externally mounted type; all others use the internally mounted type

✲✲ WARNING

Prior to any service on models with the externally mounted slave cylinder, that requires removal of the slave cylinder, such as transmission and/or clutch housing removal, the clutch master cylinder pushrod must be disconnected from the clutch pedal. Failure to do this may damage the slave cylinder if the clutch pedal is depressed while the slave cylinder is disconnected.

1. From inside the vehicle, pry the pushrod and retainer bushing from the cross shaft lever pin.

2. Disconnect the interlock switch connector plug.

3. Remove the 2 retaining nuts and support bracket connecting the clutch reservoir and master cylinder assembly to the firewall.

4. From the engine compartment, first note the clutch tube routing to the slave cylinder, then remove the attaching hardware for the hydraulic tube retaining clips.

5. From the engine compartment, remove the clutch reservoir and master cylinder assembly from the firewall. On F-Series and Bronco, when the master cylinder studs are free of the dash panel, rotate cylinder counterclockwise about 100 degrees to clear the interlock switch and remove the cylinder from the vehicle.

6. On 7.3L diesel and 7.5L gas engine vehicles, use a suitable prytool and lift the 2 retaining tabs of the slave cylinder retaining bracket. Disengage the tabs from the bell housing lugs and then slide outward and remove.

7. On 4.9L, 5.0 and 5.8L engine vehicles, depress the release ring on the tube quick disconnect and gently pull the connector free of the concentric slave cylinder fitting.

8. Remove the clutch hydraulic system from the vehicle.

To Install:

9. Position the clutch fluid reservoir and master cylinder assembly into the firewall from inside the cab install the 2 nuts.

10. Correctly route the hydraulic tubing and sleeve cylinder to the transmission bell housing.

➡ **Care must be taken during routing of the nylon line to keep away from the engine exhaust system.**

11. Reinstall the clutch tube retaining clips.

➡ **Before installing external type slave cylinders, perform the clutch system bleeding procedure.**

12. On 7.3L diesel and 7.5L gas engine vehicles, install the slave cylinder by pushing the slave cylinder pushrod into the cylinder. Engage the pushrod into the release lever and slide the slave cylinder into the bell housing lugs. Seat the cylinder into the recess in the lugs.

13. On 4.9L, 5.0 and 5.8L engine vehicles, push the tube quick disconnect back onto the concentric slave cylinder fitting.

➡ **When installing a new hydraulic system, the external slave cylinder used on 7.3L diesel and 7.5L gas engine vehicles, contains a shipping strap that pre-positions the pushrod for installation and also provides a bearing insert. When installation of the slave cylinder is completed, the first actuation of the clutch pedal will beak the shipping strap and give normal system operation.**

Concentric Slave Cylinder

♦ See Figures 39 thru 48

This type slave cylinder is internally located inside the bell housing on the transmission input shaft. Removal of the transmission is required in order to replace it.

1. Disconnect the negative battery cable.

2. Disconnect the fluid coupling at the transmission, using the clutch coupling removal tool T88T-70522-A or equivalent. Slide the white plastic sleeve toward the slave cylinder while applying a slight tug on the tube.

➡ **If the special coupling tool is not available, the fluid coupling can be uncoupled by using a flat-bladed tool. Carefully pressing in around the coupling while applying a slight tug on the tube.**

3. Remove the transmission assembly.

4. Remove the slave cylinder-to-transmission retaining bolts.

5. Remove the slave cylinder from the transmission input shaft.

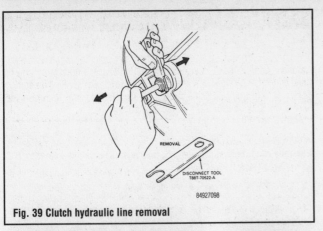

Fig. 39 Clutch hydraulic line removal

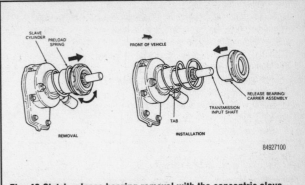

Fig. 40 Clutch release bearing removal with the concentric slave cylinder

Fig. 41 View of the concentric slave cylinder and throwout bearing assembly

Fig. 42 Removing the throwout bearing from the slave cylinder

Fig. 43 Removing the concentric slave cylinder attaching bolts

Fig. 44 Removing the concentric slave cylinder from the bell housing

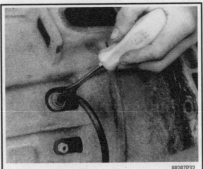

Fig. 45 If the special coupling tool is not available, the fluid coupling can be uncoupled with a flat-bladed tool

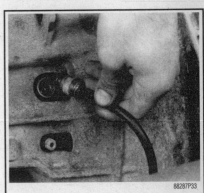

Fig. 46 Gently pull fluid hose from the fitting

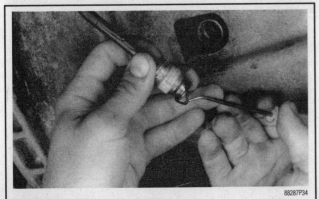

Fig. 47 Always replace the O-ring seal

Fig. 48 Use a box wrench to bleed the concentric slave cylinder at bleeder valve

To install:

6. Fit the slave cylinder over the transmission input shaft with the bleed screws and coupling facing the left side of the transmission.

7. Install the slave cylinder retaining bolts. Tighten to 14–19 ft. lbs. (19–26 Nm).

8. Install the transmission.

9. Connect the coupling to the slave cylinder.

10. Properly bleed the hydraulic system.

11. Connect the negative battery cable.

HYDRAULIC SYSTEM BLEEDING

Externally Mounted Slave Cylinder

▶ **See Figure 49**

1. Clean the reservoir cap and the slave cylinder connection.

2. Remove the slave cylinder from the housing.

3. Using a 3/32 in. punch, drive out the pin that holds the tube in place.

4. Remove the tube from the slave cylinder and place the end of the tube in a container.

5. Hold the slave cylinder so that the connector port is at the highest point, by tipping it about 30° from horizontal. Fill the cylinder with DOT 3 brake fluid through the port. It may be necessary to rock the cylinder or slightly depress the pushrod to expel all the air.

✳✳ WARNING

Pushing too hard on the pushrod will spurt fluid from the port!

6. When all air is expelled (no more bubble are seen), install the slave cylinder.

➡ **Some fluid will be expelled during installation as the pushrod is depressed.**

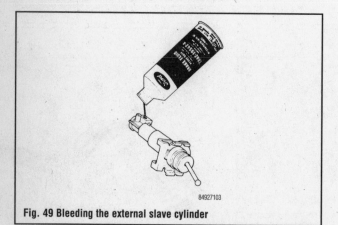

Fig. 49 Bleeding the external slave cylinder

7. Remove the reservoir cap. Some fluid will run out of the tube end into the container. Pour fluid into the reservoir until a steady stream of fluid runs out of the tube and the reservoir is filled. Quickly install the diaphragm and cap. The flow should stop.

8. Connect the tube and install the pin. Check the fluid level.

9. Check the clutch operation.

Internally Mounted Slave Cylinder

▶ **See Figure 50**

➡ **With the quick-disconnect coupling, no air should enter the system when the coupling is disconnected. However, if air should somehow enter the system, it must be bled.**

1. Remove the reservoir cap and diaphragm. Fill the reservoir with DOT 3 brake fluid.

2. Connect a piece of rubber tubing to the slave cylinder bleed screw. Place the other end in a container.

3. Loosen the bleed screw. Gravity will force fluid from the master cylinder to flow down to the slave cylinder, forcing air out of the bleed screw. When a steady stream with no bubbles flows out, the system is bled. Close the bleed screw.

➡ **Check periodically to make sure the master cylinder reservoir doesn't run dry.**

4. Add fluid to fill the master cylinder reservoir.

5. Fully depress the clutch pedal. Release it as quickly as possible. Pause for 2 seconds. Repeat this procedure 10 times.

6. Check the fluid level. Refill it if necessary. It should be kept full.

7. Repeat Steps 5 and 6 five more times.

8. Install the diaphragm and cap.

9. Have an assistant hold the pedal to the floor while you crack the bleed screw (not too far—just far enough to expel any trapped air). Close the bleed screw, then release the pedal.

10. Check, and if necessary, fill the reservoir.

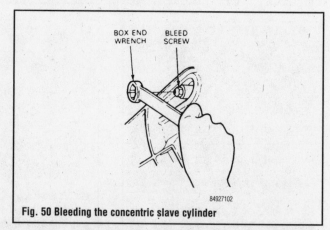

Fig. 50 Bleeding the concentric slave cylinder

AUTOMATIC TRANSMISSION

Adjustments

INTERMEDIATE BAND ADJUSTMENT

C6 Only

▶ **See Figure 51**

1. Raise the truck on a hoist or jackstands.

2. Clean all dirt away from the band adjusting screw. Remove and discard the locknut.

3. Install a new locknut and tighten the adjusting screw to 10 ft. lbs. (13 Nm).

4. Back off the adjusting screw exactly 1½ turns.

5. Hold the adjusting screw from turning and tighten the locknut to 35–40 ft. lbs. (47–54 Nm).

6. Remove the jackstands and lower the vehicle.

SHIFT LINKAGE ADJUSTMENT

Shift Rod

1. With the engine stopped, place the transmission selector lever at the steering column in the D position for the C6 or the D overdrive position for the AOD and E4OD, and hold the lever against the stop by hanging an 8 lb. weight from the lever handle.

2. Loosen the shift rod adjusting nut at the transmission lever.

3. Shift the manual lever at the transmission to the **D** position, two detents from the rear. On the F-150 with 4WD and Bronco, move the bell crank lever.

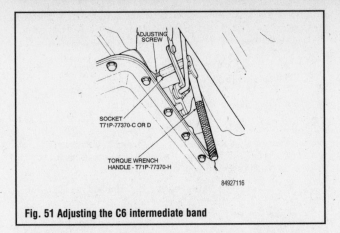

Fig. 51 Adjusting the C6 intermediate band

4. With the selector lever and transmission manual lever in the D or D over-drive position, tighten the adjusting nut to 12–18 ft. lbs. (16–24 Nm). Do not allow the rod or shift lever to move while tightening the nut. Remove the weight.

5. Check the operation of the shift linkage.

Shift Cable

1. With the engine stopped, place the transmission selector lever at the steering column in the D position for the C6 or the D overdrive position for the AODE-W, 4R70W and E4OD.

2. Hang a 3 lb. (1.4 kg) weight on the end of the shift lever.

3. Pry the end of the shift cable from the transmission control lever ball stud.

4. Unlock the adjuster body, release the lock tab on the top side of the cable by pushing down on the 2 tangs.

5. Check to be sure the cable moves freely without binding.

6. Move the lever on the transmission all the way rearward and then 3 detent positions forward.

7. Holding the cable end fitting, push the cable rearward until the end fitting lines up with the manual control lever ball stud.

8. Push up on the lock tab to lock the adjuster body in the correctly adjusted position. Be sure the locator tab is properly seated in the bracket.

9. Make certain the shift cable is clipped to the floor pan at the white cable mark and the cable is routed into the tunnel.

10. Adjust the shift indicator pointer while the transmission is still in the overdrive position.

11. Remove the weight and check the control lever in all shift positions.

THROTTLE VALVE LINKAGE ADJUSTMENT

▶ **See Figures 52, 53, 54 and 55**

AOD Transmission With Carbureted Fuel System

ADJUSTMENT AT THE CARBURETOR

The TV control linkage may be adjusted at the carburetor using the following procedure:

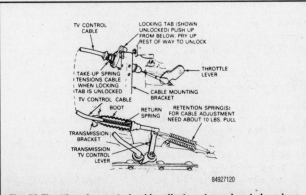

Fig. 52 Throttle valve control cable adjustment—carbureted engines

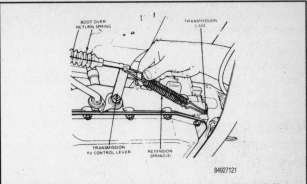

Fig. 53 Throttle valve lever retention spring on the 4.9L and 5.0L engines

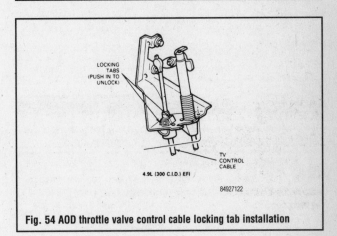

Fig. 54 AOD throttle valve control cable locking tab installation

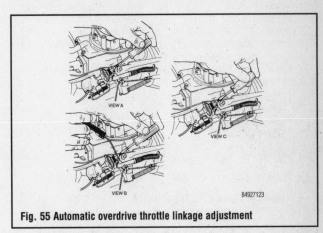

Fig. 55 Automatic overdrive throttle linkage adjustment

1. Check that engine idle speed is set at the specification.

2. De-cam the fast idle cam on the carburetor so that the throttle lever is at its idle stop. Place shift lever in **Neutral**, set park brake (engine off).

3. Back out the linkage lever adjusting screw all the way (screw end if flush with lever face).

4. Turn in adjusting screw until a thin shim (0.005 in. max.) or piece of writing paper fits snugly between end of screw and Throttle Lever. To eliminate effect of friction, push linkage lever forward (tending to close gap) and release before checking clearance between end of screw and throttle lever. Do not apply any load on levers with tools or hands while checking gap.

5. Turn in adjusting screw an additional four turns. (Four turns are preferred. Two turns minimum is permissible if screw travel is limited).

6. If it is not possible to turn in adjusting screw at least two addition turns. or if there was sufficient screw adjusting capacity to obtain an initial gap in Step 2 above, refer to Linkage Adjustment at Transmission. Whenever it is required to adjust idle speed by more than 50 rpm, the adjustment screw on the linkage lever at the carburetor should also be readjusted as shown.

Idle Speed Change/Turns on Linkage Lever Adjustment Screw
- Less than 50 rpm: No change required
- 50 to 100 rpm increase: 1½ turns out
- 50 to 100 rpm decrease: 1½ turns in
- 100 to 150 rpm increase: 2½ turns out
- 100 to 150 rpm decrease: 2½ turns in

After making any idle speed adjustments, always verify the linkage lever and throttle lever are in contact with the throttle lever at its idle stop and the shift lever is in **Neutral**.

ADJUSTMENT AT TRANSMISSION

The linkage lever adjustment screw has limited adjustment capability. It is not possible to adjust the TV linkage using this screw, the length of the TV control rod assembly must be readjusted using the following procedure. This procedure must also be followed whenever a new TV control rod assembly is installed.

This procedure requires placing the vehicle on jackstands to give access to the linkage components at the transmission TV control lever.

1. Set the engine curb idle speed to specification.
2. With engine off, de-cam the fast idle cam on the carburetor so that the throttle lever is against the idle stop. Place shift lever in **Neutral** and set park brake (engine off).
3. Set the linkage lever adjustment screw at its approximately mid-range.
4. If a new TV control rod assembly is being installed, connect the rod to the linkage lever at the carburetor.

✳✳ CAUTION

The following steps involve working in proximity to the exhaust system. Allow the exhaust system to cool before proceeding.

5. Raise the vehicle on the hoist.
6. Using a 13mm box end wrench, loosen the bolt on the sliding trunnion block on the TV control rod assembly. Remove any corrosion from the control rod and free-up the trunnion block so that it slides freely on the control rod. Insert pin into transmission lever grommet.
7. Push up on the lower end of the control rod to insure that the linkage lever at carburetor is firmly against the throttle lever. Release force on rod. Rod must stay up.
8. Push the TV control lever on the transmission up against its internal stop with a firm force (approximately 5 pounds) and tighten the bolt on the trunnion block. do not relax force on lever until nut is tightened.
9. Lower the vehicle and verify that the throttle lever is still against the idle stop. If not, repeat Steps 2 through 9.

THROTTLE VALVE CABLE ADJUSTMENT

▶ See Figures 56 and 57

AOD Transmission With Fuel Injection

ADJUSTMENT WITH ENGINE OFF

1. Set the parking brake and put the selector lever in **Neutral**.
2. Remove the protective cover from the cable.

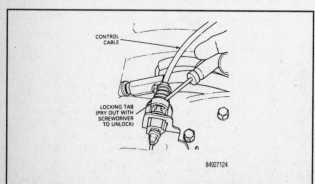

Fig. 56 Unlocking the tab at the throttle body on the 5.0L engine

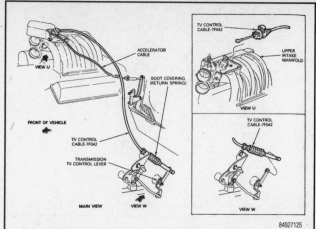

Fig. 57 Throttle valve control cable adjustment—MFI and SFI engines

3. Make sure that the throttle lever is at the idle stop. If it isn't, check for binding or interference. NEVER ATTEMPT TO ADJUST THE IDLE STOP!
4. Make sure that the cable is free of sharp bends or is not rubbing on anything throughout its entire length.
5. Lubricate the TV lever ball stud with chassis lube.
6. Unlock the locking tab at the throttle body by prying with a small screwdriver.
7. Install a spring on the TV control lever, to hold it in the rearmost travel position. The spring must exert at least 10 lbs. of force on the lever.
8. Rotate the transmission outer TV lever 10–30° and slowly allow it to return.
9. Push down on the locking tab until flush.
10. Remove the retaining spring from the lever.

THROTTLE KICKDOWN LINKAGE ADJUSTMENT

1. Move the carburetor throttle linkage to the wide open position.
2. Insert a 0.060 in. thick spacer between the throttle lever and the kickdown adjusting screw.
3. Rotate the transmission kickdown lever until the lever engages the transmission internal stop. Do not use the kickdown rod to turn the transmission lever.
4. Turn the adjusting screw until it contacts the 0.060 in. spacer.
5. Remove the spacer.

Neutral Safety/Back-up Light Switch

This is a combination switch with controls both Neutral Safety and Back-up lamp circuits.

REMOVAL & INSTALLATION

C6

▶ See Figure 58

1. Disconnect the negative battery cable.
2. Raise and safely support the vehicle on jackstands.
3. Remove the downshift linkage rod return spring at the low-reverse servo cover.
4. Coat the outer lever attaching nut with penetrating oil. Remove the nut and lever.
5. Remove the 2 switch attaching bolts, disconnect the wiring at the connectors and remove the switch.
6. Installation is the reverse of removal. Adjust the switch and tighten the bolts to 55–75 inch lbs. (6.2–8.5 Nm).
7. Remove the jackstands and lower the vehicle.
8. Connect the negative battery cable.

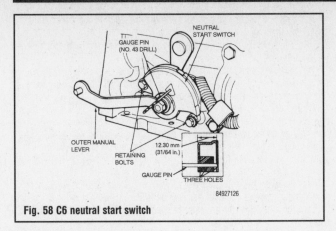

Fig. 58 C6 neutral start switch

AOD

▶ **See Figure 59**

1. Disconnect the negative battery cable.
2. Raise and safely support the vehicle on jackstands.
3. Disconnect the wiring from the switch.
4. Using a deep socket, unscrew the switch.
5. Installation is the reverse of removal. Tighten the switch to 10 ft. lbs. (14 Nm).
6. Remove the jackstands and lower the vehicle.
7. Connect the negative battery cable.

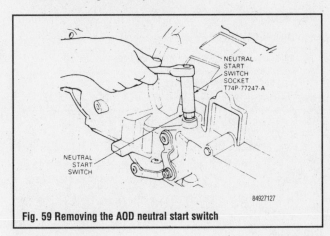

Fig. 59 Removing the AOD neutral start switch

AODE-W and 4R70W

▶ **See Figure 60**

As of 1994, the neutral safety switch is referred to as a Manual Lever Position Sensor (MLP).

1. Disconnect the negative battery cable.
2. Raise and safely support the vehicle on jackstands.
3. Disengage the harness connector from the MLP sensor.
4. Remove the 2 sensor attaching bolts and remove the sensor.

To install:

5. Install the MLP sensor and install retaining bolts. Do not tighten, the sensor requires adjustment.
6. Adjust the MLP sensor then tighten attaching screws to 80–100 inch lbs. (9–11 Nm).
7. Remove the jackstands and lower the vehicle.
8. Connect the negative battery cable.

ADJUSTMENT

C6

▶ **See Figure 58**

1. Hold the steering column transmission selector lever against the **Neutral** stop.
2. Move the sliding block assembly on the neutral switch to the **Neutral** position and insert a 0.091 in. (2.3mm) gauge pin in the alignment hole on the terminal side of the switch.
3. Move the switch assembly housing so that the sliding block contacts the actuating pin lever. Secure the switch to the outer tube of the steering column and remove the gauge pin.
4. Check the operation of the switch. The engine should only start in **Neutral** and **Park**.

AODE-W and 4R70W

▶ **See Figure 61**

➡ **Park is the last detent when the manual control lever is full forward. Return 2 detents toward the output shaft for Neutral.**

1. Position the manual control lever in **Neutral**.
2. Insert Gear Position Sensor Adjuster tool T93P-700 10-A or equivalent, into the slots.
3. Align all 3 slots on the MLP sensor with 3 tabs on the tool.
4. Tighten the attaching screws to 80–100 inch lbs. (9–11 Nm).

Vacuum Modulator

REMOVAL & INSTALLATION

C6

▶ **See Figure 62**

1. Disconnect the vacuum hose at the unit.
2. Remove the bracket bolt and bracket.
3. Pull the vacuum unit from the transmission.
4. Installation is the reverse of removal. Tighten the bolt to 12–16 ft. lbs. (16–22 Nm). Connect the vacuum hose.

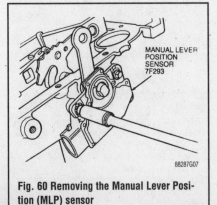

Fig. 60 Removing the Manual Lever Position (MLP) sensor

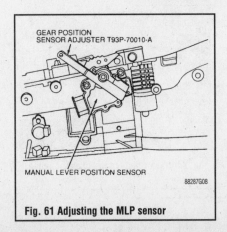

Fig. 61 Adjusting the MLP sensor

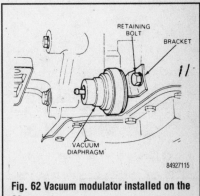

Fig. 62 Vacuum modulator installed on the C6

Shift Linkage

REMOVAL & INSTALLATION

Cable Type Linkage

1. Disconnect the negative battery cable.
2. Remove the plastic cable terminal from the shift control lever pivot ball by prying with a flat-bladed tool between the cable plastic terminal and the shift control selector lever and housing.
3. Remove the transmission shift cable from the transmission shift cable bracket by carefully lifting on the locking tab while pulling up on the fitting.
4. From the engine compartment, remove the cable and grommet from the bulkhead.
5. Remove the plastic slide adjuster from the manual lever pivot ball spring with a flat-bladed tool between the side adjuster and manual control lever.
6. Remove the transmission shift cable from the transmission shift cable bracket by carefully lifting on the locking tab while pulling up on the fitting.

To install:

7. From the instrument panel, feed the plastic terminal through the opening in the dash panel to the engine compartment.
8. Press the rubber boot on the transmission shift cable into the dash panel.
9. From the engine compartment, install the transmission shift cable into the transmission shift cable bracket and make sure the locking ears are properly located and seated into the bracket.
10. Place the transmission shift cable on the manual lever pivot ball and press into place.
11. From the passenger compartment, install the cable-to-steering column transmission shift cable bracket onto the transmission shift cable and make sure the locking tab is fully seated and locked into place.
12. Snap the cable plastic terminal to the shift control selector lever pivot ball on the steering column.
13. Properly adjust the cable as necessary. Refer to adjustment procedure in this section.
14. Remove the cable lock tab and replace the with a new lock tab.
15. Road test the vehicle and check for proper transmission operation.

Rod Type Linkage

➡**Polyurethane plastic grommets are use to connect the various rods, lever and adjusting stud. Whenever a rod is disconnected from a grommet type connector, the old grommet must be remove and a new one installed. A special tool T67P–7341-A or equivalent is required to install the grommet in the shaft lever and to install the shaft linkage rod into the grommet.**

1. To remove the rod end connected to the shift column, place the lower jaw of the tool between the shift lever and the shift rod. If working in limited space use tool T84P-341-A or equivalent.

2. Position the stop pin against the end of the shift rod and force the rod out of the grommet.
3. The grommet is removed from the lever by cutting off the large shoulder of the grommet.
4. Remove the grommet from the lever by pushing it out of the lever.
5. Disconnect the rod at the transmission manual shift lever by removing the attaching nut and remove the linkage.

To install:

6. Prior to installing a new grommet, adjust the stop pin if necessary to properly install the grommet. Coat the outside of the grommet with a Multipurpose Long Life lubricant. Then place the grommet on the stop pin and force it into the shift lever hole. Turn the grommet several times to be sure it is properly seated.
7. Re-adjust the stop pin to a length which is sufficient to install the shift rod into the grommet. If the pin height is not adjusted, the shaft rod may be pushed too far through the grommet, causing damage to the grommet retaining lip.
8. With the pin height properly adjusted, position the shift rod on the tool and force the rod into the grommet until the groove in the rod seats on the inner retaining lip of the grommet.
9. Install the shift linkage to the manual shift lever and install the retaining nut. Do not tighten.
10. Adjust the shift linkage as described in this section.

Extension Housing Seal

REMOVAL & INSTALLATION

2WD Models

▶ See Figures 63, 64 and 65

The extension seal is located at the rear of the transmission case.
1. Raise and support the vehicle safely.
2. Drain the transmission of lubricant.
3. Matchmark the driveshaft to the yoke for reassembly and remove the driveshaft.
4. Remove the old seal using a seal puller or appropriate prytool.

To install:

5. Install a new seal, coated with sealing compound, using an appropriate seal installation tool. Tool T61L-7657-A or B or equivalents are recommended.
6. Install the driveshaft, making certain to align the matchmark.
7. Fill the transmission to the level of the fill plug hole. Install the plug and lower the vehicle.

4WD Models

The extension seal on 4WD drive vehicles is located at the rear of the transfer case.

Fig. 63 Removing the extension housing seal

Fig. 64 Always replace the old seal with a new one

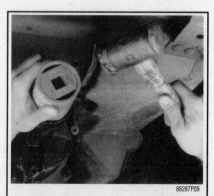

Fig. 65 Using a special tool and mallet, install the new seal

Transmission Assembly

REMOVAL & INSTALLATION

C6

1. Disconnect the negative battery cable.
2. From in the engine compartment, remove the two upper converter housing-to-engine bolts.
3. Disconnect the neutral switch wire at the in-line connector.
4. Remove the bolt securing the fluid filler tube to the engine cylinder head.
5. Raise and support the truck on jackstands.
6. Place the drain pan under the transmission fluid pan. Starting at the rear of the pan and working toward the front, loosen the attaching bolts and allow the fluid to drain. Finally remove all of the pan attaching bolts except two at the front, to allow the fluid to further drain. With fluid drained, install two bolts on the rear side of the pan to temporarily hold it in place.
7. Remove the converter drain plug access cover from the lower end of the converter housing.
8. Remove the converter-to-flywheel attaching nuts. Place a wrench on the crankshaft pulley attaching bolt to turn the converter to gain access to the nuts.
9. With the wrench on the crankshaft pulley attaching bolt, turn the converter to gain access to the converter drain plug. Place a drain pan under the converter to catch the fluid and remove the plug. After the fluid has been drained, reinstall the plug.
10. On 2WD drive models, disconnect the driveshaft from the rear axle and slide shaft rearward from the transmission. Install a seal installation tool in the extension housing to prevent fluid leakage.
11. Disconnect the speedometer cable from the extension housing.
12. Disconnect the downshift and manual linkage rods from the levers at the transmission.
13. Disconnect the oil cooler lines from the transmission.
14. Remove the vacuum hose from the vacuum diaphragm unit. Remove the vacuum line retaining clip.
15. Disconnect the cable from the terminal on the starter motor. Remove the three attaching bolts and remove the starter motor.
16. On 4WD drive models remove the transfer case.
17. Remove the two engine rear support and insulator assembly-to-attaching bolts.
18. Remove the two engine rear support and insulator assembly-to-extension housing attaching bolts.
19. Remove the six bolts securing the No. 2 crossmember to the frame side rails.
20. Raise the transmission with a transmission jack and remove both crossmembers.
21. Secure the transmission to the jack with the safety chain.
22. Remove the remaining converter housing-to-engine attaching bolts.
23. Move the transmission away from the engine. Lower the jack and remove the converter and transmission assembly from under the vehicle.
   To install:
24. Tighten the converter drain plug.
25. Position the converter on the transmission making sure the converter drive flats are fully engaged in the pump gear.
26. With the converter properly installed, place the transmission on the jack. Secure the transmission on the jack with the chain.
27. Rotate the converter until the studs and drain plug are in alignment with their holes in the flywheel.
28. Move the converter and transmission assembly forward into position, using care not to damage the flywheel and the converter pilot. The converter must rest squarely against the flywheel. This indicates that the converter pilot is not binding in the engine crankshaft.
29. Install the converter housing-to-engine attaching bolts and tighten them to 65 ft. lbs. (88 Nm) for the diesel; 50 ft. lbs. (68 Nm) for gasoline engines.
30. Remove the transmission jack safety chain from around the transmission.
31. Position the No. 2 crossmember to the frame side rails. Install and tighten the attaching bolts.
32. Install transfer case on 4WD drive models.
33. Position the engine rear support and insulator assembly above the crossmember. Install the rear support and insulator assembly-to-extension housing mounting bolts and tighten the bolts to 45 ft. lbs. (61 Nm).
34. Lower the transmission and remove the jack.
35. Secure the engine rear support and insulator assembly to the crossmember with the attaching bolts and tighten them to 80 ft. lbs. (108 Nm).
36. The balance of installation is the reverse of removal.

AOD

1. Disconnect the negative battery cable.
2. Raise the vehicle on hoist or stands.
3. Place the drain pan under the transmission fluid pan. Starting at the rear of the pan and working toward the front, loosen the attaching bolts and allow the fluid to drain. Finally remove all of the pan attaching bolts except two at the front, to allow the fluid to further drain. With fluid drained, install two bolts on the rear side of the pan to temporarily hold it in place.
4. Remove the converter drain plug access cover from the lower end of the converter.
5. Remove the converter-to-flywheel attaching nuts. Place a wrench on the crankshaft pulley attaching bolt to turn the converter to gain access to the nuts.
6. Place a drain pan under the converter to catch the fluid. With the wrench on the crankshaft pulley attaching bolt, turn the converter to gain access to the converter drain plug and remove the plug. After the fluid has been drained, reinstall the plug.
7. On 2WD drive models, matchmark and disconnect the driveshaft from the rear axle and slide shaft rearward from the transmission. Install a seal installation tool in the extension housing to prevent fluid leakage.
8. Disconnect the cable from the terminal on the starter motor. Remove the three attaching bolts and remove the starter motor. Disconnect the neutral start switch wires at the plug connector.
9. Remove the rear mount-to-crossmember attaching bolts and the two crossmember-to-frame attaching bolts.
10. Remove the two engine rear support-to-extension housing attaching bolts.
11. Disconnect the TV linkage rod from the transmission TV lever. Disconnect the manual rod from the transmission manual lever at the transmission.
12. Remove the two bolts securing the bell crank bracket to the converter housing.
13. On 4WD drive models, remove the transfer case.
14. Raise the transmission with a transmission jack to provide clearance to remove the crossmember. Remove the rear mount from the crossmember and remove the crossmember from the side supports.
15. Lower the transmission to gain access to the oil cooler lines.
16. Disconnect each oil line from the fittings on the transmission.
17. Disconnect the speedometer cable from the extension housing.
18. Remove the bolt that secures the transmission fluid filler tube to the cylinder block. Lift the filler tube and the dipstick from the transmission.
19. Secure the transmission to the jack with the chain.
20. Remove the converter housing-to-cylinder block attaching bolts.
21. Carefully move the transmission and converter assembly away from the engine and, at the same time, lower the jack to clear the underside of the vehicle.
22. Remove the converter and mount the transmission in a holding fixture.
23. Tighten the converter drain plug.
   To install:
24. Position the converter on the transmission, making sure the converter drive flats are fully engaged in the pump gear by rotating the converter.
25. With the converter properly installed, place the transmission on the jack. Secure the transmission to the jack with a chain.
26. Rotate the converter until the studs and drain plug are in alignment with the holes in the flywheel.
27. Move the converter and transmission assembly forward into position, using care not to damage the flywheel and the converter pilot. The converter must rest squarely against the flywheel. This indicates that the converter pilot is not binding in the engine crankshaft.
28. Install and tighten the converter housing-to-engine attaching bolts to 40–50 ft. lbs. (54–68 Nm).
29. The balance of installation is the reverse of removal.

AODE-W and 4R70W

1. Disconnect the negative battery cable.
2. Raise the vehicle on hoist or stands.
3. Place the drain pan under the transmission fluid pan. Starting at the rear

of the pan and working toward the front, loosen the attaching bolts and allow the fluid to drain. Finally remove all of the pan attaching bolts except two at the front, to allow the fluid to further drain. With fluid drained, install two bolts on the rear side of the pan to temporarily hold it in place.

4. Remove the converter drain plug access cover from the lower end of the converter.

5. Remove the converter-to-flywheel attaching nuts. Place a wrench on the crankshaft pulley attaching bolt to turn the converter to gain access to the nuts.

6. Place a drain pan under the converter to catch the fluid. With the wrench on the crankshaft pulley attaching bolt, turn the converter to gain access to the converter drain plug and remove the plug. After the fluid has been drained, reinstall the plug.

7. Matchmark and disconnect the driveshaft from the rear axle and slide shaft rearward from the transmission. Install a seal installation tool in the extension housing to prevent fluid leakage.

8. Disconnect the cable from the terminal on the starter motor. Remove the three attaching bolts and remove the starter motor.

9. Disconnect the harness connectors at both the Output Shaft Speed (OSS) sensor and the transmission range sensor.

10. Disconnect the shaft linkage at the manual control lever.

11. Disconnect the shaft linkage at the manual control lever.

12. Position a transmission jack under the transmission and raise it slightly.

13. Remove the engine rear support-to-frame retaining nuts and bolts.

14. If equipped, remove the right and left-hand support bracket nuts and bolts and brackets.

15. If equipped, remove the engine support insulator, engine support and engine damper mounting body brackets.

16. Lower the transmission to gain access to the fluid cooler lines.

17. Disconnect each fluid cooler line from the fittings on the transmission.

18. Remove the bolts that secure the transmission fluid filler tube to the cylinder block. Lift the filler tube and the dipstick from the transmission.

19. Secure the transmission to the jack with the chain.

20. Remove the converter housing-to-cylinder block attaching bolts.

21. Carefully move the transmission and converter assembly away from the engine and, at the same time, lower the jack to clear the underside of the vehicle.

22. Remove the converter and mount the transmission in a holding fixture.

23. Tighten the converter drain plug.

To install:

24. Position the converter on the transmission, making sure the converter drive flats are fully engaged in the pump gear by rotating the converter.

25. With the converter properly installed, place the transmission on the jack. Secure the transmission to the jack with a chain.

➡**Align the orange balancing marks on the converter stud and flywheel bolt hole if balancing marks are present.**

26. Rotate the converter until the studs and drain plug are in alignment with the holes in the flywheel.

➡**Before torque converter is bolted to the flywheel, a check should be made to ensure that the torque converter is properly seated. The torque converter should move freely with respect to the flywheel. Grasp the torque converter stud. Movement back and forth should result in a metallic clank noise if the converter is properly seated. If the torque converter will not move, the transmission must be removed and the torque converter re-position so that the impeller hub is properly engage in the pump gear.**

27. Move the converter and transmission assembly forward into position, using care not to damage the flywheel and the converter pilot. The converter must rest squarely against the flywheel. This indicates that the converter pilot is not binding in the engine crankshaft.

28. Connect the EGR tube assembly.

29. Install the converter to flywheel retaining bolts. Tighten the bolts to 37–50 ft. lbs. (50–68 Nm).

30. Install the starter motor.

31. Install and tighten the converter housing-to-engine attaching bolts to 40–50 ft. lbs. (54–68 Nm).

32. The balance of installation is the reverse of removal.

E4OD

➧ **See Figures 66 and 67**

1. Disconnect the negative battery cable.

2. Raise and support the truck on jackstands.

3. Place the drain pan under the transmission fluid pan. Starting at the rear of the pan and working toward the front, loosen the attaching bolts and allow the fluid to drain. Finally remove all of the pan attaching bolts except two at the front, to allow the fluid to further drain. With fluid drained, install two bolts on the rear side of the pan to temporarily hold it in place.

4. Remove the dipstick from the transmission.

5. On 4WD drive models, matchmark and remove the front driveshaft.

6. Matchmark and remove the rear driveshaft. Install a seal installation tool in the extension housing to prevent fluid leakage.

7. Disconnect the linkage from the transmission.

8. On 4WD drive models, disconnect the transfer case linkage.

9. Remove the heat shield and remove the manual lever position sensor connector by squeezing the tabs and pulling on the connector. NEVER ATTEMPT TO PRY THE CONNECTOR APART!

10. Remove the solenoid body heat shield.

11. Remove the solenoid body connector by pushing on the center tab and pulling on the wiring harness. NEVER ATTEMPT TO PRY APART THE CONNECTOR!

12. On 4WD drive models, remove the 4x4 switch connector from the transfer case. Be careful not to over-extend the tabs.

13. Pry the harness connector from the extension housing wire bracket.

14. On 4WD drive models, remove the wiring harness locators from the left side of the connector.

15. Disconnect the speedometer cable.

16. On 4WD drive models, remove the transfer case.

17. Remove the converter cover bolts.

18. Remove the rear engine cover plate bolts.

19. Disconnect the cable from the terminal on the starter motor. Remove the three attaching bolts and remove the starter motor. Disconnect the neutral start switch wires at the plug connector.

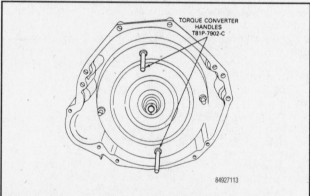

Fig. 66 Installation of the torque converter handles on the E4OD

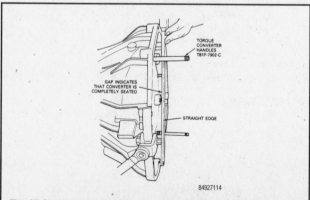

Fig. 67 Check torque converter installation with a straightedge

20. Remove the converter-to-flywheel attaching nuts. Place a wrench on the crankshaft pulley attaching bolt to turn the converter to gain access to the nuts.

21. Secure the transmission to a transmission jack. Use a safety chain.

22. Remove the rear mount-to-crossmember attaching nuts and the two crossmember-to-frame attaching bolts.

23. Disconnect each oil line from the fittings on the transmission. Cap the lines.

24. Remove the 6 converter housing-to-cylinder block attaching bolts.

25. Carefully move the transmission and converter assembly away from the engine and, at the same time, lower the jack to clear the underside of the vehicle.

26. Remove the transmission filler tube.

27. On F-Super Duty, remove the transmission-mounted brake. See Section 9.

28. Install Torque Converter Handles T81P-7902-C, or equivalent, at the 12 o'clock and 6 o'clock positions.

To install:

29. Install the converter with the handles at the 12 o'clock and 6 o'clock positions. Push and rotate the converter until it bottoms out. Check the seating of the converter by placing a straightedge across the converter and bell housing. There must be a gap between the converter and straightedge. Remove the handles.

30. On F-Super Duty, install the transmission-mounted brake. See Section 9.

31. Install the transmission filler tube.

32. Rotate the converter to align the studs with the flywheel mounting holes.

33. Carefully raise the transmission into position at the engine. The converter must rest squarely against the flywheel.

34. Install the 6 converter housing-to-cylinder block attaching bolts. Snug them alternately and evenly, then, tighten them alternately and evenly to 40–50 ft. lbs. (54–68 Nm).

35. Install the converter drain plug cover.

36. Connect each oil line at the fittings on the transmission.

37. Install the rear mount-to-crossmember attaching nuts and the two crossmember-to-frame attaching bolts. Tighten the nuts and bolts to 50 ft. lbs. (68 Nm).

38. Remove the transmission jack.

39. Install the converter-to-flywheel attaching nuts. Place a wrench on the crankshaft pulley attaching bolt to turn the converter to gain access to the nuts. Tighten the nuts to 20–30 ft. lbs. (27–41 Nm).

40. The balance of installation is the reverse of removal.

TRANSFER CASE

Control Module

REMOVAL & INSTALLATION

Borg-Warner 13–56 Electronic Shift

1. Remove the right side cowl panel kick pad.
2. Remove the 2 module retaining screws, lift out the module and unplug the wiring.
3. Installation is the reverse of removal.

Front or Rear Output Shaft Seal

REMOVAL & INSTALLATION

Borg-Warner 13–45

1. Raise and support the truck on jackstands.
2. Disconnect the driveshaft at the yoke.
3. Remove the yoke nut and washer.
4. Pull the yoke from the shaft.
5. Center-punch the seal and carefully pry it from its bore. Don't scratch the bore!

To install:

6. Clean the bore thoroughly.
7. Coat the OD of the new seal with sealer and the ID with clean Dexron®II ATF.
8. Position the seal squarely in the bore and drive it into place with a seal driver, or similar tool. Don't hammer directly on the seal.
9. Install the washer and yoke. Coat the threads of the shaft with a thread-locking compound. Install the nut and torque it to 120–150 ft. lbs. (163–203 Nm).
10. Install the driveshaft.

Borg-Warner 13–56 Manual Shift

FIXED YOKE TYPE

1. Raise and support the truck on jackstands.
2. Disconnect the driveshaft at the yoke.
3. Remove the 30mm yoke nut, washer and rubber seal.
4. Pull the yoke from the shaft.

5. Center-punch the seal and carefully pry it from its bore. Don't scratch the bore!

To install:

6. Clean the bore thoroughly.
7. Coat the OD and ID of the new seal with clean Dexron®II ATF.
8. Position the seal squarely in the bore and drive it into place with a seal driver, or similar tool. Don't hammer directly on the seal.
9. Install a new seal slinger.
10. Install the rubber seal, washer and yoke. Install the nut and torque it to 150–180 ft. lbs. (203–244 Nm).
11. Install the driveshaft.

SLIP-TYPE REAR SPLINE SEAL

▶ **See Figures 68, 69 and 70**

1. Raise and support the truck on jackstands.
2. Disconnect the driveshaft at the rear axle and slide it from the transfer case.
3. Center-punch the seal and carefully pry it from its bore. Don't scratch the bore!
4. Remove and discard the bushing from the retainer.

To install:

5. Drive a new bushing into place with a seal driver or equivalent tool
6. Position the seal in the retainer so the notch on the seal faces upwards and the drain hole in the rubber boot is downwards. Drive it into place with a seal driver, or similar tool. Don't hammer directly on the seal.
7. Install the driveshaft.

Borg-Warner 13–56 Electronic Shift

1. Raise and support the truck on jackstands.
2. Disconnect the driveshaft at the yoke.
3. Remove the 30mm yoke nut, washer and rubber seal.
4. Pull the yoke from the shaft.
5. Center-punch the seal and carefully pry it from its bore. Don't scratch the bore!

To install:

6. Clean the bore thoroughly.
7. Coat the OD and ID of the new seal with clean Dexron®II ATF.
8. Position the seal squarely in the bore and drive it into place with a seal driver, or similar tool. Don't hammer directly on the seal.
9. Install a new seal slinger.
10. Install the rubber seal, washer and yoke. Install the nut and torque it to 150–180 ft. lbs. (203–244 Nm).
11. Install the driveshaft.

Fig. 68 Removing the rear output shaft seal

Fig. 69 Always replace the old seal with a new one

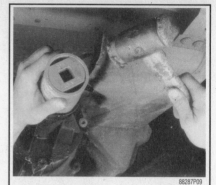

Fig. 70 Using a special tool and mallet, install the new seal

Transfer Case Assembly

REMOVAL & INSTALLATION

Borg-Warner Model 13–45

▶ See Figures 71 thru 76

1. Raise and support the truck on jackstands.
2. Drain the fluid from the transfer case.
3. Disconnect the four wheel drive indicator switch wire connector at the transfer case.
4. Remove the skid plate from the frame, if so equipped.
5. Matchmark and disconnect the front driveshaft from the front output yoke.
6. Matchmark and disconnect the rear driveshaft from the rear output shaft yoke.

7. Disconnect the speedometer driven gear from the transfer case rear bearing retainer.
8. Remove the retaining rings and shift rod from the transfer case shift lever.
9. Disconnect the vent hose from the transfer case.
10. Remove the heat shield from the frame.
11. Support the transfer case with a transmission jack.
12. Remove the bolts retaining the transfer case to the transmission adapter.
13. Lower the transfer case from the vehicle.

To install:

14. When installing place a new gasket between the transfer case and the adapter.
15. Raise the transfer case with the transmission jack so that the transmission output shaft aligns with the splined transfer case input shaft. Install the bolts retaining the transfer case to the adapter.
16. Remove the transmission jack from the transfer case.

Fig. 71 View of the transfer case lever and linkage assembly—manual type transfer case

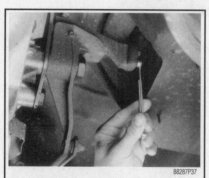

Fig. 72 Removing the transfer case shift lever-to-linkage attaching bolts—manual type transfer case

Fig. 73 Loosening the transfer case yoke-to-driveshaft clamp nuts

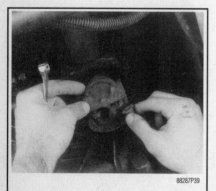

Fig. 74 Removing the transfer case yoke-to-driveshaft clamp nuts

Fig. 75 Carefully separate the driveshaft from the yoke; a prytool may be needed for this

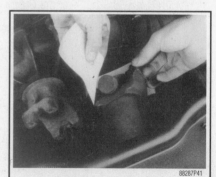

Fig. 76 To keep the U-joint cups from falling off, a good practice is to tape the U-joint together

17. Connect the rear driveshaft to the rear output shaft yoke. Tighten the bolts to 15 ft. lbs. (20 Nm).

18. Install the shift lever to the transfer case and install the retaining nut.

19. Connect the speedometer driven gear to the transfer case.

20. Connect the four wheel drive indicator switch wire connector at the transfer case.

21. Connect the front driveshaft to the front output yoke. Tighten the bolts to 15 ft. lbs. (27 Nm).

22. Position the heat shield to the frame crossmember and the mounting lug on the transfer case. Install and tighten the retaining bolts.

23. Install the skid plate to the frame.

24. Install the drain plug. Remove the filler plug and install six pints of Dexron®II type transmission fluid or equivalent.

25. Lower the vehicle.

Borg-Warner 13–56 Manual Shift

1. Raise and support the truck on jackstands.

2. Drain the fluid from the transfer case.

3. Disconnect the four wheel drive indicator switch wire connector at the transfer case.

4. Remove the skid plate from the frame, if so equipped.

5. Matchmark and disconnect the front driveshaft from the front output yoke.

6. Matchmark and disconnect the rear driveshaft from the rear output shaft yoke.

7. Disconnect the speedometer driven gear from the transfer case rear bearing retainer.

8. Remove the retaining rings and shift rod from the transfer case shift lever.

9. Disconnect the vent hose from the transfer case.

10. Remove the heat shield from the frame.

11. Support the transfer case with a transmission jack.

12. Remove the bolts retaining the transfer case to the transmission adapter.

13. Lower the transfer case from the vehicle.

To install:

14. When installing place a new gasket between the transfer case and the adapter.

15. Raise the transfer case with the transmission jack so that the transmission output shaft aligns with the splined transfer case input shaft. Install the bolts retaining the transfer case to the adapter. Tighten the bolts to 40 ft. lbs. (54 Nm) in the pattern shown.

16. Remove the transmission jack from the transfer case.

17. Connect the rear driveshaft to the rear output shaft yoke. Tighten the bolts to 15 ft. lbs. (20 Nm).

18. Install the shift lever to the transfer case and install the retaining nut.

19. Connect the speedometer driven gear to the transfer case.

20. Connect the four wheel drive indicator switch wire connector at the transfer case.

21. Connect the front driveshaft to the front output yoke. Tighten the bolts to 15 ft. lbs. (20 Nm).

22. Position the heat shield to the frame crossmember and the mounting lug on the transfer case. Install and tighten the retaining bolts.

23. Install the skid plate to the frame.

24. Install the drain plug. Remove the filler plug and install six pints of Dexron®II type transmission fluid or equivalent.

25. Lower the vehicle.

Borg-Warner 13–56 Electronic Shift

♦ See Figures 77 and 78

1. Raise and support the truck on jackstands.

2. Drain the fluid from the transfer case.

3. Disconnect the wire connector at the transfer case.

4. Remove the skid plate from the frame, if so equipped.

5. Matchmark and disconnect the front driveshaft from the front output yoke.

6. Matchmark and disconnect the rear driveshaft from the rear output shaft yoke.

7. Disconnect the speedometer driven gear from the transfer case rear bearing retainer.

8. Disconnect the vent hose from the transfer case.

9. Remove the heat shield from the frame.

10. Support the transfer case with a transmission jack.

11. Remove the bolts retaining the transfer case to the transmission adapter.

12. Lower the transfer case from the vehicle.

13. When installing place a new gasket between the transfer case and the adapter.

To install:

14. Raise the transfer case with the transmission jack so that the transmission output shaft aligns with the splined transfer case input shaft. Install the bolts retaining the transfer case to the adapter. Tighten the bolts to 40 ft. lbs. (54 Nm) in the pattern illustrated.

15. Remove the transmission jack from the transfer case.

16. Connect the rear driveshaft to the rear output shaft yoke. Tighten the bolts to 28 ft. lbs. (38 Nm).

17. Install the shift lever to the transfer case and install the retaining nut.

18. Connect the speedometer driven gear to the transfer case. Tighten the bolt to 25 inch lbs. (2.8 Nm).

19. Connect the wire connector at the transfer case.

20. Connect the front driveshaft to the front output yoke. Tighten the bolts to 15 ft. lbs. (20 Nm).

21. Position the heat shield to the frame crossmember and the mounting lug on the transfer case. Install and tighten the retaining bolts.

22. Install the skid plate to the frame.

23. Install the drain plug. Remove the filler plug and install six pints of Dexron®II type transmission fluid or equivalent.

24. Lower the vehicle.

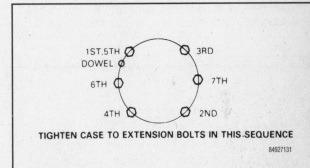

TIGHTEN CASE TO EXTENSION BOLTS IN THIS SEQUENCE

84927131

Fig. 77 13–56 electronic shift transfer case extension bolt torque sequence

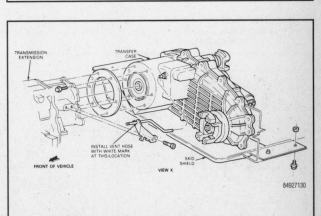

84927130

Fig. 78 Borg-Warner 13–56 electronic shift transfer case

DRIVELINE

Front Driveshaft and U-Joints

REMOVAL & INSTALLATION

Single Type U-Joint

EXCEPT F-350

▶ **See Figures 73, 74, 75, 76 and 79**

1. Matchmark the driveshaft yoke and axle pinion flange.
2. Matchmark the driveshaft yoke and transfer case flange.
3. Remove the U-bolt nuts and U-bolts attaching the yoke to the axle flange.
4. Separate the yoke from the flange. It may be necessary to pry it free with a small prybar. Immediately after separation, wrap tape around the U-joint caps to keep them from falling off.
5. Remove the U-bolts and nuts (bolts for the F-350) and disconnect the driveshaft from the transfer case. It may be necessary to pry it free with a small prybar. Immediately after separation, wrap tape around the U-joint caps to keep them from falling off.

➡ **Avoid separating the driveshaft parts at the slip joint. If the driveshaft should become separated or if you wish to separate it, see the procedure, below.**

6. Installation is the reverse of removal. Align the yoke-to-flange matchmarks. Tighten the U-bolt nuts to 15 ft. lbs. (20 Nm). Tighten the F-350 bolts to 20–28 ft. lbs. (27–38 Nm).

F-350

1. Matchmark the front yoke and front axle flange.
2. Matchmark the cardan joint and the transfer case yoke.
3. Remove the U-bolt nuts and U-bolts attaching the yoke to the axle flange.
4. Separate the yoke from the flange. It may be necessary to pry it free with a small prybar. Immediately after separation, wrap tape around the U-joint caps to keep them from falling off.
5. Remove the cardan joint-to transfer case yoke bolts and separate the cardan joint from the yoke.
6. Installation is the reverse of removal. Align the matchmarks. Tighten the U-bolt nuts to 15 ft. lbs. (20 Nm); the cardan joint bolts to 25 ft. lbs. (34 Nm).

FRONT DRIVESHAFT SEPARATION

▶ **See Figure 79**

1. Remove the driveshaft and place it on a workbench.
2. Using side cutters, cut the boot bands. Discard them.
3. Pull the 2 sections apart.
4. Remove and inspect the boot. If it is in any way damaged, replace it.

➡ **If the boot was split or torn, the grease will probably be contaminated, so thoroughly clean all old grease from the parts and replace it with fresh grease.**

5. Install the boot on the splined shaft as far as it will go.
6. Install a new small clamp and crimp it with crimping pliers. Use only crimp type clamps as hose type clamps can throw the shaft out of balance.
7. Coat the splines with chassis lube.
8. Place about 10 grams of chassis lube in the boot.
9. Place a new large crimp clamp on the rear yoke.
10. Align the blind splines and push the rear yoke onto the driveshaft splines.
11. Remove the excess grease and position the rear end of the boot in the slip yoke boot groove. On trucks with single type U-joints at each end, move the yoke in or out as required to obtain a total driveshaft length of:
   • F-150, 250 and Bronco; C6 and ZF transmissions: 892mm
   • AOD transmission: 917mm
   • M5OD transmission: 978mm
   This measurement is made between the centerlines of the U-joints.
   • F-350: C6 transmission: 819mm
   • E4OD transmission: 970mm; ZF transmission with 7.3L or 7.5L: 832mm
   • ZF transmission with 5.8L: 905.8mm
   This measurement is made between the centerlines of the U-joints with the shaft fully collapsed.
12. Make sure that the boot has stayed in its groove, dispel any trapped air from the boot and crimp the clamp in place.

U-JOINT REPLACEMENT

▶ **See Figures 79, 80, 81 and 82**

Except Double Cardan Joint

1. Remove the driveshaft from the vehicle and place it in a vise, being careful not to damage it.
2. Remove the snaprings which retain the bearings in the flange and in the driveshaft.

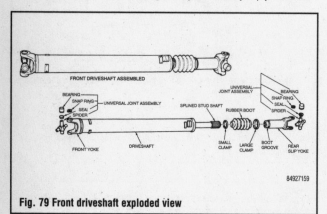

Fig. 79 Front driveshaft exploded view

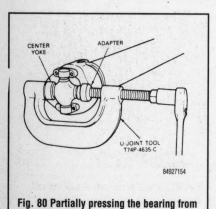

Fig. 80 Partially pressing the bearing from the center yoke

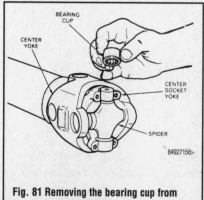

Fig. 81 Removing the bearing cup from the center yoke socket

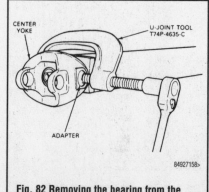

Fig. 82 Removing the bearing from the rear of the center yoke

3. Remove the driveshaft tube from the vise and position the U-joint in the vise with a socket smaller than the bearing cap on one side and a socket larger than the bearing cap on the other side.

4. Slowly tighten the jaws of the vise so that the smaller socket forces the U-joint spider and the opposite bearing into the larger socket.

5. Remove the other side of the spider in the same manner (if applicable) and remove the spider assembly from the driveshaft. Discard the spider assemblies.

6. Clean all foreign matter from the yoke areas at the end of the driveshaft(s).

7. Start the new spider and one of the bearing cap assemblies into a yoke by positioning the yoke in a vise with the spider positioned in place with one of the bearing cap assemblies positioned over one of the holes in the yoke. Slowly close the vise, pressing the bearing cap assembly in the yoke. Press the cap in far enough so that the retaining snapring can be installed. Use the smaller socket to recess the bearing cap.

8. Open the vise and position the opposite bearing cap assembly over the proper hole in the yoke with the socket that is smaller than the diameter of the bearing cap located on the cap. Slowly close the vise, pressing the bearing cap into the hole in the yoke with the socket. Make sure that the spider assembly is in line with the bearing cap as it is pressed in. Press the bearing cap in far enough so that the retaining snapring can be installed.

9. Install all remaining U-joints in the same manner.

10. Install the driveshaft and grease the new U-joints.

Double Cardan Joint

1. Working at the rear axle end of the shaft, mark the position of the spiders, the center yoke, and the centering socket yoke as related to the companion flange. The spiders must be assembled with the bosses in their original position to provide proper clearances.

2. Using a large vise or an arbor press and a socket smaller than the bearing cap on one side and a socket larger than the bearing cap on the other side, drive one of the bearings in toward the center of the universal joint, which will force the opposite bearing out.

3. Remove the driveshaft from the vise.

4. Tighten the bearing in the vise and tap on the yoke to free the bearing from the center yoke. Do not tap on the driveshaft tube.

5. Reposition the sockets on the yoke and force the opposite bearing outward and remove it.

6. Position the sockets on one of the remaining bearings and force it outward approximately ⅜ in. (9.5mm).

7. Grip the bearing in the vise and tap on the weld yoke to free the bearing from the center yoke. Do not tap on the driveshaft tube.

8. Reposition the sockets on the yoke to press out the remaining bearing.

9. Remove the spider from the center yoke.

10. Remove the bearings from the driveshaft yoke as outlined above and remove the spider from the yoke.

11. Insert a suitable tool into the centering ball socket located in the companion flange and pry out the rubber seal. Remove the retainer, three piece ball seat, washer and spring from the ball socket.

12. Inspect the centering ball socket assembly for worn or damaged parts. If any damage is evident replace the entire assembly.

13. Insert the spring, washer, three piece ball seat and retainer into the ball socket.

14. Using a suitable tool, install the centering ball socket seal.

15. Position the spider in the driveshaft yoke. Make sure the spider bosses are in the same position as originally installed. Press in the bearing cups with the sockets and vise. Install the internal snaprings provided in the repair kit.

16. Position the center yoke over the spider ends and press in the bearing cups. Install the snaprings.

17. Install the spider in the companion flange yoke. Make sure the spider bosses are in the position as originally installed. Press on the bearing cups and install the snaprings.

18. Position the center yoke over the spider ends and press on the bearing cups. Install the snaprings.

Rear Driveshaft and U-Joints

REMOVAL & INSTALLATION

Single Type U-Joint

ONE-PIECE DRIVESHAFT

▶ See Figures 83, 84, 85, 86 and 87

1. Matchmark the driveshaft yoke and axle pinion flange.

2. Remove the U-bolt nuts and U-bolts attaching the yoke to the axle flange.

3. Separate the yoke from the flange. It may be necessary to pry it free with a small prybar. Immediately after separation, wrap tape around the U-joint caps to keep them from falling off.

4. Slip the driveshaft off the transmission splines.

5. Installation is the reverse of removal. Align the yoke-to-flange matchmarks. Tighten the U-bolt nuts to 15 ft. lbs. (20 Nm).

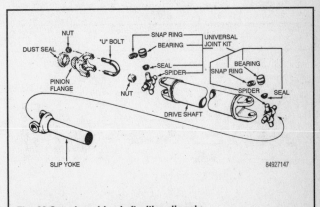

Fig. 83 One-piece driveshaft with a slip yoke

Fig. 84 Matchmark the driveshaft and yoke for balance reasons

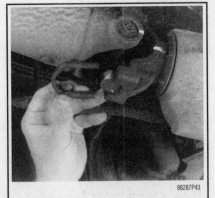

Fig. 85 Removing the U-clamp

Fig. 86 Carefully separate the driveshaft from the yoke; a prytool may be needed for this

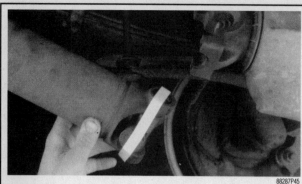

Fig. 87 To keep the U-joint cups from falling off, a good practices is to tape the U-joint together

TWO-PIECE DRIVESHAFT/COUPLING SHAFT EXCEPT F-SUPER DUTY STRIPPED CHASSIS AND MOTOR HOME CHASSIS

▶ See Figure 88

1. Matchmark the driveshaft yoke and axle pinion flange.
2. Remove the U-bolt nuts and U-bolts attaching the yoke to the axle flange.
3. Separate the yoke from the flange. It may be necessary to pry it free with a small prybar. Immediately after separation, wrap tape around the U-joint caps to keep them from falling off.
4. Slip the driveshaft off the coupling shaft splines.
5. Remove the center bearing.
6. Slide the coupling shaft from the transmission shaft splines.
7. Clean all parts and check for damage. Do not remove the blue plastic coating from the male splines.
8. Installation is the reverse of removal. Coat the splines with chassis lube. Tighten the center bearing support bolts to 50 ft. lbs. (68 Nm). Align the yoke-to-flange matchmarks. Tighten the U-bolt nuts to:
- ⁵⁄₁₆ in.—18: 15 ft. lbs. (20 Nm)
- ³⁄₈ in.—18: 17–26 ft. lbs. (23–35 Nm)
- ⁷⁄₁₆ in.—20: 30–40 ft. lbs. (41–54 Nm)

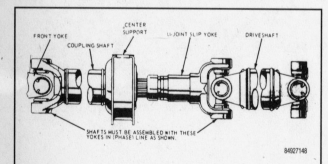

Fig. 88 Two-piece driveshaft with a slip yoke at the transmission end

TWO OR THREE-PIECE DRIVE SHAFT-SUPER DUTY STRIPPED CHASSIS AND MOTOR HOME CHASSIS

▶ See Figure 89

1. Matchmark the driveshaft yoke and axle pinion flange.
2. Remove the U-bolt nuts and U-bolts attaching the yoke to the axle flange.
3. Separate the yoke from the flange. It may be necessary to pry it free with a small prybar. Immediately after separation, wrap tape around the U-joint caps to keep them from falling off.
4. Slip the driveshaft off the coupling shaft splines.
5. Remove the rearmost center bearing.
6. Remove the center driveshaft from its mating yoke.
7. Remove the next center bearing.

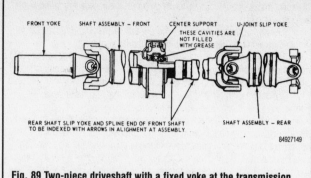

Fig. 89 Two-piece driveshaft with a fixed yoke at the transmission end

8. Remove the front driveshaft from the transmission splines.
9. Clean all parts and check for damage. Do not remove the blue plastic coating from the male splines.
10. Installation is the reverse of removal. Coat the splines with chassis lube. Tighten the center bearing support bolts to 50 ft. lbs. (68 Nm). Align the yoke-to-flange matchmarks. Tighten the U-bolt nuts to:
- ⁵⁄₁₆ in.—18: 15 ft. lbs. (20 Nm)
- ³⁄₈ in.—18: 17–26 ft. lbs. (23–35 Nm)
- ⁷⁄₁₆ in.—20: 30–40 ft. lbs. (41–54 Nm)

Double Cardan Type U-Joint

BRONCO

▶ See Figure 90

1. Matchmark the rear yoke and axle flange.
2. Matchmark the front cardan joint and the transfer case yoke.
3. Remove the U-bolt nuts and U-bolts attaching the yoke to the axle flange.
4. Separate the yoke from the flange. It may be necessary to pry it free with a small prybar. Immediately after separation, wrap tape around the U-joint caps to keep them from falling off.
5. Remove the cardan joint-to transfer case yoke bolts and separate the cardan joint from the yoke.
6. Installation is the reverse of removal. Align the matchmarks. Tighten the U-bolt nuts to 15 ft. lbs. (20 Nm); the cardan joint bolts to 25 ft. lbs. (34 Nm).

U-JOINT REPLACEMENT

▶ See Figures 80, 81 and 82

Except Double Cardan Universal

1. Remove the driveshaft from the vehicle and place it in a vise, being careful not to damage it.
2. Remove the snaprings which retain the bearings in the flange and in the driveshaft.

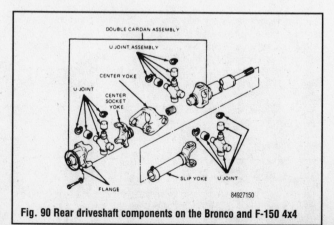

Fig. 90 Rear driveshaft components on the Bronco and F-150 4x4

3. Remove the driveshaft tube from the vise and position the U-joint in the vise with a socket smaller than the bearing cap on one side and a socket larger than the bearing cap on the other side.

4. Slowly tighten the jaws of the vise so that the smaller socket forces the U-joint spider and the opposite bearing into the larger socket.

5. Remove the other side of the spider in the same manner (if applicable) and remove the spider assembly from the driveshaft. Discard the spider assemblies.

6. Clean all foreign matter from the yoke areas at the end of the driveshaft(s).

7. Start the new spider and one of the bearing cap assemblies into a yoke by positioning the yoke in a vise with the spider positioned in place with one of the bearing cap assemblies positioned over one of the holes in the yoke. Slowly close the vise, pressing the bearing cap assembly in the yoke. Press the cap in far enough so that the retaining snapring can be installed. Use the smaller socket to recess the bearing cap.

8. Open the vise and position the opposite bearing cap assembly over the proper hole in the yoke with the socket that is smaller than the diameter of the bearing cap located on the cap. Slowly close the vise, pressing the bearing cap into the hole in the yoke with the socket. Make sure that the spider assembly is in line with the bearing cap as it is pressed in. Press the bearing cap in far enough so that the retaining snapring can be installed.

9. Install all remaining U-joints in the same manner.

10. Install the driveshaft and grease the new U-joints.

Double Cardan Joint

1. Working at the rear axle end of the shaft, mark the position of the spiders, the center yoke, and the centering socket yoke as related to the companion flange. The spiders must be assembled with the bosses in their original position to provide proper clearances.

2. Using a large vise or an arbor press and a socket smaller than the bearing cap on one side and a socket larger than the bearing cap on the other side, drive one of the bearings in toward the center of the universal joint, which will force the opposite bearing out.

3. Remove the driveshaft from the vise.

4. Tighten the bearing in the vise and tap on the yoke to free the bearing from the center yoke. Do not tap on the driveshaft tube.

5. Reposition the sockets on the yoke and force the opposite bearing outward and remove it.

6. Position the sockets on one of the remaining bearings and force it outward approximately ⅜ in. (9.5mm).

7. Grip the bearing in the vise and tap on the weld yoke to free the bearing from the center yoke. Do not tap on the driveshaft tube.

8. Reposition the sockets on the yoke to press out the remaining bearing.

9. Remove the spider from the center yoke.

10. Remove the bearings from the driveshaft yoke as outlined above and remove the spider from the yoke.

11. Insert a suitable tool into the centering ball socket located in the companion flange and pry out the rubber seal. Remove the retainer, three piece ball seat, washer and spring from the ball socket.

12. Inspect the centering ball socket assembly for worn or damaged parts. If any damage is evident replace the entire assembly.

13. Insert the spring, washer, three piece ball seat and retainer into the ball socket.

14. Using a suitable tool, install the centering ball socket seal.

15. Position the spider in the driveshaft yoke. Make sure the spider bosses are in the same position as originally installed. Press in the bearing cups with the sockets and vise. Install the internal snaprings provided in the repair kit.

16. Position the center yoke over the spider ends and press in the bearing cups. Install the snaprings.

17. Install the spider in the companion flange yoke. Make sure the spider bosses are in the position as originally installed. Press on the bearing cups and install the snaprings.

18. Position the center yoke over the spider ends and press on the bearing cups. Install the snaprings.

DRIVESHAFT BALANCING

▶ See Figures 91, 92 and 93

Driveline vibration or shudder, felt mainly on acceleration, coasting or under engine braking, can be caused, among other things, by improper driveshaft installation or imbalance.

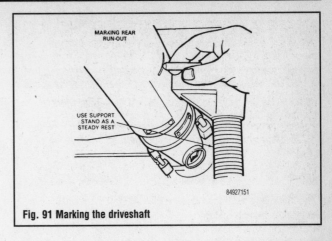
Fig. 91 Marking the driveshaft

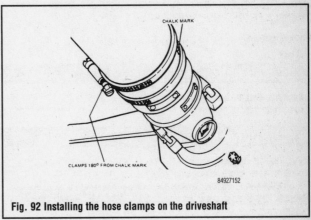
Fig. 92 Installing the hose clamps on the driveshaft

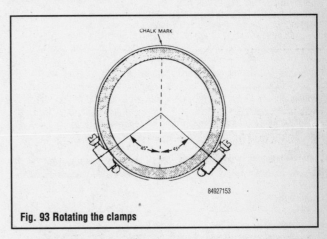
Fig. 93 Rotating the clamps

If the condition follows driveshaft replacement or installation after disconnection, try disconnecting the driveshaft at the axle and rotating it 180°. Then, reconnect it. If that doesn't work, try the following procedure:

1. Raise and support the truck on jackstands so that all wheels are off the ground and free to rotate. The truck must be as level as possible.

2. Remove the wheels. Install the lug nuts to retain the brake drums or rotors.

3. Start the engine, place the transmission in gear and increase engine speed to the point at which the vibration is most severe. Record this speedometer speed as a reference point.

4. Shift into **Neutral** and shut off the engine.

5. Check all driveshaft attachment fasteners, U-joint bearing caps, U-joint cap retaining rings or cap locating lugs. Tighten any loose fasteners, replace any missing, damaged or shaved retaining rings or lugs. If worn U-joints are suspected, replace them. If everything is normal, or if any corrections made do not solve the problem, continue.

6. Start the engine, place the transmission in gear and increase engine speed to an indicated road speed of 40–50 mph (64–80 km/h). Maintain this speed with some sort of accelerator control, such as a weight on the pedal, or have an assistant hold the pedal.

✳✳ CAUTION

The following procedure can be dangerous! Be careful when approaching the spinning driveline parts!

7. Carefully raise a piece of chalk until **just barely** touches the driveshaft at the front, middle and rear. At either end, try touching the shaft about an inch or so from the yokes. Don't touch any existing driveshaft balancing weights. The chalk marks will indicate the heavy points of the driveshaft. Shut off the engine.

➡It helps greatly to steady your hand on some sort of support.

8. Check the driveshaft end of the shaft first. If the chalk mark is continuous around the shaft proceed to the opposite end, then the middle. If the chalk mark is not continuous, install 2 screw-type hose clamps on the shaft so that their heads are 180° from the center of the chalk mark.

9. Start the engine and run it to the speed recorded previously. If the vibration persists, stop the engine and move the screw portions of the clamps 45° from each other. Try the run test again.

✳✳ WARNING

Check the engine temperature!

FRONT DRIVE AXLE

▶ **See Figures 94 thru 99**

Manual Locking Hubs

REMOVAL & INSTALLATION

1. To remove hub, first separate cap assembly from body assembly by removing the six (6) socket head capscrews from the cap assembly and slip apart.
2. Remove snapring (retainer ring) from the end of the axle shaft.
3. Remove the lock ring seated in the groove of the wheel hub. The body assembly will now slide out of the wheel hub. If necessary, use an appropriate puller to remove the body assembly.
4. Install hub in reverse order of removal. Torque socket head capscrews to 30–50 inch lbs. (3.4–5.64 Nm).

Automatic Locking Hubs

REMOVAL

1. Remove the 5 capscrews with a TX25 Torx® bit, and remove hub cap assembly from the hub.

➡Take care to avoid dropping the spring, ball bearing, bearing race or retainer!

2. Remove the rubber seal.
3. Remove the seal bridge (a small metal stamping) from the retainer ring space.
4. Remove lock ring seated in the groove of the wheel hub by compressing the ends with a needle nose pliers, while pulling the hub lock from the hub body. If body assembly does not slide out easily, use an appropriate puller.
5. If the hub and spindle are being removed:
   a. Remove the C-washer from the groove in the stub shaft.
   b. Remove the splined spacer from the shaft.
   c. Remove the outer locknut, locking washer and inner bearing locknut.
   d. Pull the hub and bearings from the spindle.
6. See the Wheel Bearing procedures for cleaning and repacking the bearings.

10. If the vibration persists, move the screw portions of the clamps apart in small increments until the vibration disappears. If this doesn't cure the problem, proceed to the other end, then the middle, performing the operation all over again. If the problem persists, investigate other driveline components.

Center Bearing

REMOVAL & INSTALLATION

1. Remove the driveshafts.
2. Remove the two center support bearing attaching bolts and remove the assembly from the vehicle.
3. Do not immerse the sealed bearing in any type of cleaning fluid. Wipe the bearing and cushion clean with a cloth dampened with cleaning fluid.
4. Check the bearing for wear or rough action by rotating the inner race while holding the outer race. If wear or roughness is evident, replace the bearing. Examine the rubber cushion for evidence of hardening, cracking, or deterioration. Replace it if it is damaged in any way.
5. Place the bearing in the rubber support and the rubber support in the U-shaped support and install the bearing in the reverse order of removal. Tighten the bearing to support bracket fasteners to 50 ft. lbs. (68 Nm).

DISASSEMBLY

1. Remove the snapring and flat washer from the inner end of the hub lock assembly
2. Pull the hub sleeve and attached parts out of the drag sleeve to unlock the tangs of the brake band, Remove the drag sleeve assembly.

➡Never remove the brake band from the drag sleeve!

ASSEMBLY

1. Wash all parts in a non-flammable solvent and let them air dry.
2. Lubricate the brake band and drag sleeve with 1.5g (0.05 oz.) of Automatic Hub Lock Grease E1TZ-19590-A (ESL-M1C193A) (Darmex Spec. DX-123-LT), or equivalent. Work the lubricant over and under the spring.
3. Dip the locking hub body (not the cap or brake band/drag sleeve) into Dexron®II ATF and allow it to drip off the excess.
4. Assemble the brake band so that one tang is on each side of the plastic outer cage, located in the window of the steel inner cage. It will probably be necessary to cock these parts to engage the tangs as the drag sleeve is positioned against the face of the cam follower.
5. Install the washer and snapring.

INSTALLATION

1. Position the hub and bearings on the spindle. Adjust the bearings as described below.
2. Install the splined spacer and C-washer.
3. Wipe off excess grease from the splines and start the locking hub assembly into the hub body. Make sure the large tangs are aligned with the lockwasher and the outside diameter, and the inside diameter splines are aligned with the hub and axle shaft splines.
4. Install the retaining ring while pushing the locking hub assembly into the hub body.
5. Install the seal bridge, narrow end first.
6. Install the rubber seal.
7. Install the cover, making sure the ball bearing, spring and race are in position.
8. Install the 5 Torx® screws and tighten them to 40–50 inch lbs. (4.5–5.65 Nm) by tighten one, then skipping one, and so on until they are all tightened.

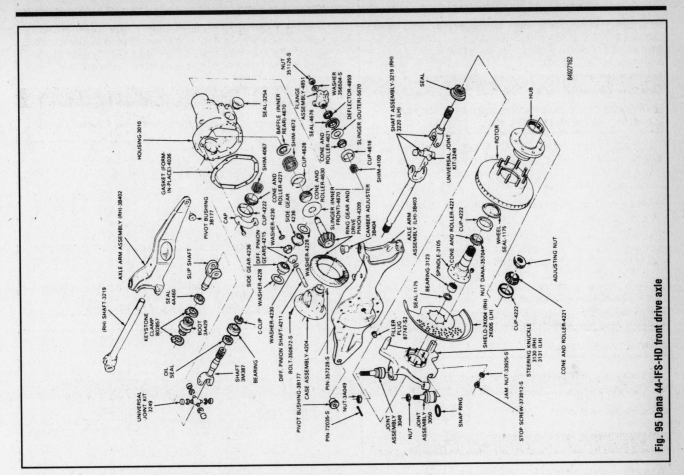

Fig. 95 Dana 44-IFS-HD front drive axle

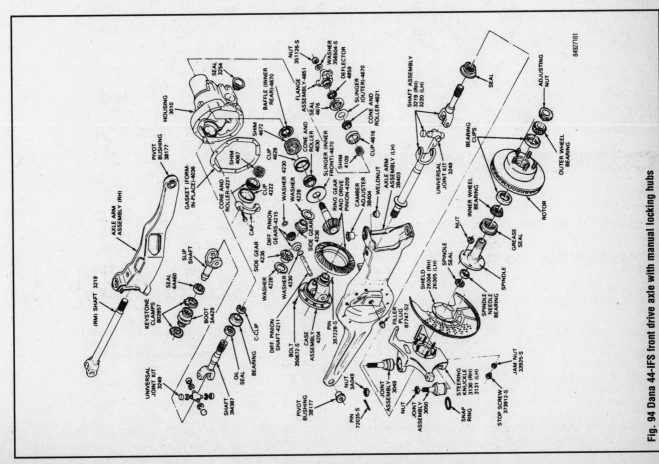

Fig. 94 Dana 44-IFS front drive axle with manual locking hubs

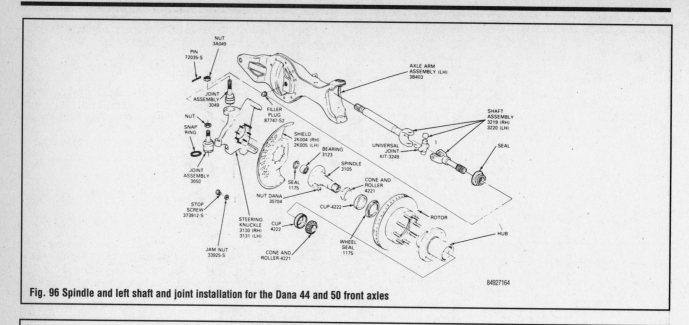

Fig. 96 Spindle and left shaft and joint installation for the Dana 44 and 50 front axles

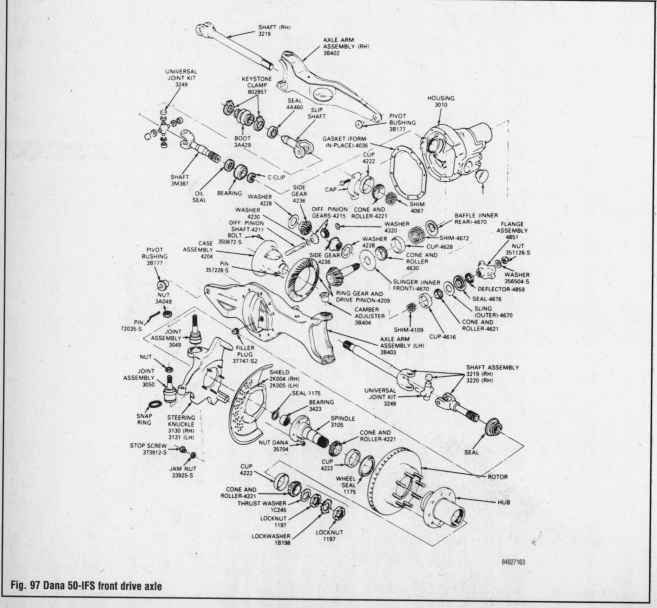

Fig. 97 Dana 50-IFS front drive axle

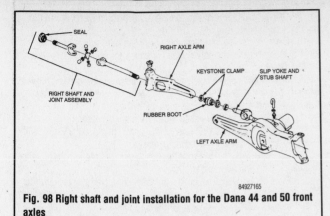

84927165

Fig. 98 Right shaft and joint installation for the Dana 44 and 50 front axles

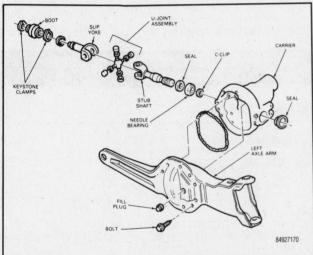

84927170

Fig. 99 Carrier and slip yoke, and stub shaft installation on the Dana 44 and 50 IFS

Front Wheel Bearings

For Removal, Repacking and Installation of front wheel bearings, see Section 1.

Right and Left Axle Shafts, Spindle and Joint

REMOVAL & INSTALLATION

Dana 44 IFS, Dana 44 IFS-HD, and Dana 50 IFS

1. Raise and support the front end on jackstands.
2. Remove the front wheels.
3. Remove the calipers.
4. Remove the hub/rotor assemblies.
5. Remove the nuts retaining the spindle to the steering knuckle. Tap the spindle with a plastic mallet to remove it from the knuckle.
6. Remove the splash shield.
7. On the left side, pull the shaft from the carrier, through the knuckle.
8. On the right side, remove and discard the keystone clamp from the shaft and joint assembly and the stub shaft. Slide the rubber boot onto the shaft and pull the shaft and joint assembly from the splines of the stub shaft.
9. Place the spindle in a soft-jawed vise clamped on the second step of the spindle.
10. Using a slide hammer and bearing puller, remove the needle bearing from the spindle.
11. Inspect all parts. If the spindle is excessively corroded or pitted it must

be replaced. If the U-joints are excessively loose or don't move freely, they must be replaced. If any shaft is bent, it must be replaced.

To install:

12. Clean all dirt and grease from the spindle bearing bore. The bore must be free of nicks and burrs.
13. Insert a new spindle bearing in its bore with the printing facing outward. Drive it into place with drive T80T–4000–S for F-150 and Bronco and F-250, or T80T–4000–R for the F-350, or their equivalents. Install a new bearing seal with the lip facing away from the bearing.
14. Pack the bearing and hub seal with grease. Install the hub seal with a driver.
15. Place the thrust washer on the axle shaft.
16. Place a new slinger on the axle shaft.
17. Install the rubber V-seal on the slinger. The seal lip should face the spindle.
18. Install the plastic spacer on the axle shaft. The chamfered side of the spacer should be inboard against the axle shaft.
19. Pack the thrust face of the seal in the spindle bore and the V-seal on the axle shaft with heavy duty, high temperature, waterproof wheel bearing grease.
20. On the right side, install the rubber boot and new keystone clamps on the stub shaft and slip yoke. The splines permit only one way of meshing so you'll have to properly align the missing spline in the slip yoke with the gapless male spline on the shaft. Slide the right shaft and joint assembly into the slip yoke, making sure that the splines are fully engaged. Slide the boot over the assembly and crimp the keystone clamp.
21. On the left side, slide the shaft and joint assembly through the knuckle and engage the splines in the carrier.
22. Install the splash shield and spindle on the knuckle. Tighten the spindle nuts to 60 ft. lbs. (81 Nm).
23. Install the rotor on the spindle. Install the outer wheel bearing into the cup. Make sure that the grease seal lip totally encircles the spindle.
24. Install the wheel bearing, locknut, thrust bearing, snapring and locking hubs. See Section 1.
25. Install the caliper.

Spindle and Front Axle Shaft

REMOVAL & INSTALLATION

Dana 60 Monobeam

▶ **See Figures 100 thru 106**

1. Raise and support the front end on jackstands.
2. Remove the caliper from the knuckle and wire it out of the way.
3. Remove the free-running hub.
4. Remove the front wheel bearing. See Section 1.
5. Remove the hub and rotor assembly.
6. Remove the spindle-to-knuckle bolts. Tap the spindle from the knuckle using a plastic mallet.
7. Remove the splash shield and caliper support.
8. Pull the axle shaft out through the knuckle.

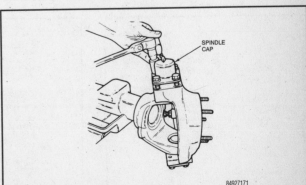

84927171

Fig. 100 Spindle cap removal for the Dana 60 Monobeam front drive axle

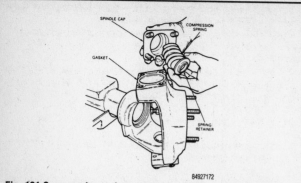

Fig. 101 Compression spring removal for the Dana 60 Monobeam front drive axle

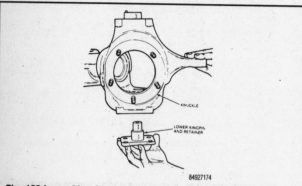

Fig. 102 Lower kingpin removal for the Dana 60 Monobeam front drive axle

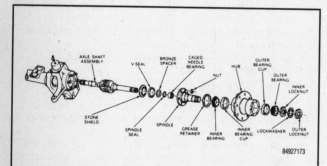

Fig. 103 Axle shift components for the Dana 60 Monobeam front drive axle

9. Using a slide hammer and bearing cup puller, remove the needle bearing from the spindle.

10. Clean the spindle bore thoroughly and make sure that it is free of nicks and burrs. If the bore is excessively pitted or scored, the spindle must be replaced.

To install:

11. Insert a new spindle bearing in its bore with the printing facing outward. Drive it into place with driver T80T–4000–R, or its equivalent. Install a new bearing seal with the lip facing away from the bearing.

12. Pack the bearing with waterproof wheel bearing grease.

13. Pack the thrust face of the seal in the spindle bore and the V-seal on the axle shaft with waterproof wheel bearing grease.

14. Carefully guide the axle shaft through the knuckle and into the housing. Align the splines and fully seat the shaft.

15. Place the bronze spacer on the shaft. The chamfered side of the spacer must be inboard.

16. Install the splash shield and caliper support.

17. Place the spindle on the knuckle and install the bolts. Tighten the bolts to 50–60 ft. lbs. (68–81 Nm).

18. Install the hub/rotor assembly on the spindle.

19. Assemble the wheel bearings.

20. Assemble the free-running hub.

Right Side Slip Yoke and Stub Shaft, Carrier, Carrier Oil Seal and Bearing

REMOVAL & INSTALLATION

Independent Front Axle

➡ This procedure requires the use of special tools.

1. Raise and support the front end on jackstands.

2. Disconnect the front driveshaft from the carrier and wire it up out of the way.

3. Remove the left and right axle shafts and both spindles.

4. Support the carrier with a floor jack and unbolt the carrier from the support arm.

5. Place a drain pan under the carrier, separate the carrier from the support arm and drain the carrier.

6. Remove the carrier from the truck.

7. Place the carrier in holding fixture T57L–500–B with adapters T80T–4000–B.

8. Rotate the slip yoke and shaft assembly from the carrier.

9. Using a slide hammer/puller remove the caged needle bearing and oil seal as a unit. Discard the oil seal and bearing.

To install:

10. Clean the bearing bore thoroughly and make sure that it is free of nicks and burrs.

11. Insert a new bearing in its bore with the printing facing outward. Drive it into place with driver T83T–1244–A, or its equivalent. Install a new bearing seal with the lip facing away from the bearing. Coat the bearing and seal with waterproof wheel bearing grease.

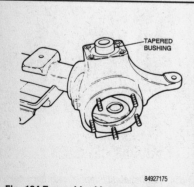

Fig. 104 Tapered bushing removal for the Dana 60 Monobeam, front drive axle

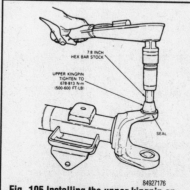

Fig. 105 Installing the upper kingpin on the Dana 60 Monobeam front drive axle

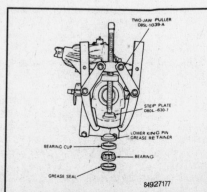

Fig. 106 Removing the lower kingpin on the Dana 60 Monobeam front drive axle

12. Install the slip yoke and shaft assembly into the carrier so that the groove in the shaft is visible in the differential case.

13. Install the snapring in the groove in the shaft. It may be necessary to force the snapring into place with a small prybar. Don't strike the snapring!

14. Remove the carrier from the holding fixture.

15. Clean all traces of sealant from the carrier and support arm. Make sure the mating surfaces are clean. Apply a ¼ in. (6mm) wide bead of RTV sealant to the mating surface of the carrier. The bead must be continuous and should not pass through or outside of the holes. Install the carrier with 5 minutes of applying the sealer.

16. Position the carrier on the jack and raise it into position using guide pins to align it if you'd like. Install and hand-tighten the bolts. Tighten the bolts in a circular pattern to 30–40 ft. lbs. (41–54 Nm).

17. Install the support arm tab bolts and tighten them to 85–100 ft. lbs. (115–136 Nm).

18. Install all other parts in reverse order of removal.

Pinion Seal

REMOVAL & INSTALLATION

Independent Front Axle

➡ **A torque wrench capable of at least 225 ft. lbs. (305 Nm) is required for pinion seal installation.**

1. Raise and safely support the vehicle with jackstands under the frame rails. Allow the axle to drop to rebound position for working clearance.

2. Mark the companion flanges and U-joints for correct reinstallation position.

REAR AXLE

Axle Shaft, Bearing and Seal

REMOVAL & INSTALLATION

▶ **See Figures 107 thru 114**

Ford 8.8 in. (223.5mm) Ring Gear With Integral Carrier; Ford 10.25 in. (260.35mm) Ring Gear With Semi-Floating Integral Carrier

▶ **See Figure 115**

1. Raise and safely support the vehicle on jackstands.

2. Remove the wheels from the brake drums.

3. Place a drain pan under the housing and drain the lubricant by loosening the housing cover.

4. Remove the locks securing the brake drums to the axle shaft flanges and remove the drums.

5. Remove the housing cover and gasket.

3. Remove the driveshaft. Use a suitable tool to hold the companion flange. Remove the pinion nut and companion flange.

4. Use a slide hammer and hook or sheet metal screw to remove the oil seal.

To install:

5. Install a new pinion seal after lubricating the sealing surfaces. Use a suitable seal driver. Install the companion flange and pinion nut. Tighten the nut to 200–220 ft. lbs. (271–298 Nm).

Monobeam Front Axle

➡ **A torque wrench capable of at least 300 ft. lbs. (407 Nm) is required for pinion seal installation.**

1. Raise and support the truck on jackstands.

2. Allow the axle to hang freely.

3. Matchmark and disconnect the driveshaft from the front axle.

4. Using a tool such as T75T–4851–B, or equivalent, hold the pinion flange while removing the pinion nut.

5. Using a puller, remove the pinion flange.

6. Use a puller to remove the seal, or punch the seal out using a pin punch.

To install:

7. Thoroughly clean the seal bore and make sure that it is not damaged in any way. Coat the sealing edge of the new seal with a small amount of 80W/90 oil and drive the seal into the housing using a seal driver.

8. Coat the inside of the pinion flange with clean 80W/90 oil and install the flange onto the pinion shaft.

9. Install the nut on the pinion shaft and tighten it to 250–300 ft. lbs. (339–407 Nm).

10. Connect the driveshaft.

6. Remove the side gear pinion shaft lockbolt and the side gear pinion shaft.

7. Push the axle shafts inward and remove the C-locks from the inner end of the axle shafts. Temporarily replace the shaft and lockbolt to retain the differential gears in position.

8. Remove the axle shafts with a slide hammer. Be sure the seal is not damaged by the splines on the axle shaft.

9. Remove the bearing and oil seal from the housing. Both the seal and bearing can be removed with a slide hammer

10. Two types of bearings are used on some axles, one requiring a press fit and the other a loose fit. A loose fitting bearing does not necessarily indicate excessive wear.

11. Inspect the axle shaft housing and axle shafts for burrs or other irregularities. Replace any work or damaged parts. A light yellow color on the bearing journal of the axle shaft is normal, and does not require replacement of the axle shaft. Slight pitting and wear is also normal.

12. Lightly coat the wheel bearing rollers with axle lubricant. Install the bearings in the axle housing until the bearing seats firmly against the shoulder.

88287P53

Fig. 107 View of the differential carrier assembly

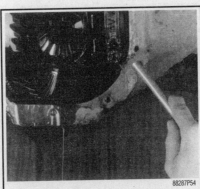
88287P54

Fig. 108 Clean the cover and housing mating surfaces good

88287P55

Fig. 109 Rotate the carrier until the pinion shaft retaining screw is exposed, then remove the screw

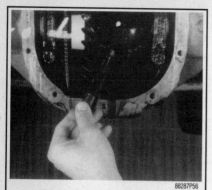

Fig. 110 After the retaining screw is out, remove the pinion shaft from the carrier

Fig. 111 Push the axle in toward the center and remove the C-lock from the end of the axle

Fig. 112 When the C-lock is removed, the axle can be pulled from the housing

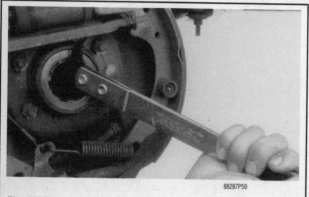

Fig. 113 Remove the old axle seal, using a suitable prytool

Fig. 114 Install a new seal using a suitable seal installer tool and mallet

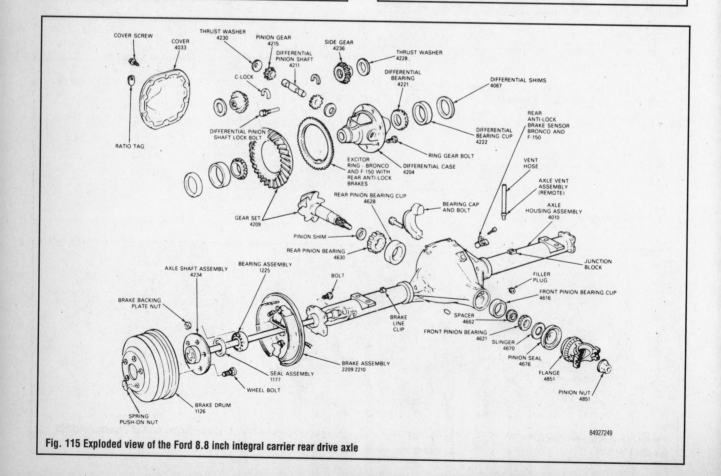

Fig. 115 Exploded view of the Ford 8.8 inch integral carrier rear drive axle

13. Wipe all lubricant from the oil seal bore, before installing the seal.

14. Inspect the original seals for wear. If necessary, these may be replaced with new seals, which are prepacked with lubricant and do not require soaking.

To install:

15. Install the oil seal.

16. Remove the lockbolt and pinion shaft. Carefully slide the axle shafts into place. Be careful that you do not damage the seal with the splined end of the axle shaft. Engage the splined end of the shaft with the differential side gears.

17. Install the axle shaft C-locks on the inner end of the axle shafts and seat the C-locks in the counterbore of the differential side gears.

18. Rotate the differential pinion gears until the differential pinion shaft can be installed. Install the differential pinion shaft lockbolt. Tighten to 15–22 ft. lbs. (20–30 Nm).

19. Install the brake drum on the axle shaft flange.

20. Install the wheel and tire on the brake drum and tighten the attaching nuts.

21. Clean the gasket surface of the rear housing and install a new cover gasket and the housing cover. Some covers do not use a gasket. On these mod-els, apply a bead of silicone sealer on the gasket surface. The bead should run inside of the bolt holes.

22. Raise the rear axle so that it is in the running position. Add the amount of specified lubricant to bring the lubricant level to ½ in. (12.7mm) below the filler hole.

Ford 10.25 in. (260.35mm) Ring Gear With Full Floating Integral Carrier

♦ See Figures 116 thru 125

The wheel bearings on the full floating rear axle are packed with wheel bearing grease. Axle lubricant can also flow into the wheel hubs and bearings, however, wheel bearing grease is the primary lubricant. The wheel bearing grease provides lubrication until the axle lubricant reaches the bearings during normal operation.

1. Set the parking brake and loosen the axle shaft bolts.

2. Raise the rear wheels off the floor and place jackstands under the rear axle housing so that the axle is parallel with the floor.

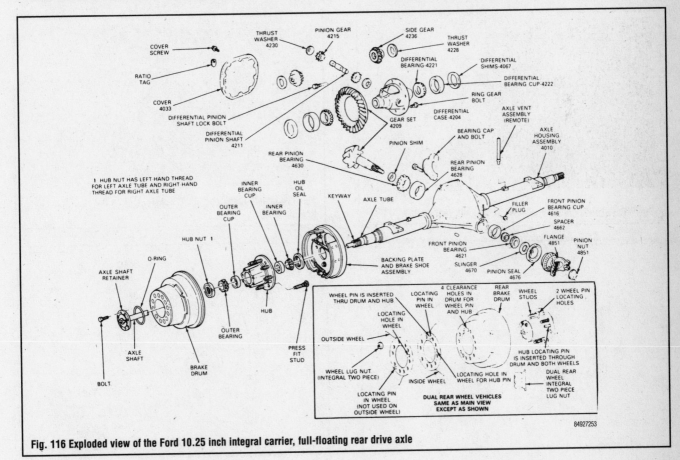

Fig. 116 Exploded view of the Ford 10.25 inch integral carrier, full-floating rear drive axle

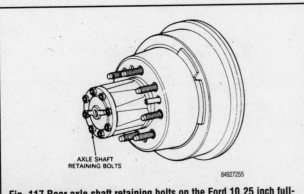

Fig. 117 Rear axle shaft retaining bolts on the Ford 10.25 inch full-floating rear axle

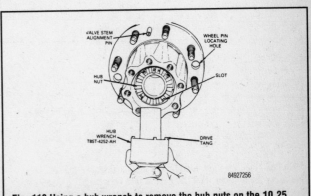

Fig. 118 Using a hub wrench to remove the hub nuts on the 10.25 inch full-floating axle

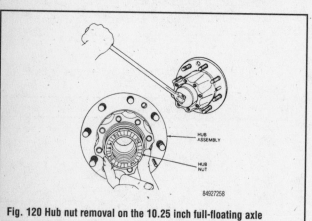

Fig. 119 Loosening the hub on the 10.25 inch full-floating axle

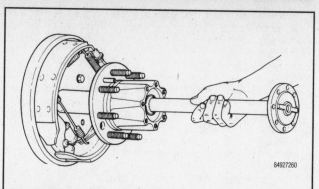

Fig. 122 Removing the axle shaft from the Ford 10.25 inch full-floating rear axle

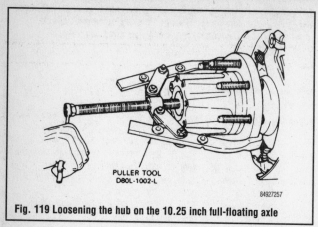

Fig. 120 Hub nut removal on the 10.25 inch full-floating axle

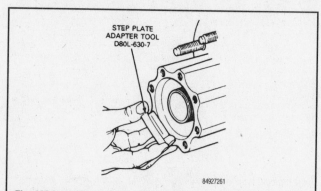

Fig. 123 Installing the step plate adapter tool on the 10.25 inch full-floating axle

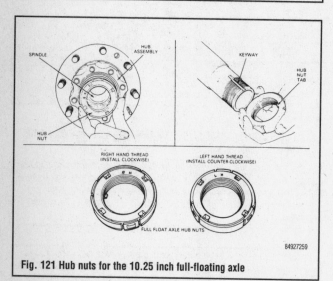

Fig. 121 Hub nuts for the 10.25 inch full-floating axle

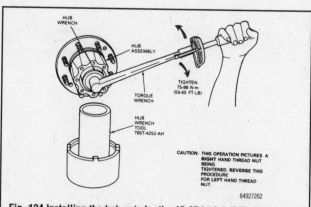

Fig. 124 Installing the hub nuts for the 10.25 inch full-floating axle

3. Remove the wheels.
4. Remove the brake drums.
5. Remove the axle shaft bolts.
6. Remove the axle shaft and discard the gaskets.
7. With the axle shaft removed, remove the gasket from the axle shaft flange studs.
8. Install Hub Wrench T85T–4252–AH, or equivalent, so that the drive tangs on the tool engage the slots in the hub nut.

➡The hub nuts are right-hand thread on the right hub and left-hand thread on the left hub. The hub nuts should be stamped RH and LH. Never use power or impact tools on these nuts! The nuts will ratchet during removal.

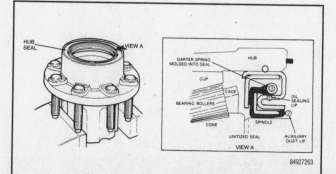

Fig. 125 Unitized rear wheel seals on the 10.25 inch full-floating axle

9. Remove the hub nut.

10. Install step plate adapter tool D80L–630–7, or equivalent, in the hub.

11. Install puller D80L–1002–L, or equivalent and loosen the hub to the point of removal. Remove the puller and step plate.

12. Remove the hub, taking care to catch the outer bearing as the hub comes off.

13. Install the hub in a soft-jawed vise and pry out the hub seal.

14. Lift out the inner bearing.

15. Drive out the inner and outer bearing races with a drift.

16. Wash all the old grease or axle lubricant out of the wheel hub, using a suitable solvent.

17. Wash the bearing races and rollers and inspect them for pitting, galling, and uneven wear patterns. Inspect the roller for end wear. Replace any bearing and race that appears in any way damaged. Always replace the bearings and races as a set.

18. Coat the race bores with a light coat of clean, waterproof wheel bearing grease and drive the races squarely into the bores until they are fully seated. A good indication that the race is seated is when you notice the grease from the bore squashing out under the race when it contact the shoulder. Another indication is a definite change in the metallic tone when you seat the race. Just be very careful to avoid damaging the bearing surface of the race!

19. Pack each bearing cone and roller with a bearing packer or in the manner outlined in Section 1 for the front wheel bearings on 2WD Drive trucks.

To install:

20. Place the inner bearing cone and roller assembly in the wheel hub.

➡When installing the new seal, the words OIL SIDE must go inwards towards the bearing!

21. Place the seal squarely in the hub and drive it into place. The best tool for the job is a seal driver such as T85T–1175–AH, which will stop when the seal is at the proper depth.

➡If the seal is misaligned or damaged during installation, a new seal must be installed.

22. Clean the spindle thoroughly. If the spindle is excessively pitted, damaged or has a predominately bluish tint (from overheating), it must be replaced.

23. Coat the spindle with 80W/90 oil.

24. Pack the hub with clean, waterproof wheel bearing grease.

25. Pack the outer bearing with clean, waterproof wheel bearing grease in the same manner as you packed the inner bearing.

26. Place the outer bearing in the hub and install the hub and bearing together on the spindle.

27. Install the hub nut on the spindle. Make sure that the nut tab is located in the keyway prior to thread engagement. Turn the hub nut onto the threads as far as you can by hand, noting the thread direction.

28. Install the hub wrench tool and tighten the nut to 55–65 ft. lbs. (75–88 Nm). Rotate the hub occasionally during nut tightening.

29. Ratchet the nut back 5 teeth. **Make sure that you hear 5 clicks!**

30. Inspect the axle shaft O-ring seal and replace it if it looks at all bad.

31. Install the axle shaft.

32. Coat the axle shaft bolt threads with waterproof seal and install them by hand until they seat. **Do not tighten them with a wrench at this time!**

33. Check the diameter across the center of the brake shoes. Check the diameter of the brake drum. Adjust the brake shoes so that their diameter is 0.030 in. (0.76mm) less than the drum diameter.

34. Install the brake drum

35. Install the wheel.

36. Loosen the differential filler plug. If lubricant starts to run out, retighten the plug. If not, remove the plug and fill the housing with 80W/90 gear oil.

37. Lower the truck to the floor.

38. Tighten the wheel lugs to 140 ft. lbs. (190 Nm).

39. Now tighten the axle shaft bolts. Tighten them to 60–80 ft. lbs. (81–108 Nm).

Dana Model 80

♦ See Figures 126 and 127

New Dual Rear Wheel models have flat-faced lug nut replacing the old cone-shaped lug nuts. NEVER replace these new nuts with the

older design! Never replace the newer designed wheels with older design wheels! The newer wheels have lug holes with special shoulders to accommodate the newly designed lug nuts.

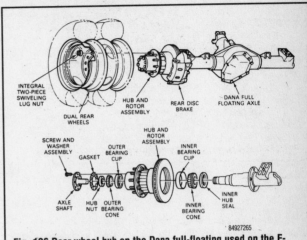

Fig. 126 Rear wheel hub on the Dana full-floating used on the F-Super Duty

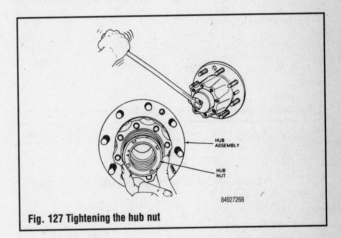

Fig. 127 Tightening the hub nut

1988–89 F-SUPER DUTY, STRIPPED CHASSIS AND MOTOR HOME CHASSIS

The wheel bearings on full floating rear axles are packed with wheel bearing grease. Axle lubricant can also flow into the wheel hubs and bearings, however, wheel bearing grease is the primary lubricant. The wheel bearing grease provides lubrication until the axle lubricant reaches the bearings during normal operation.

1. Set the parking brake and loosen, but do not remove, the axle shaft bolts.

2. Raise the rear wheels off the floor and place jackstands under the rear axle housing so that the axle is parallel with the floor. Release the parking brake.

3. Remove the axle shaft bolts and lockwashers. They should not be re-used.

4. Place a heavy duty wheel dolly under the wheels and raise them so that all weight is off the wheel bearings.

5. Remove the axle shaft and gasket(s).

6. Remove the caliper. See Section 9.

7. Using a special hub nut wrench, remove the hub nut.

➡The hub nut on the right spindle is right-hand thread; the one on the left spindle is left-hand thread. They are marked RH and LH. NEVER use an impact wrench on the hub nut!

8. Remove the outer bearing cone and pull the wheel straight off the axle.

9. With a piece of hardwood or a brass drift which will just clear the outer bearing cup, drive the inner bearing cone and inner seal out of the wheel hub.

To install:

10. Wash all the old grease or axle lubricant out of the wheel hub, using a suitable solvent.

11. Wash the bearing cups and rollers and inspect them for pitting, galling, and uneven wear patterns. Inspect the roller for end wear.

12. If the bearing cups are to be replaced, drive them out with a brass drift. Install the new cups with a block of wood and hammer or press them in.

13. If the bearing cups are properly seated, a 0.0015 in. (0.038mm) feeler gauge will not fit between the cup and the wheel hub. The gauge should not fit beneath the cup. Check several places to make sure the cups are squarely seated.

14. Pack each bearing cone and roller with a bearing packer or in the manner outlined for the front wheel bearings on 2WD trucks in Section 1. Use a multi-purpose wheel bearing grease.

15. Place the inner bearing cone and roller assembly in the wheel hub. Install a new inner seal in the hub with a seal installation tool.

16. Wrap the threads of the spindle with tape and carefully slide the hub straight on the spindle. Take care to avoid damaging the seal! Remove the tape.

17. Install the outer bearing. Start the hub nut, making sure that the hub tab is engaged with the keyway prior to threading.

18. Tighten the nut to 65–75 ft. lbs. (88–102 Nm) while rotating the wheel.

➡ **The hub will ratchet at torque is applied. This ratcheting can be avoided by using Ford tool No. T88T-4252-A. Avoiding ratcheting will give more even bearing preloads.**

19. Back off (loosen) the adjusting nut 90° (¼ turn). Then, tighten it to 15–20 ft. lbs. (20–27 Nm).

20. Using a dial indicator, check end-play of the hub. No end-play is permitted.

21. Clean the hub bolt holes thoroughly. Replace the hub if any cracks are found around the holes or if the threads in the holes are in any way damaged.

22. Install the axle shaft, new flange gasket, lock washers and new shaft retaining bolts. Coat the bolt threads with thread adhesive. Tighten them snugly, but not completely.

23. Install the caliper.

24. Install the wheels.

25. Lower the truck to the groups.

26. Tighten the wheel lug nuts.

27. Tighten the axle shaft bolts to 70–85 ft. lbs. (95–115 Nm).

1990–96 F-SUPER DUTY, STRIPPED CHASSIS AND MOTOR HOME CHASSIS

The wheel bearings on full floating rear axles are packed with wheel bearing grease. Axle lubricant can also flow into the wheel hubs and bearings, however, wheel bearing grease is the primary lubricant. The wheel bearing grease provides lubrication until the axle lubricant reaches the bearings during normal operation.

1. Set the parking brake and loosen, but do not remove, the axle shaft bolts.

2. Raise the rear wheels off the floor and place jackstands under the rear axle housing so that the axle is parallel with the floor. The axle shafts must turn freely, so release the parking brake.

3. Remove the axle shaft bolts and lockwashers. They should not be reused.

4. Place a heavy duty wheel dolly under the wheels and raise them so that all weight is off the wheel bearings.

5. Remove the axle shaft and gasket(s).

6. Remove the brake caliper. See Section 9.

7. Using a special hub nut wrench, remove the hub nut.

➡ **The hub nuts for both sides are right-hand thread and marked RH.**

8. Remove the outer bearing cone and pull the wheel straight off the axle.

9. With a piece of hardwood or a brass drift which will just clear the outer bearing cup, drive the inner bearing cone and inner seal out of the wheel hub.

To install:

10. Wash all the old grease or axle lubricant out of the wheel hub, using a suitable solvent.

11. Wash the bearing cups and rollers and inspect them for pitting, galling, and uneven wear patterns. Inspect the roller for end wear.

12. If the bearing cups are to be replaced, drive them out with a brass drift. Install the new cups with a block of wood and hammer or press them in.

13. If the bearing cups are properly seated, a 0.0015 in. (0.038mm) feeler gauge will not fit between the cup and the wheel hub. The gauge should not fit beneath the cup. Check several places to make sure the cups are squarely seated.

14. Pack each bearing cone and roller with a bearing packer or in the manner outlined for the front wheel bearings on 2WD trucks in Section 1. Use a multi-purpose wheel bearing grease.

15. Place the inner bearing cone and roller assembly in the wheel hub. Install a new inner seal in the hub with a seal installation tool.

16. Wrap the threads of the spindle with tape and carefully slide the hub straight on the spindle. Take care to avoid damaging the seal! Remove the tape.

17. Install the outer bearing. Start the hub nut, making sure that the hub tab is engaged with the keyway prior to threading.

18. Tighten the nut to 65–75 ft. lbs. (88–102 Nm) while rotating the wheel.

➡ **The hub will ratchet at torque is applied. This ratcheting can be avoided by using Ford tool No. T88T-4252-A. Avoiding ratcheting will give more even bearing preloads.**

19. Back off (loosen) the adjusting nut 90° (¼ turn). Then, tighten it to 15–20 ft. lbs. (20–27 Nm).

20. Using a dial indicator, check end-play of the hub. No end-play is permitted.

21. Clean the hub bolt holes thoroughly. Replace the hub if any cracks are found around the holes or if the threads in the holes are in any way damaged.

22. Install the axle shaft, new flange gasket, lock washers and new shaft retaining bolts. Coat the bolt threads with thread adhesive. Tighten them snugly, but not completely.

23. Install the caliper.

24. Install the wheels.

25. Lower the truck to the groups.

26. Tighten the wheel lug nuts.

27. Tighten the axle shaft bolts to 40–55 ft. lbs. (54–75 Nm).

Pinion Seal

REMOVAL & INSTALLATION

Ford 8.8 in. (223.5mm) Ring Gear With Integral Carrier Axle

▶ **See Figures 128 and 129**

➡ **A torque wrench capable of at least 225 ft. lbs. (305 Nm) is required for pinion seal installation.**

1. Raise and safely support the vehicle with jackstands under the frame rails. Allow the axle to drop to rebound position for working clearance.

2. Remove the rear wheels and brake drums. No drag must be present on the axle.

3. Mark the companion flanges and U-joints for correct reinstallation position.

4. Remove the driveshaft.

5. Using an inch pound torque wrench and socket on the pinion yoke nut

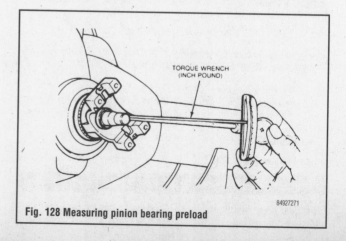

Fig. 128 Measuring pinion bearing preload

84927271

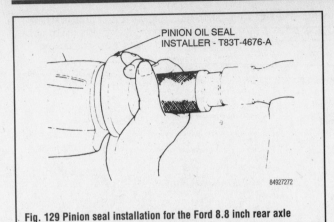

PINION OIL SEAL
INSTALLER - T83T-4676-A

84927272

Fig. 129 Pinion seal installation for the Ford 8.8 inch rear axle

measure the amount of torque needed to maintain differential rotation through several clockwise revolutions. Record the measurement.

6. Use a suitable tool to hold the companion flange. Remove the pinion nut.

7. Place a drain pan under the differential, clean the area around the seal, and mark the yoke-to-pinion relation.

8. Use a 2-jawed puller to remove the pinion.

9. Remove the seal with a small prybar.

To install:

10. Thoroughly clean the oil seal bore.

➡If you are not absolutely certain of the proper seal installation depth, the proper seal driver must be used. If the seal is misaligned or damaged during installation, it must be removed and a new seal installed.

11. Drive the new seal into place with a seal driver such as T83T–4676–A. Coat the seal lip with clean, waterproof wheel bearing grease.

12. Coat the splines with a small amount of wheel bearing grease and install the yoke, aligning the matchmarks. Never hammer the yoke onto the pinion!

13. Install a NEW nut on the pinion.

14. Hold the yoke with a holding tool. Tighten the pinion nut to at least 160 ft. lbs. (217 Nm), taking frequent turning torque readings until the original preload reading is attained. If the original preload reading, that you noted before disassembly, is lower than the specified reading of 8–14 inch lbs. (0.9–1.6 Nm) for used bearings; 16–29 inch lbs. (1.8–3,3 Nm) for new bearings, keep tightening the pinion nut until the specified reading is reached. If the original preload reading is higher than the specified values, tighten the nut just until the original reading is reached.

✳✳ WARNING

Under no circumstances should the nut be backed off to reduce the preload reading! If the preload is exceeded, the yoke and bearing must be removed and a new collapsible spacer must be installed. The entire process of preload adjustment must be repeated.

15. Install the driveshaft using the matchmarks. Tighten the nuts to 15 ft. lbs. (20 Nm).

Ford 10.25 in. (260.35mm) Ring Gear With Integral Carrier Axle

➡A torque wrench capable of at least 225 ft. lbs. (305 Nm) is required for pinion seal installation.

1. Raise and safely support the vehicle with jackstands under the frame rails. Allow the axle to drop to the rebound position for working clearance.

2. Remove the rear wheels and brake drums. No drag must be present on the axle.

3. Mark the companion flanges and U-joints for correct reinstallation position.

4. Remove the driveshaft.

5. Using an inch pound torque wrench and socket on the pinion yoke nut measure the amount of torque needed to maintain differential rotation through several clockwise revolutions. Record the measurement.

6. Use a suitable tool to hold the companion flange. Remove the pinion nut.

7. Place a drain pan under the differential, clean the area around the seal, and mark the yoke-to-pinion relation.

8. Use a 2-jawed puller to remove the pinion.

9. Remove the seal with a small prybar.

To install:

10. Thoroughly clean the oil seal bore.

➡If you are not absolutely certain of the proper seal installation depth, the proper seal driver must be used. If the seal is misaligned or damaged during installation, it must be removed and a new seal installed.

11. Drive the new seal into place with a seal driver such as T83T–4676–A. Coat the seal lip with clean, waterproof wheel bearing grease.

12. Coat the splines with a small amount of wheel bearing grease and install the yoke, aligning the matchmarks. Never hammer the yoke onto the pinion!

13. Install a NEW nut on the pinion.

14. Hold the yoke with a holding tool. Tighten the pinion nut to at least 160 ft. lbs. (217 Nm), taking frequent turning torque readings until the original preload reading is attained. If the original preload reading, that you noted before disassembly, is lower than the specified reading of 8–14 inch lbs. (0.9–1.6 Nm) for used bearings; 16–29 inch lbs. (1.8–3.3 Nm) for new bearings, keep tightening the pinion nut until the specified reading is reached. If the original preload reading is higher than the specified values, tighten the nut just until the original reading is reached.

✳✳ WARNING

Under no circumstances should the nut be backed off to reduce the preload reading! If the preload is exceeded, the yoke and bearing must be removed and a new collapsible spacer must be installed. The entire process of preload adjustment must be repeated.

15. Install the driveshaft using the matchmarks. Tighten the nuts to 15 ft. lbs. (20 Nm).

Dana 80

➡A torque wrench capable of at least 500 ft. lbs. (678 Nm) is required for pinion seal installation.

1. Raise and safely support the vehicle with jackstands under the frame rails. Allow the axle to drop to the rebound position for working clearance.

2. Remove the rear wheels and brake drums. No drag must be present on the axle.

3. Mark the companion flanges and U-joints for correct reinstallation position.

4. Remove the driveshaft.

5. Use a suitable tool to hold the companion flange. Remove the pinion nut.

6. Place a drain pan under the differential, clean the area around the seal, and mark the yoke-to-pinion relation.

7. Use a 2-jawed puller to remove the pinion.

8. Remove the seal with a small prybar.

To install:

9. Thoroughly clean the oil seal bore.

➡If you are not absolutely certain of the proper seal installation depth, the proper seal driver must be used. If the seal is misaligned or damaged during installation, it must be removed and a new seal installed.

10. Coat the new oil seal with wheel bearing grease. Install the seal using oil seal driver T56T–4676–B. After the seal is installed, make sure that the seal garter spring has not become dislodged. If it has, remove and replace the seal.

11. Install the yoke, using flange replacer tool D81T–4858–A if necessary to draw the yoke into place.

12. Install a new pinion nut and washer. Tighten the nut to 440–500 ft. lbs. (597–678 Nm).

13. Connect the driveshaft. Tighten the fasteners to 15–20 ft. lbs. (20–27 Nm).

Troubleshooting the Manual Transmission and Transfer Case

Problem	Cause	Solution
Transmission shifts hard	· Clutch adjustment incorrect · Clutch linkage or cable binding · Shift rail binding	· Adjust clutch · Lubricate or repair as necessary · Check for mispositioned selector arm roll pin, loose cover bolts, worn shift rail bores, worn shift rail, distorted oil seal, or extension housing not aligned with case. Repair as necessary.
	· Internal bind in transmission caused by shift forks, selector plates, or synchronizer assemblies · Clutch housing misalignment · Incorrect lubricant · Block rings and/or cone seats worn	· Remove, dissemble and inspect transmission. Replace worn or damaged components as necessary. · Check runout at rear face of clutch housing · Drain and refill transmission · Blocking ring to gear clutch tooth face clearance must be 0.030 inch or greater. If clearance is correct it may still be necessary to inspect blocking rings and cone seats for excessive wear. Repair as necessary.
Gear clash when shifting from one gear to another	· Clutch adjustment incorrect · Clutch linkage or cable binding · Clutch housing misalignment · Lubricant level low or incorrect lubricant · Gearshift components, or synchronizer assemblies worn or damaged	· Adjust clutch · Lubricate or repair as necessary · Check runout at rear of clutch housing · Drain and refill transmission and check for lubricant leaks if level was low. Repair as necessary. · Remove, disassemble and inspect transmission. Replace worn or damaged components as necessary.
Transmission noisy	· Lubricant level low or incorrect lubricant · Clutch housing-to-engine, or transmission-to-clutch housing bolts loose · Dirt, chips, foreign material in transmission · Gearshift mechanism, transmission gears, or bearing components worn or damaged · Clutch housing misalignment	· Drain and refill transmission. If lubricant level was low, check for leaks and repair as necessary. · Check and correct bolt torque as necessary · Drain, flush, and refill transmission · Remove, disassemble and inspect transmission. Replace worn or damaged components as necessary. · Check runout at rear face of clutch housing

86747G56

Troubleshooting the Manual Transmission and Transfer Case (cont.)

Problem	Cause	Solution
Jumps out of gear	· Clutch housing misalignment · Gearshift lever loose · Offset lever nylon insert worn or lever attaching nut loose · Gearshift mechanism, shift forks, selector plates, interlock plate, selector arm, shift rail, detent plugs, springs or shift cover worn or damaged · Clutch shaft or roller bearings worn or damaged	· Check runout at rear face of clutch housing · Check lever for worn fork. Tighten loose attaching bolts. · Remove gearshift lever and check for loose offset lever nut or worn insert. Repair or replace as necessary. · Remove, disassemble and inspect transmission cover assembly. Replace worn or damaged components as necessary. · Replace clutch shaft or roller bearings as necessary
Jumps out of gear (cont.)	· Gear teeth worn or tapered, synchronizer assemblies worn or damaged, excessive end play caused by worn thrust washers or output shaft gears · Pilot bushing worn	· Remove, disassemble, and inspect transmission. Replace worn or damaged components as necessary. · Replace pilot bushing
Will not shift into one gear	· Gearshift selector plates, interlock plate, or selector arm, worn, damaged, or incorrectly assembled · Shift rail detent plunger worn, spring broken, or plug loose · Gearshift lever worn or damaged · Synchronizer sleeves or hubs, damaged or worn	· Remove, disassemble, and inspect transmission cover assembly. Repair or replace components as necessary. · Tighten plug or replace worn or damaged components as necessary · Replace gearshift lever · Remove, disassemble and inspect transmission. Replace worn or damaged components.
Locked in one gear—cannot be shifted out	· Shift rail(s) worn or broken, shifter fork bent, setscrew loose, center detent plug missing or worn · Broken gear teeth on countershaft gear, clutch shaft, or reverse idler gear Gearshift lever broken or worn, shift mechanism in cover incorrectly assembled or broken, worn damaged gear train components	· Inspect and replace worn or damaged parts · Inspect and replace damaged part · Disassemble transmission. Replace damaged parts or assemble correctly.

86747G57

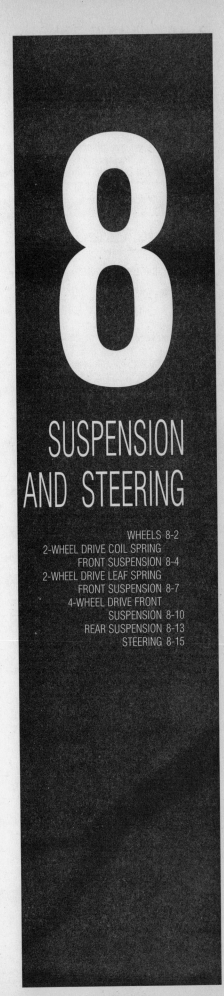

8

SUSPENSION AND STEERING

WHEELS

❄ CAUTION

Some aftermarket wheels may not be compatible with these vehicles. The use of incompatible wheels may result in equipment failure and possible personal injury! Use only approved wheels!

Front or Rear Wheels

REMOVAL & INSTALLATION

Bronco F-150 F-250 and F-350 with Single Rear Wheels

▸ **See Figure 1**

1. Set the parking brake and block the opposite wheel.
2. On trucks with an automatic transmission, place the selector lever in **PARK**. On trucks with a manual transmission, place the transmission in **REVERSE**.
3. If equipped, remove the wheel cover.
4. Break loose the lug nuts. If a nut is stuck, never use heat to loosen it or damage to the wheel and bearings may occur. If the nuts are seized, one or two heavy hammer blows directly on the end of the bolt head usually loosens the rust. Be careful as continued pounding will likely damage the brake drum or rotor.
5. Raise the truck until the tire is clear of the ground.
6. Remove the lug nuts and remove the wheel.

To install:

7. Make sure the wheel and hub mating surfaces, as well as the wheel lug studs, are clean and free of all foreign material. Always remove rust from the wheel mounting surfaces and the brake rotors/drums. Failure to do so may cause the lug nuts to loosen in service.
8. Position the wheel on the hub or drum and hand-tighten the lug nuts. Make sure that the coned ends face inward.
9. Using the lug wrench, tighten all the lugs, in a crisscross fashion until they are snug.
10. Lower the truck. Tighten the nuts, in the sequence shown, to 100 ft. lbs. (135 Nm) for 5-lug wheels; 140 ft. lbs. (190 Nm) for 8-lug and 10-lug wheels.

Fig. 1 Wheel lug torque sequence

F-350 With Dual Rear Wheels and F-Super Duty Models

▸ **See Figure 2**

➥ For vehicles with dual rear wheels, please refer to the Dual Rear Wheels procedure to remove and install rear wheels on these vehicles.

❄ CAUTION

Use only integral 2-piece, swiveling lug nuts. Do not attempt to use cone-shaped, one-piece lugs. The use of cone-shaped nuts will cause the nuts to come loose during vehicle operation! Do not attempt to use older-style wheels that use cone-shaped lug nuts. This practice will also cause the wheels to come loose!

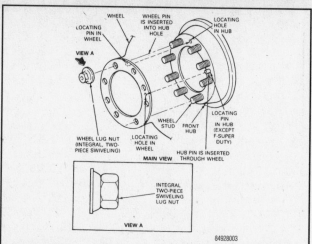

Fig. 2 Front wheel installation for F-350 with dual rear wheels and F-Super Duty. The 10-lug wheel is identical except for the number of wheel lugs

1. Set the parking brake and block the opposite wheel.
2. On trucks with an automatic transmission, place the selector lever in **P**. On trucks with a manual transmission, place the transmission in reverse.
3. If equipped, remove the wheel cover.
4. Break loose the lug nuts.
5. Raise the truck until the tire is clear of the ground.
6. Remove the lug nuts and remove the wheel.

To install:

7. Clean the wheel lugs and brake drum or hub of all foreign material.
8. Position the wheel on the hub or drum and hand-tighten the lug nuts.
9. Using the lug wrench, tighten all the lugs, in a crisscross fashion until they are snug.
10. Lower the truck. Tighten the nuts, in the sequence shown, to 140 ft. lbs. (190 Nm).

Dual Rear Wheels

REMOVAL & INSTALLATION

▸ **See Figure 3**

❄ CAUTION

Use only integral 2-piece, swiveling lug nuts. Do not attempt to use cone-shaped, one-piece lugs. The use of cone-shaped nuts will cause the nuts to come loose during vehicle operation! Do not attempt to use older-style wheels that use cone-shaped lug nuts. This practice will also cause the wheels to come loose!

➥ F-Super Duty models require the use of center-pilot type wheels.

1. Set the parking brake and block the opposite wheel.
2. On trucks with an automatic transmission, place the selector lever in PARK. On trucks with a manual transmission, place the transmission in REVERSE.
3. If equipped, remove the wheel cover.
4. Break loose the lug nuts.
5. Raise the truck until the tire is clear of the ground.
6. Remove the lug nuts and remove the wheel(s).

To install:

7. Clean the wheel lugs and brake drum or hub of all foreign material.
8. Mount the inner wheel on the hub with the dished (concave) side inward. Align the wheel with the small indexing hole—located in the wheel between the stud holes—with the alignment pin on the hub. Make sure that the wheel is flush against the hub.

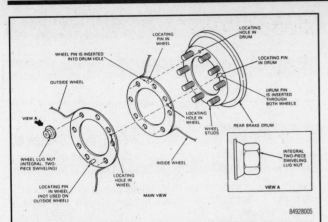

Fig. 3 Exploded view of the rear wheel drum assembly—F-350 models with dual rear wheels

9. Install the outer wheel so that the protruding (convex) side is flush against the inner wheel. Make sure that the alignment pin is protruding through the wheel index hole.

10. Hand-tighten the lug nuts.

11. Using the lug wrench, tighten all the lugs, in a crisscross fashion until they are snug.

12. Lower the truck. Tighten the nuts, in the sequence shown, to 140 ft. lbs. (190 Nm)

✳✳ CAUTION

The lug nuts on dual rear wheels should be retightened after the first 100 miles (62 km) of new-vehicle operation. The lug nuts on dual rear wheels should be retightened at an interval of 500 miles (310 km) after anytime a wheel has been removed and installed for any reason! Failure to observe this procedure may result in the wheel coming loose during vehicle operation!

INSPECTION

Check the wheels for any damage. They must be replaced if they are bent, dented, heavily rusted, have elongated bolt holes, or have excessive lateral or radial run-out. Wheels with excessive run-out may cause a high-speed vehicle vibration.

Replacement wheels must be of the same load capacity, diameter, width, offset and mounting configuration as the original wheels. Using the wrong wheels may affect wheel bearing life, ground and tire clearance, or speedometer and odometer calibrations.

Wheel Lug Studs

REPLACEMENT

Front Wheels

USING A PRESS

1. Remove the wheel.
2. Place the hub/rotor assembly in a press, supported by the hub surface. NEVER rest the assembly on the rotor!
3. Press the stud from the hub.
4. Position the new stud in the hub and align the serrations. Make sure it is square and press it into place.

USING A HAMMER AND DRIVER

▶ See Figures 4 thru 9

1. Remove the wheel.
2. Support the hub/rotor assembly on a flat, hard surface, resting the assembly on the hub. NEVER rest the assembly on the rotor!
3. Position a driver, such as a drift or broad punch, on the outer end of the stud and drive it from the hub.
4. Turn the assembly over, coat the serrations of the new stud with liquid soap, position the stud in the hole, aligning the serrations, and, using the drift and hammer, drive it into place until fully seated.

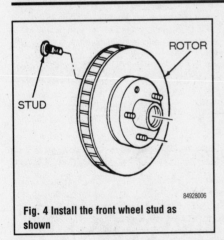

Fig. 4 Install the front wheel stud as shown

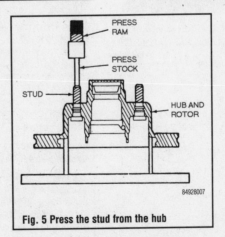

Fig. 5 Press the stud from the hub

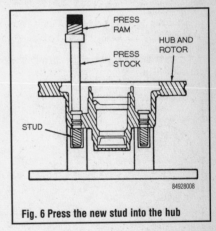

Fig. 6 Press the new stud into the hub

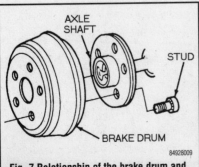

Fig. 7 Relationship of the brake drum and stud

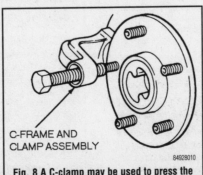

Fig. 8 A C-clamp may be used to press the stud out with a C-clamp

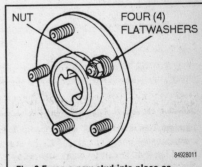

Fig. 9 Force a new stud into place as shown

Rear Wheels

1. Remove the wheel.
2. Remove the drum or rotor from the axle shaft or hub studs.
3. Using a large C-clamp and socket, press the stud from the drum or rotor.
4. Coat the serrated part of the stud with liquid soap and place it in the hole. Align the serrations.

2-WHEEL DRIVE COIL SPRING FRONT SUSPENSION

♦ See Figure 10

Trucks with 2-Wheel Drive and coil springs use two I-beam type front axles; one for each wheel. One end of each axle is attached to the spindle and a radius arm, and the other end is attached to a frame pivot bracket on the opposite side of the truck.

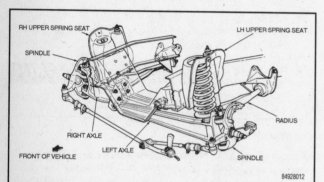

RH UPPER SPRING SEAT
LH UPPER SPRING SEAT
SPINDLE
RADIUS
RIGHT AXLE
LEFT AXLE
FRONT OF VEHICLE
SPINDLE
84928012

Fig. 10 A common 2-wheel drive Twin I-Beam front suspension, with ball joints

Coil Springs

REMOVAL & INSTALLATION

1. Raise the front of the vehicle and place jackstands under the frame and a jack under the axle.
2. Remove the wheels.
3. Disconnect the shock absorber from the lower bracket.
4. Remove one bolt and nut and remove the rebound bracket.
5. Remove the two spring upper retainer attaching bolts from the top of the spring upper seat and remove the retainer.
6. Remove the nut attaching the spring lower retainer to the lower seat and axle and remove the retainer.
7. Place a safety chain through the spring to prevent it from suddenly coming loose. Slowly lower the axle and remove the spring.

To install:

8. Place the spring in position and raise the front axle.
9. Position the spring lower retainer over the stud and lower seat, and install the two attaching bolts.
10. Position the upper retainer over the spring coil and against the spring upper seat, and install the two attaching bolts.
11. Tighten the upper retaining bolts to 13–18 ft. lbs. (18–24 Nm); the lower retainer attaching nuts to 70–100 ft. lbs. (95–135 Nm).
12. Connect the shock absorber to the lower bracket. Tighten the bolt and nut to 40–60 ft. lbs. (54–81 Nm). Install the rebound bracket.
13. Remove the jack and jackstands.

Shock Absorbers

Most of these trucks are equipped with hydraulic shock absorbers as standard equipment. Some, however, are equipped with low pressure gas shock absorbers as standard equipment and all are available with gas shocks as optional equipment.

5. Place 3 or 4 flat washers on the outer end of the stud and thread a lug nut on the stud with the flat side against the washers. Tighten the lug nut until the stud is drawn all the way in.

✳✳ WARNING

Do not use an impact wrench!

✳✳ CAUTION

Low pressure gas shocks are charged with nitrogen gas to 135 psi (931 kPa). Do not puncture, attempt to open, or apply heat to the shock absorbers.

REMOVAL & INSTALLATION

Remove the self-locking nut, steel washer, and rubber bushings at the upper end of the shock absorber. Remove the bolt and nut at the lower end and remove the shock absorber.

When installing a new shock absorber, use new rubber bushings. Position the shock absorber on the mounting brackets with the stud end at the top.

Install the rubber bushing, steel washer and self-locking nut at the upper end, and the bolt and nut at the lower end. Tighten the upper end to 25–35 ft. lbs. (34–47 Nm) and the lower end to 40–60 ft. lbs. (54–81 Nm).

TESTING

♦ See Figure 11

The purpose of the shock absorber is simply to limit the motion of the spring during compression and rebound cycles. If the vehicle is not equipped with these motion dampers, the up and down motion would multiply until the vehicle was alternately trying to leap off the ground and to pound itself into the pavement.

Contrary to popular rumor, the shocks do not affect the ride height of the vehicle. This is controlled by other suspension components such as springs and tires. Worn shock absorbers can affect handling; if the front of the vehicle is rising or falling excessively, the "footprint" of the tires changes on the pavement and steering is affected.

The simplest test of the shock absorber is simply push down on one corner of the unladen vehicle and release it. Observe the motion of the body as it is released. In most cases, it will come up beyond it original rest position, dip back below it and settle quickly to rest. This shows that the damper is controlling the spring action. Any tendency to excessive pitch (up-and-down) motion

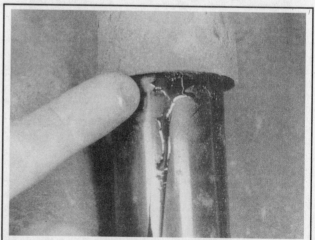

TCCA8P73

Fig. 11 When fluid is seeping out of the shock absorber, it's time to replace it

or failure to return to rest within 2-3 cycles is a sign of poor function within the shock absorber. Oil-filled shocks may have a light film of oil around the seal, resulting from normal breathing and air exchange. This should NOT be taken as a sign of failure, but any sign of thick or running oil definitely indicates failure. Gas filled shocks may also show some film at the shaft; if the gas has leaked out, the shock will have almost no resistance to motion.

While each shock absorber can be replaced individually, it is recommended that they be changed as a pair (both front or both rear) to maintain equal response on both sides of the vehicle. Chances are quite good that if one has failed, its mate is weak also.

Upper and Lower Ball Joints

INSPECTION

1. Before an inspection of the ball joints, make sure the front wheel bearings are properly packed and adjusted.
2. Jack up the front of the truck and safely support it with jackstands, placing the stands under the I-beam axle, beneath the spring.
3. Have a helper grab the lower edge of the tire and move the wheel assembly in and out.
4. While the wheel is being moved, observe the lower spindle arm and the lower part of the axle jaw (the end of the axle to which the spindle assembly attaches). If there is 1/32 in. (0.8mm) or greater movement between the lower part of the axle jaw and the lower spindle arm, the lower ball must be replaced.
5. To check upper ball joints, grab the upper edge of the tire and move the wheel in and out. If there is 1/32 in. (0.8mm) or greater movement between the upper spindle arm and the upper part of the jaw, the upper ball joint must be replaced.

REMOVAL

♦ See Figures 12 and 13

1. Remove the spindle as previously described.
2. Remove the snapring from the ball joints. Assemble the C-frame assembly T74P–4635–C and receiver cup D81T–3010–A, or equivalents, on the upper ball joint. Turn the forcing screw clockwise until the ball joint is removed from the axle.
3. Repeat Step 2 on the lower ball joint.

➡The upper ball joint must always be removed first. DO NOT heat the ball joint or spindle!

INSTALLATION

➡The lower ball joint must be installed first.

1. To install the lower ball joint, assemble the C-frame with ball joint receiver cup D81T–3010–A5 and installation cup D81T–3010–A1, and turn the forcing screw clockwise until the ball joint is seated. DO NOT heat the ball joint to aid in installation!

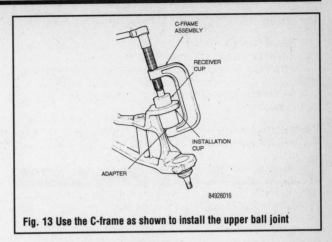

Fig. 13 Use the C-frame as shown to install the upper ball joint

2. Install the snapring onto the ball joint.
3. Install the upper ball joint in the same manner as the lower ball joint.
4. Install the spindle assembly.

Radius Arm

REMOVAL & INSTALLATION

♦ See Figure 14

➡A torque wrench with a capacity of at least 350 ft. lbs. (475 Nm) is necessary, along with other special tools, for this procedure.

1. Raise the front of the vehicle and place jackstands under the frame and a jack under the wheel or axle. Remove the wheels.
2. Disconnect the shock absorber from the radius arm bracket.
3. Remove the two spring upper retainer attaching bolts from the top of the spring upper seat and remove the retainer.
4. Remove the nut which attached the spring lower retainer to the lower seat and axle and remove the retainer.
5. Lower the axle and remove the spring.
6. Remove the spring lower seat and shim from the radius arm. The, remove the bolt and nut which attach the radius arm to the axle.
7. Remove the cotter pin, nut and washer from the radius arm rear attachment.
8. Remove the bushing from the radius arm and remove the radius arm from the vehicle.
9. Remove the inner bushing from the radius arm.

To install:

10. Position the radius arm to the axle and install the bolt and nut finger-tight.

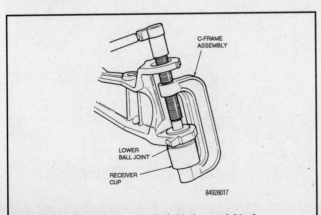

Fig. 12 Remove the lower ball joint with the special tool

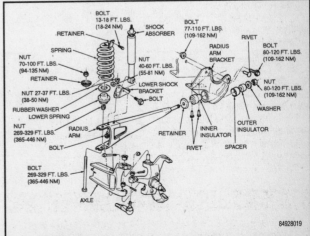

Fig. 14 Exploded view of the radius arm assembly—2-wheel drive F-150, F-250 and F-350 models

11. Install the inner bushing on the radius arm and position the arm to the frame bracket.

12. Install the bushing, washer, and attaching nut. Tighten the nut to 120 ft. lbs. (162 Nm) and install the cotter pin.

13. Tighten the radius arm-to-axle bolt to 269–329 ft. lbs. (365–446 Nm).

14. Install the spring seat and insulator on the radius arm so that the hole in the seat fits over the arm-to-axle nut.

15. Install the spring.

16. Connect the shock absorber. Tighten the nut and bolt to 40–60 ft. lbs. (54–81 Nm).

17. Install the wheels.

Stabilizer Bar

REMOVAL & INSTALLATION

1. Raise and support the front end on jackstands.
2. Disconnect the right and left stabilizer bar ends from the link assembly.
3. Disconnect the retainer bolts and remove the stabilizer bar.
4. Disconnect the stabilizer link assemblies by loosening the right and left locknuts from their respective brackets on the I-beams.

To install:

5. Loosely install the entire assembly. The links are marked with an **R** and **L** for identification.

6. Tighten the link-to-stabilizer bar and axle bracket fasteners to 70 ft. lbs. (95 Nm).

7. Check to make sure that the insulators are properly seated and the stabilizer bar is centered.

8. On the F-150, torque the 6 stabilizer bar to crossmember attaching bolts to 35 ft. lbs. (47 Nm). On the F-250 and F-350, torque the stabilizer bar-to-frame retainer bolts to 35 ft. lbs. (47 Nm). Tighten the frame mounting bracket nuts/bolts to 65 ft. lbs. (88 Nm).

Front Wheel Spindle

REMOVAL & INSTALLATION

♦ **See Figure 15**

➡**All 2-Wheel Drive pick-ups utilize upper and lower ball joints.**

1. Jack up the front of the truck and safely support it with jackstands.
2. Remove the wheels.
3. Remove the front brake caliper assembly and hold it out of the way with a piece of wire. Do not disconnect the brake line.
4. Remove the brake rotor from the spindle.
5. Remove the inner bearing cone and seal. Discard the seal, as you'll be fitting a new one during installation.
6. Remove the brake dust shield.
7. Disconnect the steering linkage from the spindle arm using a tie rod removal tool.

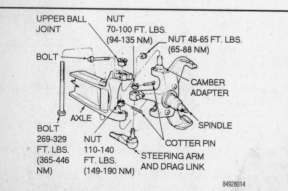

Fig. 15 Exploded view of the front wheel spindle— 2-wheel drive F-150, F-250 and F-350 with ball joints

8. Remove the cotter from the upper and lower ball joint stud nuts. Discard the cotter pins, as new ones should be installed during reassembly.

9. Remove the upper ball joint nut and loosen the lower ball joint nut to the end of the threads.

10. Strike the inside area or the spindle as shown in the illustration to pop the ball joints loose from the spindle.

⁂ WARNING

Do not use a forked ball joint removal tool to separate the ball joints as this will damage the seal and ball joint socket.

11. Remove the nut. Remove the spindle.

To install:

➡**Before reassembly, be advised that new cotter pins should be used on the ball joints, and that new bearing seal(s) should also be used. Also, make sure the upper and lower ball joint seals are in place.**

12. Place the spindle over the ball joints.

13. Install the nuts on the lower ball joint stud and partially tighten to 35 ft. lbs. (47 Nm). Turn the castellated nut until you are able to install the cotter pin.

14. Install the camber adapter in the upper spindle over the upper ball joint stud. Be sure the adapter is aligned properly.

➡**If camber adjustment is necessary special adapters must be installed.**

15. Install the nut on the upper ball joint stud. Hold the camber adapter with a wrench to keep the ball stud from turning. If the ball stud turns, tap the adapter deeper into the spindle. Tighten the nut to 110–140 ft. lbs. (149–190 Nm) and continue tightening the castellated nut until it lines up with the hole in the stud. Install the cotter pin.

16. Tighten the lower nut to 110–140 ft. lbs. (149–190 Nm). Advance the nut to install a new cotter pin.

17. Install the brake dust shield.

18. Pack the inner and outer bearing cone with a quality wheel bearing grease by hand, working the grease through the cage behind the roller.

19. Install the inner bearing cone and seal. Install the hub and rotor on the spindle.

20. Install the outer bearing cone, washer, and nut. Adjust the bearing end-play and install the nut retainer, cotter pin and dust cap.

21. Install the brake caliper. connect the steering linkage to the spindle. Tighten the nut to 70–100 ft. lbs. (95–135 Nm) and advance the nut as far necessary to install the cotter pin.

22. Install the wheels. Lower the truck and adjust toe-in if necessary.

Twin I-Beam Axles

REMOVAL & INSTALLATION

♦ **See Figures 16 and 17**

➡**A torque wrench with a capacity of at least 350 ft. lbs. (475 Nm) is necessary, along with other special tools, for this procedure.**

1. Raise and support the front end on jackstands.
2. Remove the spindles.
3. Remove the springs.
4. Remove the stabilizer bar.
5. Remove the lower spring seats from the radius arms.
6. Remove the radius arm-to-axle bolts.
7. Remove the axle-to-frame pivot bolts and remove the axles.

To install:

8. Position the axle on the pivot bracket and loosely install the bolt/nut.

9. Position the other end on the radius arm and install the bolt. Tighten the bolt to 269–329 ft. lbs. (365–446 Nm).

10. Install the spring seats.

11. Install the springs.

12. Tighten the axle pivot bolts to 120–150 ft. lbs. (163–203 Nm).

13. Install the spindles.

14. Install the stabilizer bar.

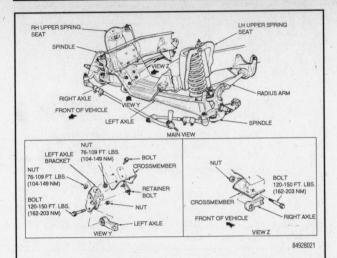

Fig. 16 Axle pivot bracket and axle arm installation—2-wheel drive F-150, F-250 and F-350 models

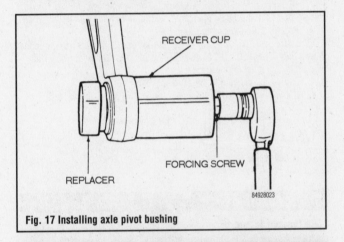

Fig. 17 Installing axle pivot bushing

Front Wheel Bearings

Because removal, repacking and installation of the front wheel bearings is considered a part of routine maintenance, this procedure is covered in Section 1 of this manual.

2-WHEEL DRIVE LEAF SPRING FRONT SUSPENSION

The F-Super Duty chassis/cab utilizes leaf springs attached to a solid, I-beam type front axle. The springs are mounted on the axle with U-bolts and attached to the frame side rails by a fixed bracket at the rear and moveable shackles at the front.

The F-Super Duty stripped chassis and motor home chassis utilize leaf springs attached to a solid, I-beam type front axle. The springs are mounted on the axle with U-bolts and attached to the frame side rails by a fixed bracket at the front and moveable shackles at the rear.

Chassis/cab models also utilize a tracking bar between the left side of the No.1 crossmember and the right side of the axle beam, inboard of the right spring pad.

Springs

REMOVAL & INSTALLATION

▶ **See Figures 18, 19 and 20**

1. Raise and support the front end on jackstands with the tires still touching the ground.

Wheel Alignment

If the tires are worn unevenly, if the vehicle is not stable on the highway or if the handling seems uneven in spirited driving, the wheel alignment should be checked. If an alignment problem is suspected, first check for improper tire inflation and other possible causes. These can be worn suspension or steering components, accident damage or even unmatched tires. If any worn or damaged components are found, they must be replaced before the wheels can be properly aligned. Wheel alignment requires very expensive equipment and involves minute adjustments which must be accurate; it should only be performed by a trained technician. Take your vehicle to a properly equipped shop.

Following is a description of the alignment angles which are adjustable on most vehicles and how they affect vehicle handling. Although these angles can apply to both the front and rear wheels, usually only the front suspension is adjustable.

CASTER

Looking at a vehicle from the side, caster angle describes the steering axis rather than a wheel angle. The steering knuckle is attached to a control arm or strut at the top and a control arm at the bottom. The wheel pivots around the line between these points to steer the vehicle. When the upper point is tilted back, this is described as positive caster. Having a positive caster tends to make the wheels self-centering, increasing directional stability. Excessive positive caster makes the wheels hard to steer, while an uneven caster will cause a pull to one side. Overloading the vehicle or sagging rear springs will affect caster, as will raising the rear of the vehicle. If the rear of the vehicle is lower than normal, the caster becomes more positive.

CAMBER

Looking from the front of the vehicle, camber is the inward or outward tilt of the top of wheels. When the tops of the wheels are tilted in, this is negative camber; if they are tilted out, it is positive. In a turn, a slight amount of negative camber helps maximize contact of the tire with the road. However, too much negative camber compromises straight-line stability, increases bump steer and torque steer.

TOE

Looking down at the wheels from above the vehicle, toe angle is the distance between the front of the wheels, relative to the distance between the back of the wheels. If the wheels are closer at the front, they are said to be toed-in or to have negative toe. A small amount of negative toe enhances directional stability and provides a smoother ride on the highway.

2. Using jacks, take up the weight of the axle, off the U-bolts.
3. Disconnect the lower end of each shock absorber.
4. Disconnect the spring from the front bracket or shackle.
5. Disconnect the spring from the rear bracket or shackle.
6. Remove the U-bolt nuts.
7. Remove the U-bolts.
8. Disconnect the jack bracket or stabilizer bar as necessary.
9. Lower the axle slightly and remove the spring. Take note of the position of the spring spacer.

To install

10. Position the spring on its seat on the axle and raise it to align the front of the spring with the bracket or shackle.
11. Coat the bushing with silicone grease.
12. Carefully guide the attaching bolt through the bracket or shackle, and the bushing.
13. Install the nut and, depending on model or which bolts you removed, torque it to:
    • chassis/cab spring-to-shackle: 120–150 ft. lbs. (163–203 Nm)
    • chassis/cab shackle-to-frame: 150–210 ft. lbs. (203–285 Nm)
    • stripped chassis or motor home chassis spring-to-bracket: 148–207 ft. lbs. (200–281 Nm)

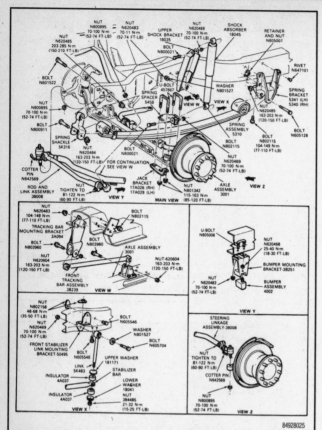

Fig. 18 Front spring and shock absorber installation for F-Super Duty chassis/cab

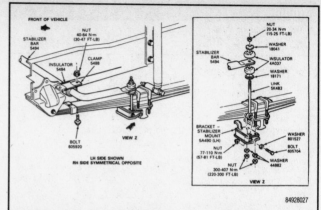

Fig. 20 Front stabilizer bar installation for F-Super Duty stripped chassis or motor home chassis

14. In a similar fashion, attach the rear of the spring. The torques are:
   • chassis/cab spring-to-bracket: 150–210 ft. lbs. (203–285 Nm)
   • stripped chassis or motor home chassis spring-to-shackle or shackle-to-bracket: 74–110 ft. lbs. (100–149 Nm)

15. Position the spacer on the spring.

16. Install the U-bolts. Install the jack bracket or stabilizer bar bracket on the forward U-bolt. Install the U-bolt nuts. Tighten the nuts, evenly and in gradual increments, in a crisscross fashion, to:
   • chassis/cab: 150–210 ft. lbs. (203–285 Nm)
   • stripped chassis and motor home chassis: 220–300 ft. lbs. (298–407 Nm)

17. Connect the shock absorbers. Tighten them to:
   • chassis/cab models, shock absorber-to-bracket nuts to 52–74 ft. lbs. (71–100 Nm).
   • stripped chassis or motor home chassis models, lower attaching bolt to 220–300 ft. lbs. (298–407 Nm)

Shock Absorbers

◆ See Figures 18 and 19

These trucks are equipped with either hydraulic shock absorbers or with low pressure gas shock absorbers depending on equipment ordered.

✳✳ CAUTION

Low pressure gas shocks are charged with nitrogen gas to 135 psi (931 kPa). Do not puncture, attempt to open, or apply heat to the shock absorbers.

TESTING AND INSPECTION

Please refer to Shock Absorber TESTING under 2–Wheel Drive Coil Spring Front Suspension in this Section.

REMOVAL & INSTALLATION

1. Remove the nut and bolt which retains the shock to the upper bracket.

2. Remove the nut (chassis/cab) or nut and bolt (stripped chassis and motor home chassis) that retains the lower end of the shock at the spring.

3. Installation is the reverse of removal. It's a good idea to lubricate the bushings with silicone grease prior to installation. Tighten the fasteners as follows:
   • chassis/cab upper and lower: 52–74 ft. lbs. (71–100 Nm)
   • stripped cab and motor home chassis upper and lower: 220–300 ft. lbs. (298–407 Nm)

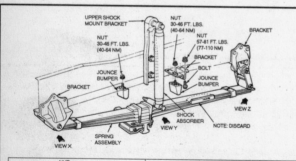

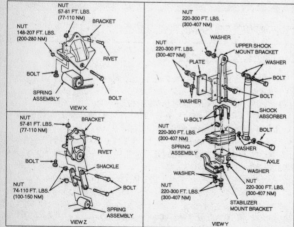

Fig. 19 Front spring and shock absorber installation for F-Super Duty stripped chassis or motor home chassis models

Spindles

REMOVAL & INSTALLATION

♦ **See Figures 21, 22 and 23**

1. Raise and support the front end on jackstands.
2. Remove the wheels.
3. Remove the caliper and suspend it out of the way (see Section 9).
4. Remove the hub and rotor assembly (see Section 9).
5. Remove the inner bearing and seal. Discard the seal.
6. Remove the dust shield.
7. Remove the cotter pin and nut, and, using a ball joint separator—the forcing screw type, not the fork type—disconnect the tie rod end from the spindle arm.
8. On stripped chassis and motor home models, disconnect the drag link from the steering arm using a forcing type ball joint separator.
9. Remove the nut and washer from the spindle bolt lock pin and remove the lock pin.
10. Remove the upper and lower spindle pin plugs.
11. Using a brass drift, drive out the spindle pin from the top and remove the spindle and thrust bearing.
12. Remove the thrust bearing and seal.

To install:

13. Clean the spindle pin bore and make sure it is free of corrosion, nicks or burrs. Light corrosion and other irregularities can be removed.
14. Lightly coat the bore with lithium based grease meeting ESA-M1C75-B rating.
15. Install a new spindle pin seal with the metal side facing up into the spindle. Gently press the seal into position being careful to avoid distorting it.
16. Install a new thrust bearing with the lip flange facing downward. Press the bearing in until firmly seated against the surface of the spindle.
17. Lightly coat the bushing surface with lithium based grease and place the spindle on the axle.
18. Hold the spindle, with the thrust bearing in place, tightly against the axle, and measure the space between the axle and spindle at the top of the axle. Determine what thickness of shims is necessary to eliminate all play. Install the shims, available from the dealer.
19. One end of the spindle pin is stamped with a **T**. Install the spindle pin, from the top, with the **T** at the top and the notch aligned with the lock pin hole.
20. Install the lock pin with the threads forward and the wedge groove facing the spindle pin notch. Drive the lock pin in all the way and install the nut. Tighten the nut to 40–50 ft. lbs. (54–68 Nm).
21. Install the spindle pin plugs. Tighten them to 35–50 ft. lbs. (47–68 Nm).
22. Lubricate the spindle pin through the fittings until grease seeps past the upper seal and the thrust bearing slip joint at the bottom. If grease can't be forced past these points, the installation was probably done incorrectly and will have to be disassembled and re-assembled.
23. Install the dust shield.

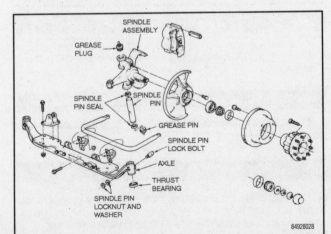

Fig. 21 Front wheel spindle installation for F-Super Duty chassis/cab models

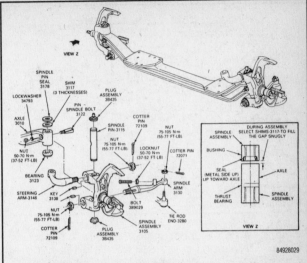

Fig. 22 Front wheel spindle installation for F-Super Duty stripped chassis or motor home chassis models

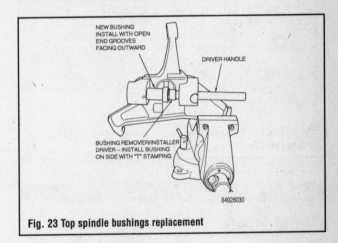

Fig. 23 Top spindle bushings replacement

24. Clean, pack and install the bearings. Install a new seal (see Section 1).
25. Install the hub and rotor assembly (see Section 9).
26. Install the caliper (see Section 9).
27. Connect the tie rod end and, if necessary, the drag link. Tighten the nuts to 50–70 ft. lbs. (68–95 Nm). Always advance the nut to align the cotter pin holes. NEVER back them off! Always use new cotter pins!
28. Install the wheels.

BRONZE SPINDLE BUSHING REPLACEMENT

♦ **See Figures 24, 25 and 26**

1. Remove the spindle and secure it in a bench vise.
2. The bushings have an inside diameter of 1.301–1.302 in. (33.05–33.07mm). Use the following tools or their equivalents:
   • Reamer T88T-3110-BH
   • Bushing Remover/Installer T88T-3110-AH
   • Driver Handle T80T-4000-W—One side of the Remover/Installer is marked with a **T**; the other side with a **B**. The **T** side is used on the top bushing; the **B** side is for the bottom bushing.
3. Remove and discard the seal from the upper bushing bore.
4. Working on the upper bushing first, install the driver handle through the bottom bore. Position a new bushing on the **T** side of the tool. The bushing must be positioned so that the open end grooves will face outward when installed. Position the bushing and tool over the old bushing, insert the handle and drive out the old bushing while driving in the new bushing. Continue driving until the tool is fully seated. The new bushing should then be seated at the proper depth of 0.08 in. (2.03mm) minimum from the bottom of the upper spindle boss.

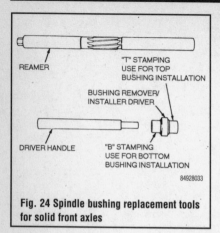

Fig. 24 Spindle bushing replacement tools for solid front axles

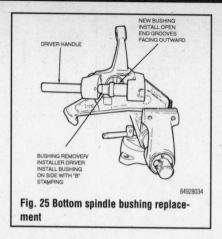

Fig. 25 Bottom spindle bushing replacement

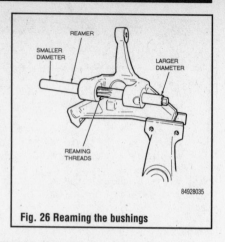

Fig. 26 Reaming the bushings

5. Working on the bottom bushing, position the driver handle through the top bushing bore. Position a new bushing on the **B** side of the tool. The bushing must be positioned so that the open end grooves will face outward when installed. Position the bushing and tool over the old bushing, insert the handle and drive out the old bushing while driving in the new bushing. Continue driving until the tool is fully seated. The new bushing should then be seated at the proper depth of 0.13 in. (3.3mm) minimum from the top of the lower spindle boss.

6. Ream the new bushings to 0.001–0.003 in. (0.025–0.076mm) larger than the diameter of the new spindle pin. Ream the top bushing first. Install the smaller diameter of the reamer through the top bore and into the bottom bore until the threads are in position is the top bushing. Ream the bushing until the threads exit the top bushing. Ream the bottom bushing. The larger diameter portion of the tool will act as a pilot in the top bushing to properly ream the bottom bushing.

7. Remove the tool and thoroughly clean all metal shavings from the bushings and surrounding parts. Coat the bushings and spindle pins with grease meeting specification ESA-M1C75-B.

8. Install a new seal on the Remover/Installer on the **T** side. Using the handle, push the seal into position in the bottom of the top bore.

Stabilizer Bar

REMOVAL & INSTALLATION

Chassis/Cab

♦ **See Figure 27**

1. Raise and support the front end on jackstands.
2. Disconnect each end of the bar from the links.
3. Disconnect the bar from the axle.
4. Unbolt and remove the links from the frame.
5. Installation is the reverse of removal. Replace any worn or cracked rubber parts. Install the bar loosely and make sure it is centered between the leaf springs. Make sure the insulators are seated in the retainers. When everything is in proper order, tighten the stabilizer bar-to-axle mounting bolts to 35–50 ft. lbs. (47–68 Nm). Tighten the end link-to-frame bolts to 52–74 ft. lbs. (71–100 Nm). Tighten the bar-to-end link nuts to 15–25 ft. lbs. (20–34 Nm).

Stripped Chassis or Motor Home Chassis

1. Raise and support the front end on jackstands.
2. Disconnect the stabilizer bar ends from the links attached to the axle.

4-WHEEL DRIVE FRONT SUSPENSION

♦ **See Figures 28, 29, 30 and 31**

The suspension of the F-150 and Bronco 4-wheel drive models consists of a Dana 44-IFS independent driving axle attached to the frame with two coil springs, two radius arms, and a stabilizer bar.

The front suspension on an F-250 4-Wheel Drive consists of a Dana 44- or

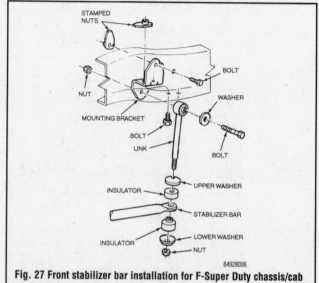

Fig. 27 Front stabilizer bar installation for F-Super Duty chassis/cab

3. Remove the bar-to-frame bolts and remove the bar.
4. Remove the links from the axle brackets.
5. Installation is the reverse of removal. Replace any worn or cracked rubber parts. Assemble all parts loosely and make sure the assembly is centered on the frame. make sure that the insulators are seated in the retainers. When everything is in proper order, tighten the bar-to-frame brackets bolts to 30–47 ft. lbs. (41–64 Nm). Tighten the link-to-axle bracket bolts to 57–81 ft. lbs. (77–110 Nm). Tighten the bar-to-link nuts to 15–25 ft. lbs. (20–34 Nm).

Front Wheel Bearings

Because removal, repacking and installation of the front wheel bearings is considered a part of routine maintenance, this procedure is covered in Section 1 of this manual.

Front End Alignment

Please refer to the procedure under the 2WD coil spring front suspension section.

50-IFS independent driving axle attached to the frame with two semi-elliptic leaf springs. Each spring is clamped to the axle with two U-bolts. The front of the spring rests in a front shackle bracket and the rear is attached to a frame bracket.

The front suspension on an F-350 4-Wheel Drive consists of a Dana 60 Monobeam one piece driving axle attached to the frame with two semi-elliptic

Fig. 28 Dual shocks and a coil spring characterize this 4x4 front suspension—1990 F-150 shown

Fig. 29 View of the 4x4 front suspension—1990 F-150 shown

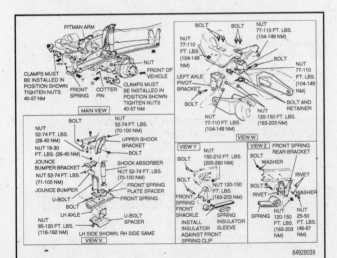

Fig. 30 F-250 4-wheel drive front suspension with Dana 44-IFS-HD or Dana IFS

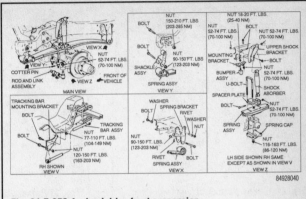

Fig. 31 F-350 4-wheel drive front suspension

leaf springs. Each spring is clamped to the axle with two U-bolts. The front of the spring rests in a front shackle bracket and the rear is attached to a frame bracket. On the right spring cap, a track bar is attached with the other end mounted on the crossmember.

Springs

REMOVAL & INSTALLATION

▶ See Figures 30 and 31

F-150 and Bronco Models

1. Raise and support the front end on jackstands.
2. Remove the shock absorber lower attaching bolt and nut.
3. Remove the spring lower retainer nuts from inside of the spring coil.
4. Remove the upper spring retainer by removing the attaching screw.
5. Position jackstands under the frame side rails and lower the axle on a floor jack just enough to relieve tension from the spring.

➡The axle must be supported on the jack throughout spring removal, and must not be permitted to hang from the brake hose. If the length of the brake hose does not provide sufficient clearance it may be necessary to remove and support the brake caliper.

6. Remove the spring lower retainer and lower the spring from the vehicle.
To install:
7. Place the spring in position and slowly raise the front axle. Make sure the springs are positioned correctly in the upper spring seats.
8. Install the lower spring retainer and torque the nut to 100 ft. lbs. (135 Nm).
9. Position the upper retainer over the spring coil and tighten the attaching screws to 13–18 ft. lbs. (18–24 Nm).
10. Position the shock absorber to the lower bracket and torque the attaching bolt and nut to 65 ft. lbs. (88 Nm).
11. Remove the jackstands and lower the vehicle.

F-250 and F-350 Models

1. Raise the vehicle frame until the weight is off the front spring with the wheels still touching the floor. Support the axle to prevent rotation.
2. Disconnect the lower end of the shock absorber from the U-bolt spacer. Remove the U-bolts, U-bolt cap and spacer. On F-350 models, remove the 2 bolts retaining the track bar to the spring cap and the track bar bracket.
3. Remove the nut from the hanger bolt retaining the spring at the rear and drive out the hanger bolt.
4. Remove the nut connecting the front shackle and spring eye and drive out the shackle bolt and remove the spring.
To install:
5. Position the spring on the spring seat. Install the shackle bolt through the shackle and spring. Tighten the nuts to 150 ft. lbs. (203 Nm).
6. Position the rear of the spring and install the hanger bolt. Tighten the nut to 150 ft. lbs. (203 Nm).
7. Position the U-bolt spacer and place the U-bolts in position through the holes in the spring seat cap. Install but do not tighten the U-bolt nut. On the F-

Fig. 32 Remove the upper nut from the shock absorber—F-150 with quad shocks

Fig. 33 Remove the lower nut from the shock absorber

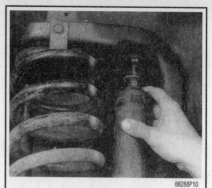

Fig. 34 Compress and remove the shock from its mounted position

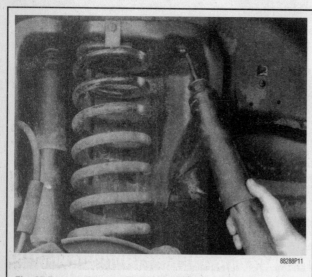

Fig. 35 Remove the shock from the vehicle

350, install the track bar. Tighten the track bar-to-bracket bolts to 200 ft. lbs. (271 Nm).

8. Connect the lower end of the shock absorber to the U-bolt spacer. Tighten the fasteners to 60 ft. lbs. (81 Nm) on the F-250; 70 ft. lbs. (95 Nm) on the F-350.

9. Lower the vehicle and tighten the U-bolt nuts to 120 ft. lbs. (163 Nm).

Shock Absorbers

TESTING AND INSPECTION

Please refer to Shock Absorber TESTING under 2–Wheel DriveCoil Spring Front Suspension in this Section.

REMOVAL & INSTALLATION

F-150 and Bronco Models Without Quad Shocks

1. Remove the upper nut while holding the shock absorber stem.
2. Remove the lower mounting bolt/nut from the bracket.
3. Compress the shock and remove it.
4. Installation is the reverse of removal. Hold the stud while tightening the upper nut to 30 ft. lbs. (41 Nm). Tighten the lower bolt/nut to 60 ft. lbs. (81 Nm).

F-150 and Bronco Models With Quad Shocks

▶ See Figures 32, 33, 34, 35 and 36

1. Remove the upper nut while holding the shock absorber stem on both forward and rearward shocks.

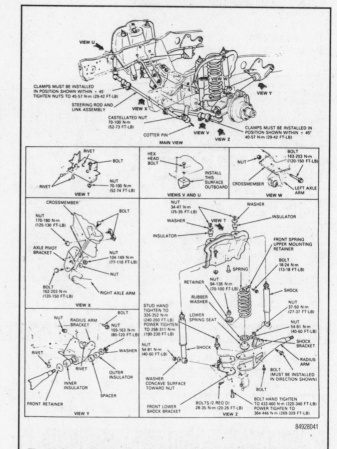

Fig. 36 Quad shock installation on the Bronco and 4-wheel drive F-150 models

2. Remove the lower mounting bolt/nut from the rearward shock bracket; the nut and washer from the forward shock bracket.
3. Compress the shocks and remove them.
4. Cut the insulators from the upper spring seat.
5. Install new one piece insulators into the top surface of the upper spring seat. Coat them with a soap solution to aid in installation.
6. Installation of the shocks is the reverse of removal. Use a new steel washer under the upper nut. Hold the stud while tightening the upper nut to 30 ft. lbs. (41 Nm). Tighten the lower bolt/nut to 60 ft. lbs. (81 Nm).

F-250 and F-350 Models

1. Remove the nut/bolt retaining the shock to the upper bracket.
2. Remove the lower mounting bolt/nut from the bracket.
3. Compress the shock and remove it.

4. Installation is the reverse of removal. Tighten the upper and lower nut/bolt to 70 ft. lbs. (95 Nm).

Front Wheel Spindle

REMOVAL & INSTALLATION

For this procedure, see Section 7 under Front Drive Axle.

Radius Arm

▶ See Figures 30 and 31

REMOVAL & INSTALLATION

F-150 and Bronco Models

1. Raise the vehicle and position jackstands under the frame side rails.
2. Remove the shock absorber lower attaching bolt and nut and pull the shock absorber free of the radius arm.
3. Remove the lower spring retaining bolt from the inside of the spring coil.
4. Loosen the axle pivot bolt.
5. Remove the nut attaching the radius arm to the frame bracket and remove the radius arm rear insulator. Lower the axle and allow the axle to move forward.

➡ The axle must be supported on a floor jack throughout this procedure, and must not be permitted to hang from the brake hose. If the length of the brake hose does not provide sufficient clearance it may be necessary to remove and support the brake caliper.

6. Remove the spring as described above.
7. Remove the bolt and stud attaching the radius arm and bracket to the axle.
8. Move the axle forward and remove the radius arm from the axle. Then, pull the radius arm from the frame bracket.
9. Install the components in the reverse order of removal. Install new bolts and stud type bolts which attach the radius arm and bracket to the axle. Tighten the bracket-to-axle bolts to 25 ft. lbs. (34 Nm). Tighten the lower radius arm-to-axle bolt to 330 ft. lbs. (447 Nm). Tighten the upper stud-type radius arm-to-axle bolt to 250 ft. lbs. (339 Nm). Tighten the radius arm rear attaching nut to 120 ft. lbs. (163 Nm). Tighten the lower spring retainer nut to 100 ft. lbs. (135

Nm). Tighten the upper spring retainer bolts to 15 ft. lbs. (20 Nm). Tighten the axle pivot bolt to 150 ft. lbs. (203 Nm). Tighten the lower shock absorber bolt to 60 ft. lbs. (81 Nm).

Stabilizer Bar

REMOVAL & INSTALLATION

F-150 and Bronco Models

1. Unbolt the stabilizer bar from the connecting links.
2. Unbolt the stabilizer bar retainers.
3. If you have to remove the stabilizer bar mounting bracket, remove the coil springs as described above.
4. Installation is the reverse of removal. Tighten the retainer nuts to 35 ft. lbs. (47 Nm)., then torque all other nuts at the links to 70 ft. lbs. (95 Nm).

F-250 and F-350 Models

1. Remove the bolts, washers and nuts securing the links to the spring seat caps. On models with the Monobeam axle, remove the nut, washer and bolt securing the links to the mounting brackets. Remove the nuts, washers and insulators connecting the links to the stabilizer bar. Remove the links.
2. Unbolt and remove the retainers from the mounting brackets.
3. Remove the stabilizer bar.
4. Installation is the reverse of removal. Tighten the connecting links-to-spring seat caps to 70 ft. lbs. (90 Nm). Tighten the nuts securing the connecting links to the stabilizer bar to 25 ft. lbs. (34 Nm). Tighten the retainer-to-mounting bracket nuts to 35 ft. lbs. (47 Nm).

Front Wheel Bearings

Because removal, repacking and installation of the front wheel bearings is considered a part of routine maintenance, this procedure is covered in Section 1 of this manual.

Front End Alignment

Please refer to the procedure under the 2WD coil spring front suspension section.

REAR SUSPENSION

Semi-elliptic, leaf type springs are used at the rear axle. The front end of the spring is attached to a spring bracket on the frame side member. The rear end of the spring is attached to the bracket on the frame side member with a shackle. Each spring is attached to the axle with two U-bolts. A spacer is located between the spring and the axle on some applications to obtain a level ride position.

Leaf Springs

REMOVAL & INSTALLATION

▶ See Figure 37

1. Remove the nuts from the spring U-bolts and drive the U-bolts from the U-bolt plate. Remove the auxiliary spring and spacer, if so equipped.
2. Remove the spring-to-bracket nut and bolt at the front of the spring.
3. Remove the upper and lower shackle nuts and bolts at the rear of the spring and remove the spring and shackle assembly from the rear shackle bracket.
4. Raise the vehicle by the frame until the weight is off the rear spring with the tires still on the floor.
5. Remove the bushings in the spring or shackle, if they are worn or damaged, and install new ones.

➡ When installing the components, snug down the fasteners. Don't apply final torque to the fasteners until the truck is back on the ground.

6. Position the spring in the shackle and install the upper shackle-to-spring nut and bolt with the bolt head facing outward.
7. Position the front end of the spring in the bracket and install the nut and bolt.
8. Position the shackle in the rear bracket and install the nut and bolt.
9. Position the spring on top of the axle with the spring center bolts centered in the hole provided in the seat. Install the auxiliary spring and spacer, if so equipped.
10. Install the spring U-bolts, plate and nuts.
11. Lower the vehicle to the floor and tighten the attaching hardware as follows:
U-bolts nuts:
- Bronco, F-150 and F-250 under 8,500 lb. GVW: 75–115 ft. lbs. (102–156 Nm)
- F-250 HD and F-350: 150–210 ft. lbs. (203–285 Nm)
- F-Super Duty chassis/cab: 200–270 ft. lbs. (272–366 Nm)
- F-Super Duty stripped chassis and motor home chassis: 220–300 ft. lbs. (298–407 Nm)

Spring to front spring hanger:
- F-150 2wd: 75–115 ft. lbs. (102–156 Nm)
- F-250 2wd, F-350 2wd and Bronco: 150–210 ft. lbs. (203–285 Nm)
- F-150, F-250 and F-350 models 4wd: 150–175 ft. lbs. (203–237 Nm)
- F-Super Duty: 255–345 ft. lbs. (346–468 Nm)

Spring to rear spring hanger:
- All except F-250 and F-350 2wd Chassis Cab: 75–115 ft. lbs.
- F-250 and F-350 2wd Chassis Cab; F-Super Duty: 150–210 ft. lbs. (203–285 Nm)

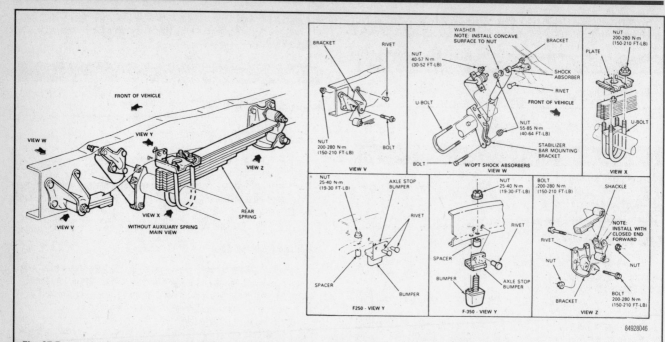

Fig. 37 Rear spring installation for F-250, 350 2-wheel Chassis Cab with Dana axles

ADJUSTMENTS

Side-to-side lean can be adjusted by about ⅜ in. (10mm) by installing a shim between the spring and axle on the low side. A truck that is low in the rear on both sides can be similarly raised by the insertion of 1 shim on each side.

If the side-to-side lean is greater than ½ in., try switching the springs from one side to the other.

Shock Absorbers

TESTING

Please refer to Shock Absorber TESTING under 2–Wheel Drive Coil Spring Front Suspension in this Section.

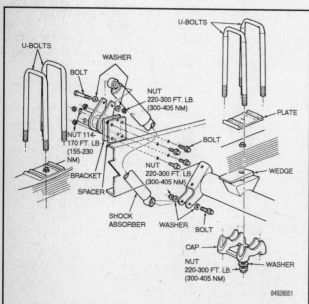

Fig. 38 Rear shock absorber for F-Super Duty stripped chassis and motor home chassis

REMOVAL & INSTALLATION

▶ **See Figures 38 and 39**

1. Raise and support the rear end on jackstands.
2. Remove the self-locking nut, steel washer and bolt from the lower end of the shock absorber. Swing the lower end away from the bracket.
3. Remove the upper mounting nut and washer.
To install:
4. Attach the upper end first, then the lower end; don't tighten the nuts yet. If you are installing new gas shocks, attach the upper end loosely, aim the lower end at its bracket and cut the strap holding the shock compressed. Once extended, these shocks are very difficult to compress by hand!
5. Once the upper and lower ends are attached, tighten the nuts, for all models, as follows:
• Lower end, except Super Duty stripped chassis and motor home chassis: 52–74 ft. lbs. (71–100 Nm)
• Upper end, except Super Duty stripped chassis and motor home chassis: 40–60 ft. lbs. (54–81 Nm)
• Super Duty stripped chassis and motor home chassis upper and lower ends: 220–300 ft. lbs. (298–407 Nm)

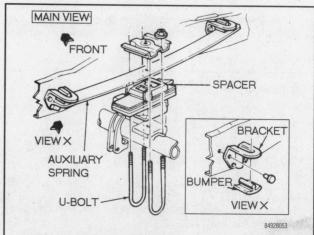

Fig. 39 Rear spring installation with auxiliary spring—4-wheel drive F-150, F-250 and F-350 models

Stabilizer Bar

REMOVAL & INSTALLATION

1. Remove the nuts from the lower ends of the stabilizer bar link.
2. Remove the outer washers and insulators.
3. Disconnect the bar from the links.
4. Remove the inner insulators and washers.
5. Unbolt the link from the frame.
6. Remove the U-bolts, brackets and retainers.
7. Installation is the reverse of removal. Replace all worn or cracked rubber

parts. Coat all new rubber parts with silicone grease. Assemble all parts loosely and make sure the bar assembly is centered before tightening the fasteners. Observe the following torque figures:

- Stabilizer bar-to-axle nut, except Super Duty: 30–42 ft. lbs. (41–57 Nm)
- Stabilizer bar-to-axle bolt, Super Duty chassis/cab: 27–37 ft. lbs. (37–50 Nm)
- Stabilizer bar-to-axle bolt, Super Duty stripped chassis and motor home chassis: 30–47 ft. lbs. (41–64 Nm)
- Link bracket-to-frame nut, 4wd: 30–42 ft. lbs. (41–57 Nm)
- Link-to-bracket nut, 4wd: 60 ft. lbs. (81 Nm)
- Link-to-frame nut, 2wd: 60 ft. lbs. (81 Nm)
- Stabilizer bar-to-link: 15–25 ft. lbs. (20–34 Nm)

STEERING

Steering Wheel

REMOVAL & INSTALLATION

Without Air Bag

EXCEPT F-SUPER DUTY STRIPPED CHASSIS MODELS AND MOTOR HOME CHASSIS MODELS

▶ **See Figures 40 thru 47**

➡ **The factory recommends that the front wheels be set in the straight-ahead position and you paint or make chalk marks on the column and steering wheel hub for alignment purposes during installation. Of these two safeguards, it is more important to mark the column so even if the column is moved slightly, the steering wheel can still be repositioned in its original position.**

1. Disconnect the negative battery cable.

2. Remove the one screw from the underside of each steering wheel spoke, and lift the horn switch assembly (steering wheel pad) from the steering wheel. On vehicles equipped with the sport steering wheel option, pry the button cover off with a suitable prytool.

3. Disconnect the horn switch wires at the connector and remove the switch assembly. On trucks equipped with speed control, squeeze the J-clip ground wire terminal firmly and pull it out of the hole in the steering wheel. Don't pull the wire out without squeezing the clip.

4. Remove the horn switch assembly.

5. Remove the steering wheel retaining nut and remove the steering wheel with a puller.

✳✳ WARNING

Never hammer on the wheel or shaft to remove it! Never use a knock-off type puller.

6. Install the steering wheel in the reverse order of removal. Tighten the shaft nut to 40 ft. lbs. (54 Nm)

Fig. 40 Remove the screws from behind the wheel—F-150 model without air bag

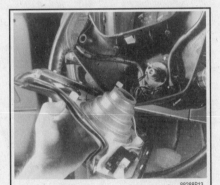

Fig. 41 Pull away the cover with the wiring still connected

Fig. 42 Disconnect the wiring at the steering wheel

Fig. 43 Matchmark the steering wheel

Fig. 44 Remove the center nut from the steering wheel

Fig. 45 Use a steering wheel puller to remove the wheel

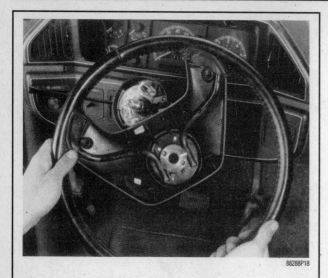

Fig. 46 Remove the steering wheel from the shaft

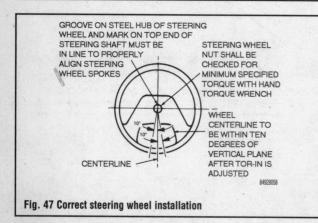

Fig. 47 Correct steering wheel installation

F-SUPER DUTY STRIPPED CHASSIS MOTOR HOME CHASSIS MODELS

1. Set the front wheel in the straight-ahead position and make chalk marks on the column and steering wheel hub for alignment purposes during installation.
2. Disconnect the negative battery cable.
3. Remove the one screw from the underside of each steering wheel spoke, and lift the horn switch assembly (steering wheel pad) from the steering wheel.
4. Disconnect the horn switch wires at the connector and remove the switch assembly.
5. Remove the horn switch assembly.
6. Remove the steering wheel retaining nut and remove the steering wheel with a puller.

✳✳ WARNING

Never hammer on the wheel or shaft to remove it! Never use a knock-off type puller.

7. Install the steering wheel in the reverse order of removal. Tighten the shaft nut to 30–42 ft. lbs. (41–57 Nm).

With Air Bag

▶ See Figure 48

✳✳ CAUTION

Read the air bag service precautions in Section 6 prior to doing work involving an air bag equipped steering column component. Always wear safety glasses when servicing an air bag vehicle and handling the air bag to avoid possible injury.

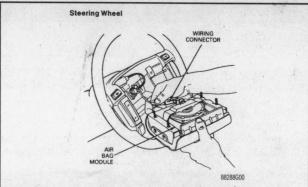

Fig. 48 Remove the air bag module and disconnect the wiring harnesses

1. Turn the front wheels to the straight-ahead position.
2. Disconnect the battery-to-starter relay cable for at least one minute to let the air bag back-up power supply discharge.
3. Remove the air bag module from the steering wheel (refer to Section 6).
4. Disconnect the horn/speed control wiring from the steering wheel.
5. Remove the steering wheel retaining bolt.
6. Install the Differential Bearing Cone Remover/Replacer, No. T77F–4220B1, or equivalent, and remove the steering wheel. Route the contact assembly harnesses through the steering wheel as it is lifted off of the shaft.

To install:

➡**Make sure the front wheels are still in the straight-ahead position prior to installation.**

7. Route the air bag sliding contact wiring through the steering wheel at the 3 o'clock position. Position the steering wheel on the shaft an align the marks. Make sure not to pinch the contact wire.

✳✳ WARNING

Make sure no air gets trapped between the steering wheel and air bag sliding contact.

8. Install a new steering wheel retaining bolt, then tighten to 23–33 ft. lbs. (31–45 Nm).
9. Connect the horn/speed control wiring and clip in place. Connect the air bag wire harness. Tighten the module retaining nuts to 35–53 inch lbs. (4–6 Nm).

➡**When the battery cable has been disconnected, then reconnected, some abnormal driving symptoms may occur for the first 10 miles (16 km) until the PCM re-learns it adaptive strategy.**

10. Connect the battery to starter cable. Verify the air bag warning indicator light on the instrument panel.

Turn Signal Switch

REMOVAL & INSTALLATION

✳✳ CAUTION

Read the air bag service precautions in Section 6 prior to doing work involving an air bag equipped steering column component. Always wear safety glasses when servicing an air bag vehicle and handling the air bag to avoid possible injury.

1. Disconnect the battery ground cable.
2. Remove the steering wheel.
3. Remove the turn signal lever by unscrewing it from the steering column.
4. Disconnect the turn signal indicator switch wiring connector plug by lifting up the tabs on the side of the plug and pulling it apart.
5. Remove the switch assembly attaching screws.
6. On trucks with a fixed column, lift the switch out of the column and guide the connector plug through the opening in the shift socket.

7. On trucks with a tilt column, remove the connector plug before removing the switch from the column. The shift socket opening is not large enough for the plug connector to pass through.

8. Install the turn signal switch in the reverse order of removal.

Ignition Switch

REMOVAL & INSTALLATION

✳✳ CAUTION

Read the air bag service precautions in Section 6 prior to doing work involving an air bag equipped steering column component. Always wear safety glasses when servicing an air bag vehicle and handling the air bag to avoid possible injury.

1. Disconnect the battery ground cable.
2. Remove the steering column shroud and lower the steering column.
3. Disconnect the switch wiring at the multiple plug.
4. Remove the two nuts that retain the switch to the steering column.
5. Lift the switch vertically upward to disengage the actuator rod from the switch and remove the switch.
6. When installing the ignition switch, both the locking mechanism at the top of the column and the switch itself must be in the LOCK position for correct adjustment. To hold the mechanical parts of the column in the LOCK position, move the shift lever into PARK (with automatic transmissions) or REVERSE (with manual transmissions), turn the key to the LOCK position, and remove the key. New replacement switches, when received, are already pinned in the LOCK position by a metal shipping pin inserted in a locking hole on the side of the switch.
7. Engage the actuator rod in the switch.
8. Position the switch on the column and install the retaining nuts, but do not tighten them.
9. Move the switch up and down along the column to locate the mid-position of rod lash, and then tighten the retaining nuts.
10. Remove the locking pin, connect the battery cable, and check for proper start in PARK or NEUTRAL.—Also check to make certain that the start circuit cannot be actuated in the DRIVE and REVERSE position.
11. Raise the steering column into position at instrument panel. Install steering column shroud.

Ignition Lock Cylinder

REMOVAL & INSTALLATION

With Key

1. Disconnect the battery ground.
2. On tilt columns, remove the upper extension shroud by unsnapping the shroud from the retaining clip at the 9 o'clock position.

3. Remove the trim shroud halves.
4. Unplug the wire connector at the key warning switch.
5. Place the shift lever in PARK and turn the key to **ON**.
6. Place a ⅛ in. (3mm) wire pin in the hole in the casting surrounding the lock cylinder and depress the retaining pin while pulling out on the cylinder.
7. When installing the cylinder, turn the lock cylinder to the **RUN** position and depress the retaining pin, then insert the lock cylinder into its housing in the flange casting. Assure that the cylinder is fully seated and aligned in the interlocking washer before turning the key to the **OFF** position. This will allow the cylinder retaining pin to extend into the cylinder cast housing hole.
8. The remainder of installation is the reverse of removal.

Non-Functioning Cylinder or No Key Available

FIXED COLUMNS

1. Disconnect the battery ground.
2. Remove the steering wheel.
3. Remove the turn signal lever.
4. Remove the column trim shrouds.
5. Unbolt the steering column and lower it carefully.
6. Remove the ignition switch and warning buzzer and pin the switch in the **LOCK** position.
7. Remove the turn signal switch.
8. Remove the snapring and T-bolt nuts that retain the flange casting to the column outer tube.
9. Remove the flange casting, upper shaft bearing, lock cylinder, ignition switch actuator and the actuator rod by pulling the entire assembly over the end of the steering column shaft.
10. Remove the lock actuator insert, the T-bolts and the automatic transmission indicator insert or, with manual transmissions, the key release lever.
11. Upon reassembly, the following parts must be replaced with new parts:
   • Flange
   • Lock cylinder assembly
   • Steering column lock gear
   • Steering column lock bearing
   • Steering column upper bearing retainer
   • Lock actuator assembly
12. Assembly is a reversal of the disassembly procedure. It is best to install a new upper bearing. Check that the truck starts only in PARK and NEUTRAL.

TILT COLUMNS

▶ See Figures 49, 50, 51, 52 and 53

1. Disconnect the battery ground.
2. Remove the steering column shrouds.
3. Using masking tape, tape the gap between the steering wheel hub and the cover casting. Cover the entire circumference of the casting. Cover the seat and floor area with a drop-cloth.
4. Pull out the hazard switch and tape it in a downward position.
5. The lock cylinder retaining pin is located on the outside of the steering column cover casting adjacent to the hazard flasher button.

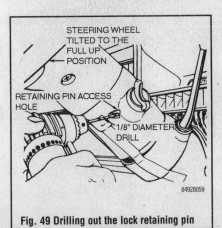

Fig. 49 Drilling out the lock retaining pin

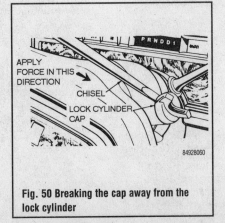

Fig. 50 Breaking the cap away from the lock cylinder

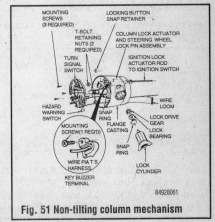

Fig. 51 Non-tilting column mechanism

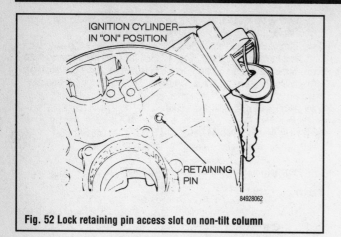

Fig. 52 Lock retaining pin access slot on non-tilt column

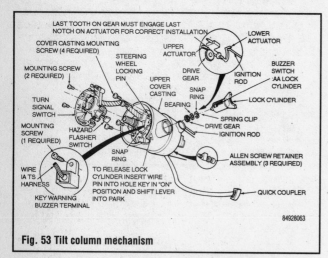

Fig. 53 Tilt column mechanism

6. Tilt the steering column to the full up position and pre-punch the lock cylinder retaining pin with a sharp punch.

7. Using a ⅛ in. (3mm) drill bit, mounted in a right angle drive drill adapter, drill out the retaining pin, going no deeper than ½ in. (13mm).

8. Tilt the column to the full down position. Place a chisel at the base of the ignition lock cylinder cap and using a hammer break away the cap from the lock cylinder.

9. Using a ⅜ in. (10mm) drill bit, drill down the center of the ignition lock cylinder key slot about 1¾ in. (44mm), until the lock cylinder breaks loose from the steering column cover casting.

10. Remove the lock cylinder and the drill shavings.
11. Remove the steering wheel.
12. Remove the turn signal lever.
13. Remove the turn signal switch attaching screws.
14. Remove the key buzzer attaching screw.
15. Remove the turn signal switch up and over the end of the column, but don't disconnect the wiring.
16. Remove the 4 attaching screws from the cover casting and lift the casting over the end of the steering shaft, allowing the turn signal switch to pass through the casting. The removal of the casting cover will expose the upper actuator. Remove the upper actuator.
17. Remove the drive gear, snapring and washer from the cover casting along with the upper actuator.
18. Clean all components and replace any that appear damaged or worn.
19. Installation is the reverse of removal.

Steering Linkage

REMOVAL & INSTALLATION

▶ See Figures 54, 55 and 56

Pitman Arm

EXCEPT F-SUPER DUTY STRIPPED CHASSIS AND MOTOR HOME CHASSIS

1. Place the wheels in a straight-ahead position.
2. Disconnect the drag link at the Pitman arm. You'll need a puller such as a tie rod end remover.
3. Remove the Pitman arm-to-gear nut and washer.
4. Matchmark the Pitman arm and gear housing for installation purposes.
5. Using a 2-jawed puller, remove the Pitman arm from the gear.
6. Installation is the reverse of removal. Align the matchmarks when installing the Pitman arm. Tighten the Pitman arm nut to 170–230 ft. lbs. (230–312 Nm); torque the drag link ball stud nut to 50–75 ft. lbs. (68–102 Nm), advancing the nut to align the cotter pin hole. Never back off the nut to align the hole.

F-SUPER DUTY STRIPPED CHASSIS MOTOR HOME CHASSIS

1. Matchmark the Pitman arm and sector shaft.
2. Disconnect the drag link from the Pitman arm.
3. Remove the bolt and nut securing the Pitman arm to the sector shaft.
4. Using a 2-jawed gear puller, remove the Pitman arm from the sector shaft.

To install:

5. Aligning the matchmarks, slide the Pitman arm onto the sector shaft. If the arm won't slide on easily, use a cold chisel to spread the separation. NEVER

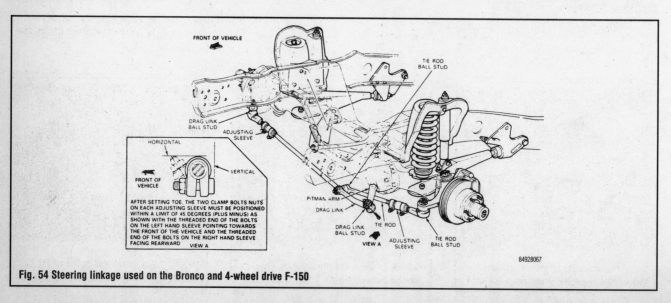

Fig. 54 Steering linkage used on the Bronco and 4-wheel drive F-150

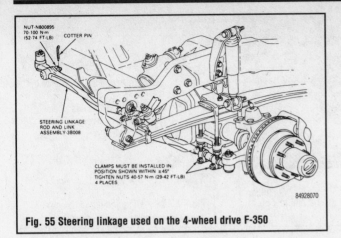

Fig. 55 Steering linkage used on the 4-wheel drive F-350

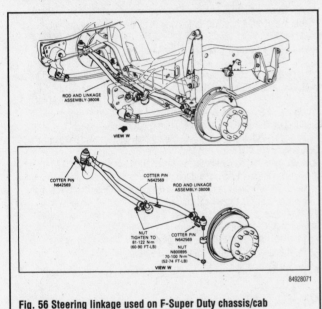

Fig. 56 Steering linkage used on F-Super Duty chassis/cab

HAMMER THE ARM ONTO THE SHAFT! Hammering on the arm will damage the steering gear!

6. Install the nut and bolt. Tighten the nut to 220–300 ft. lbs. (298–407 Nm).
7. Connect the drag link.

Tie Rod and Drag Link

EXCEPT RUBBERIZED BALL SOCKET LINKAGE

1. Place the wheels in a straight-ahead position.
2. Remove the cotter pins and rust from the drag link and tie rod ball studs.

3. Remove the drag link ball studs from the right-hand spindle and Pitman arm.
4. Remove the tie rod ball studs from the left-hand spindle and drag link.
5. Installation is the reverse of removal. Seat the studs in the tapered hole before tightening the nuts. This will avoid wrap-up of the rubber grommets during tightening of the nuts. Tighten the nuts to 70 ft. lbs. (95 Nm). Always use new cotter pins.
6. Have the front end alignment checked.

RUBBERIZED BALL SOCKET LINKAGE

1. Raise and support the front end on jackstands.
2. Place the wheels in the straight-ahead position.
3. Remove the nuts connecting the drag link ball studs to the connecting rod and Pitman arm.
4. Disconnect the drag link using a tie rod end remover.
5. Loosen the bolts on the adjuster clamp. Count the number of turns it take to remove the drag link from the adjuster.

To install:

6. Installation is the reverse of the removal procedure. Install the drag link with the same number of turns it took to remove it. Make certain that the wheels remain in the straight-ahead position during installation. Seat the studs in the tapered hole before tightening the nuts. This will avoid wrap-up of the rubber grommets during tightening of the nuts. Tighten the adjuster clamp nuts to 40 ft. lbs. (54 Nm). Tighten the ball stud nuts to 75 ft. lbs. (102 Nm).
7. Have the front end alignment checked.

Connecting Rod

RUBBERIZED BALL SOCKET LINKAGE

1. Raise and support the front end on jackstands.
2. Place the wheels in the straight-ahead position.
3. Disconnect the connecting rod from the drag link by removing the nut and separating the two with a tie rod end remover.
4. Loosen the bolts on the adjusting sleeve clamps. Count the number of turns it takes to remove the connecting rod from the connecting rod from the adjuster sleeve and remove the rod.
5. Installation is the reverse of removal. Install the connecting rod the exact number of turns noted during removal. Tighten the tie rod nuts to 40 ft. lbs. (54 Nm); the ball stud nut to 75 ft. lbs. (102 Nm).
6. Have the front end alignment checked.

Tie Rod Ends

RUBBERIZED BALL SOCKET LINKAGE

◆ See Figures 57 thru 62

1. Raise and support the front end on jackstands.
2. Place the wheels in a straight-ahead position.
3. Remove the ball stud from the Pitman arm using a tie rod end remover.

➡**Optional: paint a mark or measure the length of the tie rod end threads to ease reinstallation in as close to the original position as possible.**

Fig. 57 Remove the cotter pin from the castellated nut at the ball stud

Fig. 58 Remove the nut from the ball stud

Fig. 59 Use a tie rod end puller tool to remove the ball stud from the Pitman arm

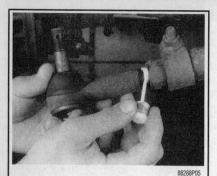

Fig. 60 Liquid correction fluid makes excellent paint to mark the threads of the tie rod end

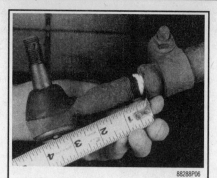

Fig. 61 For a more accurate reinstallation, you may measure the tie rod end prior to removal

Fig. 62 After having loosened the nut, unscrew and remove the tie rod end

4. Loosen the nuts on the adjusting sleeve clamp. Remove the ball stud from the adjuster, or the adjuster from the tie rod. Count the number of turns it takes to remove the sleeve from the tie rod or ball stud from the sleeve.

To install:

5. Install the sleeve on the tie rod, or the ball in the sleeve the same number of turns noted during removal. Make sure that the adjuster clamps are in the correct position, illustrated, and torque the clamp bolts to 40 ft. lbs. (54 Nm).

6. Keep the wheels facing straight-ahead and install the ball studs. Tighten the nuts to 75 ft. lbs. (102 Nm). Use new cotter pins.

7. Install the drag link and connecting rod.

8. Have the front end alignment checked.

Ford Integral Power Steering Gear

♦ See Figure 63

The Ford Integral Power Steering Gear is used on all 1987–92 models except the F-Super Duty stripped chassis and motor home chassis.

ADJUSTMENTS

Meshload

1. Raise and support the front end on jackstands.
2. Matchmark the Pitman arm and gear housing.
3. Set the wheels in a straight-ahead position.
4. Disconnect the Pitman arm from the sector shaft.
5. Disconnect the fluid RETURN line at the pump reservoir and cap the reservoir nipple.
6. Place the end of the return line in a clean container and turn the steering wheel lock-to-lock a few times to expel the fluid from the gear.
7. Turn the steering wheel all the way to the right stop. Place a small piece of masking tape on the steering wheel rim as a reference and rotate the steering wheel 45° from the right stop.
8. Disconnect the battery ground.

9. Remove the horn pad.

10. Using an inch pound torque wrench on the steering wheel nut, record the amount of torque needed to turn the steering wheel ⅛ turn counterclockwise. The preload reading should be 4–9 inch lbs. (0.45–1 Nm).

11. Center the steering wheel (½ the total lock-to-lock turns) and record the torque needed to turn the steering wheel 90° to either side of center. On a truck with fewer than 5,000 miles (8050 km), the meshload should be 15–25 inch lbs. (1.7–2.82 Nm) on trucks with 5,000 or more miles, the meshload should be 7 inch lbs. (0.8 Nm) more than the preload torque. On trucks with fewer than 5,000 miles, if the meshload is not within specifications, it should be reset to a figure 14–18 inch lbs. (1.58–2 Nm) greater than the recorded preload torque. On trucks with 5,000 or more miles (8050 km), if the meshload is not within specifications, it should be reset to a figure 10–14 inch lbs. (1.13–1.58 Nm) greater than the recorded preload torque.

12. If an adjustment is required, loosen the adjuster locknut and turn the sector shaft adjuster screw until the necessary torque is achieved.

13. Once adjustment is completed. hold the adjuster screw and tighten the locknut to 45 ft. lbs. (61 Nm).

14. Recheck the adjustment readings and reset if necessary.

15. Connect the return line and refill the reservoir.

16. Install the Pitman arm.

17. Install the horn pad.

REMOVAL & INSTALLATION

♦ See Figure 64

1. Raise and support the front end on jackstands.
2. Place the wheels in the straight-ahead position.

Fig. 63 Ford integral power steering gear

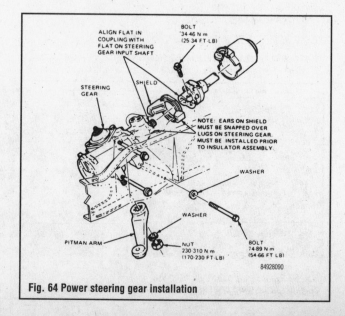

Fig. 64 Power steering gear installation

3. Place a drain pan under the gear and disconnect the pressure and return lines. Cap the openings.

4. Remove the splash shield from the flex coupling.

5. Disconnect the flex coupling at the gear.

6. Matchmark and remove the Pitman arm from the sector shaft.

7. Support the steering gear and remove the mounting bolts.

8. Remove the steering gear. It may be necessary to work it free of the flex coupling.

To install:

9. Place the splash shield on the steering gear lugs.

10. Slide the flex coupling into place on the steering shaft. Make sure the steering wheel spokes are still horizontal.

11. Center the steering gear input shaft with the indexing flat facing downward.

12. Slide the steering gear input shaft into the flex coupling and into place on the frame side rail. Install the flex coupling bolt and torque it to 30 ft. lbs. (41 Nm).

13. Install the gear mounting bolts and torque them to 65 ft. lbs. (88 Nm).

14. Make sure that the wheels are still straight-ahead and install the Pitman arm. Tighten the nut to 230 ft. lbs. (312 Nm).

15. Connect the pressure, then, the return lines. Tighten the pressure line to 25 ft. lbs. (34 Nm).

16. Snap the flex coupling shield into place.

17. Fill the steering reservoir.

18. Run the engine and turn the steering wheel lock-to-lock several times to expel air. Check for leaks.

Ford XR-50 Power Steering Gear

The XR-50 Power Steering Gear is used on all 1993–96 models except the F-Super Duty stripped chassis and motor home chassis.

ADJUSTMENTS

▶ **See Figure 65**

Meshload

1. Raise and support the front end on jackstands.

2. Matchmark the Pitman arm and gear housing.

3. Set the wheels in a straight-ahead position.

4. Disconnect the Pitman arm from the sector shaft.

5. Disconnect the fluid RETURN line at the pump reservoir and cap the reservoir nipple.

6. Place the end of the return line in a clean container and turn the steering wheel lock-to-lock a few times to expel the fluid from the gear.

7. Turn the steering wheel all the way to the right stop. Place a small piece of masking tape on the steering wheel rim as a reference and rotate the steering wheel 45° from the right stop.

8. Disconnect the battery ground.

9. Remove the horn pad.

10. Using an inch pound torque wrench on the steering wheel nut, record the amount of torque needed to turn the steering wheel ⅛ turn counterclock-

wise. The preload reading should be 4–9 inch lbs. (0.45–1 Nm).

11. Center the steering wheel (½ the total lock-to-lock turns) and record the torque needed to turn the steering wheel 90° to either side of center. On a truck with less than 5000 miles (less than 6779 km), the meshload should be 15–25 inch lbs. (1.70–2.8 Nm). On a truck with 5000 or more miles (more than 6779 km), the meshload should be 7 inch lbs. (0.8 Nm) more than the preload torque. On trucks with less than 5000 miles (less than 6779 km), if the meshload is not within specifications, it should be reset to a figure 14–18 inch lbs. (1.58–2 Nm) greater than the recorded preload torque.—On trucks with 5000 or more miles (more than 6779 km), if the meshload is not within specifications, it should be reset to a figure 10–14 inch lbs. (1.35–1.6 Nm) greater than the recorded preload torque

12. If an adjustment is required, loosen the adjuster locknut and turn the sector shaft adjuster screw until the necessary torque is achieved.

13. Once adjustment is completed. hold the adjuster screw and tighten the locknut to 45 ft. lbs. (61 Nm).

14. Recheck the adjustment readings and reset if necessary

15. Connect the return line and refill the reservoir.

16. Install the Pitman arm.

17. Install the horn pad.

REMOVAL & INSTALLATION

▶ **See Figure 66**

1. Raise and support the front end on jackstands.

2. Place the wheels in the straight-ahead position.

3. Place a drain pan under the gear and disconnect the pressure and return lines. Cap the openings.

4. Remove the splash shield from the flex coupling.

5. Disconnect the flex coupling at the gear.

6. Matchmark and remove the Pitman arm from the sector shaft.

7. Support the steering gear and remove the mounting bolts.

8. Remove the steering gear. It may be necessary to work it free of the flex coupling.

To install:

9. Place the splash shield on the steering gear lugs.

10. Slide the flex coupling into place on the steering shaft. Make sure the steering wheel spokes are still horizontal.

11. Center the steering gear input shaft with the indexing flat facing downward.

12. Slide the steering gear input shaft into the flex coupling and into place on the frame side rail. Install the flex coupling bolt and torque it to 30–42 ft. lbs. (41–57 Nm).

13. Install the gear mounting bolts and torque them to 65 ft. lbs. (88 Nm).

14. Make sure that the wheels are still straight-ahead and install the Pitman arm. Tighten the nut to 170–288 ft. lbs. (230–390 Nm).

15. Connect the pressure, then, the return lines. Tighten the pressure line to 25 ft. lbs. (34 Nm).

16. Snap the flex coupling shield into place.

17. Fill the steering reservoir.

18. Run the engine and turn the steering wheel lock-to-lock several times to expel air. Check for leaks.

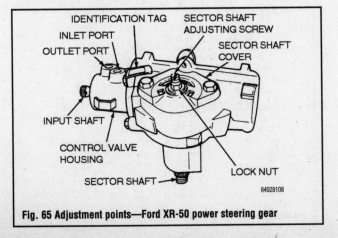

Fig. 65 Adjustment points—Ford XR-50 power steering gear

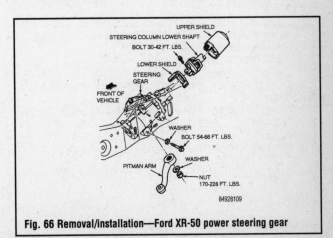

Fig. 66 Removal/installation—Ford XR-50 power steering gear

Bendix C-300N Power Steering Gear

The Bendix gear is used on F-Super Duty stripped chassis models and motor home chassis models.

ADJUSTMENTS

Adjustments must be made with the steering gear removed and mounted in a vise.

Piston-to-Output Shaft Gear Backlash Adjustment

▶ See Figure 67

➡Backlash is correct when a 4–18 inch lb. (0.45–2 Nm) increase in rotational torque is noted at the input shaft as it is rotated and the piston passes the mid-point of its total travel in the housing. The torque increase should occur only at mid-point and should disappear after mid-point.

1. Loosen the locknut and turn the adjusting screw counterclockwise as far as it will go.
2. Using an inch pound torque wrench, rotate the input shaft as far as it will go in one direction, then, counting the number of full turns and noting the rotational torque, rotate it to the opposite stop.
3. Turn the shaft back ½ the total number of turns to the mid-point.
4. Rotate the shaft 180° to both sides of the mid-point, noting the change in rotational torque. Turn the adjusting screw ⅛–¼ turn at a time until the proper reading of 4–18 inch lbs. (0.45–2 Nm) increase in torque is noted over the mid-point. This increase in torque must be plus the total rotational torque.
5. When the adjustment is correct, hold the adjusting screw and, using a crow's foot adapter, torque the locknut to 74–88 ft. lbs. (100–119 Nm).
6. Check the adjustment to make sure it hasn't changed. Rotate the shaft through its entire travel. It must rotate smoothly.

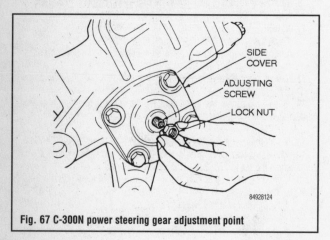

Fig. 67 C-300N power steering gear adjustment point

REMOVAL & INSTALLATION

1. Raise and support the front end on jackstands.
2. Thoroughly clean all connections.
3. Place a drain pan under the area.
4. Disconnect the hydraulic lines at the gear. Cap all openings at once.
5. Remove the retaining bolt and nut and disconnect the Pitman arm from the sector shaft.
6. Remove the bolt and nut securing the input shaft and U-joint.
7. Support the gear and remove the gear-to-frame bolts and nuts.
To install:
8. Position the gear on the frame and install the bolts and nuts. Tighten the nuts to 150–200 ft. lbs. (203–271 Nm).
9. Install the U-joint bolt and nut. Tighten the nut to 50–70 ft. lbs. (68–95 Nm).
10. Install the Pitman arm.

✳✳ CAUTION

Never hammer the Pitman shaft onto the sector shaft! Hammering will damage the gear. Use a cold chisel to separate the Pitman arm opening.

11. Install the bolt and nut. Tighten the nut to 220–300 ft. lbs. (298–407 Nm).
12. Connect the hydraulic lines, fill the reservoir, run the engine and check for leaks.

Quick-Connect Pressure Line

▶ See Figure 68

Some pumps will have a quick-connect fitting for the pressure line. This fitting may, under certain circumstances, leak and/or be improperly engaged, resulting in unplanned disconnection.

The leak is usually caused by a cut O-ring, imperfections in the outlet fitting inside diameter, or an improperly machined O-ring groove.

Improper engagement can be caused by an improperly machined tube end, tube nut, snapring, outlet fitting or gear port.

If a leak occurs, the leaking O-ring should be replaced. Special O-rings are made for quick-disconnect fittings. Standard O-rings should never be used in their place. If the new O-ring(s) do not solve the leak problem, replace the outlet fitting. If that doesn't work, replace the pressure line.

Improper engagement due to a missing or bent snapring, or improperly machined tube nut, may be corrected with a Ford snapring kit made for the purpose. If that doesn't work, replace the pressure hose.

When tightening a quick-connect tube nut, always use a tube nut wrench; never use an open-end wrench! Use of an open-end wrench will result in deformation of the nut! Tighten quick-connect tube nuts to 15 ft. lbs. (20 Nm).

Swivel and/or end-play of quick-connect fittings is normal.

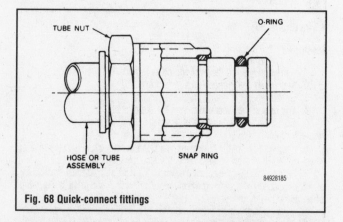

Fig. 68 Quick-connect fittings

Ford C-II Power Steering Pump

This pump is used by all models except the F-Super Duty stripped chassis and motor home models.

REMOVAL & INSTALLATION

1. Disconnect the return line at the pump and drain the fluid into a container.
2. Disconnect the pressure line from the pump.
3. Loosen the pump bracket nuts and remove the drive belt. On the 4.9L engine or 5.0L engine with a serpentine drive belt, remove belt tension by lifting the tensioner out of position.
4. Remove the nuts and lift out the pump/bracket assembly.
5. If a new pump or bracket is being installed, you'll have to remove the pulley from the present pump. This is best done with a press and adapters.
6. Installation is the reverse of removal. Note the following torques:
• Pivot bolt (4.9L and 5.0L): 45 ft. lbs. (61 Nm)
• Pump-to-adjustment bracket: 45 ft. lbs. (61 Nm)

- Support bracket-to-engine (5.8L): 65 ft. lbs. (88 Nm)
- Support bracket-to-water pump housing (4.9L): 17 ft. lbs. (23 Nm)
- Support bracket-to-water pump housing (5.0L, 5.8L): 45 ft. lbs. (61 Nm)
- Pressure line-to-fitting: 29 ft. lbs. (39 Nm)
- Adjustment bracket-to-support bracket: 4.9L, 5.0L, 5.8L: 45 ft. lbs. (61 Nm); 7.5L and Diesel: Long bolt—65 ft. lbs. (88 Nm)
- Short bolt—45 ft. lbs. (61 Nm)

ZF Power Steering Pump

This pump is used on the F-Super Duty stripped chassis and motor home models.

REMOVAL & INSTALLATION

1. Place a drain pan under the pump, remove the return hose and drain the reservoir.
2. Disconnect the pressure line from the pump and tie up the ends of both hoses in a raised position. Cap the openings.
3. Loosen the pump pivot and adjusting bolts, then remove the drive belt.
4. Remove the bolts and lift out the pump.
5. Installation is the reverse of removal. Adjust the belt tension. Tighten the bolts to 30–45 ft. lbs. (40–61 Nm). Connect the hoses. Refill the reservoir. Run the engine and check for leaks.

TORQUE SPECIFICATIONS

Component	U.S.	Metric
WHEELS		
Front or rear wheels		
5-lug	100 ft. lbs.	136 Nm
All others	140 ft. lbs.	190 Nm
2-WHEEL DRIVE COIL SPRING FRONT SUSPENSION		
Front Wheel Spindle		
Lower ball joint stud	35 ft. lbs.	48 Nm
Steering linkage to spindle nut	70–100 ft. lbs.	95-136 Nm
Upper ball joint stud	110–140 ft. lbs.	150-190 Nm
I-beam axle pivot bolts	120–150 ft. lbs.	163-204 Nm
Radius Arm		
Bushing nut	120 ft. lbs.	163 Nm
Radius arm-to-axle bolt	269–329 ft. lbs.	366-447 Nm
Shock Absorbers		
Lower end	40–60 ft. lbs.	54-82 Nm
Upper end	25–35 ft. lbs.	34-48 Nm
Springs		
Lower retainer attaching nuts	70–100 ft. lbs.	95-136 Nm
Upper retaining bolts	13–18 ft. lbs.	18-24 Nm
Stabilizer Bar		
Frame mounting bracket nuts/bolts		
F-250 and F-350	65 ft. lbs.	88 Nm
Link-to-stabilizer bar and axle bracket	70 ft. lbs.	95 Nm
Stabilizer bar-to-crossmember attaching bolts		
F-150	35 ft. lbs.	48 Nm
Stabilizer bar-to-frame retainer bolts		
F-250 and F-350	35 ft. lbs.	48 Nm
2-WHEEL DRIVE LEAF SPRING FRONT SUSPENSION		
Shock Absorbers		
Chassis/cab upper and lower	52–74 ft. lbs.	71-101 Nm
Stripped cab and motor home chassis upper and lower	220–300 ft. lbs.	299-408 Nm
Spindles		
Drag link nut	50–70 ft. lbs.	68-95 Nm
Lock pin nut	40–50 ft. lbs.	54-68 Nm
Spindle pin plugs	35–50 ft. lbs.	48-68 Nm
Tie rod end nut	50–70 ft. lbs.	68-95 Nm
Springs		
Front end of spring		
Chassis/cab spring-to-shackle	120–150 ft. lbs.	163-204 Nm
Chassis/cab shackle-to-frame	150–210 ft. lbs.	204-286 Nm
Stripped chassis or motor home chassis spring-to-bracket	148–207 ft. lbs.	201-282 Nm
Rear end of spring		
Chassis/cab spring-to-bracket	150–210 ft. lbs.	204-286 Nm
Stripped chassis or motor home chassis spring-to-shackle or shackle-to-bracket	74–110 ft. lbs.	101-150 Nm
U-bolts		
Chassis/cab	150–210 ft. lbs.	204-286 Nm
Stripped chassis and motor home chassis	220–300 ft. lbs.	299-408 Nm

84928193

TORQUE SPECIFICATIONS

Component	U.S.	Metric
2-WHEEL DRIVE LEAF SPRING FRONT SUSPENSION		
Stabilizer Bar		
Chassis/Cab		
End link-to-frame bolts	52–74 ft. lbs.	71-101 Nm
Stabilizer bar-to-axle mounting bolts	35–50 ft. lbs.	48-68 Nm
Stabilizer bar-to-end link nuts	15–25 ft. lbs.	20-34 Nm
Stripped Chassis or Motor Home Chassis		
Link-to-axle bracket bolts	57–81 ft. lbs.	78-110 Nm
Stabilizer bar-to-frame brackets bolts	30–47 ft. lbs.	41-64 Nm
Stabilizer bar-to-link nuts	15–25 ft. lbs.	20-34 Nm
Track Bar		
Chassis/Cab Models	120–150 ft. lbs.	163-204 Nm
4-WHEEL DRIVE FRONT SUSPENSION		
Axle pivot bolt	150 ft. lbs.	204 Nm
Radius Arm		
F-150 and Bronco		
Bracket-to-axle bolts	25 ft. lbs.	34 Nm
Radius arm-to-axle bolt	330 ft. lbs.	449 Nm
Radius arm rear attaching nut	120 ft. lbs.	163 Nm
Upper stud-type radius arm-to-axle bolt	250 ft. lbs.	340 Nm
Shock Absorbers		
F-150 and Bronco		
Upper nut	30 ft. lbs.	41 Nm
Lower bolt/nut	60 ft. lbs.	82 Nm
F-250, F-350, F-Super Duty		
Upper and lower nut/bolt	70 ft. lbs.	95 Nm
Springs		
U-bolt nuts 120 ft. lbs.	163 Nm	
F-150 and Bronco		
Lower spring retainer nut	100 ft. lbs.	136 Nm
Upper retainer bolts	13–18 ft. lbs.	18-24 Nm
F-250, F-350		
Shackle bolt nuts	150 ft. lbs.	204 Nm
Hanger bolt nut	150 ft. lbs.	204 Nm
Stabilizer Bar		
F-150 and Bronco		
Retainer nuts	35 ft. lbs.	48 Nm
All other nuts at the links	70 ft. lbs.	95 Nm
F-250 and F-350		
Connecting links-to-spring seat caps	70 ft. lbs.	95 Nm
Connecting links-to-stabilizer bar	25 ft. lbs.	34 Nm
Retainer-to-mounting bracket nuts	35 ft. lbs.	48 Nm
Track bar-to-bracket bolts		
F-350	200 ft. lbs.	272 Nm
REAR SUSPENSION		
Shock Absorbers		
Lower end		
exc. Super Duty stripped chassis & motor home	52–74 ft. lbs.	71-101 Nm
Upper end		
exc. Super Duty stripped chassis & motor home	40–60 ft. lbs.	54-82 Nm
Super Duty stripped chassis & motor home chassis		
Upper & lower ends	220–300 ft. lbs.	299-408 Nm

TORQUE SPECIFICATIONS

Component	U.S.	Metric
REAR SUSPENSION		
Springs		
Spring-to-front spring hanger		
F-150 2-wd	75–115 ft. lbs.	102-156 Nm
F-250 2-wd, F-350 2-wd and Bronco	150–210 ft. lbs.	204-286 Nm
F-150, 250, 350 4-wd	150–175 ft. lbs.	204-238 Nm
F-Super Duty	255–345 ft. lbs.	345-469 Nm
Spring-to-rear spring hanger		
All except F-250 and F-350 2-wd Chassis Cab	75–115 ft. lbs.	102-156 Nm
F-250 and F-350 2-wd Chassis Cab; F-Super Duty	150–210 ft. lbs.	204-286 Nm
U-bolts		
Bronco, F-150 and F-250 under 8,500 lb. GVW	75–115 ft. lbs.	102-156 Nm
F-250 HD and F-350	150–210 ft. lbs.	204-286 Nm
F-Super Duty chassis/cab	200–270 ft. lbs.	272-367 Nm
F-Super Duty stripped chassis and motor home chassis	220–300 ft. lbs.	299-408 Nm
Stabilizer Bar		
Link bracket-to-frame nut, 4-wd	30–42 ft. lbs.	41-57 Nm
Link-to-bracket nut, 4-wd	60 ft. lbs.	84 Nm
Link-to-frame nut, 2-wd	60 ft. lbs.	84 Nm
Stabilizer bar-to-axle bolt		
Super Duty stripped chassis and motor home chassis	30–47 ft. lbs.	41-64 Nm
Stabilizer bar-to-axle nut		
exc. Super Duty	30–42 ft. lbs.	41-57 Nm
Stabilizer bar-to-axle bolt		
Super Duty chassis/cab	27–37 ft. lbs.	37-50 Nm
Stabilizer bar-to-link	15–25 ft. lbs.	20-34 Nm
STEERING		
Bendix C-300N Power Steering Gear		
Adjusting screw locknut	74–88 ft. lbs.	101-120 Nm
Gear mounting bolts	150–200 ft. lbs.	204-272 Nm
Meshload	4–18 inch lb.*	0.5-2.0 Nm*
Piston and valve body bolts	80–88 ft. lbs.	109-120 Nm
Pressure relief plug	66–73 ft. lbs.	90-99 Nm
Pressure relief valve seat	15–18 ft. lbs.	20-24 Nm
Side cover bolts	80–88 ft. lbs.	109-120 Nm
Steering limiting valve seat	9–11 ft. lbs.	12-15 Nm
U-joint bolt and nut	50–70 ft. lbs.	68-95 Nm
Valve nut	221–257 ft. lbs.	301-350 Nm
	* plus the total rotational torque	
Connecting rod ball stud nut	75 ft. lbs.	102 Nm
Drag link ball stud nut	50–75 ft. lbs.	68-102 Nm
Ford C-II Power Steering Pump		
Adjustment bracket-to-support bracket		
6-4.9L, 8-5.0L, 8-5.8L	45 ft. lbs.	61 Nm
8-7.5L and Diesel		
Long bolt	65 ft. lbs.	88 Nm
Short bolt	45 ft. lbs.	61 Nm
Pivot bolt		
6-4.9L and 8-5.0L	45 ft. lbs.	61 Nm
Pressure line-to-fitting	29 ft. lbs.	39 Nm
Pump-to-adjustment bracket	45 ft. lbs.	61 Nm
Support bracket-to-engine		
8-5.8L	65 ft. lbs.	88 Nm
Support bracket-to-water pump housing		
6-4.9L	17 ft. lbs.	23 Nm
8-5.0L, 5.8L	45 ft. lbs.	61 Nm

84928195

TORQUE SPECIFICATIONS

Component	U.S.	Metric
STEERING		
Ford Integral Power Steering Gear		
Adjuster screw locknut	45 ft. lbs.	61 Nm
Ball clamps	42–70 inch lbs.	4.7-7.8 Nm
Flex coupling bolt	30 ft. lbs.	41 Nm
Gear mounting bolts	65 ft. lbs.	88 Nm
Meshload		
Fewer than 5,000 miles	15–25 inch lbs.	1.7-2.8 Nm
5,000 or more miles	7 inch lbs.*	0.8 Nm*
Preload	4–9 inch lbs.	0.5-1.0
Pressure line	25 ft. lbs.	34 Nm
Race nut	55–90 ft. lbs.	75-122 Nm
Sector shaft bolts	55–70 ft. lbs.	75-95 Nm
*more than the preload		
Ford XR-50 Power Steering Gear		
Adjuster screw locknut	45 ft. lbs.	61 Nm
Ball clamps and tighten	42–70 inch lbs.	4.7-7.8 Nm
Flex coupling bolt	30–42 ft. lbs.	41-57 Nm
Gear mounting bolts	65 ft. lbs.	88 Nm
Meshload		
Fewer than 5,000 miles	15–25 inch lbs.	1.7-2.8 Nm
5,000 or more miles	7 inch lbs.*	0.8 Nm*
Preload	4–9 inch lbs.	0.5-1.0 Nm
Pressure line	25 ft. lbs.	34 Nm
Race nut	55–90 ft. lbs.	75-122 Nm
Sector bolts	55–70 ft. lbs.	75-95 Nm
* more than preload		
Manual Steering Gear		
Adjusting screw locknut	25 ft. lbs.	34 Nm
Flex coupling-to-gear bolt	30 ft. lbs.	41 Nm
Gear mounting bolts	65 ft. lbs.	88 Nm
Meshload	9–14 inch lbs.	1.0-1.5 Nm
Preload	5-9 inch lbs.	0.5-1.0 Nm
Sector cover bolts	40 ft. lbs.	54 Nm
Pitman arm nut		
All Except F-Super Duty Stripped Chassis & Motor Home	170–230 ft. lbs.	231-313 Nm
F-Super Duty Stripped Chassis & Motor Home	220–300 ft. lbs.	299-408 Nm
Quick-Connect Pressure Line		
Tube nuts	15 ft. lbs. max.	20 Nm max.
Steering Column		
All Models Except F-Super Duty Stripped Chassis and Motor Home		
Column support bracket nuts	35 ft. lbs.	48 Nm
Cover plate clamp bolt	18 ft. lbs.	24 Nm
Floor cover bolts	10 ft. lbs.	14 Nm
Intermediate shaft bolt	50 ft. lbs.	68 Nm
Shroud bottom screw	15 inch lbs.	1.7 Nm
Support bracket bolts	25 ft. lbs.	34 Nm
F-Super Duty Stripped Chassis & Motor Home		
Column-to-support bracket bolts	19–27 ft. lbs.	26-37 Nm
Floor cover bolts	10 ft. lbs.	14 Nm
Intermediate shaft bolt	20–35 ft. lbs.	27-48 Nm

84928196

TORQUE SPECIFICATIONS

Component	U.S.	Metric
STEERING		
Steering wheel nut		
All Except F-Super Duty Stripped Chassis models & Motor Home	40 ft. lbs.	54 Nm
F-Super Duty Stripped Chassis & Motor Home	30–42 ft. lbs.	41-57 Nm
Tie Rod		
Adjuster clamp nuts	40 ft. lbs.	54 Nm
Except Rubberized Ball Socket Linkage	70 ft. lbs.	95 Nm
Rubberized Ball Socket Linkage	75 ft. lbs.	102 Nm
ZF Power Steering Pump		
Mounting bolts	30–45 ft. lbs.	41-61 Nm

84928197

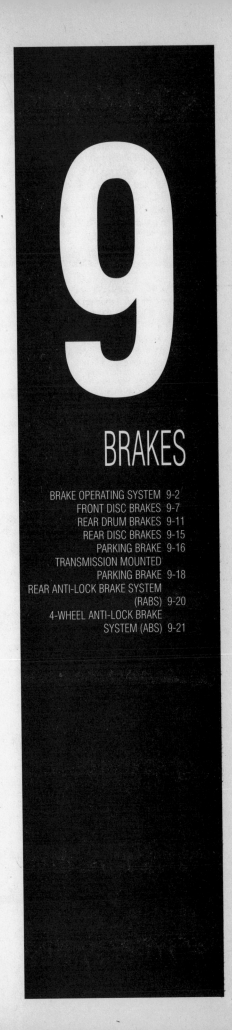

9
BRAKES

BRAKE OPERATING SYSTEM

✳✳ WARNING

Clean, high quality brake fluid is essential to the safe and proper operation of the brake system. You should always buy the highest quality brake fluid that is available. If the brake fluid becomes contaminated, drain and flush the system and fill the master cylinder with new fluid. Never reuse any brake fluid. Any brake fluid that is removed from the system should be discarded.

Brake Light Switch

REMOVAL & INSTALLATION

♦ See Figure 1

1. Lift the locking tab on the switch connector and disconnect the wiring.
2. Remove the hairpin retainer, slide the stop lamp switch, pushrod and nylon washer off of the pedal. Remove the washer, then the switch by sliding it up or down.

➡**On trucks equipped with speed control, the spacer washer is replaced by the dump valve adapter washer.**

3. To install the switch, position it so that the U-shaped side is nearest the pedal and directly over/under the pin.
4. Slide the switch up or down, trapping the master cylinder pushrod and bushing between the switch side plates.
5. Push the switch and pushrod assembly firmly towards the brake pedal arm. Assemble the outside white plastic washer to the pin and install the hairpin retainer.

✳✳ CAUTION

Don't substitute any other type of retainer. Use only the Ford specified hairpin retainer.

6. Assemble the connector on the switch.
7. Check stop lamp operation.

✳✳ CAUTION

Make sure that the stop lamp switch wiring has sufficient travel during a full pedal stroke!

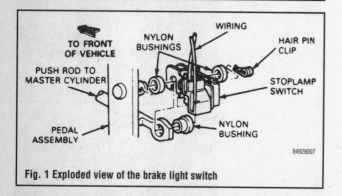

Fig. 1 Exploded view of the brake light switch

Pressure Differential Valve

REMOVAL & INSTALLATION

1. Disconnect the electrical leads from the valve.
2. Unscrew the valve from the master cylinder.
3. Install the valve in the reverse order of removal.
4. Bleed the master cylinder.

Height Sensing Proportioning Valve

REMOVAL & INSTALLATION

F-Super Duty Only

♦ See Figures 2 and 3

➡**If the linkage is disconnected from the valve, the proper setting of the valve will be lost and a new valve will have to be installed. The new valve will have the shaft preset and secured internally. If the shaft of the new valve turns freely, DO NOT USE IT!—The valve cannot be repaired or disassembled. It is to be replaced as a unit.—If the linkage is damaged or broken and requires replacement, a new sensing valve will also be required.**

1. Raise and support the rear end on jackstands.
2. Raise the frame to obtain a clearance of 6 ⅝ in. (168.3mm) between the bottom edge of the rubber jounce bumper and the top of the axle tube—on BOTH sides of the axle. The is the correct indexing height for the valve.

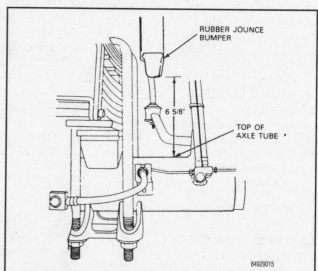

Fig. 2 Setting the correct indexing height for the height sensing proportioning valve

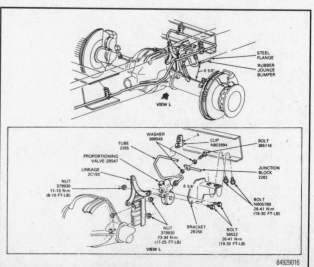

Fig. 3 A common height sensing proportioning valve—F-Super Duty models

3. Remove the nut holding the linkage arm to the valve and disconnect the arm.
4. Remove the bolt holding the flexible brake hose to the valve.
5. Disconnect the brake line from the valve.
6. Remove the 2 mounting bolts and remove the valve from its bracket.

To install:

7. Place the new valve on the bracket and tighten the mounting bolts to 12–18 ft. lbs. (16–24 Nm).
8. Install the brake hose, using new copper gaskets and tighten the bolt to 28–34 ft. lbs. (38–46 Nm).
9. Attach the brake line to the lower part of the valve.
10. Connect the linkage arm to the valve and tighten the nut to 8–10 ft. lbs. (11–13 Nm).
11. Bleed the brakes.

➡When servicing axle or suspension parts which would require disconnection of the valve, instead, remove the 2 nuts that attach the linkage arm to the axle cover plate. This will avoid disconnecting the valve and avoid having to replace the valve.

Master Cylinder

REMOVAL & INSTALLATION

♦ **See Figures 4 thru 16**

1. Disconnect the negative battery cable.
2. Apply the brake pedal several times to exhaust all the vacuum in the system.
3. Detach and cap the brake lines from the master cylinder.
4. If equipped, detach the brake warning indicator connector.

➡A turkey baster (tapered tube with a squeeze ball on top) works well for removing fluid from the reservoir (see photo).

5. Siphon off the fluid from the master cylinder reservoir to minimize spillage when lines are disconnected.
6. If applicable, disconnect and cap the Hydraulic Control Unit (HCU) supply hose at the master cylinder reservoir and secure in a position to prevent loss of fluid.
7. Unfasten the 2 nuts and lockwashers that attach the master cylinder to the brake booster.
8. Remove the master cylinder from the booster by sliding it forward and upward from the vehicle.

To install:

9. Install a new seal in the groove in the master cylinder mounting face.
10. Position the master cylinder assembly over the booster pushrod and onto the 2 studs on the booster assembly.

11. Install the retaining nuts, then tighten to 18–25 ft. lbs. (24–34 Nm).
12. Uncap and connect the brake lines to the master cylinder. Tighten the front fitting to 16–21 ft. lbs. (21–29 Nm), and the rear fitting to 10–15 ft. lbs. (15–20 Nm).
13. Uncap and connect the HCU hose to the master cylinder reservoir fitting and secure with a hose clamp.
14. If equipped, connect the brake warning indicator.
15. Fill the master cylinder with Heavy Duty Brake Fluid C6AZ-19542-AA or equivalent DOT 3 brake fluid from a clean, sealed container. Bleed the entire brake system, as outlined in this section.
16. Connect the negative battery cable.
17. Operate the brake several times, then check for external hydraulic leaks.

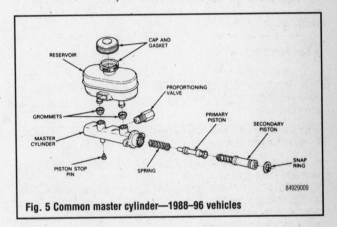

Fig. 5 Common master cylinder—1988–96 vehicles

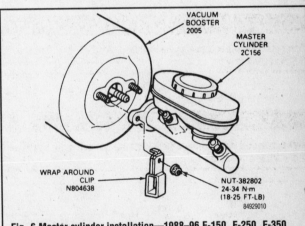

Fig. 6 Master cylinder installation—1988–96 F-150, F-250, F-350 and Bronco models

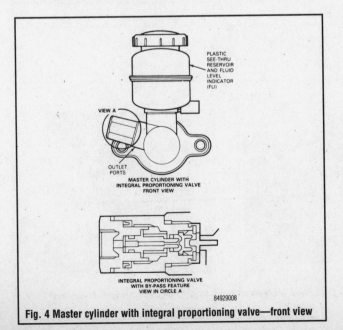

Fig. 4 Master cylinder with integral proportioning valve—front view

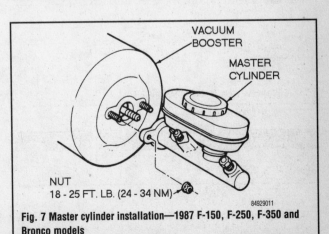

Fig. 7 Master cylinder installation—1987 F-150, F-250, F-350 and Bronco models

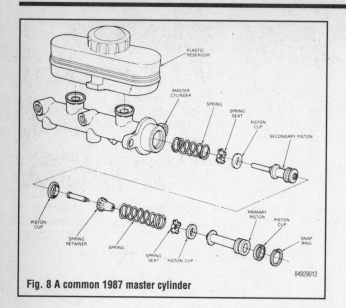

Fig. 8 A common 1987 master cylinder

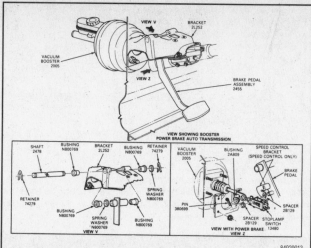

Fig. 9 Brake pedal installation—models equipped with automatic transmission

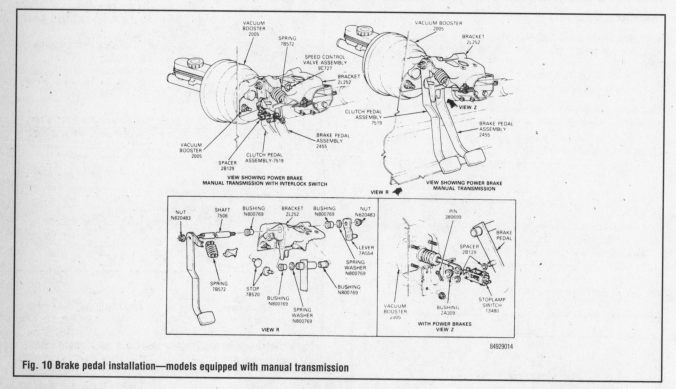

Fig. 10 Brake pedal installation—models equipped with manual transmission

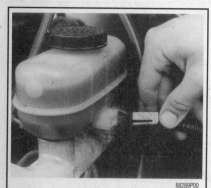

Fig. 11 Disconnect the warning indicator at the master cylinder

Fig. 12 Remove the fluid to minimize the amount that would otherwise inevitably be spilled

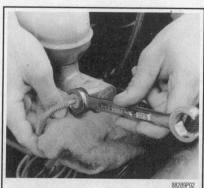

Fig. 13 Unscrew the line fittings at the master cylinder

Fig. 14 Hold a rag under the fittings to keep fluid from dripping all over things

Fig. 15 Unbolt the master cylinder from the brake booster

Fig. 16 Remove the master cylinder from the vehicle and set it in a clean location

Power Brake Booster

REMOVAL & INSTALLATION

▶ See Figure 17

2-Wheel Drive F-150 and F-250, 4-Wheel Drive F-150 and F-250, and Bronco Models

1. Disconnect the brake light switch wires.
2. Support the master cylinder from below, with a prop of some kind.
3. Loosen the clamp and remove the booster check valve hose.
4. Remove the master cylinder from the booster. Keep it supported. It will not be necessary to disconnect the brake lines.
5. Working inside the truck below the instrument panel, disconnect the booster valve operating rod from the brake pedal assembly.
6. Remove the 4 bracket-to-dash panel attaching nuts.
7. Remove the booster and bracket assembly from the dash panel, sliding the valve operating rod out from the engine side of the dash panel.

To install:

8. Mount the booster and bracket assembly on the dash panel by sliding the valve operating rod in through the hole in the dash panel, and installing the attaching nuts. Tighten the nuts to 18–25 ft. lbs. (24–34 Nm).
9. Connect the manifold vacuum hose to the booster.
10. Install the master cylinder. Tighten the nuts to 18–25 ft. lbs. (24–34 Nm).
11. Connect the stop light switch wires.
12. Working inside the truck below the instrument panel, connect the pushrod and stoplight switch.

F-250 HD 2 & 4-Wheel Drive F-350 2 & 4-Wheel Drive

1. Disconnect the brake light switch wires.
2. Support the master cylinder from below, with a prop of some kind.
3. Loosen the clamp and remove the booster check valve hose.
4. Remove the wraparound clip from the booster inboard stud.
5. Remove the master cylinder from the booster. Keep it supported. It will not be necessary to disconnect the brake lines.
6. Working inside the truck below the instrument panel, disconnect the booster valve operating rod from the brake pedal assembly.
7. Remove the 4 bracket-to-dash panel attaching nuts.
8. Remove the booster and bracket assembly from the dash panel, sliding the valve operating rod out from the engine side of the dash panel.

To install:

9. Mount the booster and bracket assembly on the dash panel by sliding the valve operating rod in through the hole in the dash panel, and installing the attaching nuts. Tighten the nuts to 18–25 ft. lbs. (24–34 Nm).
10. Connect the manifold vacuum hose to the booster.
11. Install the master cylinder. Tighten the nuts to 18–25 ft. lbs. (24–34 Nm).
12. Install the wraparound clip.
13. Connect the stop light switch wires.
14. Working inside the truck below the instrument panel, connect the pushrod and stoplight switch.

BRAKE BOOSTER PUSHROD ADJUSTMENT

▶ See Figure 18

The pushrod has an adjustment screw to maintain the correct relationship between the booster control valve plunger and the master cylinder piston. If the plunger is too long it will prevent the master cylinder piston from completely releasing hydraulic pressure, causing the brakes to drag. If the plunger is too short it will cause excessive pedal travel and an undesirable clunk in the booster area. Remove the master cylinder for access to the booster pushrod.

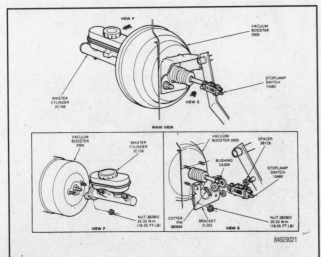

Fig. 17 A common brake booster—F-150, F-250, F-350 and Bronco models

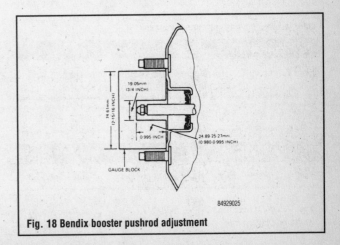

Fig. 18 Bendix booster pushrod adjustment

To check the adjustment of the screw, fabricate a gauge (from cardboard, following the dimensions in the illustration) and place it against the master cylinder mounting surface of the booster body. Adjust the pushrod screw by turning it until the end of the screw just touches the inner edge of the slot in the gauge. Install the master cylinder and bleed the system.

Diesel Brake Booster Vacuum Pump

Unlike gasoline engines, diesel engines have little vacuum available to power brake booster systems. The diesel is thus equipped with a vacuum pump, which is driven by a single belt off of the alternator. This pump is located on the top right side of the engine.

Diesel pickups are also equipped with a low vacuum indicator switch which actuates the BRAKE warning lamp when available vacuum is below a certain level. The switch senses vacuum through a fitting in the vacuum manifold that intercepts the vacuum flow from the pump. The low vacuum switch is mounted on the right side of the engine compartment, adjacent to the vacuum pump on F-250 and F-350 models.

➡The vacuum pump cannot be disassembled. It is only serviced as a unit (the pulley is separate).

REMOVAL & INSTALLATION

1. Remove the hose clamp and disconnect the pump from the hose on the manifold vacuum outlet fitting.
2. Loosen the vacuum pump adjustment bolt and the pivot bolt. Slide the pump downward and remove the drive belt from the pulley.
3. Remove the pivot and adjustment bolts and the bolts retaining the pump to the adjustment plate. Remove the vacuum pump and adjustment plate.
To install:
4. Install the pump-to-adjustment plate bolts and tighten to 11–18 ft. lbs. (15–24 Nm). Position the pump and plate on the vacuum pump bracket and loosely install the pivot and adjustment bolts.
5. Connect the hose from the manifold vacuum outlet fitting to the pump and install the hose clamp.
6. Install the drive belt on the pulley. Place a ⅜ in. drive breaker bar or ratchet into the slot on the vacuum pump adjustment plate. Lift up on the assembly until the proper belt tension is obtained. Tighten the pivot and adjustment bolts to 11–18 ft. lbs. (15–24 Nm).
7. Start the engine and make sure the brake system functions properly.

➡The BRAKE light will glow until brake vacuum builds up to the normal level.

F-Super Duty Hydro-Boost Brake Booster

A hydraulically powered brake booster is used on the F-Super Duty truck. The power steering pump provides the fluid pressure to operate both the brake booster and the power steering gear.

The Hydro-Boost assembly contains a valve which controls pump pressure while braking, a lever to control the position of the valve and a boost piston to provide the force to operate a conventional master cylinder attached to the front of the booster. The Hydro-Boost also has a reserve system, designed to store sufficient pressurized fluid to provide at least 2 brake applications in the event of insufficient fluid flow from the power steering pump. The brakes can also be applied unassisted if the reserve system is depleted.

✳✳ WARNING

Before removing the Hydro-Boost, discharge the accumulator by making several brake applications until a hard pedal is felt.

REMOVAL & INSTALLATION

✳✳ CAUTION

Do not depress the brake pedal with the master cylinder removed!

1. Remove the master cylinder from the Hydro-Boost unit. Do not disconnect the brake lines from the master cylinder! Position the master cylinder out of the way.

2. Disconnect the 3 hydraulic lines from the Hydro-Boost unit.
3. Disconnect the pushrod from the brake pedal.
4. Remove the booster mounting nuts and lift the booster from the firewall.

✳✳ CAUTION

The booster should never be carried by the accumulator. The accumulator contains high pressure nitrogen and can be dangerous if mishandled! If the accumulator is to be disposed of, do not expose it to fire or other forms of incineration! Gas pressure can be relieved by drilling a ¹⁄₁₆ in. (1.5mm) hole in the end of the accumulator can. Always wear safety goggles during the drilling!

5. Installation is the reverse of removal. Tighten the booster mounting nuts to 25 ft. lbs. (34 Nm); the master cylinder nuts to 25 ft. lbs. (34 Nm); connect the hydraulic lines, refill and bleed the booster as follows:
   a. Fill the pump reservoir with Dexron®II ATF.
   b. Disconnect the coil wires and crank the engine for several seconds.
   c. Check the fluid level and refill, if necessary.
   d. Connect the coil wires and start the engine.
   e. With the engine running, turn the steering wheel lock-to-lock twice. Shut off the engine.
   f. Depress the brake pedal several times to discharge the accumulator.
   g. Start the engine and repeat Step E.
   h. If foam appears in the reservoir, allow the foam to dissipate.
   i. Repeat Step E as often as necessary to expel all air from the system.

➡The system is, in effect, self-bleeding and normal vehicle operation will expel any further trapped air.

Bleeding the Brakes

◆ See Figures 19, 20, 21 and 22

When any part of the hydraulic system has been disconnected for repair or replacement, air may get into the lines and cause spongy pedal action (because air can be compressed and brake fluid cannot). To correct this condition, it is necessary to bleed the hydraulic system after it has been properly connected to be sure that all air is expelled from the brake cylinders and lines.

When bleeding the brake system, bleed one brake cylinder at a time, beginning at the cylinder with the longest hydraulic line (farthest from the master cylinder) first. Keep the master cylinder reservoir filled with brake fluid during bleeding operation. Never use brake fluid that has been drained from the hydraulic system, no matter how clean it is.

It will be necessary to centralize the pressure differential valve after a brake system failure has been corrected and the hydraulic system has been bled.

The primary and secondary hydraulic brake systems are individual systems and are bled separately. During the entire bleeding operation, do not allow the reservoir to run dry. Keep the master cylinder reservoirs filled with brake fluid.

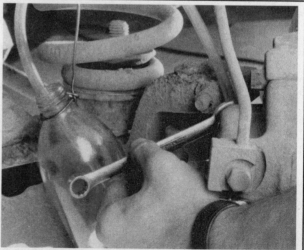

Fig. 19 Bleeding the front brakes

Fig. 20 Bleeding the rear brakes

Fig. 21 Use a shatter resistant container and secure it in a manner as shown

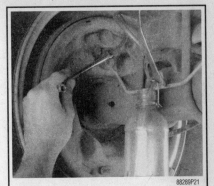

Fig. 22 Use a flare wrench or box end wrench to better grasp the bleeder valve

WHEEL CYLINDERS AND CALIPERS

1. Clean all dirt from around the master cylinder fill cap, remove the cap and fill the master cylinder with brake fluid until the level is within ¼ in. (6mm) of the top of the edge of the reservoir.

2. Clean off the bleeder screws at the wheel cylinders and calipers.

3. Attach the length of rubber hose over the nozzle of the bleeder screw at the wheel to be done first. Place the other end of the hose in a glass jar, submerged in brake fluid.

4. Open the bleed screw valve ½–¾ turn.

5. Have an assistant slowly depress the brake pedal. Close the bleeder screw valve and tell your assistant to allow the brake pedal to return slowly. Continue this pumping action to force any air out of the system. When bubbles cease to appear at the end of the bleeder hose, close the bleed valve and remove the hose.

6. Check the master cylinder fluid level and add fluid accordingly. Do this after bleeding each wheel.

7. Repeat the bleeding operation at the remaining 3 wheels, ending with the one closest to the master cylinder. Fill the master cylinder reservoir.

MASTER CYLINDER

1. Fill the master cylinder reservoirs.

2. Place absorbent rags under the fluid lines at the master cylinder.

3. Have an assistant depress and hold the brake pedal.

4. With the pedal held down, slowly crack open the hydraulic line fitting, allowing the air to escape. Close the fitting and have the pedal released.

5. Repeat Steps 3 and 4 for each fitting until all the air is released.

FRONT DISC BRAKES

✳ CAUTION

Brake shoes may contain asbestos, which has been determined to be a cancer causing agent. Never clean the brake surfaces with compressed air! Avoid inhaling any dust from any brake surface! When cleaning brake surfaces, use a commercially available brake cleaning fluid.

There are two types of sliding calipers, the LD sliding caliper unit is operated by one piston per caliper. The caliper and steering arm are cast as one piece and combined with the spindle stem to form an integral spindle assembly.

The light duty system is used on all F-150 and Bronco models.

The HD slider caliper unit contains 2 pistons on the same side of the rotor. The caliper slides on the support assembly and is retained by a key and spring.

The heavy duty system is used on all F-250, F-350 and F-Super Duty models.

Brake Pads

REMOVAL & INSTALLATION

➡ **Never replace the pads on one side only! Always replace pads on both wheels as a set!**

LD Sliding Caliper (Single Piston)

◗ **See Figures 23 thru 31**

1. To avoid overflowing of the master cylinder when the caliper pistons are pressed into the caliper cylinder bores, siphon or dip some brake fluid out of the larger reservoir.

2. Jack up the front of the truck, support it on jackstands, and remove the wheels.

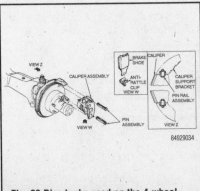

Fig. 23 Disc brake used on the 4-wheel drive F-150 and Bronco models

Fig. 24 Compressing the pin tabs on LD calipers

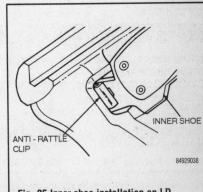

Fig. 25 Inner shoe installation on LD calipers

Fig. 26 Correct caliper pin installation

SPINDLE FLANK

AFTER INSTALLATION, INSPECT TO INSURE THAT PIN TABS ARE FREE TO CONTACT SPINDLE FLANKS ON EACH END OF PIN

84929040

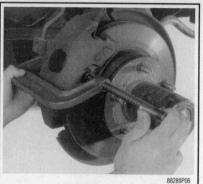

Fig. 27 Use a C-clamp to push the caliper piston back into the bore

88289P06

Fig. 28 Drive the upper caliper pin inward until the tabs on the pin touch the spindle

88289P07

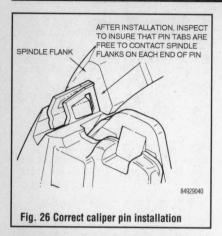

Fig. 29 Remove the caliper from its carrier

88289P08

Fig. 30 Remove the brake pads from the caliper

88289P09

Fig. 31 Install the new pad with wear indicators in the same position as on the old pad

88289P10

3. Place an 8 in. (203mm) C-clamp on the caliper and tighten the clamp to bottom the caliper piston in the cylinder bore. Bear the clamp on the outer pad. NEVER PRESS DIRECTLY ON THE PISTON! Remove the C-clamp.

4. Clean the excess dirt from around the caliper pin tabs.

5. Drive the upper caliper pin inward until the tabs on the pin touch the spindle.

6. Insert a small prybar into the slot provided behind the pin tabs on the inboard side of the pin.

7. Using needlenose pliers, compress the outboard end of the pin while, at the same time, prying with the prybar until the tabs slip into the groove in the spindle.

8. Place the end of a 7/16 in. (11mm) punch against the end of the caliper pin and drive the pin out of the caliper slide groove.

9. Repeat this procedure for the lower pin.

10. Lift the caliper off of the rotor.

11. Remove the brake pads and anti-rattle spring.

➡ Do not allow the caliper to hand by the brake hose.

To install:

12. Thoroughly clean the areas of the caliper and spindle assembly which contact each other during the sliding action of the caliper.

13. Place a new anti-rattle clip on the lower end of the inboard shoe. Make sure that the tabs on the clip are positioned correctly and the loop-type spring is away from the rotor.

14. Place the lower end of the inner brake pad in the spindle assembly pad abutment, against the anti-rattle clip, and slide the upper end of the pad into position. Be sure that the clip is still in position.

15. Check and make sure that the caliper piston is fully bottomed in the cylinder bore. Use a large C-clamp, bearing on a piece of wood, to bottom the piston, if necessary.

16. Position the outer brake pad on the caliper, and press the pad tabs into place with your fingers. If the pad cannot be pressed into place by hand, use a C-clamp. Be careful not to damage the lining with the clamp. Bend the tabs to prevent rattling.

17. Position the caliper on the spindle assembly. Lightly lubricate the caliper sliding grooves with caliper pin grease.

18. Position the a new upper pin with the retention tabs next to the spindle groove.

➡ Don't use the bolt and nut with the new pin.

19. Carefully drive the pin, at the outboard end, inward until the tabs contact the spindle face.

20. Repeat the procedure for the lower pin.

✻✻ WARNING

Don't drive the pins in too far, or it will be necessary to drive them back out until the tabs snap into place. The tabs on each end of the pin MUST be free to catch on the spindle sides!

21. Install the wheels.

HD Sliding Caliper (Two Piston)

◗ See Figures 32, 33, 34 and 35

1. To avoid overflowing of the master cylinder when the caliper pistons are pressed into the caliper cylinder bores, siphon or dip some brake fluid out of the larger reservoir.

2. Raise and support the front end on jackstands.

3. Remove the wheels.

4. Place an 8 in. (203mm) C-clamp on the caliper and, with the clamp bearing on the outer pad, tighten the clamp to bottom the caliper pistons in cylinder bores. Remove the C-clamp.

5. Clean the excess dirt from around the caliper pin tabs.

6. Drive the upper caliper pin inward until the tabs on the pin touch the spindle.

7. Insert a small prybar into the slot provided behind the pin tabs on the inboard side of the pin.

8. Using needlenose pliers, compress the outboard end of the pin while, at the same time, prying with the prybar until the tabs slip into the groove in the spindle.

9. Place the end of a 7/16 in. (11mm) punch against the end of the caliper pin and drive the pin out of the caliper slide groove.

10. Repeat this procedure for the lower pin.

11. Lift the caliper off of the rotor.

12. Remove the brake pads and anti-rattle spring.

➡ **Do not allow the caliper to hand by the brake hose.**

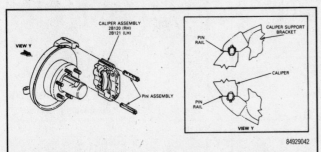

Fig. 32 Disc brake used on the 4-wheel drive F-250 and F-350

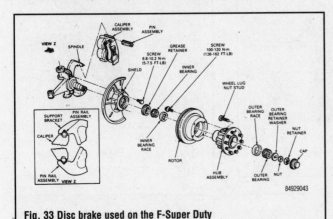

Fig. 33 Disc brake used on the F-Super Duty

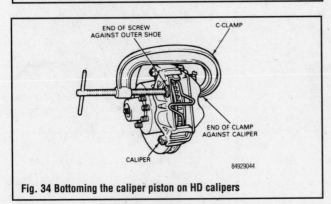

Fig. 34 Bottoming the caliper piston on HD calipers

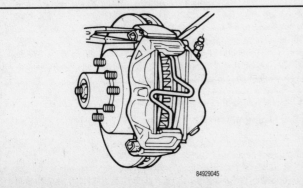

Fig. 35 Compressing the spring tabs on HD calipers

To install:

13. Thoroughly clean the areas of the caliper and spindle assembly which contact each other during the sliding action of the caliper.

14. Place a new anti-rattle clip on the lower end of the inboard shoe. Make sure that the tabs on the clip are positioned correctly and the loop-type spring is away from the rotor.

15. Place the lower end of the inner brake pad in the spindle assembly pad abutment, against the anti-rattle clip, and slide the upper end of the pad into position. Be sure that the clip is still in position.

16. Check and make sure that the caliper piston is fully bottomed in the cylinder bore. Use a large C-clamp to bottom the piston, if necessary.

17. Position the outer brake pad on the caliper, and press the pad tabs into place with your fingers. If the pad cannot be pressed into place by hand, use a C-clamp: Be careful not to damage the lining with the clamp. Bend the tabs to prevent rattling.

18. Position the caliper on the spindle assembly. Lightly lubricate the caliper sliding grooves with caliper pin grease.

19. Position the a new upper pin with the retention tabs next to the spindle groove.

➡ **Don't use the bolt and nut with the new pin.**

20. Carefully drive the pin, at the outboard end, inward until the tabs contact the spindle face.

21. Repeat the procedure for the lower pin.

✳✳ WARNING

Don't drive the pins in too far, or it will be necessary to drive them back out until the tabs snap into place. The tabs on each end of the pin MUST be free to catch on the spindle sides!

22. Install the wheels.

INSPECTION

Remove the brake pads and measure the thickness of the lining. If the lining at any point on the pad assembly is less 1/16 in. (1.5mm) for LD brakes or 1/32 in. (0.8mm) for HD brakes, thick (above the backing plate or rivets), or there is evidence of the lining being contaminated by brake fluid or oil, replace the brake pad.

Brake Caliper

REMOVAL & INSTALLATION

▶ **See Figure 36**

1. Raise and support the front end on jackstands.

2. Remove the wheels.

3. Remove the caliper and the brake pads as outlined under Disc Brake Pad Removal and Installation.

4. Disconnect the brake hose from the caliper.

To install:

5. Connect the brake hose to the caliper. When connecting the brake fluid hose to the caliper, it is recommended that a new copper washer be used at the connection of the brake hose and caliper.

6. Install the brake caliper and pads onto the vehicle as outlined in this section.

7. Install the wheels and lower the vehicle. Bleed the brake system.

OVERHAUL

LD Sliding Caliper (Single Piston)

▶ **See Figures 37 thru 44**

1. Clean the outside of the caliper in alcohol after removing it from the vehicle and removing the brake pads.

2. Drain the caliper through the inlet port.

3. Roll some thick shop cloths or rags and place them between the piston and the outer legs of the caliper.

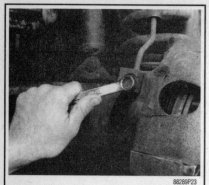

Fig. 36 Unbolt the brake hose fitting at the caliper

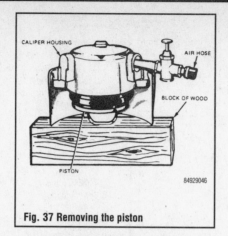

Fig. 37 Removing the piston

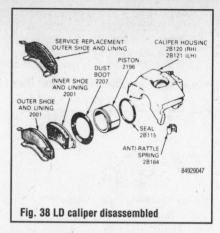

Fig. 38 LD caliper disassembled

Fig. 39 Piston and dust boot

Fig. 40 Position a piece of wood as a stop, then use compressed air to expel the piston from its bore

Fig. 41 The piston should gently bottom against the piece of wood

Fig. 42 Remove the piston for inspection

Fig. 43 Pry out the outer seal without gouging the surface

Fig. 44 Remove the inner seal with a thin prytool

4. Apply compressed air to the caliper inlet port until the piston comes out of the caliper bore. Use low air pressure to avoid having the piston pop out too rapidly and possible causing injury.

5. If the piston becomes cocked in the cylinder bore and will not come out, remove the air pressure and tap the piston with a soft hammer to try and straighten it. Do not use a sharp tool or pry the piston out of the bore. Reapply the air pressure.

6. Remove the boot from the piston and seal from the caliper cylinder bore.

7. Clean the piston and caliper in alcohol.

To install:

8. Lubricate the piston seal with clean brake fluid, and position the seal in the groove in the cylinder bore.

9. Coat the outside of the piston and both of the beads of dust boot with clean brake fluid. Insert the piston through the dust boot until the boot is around the bottom (closed end) of the piston.

10. Hold the piston and dust boot directly above the caliper cylinder bore, and use your fingers to work the bead of dust boot into the groove near the top of the cylinder bore.

11. After the bead is seated in the groove, press straight down on the piston until it bottoms in the bore. Be careful not to cock the piston in the bore. Be careful not to cock the piston in the bore. Use a C-clamp with a block of wood inserted between the clamp and the piston to bottom the piston, if necessary.

12. Install the brake pads and install the caliper. Bleed the brake hydraulic system and recenter the pressure differential valve. Do not drive the vehicle until a firm brake pedal is obtained.

HD Sliding Caliper (Two Piston)

▶ See Figures 45 and 46

1. Disconnect and plug the flexible brake hose.
2. Remove the front shoe and lining assemblies.
3. Drain the fluid from the cylinders.
4. Secure the caliper in a vise and place a block of wood between the caliper bridge and the cylinders.

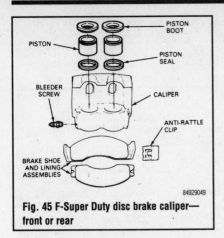

Fig. 45 F-Super Duty disc brake caliper—front or rear

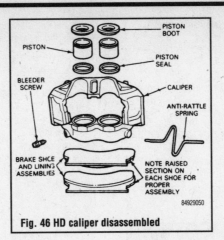

Fig. 46 HD caliper disassembled

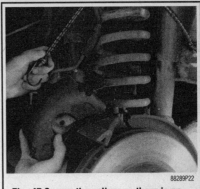

Fig. 47 Secure the caliper so there is no tension on the brake hose

5. Apply low pressure air to the brake hose inlet and the pistons will be forced out to the wood block.

6. Remove the block of wood and remove the pistons.

7. Remove the piston seals.

8. Lubricate the new piston seals with clean brake fluid and install them in the seal grooves in the cylinder bores.

9. Lubricate the retaining lips of the dust boots with clean brake fluid and install them in the grooves of the cylinder bores.

10. Apply a film of clean brake fluid to the pistons.

11. Insert the pistons into the dust boots and start them into the cylinders by hand until they are beyond the piston seals. Be careful not to dislodge or damage the piston seals.

12. Place a block of wood over one piston and press the piston into the cylinder. Be careful not to cock the piston in the cylinder bore.

13. Install the second piston in the same manner.

14. Install the brake shoe assemblies and anti-rattle clip in the caliper assembly.

15. Install the brake hose. Tighten the fitting to 25 ft. lbs. (34 Nm).

16. Install the caliper and bleed the system.

Brake Disc (Rotor)

REMOVAL & INSTALLATION

Except F-Super Duty with 4-Wheel Disc Brakes

♦ See Figure 47

1. Jack up the front of the truck and support it with jackstands. Remove the front wheel.

REAR DRUM BRAKES

✲ CAUTION

Brake shoes may contain asbestos, which has been determined to be a cancer causing agent. Never clean the brake surfaces with compressed air! Avoid inhaling any dust from any brake surface! When cleaning brake surfaces, use a commercially available brake cleaning fluid.

Brake Drums

INSPECTION

Check that there are no cracks or chips in the braking surface. Excessive bluing indicates overheating and a replacement drum is needed. The drum can be machined to remove minor damage and to establish a rounded braking surface on a warped drum. Never exceed the maximum oversize of the drum when machining the braking surface. The maximum inside diameter is stamped on the rim of the drum.

2. Remove the caliper assembly and support it on the frame with a piece of wire (or something equally secure) without disconnecting the brake fluid hose.

3. Remove the hub and rotor assembly.

4. Install the rotor in the reverse order of removal, and adjust the wheel bearing as outlined in Section 1.

F-Super Duty with 4-Wheel Disc Brakes

The hub and rotor are individual pieces, allowing the rotor to be replaced independently. The front and rear rotors are the same and are attached with 10 bolts and washers. The bolts are tightened a little at a time, in a crisscross fashion, to an ultimate torque of 74–89 ft. lbs. (100–121 Nm).

INSPECTION

If the rotor is deeply scarred or has shallow cracks, it may be refinished on a disc brake rotor lathe. Also, if the lateral run-out exceeds 0.010 in. (0.25mm) within a 6 in. (152mm) radius when measured with a dial indicator, with the stylus 1 in. (25mm) in from the edge of the rotor, the rotor should be refinished or replaced.

A maximum of 0.020 in. (0.5mm) of material may be removed equally from each friction surface of the rotor. If the damage cannot be corrected when the rotor has been machined to the minimum thickness shown on the rotor, it should be replaced.

The finished braking surfaces of the rotor must be parallel within 0.007 in. (0.18mm) and lateral run-out must not be more than 0.003 in. (0.076mm) on the inboard surface in a 5 in. (127mm) radius.

REMOVAL & INSTALLATION

Bronco, F-150, and F-250 Light Duty Models

1. Raise the vehicle so that the wheel to be worked on is clear of the floor and install jackstands under the vehicle.

2. Remove the wheel. Remove the three retaining nuts and remove the brake drum. It may be necessary to back off the brake shoe adjustment in order to remove the brake drum. This is because the drum might be grooved or worn from being in service for an extended period of time.

3. Before installing a new brake drum, be sure to remove any protective coating with brake cleaner or a suitable fast-drying degreaser.

4. Install the brake drum in the reverse order of removal and adjust the brakes.

F-250HD and F-350 Models

1. Raise the vehicle and install jackstands.

2. Remove the wheel. Loosen the rear brake shoe adjustment.

3. Remove the rear axle retaining bolts and lockwashers, axle shaft, and gasket.

4. Remove the wheel bearing locknut, lockwasher, and adjusting nut.

5. Remove the hub and drum assembly from the axle.

6. Remove the brake drum-to-hub retaining screws, bolts or bolts and nut. Remove the brake drum from the hub.

To install:

7. Place the drum on the hub and attach it to the hub with the attaching nuts and bolts.

8. Place the hub and drum assembly on the axle and start the adjusting nut.

9. Adjust the wheel bearing nut and install the wheel bearing lockwasher and locknut.

10. Install the axle shaft with a new gasket and install the axle retaining bolts and lockwashers.

11. Install the wheel and adjust the brake shoes. Remove the jackstands and lower the vehicle.

Brake Shoes

REMOVAL & INSTALLATION

Bronco, F-150 and F-250 Light Duty Models

▶ See Figures 48 thru 60

1. Raise and support the vehicle and remove the wheel and brake drum from the wheel to be worked on.

➡ If you have never replaced the brakes on a truck before and you are not too familiar with the procedures involved, only dissemble and assemble one side at a time, leaving the other side intact as a reference during reassembly.

2. Install a clamp over the ends of the wheel cylinder to prevent the pistons of the wheel cylinder from coming out, causing loss of fluid and much grief.

3. Contract the brake shoes by pulling the self-adjusting lever away from the starwheel adjustment screw and turn the starwheel up and back until the pivot nut is drawn onto the starwheel as far as it will come.

4. Pull the adjusting lever, cable and automatic adjuster spring down and toward the rear to unhook the pivot hook from the large hole in the secondary shoe web. Do not attempt to pry the pivot hook from the hole.

5. Remove the automatic adjuster spring and the adjusting lever.

6. Remove the secondary shoe-to-anchor spring with a brake tool. (Brake tools are very common implements and are available at auto parts stores). Remove the primary shoe-to-anchor spring and unhook the cable anchor. Remove the anchor pin plate.

7. Remove the cable guide from the secondary shoe.

8. Remove the shoe hold-down springs, shoes, adjusting screw, pivot nut, and socket. Note the color of each hold-down spring for assembly. To remove the hold-down springs, reach behind the brake backing plate and place one finger on the end of one of the brake hold-down spring mounting pins. Using a pair of pliers, grasp the washer type retainer on top of the hold-down spring that corresponds to the pin which you are holding. Push down on the pliers and turn them 90° to align the slot in the washer with the head on the spring mounting pin. Remove the spring and washer retainer and repeat this operation on the hold down spring on the other shoe.

9. Remove the parking brake link and spring. Disconnect the parking brake cable from the parking brake lever.

10. After removing the rear brake secondary shoe, disassemble the parking brake lever from the shoe by removing the retaining clip and spring washer.

11. Assemble the parking brake lever to the secondary shoe and secure it with the spring washer and retaining clip.

12. Apply a light coating of Lubriplate®, or equivalent, at the points where the brake shoes contact the backing plate.

13. Position the brake shoes on the backing plate, and install the hold-down spring pins, springs, and spring washer type retainers. On the rear brake, install the parking brake link, spring and washer. Connect the parking brake cable to the parking brake lever.

14. Install the anchor pin plate, and place the cable anchor over the anchor pin with the crimped side toward the backing plate.

15. Install the primary shoe-to-anchor spring with the brake tool.

16. Install the cable guide on the secondary shoe web with the flanged holes fitted into the hole in the secondary shoe web. Thread the cable around the cable guide groove.

17. Install the secondary shoe-to-anchor (long) spring. Be sure that the cable end is not cocked or binding on the anchor pin when installed. All of the parts should be flat on the anchor pin. Remove the wheel cylinder piston clamp.

18. Apply Lubriplate®, or equivalent, to the threads and the socket end of the adjusting starwheel screw. Turn the adjusting screw into the adjusting pivot nut to the limit of the threads and then back off ½ turn.

➡ Interchanging the brake shoe adjusting screw assemblies from one side of the vehicle to the other would cause the brake shoes to retract rather than expand each time the automatic adjusting mechanism is

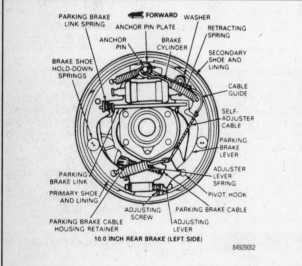

PARKING BRAKE LINK SPRING — FORWARD — WASHER
ANCHOR PIN PLATE
RETRACTING SPRING
ANCHOR PIN
BRAKE CYLINDER
SECONDARY SHOE AND LINING
BRAKE SHOE HOLD-DOWN SPRINGS
CABLE GUIDE
SELF-ADJUSTER CABLE
PARKING BRAKE LEVER
PARKING BRAKE LINK
ADJUSTER LEVER SPRING
PRIMARY SHOE AND LINING
PIVOT HOOK
ADJUSTING SCREW
PARKING BRAKE CABLE
PARKING BRAKE CABLE HOUSING RETAINER
ADJUSTING LEVER

10.0 INCH REAR BRAKE (LEFT SIDE)

84929052

Fig. 48 Standard rear brakes used on the F-150 and Bronco models

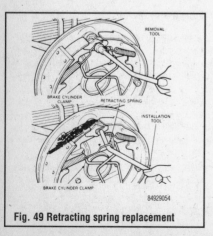

REMOVAL TOOL
BRAKE CYLINDER CLAMP
RETRACTING SPRING
INSTALLATION TOOL
BRAKE CYLINDER CLAMP

84929054

Fig. 49 Retracting spring replacement

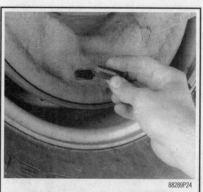

88289P24

Fig. 50 Remove the plug to access the starwheel adjuster

88289P25

Fig. 51 Contract the shoes by turning back the starwheel

Fig. 52 Disconnect the brake shoe retracting springs at the anchor pin using a brake tool

Fig. 53 As you remove parts be sure to keep them organized where they won't get scattered

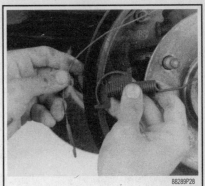

Fig. 54 Remove the brake shoe adjusting cable from the cable guide

Fig. 55 Remove the brake shoe anchor pin guide plate

Fig. 56 Use a suitable tool to push in and turn, then release the brake shoe hold-down spring

Fig. 57 Remove the brake shoes (and other related parts) and set them aside

Fig. 58 Detach the parking brake cable from the lever arm

Fig. 59 Use Lubriplate®, or equivalent, to the brake shoe contact points on the guide plate

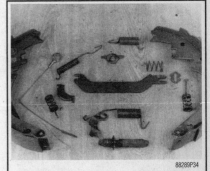

Fig. 60 Use this exploded view of brake shoe assembly as a reference (if needed) for reinstallation

operated. To prevent this, the socket end of the adjusting screw is stamped with an "R" or an "L" for "RIGHT" or "LEFT". The adjusting pivot nuts can be distinguished by the number of lines machined around the body of the nut; one line indicates left hand nut and two lines indicate a right hand nut.

19. Place the adjusting socket on the screw and install this assembly between the shoe ends with the adjusting screw nearest to the secondary shoe.

20. Place the cable hook into the hole in the adjusting lever from the backing plate side. The adjusting levers are stamped with an **R** (right) or a **L** (left) to indicate their installation on the right or left hand brake assembly.

21. Position the hooked end of the adjuster spring in the primary shoe web and connect the loop end of the spring to the adjuster lever hole.

22. Pull the adjuster lever, cable and automatic adjuster spring down toward the rear to engage the pivot hook in the large hole in the secondary shoe web.

23. After installation, check the action of the adjuster by pulling the section of the cable guide and the adjusting lever toward the secondary shoe web far enough

to lift the lever past a tooth on the adjusting screw starwheel. The lever should snap into position behind the next tooth, and release of the cable should cause the adjuster spring to return the lever to its original position. This return action of the lever will turn the adjusting screw starwheel one tooth. The lever should contact the adjusting screw starwheel one tooth above the centerline of the adjusting screw.

If the automatic adjusting mechanism does not perform properly, check the following:

24. Check the cable and fittings. The cable ends should fill or extend slightly beyond the crimped section of the fittings. If this is not the case, replace the cable.

25. Check the cable guide for damage. The cable groove should be parallel to the shoe web, and the body of the guide should lie flat against the web. Replace the cable guide if this is not so.

26. Check the pivot hook on the lever. The hook surfaces should be square with the body on the lever for proper pivoting. Repair or replace the hook as necessary.

27. Make sure that the adjusting screw starwheel is properly seated in the notch in the shoe web.

F-250 HD and F-350 Models

♦ **See Figures 61, 62 and 63**

1. Raise and support the vehicle.
2. Remove the wheel and drum.
3. Remove the parking brake lever assembly retaining nut from behind the backing plate and remove the parking brake lever assembly.
4. Remove the adjusting cable assembly from the anchor pin, cable guide, and adjusting lever.
5. Remove the brake shoe retracting springs.
6. Remove the brake shoe hold-down spring from each shoe.
7. Remove the brake shoes and adjusting screw assembly.
8. Disassemble the adjusting screw assembly.
9. Clean the ledge pads on the backing plate. Apply a light coat of Lubriplate®, or equivalent, to the ledge pads (where the brake shoes rub the backing plate).

To install:

10. Apply Lubriplate® to the adjusting screw assembly and the hold-down and retracting spring contacts on the brake shoes.
11. Install the upper retracting spring on the primary and secondary shoes and position the shoe assembly on the backing plate with the wheel cylinder pushrods in the shoe slots.

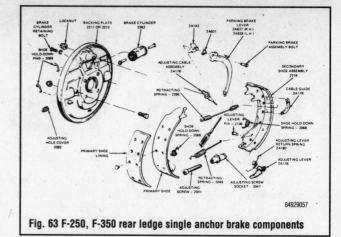

Fig. 63 F-250, F-350 rear ledge single anchor brake components

12. Install the brake shoe hold-down springs.
13. Install the brake shoe adjustment screw assembly with the slot in the head of the adjusting screw toward the primary shoe, lower retracting spring, adjusting lever spring, adjusting lever assembly, and connect the adjusting cable to the adjusting lever. Position the cable in the cable guide and install the cable anchor fitting on the anchor pin.
14. Install the adjusting screw assemblies in the same locations from which they were removed. Interchanging the brake shoe adjusting screws from one side of the vehicle to the other will cause the brake shoes to retract rather than expand each time the automatic adjusting mechanism is operated. To prevent incorrect installation, the socket end of each adjusting screw is stamped with an **R** or an **L** to indicate their installation on the right or left side of the vehicle. The adjusting pivot nuts can be distinguished by the number of lines machined around the body of the nut. Two lines indicate a right hand nut; one line indicates a left hand nut.
15. Install the parking brake assembly in the anchor pin and secure with the retaining nut behind the backing plate.
16. Adjust the brakes before installing the brake drums and wheels. Install the brake drums and wheels.
17. Lower the vehicle and road test the brakes. New brakes may pull to one side or the other before they are seated. Continued pulling or erratic braking should not occur.

ADJUSTMENT

♦ **See Figures 64, 65, 66 and 67**

The drum brakes are self-adjusting and require a manual adjustment only after the brake shoes have been replaced, or when the length of the adjusting screw has been changed while performing some other service operation, as, for example, when taking off brake drums.

To adjust the brakes, perform the procedures that follow:

Drum Installed

1. Raise and support the rear of the vehicle on jackstands.
2. Remove the rubber plug from the adjusting slot on the backing plate.
3. Insert a brake adjusting spoon into the slot and engage the lowest possible tooth on the starwheel. Move the end of the brake spoon downward to move the starwheel upward and expand the adjusting screw. Repeat this operation until the brakes lock the wheels.
4. Insert a small screwdriver or piece of firm wire (coat hanger wire) into the adjusting slot and push the automatic adjusting lever out and free of the starwheel on the adjusting screw and hold it there.
5. Engage the topmost tooth possible on the starwheel with the brake adjusting spoon. Move the end of the adjusting spoon upward to move the adjusting screw starwheel downward and contract the adjusting screw. Back off the adjusting screw starwheel until the wheel spins freely with a minimum of drag. Keep track of the number of turns that the starwheel is backed off, or the number of strokes taken with the brake adjusting spoon.

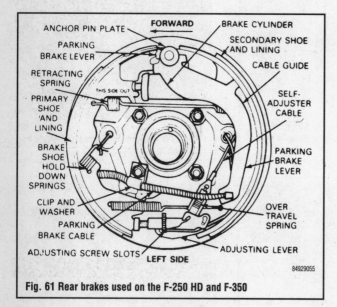

Fig. 61 Rear brakes used on the F-250 HD and F-350

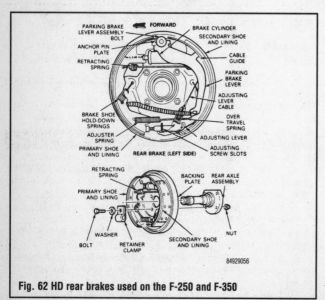

Fig. 62 HD rear brakes used on the F-250 and F-350

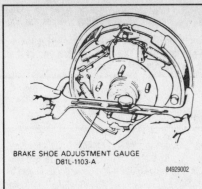

Fig. 64 Use a gauge as shown to measure the brake shoes

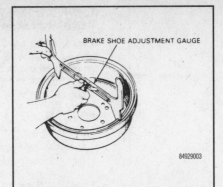

Fig. 65 Use a gauge as shown to measure the drum

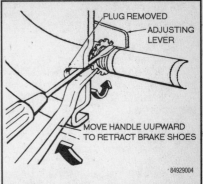

Fig. 66 Rear brake adjustment—F-150 and Bronco models

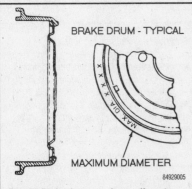

Fig. 67 Brake drum maximum diameter location

Fig. 68 With the brake line loosened, remove the attaching bolts to the wheel cylinder

Fig. 69 Once detached, remove the wheel cylinder from the vehicle

6. Repeat this operation for the other side. When backing off the brakes on the other side, the starwheel adjuster must be backed off the same number of turns to prevent side-to-side brake pull.

7. When the brakes are adjusted make several stops while backing the vehicle, to equalize the brakes at both of the wheels.

8. Remove the jackstands and lower the vehicle. Road test the vehicle.

Drum Removed

✳✳ CAUTION

Brake shoes may contain asbestos, which has been determined to be a cancer causing agent. Never clean the brake surfaces with compressed air! Avoid inhaling any dust from any brake surface! When cleaning brake surfaces, use a commercially available brake cleaning fluid.

1. Make sure that the shoe-to-contact pad areas are clean and properly lubricated.

REAR DISC BRAKES

▶ **See Figure 70**

F-Super Duty models are equipped with the heavy duty, sliding 2-piston caliper similar to that used on the front axle.

Brake Pads

REMOVAL & INSTALLATION

➡**Never replace the pads on one side only! Always replace pads on both wheels as a set!**

2. Using an inside caliper check the inside diameter of the drum. Measure across the diameter of the assembled brake shoes, at their widest point.

3. Turn the adjusting screw so that the diameter of the shoes is 0.030 in. (0.76mm) less than the brake drum inner diameter.

4. Install the drum.

Wheel Cylinders

REMOVAL & INSTALLATION

▶ **See Figures 68 and 69**

1. Remove the brake drum.
2. Remove the brake shoes.
3. Loosen the brake line at the wheel cylinder.
4. Remove the wheel cylinder attaching bolt and unscrew the cylinder from the brake line.
5. Installation is the reverse of removal.

1. To avoid overflowing of the master cylinder when the caliper pistons are pressed into the caliper cylinder bores, siphon or dip some brake fluid out of the larger reservoir.

2. Raise and support the rear end on jackstands.

3. Remove the wheels.

4. Place an 8 in. (203mm) C-clamp on the caliper and tighten the clamp to bottom the caliper pistons in the cylinder bores. Remove the C-clamp.

5. Clean the excess dirt from around the caliper pin tabs.

6. Drive the upper caliper pin inward until the tabs on the pin touch the caliper support.

7. Insert a small prybar into the slot provided behind the pin tabs on the inboard side of the pin.

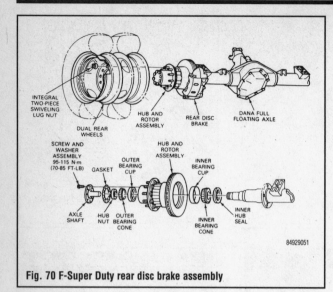

INTEGRAL TWO-PIECE SWIVELING LUG NUT
DUAL REAR WHEELS
SCREW AND WASHER ASSEMBLY 95-115 N·m (70-85 FT-LB)
GASKET
OUTER BEARING CUP
HUB AND ROTOR ASSEMBLY
REAR DISC BRAKE
DANA FULL FLOATING AXLE
HUB AND ROTOR ASSEMBLY
INNER BEARING CUP
AXLE SHAFT
HUB NUT
OUTER BEARING CONE
INNER BEARING CONE
INNER HUB SEAL

84929051

Fig. 70 F-Super Duty rear disc brake assembly

8. Using needlenose pliers, compress the outboard end of the pin while, at the same time, prying with the prybar until the tabs slip into the groove in the caliper support.

9. Place the end of a 7/16 in. (11mm) punch against the end of the caliper pin and drive the pin out of the caliper slide groove.

10. Repeat this procedure for the lower pin.

11. Lift the caliper off of the rotor.

12. Remove the brake pads and anti-rattle spring.

➡**Do not allow the caliper to hand by the brake hose.**

13. Thoroughly clean the areas of the caliper and caliper support assembly which contact each other during the sliding action of the caliper.

To install:

14. Place a new anti-rattle clip on the lower end of the inboard shoe. Make sure that the tabs on the clip are positioned correctly and the loop-type spring is away from the rotor.

15. Place the lower end of the inner brake pad in the caliper support assembly pad abutment, against the anti-rattle clip, and slide the upper end of the pad into position. Be sure that the clip is still in position.

16. Check and make sure that the caliper pistons are fully bottomed in the cylinder bores. Use a large C-clamp to bottom the pistons, if necessary.

17. Position the outer brake pad on the caliper, and press the pad tabs into place with your fingers. If the pad cannot be pressed into place by hand, use a C-clamp. Be careful not to damage the lining with the clamp. Bend the tabs to prevent rattling.

18. Position the caliper on the caliper support. Lightly lubricate the caliper sliding grooves with caliper pin grease.

19. Position the a new upper pin with the retention tabs next to the support groove.

➡**Don't use the bolt and nut with the new pin.**

20. Carefully drive the pin, at the outboard end, inward until the tabs contact the caliper support face.

21. Repeat the procedure for the lower pin.

Don't drive the pins in too far, or it will be necessary to drive them back out until the tabs snap into place. The tabs on each end of the pin MUST be free to catch on the support sides!

22. Install the wheels.

INSPECTION

Remove the brake pads and measure the thickness of the lining. If the lining at any point on the pad assembly is less than 1/16 in. (0.8mm) thick (above the backing plate or rivets), or there is evidence of the lining being contaminated by brake fluid or oil, replace the brake pad.

Brake Caliper

REMOVAL & INSTALLATION

1. Raise and support the rear end on jackstands.
2. Remove the wheels.
3. Remove the caliper and the brake pads as outlined under Disc Brake Pad Removal and Installation.
4. Disconnect the brake hose from the caliper. Cap the openings at once!
5. When connecting the brake fluid hose to the caliper, it is recommended that a new copper washer be used at the connection of the brake hose and caliper.
6. Bleed the brake system and install the wheels. Lower the truck.

OVERHAUL

1. Disconnect and plug the flexible brake hose.
See Front Brake Caliper Overhaul in this Section.

Brake Disc (Rotor)

REMOVAL & INSTALLATION

1. Jack up the rear of the truck and support it with jackstands. Remove the wheel.
2. Remove the caliper assembly and support it to the frame with a piece of wire without disconnecting the brake fluid hose.
3. Remove the axle hub and rotor assembly. See Section 7 under Dana 80 rear axle.
4. Install the rotor using the procedures found in Section 7.

INSPECTION

If the rotor is deeply scarred or has shallow cracks, it may be refinished on a disc brake rotor lathe. Also, if the lateral run-out exceeds 0.008 in. (0.20mm) within a 6 in. (152mm) radius when measured with a dial indicator, with the stylus 1 in. (25mm) in from the edge of the rotor, the rotor should be refinished or replaced.

A maximum of 0.020 in. (0.5mm) of material may be removed equally from each friction surface of the rotor. If the damage cannot be corrected when the rotor has been machined to the minimum thickness shown on the rotor, it should be replaced.

The finished braking surfaces of the rotor must be parallel within 0.0010 in. (0.025mm) and lateral run-out must not be more than 0.008 in. (0.20mm) on the inboard surface in a 5 in. (127mm) radius.

PARKING BRAKE

Except F-Super Duty Model

▶ **See Figures 71, 72 and 73**

➡**Before making any parking brake adjustment, make sure that the drum brakes are properly adjusted.**

ADJUSTMENT

▶ **See Figure 74**

1. Raise and support the rear end on jackstands.
2. The brake drums should be cold.

3. Make sure that the parking brake pedal is fully released.

4. While holding the tension equalizer, tighten the equalizer nut 6 full turns past its original position.

5. Fully depress the parking brake pedal. Using a cable tension gauge, check rear cable tension. Cable tension should be 350 lbs. minimum.

6. Fully release the parking brake. No drag should be noted at the wheels.

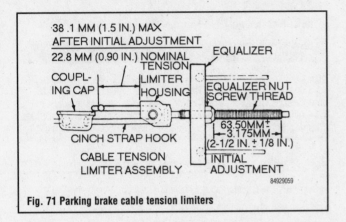

Fig. 71 Parking brake cable tension limiters

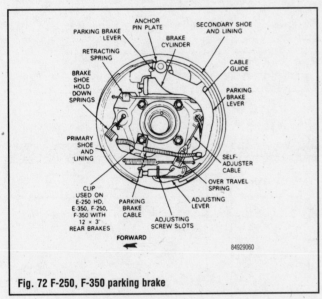

Fig. 72 F-250, F-350 parking brake

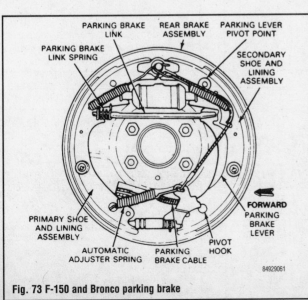

Fig. 73 F-150 and Bronco parking brake

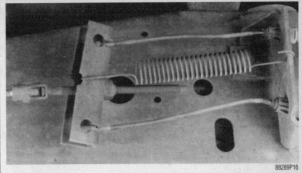

Fig. 74 Turn the nut on the threaded rod to adjust the parking brake tension equalizer

7. If drag is noted on F-250 and F-350 models, you'll have to remove the drums and adjust the clearance between the parking brake lever and cam plate. Clearance should be 0.015 in. (0.38mm). Clearance is adjusted at the parking brake equalizer adjusting nut.

➡If the tension limiter on the F-150 and Bronco models doesn't release the drag, the tension limiter will have to be replaced.

Initial Adjustment After Tension Limiter Has Been Replaced

1. Raise and support the front end on jackstands.
2. Depress the parking brake pedal fully.
3. Hold the tension limiter, install the equalizer nut and tighten it to a point 2⅜–2⅝ in. (60.325–66.675mm) up the rod.
4. Check to make sure that the cinch strap has 1⅜ in. (35mm) remaining.

REMOVAL & INSTALLATION

Parking Brake Control

1. Raise and support the rear end on jackstands.
2. Loosen the adjusting nut at the equalizer.
3. Working in the engine compartment, remove the nuts attaching the parking brake control to the firewall.
4. Remove the cable from the control assembly clevis by compressing the conduit end prongs.
5. Installation is the reverse of removal. Tighten the attaching nuts to 15 ft. lbs. (20 Nm).

Equalizer-to-Control Assembly Cable

1. Raise and support the rear end on jackstands.
2. Back off the equalizer nut and disconnect the cable from the tension limiter.
3. Remove the parking brake cable from the mount.
4. Disconnect the forward end of the cable from the control assembly.
5. Using a cord attached to the upper end of the cable, pull the cable from the truck.
6. Installation is the reverse of removal. Adjust the parking brake.

Equalizer-to-Rear Wheel Cable

1. Raise and support the rear end on jackstands.
2. Remove the wheels and brake drums.
3. Remove the tension limiter.
4. Remove the locknut from the threaded rod and disconnect the cable from the equalizer.
5. Disconnect the cable housing from the frame bracket and pull the cable and housing out of the bracket.
6. Disconnect the cables from the brake backing plates.
7. With the spring tension removed from the lever, lift the cable out of the slot in the lever and remove the cable through the backing plate hole.
8. Installation is the reverse of removal. On the F-250 and F-350, check the clearance between the parking brake operating lever and the cam plate. Clearance should be 0.015 in. (0.38mm) with the brakes fully released.
9. Adjust the brakes.

TRANSMISSION MOUNTED PARKING BRAKE

F-Super Duty Model

→To replace the brake shoes, or any other component, the unit must be disassembled.

REMOVAL

▶ See Figures 75 thru 81

1. Place the transmission in gear.
2. Fully release the parking brake pedal.
3. Raise and support the truck on jackstands.
4. Disconnect the speedometer cable.
5. Spray penetrating oil on the adjusting clevis, jam nut and threaded end of the cable.
6. Loosen the jam nut and remove the locking pin from the clevis pin.

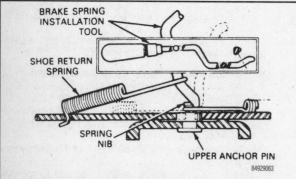

Fig. 75 F-Super Duty parking brake shoe return spring installation

7. Remove the clevis pin, clevis and jam nut from the cable.
8. Remove the cable from the bracket on the case.
9. Matchmark the driveshaft and disconnect it from the flange.
10. Remove the 6 hex-head bolts securing the parking brake unit to the transmission extension housing and lift off the unit.

→The unit is filled with Ford Type H ATF.

※※ CAUTION

Brake shoes may contain asbestos, which has been determined to be a cancer causing agent. Never clean the brake surfaces with compressed air! Avoid inhaling any dust from any brake surface! When cleaning brake surfaces, use a commercially available brake cleaning fluid.

DISASSEMBLY

→Several special tools and a hydraulic press are necessary.

1. Remove the unit from the truck.
2. Remove the 4 bolts securing the yoke flange and drum, and remove the flange and drum.
3. Remove the 75mm hex nut from the mainshaft, using tool T88T–2598–G, or equivalent.
4. Press the mainshaft, drum and output flange from the case.
5. Remove the speedometer drive gear from the case.
6. Using tools D80L–1002–2, D79L–4621–A and D80L–630–6, remove the outer bearing cone from the mainshaft.
7. Place the threaded end of the output shaft in a soft-jawed vise.
8. Matchmark the drum, flange/yoke and mainshaft. Remove the 4 nuts securing the flange and drum to the output shaft and remove the flange and drum.

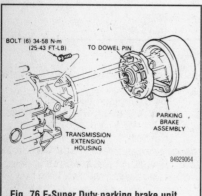

Fig. 76 F-Super Duty parking brake unit removal

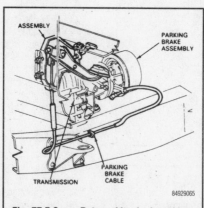

Fig. 77 F-Super Duty parking brake cables

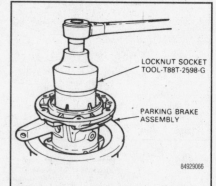

Fig. 78 Removing the parking brake mainshaft locknut

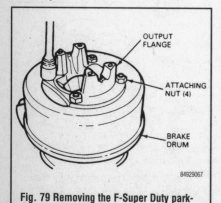

Fig. 79 Removing the F-Super Duty parking brake output flange

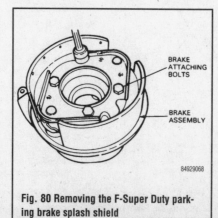

Fig. 80 Removing the F-Super Duty parking brake splash shield

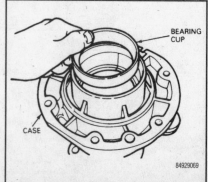

Fig. 81 Removing the F-Super Duty parking brake outer bearing cup

9. Using tool T77F–1102–A, remove the input shaft oil seal, spacer, O-ring, bearing cone and race from the input shaft end of the case.

10. Remove the 4 bolts securing the splash shield and brake assembly from the case. Remove the brake assembly and splash shield.

11. Remove the brake actuating lever and spring from the case.

12. Using tool T77F–1102–A, remove the outer bearing cup and oil seal.

13. Unscrew the vent from the case.

14. Hold the brake assembly securely and remove the 2 brake sure return springs.

15. Spread the free ends of the shoes and remove the shoes from the lower anchor pin. Remove the shoe-to-shoe spring.

ASSEMBLY

▶ **See Figures 82 and 83**

1. Clean the brake assembly thoroughly with a brake cleaning solvent.

2. Using a brake caliper grease, place a light coating on:
- Camshaft lugs and ball on the actuating lever
- Shoe guide lugs and support pads on the support plate
- Upper and lower anchor pins
- Brake shoe anchor pin contact points

3. Connect a NEW shoe-to-shoe spring between the brake shoes, spread the shoes and position them on the lower anchor pin.

4. Position the upper ends on the upper anchor pin, inserting the show webs between the shoe guide lugs and the pads on the support plate.

5. Install 2 NEW return springs.

6. Drive a new inner bearing race into place.

7. Drive a new outer bearing race into the case making sure it bottoms evenly.

8. Install a new outer bearing.

9. Coat the outer edge of a new outer oil seal with sealer and drive the seal into place with the lip facing inward. The seal must be flush with the bore surface.

10. Install the actuating lever spring.

11. Apply a light coating of brake grease on the actuating lever ball and install the lever through the coiled end of the spring.

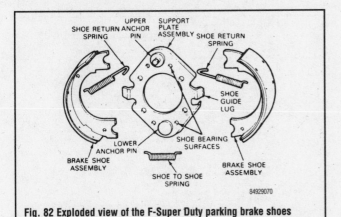

Fig. 82 Exploded view of the F-Super Duty parking brake shoes

12. Position the brake assembly into the case. Insert the lever into position in the brake assembly.

13. Tighten the 4 brake assembly attaching bolts to 90 ft. lbs. (122 Nm).

14. Attach the retracting spring to the actuating lever while bending the long end to snap over the lever.

15. Place the mainshaft in a soft-jawed vise with the flanged end upward.

16. Install the brake drum and output flange onto the mainshaft, being aware of the matchmarks.

17. Install the 4 nuts and tighten them to 85 ft. lbs. (115 Nm).

18. Turn the mainshaft over and clamp it in the vise.

19. Install the case, with the outer bearing installed loosely on the mainshaft, guiding the mainshaft through the oil seal and bearing cone.

20. Install the outer bearing cone on the mainshaft using tool T88T–2598–F, or equivalent, to seat the bearing on the shaft.

21. Install the speedometer gear and snapring.

22. Install the shim on the mainshaft.

➡ **This shim determines end-play. It is available in several thicknesses with variations of 0.0019 in. (0.05mm).**

23. Install the inner bearing cone and spacer on the mainshaft.

➡ **To check end-play, first install the inner bearing spacer without the O-ring.**

24. Thread the 75mm nut onto the shaft and tighten it to 215 ft. lbs. (292 Nm).

25. Mount a dial indicator and bracket with the dial indicator between the mainshaft and case to check end-play. While rotating the case assembly on the mainshaft to center the bearings, apply pressure up and down. An end-play reading of 0.0019–0.0039 in. (0.05–0.10mm) is desired. Shim as necessary.

26. Remove the 75mm nut, spacer and bearing to install the shim(s).

27. Install the bearing.

28. Coat the outer edge of a new seal with sealer and seat it in the case bore with the lip facing inward.

29. Install a new O-ring in the spacer and install the spacer on the mainshaft until it butts against the shoulder of the shaft.

30. Install a NEW 75mm nut and tighten it to 215 ft. lbs. (292 Nm).

31. Install the vent.

INSTALLATION

▶ **See Figures 84, 85, 86 and 87**

1. Refill the unit through the filler plug to the bottom of the plug hole. Install the plug and tighten it to 45 ft. lbs. (61 Nm).

2. Position the unit on the extension housing using 2 guide pins.

3. Using 6 NEW hex-bolts, attach the unit and tighten the bolts to 40 ft. lbs. (54 Nm).

4. Connect the driveshaft and tighten the bolts to 20 ft. lbs. (27 Nm).

5. Assemble the cable components. Screw on the clevis until the pin can be inserted while the lever and cable are held tightly in the applied position. Then, remove the pin, let go of the cable and lever, and turn the clevis 10 full turns counterclockwise (loosen).

6. Install the pin.

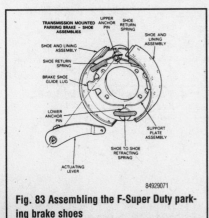

Fig. 83 Assembling the F-Super Duty parking brake shoes

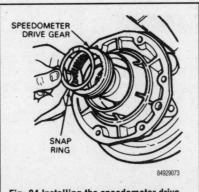

Fig. 84 Installing the speedometer drive gear on the F-Super Duty parking brake

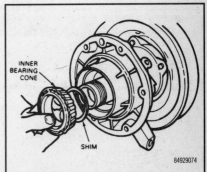

Fig. 85 Installing the inner bearing cone and shim on the F-Super Duty parking brake

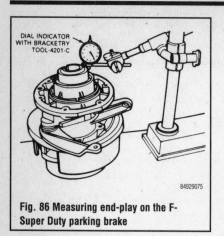

Fig. 86 Measuring end-play on the F-Super Duty parking brake

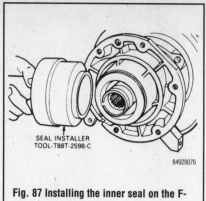

Fig. 87 Installing the inner seal on the F-Super Duty parking brake

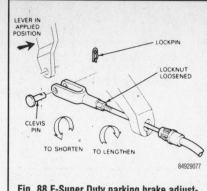

Fig. 88 F-Super Duty parking brake adjustment points

ADJUSTMENT

▶ See Figure 88

1. Fully release the brake pedal.
2. Spray penetrating oil on the adjusting clevis, jam nut and threaded end of the cable.

3. Loosen the jam nut and remove the locking pin from the clevis.
4. Back off on the clevis until there is slack in the cable.
5. Screw on the clevis until the pin can be inserted while the lever and cable are held tightly in the applied position. Then, remove the pin, let go of the cable and lever, and turn the clevis 10 full turns counterclockwise (loosen).
6. Install the pin.

REAR ANTI-LOCK BRAKE SYSTEM (RABS)

Operation

The RABS system is found on all models except the F-Super Duty and 1993–96 Bronco models.

The system constantly monitors rear wheel speed and, in the event of impending rear wheel lock-up in a sudden stop, regulates the brake fluid hydraulic pressure at the rear brakes to prevent total wheel lock-up, thus reducing the possibility of skidding.

Trouble Codes

▶ See Figure 89

RABS Hydraulic Control Valve

REMOVAL & INSTALLATION

▶ See Figure 90

The valve is located in the brake lines, below the master cylinder.
1. Disconnect the brake lines from the valve and plug the lines.
2. Disconnect the wiring harness at the valve.
3. Remove the 3 nuts retaining the valve to the frame rail and lift out the valve.
4. Installation is the reverse of removal. Don't overtighten the brake lines. Bleed the brakes.

Control Module

REMOVAL & INSTALLATION

▶ See Figure 91

The module is located on the firewall just inboard of the master cylinder.
1. Disconnect the wiring harness.

FLASHOUT CODES CHART
CONDITION
No Flashout Code
Yellow REAR ABS Light Flashes 1 Time This Code Should Not Occur
Yellow REAR ABS Light Flashes 2 Times Open Isolate Circuit
Yellow REAR ABS Light Flashes 3 Times Open Dump Circuit
Yellow REAR ABS Light Flashes 4 Times Red Brake Warning Light Illuminated RABS Valve Switch Closed
Yellow REAR ABS Light Flashes 5 Times System Dumps Too Many Times in 2WD (2WD and 4WD vehicles). Condition Occurs While Making Normal or Hard Stops. Rear Brake May Lock
Yellow REAR ABS Light Flashes 6 Times (Sensor Signal Rapidly Cuts In and Out). Condition Only Occurs While Driving
Yellow REAR ABS Light Flashes 7 Times No Isolate Valve Self Test
Yellow REAR ABS Light Flashes 8 Times No Dump Valve Self Test
Yellow REAR ABS Light Flashes 9 Times High Sensor Resistance
Yellow REAR ABS Light Flashes 10 Times Low Sensor Resistance
Yellow REAR ABS Light Flashes 11 Times Stoplamp Switch Circuit Defective. Condition Indicated Only When Driving Above 35 mph
Yellow REAR ABS Light Flashes 12 Times Fluid Level Switch Grounded During a RABS Stop.
Yellow REAR ABS Light Flashes 13 Times Speed Processor Check
Yellow REAR ABS Light Flashes 14 Times Program Check
Yellow REAR ABS Light Flashes 15 Times Memory Failure
Yellow REAR ABS Light Flashes 16 Times or More 16 or More Flashes Should Not Occur

CAUTION: WHEN CHECKING RESISTANCE IN THE RABS SYSTEM, ALWAYS DISCONNECT THE BATTERY. IMPROPER RESISTANCE READINGS MAY OCCUR WITH THE VEHICLE BATTERY CONNECTED.

Fig. 89 Rear ABS Flash codes chart—except 1993–96 Bronco models

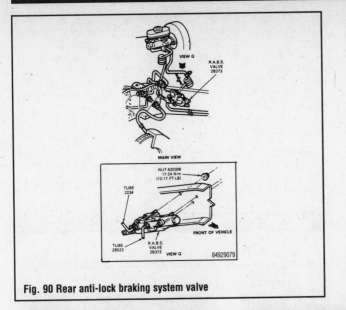

Fig. 90 Rear anti-lock braking system valve

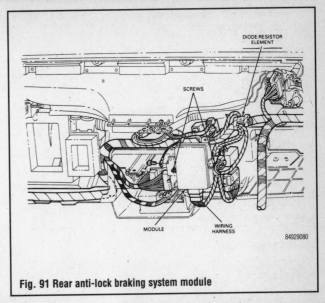

Fig. 91 Rear anti-lock braking system module

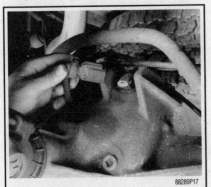

Fig. 92 Remove the connector from the RABS sensor at the axle housing

Fig. 93 Remove the RABS sensor hold-down bolt

Fig. 94 Remove the RABS sensor from the vehicle

2. Remove the 2 attaching screws and lift out the module.
3. Installation is the reverse of removal.

RABS Sensor

REMOVAL & INSTALLATION

▶ See Figures 92, 93 and 94

The sensor is located on the rear axle housing.
1. Remove the sensor hold-down bolt.

4-WHEEL ANTI-LOCK BRAKE SYSTEM (ABS)

General Information

The 4-Wheel Anti-lock Brake System (ABS) used on 1993–96 Bronco models is an electronically operated, all wheel brake control system. Major components include the master cylinder, vacuum power brake booster, ABS Control Module, Hydraulic Control Unit (HCU) and various control sensors and switches.

The brake system is a three channel design. The front brakes are controlled individually and the rear brakes in tandem.

The system is designed to retard wheel lockup during periods of high wheel slip when braking. Retarding wheel lockup is accomplished by modulating fluid pressure to the wheel brake units.

2. Remove the sensor.
3. Carefully clean the axle surface to keep dirt from entering the housing.
4. If a new sensor is being installed, lubricate the O-ring with clean engine oil. Carefully push the sensor into the housing aligning the mounting flange hole with the threaded hole in the housing. Tighten the hold-down bolt to 30 ft. lbs. (41 Nm)—If the old sensor is being installed, clean it thoroughly and install a new O-ring coated with clean engine oil.

Exciter Ring

The ring is located on the differential case inside the axle housing. Once it is pressed of the case it cannot be reused. See Section 7 for the procedure.

SYSTEM COMPONENTS

Power Brake Booster

The diaphragm-type power brake booster is self contained, and is mounted on the engine compartment side of the dash panel. The booster uses engine intake manifold vacuum and atmospheric pressure for its power. It is serviced as an assembly only, except for the power brake booster check valve.

Master Cylinder

The brake master cylinder is a tandem master cylinder. The primary (rear) circuit feeds the right side front and left side rear brakes. The secondary (front) circuit feeds the left side front and right side rear brakes. The master cylinder is serviced as a complete assembly.

Brake Pressure Control Valve

The brake pressure control valve regulates pressure to the rear brakes to create a balance between the front and rear brakes.

Brake Master Cylinder and Brake Fluid Level Switch

The master cylinder reservoir is a clear, translucent plastic container with three main chambers:
- An integral fluid level switch is part of the master cylinder reservoir assembly.
- A low pressure hose is attached to the master cylinder reservoir which feeds brake fluid to the hydraulic control unit reservoir.
- The brake master cylinder reservoir and brake master cylinder filler cap gasket are serviced separately

Hydraulic Control Unit (HCU)

The Hydraulic Control Unit (HCU) is located outside of the engine compartment on a bracket which attaches to the left frame rail. It consists of the following:
- Brake pressure control valve block assembly
- Pump motor
- Hydraulic control unit reservoir which a fluid level indicator assembly

During normal braking, fluid from the master cylinder enters the HCU through two inlet ports located at the rear of the HCU. The fluid then passes through four normally open inlet valve, one to each wheel. The anti-lock brake control module senses that a wheel is about to lock, the control module closes the appropriate inlet valve. This prevents any more fluid from entering the affected brake.

The anti-lock brake control module then looks at that wheel again. If it is still decelerating, then anti-lock brake control module opens the normally closed outlet valve which decreased the pressure trapped in the line. If equipped, the Traction Assist (TA) valve body contains two isolation valves for traction assist function: one for the primary circuit and one for the secondary circuit. The isolation valves close during traction assist operation to prevent front brake operation.

The following components are serviced separately:
- Brake pressure control valve block
- Pump motor
- Hydraulic control unit reservoir

Anti-Lock Brake Control Module

The anti-lock brake control module is located on the anti-lock brake hydraulic control bracket mounting bracket located outside of the engine compartment attached to the outer frame rail.

The module is an on-board diagnostic non-repairable unit consisting of two microprocessors and the necessary circuitry for their operation. These microprocessors are programmed identically. The anti-lock brake control module monitors system operation during normal driving operation as wheel as during anti-lock braking and traction assist cycling, if equipped.

Under normal driving conditions, the microprocessors produce short test pulses to the solenoid valves that check the electrical system without any mechanical reaction. Impending wheel lock conditions trigger signals from the anti-lock brake control module that open and close the appropriate solenoid valves. This results in moderate pulsations in the brake pedal.

If brake pedal travel exceeds a preset dimension determined by the ABS sensor switch setting, the control module will send a signal to the pump to turn on and provide high pressure to the brake system. When the pump motor starts to run, a gradual rise in pedal height will be noticed. This rise will continue until the anti-lock brake pedal sensor switch closes and the pump motor will shut off until the pedal travel exceeds the sensor switch setting again. During normal braking, the brake pedal feel will be identical to a standard brake system.

Anti-Lock Brake Sensors

The anti-lock brake system uses three variable reluctance brake anti-lock sensors to determine the rotational speed of each of the two front wheels and the rear wheels as a pair. The sensors operate on the magnetic induction princi-

ple. As the teeth on the sensor rotate past the sensor indicator, a signal proportional to the speed of the rotation is generated and sent to the anti-lock brake control module through a coaxial cable and shielded wiring harness.

The front brake anti-lock sensors are attached to the front wheel spindles, and the front brake anti-lock sensor indicators are pressed onto the wheel hub assembly. The rear brake anti-lock sensors are attached to the rear axle housing.

The front and rear anti-lock sensors are not adjustable. The rear brake anti-lock sensors and sensor indicators are serviced separately.

Stop Light Switch

The anti-lock brake system uses a brake pedal sensor switch which monitors brake pedal travel and sends this information to the anti-lock brake control module through the wire harness. The anti-lock brake pedal sensor switch adjustment is critical to pedal feel during ABS cycling.

Hydraulic Control Unit

REMOVAL & INSTALLATION

1. Disconnect the battery ground cable.
2. Unplug the 8-pin connector from the unit, and the 4-pin connector from the pump motor.
3. Disconnect the 5 inlet and outlet tubes from the unit. Immediately plug the ports.
4. Remove the 3 unit attaching nuts and lift out the unit.
5. Installation is the reverse of removal. Tighten the mounting nuts to 12–18 ft. lbs. (16–24 Nm) and the tube fittings to 10–18 ft. lbs. (13–24 Nm).

➡**After reconnecting the battery, it may take 10 miles or more of driving for the Powertrain Control Module to relearn its driveability codes.**

6. Bleed the brakes.

Electronic Control Unit

REMOVAL & INSTALLATION

1. Disconnect the battery ground cable.
2. Unplug the wiring from the ECU.
3. Remove the mounting bolts, slide the ECU off its bracket.
4. Installation is the reverse of removal. Tighten the mounting screw to 60–72 inch lbs. (5–6 Nm) and the connector bolt to 48–60 inch lbs. (4–5 Nm).

➡**After reconnecting the battery, it may take 10 miles (16 km) or more of driving for the Powertrain Control Module to relearn its driveability codes.**

Front Wheel Speed Sensor

REMOVAL & INSTALLATION

1. Inside the engine compartment, disconnect the sensor from the harness.
2. Unclip the sensor cable from the brake hose clips.
3. Remove the retaining bolt from the spindle and slide the sensor from its hole.
4. Installation is the reverse of removal. Tighten the retaining bolt to 40–60 inch lbs. (3.5–5 Nm).

Rear Speed Sensor

REMOVAL & INSTALLATION

1. Disconnect the wiring from the harness.
2. Remove the sensor hold-down bolt and remove the sensor from the axle.
To install:
3. Thoroughly clean the mounting surfaces. Make sure no dirt falls into the axle. Clean the magnetized sensor pole piece. Metal particles can cause sensor problems. Replace the O-ring.

4. Coat the new O-ring with clean engine oil.

5. Position the new sensor on the axle. It should slide into place easily. Correct installation will allow a gap of 0.005-0.045 in. (0.127–1.143mm).

6. Tighten the hold-down bolt to 25–30 ft. lbs. (34–41 Nm).

7. Connect the wiring.

Front Speed Sensor Ring

REMOVAL & INSTALLATION

▶ **See Figure 95**

1. Raise and support the front end on jackstands.
2. Remove the wheels.
3. Remove the caliper, rotor and hub.
4. Using a 3-jawed puller, remove the ring from the hub. The ring cannot be reused; it must be replaced.

To install:

5. Support the hub in a press so that the lug studs do not rest on the work surface.

6. Position the **new** sensor ring on the hub. Using a cylindrical adapter 98mm IDx106mm OD, press the ring into place. The ring **must** be fully seated!

7. The remainder of installation is the reverse of removal.

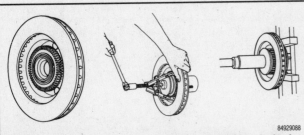

84929088

Fig. 95 Front wheel sensor ring removal and installation—4-wheel ABS

Rear Speed Sensor Ring

REMOVAL & INSTALLATION

This procedure requires the removal of the differential (see Section 7).

Bleeding The ABS System

▶ **See Figure 96**

The 4-wheel anti-lock brake system can be bled in the conventional manner unless the Hydraulic Control Unit (HCU) has been replaced. Only perform this procedure if the HCU has been replaced.

➡**Brake fluid absorbs moisture from the air. Don't leave the master cylinder or the fluid container uncovered any longer than necessary. Be careful handling the fluid—it will damage the vehicle's paint.**

1. Pressure bleed the brake system.

2. Connect Anti-Lock Brake Adapter T90P-50-ALA (bleeder box) and Anti-Lock Adapter T93T-50-ALA (jumper cable).

3. Press down on the brake pedal and depress the VALVES button on the bleeder box (brake pedal will fall.

4. Release the VALVES button and release the brake pedal.

5. Repeat Steps 3 and 4 once more.

6. Depress the MOTOR START button and let the pump motor run for 1 minute.

7. Pressure bleed the brake system.

Check the level of the fluid often when bleeding, and refill the reservoirs as necessary. Don't let them run dry, or you will have to repeat the process.

8. Have an assistant push the brake pedal down slowly through its full travel. Close the bleeder fitting and allow the pedal to slowly return to its full release position. Wait 5 seconds and repeat the procedure until no bubbles appear at the submerged end of the bleeder tube. Secure the bleeder fitting and remove the bleeder tube. Install the rubber dust cap on the bleeder fitting.

9. Repeat the bleeding procedure at the left front, left rear and right front (in that order). Refill the master cylinder reservoir after each caliper has been bled, and install the master cylinder cap and gasket. When brake bleeding is completed, the fluid level should be filled to the maximum level indicated on the reservoir.

10. Always make sure the disc brake pistons are returned to their normal positions by depressing the brake pedal several times until normal pedal travel is established. If the pedal feels spongy, repeat the bleeding procedure.

After finishing, there should be no feeling of sponginess in the brake pedal. If there is, either there is still air in the line, in which case the process must be repeated, or there is a leak somewhere, which, of course, must be corrected before the vehicle is moved. After all repairs and service work is finished, road test the vehicle to verify proper brake system operation.

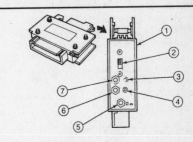

1. Anti-lock brake adapter
2. Bleed/harness selector
3. Green MOTOR ON lamp
4. Red MOTOR off lamp
5. Valve button
6. Abort button
7. Motor start button

88289G00

Fig. 96 Details of the ABS adapter controls

BRAKE SPECIFICATIONS
All measurements in inches unless noted

Year	Model		Master Cylinder Bore	Brake Disc Original Thickness	Brake Disc Minimum Thickness	Brake Disc Maximum Runout	Brake Drum Original Inside Diameter	Brake Drum Max Wear Limit	Brake Drum Maximum Machine Diameter	Min Lining Thickness Front	Min Lining Thickness Rear
1987	Bronco		1.000	1.160	1.120	0.003	11.03	11.12	11.09	④	④
	F-150		1.000	1.160	1.120	0.003	11.03	11.12	11.09	④	④
	F-250		①	1.220	1.180	0.003	12.00	12.09	12.06	④	④
	F-350 DRW		1.125	1.220	1.180	0.005	12.12	12.21	12.18	④	④
	F-350 SRW		1.125	1.220	1.180	0.003	12.00	12.09	12.06	④	④
	F-Super Duty	F	NA	NA	1.430	0.008	-	-	-	④	④
		R	NA	NA	1.430	0.008	-	-	-	④	④
1988	Bronco		1.000	1.160	1.120	0.003	11.03	11.12	11.09	④	④
	F-150		1.000	1.160	1.120	0.003	11.03	11.12	11.09	④	④
	F-250		①	1.220	1.180	0.003	12.00	12.09	12.06	④	④
	F-350 DRW		1.125	1.220	1.180	0.005	12.12	12.21	12.18	④	④
	F-350 SRW		1.125	1.220	1.180	0.003	12.00	12.09	12.06	④	④
	F-Super Duty	F	NA	NA	1.430	0.008	-	-	-	④	④
		R	NA	NA	1.430	0.008	-	-	-	④	④
1989	Bronco		1.000	1.160	1.120	0.003	11.03	11.12	11.09	④	④
	F-150		1.000	1.160	1.120	0.003	11.03	11.12	11.09	④	④
	F-250		①	1.220	1.180	0.003	12.00	12.09	12.06	④	④
	F-350 DRW		1.125	1.220	1.180	0.005	12.12	12.21	12.18	④	④
	F-350 SRW		1.125	1.220	1.180	0.003	12.00	12.09	12.06	④	④
	F-Super Duty	F	NA	NA	1.430	0.008	-	-	-	④	④
		R	NA	NA	1.430	0.008	-	-	-	④	④
1990	Bronco		1.000	1.160	1.120	0.003	11.03	11.12	11.09	④	④
	F-150		1.000	1.160	1.120	0.003	11.03	11.12	11.09	④	④
	F-250		①	1.220	1.180	0.003	12.00	12.09	12.06	④	④
	F-350 DRW		1.125	1.220	1.180	0.005	12.12	12.21	12.18	④	④
	F-350 SRW		1.125	1.220	1.180	0.003	12.00	12.09	12.06	④	④
	F-Super Duty	F	NA	NA	1.430	0.008	-	-	-	④	④
		R	NA	NA	1.430	0.008	-	-	-	④	④
1991	Bronco		1.000	1.160	1.120	0.003	11.03	11.12	11.09	④	④
	F-150		1.000	1.160	1.120	0.003	11.03	11.12	11.09	④	④
	F-250		①	1.220	1.180	0.003	12.00	12.09	12.06	④	④
	F-350 DRW		1.125	1.220	1.180	0.005	12.12	12.21	12.18	④	④
	F-350 SRW		1.125	1.220	1.180	0.003	12.00	12.09	12.06	④	④
	F-Super Duty	F	NA	NA	1.430	0.008	-	-	-	④	④
		R	NA	NA	1.430	0.008	-	-	-	④	④
1992	Bronco		1.000	1.160	1.120	0.003	11.03	11.12	11.09	④	④
	F-150		1.000	1.160	1.120	0.003	11.03	11.12	11.09	④	④
	F-250		①	1.220	1.180	0.003	12.00	12.09	12.06	④	④
	F-350 DRW		1.125	1.220	1.180	0.005	12.12	12.21	12.18	④	④
	F-350 SRW		1.125	1.220	1.180	0.003	12.00	12.09	12.06	④	④
	F-Super Duty	F	NA	NA	1.430	0.008	-	-	-	④	④
		R	NA	NA	1.430	0.008	-	-	-	④	④
1993	Bronco		1.000	1.160	1.120	0.003	11.03	11.12	11.09	④	④
	F-150		1.000	1.160	1.120	0.003	11.03	11.12	11.09	④	④
	F-250		①	1.220	1.180	0.003	12.00	12.09	12.06	④	④

NA - Not Available
F - Front
R - Rear
DRW - Dual Rear Wheels
SRW - Single Rear Wheels

88289C01

BRAKE SPECIFICATIONS
All measurements in inches unless noted

Year	Model		Master Cylinder Bore	Brake Disc Original Thickness	Brake Disc Minimum Thickness	Brake Disc Maximum Runout	Brake Drum Original Inside Diameter	Brake Drum Max Wear Limit	Brake Drum Maximum Machine Diameter	Min Lining Thickness Front	Min Lining Thickness Rear
1993	F-350 DRW		1.125	1.220	1.180	0.005	12.12	12.21	12.18	⑧	⑧
	F-350 SRW		1.125	1.220	1.180	0.003	12.00	12.09	12.06	⑧	⑧
	F-Super Duty	F	NA	NA	1.430	0.008	-	-	-	⑧	⑧
		R	NA	NA	1.430	0.008	-	-	-	⑧	⑧
1994	Bronco		1.000	1.160	0.963	0.003	11.03	⑧	11.09	⑧	⑧
	F-150		1.000	1.160	0.963	0.003	11.03	⑧	11.09	⑧	⑧
	F-250		①	1.220	1.180	0.003	12.00	⑦	12.06	⑧	⑧
	F-350 DRW		1.125	1.220	1.180	0.005	12.12	⑧	12.18	⑧	⑧
	F-350 SRW		1.125	1.220	1.180	0.003	12.00	⑧	12.06	⑧	⑧
	F-Super Duty	F	NA	NA	1.430	0.008	-	-	-	⑧	⑧
		R	NA	NA	1.430	0.008	-	-	-	⑧	⑧
1995	Bronco		1.000	1.160	0.963	0.003	11.03	⑧	11.09	⑧	⑧
	F-150		1.000	1.160	0.963	0.003	11.03	⑧	11.09	⑧	⑧
	F-250		1.125	1.220	⑥	⑥	12.00	⑧	12.06	⑧	⑧
	F-350 DRW		1.125	1.220	1.180	⑥	12.12	⑧	12.18	⑧	⑧
	F-350 SRW		1.125	1.220	1.180	⑥	12.00	⑧	12.06	⑧	⑧
1996	Bronco		1.000	1.160	1.430	—	NA	⑧	11.09	⑧	⑧
	F-150		1.000	1.160	0.963	0.003	11.03	⑧	11.09	⑧	⑧
	F-250		①	1.220	0.963	⑥	12.00	⑧	12.06	⑧	⑧
	F-350 DRW		1.125	1.220	②	⑥	12.12	⑧	12.18	⑧	⑧
	F-350 SRW		1.125	1.220	②	⑥	12.00	⑧	12.06	⑧	⑧
	F-Super Duty	F	NA	NA	1.430	0.008	-	-	-	⑧	⑧
		R	NA	NA	1.430	0.008	-	-	-	⑧	⑧

① F-250: 1.002
② 2WD: 1.100; 4WD: 1.120

⑥ 2WD with 1 piece rotor: 0.003 in.; 2WD with 2 piece rotor: 0.001 in.; 4WD: 0.005 in.
⑦ 0.030 in. over rivet head. For bonded lining use 0.062 in.
⑧ With 2 piece rotor: 0.005 in.
② With 1 piece rotor; ⑦ 2WD shown, 4WD use 0.006 in. Maximum wear limit is stamped on drum.

88289C02

TORQUE SPECIFICATIONS

Component	U.S.	Metric
ABS Hydraulic Control Unit		
Mounting nuts	12-18 ft. lbs.	16-24 Nm
Tube fittings	10-18 ft. lbs.	14-24 Nm
ABS Electronic Control Unit		
Connector bolt	4-5 ft. lbs.	5-7 Nm
Mounting screw	5-6 ft. lbs.	7-8 Nm
ABS Front Wheel Speed Sensor bolt	40-60 inch lbs.	4-7 Nm
ABS Rear Speed Sensor bolt	25-30 ft. lbs.	34-41 Nm
Brake tubing hydraulic connections	10-15 ft. lbs. *	14-20 Nm *
Booster bracket-to-dash panel nuts	18-25 ft. lbs.	24-34 Nm
Diesel Brake Booster Vacuum Pump		
Pivot adjustment bolts	11-18 ft. lbs.	15-25 Nm
Pump-to-adjustment plate bolts	11-18 ft. lbs.	15-24 Nm
Height Sensing Proportioning Valve		
F-Super Duty Only		
Brake hose bolt	28-34 ft. lbs.	38-46 Nm
Linkage arm-to-valve nut	8-10 ft. lbs.	11-14 Nm
Valve-to-bracket bolts	12-18 ft. lbs.	16-24 Nm
Hydro-Boost Brake Booster		
Booster mounting nuts	25 ft. lbs.	34 Nm
Master cylinder-to-booster	18-25 ft. lbs.	24-34 Nm
Parking brake control-to-firewall	15 ft. lbs.	20 Nm
RABS sensor holddown bolt	30 ft. lbs.	41 Nm
Rotor attaching bolts		
F-Super Duty		
Front or rear	74-89 ft. lbs.	101-121 Nm
Transmission Mounted Parking Brake		
F-Super Duty		
Brake assembly-to-case	90 ft. lbs.	122 Nm
Brake drum and output flange nuts	85 ft. lbs.	116 Nm
Brake unit-to-extension housing	40 ft. lbs.	54 Nm
Driveshaft bolts	20 ft. lbs.	27 Nm
Filler plug	45 ft. lbs.	61 Nm
Mainshaft 75mm nut	215 ft. lbs.	292 Nm

*Except front master cylinder brake tube fitting, tighten to 16-21 ft.lbs. (22-28 Nm).

84929192

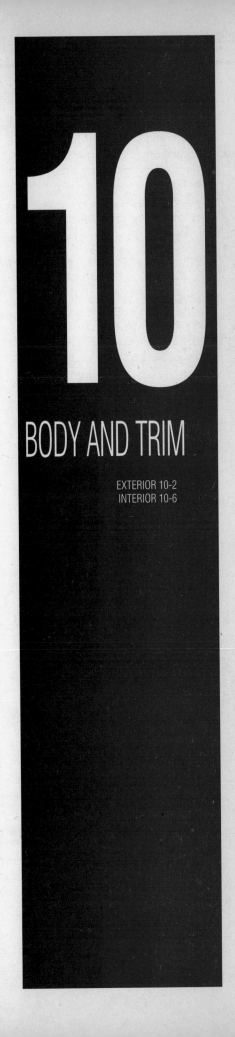

10

BODY AND TRIM

EXTERIOR 10-2
INTERIOR 10-6

EXTERIOR

Doors

ADJUSTMENT

♦ **See Figures 1 and 2**

➡ **Loosen the hinge-to-door bolts for lateral adjustment only. Loosen the hinge-to-body bolts for both lateral and vertical adjustment.**

1. Determine which hinge bolts are to be loosened and back them out just enough to allow movement.

2. To move the door safely, use a padded prybar. When the door is in the proper position, tighten the bolts to 19–25 ft. lbs. (25.5–34.5 Nm) and check the door operation. There should be no binding or interference when the door is closed and opened.

3. Door closing adjustment can also be affected by the position of the lock striker plate. Loosen the striker plate bolts and move the striker plate just enough to permit proper closing and locking of the door.

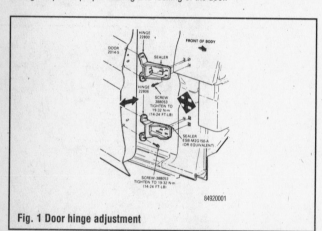

Fig. 1 Door hinge adjustment

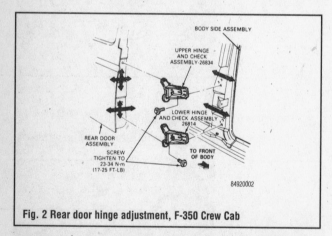

Fig. 2 Rear door hinge adjustment, F-350 Crew Cab

Hood

REMOVAL & INSTALLATION

➡ **You'll need an assistant for this job.**

1. Open the hood.
2. Remove the 2 link assembly bolts.
3. Matchmark the hood-to-hinge position.
4. Remove the hood-to-hinge bolts and lift off the hood.
5. Installation is the reverse of removal. Loosely install the hood and align the matchmarks. Torque all bolts to 13–19 ft. lbs. (17–27 Nm).

ADJUSTMENT

1. Open the hood and matchmark the hinge and latch positions.
2. Loosen the hinge-to-fender bolts just enough to allow movement of the hood.
3. Loosen the 2 latch attaching bolts.
4. Loosen the hinge-to-hood bolts just enough to allow movement of the hood.
5. Move the hood as required to obtain the proper fit and alignment between the hood and the top of the cowl panel.
6. Move the hood forward/backward and/or side-to-side to obtain a proper hood fit.
7. Tighten the hood-to-hinge bolts to 13–19 ft. lbs. (17–27 Nm).
8. Move the latch from side-to-side to align the latch with the striker. Tighten the latch bolts to 13–19 ft. lbs. (17–27 Nm).
9. Lubricate the latch and hinges and check the hood fit several times.

Tailgate

REMOVAL & INSTALLATION

Bronco

1. Lower the tailgate.
2. Disconnect the cable at each end.
3. Disconnect the tailgate wiring at the connector.
4. Pull the wiring from the tailgate body rail.
5. Have someone support the tailgate and remove the torsion bar retainer from the body.
6. Matchmark the hinge-to-body positions and unbolt the hinges from the body.
7. Installation is the reverse of removal. Torque the hinge nuts and cable bolts to 20–30 ft. lbs. (28–40 Nm)

Pick-Ups

1987 STYLESIDE

1. Unhook the chain.
2. Remove the movable pivot-to-body bolts and remove the pivot.
3. Slide the tailgate off the stationary pivot.
4. Installation is the reverse of removal.

1988–96 FLARESIDE AND STYLESIDE

1. Remove the tailgate support or strap or cable at the pillar T-head pivot.
2. Lift off the tailgate at the right hinge.
3. Pull off the left hinge.
4. Installation is the reverse of removal.

Tailgate Latch Release Handle and Lock Release Control Assemblies

REMOVAL & INSTALLATION

Bronco

1. Lower the tailgate and remove the inner access cover.
2. Remove the 2 screws securing the handle to the tailgate.
3. Remove the rod from the clip that holds the handle rod to the lock control.
4. Remove the handle and rod assembly.
5. Disconnect the latch release links and latch control rod.
6. Disconnect the wiring from the interlock switch.
7. Remove the 3 lock control-to-tailgate retaining screws.
8. Remove the lock control from the tailgate.

To install:

9. Install the lock control and tighten the screws to 11 ft. lbs. (15 Nm).

10. Connect the wires.
11. Place the latch control rod in position and install the clip.
12. Place the latch release links in position and install the clips.
13. Place the handle and rod assembly in the tailgate. Connect the rod to the lock control and install the clip.
14. Install and tighten the handle attaching screws.
15. Install the access cover.

Front or Rear Bumper

REMOVAL & INSTALLATION

All Except F-Super Duty Stripped/Commercial Chassis Front Bumper

▶ See Figures 3 and 4

1. Support the bumper.
2. Remove the nuts and bolts attaching the bumper to the frame.
3. Installation is the reverse of removal. Tighten the bracket-to-frame bolts for both front and rear bumpers to 71–103 ft. lbs. (95–140 Nm) for 1987–93 vehicles. For 1994–96 vehicles tighten the bracket-to-frame bolts for the front bumper to 65–87 ft. lbs. (88–118 Nm) and for the rear bumper to 72–98 ft. lbs. (98–132 Nm).

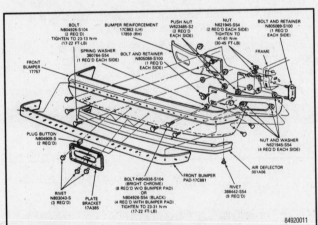

Fig. 3 1988–93 front bumper installation, except stripped/commercial chassis

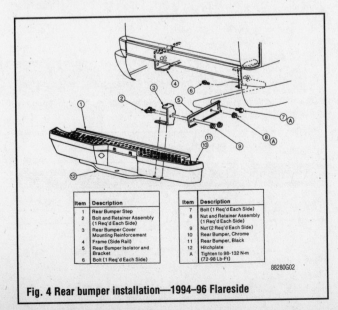

Fig. 4 Rear bumper installation—1994–96 Flareside

F-Super Duty Stripped/Commercial Chassis Front Bumper

1. Support the bumper.
2. Remove the nuts and bolts attaching the bumper to the reinforcement brackets.
3. Installation is the reverse of removal. Torque the bumper-to-bracket bolts to 59–88 ft. lbs. 80–120 Nm).

Grille

REMOVAL & INSTALLATION

All 1987 Models

▶ See Figure 5

1. Remove the 4 screws, one at each corner, attaching the grille to the headlight housings.
2. Carefully push inward on the 4 snap-in retainers and disengage the grille from the headlight housings.
3. Installation is the reverse of removal.

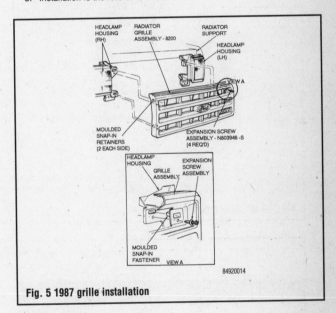

Fig. 5 1987 grille installation

1988–93 Models

▶ See Figure 6

1. Remove the 2 expansion screws that retain the grille to the headlamp housings.
2. Using a standard screwdriver, carefully depress the 4 molded snap-in retainers to disengage the grille from the headlamp housings.
3. Remove the grille.

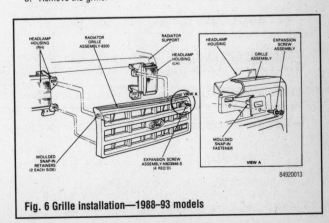

Fig. 6 Grille installation—1988–93 models

To install:

4. Install the grille on the vehicle.
5. Using hand pressure, engage the snap-in retainers. Push the expansion screws into the nuts until they are fully seated.

1994–96 Models

▶ **See Figure 7**

1. Open the hood.
2. Remove the screws securing the top of the grille to the front valance panel.
3. Remove the screws securing the top of the grille to the radiator grille opening panel reinforcement.
4. Remove the grille.

To install:

5. Position the grille on the vehicle.
6. Reverse the removal steps and tighten the retaining screws to 9–17 inch lbs. (1–2 Nm).

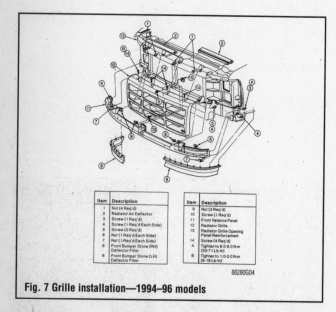

Item	Description	Item	Description
1	Nut (4 Req'd)	9	Nut (3 Req'd)
2	Radiator Air Deflector	10	Screw (1 Req'd)
3	Screw (1 Req'd)	11	Front Valance Panel
4	Screw (1 Req'd Each Side)	12	Radiator Grille
5	Screw (3 Req'd)	13	Radiator Grille Opening Panel Reinforcement
6	Nut (1 Req'd Each Side)	14	Screw (4 Req'd)
7	Nut (1 Req'd Each Side)	A	Tighten to 6.0-8.0 N·m (53-71 Lb-In)
8	Front Bumper Stone (RH) Deflector Filler	B	Tighten to 1.0-2.0 N·m (9-18 Lb-In)
8	Front Bumper Stone (LH) Deflector Filler		

88280G04

Fig. 7 Grille installation—1994–96 models

Pick-Up Box

▶ **See Figure 8**

REMOVAL & INSTALLATION

Flareside and Styleside

1. Remove the tailgate from the pick-up box as outlined in this section.
2. Remove the rear lamps from the box. Reroute the wiring assembly for the rear lamps through the tail lamp housing so that the wiring does not interfere with the removal of the pick-up box.
3. From underside of the vehicle, remove the eight nuts attaching the pick-up box to the frame rails.
4. Remove the eight bolts and shims (if any) from the pick-up box, while noting their positions for reinstallation.
5. Remove the fuel filler neck attaching screws from the box.

➡ **Because of the weight of the pick-up box it may be necessary to have at least two people on each side of the box to aid in removal.**

6. With assistance from helpers or a crane, remove the pick-up box from the frame.

To install:

7. With assistance from helpers or a crane, position the pick-up box to the frame.
8. Install the eight bolts and shims as required, to the pick-up box in their proper positions.

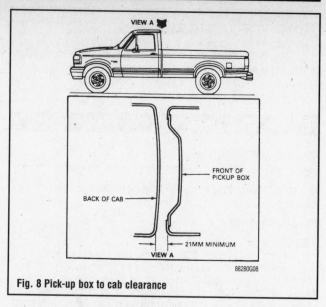

Fig. 8 Pick-up box to cab clearance

9. Move the box so that the front of the pick-up box is centered on the rear of the cab.

➡ **Make sure the cab-to-box margin at the outboard edge of the box is no less than 0.827 in. (21 mm). Less than minimum clearance may result in cab-to-box contact during severe usage.**

10. From underside of the vehicle, install the eight nuts attaching the pick-up box to the frame rails and tighten to 40–70 ft. lbs. (54–95 Nm).
11. Install the rear lamps to the pick-up box.
12. Install the tailgate to the pick-up box as outlined in this section.

Mirrors

REMOVAL & INSTALLATION

All mirrors are remove by removing the mounting screws and lifting off the mirror and gasket.

Antenna

REMOVAL & INSTALLATION

▶ **See Figures 9, 10, 11, 12 and 13**

1. Remove the cowl top grille panel.
2. Remove the antenna mast from the base.
3. Outside, unsnap the cap from the antenna base.
4. Disconnect the antenna cable at the radio by pulling it straight out of the set.
5. Working under the instrument panel, disengage the cable from its retainers.

➡ **On some models, it may be necessary to remove the instrument panel pad to get at the cable. See Section 6.**

6. Remove the 4 screws and lift off the antenna, pulling the cable with it, carefully.
7. Installation is the reverse of removal.

Bronco Fiberglass Roof

REMOVAL & INSTALLATION

Roof

▶ **See Figure 14**

1. Lower the tailgate.
2. Remove the lower trim moldings from the roof panels.

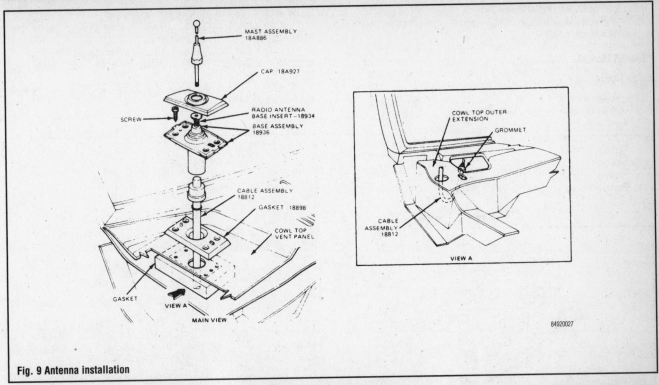

Fig. 9 Antenna installation

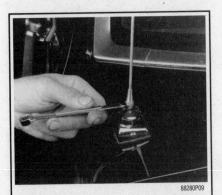

Fig. 10 Remove the antenna mast from the base

Fig. 11 Unsnap the antenna base cap and remove the cap from the antenna base

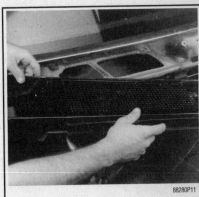

Fig. 12 Removing the cowl top grille panel

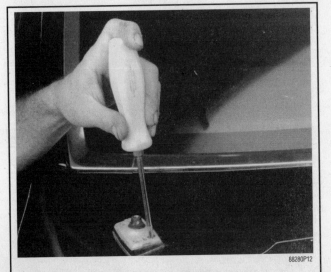

Fig. 13 Removing the four antenna base attaching screws

3. Scribe the locations of each trim molding bracket and number each bracket as it is removed.

4. Remove all the roof attaching bolts and trim bolts.

5. With at least one other person, carefully lift the roof off of the body. Be careful to avoid tearing the weather-stripping. Be careful to avoid over-flexing the roof. The roof weighs about 120 lbs.

6. Installation is the reverse of removal. Torque the roof retaining bolts to 72–84 inch lbs. (8–9 Nm).

Stationary Window

➡You'll need an assistant for this job.

1. Have your assistant stand outside and support the glass.

2. Working from the inside truck, start at one upper corner and work the weather-stripping across the top of the glass, pulling the weather-stripping down and pushing outward on the glass until your assistant can grab the glass and lift it out.

3. Remove the moldings.

4. Remove the weather-stripping from the glass.

To install:

5. Clean the weather-stripping, glass and glass opening with solvent to remove all old sealer.

6. Apply liquid butyl sealer C9AZ–19554–B, or equivalent, in the glass channel of the weather-stripping and install the weather-stripping on the glass.

7. Install the moldings.

8. Apply a bead of sealer to the opening flange and in the inner flange crevice of the weather-stripping lip.

9. Place a length of strong cord, such as butcher's twine, in the flange crevice of the weather-stripping. The cord should go all the way around the weather-stripping with the ends, about 18 in. (457mm) long each, hanging down together at the bottom center of the window.

10. Apply soapy water to the weather-stripping lip.

11. Have your assistant position the window assembly in the channel from the outside, applying firm inward pressure.

12. From inside, you guide the lip of the weather-stripping into place using the cord, working each end alternately, until the window is locked in place.

13. Remove the cord, clean the glass and weather-stripping of excess sealer and leak test the window.

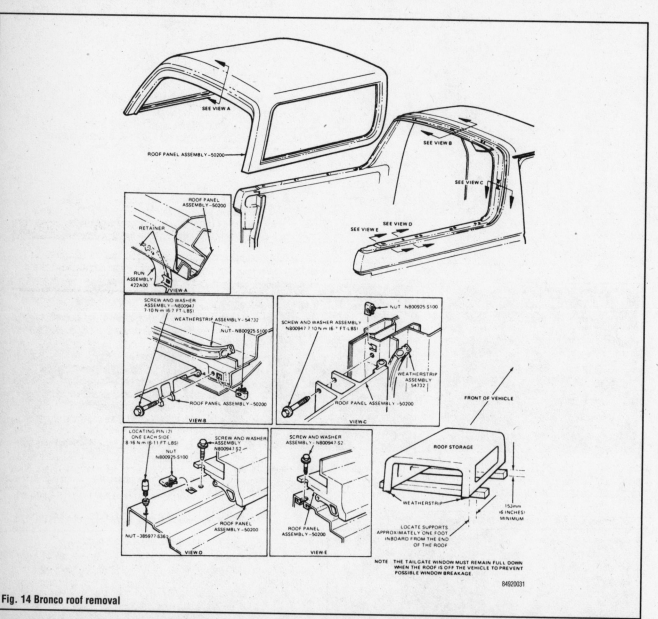

Fig. 14 Bronco roof removal

INTERIOR

Precautions

Electronic modules, such as instrument clusters, powertrain controls and sound systems are sensitive to static electricity and can be damaged by static discharges which are below the levels that you can hear "snap" or detect on your skin. A detectable snap or shock of static electricity is in the 3,000 volt range. Some of these modules can be damaged by a charge of as little as 100 volts.

The following are some basic safeguards to avoid static electrical damage:
• Leave the replacement module in its original packing until you are ready to install it.
• Avoid touching the module connector pins
• Avoid placing the module on a non-conductive surface
• Use a commercially available static protection kit. These kits contain such things as grounding cords and conductive mats.

Instrument Panel

REMOVAL & INSTALLATION

1987–91 Vehicles

▶ **See Figures 15 and 16**

1. Disconnect the battery(ies).
2. Remove the nut attaching the panel to the brake pedal, or, brake and clutch pedal, support.
3. Remove the bolt attaching the panel to the firewall brace.
4. Remove the 4 quarter-turn pins which attach the steering column opening cover and remove the cover.
5. Remove the 2 panel-to-side cowl attaching screws.
6. Unplug the wiring connectors at:
- blower switch
- air conditioner control switch
- heater/air conditioner control bulb
7. Disconnect the hoses at the vacuum valve.
8. Disconnect the control cables at the heater/air conditioner control assembly.

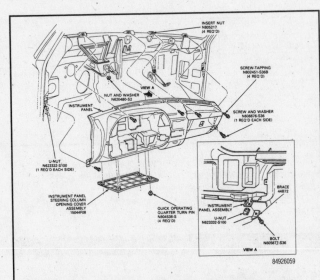

Fig. 15 Exploded view of the instrument panel—1989–91 models

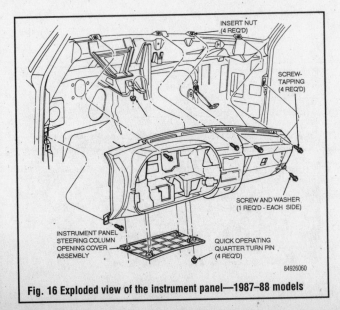

Fig. 16 Exploded view of the instrument panel—1987–88 models

9. Remove the 4 screws securing the upper, leading edge of the panel to the dash.
10. Lift the panel assembly up and over the steering wheel and out of the truck.

To install:

11. Position the panel assembly in the truck and align the 4 upper edge screw holes.
12. Install the 4 screws securing the upper, leading edge of the panel to the dash.
13. Connect the control cables at the heater/air conditioner control assembly.
14. Connect the hoses at the vacuum valve.
15. Connect the wiring at:
- blower switch
- air conditioner control switch
- heater/air conditioner control bulb
16. Install the 2 panel-to-side cowl attaching screws.
17. Install the steering column opening cover.
18. Install the bolt attaching the panel to the firewall brace.
19. Install the nut attaching the panel to the brake pedal, or, brake and clutch pedal, support.
20. Connect the battery(ies).

1992–96 Vehicles

▶ **See Figure 17**

> **※ CAUTION**
>
> **On vehicles equipped with air bags, please refer to section 6 for arming, disarming and precautions. Accidental deployment of the air bag system can cause serious personal injury.**

1. Disconnect the negative battery cable.
2. Unplug the connectors from the instrument panel rear lamp wiring and the engine control sensor wiring in the engine compartment by loosening the bolts and separating the connectors.
3. Remove the radio as outlined in Section 6.
4. Remove the right and left side windshield side garnish moldings.
5. Remove the 4 screws attaching the top of the instrument panel to the cowl.
6. Remove the 2 screws attaching the instrument panel steering column opening cover assembly to the underside of the instrument panel.
7. Remove the cover by pulling up at the top of the cover and unsnapping the 4 retaining clips.
8. Pull the antenna lead-in cable down and unsnap the wire from the bottom of the instrument panel and lay the wire down on the floor out of the way.
9. Remove the bolt attaching the instrument panel to the panel brace. Some vehicles may have 2 lower braces.
10. Remove the screw and washer assembly located at the lower corner on the right side of the instrument panel.
11. Unplug the wiring connectors from the main wiring harness at the right cowl side panel.
12. Unplug the wiring connector from the parking brake control.
13. Remove the 3 nuts attaching the parking brake control to the left side cowl panel and lay on the floor. Do not disconnect the parking brake cable.
14. On vehicles with column shift; disconnect the shift cable from the steering column shift cable bracket.
15. Unplug the wiring connector from the brake light switch.
16. On vehicles with manual transmission; unplug the wiring connector from the clutch interlock switch.
17. Unplug the wiring connectors from the main wiring harness at the left cowl side panel.
18. Remove the pinch bolt from the steering column to the lower steering column shaft. Move the lower steering column shaft toward the engine and separate from the column U-joint.
19. With the aid of an assistant, support the instrument panel and remove the 3 bolts and 1 nut attaching the left side of the instrument panel.
20. With the aid of an assistant, pull the instrument panel rearward and disconnect the heater controls and air conditioner vacuum line connector, if equipped. Unplug any remaining wiring harnesses.
21. With the aid of an assistant, carefully remove the instrument panel through the front door.

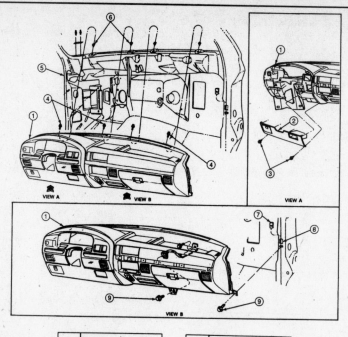

Item	Description
1	Instrument Panel
2	Steering Column Opening Cover
3	Screw(s) 2.0-3.0 N·m (19.0-26.0 In-Lb)
4	Screw(s) 2.0-2.4 N·m (18.0-21.0 In-Lb)

Item	Description
5	Cowl Side Panel (LH)
6	Nut Insert (4 Req'd)
7	U-Nut
8	Cowl Side Panel (RH)
9	Screw(s) 2.0-2.4 N·m (18.0-21.0 In-Lb)

88280G13

Fig. 17 Instrument panel installation—1992–96 vehicles

To install:

22. With the aid of an assistant, carefully position the instrument panel through the front door.

23. With the aid of an assistant, position the instrument panel forward and connect the heater controls and air conditioner vacuum line connector, if equipped. Engage any wiring harnesses

24. With the aid of an assistant to support the instrument panel, install the 3 bolts and 1 nut attaching the left side of the instrument panel.

25. Move the lower steering column shaft toward the column U-joint and install the steering column pinch bolt to the lower steering column shaft. Tighten to 30–42 ft. lbs. 41–57 Nm).

26. Engage the wiring connectors to the main wiring harness at the left cowl side panel.

27. On vehicles with manual transmission; engage the wiring connector to the clutch interlock switch.

28. Engage the wiring connector to the brake light switch.

29. On vehicles with column shift; connect the shift cable to the steering column shift cable bracket.

30. Install the 3 nuts attaching the parking brake control to the left side cowl panel.

31. Engage the wiring connector to the parking brake control.

32. Engage the wiring connectors to the main wiring harness at the right cowl side panel.

33. Install the screw and washer assembly located at the lower corner on the right side of the instrument panel.

34. Install the bolt attaching the instrument panel to the panel brace. Some vehicles may have 2 lower braces.

35. Position the antenna lead-in cable up and snap the wire to the bottom of the instrument panel.

36. Install the 2 screws attaching the instrument panel steering column opening cover assembly to the underside of the instrument panel.

37. Install the top of the instrument panel to the cowl with the 4 retaining screws.

38. Install the right and left side windshield side garnish moldings.

39. Install the radio as outlined in Section 6.

40. Install the connectors to the instrument panel rear lamp wiring and the engine control sensor wiring in the engine compartment by engaging the connectors and tightening the retaining bolts.

41. Connect the negative battery cable and arm the air bag system. Refer to Section 6.

Door Trim Panels

REMOVAL & INSTALLATION

♦ **See Figures 18 thru 24**

1. Remove the armrest pad retaining screw.
2. Remove the retaining screw and washer from the trim panel upper corner.
3. Remove the door handle screw and pull off the handle.

88280P16

Fig. 18 Removing the armrest screw

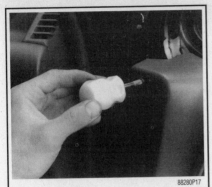

Fig. 19 Remove the retaining screw and washer from the trim panel upper corner

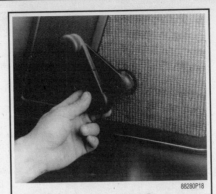

Fig. 20 Remove the window regulator handle retaining screw cover

Fig. 21 Remove the window regulator handle retaining screw

Fig. 22 Removing the window regulator handle washer

Fig. 23 Remove the retaining screw and washer from the trim panel lower corner

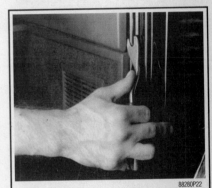

Fig. 24 Using a special trim panel tool to pry the push pins away from the door

4. If equipped with manual windows, remove the window regulator handle screw and pull off the handle and washer. On vehicles with power windows, remove the power window switch housing.

5. If equipped with manual door locks, remove the door lock control. On vehicles with power door locks, remove the power door lock switch housing.

6. On models with electric outside rear view mirrors, remove the power mirror switch housing.

7. Remove the retaining screw and washer from the trim panel lower corner.

8. Using a special door trim panel removal tool or a flat wood spatula, insert it carefully behind the panel and slide it along to find the push-pins. When you encounter a pin, pry the pin outward. Do this until all the pins are out. NEVER PULL ON THE PANEL TO REMOVE THE PINS!

9. Installation is the reverse of removal.

Console

REMOVAL & INSTALLATION

1. To remove the floor-mounted console, remove the bolts from the base of the console panel.

2. To remove the seat-mounted console, lift the console up and forward to disengage from the shoulder bolts.

3. Installation is the reverse of removal.

Interior Trim Panels

REMOVAL & INSTALLATION

All interior trim panels are retained by either screws or push pins. Illustrations show the panels and their positioning. In the case of push pins, use a flat bladed tool such as a spatula and pry out on the panel next to each pin.

Manual Door Locks

REMOVAL & INSTALLATION

Front Door Latch

ALL MODELS

1. Remove the door trim panel and watershield.

2. Disconnect the rods from the handle and lock cylinder, and from the remote control assembly.

3. Remove the latch assembly attaching screws and remove the latch from the door.

4. Installation is the reverse of removal.

Rear Door Latch

F-350 CREW CAB

1. Remove the door trim panel and watershield.

2. Disconnect the rods from the handle and lock cylinder, and from the remote control assembly.

3. Remove the latch assembly attaching screws and remove the latch from the door.

4. Installation is the reverse of removal.

Door Lock Linkage

1. Remove the door trim panels.

2. Remove the door lock control attaching screws and remove the control from the door.

3. Disconnect the linkage rod from the control.

4. Installation is the reverse of removal. Transfer the clip to the new linkage.

Door Lock Cylinder

1. Place the window in the UP position.
2. Remove the trim panel and watershield.
3. Disconnect the actuating rod from the lock control link clip.
4. Slide the retainer away from the lock cylinder.
5. Pull the cylinder from the door.
6. Installation is the reverse of removal.

Tailgate Lock Cylinder

1. Remove the tailgate access cover.
2. Raise the glass. If the glass can't be raised, remove it as described below.
3. Remove the lock cylinder retainer.
4. Disengage the lock cylinder from the switch and remove it from the tailgate.
5. Installation is the reverse of removal.

Power Door Locks

REMOVAL & INSTALLATION

Actuator Motor

▶ **See Figure 25**

1. Remove the door trim panel.
2. Disconnect the motor from the door latch.
3. Remove the motor and swivel bracket from the door by drilling out the pop rivet.
4. Disconnect the wiring harness.
5. Installation is the reverse of removal. Make sure that the pop rivet is tight.

Control Switch

1. Insert a small, thin-bladed screwdriver into the spring tab slots at the front and rear of the switch housing, and pop the housing out.
2. Remove the 3 connector attaching screws from the switch housing.
3. The switch is held in place by the electrical contact pins. Carefully pry the switch away from the connector to remove it.
4. Installation is the reverse of removal. The switch can be install only one way.

Vent Window

REMOVAL & INSTALLATION

1. Remove the door trim panel.
2. Remove the division bar-to-door panel screw.
3. Remove the 2 screws retaining the vent window to the door leading edge.
4. Lower the door window all the way.
5. Pull the glass run part of the way out of the door run retainer in the area of the division bar.
6. Tilt the vent window and division bar rearwards and pull the vent window assembly from the door.
7. Remove the 2 pivot-to-frame screws.
8. Remove the nut and spring from the lower pivot.
9. Separate the glass retainer and the pivot stops from the frame and weather-stripping.
   To install:
10. Re-assemble the parts of the window and install the 2 pivot-to-frame screws.
11. Install the spring and nut. The spring tension should be adjusted so that the window will stay open at highway speeds.
12. Place the run assembly in the vent assembly.
13. Place the window and division bar in the door. Make sure the spacer is in position.
14. Install the window-to-door edge screws.
15. Install the division bar screw. Adjust the run for proper window operation.
16. Install the door trim.

Windshield and Fixed Glass

REMOVAL & INSTALLATION

If your windshield, or other fixed window, is cracked or chipped, you may decide to replace it with a new one yourself. However, there are two main reasons why replacement windshields and other window glass should be installed only by a professional automotive glass technician: safety and cost.

The most important reason a professional should install automotive glass is for safety. The glass in the vehicle, especially the windshield, is designed with safety in mind in case of a collision. The windshield is specially manufactured

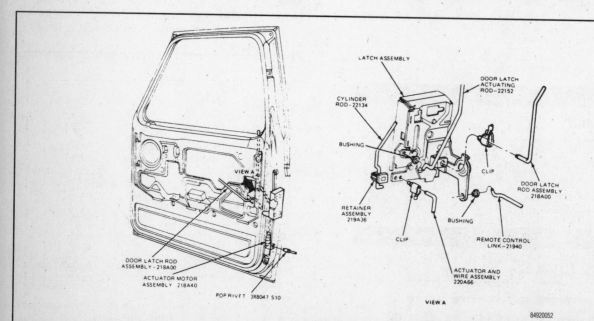

Fig. 25 Electric door lock installation

from two panes of specially-tempered glass with a thin layer of transparent plastic between them. This construction allows the glass to "give" in the event that a part of your body hits the windshield during the collision, and prevents the glass from shattering, which could cause lacerations, blinding and other harm to passengers of the vehicle. The other fixed windows are designed to be tempered so that if they break during a collision, they shatter in such a way that there are no large pointed glass pieces. The professional automotive glass technician knows how to install the glass in a vehicle so that it will function optimally during a collision. Without the proper experience, knowledge and tools, installing a piece of automotive glass yourself could lead to additional harm if an accident should ever occur.

Cost is also a factor when deciding to install automotive glass yourself. Performing this could cost you much more than a professional may charge for the same job. Since the windshield is designed to break under stress, an often life saving characteristic, windshields tend to break VERY easily when an inexperienced person attempts to install one. Do-it-yourselfers buying two, three or even four windshields from a salvage yard because they have broken them during installation are common stories. Also, since the automotive glass is designed to prevent the outside elements from entering your vehicle, improper installation can lead to water and air leaks. Annoying whining noises at highway speeds from air leaks or inside body panel rusting from water leaks can add to your stress level and subtract from your wallet. After buying two or three windshields, installing them and ending up with a leak that produces a noise while driving and water damage during rainstorms, the cost of having a professional do it correctly the first time may be much more alluring. We here at Chilton, therefore, advise that you have a professional automotive glass technician service any broken glass on your vehicle.

WINDSHIELD CHIP REPAIR

▶ See Figures 26 and 27

➡Check with your state and local authorities on the laws for state safety inspection. Some states or municipalities may not allow chip repair as a viable option for correcting stone damage to your windshield.

Although severely cracked or damaged windshields must be replaced, there is something that you can do to prolong or even prevent the need for replacement of a chipped windshield. There are many companies which offer windshield chip repair products, such as Loctite's® Bullseye™ windshield repair kit. These kits usually consist of a syringe, pedestal and a sealing adhesive. The syringe is mounted on the pedestal and is used to create a vacuum which pulls the plastic layer against the glass. This helps make the chip transparent. The adhesive is then injected which seals the chip and helps to prevent further stress cracks from developing

➡Always follow the specific manufacturer's instructions.

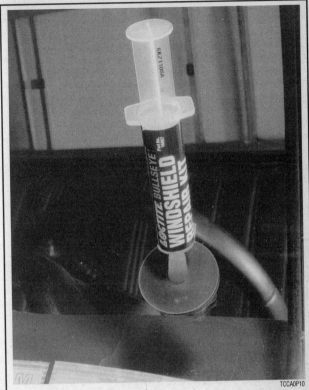

Fig. 27 Most kits us a self-stick applicator and syringe to inject the adhesive into the chip or crack

Manual Door Glass Regulator

REMOVAL & INSTALLATION

▶ See Figure 28

1. Remove the door trim panel.
2. Support the glass in the full UP position.
3. Drill out the regulator attaching rivets using a ¼ in. (6mm) drill bit.
4. Disengage the regulator arm from the glass bracket and remove the regulator.
5. Installation is the reverse of removal. ¼ in.–20 × ½ in. bolts and nuts may be used in place of the rivets to attach the regulator.

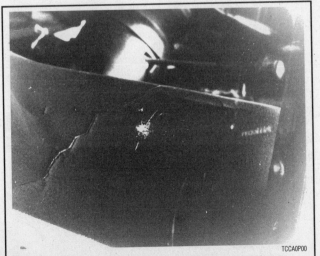

Fig. 26 Small chips on your windshield can be fixed with an aftermarket repair kit, such as the one from Loctite_

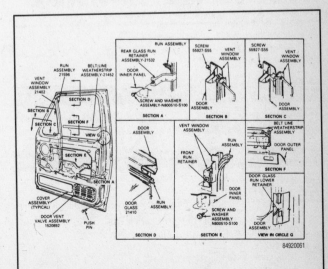

Fig. 28 Door glass and vent window installation

Power Door Glass Regulator Motor

REMOVAL & INSTALLATION

1. Disconnect the battery ground.
2. Remove the door trim panel.
3. Disconnect the window motor wiring harness.
4. There are 2 dimples in the door panel, opposite the 2 concealed motor retaining bolts. Using a ½ in. (13mm) drill bit, drill out these dimples to gain access to the motor bolts. Be careful to avoid damage to the wires.
5. Remove the 3 motor mounting bolts.
6. Push the motor towards the outside of the door to disengage it from the gears. You'll have to support the window glass once the motor is disengaged.
7. Remove the motor from the door.
8. Installation is the reverse of removal. To avoid rusting in the drilled areas, prime and paint the exposed metal, or, cover the holes with waterproof body tape. Torque the motor mounting bolts to 50–85 inch lbs. (6–10 Nm). Make sure that the motor works properly before installing the trim panel.

Bronco Tailgate Window Glass

ADJUSTMENT

1. Fore-aft adjustment is made by loosening the glass run attaching screws and positioning the glass as required. Tighten the screws to 10 ft. lbs. (14 Nm).
2. Side-to-side adjustment is made by loosening the glass-to-window bracket nuts and positioning the glass as required. Torque the nuts to 10 ft. lbs. (14 Nm).

Bronco Tailgate Window Regulator and Motor

REMOVAL & INSTALLATION

1. Lower the tailgate and remove the access panel. If the glass cannot be lowered, remove the access panel and depress the lockout rod located in the bottom center of the tailgate.
2. Using a jumper to the tailgate motor, raise the glass to the full up position. If the glass cannot be raised it will have to be removed as outlined above.
3. Remove the regulator mounting bolts and nuts and lift out the regulator.
4. Disconnect the motor harness.

✳✳ CAUTION

The counterbalance spring is under considerable tension. To prevent injury from sudden movement of the regulator components, clamp or lock the gear sectors prior to removing the components!

5. Detach the motor from the tailgate and remove it.
6. Installation is the reverse of removal. Torque the regulator mounting bolts to 10 ft. lbs. (14 Nm).

Inside Rear View Mirror

The mirror is held in place with a single setscrew. Loosen the screw and lift the mirror off. Repair kit for damaged mirrors are available and most auto parts stores.

Front Bench Seat

REMOVAL & INSTALLATION

1. Remove the 4 seat track-to-floor pan bolts or nuts.
2. Carefully lift the seat and remove from the vehicle.
To install:
3. Apply sealer to the mounting hole areas.
4. Install the seat in the vehicle and adjust position.
5. Install the mounting bolts and tighten as follows:
- Standard bench seats (1987–94)—25–34 ft. lbs. (34–46 Nm)

- Standard bench seats (1995–96)—35–46 ft. lbs. (47–63 Nm)
- 40/20/40 bench seats—35–46 ft. lbs. (47–63 Nm)

Driver's Bucket Seat

REMOVAL & INSTALLATION

1. Remove the 4 seat track-to-floor pan bolts.
2. Lift the seat and remove from the vehicle.
3. To install, apply sealer to the hole areas and position seat in the vehicle. Install and torque the mounting bolts to 30 ft. lbs. (41 Nm).

Driver's Captain's Chair

REMOVAL & INSTALLATION

1. Remove the 4 seat track-to-floor pan bolts and lift out the seat.
2. Apply sealer to the hole areas and install the seat. Torque the bolts to 30 ft. lbs. (41 Nm).

Passenger's Bucket Seat or Captain's Chair

REMOVAL & INSTALLATION

1987–89 MODELS

1. Remove the 2 front bolts retaining the passenger's seat and support assembly to the floor pan.
2. Move the seat release lever rearward allowing the seat to pop-up and fold forward.
3. Remove the 2 rear seat assembly-to-floor pan bolts.
4. Disengage one end of the passenger's seat support stop cable.
5. Move the seat and support assembly rearward until the seat back clears the instrument panel when folded forward.
6. Fold the seat fully forward and disengage the ends of the 3 assist springs from their retainers. NEVER TRY TO REMOVE THE SEAT WITH THE SPRINGS ATTACHED!
7. Return the seat to the upright position and push the seat back down firmly until the seat is latched.
8. Remove the seat from the truck.
To install:
9. Position the seat in the truck far enough rearward to enable the seat to clear the instrument panel when folded forward.
10. Fold the seat forward.
11. Attach the assist springs to their retainers.
12. Place the seat in the upright position. Push the seat down firmly to latch it.
13. Position the seat and install the 2 front holddown bolt. Hand-tighten them only at this time.
14. Connect the end of the passenger's seat support stop cable.
15. Pop the seat up and fold it forward.
16. Install the 2 rear seat bolts and tighten all 4 bolts to 30 ft. lbs. (41 Nm).
17. Position the seat upright again and latch it into place.

✳✳ WARNING

To insure that the seat support assembly is in an unlatched position, a measured distance of 102mm, or more, is required between the bumper and the lower support.

18. For captain's chairs:
    a. Push the seat support release lever rearward.
    b. Make sure that the seat back adjuster is actuated allowing the seat back to fold forward at approximately the same time that the seat support assembly pops up.
    c. If the seat assembly and/or the seat back does not release properly, it will be necessary to adjust the release cable by moving the slotted cable retainer fore or aft as needed.

1990–96 MODELS

1. Remove the seat track-to-floor pan bolts and lift the seat and track out of the truck.
2. Installation is the reverse of removal. Apply sealer to the area of the bolt holes. Torque the bolts to 25–34 ft. lbs. (34–46 Nm) for 1990–94 vehicles and 35–46 ft. lbs. (47–63 Nm) for 1995–96 vehicles.

Rear Bench Seat

REMOVAL & INSTALLATION

F-350 Crew Cab

1. Remove the seat track-to-floor pan bolts and lift the seat and track out of the truck.
2. Installation is the reverse of removal. Apply sealer to the area of the bolt holes. Torque the bolts to 18–32 ft. lbs. (25–44 Nm).

Folding Rear Seat

REMOVAL & INSTALLATION

F-Series Pick-Ups

The side-facing seats are held in place with 2 bolts. The forward facing seat is held down with 4 bolts. When replacing the seat, use sealer in the bolt hole areas. Torque the bolts to 18–32 ft. lbs. (25–44 Nm).

Bronco

To remove the folding rear seat, fold down the seat back and unlatch the seat from the floor. Fold the seat forward and remove the seat track-to-floor bolts. Torque the bolts to 45–60 ft. lbs. (62–81 Nm).

TORQUE SPECIFICATIONS

Component	U.S.	Metric
Bumpers (Front)		
Brace-to-frame bolts		
1987-93 except F-Super Duty stripped/ Comm. chassis:	71-103 ft. lbs.	95-140 Nm
1994-96 except F-Super Duty stripped/ Comm. chassis:	65-87 ft. lbs.	88-118 Nm
Super Duty stripped/Comm chassis:	59-88 ft. lbs.	80-120 Nm
Bumpers (Rear)		
1987-93:	71-103 ft. lbs.	95-140 Nm
1994-96:	72-98 ft. lbs.	98-132 Nm
Doors		
Hinge bolts	19-25 ft. lbs.	25.5-34.5 Nm
Fiberglass Roof		
Bronco		
Roof retaining bolts	72-84 inch lbs.	8-9 Nm
Hood		
Hood-to-hinge bolts	13-19 ft. lbs.	17-27 Nm
Hood hinge-to-cowl panel bolts	34 ft. lbs.	46 Nm
Pick-up Box-to-frame bolts:	40-70 ft. lbs.	54-95 Nm
Power door glass regulator motor mounting bolts:	50-85 inch lbs.	6-10 Nm
Seats		
Front Bench Seat Mounting bolts		
1987-94 with standard seat:	25-34 ft. lbs.	34-46 Nm
1995-96 with standard seat:	35-46 ft. lbs.	47-63 Nm
40/20/40 seat:	35-46 ft. lbs.	47-63 Nm
Bucket and Captain's chair bolts:		
Driver's side:	30 ft. lbs.	41 Nm
Passenger's side (1987-89):	30 ft. lbs.	41 Nm
Passenger's side (1990-94):	25-34 ft. lbs.	34-45 Nm
Passenger's side (1995-96):	35-46 ft. lbs.	47-63 Nm
Rear Bench seat bolts	18-32 ft. lbs.	25-44 Nm
Folding Rear seat:		
F-Series Pick-ups:	18-32 ft. lbs.	25-44 Nm
Bronco	45-60 ft. lbs.	62-81 Nm
Seat belt anchor bolts:	22.29 ft. lbs.	30-40 Nm
Swing-Away Spare Tire Carrier		
Bronco		
Hinge-to-body bolts	20 ft. lbs.	27 Nm
Tailgate		
Bronco		
Hinge bolts	20-30 ft. lbs.	28-40 Nm
Cable bolts	20-30 ft. lbs.	28-40 Nm
Lock control screws	11 ft. lbs.	15 Nm
Tailgate Window Glass		
Bronco		
Glass run attaching screws	10 ft. lbs.	14 Nm
Glass-to-window bracket nuts	10 ft. lbs.	14 Nm
Regular mounting bolts	10 ft. lbs.	14 Nm

88280C01

GLOSSARY

AIR/FUEL RATIO: The ratio of air-to-gasoline by weight in the fuel mixture drawn into the engine.

AIR INJECTION: One method of reducing harmful exhaust emissions by injecting air into each of the exhaust ports of an engine. The fresh air entering the hot exhaust manifold causes any remaining fuel to be burned before it can exit the tailpipe.

ALTERNATOR: A device used for converting mechanical energy into electrical energy.

AMMETER: An instrument, calibrated in amperes, used to measure the flow of an electrical current in a circuit. Ammeters are always connected in series with the circuit being tested.

AMPERE: The rate of flow of electrical current present when one volt of electrical pressure is applied against one ohm of electrical resistance.

ANALOG COMPUTER: Any microprocessor that uses similar (analogous) electrical signals to make its calculations.

ARMATURE: A laminated, soft iron core wrapped by a wire that converts electrical energy to mechanical energy as in a motor or relay. When rotated in a magnetic field, it changes mechanical energy into electrical energy as in a generator.

ATMOSPHERIC PRESSURE: The pressure on the Earth's surface caused by the weight of the air in the atmosphere. At sea level, this pressure is 14.7 psi at 32°F (101 kPa at 0°C).

ATOMIZATION: The breaking down of a liquid into a fine mist that can be suspended in air.

AXIAL PLAY: Movement parallel to a shaft or bearing bore.

BACKFIRE: The sudden combustion of gases in the intake or exhaust system that results in a loud explosion.

BACKLASH: The clearance or play between two parts, such as meshed gears.

BACKPRESSURE: Restrictions in the exhaust system that slow the exit of exhaust gases from the combustion chamber.

BAKELITE: A heat resistant, plastic insulator material commonly used in printed circuit boards and transistorized components.

BALL BEARING: A bearing made up of hardened inner and outer races between which hardened steel balls roll.

BALLAST RESISTOR: A resistor in the primary ignition circuit that lowers voltage after the engine is started to reduce wear on ignition components.

BEARING: A friction reducing, supportive device usually located between a stationary part and a moving part.

BIMETAL TEMPERATURE SENSOR: Any sensor or switch made of two dissimilar types of metal that bend when heated or cooled due to the different expansion rates of the alloys. These types of sensors usually function as an on/off switch.

BLOWBY: Combustion gases, composed of water vapor and unburned fuel, that leak past the piston rings into the crankcase during normal engine operation. These gases are removed by the PCV system to prevent the buildup of harmful acids in the crankcase.

BRAKE PAD: A brake shoe and lining assembly used with disc brakes.

BRAKE SHOE: The backing for the brake lining. The term is, however, usually applied to the assembly of the brake backing and lining.

BUSHING: A liner, usually removable, for a bearing; an anti-friction liner used in place of a bearing.

CALIPER: A hydraulically activated device in a disc brake system, which is mounted straddling the brake rotor (disc). The caliper contains at least one piston and two brake pads. Hydraulic pressure on the piston(s) forces the pads against the rotor.

CAMSHAFT: A shaft in the engine on which are the lobes (cams) which operate the valves. The camshaft is driven by the crankshaft, via a belt, chain or gears, at one half the crankshaft speed.

CAPACITOR: A device which stores an electrical charge.

CARBON MONOXIDE (CO): A colorless, odorless gas given off as a normal byproduct of combustion. It is poisonous and extremely dangerous in confined areas, building up slowly to toxic levels without warning if adequate ventilation is not available.

CARBURETOR: A device, usually mounted on the intake manifold of an engine, which mixes the air and fuel in the proper proportion to allow even combustion.

CATALYTIC CONVERTER: A device installed in the exhaust system, like a muffler, that converts harmful byproducts of combustion into carbon dioxide and water vapor by means of a heat-producing chemical reaction.

CENTRIFUGAL ADVANCE: A mechanical method of advancing the spark timing by using flyweights in the distributor that react to centrifugal force generated by the distributor shaft rotation.

CHECK VALVE: Any one-way valve installed to permit the flow of air, fuel or vacuum in one direction only.

CHOKE: A device, usually a moveable valve, placed in the intake path of a carburetor to restrict the flow of air.

CIRCUIT: Any unbroken path through which an electrical current can flow. Also used to describe fuel flow in some instances.

CIRCUIT BREAKER: A switch which protects an electrical circuit from overload by opening the circuit when the current flow exceeds a predetermined level. Some circuit breakers must be reset manually, while most reset automatically.

COIL (IGNITION): A transformer in the ignition circuit which steps up the voltage provided to the spark plugs.

COMBINATION MANIFOLD: An assembly which includes both the intake and exhaust manifolds in one casting.

COMBINATION VALVE: A device used in some fuel systems that routes fuel vapors to a charcoal storage canister instead of venting them into the atmosphere. The valve relieves fuel tank pressure and allows fresh air into the tank as the fuel level drops to prevent a vapor lock situation.

COMPRESSION RATIO: The comparison of the total volume of the cylinder and combustion chamber with the piston at BDC and the piston at TDC.

CONDENSER: 1. An electrical device which acts to store an electrical charge, preventing voltage surges. 2. A radiator-like device in the air conditioning system in which refrigerant gas condenses into a liquid, giving off heat.

CONDUCTOR: Any material through which an electrical current can be transmitted easily.

CONTINUITY: Continuous or complete circuit. Can be checked with an ohmmeter.

COUNTERSHAFT: An intermediate shaft which is rotated by a mainshaft and transmits, in turn, that rotation to a working part.

CRANKCASE: The lower part of an engine in which the crankshaft and related parts operate.

CRANKSHAFT: The main driving shaft of an engine which receives reciprocating motion from the pistons and converts it to rotary motion.

CYLINDER: In an engine, the round hole in the engine block in which the piston(s) ride.

CYLINDER BLOCK: The main structural member of an engine in which is found the cylinders, crankshaft and other principal parts.

CYLINDER HEAD: The detachable portion of the engine, usually fastened to the top of the cylinder block and containing all or most of the combustion chambers. On overhead valve engines, it contains the valves and their operating parts. On overhead cam engines, it contains the camshaft as well.

DEAD CENTER: The extreme top or bottom of the piston stroke.

DETONATION: An unwanted explosion of the air/fuel mixture in the combustion chamber caused by excess heat and compression, advanced timing, or an overly lean mixture. Also referred to as "ping".

DIAPHRAGM: A thin, flexible wall separating two cavities, such as in a vacuum advance unit.

DIESELING: A condition in which hot spots in the combustion chamber cause the engine to run on after the key is turned off.

DIFFERENTIAL: A geared assembly which allows the transmission of motion between drive axles, giving one axle the ability to turn faster than the other.

DIODE: An electrical device that will allow current to flow in one direction only.

DISC BRAKE: A hydraulic braking assembly consisting of a brake disc, or rotor, mounted on an axle, and a caliper assembly containing, usually two brake pads which are activated by hydraulic pressure. The pads are forced against the sides of the disc, creating friction which slows the vehicle.

DISTRIBUTOR: A mechanically driven device on an engine which is responsible for electrically firing the spark plug at a predetermined point of the piston stroke.

DOWEL PIN: A pin, inserted in mating holes in two different parts allowing those parts to maintain a fixed relationship.

DRUM BRAKE: A braking system which consists of two brake shoes and one or two wheel cylinders, mounted on a fixed backing plate, and a brake drum, mounted on an axle, which revolves around the assembly.

DWELL: The rate, measured in degrees of shaft rotation, at which an electrical circuit cycles on and off.

ELECTRONIC CONTROL UNIT (ECU): Ignition module, module, amplifier or igniter. See Module for definition.

ELECTRONIC IGNITION: A system in which the timing and firing of the spark plugs is controlled by an electronic control unit, usually called a module. These systems have no points or condenser.

END-PLAY: The measured amount of axial movement in a shaft.

ENGINE: A device that converts heat into mechanical energy.

EXHAUST MANIFOLD: A set of cast passages or pipes which conduct exhaust gases from the engine.

FEELER GAUGE: A blade, usually metal, or precisely predetermined thickness, used to measure the clearance between two parts.

FIRING ORDER: The order in which combustion occurs in the cylinders of an engine. Also the order in which spark is distributed to the plugs by the distributor.

FLOODING: The presence of too much fuel in the intake manifold and combustion chamber which prevents the air/fuel mixture from firing, thereby causing a no-start situation.

FLYWHEEL: A disc shaped part bolted to the rear end of the crankshaft. Around the outer perimeter is affixed the ring gear. The starter drive engages the ring gear, turning the flywheel, which rotates the crankshaft, imparting the initial starting motion to the engine.

FOOT POUND (ft. lbs. or sometimes, ft.lb.): The amount of energy or work needed to raise an item weighing one pound, a distance of one foot.

FUSE: A protective device in a circuit which prevents circuit overload by breaking the circuit when a specific amperage is present. The device is constructed around a strip or wire of a lower amperage rating than the circuit it is designed to protect. When an amperage higher than that stamped on the fuse is present in the circuit, the strip or wire melts, opening the circuit.

GEAR RATIO: The ratio between the number of teeth on meshing gears.

GENERATOR: A device which converts mechanical energy into electrical energy.

HEAT RANGE: The measure of a spark plug's ability to dissipate heat from its firing end. The higher the heat range, the hotter the plug fires.

HUB: The center part of a wheel or gear.

HYDROCARBON (HC): Any chemical compound made up of hydrogen and carbon. A major pollutant formed by the engine as a byproduct of combustion.

HYDROMETER: An instrument used to measure the specific gravity of a solution.

INCH POUND (inch lbs.; sometimes in.lb. or in. lbs.): One twelfth of a foot pound.

INDUCTION: A means of transferring electrical energy in the form of a magnetic field. Principle used in the ignition coil to increase voltage.

INJECTOR: A device which receives metered fuel under relatively low pressure and is activated to inject the fuel into the engine under relatively high pressure at a predetermined time.

INPUT SHAFT: The shaft to which torque is applied, usually carrying the driving gear or gears.

INTAKE MANIFOLD: A casting of passages or pipes used to conduct air or a fuel/air mixture to the cylinders.

JOURNAL: The bearing surface within which a shaft operates.

KEY: A small block usually fitted in a notch between a shaft and a hub to prevent slippage of the two parts.

MANIFOLD: A casting of passages or set of pipes which connect the cylinders to an inlet or outlet source.

MANIFOLD VACUUM: Low pressure in an engine intake manifold formed just below the throttle plates. Manifold vacuum is highest at idle and drops under acceleration.

MASTER CYLINDER: The primary fluid pressurizing device in a hydraulic system. In automotive use, it is found in brake and hydraulic clutch systems and is pedal activated, either directly or, in a power brake system, through the power booster.

MODULE: Electronic control unit, amplifier or igniter of solid state or integrated design which controls the current flow in the ignition primary circuit based on input from the pick-up coil. When the module opens the primary circuit, high secondary voltage is induced in the coil.

NEEDLE BEARING: A bearing which consists of a number (usually a large number) of long, thin rollers.

OHM: (Ω) The unit used to measure the resistance of conductor-to-electrical flow. One ohm is the amount of resistance that limits current flow to one ampere in a circuit with one volt of pressure.

OHMMETER: An instrument used for measuring the resistance, in ohms, in an electrical circuit.

OUTPUT SHAFT: The shaft which transmits torque from a device, such as a transmission.

OVERDRIVE: A gear assembly which produces more shaft revolutions than that transmitted to it.

OVERHEAD CAMSHAFT (OHC): An engine configuration in which the camshaft is mounted on top of the cylinder head and operates the valve either directly or by means of rocker arms.

OVERHEAD VALVE (OHV): An engine configuration in which all of the valves are located in the cylinder head and the camshaft is located in the cylinder block. The camshaft operates the valves via lifters and pushrods.

OXIDES OF NITROGEN (NOx): Chemical compounds of nitrogen produced as a byproduct of combustion. They combine with hydrocarbons to produce smog.

OXYGEN SENSOR: Use with the feedback system to sense the presence of oxygen in the exhaust gas and signal the computer which can reference the voltage signal to an air/fuel ratio.

PINION: The smaller of two meshing gears.

PISTON RING: An open-ended ring with fits into a groove on the outer diameter of the piston. Its chief function is to form a seal between the piston and cylinder wall. Most automotive pistons have three rings: two for compression sealing; one for oil sealing.

PRELOAD: A predetermined load placed on a bearing during assembly or by adjustment.

PRIMARY CIRCUIT: the low voltage side of the ignition system which consists of the ignition switch, ballast resistor or resistance wire, bypass, coil, electronic control unit and pick-up coil as well as the connecting wires and harnesses.

PRESS FIT: The mating of two parts under pressure, due to the inner diameter of one being smaller than the outer diameter of the other, or vice versa; an interference fit.

RACE: The surface on the inner or outer ring of a bearing on which the balls, needles or rollers move.

REGULATOR: A device which maintains the amperage and/or voltage levels of a circuit at predetermined values.

RELAY: A switch which automatically opens and/or closes a circuit.

RESISTANCE: The opposition to the flow of current through a circuit or electrical device, and is measured in ohms. Resistance is equal to the voltage divided by the amperage.

RESISTOR: A device, usually made of wire, which offers a preset amount of resistance in an electrical circuit.

RING GEAR: The name given to a ring-shaped gear attached to a differential case, or affixed to a flywheel or as part of a planetary gear set.

ROLLER BEARING: A bearing made up of hardened inner and outer races between which hardened steel rollers move.

ROTOR: 1. The disc-shaped part of a disc brake assembly, upon which the brake pads bear; also called, brake disc. 2. The device mounted atop the distributor shaft, which passes current to the distributor cap tower contacts.

SECONDARY CIRCUIT: The high voltage side of the ignition system, usually above 20,000 volts. The secondary includes the ignition coil, coil wire, distributor cap and rotor, spark plug wires and spark plugs.

SENDING UNIT: A mechanical, electrical, hydraulic or electro-magnetic device which transmits information to a gauge.

SENSOR: Any device designed to measure engine operating conditions or ambient pressures and temperatures. Usually electronic in nature and designed to send a voltage signal to an on-board computer, some sensors may operate as a simple on/off switch or they may provide a variable voltage signal (like a potentiometer) as conditions or measured parameters change.

SHIM: Spacers of precise, predetermined thickness used between parts to establish a proper working relationship.

SLAVE CYLINDER: In automotive use, a device in the hydraulic clutch system which is activated by hydraulic force, disengaging the clutch.

SOLENOID: A coil used to produce a magnetic field, the effect of which is to produce work.

SPARK PLUG: A device screwed into the combustion chamber of a spark ignition engine. The basic construction is a conductive core inside of a ceramic insulator, mounted in an outer conductive base. An electrical charge from the spark plug wire travels along the conductive core and jumps a preset air gap to a grounding point or points at the end of the conductive base. The resultant spark ignites the fuel/air mixture in the combustion chamber.

SPLINES: Ridges machined or cast onto the outer diameter of a shaft or inner diameter of a bore to enable parts to mate without rotation.

TACHOMETER: A device used to measure the rotary speed of an engine, shaft, gear, etc., usually in rotations per minute.

THERMOSTAT: A valve, located in the cooling system of an engine, which is closed when cold and opens gradually in response to engine heating, controlling the temperature of the coolant and rate of coolant flow.

TOP DEAD CENTER (TDC): The point at which the piston reaches the top of its travel on the compression stroke.

TORQUE: The twisting force applied to an object.

TORQUE CONVERTER: A turbine used to transmit power from a driving member to a driven member via hydraulic action, providing changes in drive ratio and torque. In automotive use, it links the driveplate at the rear of the engine to the automatic transmission.

TRANSDUCER: A device used to change a force into an electrical signal.

TRANSISTOR: A semi-conductor component which can be actuated by a small voltage to perform an electrical switching function.

TUNE-UP: A regular maintenance function, usually associated with the replacement and adjustment of parts and components in the electrical and fuel systems of a vehicle for the purpose of attaining optimum performance.

TURBOCHARGER: An exhaust driven pump which compresses intake air and forces it into the combustion chambers at higher than atmospheric pressures. The increased air pressure allows more fuel to be burned and results in increased horsepower being produced.

VACUUM ADVANCE: A device which advances the ignition timing in response to increased engine vacuum.

VACUUM GAUGE: An instrument used to measure the presence of vacuum in a chamber.

VALVE: A device which control the pressure, direction of flow or rate of flow of a liquid or gas.

VALVE CLEARANCE: The measured gap between the end of the valve stem and the rocker arm, cam lobe or follower that activates the valve.

VISCOSITY: The rating of a liquid's internal resistance to flow.

VOLTMETER: An instrument used for measuring electrical force in units called volts. Voltmeters are always connected parallel with the circuit being tested.

WHEEL CYLINDER: Found in the automotive drum brake assembly, it is a device, actuated by hydraulic pressure, which, through internal pistons, pushes the brake shoes outward against the drums.

MASTER INDEX